THE NORTHERN WARS

MODERN WARS IN PERSPECTIVE

General Editors: *H.M. Scott and B.W. Collins*

This ambitious new series offers wide-ranging studies of specific wars, and distinct phases of warfare, from the close of the Middle Ages to the present day. It aims to advance the current integration of military history into the academic mainstream. To that end, the books are not merely traditional campaign narratives, but examine the causes, course and consequences of major conflicts, in their full international, political, social and ideological contexts.

Already published:

THE NORTHERN WARS

War, State and Society in Northeastern Europe, 1558–1721

Robert I. Frost

An imprint of **Pearson Education**

Harlow, England · London · New York · Reading, Massachusetts · San Francisco
Toronto · Don Mills, Ontario · Sydney · Tokyo · Singapore · Hong Kong · Seoul
Taipei · Cape Town · Madrid · Mexico City · Amsterdam · Munich · Paris · Milan

FOR KARIN

Pearson Education Limited
Edinburgh Gate
Harlow
Essex CM20 2JE
England

and Associated Companies throughout the world

Visit us on the World Wide Web at:
http://www.pearsoneduc.com

———————————

First published 2000

ISBN 0 582 06429 5
ISBN 0 582 06430 9

British Library Cataloguing-in-Publication Data
A catalogue record for this book is available from the British Library

Library of Congress Cataloging-in-Publication Data
A catalog record for this book is available from the Library of Congress

10 9 8 7 6 5 4 3 2 1
04 03 02 01 00

Typeset by 35 in 11/13pt Baskerville MT
Produced by Pearson Education Asia Pte Ltd.
Printed in Singapore

CONTENTS

LIST OF ILLUSTRATIONS

PREFACE

The linguistic complexity of northeastern Europe and the political changes which have taken place since 1721 mean that several variants of place names exist, and the preference for one form over others is inevitably controversial. Since whatever choice is made will upset somebody, I have tried to balance consistency with the requirements of writing for a largely anglophone readership. Where there is a generally-recognised English form, modern or early modern, I have used it (Cracow, Moscow, Kiev, Malmo, Copenhagen, Samogitia, Livonia). Otherwise I have mainly preferred the form as it appears most frequently in contemporary documents. The greatest problems are posed by Livonia and Estonia, where I have preferred German to Estonian or Latvian forms, and Poland-Lithuania, where I have used the Polish form except for Royal Prussia (thus Danzig, not Gdańsk) and the Ukraine (which in this book denotes the palatinates of Kiev, Volhynia, Bratslav and Chernihiv), where I have used Ukrainian forms. I have used the term 'Muscovy' to refer to the Russian state until 1667, when the acquisition of the right-bank Ukraine and Kiev marked the start of the transition to the modern Russian empire. The choices are made entirely on academic grounds. Where strict adherence to these principles would involve absurdities, or where a particular form is solidly grounded in the English-language scholarship, I have departed from them. Thus the battle of Fraustadt (1706) does not become the battle of Wschowa, and I prefer Brest (Litovsk) (the Russian form) to Brześć (Litewski) (Polish). Nationalists may curse me and pedants may excommunicate me if they wish, but I am not writing for them. To help the reader, I have included a gazetteer which gives the forms used in the book and the equivalents in other languages. With regard to personal names, I have taken the English form for names of members of ruling houses, except where it sounds archaic or ridiculous – thus Louis not Lewis, Władysław not Ladislas, Vasilii not Basil, Fedor not Theodore. Transliteration from the cyrillic is according to the Library of Congress system, modified to avoid diacriticals. In the case of Ukrainian surnames, I have preferred the ending -sky to -skyi.

I am immensely grateful for the patient help and advice of many people without whose generous help this book could never have been written. In particular, Professor Józef Gierowski and Professor Jacek Staszewski invited me to address their seminars in Cracow and Toruń, and were extremely generous with their advice and assistance. I learned an enormous amount from discussions with the late Professor Ragnhild Hatton, whose encouragement and help I much appreciated. Professor Geoffrey Parker sparked my interest in the Military Revolution twenty years ago, and has encouraged my work ever since. I would also like to offer my warmest thanks to Professor Stanisław Aleksandrowicz, Dr Jolanta Choinska-Mika, Dr Brian Davies, Dr Bogusław Dybaś, Dr Igor Kąkolewski, Dr Andrzej Link-Lenczowski, Professor Antoni Mączak, Dr Mariusz Markiewicz, Dr Krzysztof Mikulski, Dr Tom Munch-Petersen, Dr Steve Murdoch, Dr Mirosław Nagielski, Dr Andrzej Nieuważny, Dr Edward Opaliński, Dr David Parrott, Professor Helmut Piirimäe, Dr Jarosław Poraziński, Dr Andrzej Rachuba, Dr Henryk Rietz, Dr Carol Stevens, Professor Stefan Troebst and Dr Katarzyna Zielińska, all of whom helped me in many different ways. Dr Henadz' Sahanovich very kindly sent me a copy of his book, for which I am extremely grateful. Professor Tony Upton read the typescript, and made many helpful suggestions which improved it immeasurably. I am grateful to the Nordic History Group for listening so politely to a Polonist trying to make sense of Scandinavian history, and for offering much helpful advice. I would also like to thank Dr Roger Mettam and members of the seminar in European History 1500–1800 at the Institute of Historical Research of London University for providing such a stimulating scholarly environment in which to try out my ideas. To mgr Stefan Czaja, director of the Library of the Nicholas Copernicus University in Toruń, I owe a great deal, and I appreciate his generous help and assistance.

Many institutions and other bodies have provided invaluable help and support. King's College London allowed me a year's leave in 1994 to complete my research. Thanks to the generosity of the Twenty Seven Foundation (now the Scouloudi Foundation) of the Institute of Historical Research, University of London, I was able to spend a month at the Herder Institute in Marburg in 1990. The British Academy kindly funded two research trips to Stockholm, and I am immensely grateful to the Estonian Academy of Sciences in Tallinn, the University of Tartu, the Nicholas Copernicus University in Toruń, the University of Warsaw, the Jagiellonian University in Cracow and the Geisteswissenschaftliche Centrum für Geschichte Ostmitteleuropas of Leipzig University for extending me their generous hospitality. I would also like to thank the staff of the many libraries and archives in which I worked, in particular the Library of the Nicholas Copernicus University in Toruń, the British Library, the Royal Library in Stockholm, the Herder Institute in Marburg, and the State Archive in Toruń, whose director, Dr Jarosław Poraziński, runs one of the friendliest archives I have come across.

I am deeply indebted to Andrew MacLennan, late of Longman, for commissioning this book, and for his constant interest and encouragement, and to Professor Hamish Scott, who first suggested the idea, who kept me going, and who read the typescript with characteristic care, making countless important suggestions for improvement. He is the best of editors. I would also like to thank Alistair Graham, Carol Gardiner and the staff of Pearson Education for the care with which they have produced this book. My greatest debt is to my wife, Dr Karin Friedrich, who contributed more to this book than she can ever know. For its shortcomings, I alone am responsible.

Leipzig, August 1999

ABBREVIATIONS

ABS	*Acta Baltico-Slavica*
AOIIuZR	*Akty otnosiashiesia k Istorii Iuzhnoi i Zapadnoi Rossii*
AOSB	*Rikskansleren Axel Oxenstiernas skrifter och brefväxling* Series I–II (Stockholm, 1888–1978)
APG	*Archiwum Państwowe w Gdańsku* (State Archive in Gdańsk)
APT	*Archiwum Państwowe w Toruniu* (State Archive in Toruń)
ASBARIAEIAN	*Akty, sobrannye v bibliotekakh i arkhivakh Rossiiskoi Imperii Arkheograficheskoiu ekspeditsieiu Imperatorskoi Akademii Nauk*
AW	*Ateneum Wilenskie*
BKE	*Beiträge zur Kunde Estlands*
BKELK	*Beiträge zur Kunde Ehst- Liv- und Kurlands*
CASS	*Canadian-American Slavic Studies*
CSSH	*Comparative Studies in Society and History*
Czart.	Biblioteka im. ks. Czartoryskich, Cracow
EFE	Elementa ad Fontium Editiones
EHQ	*European History Quarterly*
EHR	*English Historical Review*
ESAT	Estonian State Archive, Tartu
ESR	*European Studies Review*
FOG	*Forschungen zur Osteuropäischen Geschichte*
HB	*Historiskt Bibliotek*
HH	*Historiska Handlingar*
HS	*Historiska Samlingar*
HTD	*Historisk Tidsskrift* (Denmark)
HTS	*Historisk Tidskrift* (Sweden)
ISKS	*Institut Slavianovedeniia. Kratkie Soobshcheniia*
IZ	*Istoricheskie Zapiski*
JMH	*Journal of Modern History*
JGO	*Jahrbücher für Geschichte Osteuropas*
KFÅ	*Karolinska Förbundets Årsbok*

KH	*Kwartalnik Historyczny*
KKD	*Karolinska Krigares Dagböcker*
MGGLEK	*Mittheilungen aus dem Gebiete der Geschichte Liv-, Est- und Kurlands*
MHD	*Monumenta Historica Daniae*
MLGM	*Mitteilungen der Litterarischen Gesellschaft Masovia*
MM	*Militärgeschichtliche Mitteilungen*
MT	*Militärhistorisk Tidskrift*
MVGOWP	*Mitteilungen der Vereins für Gesellschaft von Ost- und Westpreußen*
NASGA	*Neues Archiv für Sächsische Geschichte und Altertumskunde*
NS	New Style
OS	Old Style
PH	*Przegląd Historyczny*
PHum	*Przegląd Humanistyczny*
PHW	*Przegląd Historyczno-Wojskowy*
PiB	*Pis'ma i Bumagi Imperatora Petra Velikogo* 13 vols (St Petersburg, Moscow, 1887–1992)
PODWP	K. Lepszy (ed.) *Polska w okresie drugiej wojny północnej* 4 vols (Warsaw, 1957)
PR	Preussiska Räkenskaper från Karl X Gustavs Krig 1655–1660
PSRL	*Polnoe Sobranie Russkikh Letopisei*
PW	*Przegląd Współczesny*
RA, Kamm.	Riksarkivet, Stockholm, Kammerarkivet
RB	*Rocznik Białystocki*
RH	*Russian History*
RHS	*Roczniki Historii Sztuki*
RR	*Russian Review*
RZNO	*Rocznik Zakładu Narodowego im Ossolińskich*
SAGP	*Sitzungsberichte der Altertumforschenden Gesellschaft zu Pernau*
SEER	*Slavonic and East European Review*
SEHR	*Scandinavian Economic History Review*
SGECRN	*Study Group on Eighteenth Century Russia Newsletter*
SIRIO	*Sbornik Imperatorskogo Russkogo Istoricheskogo Obshchestva*
SJH	*Scandinavian Journal of History*
SMHW	*Studia i Materiały do Historii Wojskowości*
SMHSW	*Studia i Materiały do Historii Sztuki Wojennej*
SR	*Slavic Review*

SS	*Scandinavian Studies*
TCA	Tallinn City Archive
THA	*Turun Historiallinen Arkisto*
UUÅ	*Upsala Universitets Årsskrift*
VL	*Volumina Legum* vols 2–5 (St Petersburg, 1859–60)
VIS	*Voenno-Istoricheskii Sbornik*
VS	*Voennyi Sbornik*
WH	*War in History*
ZH	*Zapiski Historyczne*
ZHF	*Zeitschrift für Historische Forschung*
ZHGPP	*Zeitschrift der historische Gesellschaft für die Provinz Posen*
ZNTS	*Zapiski Naukovoho Tovaristva imeni Shevchenka*
ZNUAM	*Zeszyty Naukowe Uniwersytetu im. Adama Mickiewicza*

CHAPTER ONE

Introduction

Prelude

On 2 August 1560, 465 years after Urban II launched his great call to recover Jerusalem for Christendom at the Council of Claremont, the crusading movement made its last stand. It did not last long. Unlike so many of the battles which provide convenient symbolic markers for the passing of an age or a civilisation, it was not a momentous affair. It was fought far from the Palestinian sun, amidst the dark forests of northern Europe, against a Christian enemy. With a few hundred members of the Livonian Order of the Knights of the Sword and 500 auxiliaries, Philipp Schall von Bell boldly attacked a Muscovite force several thousand strong near Ermes in Livonia. Schall von Bell was confident of the superior quality of his knights, for he did not attempt to join Jan Chodkiewicz's Lithuanian force standing to the south along the Dvina. Precedent did seem to be on his side: fifty-eight years earlier, the last great Muscovite onslaught had been repulsed by Grand Master Wolter von Plettenberg at the battles of Seritsa (January 1501) and Lake Smolino (September 1502). Schall von Bell's reconnaissance was poor, however, and he did not appreciate the extent to which he was outnumbered.[1] Although the Muscovites were initially surprised by a furious onslaught, they quickly rallied to overwhelm their enemy. Half the Order's force was killed or captured; 120 knights fell into Muscovite hands, including Schall von Bell, his brother Werner, and three other members of the Order's hierarchy. Dragged to Moscow, these proud dignitaries were executed on the orders of tsar Ivan IV; their bodies were left to rot in the street. It was a miserable end to a great ideal.

For Ermes sealed the fate of the Order, which had long since lost its *raison d'être*. The Knights of the Sword were a branch of the Teutonic Order, which had conquered the southeastern Baltic shore from Danzig to Estonia since the twelfth century, subjugating the pagan Prussians, Livs and Ests. With the conversion of Lithuania's pagan rulers to Catholicism in the 1380s, however, the purpose of the Crusade was achieved; it was difficult thereafter to justify the wars fought against Catholic Poland and Lithuania, who entered a dynastic union in 1385–6 under the Lithuanian Grand Duke Jogaila, baptised as Władysław Jagiełło. Jagiełło's great victory at Grunwald (Tannenberg) in 1410 marked the start of the Order's decline, as it came into increasing conflict with the wave of German settlers who depended upon the Knights for defence, but whose interests frequently clashed with those of the Order. As the supply of recruits for the celibate Order began to dry up in the fifteenth century, Poland-Lithuania and the emerging power of Muscovy under Ivan III (1462–1505) represented growing threats. The pressure was greatest in Prussia, where a revolt by Danzig, Thorn and Elbing, supported by much of the local nobility, sparked off the Thirteen Years War (1454–66), in which the Order lost to Poland the western part of Prussia. By the early 1520s the spread of the Reformation in northern Germany was already undermining the Order in its traditional recruiting ground. In 1525, the Order's remaining Prussian lands were secularised by its last Grand Master, Albrecht von Hohenzollern, who converted to Lutheranism and established the Duchy of Prussia as a fief of the Polish Crown. It was Europe's first Protestant state.

The collapse of the Teutonic Order in Prussia created serious problems for the Livonian Knights. Ivan III's conquest of Novgorod between 1471 and 1489, and the subjugation of Pskov by his son Vasilii III (1505–33) in 1510 brought Muscovite power to Livonia's borders. Although von Plettenberg repulsed Ivan's attacks in 1501–3, and Vasilii became involved in a series of wars against Lithuania, the Knights, in an increasingly fractious relationship with the loose Livonian Confederation, were highly vulnerable. Deprived of Prussian support, the Order faced a new threat from Albrecht von Hohenzollern, who feared that the Livonians would seek to recover his new duchy. In 1530 he secured the coadjutorship of the archbishopric of Riga for his brother Wilhelm, who became archbishop in 1539. The most dangerous factor, however, was the Reformation, as the spread of Protestantism widened the Livonian Confederation's political divisions by establishing itself in the cities. Racked with internal bickering and threatened by the political machinations of its neighbours, Livonia was in no state to resist an attack; after 1558, as opinion divided over who was best able to provide protection against the Muscovites, the Livonian conflict rapidly became a civil war.[2]

Causes

The Order's decline created a dangerous political vacuum in a region which was proving of increasing interest to all northern Europe. The great surge in Baltic trade from the mid-fifteenth century promised lucrative rewards to those who controlled the ports which channelled goods and raw materials from the vast hinterlands of Poland, Lithuania and Muscovy. In the fifteenth century, this trade had been dominated by the Hanse, led by Lübeck and the cities of the Wendish League, which at its height formed a network of several hundred cities and towns, with privileged trading offices from London to Novgorod. By 1500, however, the Hanse's very success in developing the Baltic trade was stimulating important challenges to its monopoly, particularly from states and communities along the North Sea littoral; as rival traders arrived in Baltic ports in increasing numbers, cities such as Reval, Riga and Danzig began to chafe at Hanse restrictions, while local rulers sought to tap into the wealth flowing out of their lands. The Hanse office in Novgorod was closed by Ivan III in 1493, while Riga and Reval opposed the admission of Narva to the Hanseatic League and in 1539 banned foreign merchants from trading directly with Russians.

Although the decline of the Hanse was more a political than an economic phenomenon – the tonnage of Hanse vessels visiting Baltic ports was 50 per cent greater at the end of the century than it had been 100 years earlier[3] – it was to have important consequences, as demand for Baltic goods escalated after 1500. Ever-increasing quantities of grain, timber, pitch, potash, hemp, flax, wax, hides and furs were shipped westwards. This lucrative trade was accompanied by a surge in the internal market, as the Polish-Lithuanian and Muscovite populations expanded. Although historians have often exaggerated the importance of the Baltic trade for the economies of eastern Europe – only 2.5 per cent of Poland's total grain production was exported in the sixteenth century[4] – there is little doubt that the boom in international trade was highly significant. The price of Polish rye rose 313 per cent between 1500 and 1580, that of wheat by 360 per cent; yet the terms of trade ensured that Polish grain was extremely profitable for western merchants: in 1585 one last of rye cost 685 grammes of silver in Danzig, but was worth 873 grammes in Amsterdam. (One Danzig last equals 2264 litres.) This was reflected in the rapid expansion of shipping: whereas 666 foreign ships arrived in Danzig in 1475–6, and 674 departed the port in 1530, 2,220 arrived and 2,099 departed in 1583; they came from France, England, Scotland, the Netherlands, Scandinavia and northern Germany, with by far the greatest number from the Netherlands, with 1,070 arrivals and 1,045 departures in 1581.[5]

Western merchants were, however, highly dependent on the attitudes of local rulers. The narrowness of the entry to the Baltic from the North Sea gave the kings of Denmark, who ruled both sides of the Sound, the principal channel into the Baltic, the opportunity to control trade.[6] From the late 1420s until 1857, the Danish monarchy levied the famous Sound Dues on ships entering and leaving the Baltic, sometimes blocking the passage of vessels from states with which Denmark was in dispute, as in 1543, when not a single Dutch ship entered or left the Baltic.[7] By 1560, despite fierce resistance from interested parties, the Sound Dues were well established, while attempts to circumvent Danish control of the Sound by establishing an alternative route to Russia via Archangel made little impact. If other Baltic powers did not enjoy such a favourable geographical situation, the decline of the Teutonic Knights gave them the opportunity to win control over the vital ports at the mouths of the great rivers down which trade flowed. The Poles had already secured Danzig in 1466, but at the price of granting it extensive privileges. With the crumbling of the Livonian Order and the undermining of the Hanseatic monopoly, Riga, Reval and Narva were particularly vulnerable.

Peace held for fifty years after 1503, however. Vasilii III's wars against Lithuania were followed by the long regency for his successor, Ivan IV (1533–84), who only began to exercise personal authority in the late 1540s, and who devoted most of the 1550s to the conquest of the Tatar khanates of Kazan and Astrakhan. The pace began to pick up in the 1540s, when Christian III (1534–59) claimed that although Denmark had sold Harrien and Wierland to the Order in 1346, it had not ceded sovereignty. Muscovites reacted sharply to the 1539 Livonian ban on direct trade between Muscovite and western merchants: in the early 1550s, Ivan demanded that all restrictions be removed and that foreign artisans and soldiers be allowed free passage into Muscovy; he also revived a longstanding claim to receive tribute from Dorpat. It was Albrecht von Hohenzollern, however, who played the central role in the crisis which led to war. The appointment of duke Christopher of Mecklenburg as coadjutor to the Riga archbishopric by Wilhelm von Hohenzollern was the immediate spark: the Livonian estates had already blocked Wilhelm's attempt to introduce a Lutheran church order in his archdiocese, and they saw Christopher's appointment as presaging a new onslaught on Catholicism. When the two were arrested by the estates in 1556, Denmark intervened to promote a settlement, but Sigismund Augustus of Poland-Lithuania mustered an army to force the Livonians to release them and accept his protection at the treaty of Pozwol (September 1557).[8]

Pozwol was seen by Ivan as a direct provocation. He rapidly ended a brief frontier war against Sweden in Ingria and Karelia (1554–7) to increase pressure on Dorpat to pay tribute. In January 1558 a small, largely Tatar, force invaded Livonia, followed by a larger army in the summer. As the fall of Narva and then Dorpat demonstrated the Order's manifest inability to defend Livonia, Muscovy's rivals hurried to stake their claims. Denmark briefly stepped in between July and December as protector of Reval and took control of the island of Ösel a year later; in June 1561 Reval and part of the Estonian nobility accepted Swedish protection. The final act soon followed. In November 1561 the new Grand Master Gotthard Kettler secularised the Order and surrendered Livonia to Sigismund Augustus, retaining the Duchy of Courland for himself as a Polish-Lithuanian vassal. The Northern Crusade was over; the Northern Wars had begun.

The combatants

If Ermes marked the passing of one world, it was by no means clear what the contours of the new were to be. None of the states competing for influence in Livonia was powerful enough to dominate the region. The four major combatants were very different in size, population and political structure. Denmark and Sweden were inferior in population and economic resources compared to Poland-Lithuania and Muscovy, but enjoyed certain geographical advantages. The Scandinavian powers had been linked between 1397 and 1523 in the loose Union of Kalmar, yet their political institutions, despite similarities of nomenclature, operated in very different ways. Despite Sweden's success in breaking the Kalmar Union in 1523, there was little doubt that Denmark-Norway was undoubtedly the more important power at the accession of Frederik II (1559–96) from the Oldenburg dynasty. His inheritance included Greenland, Iceland, and the Baltic islands of Bornholm and Gotland. Through possession of the duchy of Holstein, which they held along with Schleswig, the Oldenburgs were also princes of the Holy Roman Empire and played an important political role in the Lower Saxon Circle. Most importantly, their possession of Scania, Blekinge and Halland on the southern Scandinavian peninsula delivered control of the Sound and provided, along with Norway, convenient launching-pads for attacks on Sweden, whose precarious outlet to the North Sea at Älvsborg was highly vulnerable.

Denmark's new prominence in European politics was largely due to its rapid development as a naval power. The Hanseatic League had dominated the Baltic in an age when merchant vessels could easily be converted into warships and could, to a large extent, defend themselves against privateers or pirates by sailing in convoy and carrying a complement of soldiers. Recent developments in naval technology, however, with the construction of ever-larger warships designed to carry a growing number of heavy guns, shifted

the balance decisively. The new warships were unsuitable for use as merchantmen, and Hanseatic merchants, who had largely protected themselves
in the past, could not afford the vast expense of maintaining dedicated
warships on a large scale.[9] The lucrative revenues from the Sound Dues
enabled the Oldenburgs to construct and maintain a substantial warfleet
which was the basis for their famous claim to *Dominium Maris Baltici* (control
of the Baltic Sea). By 1559, the fleet comprised 15 large and 21 smaller
ships.[10]

Denmark's geographical position and growing naval power involved it
in the wider world of European politics. The Oldenburgs were dynastically
linked with a number of north German princely families, and had long
sought to expand their bridgehead in the Empire. Although Lutheran,
Christian III held aloof from the Schmalkaldic Wars and maintained good
relations with emperor Charles V. Nevertheless, the Oldenburgs kept a keen
eye on the many vulnerable north German prince-bishoprics, with a view
to expanding towards the mouth of the Elbe, the one major river draining
the central European plain which flowed into the North Sea and therefore
allowed merchants to escape the Sound Dues; if the Oldenburgs could
secure Bremen and Hamburg their power would be substantially enhanced.
This involvement in North Sea politics brought dynastic links with the
Stuarts in the late sixteenth and early eighteenth century, and was to ensure
that Denmark's rulers always maintained horizons wider than the Baltic.

The Sound Dues, which were often raised unilaterally, ensured that
Denmark remained unpopular. The Oldenburgs not only claimed *Dominium
Maris Baltici*, but sought to extend their rights in the North Sea, maintaining
after 1553 that Danish control of Iceland and the Faroe Islands gave them the
right to levy tolls on ships sailing to Archangel, a claim they could not enforce
and which alienated England. Such assertiveness could prove dangerous,
for Denmark lacked the resources to play a leading role in European politics.
Its population was no more than 600,000 in 1600; even including Norway
and the rest of the Oldenburg empire, it was no more than 1.5 million.[11]
Denmark had no significant mineral resources, and its economy was heavily
dependent upon agriculture – primarily the export of grain and cattle – and
fishing, in particular round Iceland and Greenland; attempts to keep
foreign vessels out of these teeming waters merely added to the number of
Denmark's enemies, which included Lübeck and the Dutch.

Moreover, the Oldenburgs could not count on domestic support for their
more ambitious foreign adventures. The Sound Dues flowed into royal, not
state, coffers, and while this gave individual monarchs a measure of financial
independence, enabling them to conduct an independent foreign policy,
this frequently provoked suspicion in Denmark. In the Danish system of
government, known as *adelsvælden* ('noble rule'), the elective monarchy had

to take account of the views of the Danish Council, the *Rigsråd*, which in theory shared sovereignty with the Crown, representing the interests of the nation, and in particular of the nobility. The Danish Estates, the *Rigsdag*, met only occasionally, usually in moments of crisis, and the Council played the central role in political life. It was foreign policy which was to prove the greatest source of disagreement between king and council, something which was to limit Denmark's role in the Northern Wars before 1660: the Council was happy for the monarchy to maintain a powerful navy to protect Danish commerce, but resisted wider military ambitions.

Though its independence was well-established by 1558, Sweden still lived in Denmark's shadow. Lacking Denmark's easy access to Germany and western Europe, Sweden was very much a Baltic power lying on the fringes of Europe. It was poor and sparsely-populated: in 1500, the total population was barely 750,000, a substantial majority of whom were peasant farmers.[12] The climate was harsh, and vast areas in the north and in Finland were all but unpopulated. The growing-season was short, and the economy was chronically short of specie, with rents and taxes often being paid in kind. With only a narrow and precarious outlet to the North Sea, trade with Europe was difficult, and the fact that most Swedish ports were ice-bound throughout the winter made naval operations impossible for much of the year, while Danish possession of Gotland and Bornholm formed a potential barrier to Swedish links with Germany.

Yet Sweden did possess certain advantages, including its important natural and mineral resources, particularly timber, iron and copper. Although they were as yet poorly developed, these began to attract a series of European entrepreneurs who brought their expertise to bear on the primitive Swedish mining industry. Sweden's virtual monopoly of European copper production was to be lucrative in an age when Spain led the way in establishing a copper coinage, and copper formed a vital raw material for the European arms industry. Moreover, Sweden's remote geographical situation lent it important defensive advantages. Much of its long frontier with Muscovy ran through the empty wastelands of eastern Finland, Karelia and Ingria, heavily forested and cut through by a vast network of lakes and rivers, which made land-based operations extremely difficult, as Ivan IV found during the 1554–7 war. For all that Denmark was to prove that it was relatively easy to take Älvsborg and cut Sweden off from the North Sea, Sweden's growing navy, which numbered 19 warships displacing 7,000 tons in 1560, represented an increasing threat.[13]

Sweden, like Denmark, had a consensual political system, but one which operated rather differently. Gustav Vasa, the Swedish nobleman who became king in 1523 after masterminding the destruction of the Kalmar Union, developed a populist form of government in which the *Riksdag*, composed of the four estates of nobles, clergy, burghers and free peasants, played a much more prominent role than its Danish counterpart. Thus although the narrow circle of noble families who dominated the Swedish Council (*Riksråd*) formed a powerful aristocratic force, there was always an alternative forum to which the monarchy could appeal, as it did in 1544, when Gustav Vasa persuaded the *Riksdag* to confirm the monarchy as hereditary, or in 1599, when his youngest son, duke Charles of Södermanland, secured its agreement for the deposition of his nephew Sigismund. Over the next 150 years, the *Riksdag* was to play a vital role in sanctioning Sweden's military adventures and agreeing to the taxes and other measures necessary to sustain them.

Sweden and Denmark faced formidable rivals in Poland-Lithuania and Muscovy, each of which far outstripped them in population and resources. Since the personal union of 1385–6, Poland-Lithuania had emerged as a dynamic multiple kingdom. Relatively untouched by the Black Death which devastated much of Europe in the fourteenth century, the population had continued to expand, perhaps doubling between 1300 and 1500, when it reached 7.5 million, rising to 11 million in 1650. The vast Jagiellon possessions, which covered over a million square kilometres in 1500, stretched from the Baltic in the north almost to the Black Sea in the south, incorporating modern Belarus and much of modern Ukraine. The favourable economic conjuncture from the late fifteenth century brought a rising standard of living and economic development to wide areas. The basis of the economic boom was the export trade in grain and raw material. The Polish-Lithuanian economy was dominated by agriculture; nevertheless the common stereotype of a primitive, backward society should be approached with caution. It is true that population density was low (6.6 per square kilometre in 1500, rising to 11.1 in 1650), and that the agricultural economy was increasingly dominated by serfdom, but population density was much higher in Poland than in the heavily-forested eastern lands or the steppelands of the Ukraine. Serfdom was by no means universal, and was in itself a rational economic response to the problems of agriculture in areas of low population density that was common to Europe east of the Elbe.

Moreover, despite the common perception that eastern Europe was poorly-urbanised, by the end of the sixteenth century Poland-Lithuania had more large cities than many European states: Danzig, whose population reached 50,000 by 1600, was wealthy and populous by any contemporary standard, but if Cracow (22,000), Lwów (20,000), Poznań (18–20,000), Elbing (15,000), Thorn (12,000), Warsaw (10–12,000) and Wilno (14,000) were not particularly large on the European scale, they were still substantial urban centres, and were growing in the early seventeenth century. If one judges urbanisation in eastern Europe by its own standards rather than those of more densely-populated western Europe, then the urban population was by no means negligible: most Polish town-dwellers lived in small settlements of 1–2,000 people; in 1578, 28 per cent of the population in Wielkopolska, 30 per cent in Małopolska and 18 per cent in Mazovia lived in towns; by 1600 the urban population of Royal Prussia reached 36.5 per cent. The creation of new towns continued throughout the sixteenth and early seventeenth centuries, with 300 being established between 1500 and 1650 in the Kingdom of Poland excluding the Ukraine.[14]

It is true that from the mid-sixteenth century cities played no direct part in the state's central political institutions, being excluded from participation in the central diet (the *Sejm*), and the principal local political assemblies, the dietines (*sejmiki*), except in Royal Prussia, where representatives of Danzig, Elbing and Thorn sat in the upper house of the *Landtag*, with the lesser cities represented in the lower house until 1662. Yet their formal exclusion from the most important political institutions did not mean they were without influence: Cracow (1493), Wilno (1568) and Lwów (1658) were granted noble status as corporate entities, and several cities had the right to participate in royal elections. The most important sent observers to sessions of the *Sejm*, which were held in public, and were often able to lobby effectively behind the scenes.

Poland-Lithuania remained a noble-dominated society, however, in which the state's most important institutions were exclusively noble. The *szlachta* (nobility) constituted 6–7.5 per cent of the population, although the proportion was substantially higher in certain areas, including Mazovia in Poland or Samogitia in Lithuania, and the political system rested from the mid-fifteenth century on the *sejmiki*, which increasingly strengthened their claims to scrutinise new legislation, and without whose consent the king could not summon the noble levy after 1454. By the 1490s, the bicameral *Sejm* had emerged, with an upper chamber, the Senate, composed of Catholic bishops, palatines (provincial governors), castellans and government ministers, and a lower chamber, the Chamber of Envoys, composed of envoys elected by the *sejmiki*. The emergence of the *Sejm* and the statute of *Nihil Novi* (1505), by which no new legislation was to be passed without its consent, laid the foundations of a system which was gradually extended to Lithuania during the sixteenth century, before the Union of Lublin (1569) created a common *Sejm* for what was henceforth known as the Commonwealth of the Two Nations. This principle of consensus was to provide a potent weapon – if a double-edged one – in the first phase of the Northern Wars.

Muscovy, the new Commonwealth's major rival, was also undergoing a period of rapid change. Its population and economic performance are difficult to evaluate, partly owing to the relative scarcity of useful sources, and partly because of the habit of historians of speaking of a 'Russian' economy in the sixteenth and seventeenth centuries according to the borders of the nineteenth: the nationalist Great Russian assumption that the lands of modern Belarus and Ukraine are eternally parts of Russia is still alive and well.[15] During the fifteenth century, Muscovy emerged as the most powerful of the northern Russian principalities, gradually absorbing its rivals and expanding from under 47,000 km^2 in 1300 to 430,000 km^2 in 1462 and 2,800,000 km^2 in 1533. Estimates of its population in its contemporary borders range from as low as 2–3 million to as high as 9–10 million in 1550; a figure of 6–6.5 million at a density of 4–4.5 per square kilometre is perhaps more likely. Whatever the reality, the population had expanded three- to fourfold in the fifteenth century, and continued to grow rapidly thereafter, partly through the conquest of vast territories in the south and east, and partly through natural growth.[16] By 1510, the last remnants of Tatar control had been swept away, while the absorption of Novgorod and Pskov had established Muscovy on the Gulf of Finland. Muscovite goods flowed westwards through Riga, Reval and Narva, on the other side of the river from which the Muscovites constructed the town of Ivangorod.

Muscovy's political system was very different from those of its rivals, and west Europeans were struck by what they took to be the despotic power enjoyed by its rulers. The destruction of much of the autonomy of the appanage princes in the fifteenth century had certainly increased the tsar's power, and Muscovy lacked the independent institutions of self-government which formed the basis of the Polish-Lithuanian system, yet it would be a mistake to view its political system as the embodiment of tyrannical domination by one man. Muscovy was undergoverned in comparison to other contemporary states, and its rapid territorial expansion brought significant problems of control. Despite the rapidity of this expansion, Muscovite politics retained much of the face-to-face quality that had been their hallmark when Muscovy had been one of many small Russian principalities under Mongol domination. The system was dominated by a small, closely-knit network of boyar (aristocratic) families, in which kinship groupings were the most important focus of loyalty alongside the prince. Despite the political upheavals which regularly punctuated Muscovite political life, it was a system which favoured cooperation, not conflict, and the relative stability of the boyar elite over several centuries is striking.[17]

The boyars had originally formed the military retinue of the Muscovite princes. The success of the tsars, as the Grand Dukes began calling themselves from the late fifteenth century, was dependent upon the service they offered their elites and the rewards that this service brought. Despite Muscovy's great potential wealth, the vast distances involved in bringing agricultural and forest products to foreign markets, and the chronic shortage of labour in a land where population density was even lower than in Poland-Lithuania, ensured that profitability was marginal and Muscovy's elites had to supplement their agricultural pursuits with service, which brought rewards in cash, or grants of populated land. The power of a state whose growing bureaucracy kept increasingly detailed lists of servitors and estates, was useful to middling and petty servitors in the eternal battle to ensure the supply of labour without which land was worthless. The state played a central role in developing and policing the institution of serfdom between the late fifteenth century and the completion of the legal framework in 1649.

Sixteenth-century Muscovite society was based on a complex ranking system in which an individual's status (*chin*) depended partly on birth and partly on his military or administrative service record. Servitors were divided into hereditary servitors (*sluzhilye liudi po otechestvu*) who ranged from the boyars at the top through the *dvorianstvo* in the middle to those at the bottom of the pile, the *deti boiarskie* (literally 'children of the boyars') who served from provincial towns, and non-hereditary servitors (*sluzhilye liudi po priboru*).[18] The system of place (*mestnichestvo*) was the essential regulator of social and official life, documented in huge official registers which minutely detailed lineage and made possible the elaborate precedence disputes in which servitors upheld the honour of their families by refusing to serve under anyone whose ancestors had been inferior to their own.

The system was based on the increasingly close association of land tenure with service. Following the seizure of Novgorod in the late fifteenth century, much of its land was distributed in the form of conditional service estates (*pomest'ia*) to Muscovite servitors. Over the next two centuries, tsars sought consistently to erode the distinction between service (*pomest'e*) land and hereditary allodial land (*votchina*). Most hereditary servitors were dependent upon *pomest'ia*, whose distribution was carefully controlled by the Service Land Chancery (*Pomest'nyi Prikaz*); such was the system's success, however, that the demand for estates rapidly outstripped supply, as *pomeshchiki* had to provide for their sons. As with the Ottoman Empire, to whose system of *timar* lands the *pomest'e* system bore many similarities, the success of the system fuelled territorial expansion to satisfy demand. The conquest of Kazan and Astrakhan in the 1550s brought huge territories under Muscovite control, but they were sparsely populated. The real prize lay to the west, in the shape of Lithuania, which contained most of the 'Russias' to which the 'tsars of the all the Russias' laid claim, and Livonia, whose possession would give better access to European markets.

The Northern Wars

The collapse of the Livonian Order destabilised northeastern Europe, creating problems and opportunities for all local rulers. Denmark wished above all to protect its control of the Sound, and its claims to *Dominium Maris Baltici*. Christian III also had hopes of restoring the Kalmar Union, in which Denmark had played the leading role, or at the very least upholding Danish ascendancy over the upstart Vasas: in the 1550s, he began quartering the three crowns of Sweden in his armorial bearings. Gustav Vasa objected strongly to this assertion of superiority and the reminder that Denmark had not accepted the Union's dissolution. Thus was launched a battle over history and symbol which long bedevilled Danish-Swedish relations, strengthening Swedish determination to assert its independence, to break Denmark's economic and naval stranglehold in the Baltic, and to challenge it for control of the north Scandinavian wilderness. For Denmark, the situation in the eastern Baltic was not of such pressing concern, so long as it maintained control of the Sound. Yet Sweden could not ignore developments to the south of the Gulf of Finland: the 1554–7 war with Muscovy had demonstrated only too clearly the need to strengthen its eastern frontier. Thus Sweden was to press its claims in Estonia and Livonia far more resolutely than Denmark; this inevitably dragged it into conflict with Poland-Lithuania and Muscovy.

Although Poland-Lithuania and Muscovy both laid claim to Livonia and Estonia, the clash in Livonia reignited the long-established Lithuanian-Muscovite rivalry over the heritage of the Kievan Rus' state which had collapsed during the thirteenth-century Mongol invasions. Despite the conversion of Lithuania's rulers to Catholicism, the majority of the Jagiellons' subjects were Orthodox Slavs rather than Baltic Lithuanians, and the dominant ethos of the state gradually became Slavic. The official language was Chancery Ruthenian, written in cyrillic script, and the Orthodox Church remained a dynamic force which rejected the claims of the Metropolitan – from 1589 the Patriarch – of Moscow to superiority. Thus Lithuanian-Muscovite rivalry was as much – if not more – concerned with leadership of the eastern-Slavic, Orthodox world as with trade routes, and the wars between the Commonwealth and Muscovy over the next 150 years were to be fought on a wide front from Livonia in the north to the Ukraine in the south.[19] Each faced the constant threat of war on two fronts, since they bordered on the Ottoman Empire and its vassal states, in particular the Crimean Tatars, who launched devastating raids on an almost annual basis into the Ukraine or southern Muscovy. At several points the Islamic powers were to play a significant role in the Northern Wars.[20]

After 1558, northeastern Europe was a highly unstable region, with frequent and prolonged bouts of fighting and hardly a year of peace until 1667, which opened a period of relative calm, even if it did not restore stability, as the Scanian War (1674–9) and the rapid formation of the anti-Swedish coalition in the late 1690s amply demonstrated. The taxonomy of conflict is confusing to say the least, and there is no agreed nomenclature for the various wars which were fought. The term 'First Northern War' is applied to at least three quite separate conflicts: for German, Russian, Scandinavian and Anglo-Saxon scholars it traditionally refers to the war of 1655–60, although Viljanti eccentrically calls the 1554–7 Swedish-Muscovite war the 'First Northern War', and historians of Russia sometimes use the term for the Thirteen Years War between Muscovy and Poland-Lithuania (1654–67).[21] Yet such usage ignores the essential continuity of the series of wars between 1558 and 1721. Polish historians have usually applied the term 'Northern War' to the three periods of general conflict which occurred in northeastern Europe in this period. The First Northern War is taken to have begun with the collapse of the Polish-Muscovite truce in 1562, and ended with the peace of Stettin in 1570. The term 'Second Northern War' is applied to the conflict which opened with the Swedish invasion of Poland-Lithuania in July 1655, and which ended in 1660 with the treaties of Oliva and Copenhagen. Thus the Great Northern War (1700–21) is the Third Northern War. German scholarship is increasingly adopting this nomenclature following the cogent advocacy of Klaus Zernack, although he uses the term 'First Northern War' to cover the whole of what was traditionally labelled the Livonian War (1558–83).[22] This study will adopt Zernack's nomenclature, limiting the appellation 'Northern War' to the three major conflicts which saw the involvement of three or more of the leading Baltic powers, while recognising that the numerous bilateral conflicts between 1558 and 1721 formed part of the Northern Wars in a more general sense.

The importance of the Northern Wars for modern European history is self-evident. The destruction of Sweden's Baltic empire and the eclipse of Poland-Lithuania secured Russia's position as a great power and transformed the European states system. Although Sweden made several efforts after the 1721 peace of Nystad to recapture some of what it had lost, it was never in a position thereafter seriously to challenge the position of Russia, which was sealed with the partitions of Poland-Lithuania (1772–95) and the conquest of Finland (1809). The brief conflicts after Nystad were merely a postscript, and 1721 was a date of as much significance in European history as 1648, when the treaty of Westphalia established a new international power-system in central Europe. Yet if, as Zernack argues, the period 1558–1721 forms a vital and coherent epoch in the history of northeastern Europe,[23] there is a shortage of synthetic treatments in any language. This is hardly surprising given the complexity of studying a region containing so many cultural, linguistic, religious and national borderlands. Most work on the Northern Wars has been confined within the narrow bounds of inward-looking national history. While there is a vast amount of material in several languages devoted to individual aspects of the wars, few have attempted an overview, and the general works that exist sketch in broad outlines. The situation is little better with regard to individual conflicts: the number of syntheses of even the more important of these wars is surprisingly few; most of those that do exist are one-sided and outdated, and have long been overtaken by detailed research. If there are several nineteenth-century studies, now supplemented by Jensen's account, of the Nordic Seven Years War (1563–70), these are essentially concerned with the fighting on the Swedish-Danish front, and there is no monograph in any language which deals with the First Northern War (1558–83) as a whole.[24] Estonian and Latvian accounts of the Livonian war tend to concentrate heavily on the first phase, from 1558 until 1561, even when they claim to cover the whole conflict.[25] There is no satisfactory modern account of the Second Northern War or the Thirteen Years War between Poland-Lithuania and Muscovy,[26] or the Great Northern War.

The situation is worse with regard to works in English. History, it is often suggested, is written by the winners. Yet losers also write history; they just don't get translated. Thus Anglo-Saxon historiography is dominated by accounts of the period from the Swedish viewpoint in the seventeenth century, and from the Russian viewpoint in the eighteenth.[27] Otherwise, anglophones only have access to partial accounts of individual aspects and episodes. Thanks to Michael Roberts, Ragnhild Hatton and Anthony Upton, much of Sweden's achievement in the period is familiar, but even here the coverage is patchy. The towering figures of Gustav Adolf and Charles XII have attracted most attention, but the crucial period between Gustav Adolf's death in 1632 and the accession of Charles XI in 1660 is all but ignored. There is a great deal available in English on Russia, but historians have often displayed more interest in domestic than foreign policy, and the seventeenth century has been relatively neglected. With regard to Poland and Denmark, anglophones have only been able to catch glimpses of the rich native historiographies of the period.

It is vital, however, to look at the experience of the losers as well as the victors. The domination of nineteenth- and twentieth-century European politics by Russia and Germany has too often persuaded historians to assume that their rise, the eclipse of Poland-Lithuania and the failure of Sweden to maintain its great-power status were inevitable. This view, originally fuelled by nineteenth-century German and Russian nationalist historians with their teleological vision of the destiny of certain supposedly historic nations, was subsequently underpinned by the equally teleological insights of materialist historians, who argued that Russia's expansion to its 'natural' geographic frontiers on the Baltic was predetermined: control of the mouths of the Baltic rivers could not long remain in non-Russian hands, and economic forces would sooner or later drive Russia to the Baltic coast.[28] Such views, which treat the German and Russian 'nations' as historical absolutes, peoples destined to rise and dominate, rather than historical constructs which developed and changed over time, are all too prevalent. Why Germans and Russians rather than Poles, Danes or Swedes should be so destined is not deemed worthy of explanation.[29] As late as 1700 it was by no means evident that Russia would eclipse Poland-Lithuania; neither was it obvious that Poland-Lithuania was to lose control of its Baltic coastline: the 'German' inhabitants of Royal Prussia remained loyal to the Commonwealth and resisted incorporation into Brandenburg-Prussia throughout the seventeenth and eighteenth centuries.[30]

Materialist explanations are equally unsatisfactory, especially those developed in the Soviet Union, where Marxist-Leninist materialism was in thrall to a Great Russian nationalism as mystical and chauvinistic as anything developed under the tsars. This was no doubt necessary, for it is by no means obvious why blind economic forces should have favoured one combatant over another: why, for example, should economic necessity determine that Russia won control of Riga and Reval, but not that Poland-Lithuania should hold on to Danzig, of critical importance to Polish trade, or to Riga which was more the outlet for Lithuanian than Muscovite trade? Such questions were not addressed: Poland-Lithuania was dismissed as reactionary; Russia was declared 'progressive', though why Polish 'feudalism' was reactionary, while Russian 'feudalism' was 'progressive' was never explained. The unfortunate result of this conjunction of dogmatic materialism and nationalist fervour is that many Soviet accounts of the wars, especially those written under Stalin, are worthless chauvinist rants. Much of the substantial work on the Baltic wars carried out by Soviet scholars consists of traditional diplomatic history, in which personalities play the central role, usually being judged for their perspicacity (or lack of it) in recognising the direction of 'objective' historical forces.[31] There was, for example, a great deal of attention devoted to the problem of whether Ivan IV was a forerunner of Peter I (1682–1725) in having good mercantilist reasons for his Livonian wars, and many passionate attempts to refute those who argued he was more concerned with honour, prestige and historical claims than trade.[32]

This book attempts to dispel these mystical, teleological visions, and to provide a basic guide to the complexities of this long series of wars. It is not a narrative account, and will not concern itself unduly with the reasons for the outbreak and continuation of war at the level of statecraft and diplomacy; rather it will look at how the wars were fought, and the ways in which the very different social and political structures of northeastern Europe coped with the new demands of warfare. For it is perhaps here, rather than in concentrating on the supposed genius of the traditional heroes of the period – Ivan IV, Gustav Adolf or Peter I – that the historian should seek the reasons for the outcome of this long period of fighting. By 1721, it was manifest that certain states had proved more able to adapt to the military demands posed by fighting in conditions very different from those of western Europe. In the new military world Poland-Lithuania failed to keep up with its neighbours, paying the ultimate price between 1772 and 1795, while Sweden showed in the early eighteenth century that its military capacity was stretched to the very limits by the need to defend the empire it had won in the seventeenth. From the wreckage of conflict, Russia emerged victorious. To explain why this should have occurred is the main aim of this study.

A Military Revolution?

Peter Englund begins his book *Ofredsår*, based on the experiences of the Swedish soldier, artist and diarist Erik Dahlberg in the 1640s and 1650s, with a vivid description of the battle of Warsaw (28–30 July 1656). In a chapter entitled 'the last eighty metres of the Middle Ages' he describes the charge of Aleksander Połubiński's hussars against the left wing of the Swedish and Brandenburg forces on the second day of the battle. He depicts in loving detail their magnificent appearance, with their long lances, their glistening helmets and breastplates, the tiger, leopard and lion skins worn by the officers, and their most famous accoutrement: the eagle and heron-feathers, mounted on wooden frames fixed to their backs, which rustled and fluttered when they charged. Yet for all their finery the hussars were, according to Englund, a hopelessly anachronistic relic of a form of warfare that reached back over a millennium. The tactic of the cavalry charge was long outmoded, and the hussars were merely the magnificent remnants of a long-dead tradition, kept alive by a moribund noble-dominated society. The future was standing in front of them, in the shape of the serried ranks of professional Swedish and Brandenburg infantry and reiters; commoners, whose services were paid for by the toil of good honest burghers. Experienced and well-drilled, these disciplined modern soldiers loosed coordinated volleys which ploughed bloody furrows through the glittering ranks of the hussars. Within a few short minutes, the spectacle was at an end. Połubiński's men took to their heels, leaving shattered, twitching piles of men and horses on the dusty Vistula plain. Discipline had conquered individualism; modern technology had drawn a firm, black line under the Middle Ages.[33]

Or had it? This is not yet the place for an analysis of Połubiński's charge, the results of which were much as Englund describes them. Nevertheless, his account has serious shortcomings. It draws on his expert knowledge of the Swedish army in its age of greatness, which he uses to great effect in his classic account of the battle of Poltava.[34] Yet the set of assumptions which it contains is symptomatic of a fundamental problem which has bedevilled the historiography of warfare in eastern Europe. Englund's account of the battle is seen entirely from one side, and is based wholly on Swedish or German sources; it therefore reflects their prejudices and preconceptions. In describing the Polish forces, he is content to rely on tired stereotypes of valiant, romantic Poles locked in a chivalric timewarp, oblivious to techno-logical progress and convinced that courage and cold steel could overcome the greatest odds. The tradition which presents the Poles as military Don Quixotes, and reduces Polish military history to the hopeless attack on Wellington's guns at Somosierra in 1808 and legends about Polish cavalry charging German tanks in 1939 is again deployed.

Englund's account aptly demonstrate the dangers of relying on only one side of the story. For the hussars were no outmoded, archaic formation, or the last remnants of the Middle Ages. Far from it: hussars had only appeared in the Polish army in the early sixteenth century, and their sophisticated techniques and weaponry were as much a response to the changes in con-temporary warfare as were those of the Swedish and Brandenburg infantry they faced at Warsaw. Each man was mounted on a relatively small, nimble, swift horse that was very different from the medieval charger or the slower, heavier mounts used by contemporary western reiters. Their principal weapon was the lance, which was about one-and-a-half metres longer than its medi-eval counterpart; this was possible because it was much lighter. Although strength was sacrificed for weight – lances frequently shattered on contact – this did not matter. They were designed to be decisive on first impact against either cavalry or the pikemen who are supposed to have ended the reign of the mounted knight on the European battlefield by 1560.[35]

The hussar was by no means helpless once his lance had shattered. He was also armed with a *koncerz* – a straight, pointed sword, rather like a rapier, but rigid and much longer; this was used as a kind of lance, held out and braced in front of the trooper. Each hussar also wielded a curved sabre with which they inflicted devastating slashing wounds, especially on unprotected infantry. Finally, many hussars carried bows. Far lighter than the cumber-some firearms used by western cavalry, they were also far more effective: bows could be fired at the gallop by a skilled rider; they could be fired in any direction, and they could be fired over the heads of the front ranks of a formation, which a firearm could not. A bow was more likely to hit the target than a heavy carbine or pistol, which were only useful in close mêlées.

The hussars proved in a series of encounters that they were far from an obsolete force; indeed they had solved many of the problems with regard to the deployment of cavalry which western armies had failed even to address. Yet all too often, the predominance of cavalry in Polish-Lithuanian and Muscovite armies is taken – as Englund takes it – to be a sign of backwardness. If further explanation is felt necessary, then geography is usually deployed: the great, open plains of eastern Europe were, it is suggested, terrain ideally suited to cavalry; moreover, the nature of their enemies in the east – the Tatars and the Turks – required the use of cavalry. In fact, much of the terrain of northeastern Europe, while indeed flat, was either bog or forest in the early modern period, neither of which was particularly suited to the deployment of cavalry, and while it is true that Tatars fought almost exclusively on horseback, Turkish armies relied heavily on infantry and firepower.

The assumption that eastern warfare was primitive has meant that the Northern Wars have largely been ignored in the debate over the Military Revolution, launched by Michael Roberts in the 1950s and given a new lease of life by Geoffrey Parker in the 1970s.[36] Most accept Parker's verdict that 'the wars fought on the eastern half of the Great European Plain ... remained deeply resistant to military innovation', and therefore accord them minimal attention.[37] Eastern Europe, with its cavalry-based warfare and its relative lack of modern fortifications, is seen to have avoided the key changes at the heart of the Military Revolution: the eclipse of cavalry by infantry and the increasingly important role of siege warfare. According to Roberts these 'purely military developments, of a strictly technical kind, did exert a lasting influence upon society at large. They were the agents and auxiliaries of constitutional and social change; and they bore with them a main share of responsibility for the coming of the new world which was to be so very unlike the old.'[38]

It is worth pausing to consider Roberts's words, for many historians have ignored them, preferring to understand the Revolution as a purely military phenomenon, arguing over whether particular innovations – the pike, the musket, the countermarch, the angle bastion, the bayonet – revolutionised warfare, or suggesting that military change was evolutionary not revolutionary.[39] Yet such arguments miss the point: Roberts was concerned not with warfare as such, seeing changes in military technology – many of which had begun long before 1560 – as merely the precipitants of the true revolution, which was social and political: thus it was the advent of pike and musket, and the advantage they gave to infantry, which sounded the death-knell for old, noble-dominated social systems. Only monarchs and the state could afford the massive new armies which could be deployed once the dependence on scarce heavy cavalry was destroyed, or the huge siege-trains which shattered the medieval castles which had been the strongholds of the military aristocracy. As the expense of warfare grew exponentially, a new fiscal-military state emerged and new social groups – especially the urban middle classes – became ever more influential.

Even if one understands the Military Revolution in this sense, it still appears at first sight as if it bypassed eastern Europe. For if the theory can clearly be applied to the history of Sweden – Roberts's special field of expertise – it appears that Poland-Lithuania and Russia, even taking into account the reforms of Peter I, failed to undergo the transformation which Roberts saw at the heart of the Military Revolution: in 1720, let alone 1660, both remained noble-dominated societies whose economies were based on serfdom, despite importing a steady stream of western military experts. Even if Peter managed at last to harness modern technology and modern military techniques to Russia's vast human and natural resources, it did not transform Russian society, and although there were substantial changes in Russia's political system, the basic structure was left intact.

Thus historians of eastern European warfare in the early modern period, while accepting the centrality of western military technology to Russia's eventual victory in the Northern Wars, have largely ignored the debate on the Military Revolution. Since, in Marxism-Leninism, it is economic forces which decide the development of social and political systems, little attention was paid by scholars in the Soviet period to suggestions that social and political changes were brought about by the new demands of warfare. For Soviet historians, military structures were merely the reflection of the socio-economic structure in which they appeared; they could not play a central role in the transformation of that structure. Thus military history in the Soviet Union was relatively neglected, apart from a highly traditional re-counting of campaigns and battles, often merely to illustrate the eternal martial and patriotic qualities of the Russian people, with little analysis of the impact of military change on state and society. Even non-Soviet scholars have, until recently, ignored the debate. Richard Hellie has argued brilliantly that major social change in Russia – the rise of serfdom – was a direct result of military change, but his book was published before Parker relaunched the Military Revolution debate, and he relied on nineteenth-century Russian military historians for his account of western military change. Recent work has begun to address this problem, but much remains to be done.[40]

Yet it is important to look at eastern Europe for a true understanding of the nature of military change and its relationship to social and political change in the early modern period. For eastern Europe was not an ignorant backwater, and eastern Europeans knew a great deal throughout this period about western technological developments; why, then, did the Poles remain so wedded to cavalry, apparently spurning the infantry revolution? Why did it take so long for Russia to transform its army into an effective force? This book examines such questions in an attempt to gauge the impact of military change on the very different societies and political systems of the powers that fought the Northern Wars. It seeks to avoid writing the history of the region on the basis of assumptions derived from knowledge of the very different social, economic and military conditions of western Europe.

Notes

1 Gotthard Kettler to Jan Chodkiewicz, Dünamünde, 11.VIII.1560; *Quellen zur Geschichte des Untergangs livländischer Selbständigkeit aus dem schwedischen Reichsarchive zu Stockholm* C. Schirren (ed.) (Reval, 1865) pp. 279–80; B. Rüssow, *Chronica der Provintz Lyfflandt* (Riga, 1853) p. 60.

2 See E. Christiansen, *The Northern Crusades* (London, 1980) pp. 219–53; M. Burleigh, *Prussian Society and the German Order* (Cambridge, 1984).

3 D. Kirby, *Northern Europe in the Early Modern Period. The Baltic World 1492–1772* (London, 1990) p. 7.

4 J. Topolski, 'Sixteenth-century Poland and the turning-point in European economic development' in J.K. Fedorowicz (ed.), *A Republic of Nobles* (Cambridge, 1982) p. 84.

5 A. Wyczański, *Studia nad folwarkiem szlacheckim w Polsce w latach 1500–1580* (Warsaw, 1960) p. 222; A. Mączak, *Między Gdańskiem a Sundem* (Warsaw, 1972) table 25, p. 81; A. Attman, *The Russian and Polish Markets in International Trade 1500–1650* (Göteborg, 1973) p. 62.

6 Denmark could effectively block the alternative passages through the Great and Little Belts, and few tried these routes.

7 C.E. Hill, *The Danish Sound Dues and the Command of the Baltic* (Durham, NC, 1926) p. 52.

8 K. Rasmussen, *Die livländische Krise 1554–1561* (Copenhagen, 1973) pp. 19–22.

9 J. Glete, *Navies and Nations* (Stockholm, 1993) I pp. 104–6; 110–11.

10 J.H. Barfod, 'Den danske orlogsflåde før 1560' *HTD* (1994) pp. 261–70.

11 P.D. Lockhart, *Denmark in the Thirty Years' War, 1618–1648* (Cranbury, NJ, 1996) pp. 28–9.

12 M. Roberts, *The Early Vasas* (Cambridge, 1968) p. 29.

13 Glete, *Navies* p. 134.

14 E. Cieślak (ed.), *Historia Gdańska* II (Gdańsk, 1982) p. 444; M. Bogucka, H. Samsonowicz, *Dzieje miast i mieszczaństwa w Polsce przedrozbiorowej* (Wrocław, 1986) pp. 332, 361, 364, 370–2; M. Łowmiańska, *Wilno przed najazdem moskiewskim 1655 roku* (Wilno, 1929) p. 77.

15 When Attman talks of the 'Russian', as distinct from the 'Polish' market, for example, he explicitly includes modern Belarus and the Ukraine, which were then part of Poland-Lithuania: Attman, *The Russian* pp. 44, 184. Given the importance ascribed to economic motives in the formation of policy by many historians, it is important to reject such anachronistic assumptions: as Tiberg rightly observes, it was Lithuania, not Muscovy, which was cut off from the Baltic in 1558: E. Tiberg, *Zur Vorgeschichte des livländischen Krieges* (Uppsala, 1984) pp. 8, 11, 14.

16 G. Alef, 'Muscovite military reforms in the second half of the fifteenth century' *FOG* 18 (1973) p. 84; R. Hellie, *Enserfment and Military Change in Muscovy* (Chicago, Ill., 1971) pp. 21, 305, n. 9; C. Goehrke, 'Zum Problem von Bevölkerungsziffer

und Bevölkerungsdichte des Moskauer Reiches im 16. Jahrhundert' *FOG* 24 (1973) p. 85.

17 For good introductions to the Muscovite system on the eve of the Northern Wars see N.S. Kollmann, *Kinship and Politics* (Stanford, Cal., 1987) and R. Crummey, *The Formation of Muscovy 1304–1613* (London, 1987).

18 See J.L. Keep, *Soldiers of the Tsar* (Oxford, 1985) pp. 21–37 and V.A. Kivelson, *Autocracy in the Provinces* (Stanford, Cal., 1996) pp. 26–45.

19 Tiberg's polemical attempt to deny that Muscovite policy had anything to do with trade is overstated, but provides a useful corrective to those who regard trade as the sole motivating force for the war: Tiberg, *Zur Vorgeschichte* pp. 1–18, 208–14.

20 Thus it is more appropriate to refer to the 'Northern Wars' rather than the 'Baltic Wars'. This terminology reflects the contemporary division of Europe into northern and southern (rather than western and eastern). This study will adopt Klaus Zernack's concept of 'northeastern Europe' to designate a region which is wider than the Baltic, including Scandinavia, Poland-Lithuania and European Russia: K. Zernack, 'Grundfragen der Geschichte Nordosteuropas' in Zernack, *Nordosteuropa* (Lüneburg, 1993) pp. 9–22.

21 A. Viljanti, *Gustav Vasas ryska krig 1554–1557* (Stockholm, 1957) I p. 9.

22 K. Zernack, 'Schweden als europäische Grossmacht der Frühen Neuzeit' in Zernack, *Nordosteuropa* p. 208, and 'Der Große Nordische Krieg' ibid. p. 159; idem., *Polen und Rußland. Zwei Wege in der europäischen Geschichte* (Berlin, 1994) pp. 166, 178.

23 Idem. 'Das Zeitalter der nordischen Kriege als frühneuzeitliche Geschichtsepoche' *ZHF* 1 (1974) pp. 54–79.

24 G.O.F. Westling, *Det nordiska sjuårskrigets historia* (Stockholm, 1879–80); O. Vaupell, *Den nordiske syvaarskrig 1563–1570* (Copenhagen, 1891); L.G.T. Tidander, *Nordiska sjuårskrigets historia* (Westervik, 1892); F.P. Jensen, *Danmarks konflikt med Sverige 1563–1570* (Copenhagen, 1982); L.G.T. Tidander, *Krigsföretagen i Livland under Erik XIV:s regering* (Westervik, 1891); S. Arnell, *Bidrag till belysning av den baltiska fronten under det nordiska sjuårskriget 1563–1570* (Stockholm, 1977).

25 The most detailed Estonian account is H. Kruus, *Vene-Liivi sõda (1558–1561)* (Tartu, 1924). H. Palamets, *Luvi sõda 1558–1583* (Tartu, 1973) and J. Zutis, *Livonijas karš (1558–1582)* (Riga, 1949) are very brief.

26 The short account by Sahanovich is a brave attempt; as it is written in Belarus'ian, however, its readership will remain small: H. Sahanovich, *Neviadomaia Vaina 1654–1667* (Minsk, 1995).

27 S. Oakley, *War and Peace in the Baltic 1560–1790* (London, 1992) provides an unsatisfactory narrative account; his perspective is essentially Scandinavian, and the work is error-strewn. Kirby, *Northern Europe* provides an excellent overview, but cannot devote too much space to war in a work of much broader scope. J. Lisk, *The Struggle for Supremacy in the Baltic 1600–1725* (London, 1967) and A. Stiles, *Sweden and the Baltic 1523–1721* (London, 1992) are non-specialist works based on limited secondary material in English.

28 For example W. Kirchner, *The Rise of the Baltic Question* (Newark, NJ, 1954) p. 105.

29 Kirchner, like many historians of Russia, ignores Polish historiography; where he does mention Poland he reflects the prejudices of nineteenth-century German and Russian nationalists.

30 See K. Friedrich, *The Other Prussia: Poland, Prussia and Liberty, 1569–1772* (Cambridge, 2000).

31 There were some honourable exceptions, including B.N. Floria and L.V. Zaborovskii, but the best Russian account of the early phases of the Northern Wars remains G.V. Forsten, *Baltiiskii vopros v XVI–XVII st. (1544–1648)* 2 vols (St Petersburg, 1893–4).

32 See S. Svensson, *Den merkantila bakgrunden till Rysslands anfall på den livländska ordensstaten 1558* (Lund, 1951).

33 P. Englund, *Ofredsår. Om den svenska stormaktstiden och en man i dess mitt* (Stockholm, 1993) pp. 32–46.

34 Idem. *The Battle of Poltava* (London, 1992).

35 As late as the 1660s, Andrzej Maksymilian Fredro stressed that it was important that the lance was longer than infantry pikes.

36 M. Roberts, 'The Military Revolution 1560–1660', reprinted in Roberts, *Essays in Swedish History* (Minneapolis, 1967) pp. 195–225; G. Parker, *The Military Revolution* (2nd edn, Cambridge, 1996). See also C.J. Rogers (ed.), *The Military Revolution Debate* (Boulder, Col., 1995).

37 Parker, *Military Revolution* p. 37.

38 Roberts, 'Military Revolution' pp. 195–6.

39 Sceptics have discerned a series of military revolutions from the Middle Ages to the Napoleonic era, leading Rogers to propose a model of 'punctuated equilibrium evolution' in an attempt to reconcile the supporters of evolutionary and revolutionary models of military change: Rogers, 'The Military Revolutions of the Hundred Years War' in Rogers (ed.), *Military Revolution Debate* pp. 76–7.

40 In *Enserfment* Hellie talks of a 'gunpowder revolution', but does not engage with the idea of the Military Revolution. He mentions the concept in a later article, but does not examine the real problems: Hellie, 'Warfare, changing military technology and the evolution of Muscovite society' in J.A. Lynn (ed.), *Tools of War: Instruments, Ideas and Institutions of Warfare, 1445–1871* (Urbana, Ill., 1990) pp. 74–99. See M. Poe, 'The consequences of the Military Revolution in Muscovy: a comparative perspective' *CSSH* 38 (1996) pp. 603–18 and the excellent discussion in C.B. Stevens, *Soldiers on the Steppe* (DeKalb, Ill., 1995).

CHAPTER TWO

The First Northern War

The military challenge

Whatever else was to blame for the collapse of Livonian resistance after 1558, it was not ignorance of western military technology. By 1500, the Order controlled sixty castles in Livonia, while there were a further fifty in the archbishopric of Riga and the bishoprics of Courland, Dorpat and Ösel-Wieck. They provided the base from which the German colonists ruled the native populations and organised defence against external threats. Livonia's rulers had close ties to northern Germany and the Netherlands, where gunpowder technology developed rapidy in the fifteenth century, and were far from oblivious to the new problems posed for fortification systems by the development of increasingly sophisticated firearms. Although many castles were in decay by 1558, including the vital strongpoint of Dünaburg, considerable efforts had been made elsewhere.[1] Lais was one of a network of castles built or adapted after 1450, incorporating the massive, round towers with thick walls pierced by embrasures and musket loops which represented the north German solution to the problem of defence against cannon. There was a spate of building and reconstruction between 1494 and 1535, when the fortifications of Wenden, the Order's headquarters, and Riga were extensively altered. Reval built several gun-towers, including 'Kiek in de Kök', a massive six-storey cannon tower, and the Great Coast Gate, which contained a huge, squat roundel known as 'Fat Margaret'.[2] By 1560 Narva's fortifications included three angle-bastions, indicating that Italian influences had already reached the Baltic. Most important strongpoints were well armed: when Dorpat fell in July 1558, the Muscovites found 552 guns in the city armoury.[3]

It was not just the Livonians who had changed. By 1550, firearms had been widely adopted throughout eastern Europe; indeed one of the points at issue between the Livonians and Ivan IV was the attempt to block Muscovy's import of western arms and military experts.[4] The first documented use of firearms by the Poles was in 1383; in the same year the Lithuanians used guns at the siege of Troki.[5] The relative ineffectiveness of early firearms, however, prevented their widespread adoption, and it was not until the mid-fifteenth century that Polish infantry began to use handguns to any extent. The Polish-Lithuanian army which defeated the Muscovites at Orsha in September 1514, however, deployed field artillery and contained 3,000 infantry, many armed with firearms. Cavalry remained the basis of the Polish-Lithuanian army, and Polish deficiencies in artillery were revealed between 1519 and 1521 during the short war against the Teutonic Order; nevertheless, strenuous efforts were made thereafter to build up the artillery. In 1520, the office of Master of the Ordnance was created, and cannon-foundries were established at Cracow, Lwów and Wilno; by the 1550s, there were 245 guns in the Wilno arsenal.

Muscovy's development ran exactly parallel to its western neighbour. The first clear reference to the use of guns dates to 1380. Muscovite guns breached the walls of Fellin in 1481, by which time Muscovy was casting bronze cannon in substantial numbers. Nevertheless, most were deployed defensively, and were not usually taken on campaign. To meet the new threat posed by artillery, fortresses were transformed in the late fifteenth century: the Moscow Kremlin was remodelled between 1485 and 1495, as were the most important border strongpoints. Stone walls were thickened, towers pierced with embrasures and loopholes, and wooden pallisades doubled and reinforced with earth. The shape of fortresses was altered: Ivangorod was built on a modern square plan; altogether thirty new fortresses were built in the sixteenth century.[6] The field army was still largely composed of cavalry, raised largely among the *dvorianstvo* and *deti boiarskie*, officered by boyars. Although units of arquebusiers (*pishchal'niki*) had appeared in the early fifteenth century, they were not permanent formations. Following the failure of the 1549–50 Kazan campaign, Ivan initiated sweeping reforms. He established the *strel'tsy*, a permanent corps of 3,000 infantry raised from non-hereditary servitors, armed with arquebuses (and later muskets), which expanded steadily: there were already 13,000 at Połock in 1563.[7] The reforms soon brought results, as the new formations proved their worth in the capture of Kazan (1552) and Astrakhan (1556).

Thus when the Muscovites entered Livonia with a large siege-train in the summer of 1558, the Order was facing an enemy who conceded nothing to it in terms of military technology. The results were dramatic: fortress after fortress surrendered without a shot fired. Narva fell in May; Dorpat in July.

Despite the arrival of 1,200 *Landsknechte* from Germany in September, together with 100 gunners and supplies of powder and shot, the recapture of Wesenberg in October by a force of Livonian nobles, and a retaliatory Livonian raid which burnt and harried round Krosnogora, the Muscovites retained Narva and Dorpat and many lesser strongpoints.

Yet Ivan could not win the war, despite campaigns in 1559 and 1560 in which his armies devastated wide areas, capturing further important strongpoints, including Fellin, thought to be impregnable. Despite the crushing victory at Ermes (August 1560), they failed to capture Riga, Reval or Pernau, the most valuable prizes. Ivan could defeat the Order, but not the other powers who had become involved. Reval accepted Swedish overlordship in 1561; Riga was under Polish-Lithuanian protection from 1562; Courland was now a Polish-Lithuanian fief, and Sigismund Augustus had inserted garrisons into several important fortresses in central Livonia. Frederik II had accepted the Bishop of Ösel-Wieck's offer to sell his diocese to Denmark, grasping this opportunity to be rid of his troublesome younger brother Magnus, Duke of Holstein, who arrived on Ösel in 1560. Magnus immediately demonstrated his unique talent for dubious political manoeuvre by purchasing the bishopric of Courland – Frederik refused to pay the bill – and schemed to expand into Harrien and Wierland, which won him the enmity of Sweden's new king Erik XIV (1560–8). Frederik may have regarded his brother's actions as unwise, but did not wish to see Sweden establish a bridgehead in Estonia: in July 1561 he protested at Sweden's occupation of Reval, claiming it violated Denmark's historical claim to Estonia.

It briefly seemed as if the uneasy military stalemate might lead to an agreement on partition, but tentative negotiations soon collapsed and the conflict rapidly spread along older fault-lines. Estonia was but one issue among many souring relations between Erik and Frederik. Historians have often blamed Frederik, accusing him of belligerency, but it is hard to see Erik as an injured innocent. Relations had been deteriorating since the 1550s, when a large number of border disputes had disturbed relations, and the vexed issue of the Three Crowns had arisen. Neither man was much given to compromise, and a Swedish blockade of Narva in an attempt to force trade through Reval angered both Denmark and Lübeck, who signed an alliance in June 1563. At the end of the month, a Danish squadron clashed with a much larger Swedish fleet off Bornholm; three Danish ships were captured and taken in triumph to Stockholm. In August, Frederik declared war.[8]

Meanwhile, a sharpening of relations between Lithuania and Poland, which were only linked tenuously by the person of the childless Sigismund Augustus, gave Ivan hope that Muscovy might benefit. Poles were not as concerned as Lithuanians with Livonia, but increasing Polish pressure for a closer political relationship to ensure that the union would not collapse on Sigismund Augustus's death was resented by many Lithuanians. There was some support for an offer of the Lithuanian crown to Ivan; the broaching of this idea by Ivan himself may well have been an attempt to play for time. Whether or not Ivan took it seriously, he made no move against Lithuania in 1561; it was only after the steady build-up of Lithuanian forces in Livonia that he acted, rejecting Sigismund Augustus's 1562 attempt to extend the truce which was to expire that year. After a Muscovite raid on Witebsk, Muscovite and Lithuanian forces clashed along the border and Ivan thrust not into Livonia, but against Połock, which fell after a two-week siege in February 1563.

In 1563, therefore, fighting opened on two new fronts, far from Livonia. Yet Livonia remained an important theatre of conflict, and it was Livonia which ensured that the war became a general conflict, with the emergence of two loose diplomatic alignments. Despite his best efforts, it proved impossible for Sigismund Augustus to avoid war with Sweden. Erik wished to extend Swedish control in Estonia beyond the narrow bridgehead of Reval, while the independent policy of Erik's brother John, Duke of Finland, an active supporter of a Polish alliance, did little to help the cause he sought to promote. Although Erik allowed John to marry Sigismund Augustus's sister Katarzyna in April 1562, his attempt to persuade Riga to accept Swedish protection was not appreciated by Sigismund Augustus; neither was the Swedish seizure of Pernau in June. John's wedding, celebrated in October, did nothing to improve relations. John angered Erik by lending Sigismund Augustus 120,000 riksdalers, receiving seven Livonian castles as security; he was arraigned before the *Riksdag*, found guilty of plotting against Erik and, after a brief siege of his Finnish stronghold of Åbo, was captured and imprisoned in August 1563. Sigismund Augustus immediately turned to Lübeck and Denmark, proposing an alliance against Sweden which was finalised in October 1563.

Yet these alliances brought little close cooperation. Sigismund Augustus made no real effort to draw Swedish troops from Scandinavia to Livonia, while Erik's hopes of cooperation with Muscovy were cruelly disappointed. In 1565, after two crushing Lithuanian victories at Czasniki and on the Ula river the previous year and the defection of prince Andreii Kurbskii, one of his ablest commanders, Ivan's fragile mental health collapsed. Withdrawing to Aleksandrova Sloboda, he launched a blistering attack on the boyars and clergy for having betrayed him, and announced he was establishing a separate court and administration (*Oprichnina*). He divided Muscovy into two parts, the *Oprichnina* and *Zemshchina*, each with separate armies and administrations. Over the next seven years, Muscovy descended into political chaos, as Ivan's *oprichniki* carried out a series of bloody purges. Metropolitan Filip was deposed; in 1570 Novgorod was sacked and thousands of its inhabitants slaughtered. It was not until the summer of 1571, when the political chaos and division of Muscovy's armed forces allowed the Crimean Tatars to sack Moscow, that Ivan changed course, liquidating the *Oprichnina* in 1572. Although Ivan's interest in Livonia revived in 1569–70, it was too late to save Erik.

For Erik's increasingly bizarre behaviour, which culminated in his murder of several members of the Sture family in May 1567, led to his deposition in 1568 by his brother, who ascended the throne as John III (1568–92). John's Lithuanian wife and long association with Finland had convinced him that Muscovy was a greater threat than Poland-Lithuania, and he began the negotiations which led to peace with Poland and Denmark at Stettin (December 1570). Ivan now looked for support to Frederik's maverick brother Magnus, who was attracted by Ivan's 1569 approach offering him the chance to rule Livonia and Estonia as Muscovy's vassal. Magnus was declared King of Livonia in June 1570; all he received as a basis for his new realm was Oberpahlen, although in August he began an unsuccessful eight-month siege of Reval at the head of a Muscovite army.[9]

The siege of Reval opened a new phase of the Livonian War. With Erik's overthrow and the end of the Nordic Seven Years War in December 1570, Ivan faced the threat of a Polish-Swedish rapprochement. In September 1572 Muscovite troops crossed into Livonia, capturing Weissenstein in January 1573. The campaign was accompanied by substantial devastation, but concern about the southern front meant that for the rest of 1573 and into 1574, Ivan was content to defend his positions against an abortive Swedish attempt to besiege Wesenberg; only in 1575 did the tempo pick up. The Muscovites again appeared under the walls of Reval, although there was no attempt to besiege it; instead, a Muscovite force captured Pernau from the Poles in July. Further Muscovite devastation in 1576 was followed by the most substantial campaign of the war.

Between January and March 1577, the Muscovites conducted another unsuccessful siege of Reval as the prelude to a summer onslaught led by Ivan personally. The Transylvanian prince Stefan Batory (1576–86), the new king of Poland-Lithuania, was engaged in a brief war with Danzig over the city's privileges, and was unable to respond to desperate Livonian pleas for help. Ivan crossed the border with 30,000 men; after taking a series of fortresses, he attacked Dünaburg, whose small Polish garrison capitulated without a fight. Kokenhausen attempted to ward off its fate by putting itself under Magnus's protection. Ivan, annoyed that Magnus had not consulted him, sent a strong force to take the town. Its German commanders did not wish to surrender; they were executed for their pains, and a powerful garrison of 1,000 was left in this key fortress guarding the road into Courland

and Lithuania. In late August, Ivan arrived at Wenden, the Order's former capital, where he arrested Magnus, who had been conducting a desultory siege. The town was soon taken, but the castle held out; while Ivan was inspecting its defences, he was narrowly missed by a cannonball, an incident which enraged him, provoking a promise of a terrible fate for the defenders. The garrison did not wait to discover whether he was serious. Three hundred men, women and children locked themselves in a tower and blew themselves up with four tons of gunpowder.[10]

The symbolic significance of Wenden's fall was immense; thereafter there was little resistance. Only Reval, Riga and Ösel held out, but Ivan was unable to secure his gains. After settling with Danzig in December, Batory turned his attention to Livonia, looking to Sweden for aid. John III, who had long sought a Polish alliance, had clung doggedly to his toehold in Livonia, sending significant aid to Reval in early 1577. Despite the continued presence of a 22,000-strong Muscovite force the new allies gradually won the upper hand. In November the Lithuanians recaptured Dünaburg by subterfuge; Wenden soon followed, and a Muscovite attempt to retake it in February 1578 was beaten back. Meanwhile, the Swedes took the offensive, attacking Leal, Lode and Hapsal and devastating the area round Pernau; they brought so many cattle back to Reval they were impossible to sell.[11] In July, they burned the Dorpat suburbs, defeated a Muscovite force near Pernau and raided Muscovy itself, penetrating as far as Novgorod.

The greatest shock was yet to come. In September 1578, a Muscovite army – Rüssow claims it was 18,000 strong – marched on Wenden, pausing only to take Oberpahlen from the Swedes. A small force of 5–6,000 Swedes, Poles and Germans improvised an attack on the Muscovite besiegers. The Muscovite cavalry was driven off, leaving the infantry exposed in the trenches. Casualties were substantial; several high-ranking boyars, over twenty guns and a thousand horses were captured, and the entire Swedish infantry rode back to Reval in triumph; as Kettler punningly observed, Wenden was a turning point.[12]

Ivan's failure to secure his 1577 conquests reveals the problems faced by all sides in the Livonian War. For the fighting had demonstrated the limitations of the new technology. It was relatively easy to capture castles, towns and cities, most of which had decayed or obsolete fortifications, but they were difficult to hold once an enemy returned in force. Infantry was precious, and neither Ivan nor his enemies had enough experienced, trained men to garrison the fortresses they captured; thus castles and towns swapped back and forth between the combatants at regular intervals. The Muscovites could bring significant forces on campaign, but most of the army consisted of *pomest'e* cavalry, who returned to their estates at the end of the campaign. The speciality of these forces was devastation and destruction: the very attraction of military service was the opportunity it afforded for booty. Yet such actions alienated the local population and made it difficult to support the army on a long campaign. The application of new technology might have made it easy enough to capture castles, but improved fortifications round Riga and Reval kept the greatest prizes out of Muscovy's reach; without a navy, Ivan was unable to prevent supply by sea. Reval survived the eight-month siege in 1570 without difficulty. New technology was not enough; armies had to adapt to make best use of it. Yet as the experience of Sweden and Denmark in the Nordic Seven Years War demonstrated, adaptation was no easy matter.

The Nordic Seven Years War (1563–70)

The Nordic Seven Years War is not the sort of war which pleases military historians. It did not have what wars are supposed to have. There was only one battle, at Axtorna in 1565, unless one counts the undignified scramble at Mared (1564) which scarcely merits the name. Seven years of fighting saw, it is true, some notable successes for both sides, including Denmark's capture of Älvsborg in 1563, Sweden's capture of Trondheim (1564) and Varberg (1565), and the Swedish naval victories under Klas Kristersson Horn. When peace came at Stettin in December 1570, however, little had changed. If Frederik had really planned to reconquer Sweden, his achievement fell far short of his ambition. The capture of Älvsborg – which was handed back to Sweden after 1570 in return for a 150,000-riksdaler ransom – was as close as he came, though his armies devastated wide swathes of Swedish territory. The Stettin treaty insisted on the freedom of the Narva trade and recognised Frederik as protector of Estonia, leaving Sweden technically in possession only of Reval and Weissenstein, but Frederik was unable to make good his claim.

The attention of military historians has been caught by the mercurial figure of Erik XIV, widely portrayed as a military genius whose talent was betrayed by incompetent underlings. Yet if Erik did possess notable organ-isational ability – his leadership had a remarkable galvanising effect on the Swedish forces after his recovery from his first bout of madness in 1567 – his military talent was largely that of the theoretician. As such he has received extensive praise. Roberts accords him an important place in the development of the military art, not just for falling under the influence of the Ancients, but for being 'the very first commander of modern times to translate their precepts into practice', arguing that he was 'the first . . . since the coming of firearms to employ a true linear formation, instead of the massive blocks which were fashionable on the continent' and claiming that he anticipated the reforms of Maurice of Orange and Gustav Adolf. Sweden's failure in battle is explained by pointing to inferior subordinates who failed to appreciate Erik's genius and the obtuseness of the Swedish peasant soldier who, in Roberts's vivid phrase, cast aside Erik's pikes and heavy body armour 'and robustly asserted their right to be slaughtered in their own fashion, unconstrained by royal tyranny.'[13]

The rarity of pitched battles during the Danish-Swedish war suggests, however, that the inordinate attention paid to such matters as the number of ranks in the Swedish battle-formation at Axtorna (the evidence is ambiguous) is misdirected. That Erik was an intelligent thinker on military matters is undeniable, and he indeed made great efforts to train his troops in the use of pike and musket; nevertheless, Roberts exaggerates his originality and overestimates the extent to which such tactics were effective in the conditions in which Sweden was fighting in the 1560s. Erik did not need to look to the Ancients for lessons on the potential of the pike: it was a weapon which had been known in Sweden from at least the 1520s, when Gustav Vasa had received support from Lübeck in the war of independence; he had also employed large numbers of German mercenaries against Christian II in the 1530s. Finnish infantry, which had to face cavalry-based Muscovite armies, already contained a high proportion of pikes during the 1554–7 war. Much of the initiative for increasing the proportion of pikes in Swedish units sent to Finland, and in organising infantry battalions into smaller tactical units – usually attributed to Erik – came from Gustav Vasa and his commanders, and owed more to practical requirements than a theoretical interest in the campaigns of the Romans. Gustav Vasa consulted Erik to an increasing extent, but many of the organisational changes date from 1551, when Erik was only seventeen.[14] That Erik built energetically on these foundations is undeniable; it is not credible, however, to consider him the inspirational genius who singlehandedly transformed the Swedish army. Moreover, Continental infantry was not necessarily suited to warfare under Scandinavian conditions. When Gustav Vasa's foreign mercenaries confronted the peasants of Småland in the Dackefejden rising of the mid-1530s, pikes proved too cumbersome to be of much use in the thickly-forested terrain.[15] Native troops armed with crossbows or firearms proved far more adaptable in coping with the peasant bands. Viljanti suggests that the Dackefejden was not a 'normal' war, but much of the fighting between 1563 and 1570 was conducted in just such terrain.

Although both Erik and Frederik conceived ambitious and aggressive strategies, the armies with which they pursued them were fundamentally different. Denmark was much closer to the recruiting-grounds of north-western Germany and was therefore able rapidly to assemble a professional mercenary army. The force which embarked on the Älvsborg campaign in August 1563 was 25–28,000 strong, supported by the powerful fleet of twenty-seven large warships which left Copenhagen on 5 August with a further 4,600 men.[16] Initially, everything went according to plan. Älvsborg was protected by powerful fortifications, recently improved, and a garrison of 700, with two months' supplies and 148 guns. Nevertheless, after a three-day bombardment which opened a breach large enough for a storm, it surrendered on 4 September.

Denmark had recruited a large army of professional mercenaries in the hope of winning the war at a stroke. Sweden, however, could not afford such a strategy. Älvsborg's fall deprived it of its only direct outlet to the North Sea, and it faced a tight blockade by the Danish and Lübeck fleets which prevented it from recruiting abroad on a large scale. In these circumstances, to which might be added considerations of cost, Sweden had to rely on native levies and fight the sort of defensive war to which traditional Swedish methods were well suited: peasant infantry, armed largely with crossbows or firearms used the difficult terrain of southern Sweden to hamper the Danish invaders by preparing ambushes, in which roads through the thick forests and deep ravines were blocked with barricades of boulders or trees. Yet if these tactics were applied to great effect, Erik had bolder ambitions. He did not intend merely to fight a defensive war of attrition, but devised an ambitious offensive vision, in which he sought to break the Danish stranglehold on southern Scandinavia by recapturing Älvsborg and seizing Bohuslän and Halland, or by striking through Norway to Trondheim in order to win a direct outlet to the North Sea. Such a strategy demanded infantry capable of taking the offensive; it was to this end that Erik's ambitious reforms were directed.

His first counterattack after Älvsborg's fall seemed to demonstrate the value of professionals. Erik had at his disposal 20,452 infantry and 5,424 cavalry, of which 2,476 foot and 907 horse were stationed in Livonia. Most of the troops were native conscripts, although there was a stiffening of foreign mercenary officers.[17] Besieging Halmstad in October, Erik immediately experienced supply problems and difficulty in assembling his heavy artillery. Although the walls were breached on 5 November, two attempts to storm the town were beaten back. With disease spreading through the army, Erik surrendered command to the French mercenary de Mornay. On 9 November, the army was caught by a small Danish force of cavalry and 2,000 arquebusiers at Mared. Despite heavily outnumbering the Danes and fighting on ground of their own choosing, the Swedes did badly: the cavalry was pushed back without offering serious resistance, the infantry was left with its flanks exposed and was unable to protect its artillery, which fell into Danish hands. If the Danes could have brought their whole force to bear, the

Swedes might have been annihilated, but the Danish infantry only arrived at the end of the day; having lost a considerable number of men, Mornay was able to escape under cover of darkness, abandoning forty-one guns.[18]

Despite this apparent confirmation of the value of professional troops Frederik was facing enormous problems. His army might have proved itself superior to the Swedes in siege and battle, but it was incapable of delivering a decisive blow. Frederik had originally intended to besiege both Älvsborg and Kalmar. As his commanders pointed out, however, Denmark lacked sufficient artillery for simultaneous strikes at both cities, and the attack on Kalmar was therefore abandoned. The capture of Älvsborg was a notable success, but its strategic importance should not be exaggerated. The possession of a harbour on the Kattegat could not solve the problems of blockade faced by Sweden in the war: communication-lines to Stockholm from Älvsborg were too long and too insecure for its loss to make a substantial difference.[19] The attack on Älvsborg had been launched late in the year; despite its rapid fall it was out of the question to advance overland on Stockholm: Daniel Rantzau, Frederik's ablest commander, was highly sceptical of the possibility of crossing such difficult terrain with any chance of success, and Frederik withdrew to winter quarters in the rich grain-growing province of Scania.

It was now that the dangers of relying on foreign mercenaries were starkly demonstrated. Frederik could not afford to have such a large force lying idle at a cost of 40,000 rigsdalers per month in wages alone. Almost immediately, he had to reduce it considerably: the infantry was cut from sixty to thirty-seven companies, and the cavalry from nine to six. Even these desperate measures failed to fend off a growing crisis which was gradually to paralyse the Danish war effort. Government income had been some 200,000 rigsdalers per annum on the eve of the war, a figure that was pitifully inadequate for the support of a mercenary army even without taking into consideration the huge sums required to maintain the fleet. Frederik raised substantial loans from Danish nobles and burghers, and from friendly German princes, church silver was melted down, crown estates mortgaged and the coinage debased, with around one million rigsdalers being minted in the first year of the war alone. By such desperate measures, 6–7,000,000 rigsdalers were raised in the first half of the war.[20]

It was not enough. For the rest of the war, Frederik was the proud possessor of a cripplingly expensive army which he could neither pay nor pay off, and which would not fight until it was paid. Already in January 1564 troops in winter quarters in Scania protested strongly at the shortage of supplies; in all subsequent campaigns, Frederik had to conduct long, tedious negotiations to persuade his troops to take the field. Never again would he have as many troops at his disposal. When he eventually cajoled his army into the field in the summer of 1564, it comprised two incomplete infantry regiments and seven companies of cavalry; the original plan of besieging Kalmar was soon abandoned in favour of a strike against Stockholm, but this came to nothing after the cavalry, on the point of mutiny, had to be sent back to Halmstad. In 1565, the army refused to accept pay in debased Danish coinage, and the force which Rantzau led to victory at Axtorna was only 7,400 strong.[21] In 1567, the army he took on a famous trail of devastation through central Sweden numbered barely 4,000.[22]

Although Sweden could field larger armies because it relied largely on native troops, it was equally unable to force a decision. Cavalry was recruited through *rusttjänst*, the obligation on all nobles to serve on horseback in respect of their privileged status. With regard to the infantry, the situation was more complex, and, since it is frequently misinterpreted in the non-Swedish literature, it deserves close analysis. The system's origins lay in the failure of Gustav Vasa's mercenaries during the Dackefejden. This prompted Gustav to persuade the 1544 *Riksdag* to establish a native force which would be cheaper than foreign mercenaries. On this basis, many historians have presented Sweden as the first European state to found its defence on a universal duty to defend the realm and to maintain a native standing army in peacetime.[23] This view is not groundless, but it is important not to telescope the development of the Swedish system; it did not emerge fully-formed from the defence ordinance of 1544, which merely envisaged recruitment of native rather than foreign troops to meet the immediate military crisis: there was no question of the *Riksdag* sanctioning a native standing army.

There was no need to establish by law any universal military obligation, since it already existed in the form of the *uppbåd*, the traditional royal prerogative allowing the king to call up every fifth man in Småland, and every sixth man in other provinces, for the defence of his realm. It was this ancient right – by no means peculiar to Sweden – which formed the basis of the system of *utskrivning*. Its origins lay in the 1554–7 Muscovite war, when Gustav Vasa ordered the preparation of registers of the population to facilitate mobilisation of the *uppbåd*. *Utskrivning* – literally 'writing out' – originally meant registration rather than conscription; initially, it represented an extension of the *uppbåd*, and for a considerable period there was much confusion over the exact status of the new system, which raised a stated number of troops for a specific purpose, agreed by the *Riksdag*. Rudimentary lists had been kept while recruitment was still voluntary, but the new registers made it possible to institute a more permanent system, although its development was more due to the fact that Sweden was almost constantly at war after 1563 than to any intention to establish a standing army.

The new registers enabled the government to keep a closer watch on those recruited, whom it may have regarded as part of a permanent military establishment, and granted tax concessions to keep them willing to serve, but it took time for the *uppbåd* mentality to disappear. While peasants seem, on the whole, to have accepted their duty to defend the realm, they were reluctant to serve once the immediate crisis had passed. The problems of John III, often castigated for abandoning the visionary reforms of his brother, stemmed more from the fact that his wars were fought outside Sweden, something which peasants were more reluctant to accept, since the *uppbåd* required only service in defence of the realm. Such problems were to plague Swedish rulers well into Gustav Adolf's reign.

Moreover, Erik's much-vaunted reforms failed to create a native force capable of matching continental mercenaries. The Swedish army was still essentially a peasant militia, not a regular, professional force. Erik was able to mobilise larger armies than Frederik, and his aggressive campaigns did cause considerable problems for Denmark, even if he was ultimately incapable of building on any of his successes. His most notable victory was the capture of Varberg, on the Halland coast, stormed in August 1565 after a six-day siege. Although this was followed by the defeat at Axtorna (20 October), Varberg gave the Swedes a foothold on the Kattegat once more; if it was ultimately lost in November 1569, its fall showed that the Swedes were capable of doing more than holding up the Danes in the Småland forests.

Yet Erik's army was incapable of realising his wider plans. In February 1564, he sent two armies into Norway; one under Klas Horn besieged Bohus castle in an attempt to break through to the coast, but soon had to withdraw. The other, 4,000-strong including 300 ski-troops, under the French mercenary Collart, broke into Jämtland and succeeded in capturing Trondheim, but although Collart began extracting oaths of loyalty from the Norwegian peasantry, it was unrealistic to suppose that such a small force, without naval support, could hope to subdue the whole of Norway. When a Danish army of 4,000 arrived by sea in May, Collart was forced to surrender. It was a pattern that was to be repeated throughout the war. The Swedes struck time and again at Danish provinces from Blekinge, Scania and Halland in the south, to Bohuslän and the other Norwegian provinces in the north. They certainly succeeded in disrupting Danish plans, and frequently managed to seize the initiative, but, apart from the capture of Varberg, had little to show for the effort, while the defeats at Mared and Axtorna demonstrated that Erik's native army could not make its numerical superiority tell against experienced mercenaries, although in both cases the Swedish infantry performed creditably enough; it was the abject performance of the Swedish horse which determined the course of the battle.

Neither side was capable of forcing a decision. This was already clear by 1564; thereafter the war degenerated into grim attrition, in which the Swedes laid waste the narrow Danish provinces in the south, while the Danes devastated Västergötland and Småland. This strategy did much to exacerbate the already acute problems of supply faced by both sides, but it did little to bring a decision closer, except by exhaustion. Great hopes were invested by both combatants in their respective navies, but ambitious plans for supporting land-based campaigns proved impossible to coordinate. Nevertheless, the war at sea proved more decisive than the struggle on land, not least because the Swedes, who based their tactics on naval gunnery rather than the boarding strategy still favoured by the Danes and Lübeckers, gradually won the upper hand and succeeded in breaking the Danish blockade.[24] The fleets clashed in September 1563 between Gotland and Medelsten; both were damaged, but although the Swedes withdrew to Stockholm, leaving the sea to the Danes, the Danish-Lübeck fleet, which contained at least twenty-seven large warships and a large number of smaller vessels, was simply too small to implement an effective blockade; moreover, it was bedevilled by disputes between the Danish and Lübecker commanders. Throughout October, Swedish vessels were able to sail back and forth to Germany largely unhindered. In May 1564 near Bornholm, the Swedish flagship, the *Mars*, was destroyed, but the Danes had also been badly mauled, and sickness raged through the fleet. Another Danish success in August, after which the Swedish fleet withdrew, ensured that a more effective blockade was established: only thirty-six ships reached Stockholm in 1564, where shortage of salt was causing concern.

The balance shifted in 1565, as Erik's efforts to build up his fleet began to bear dividends. One should not, however, believe too much of the hyperbole which surrounds Erik's transformation of the navy, and the supposed genius of Klas Kristersson Horn, though a competent commander he certainly was. Two bloody battles in 1565 (4 June and 7 July) can certainly be counted as Swedish successes: the first saw the death of the Danish admiral Trolle, while the allied flagship was captured in the second, but neither was as clear-cut as is sometimes suggested, and even if the Swedes were able to defy the Danish blockade, they did not command the Baltic. Roberts claims that the Danes were swept from the sea.[25] In fact this was the temporary result of an act by a higher authority: the one major sea-battle of 1566 (26 July) was sufficiently inconclusive to be claimed as a victory by both sides. It was the negligence of the Danish admiral Lauridsen, who was to die with 7,000 of his men, which led to the destruction of a large part of the allied fleet in a massive storm two days later. It was this disaster, rather than the superiority of the Swedish fleet, itself scattered by the storm, that ended Danish dreams of victory by blockade, and enabled the Swedish capture of the Dutch salt fleet which helped solve Sweden's most pressing supply problem. Frederik had managed to rebuild his fleet by the summer of 1567, although caution on both sides meant that there were no naval engagements that year, while the acute financial and manpower problems of both powers ensured that naval activity was scaled down for the rest of the war. If the Danes had been swept from the sea, nobody had told Per Munck, who made a bold attempt to seize the initiative in July 1569 by sailing an allied fleet to the eastern Baltic, far from the usual Danish waters, to bombard Reval undisturbed for eleven days.[26]

The war was winding down, as the strains on both sides ensured that thoughts of conciliation replaced dreams of conquest. Erik's overthrow brought a decisive change, as John moved towards alignment with Poland-Lithuania. Denmark, too, was changing its priorities: the Polish alliance had been a disappointment, as Sigismund Augustus had devoted far more energy to fighting the Muscovites in Lithuania than to challenging the Swedes in Livonia. As Ivan once more took an interest in Livonia in 1569–70, Frederik seized the opportunity to make peace. The uncertain political situation in Sweden helped Denmark achieve a favourable settlement, although its concrete gains were minimal.

The Nordic Seven Years War was largely a costly and futile exercise, in which the ambitions of both combatants greatly outweighed their military capacity. Frederik gambled everything on a quick victory with experienced foreign mercenaries, but although they indeed proved superior in sieges and in battle, they were simply too expensive to be sustained in sufficient numbers to prove decisive. They were reluctant to enter the field: arriving with wives and children in tow, they preferred paid inactivity to campaigning. Erik attempted to train his amateurs, but his tactics required training, drill and experience to succeed. While he was by no means completely unsuccessful, his troops remained essentially irregulars, and their abilities were shown to best effect in the dogged defence of the difficult terrain of central-southern Sweden which was their forté.

Nevertheless, if the more extravagant claims for Erik's achievements must be discounted, and if the military and political structures of both Sweden and Denmark proved incapable of carrying the load generated by the ambitious plans of their rulers, both sides managed to sustain a significant military effort over a relatively long period, in difficult terrain. In this respect, the Nordic Seven Years War did mark a significant change: never before had sustained campaigns been maintained in Scandinavia on such a wide front for so long. Furthermore, both sides had devoted significant resources to naval warfare, which was vastly expensive, and it was at sea that the major battles of the war took place. While the fleets proved incapable of providing the sort of close support of land-based campaigns that both monarchs conceived, and the Danes were ultimately incapable of enforcing the blockade which might have obliged Sweden to sue for peace earlier, nevertheless the importance of the navy to both Scandinavian powers had been clearly demonstrated. If the war at sea, as on land, posed more challenges than it provided solutions, lessons were learned which were to prove important later.

Political fallout

The peace of Stettin marked a shift in focus rather than a general settlement. All the combatants were feeling the strain. Although it did not experience a political crisis quite as dramatic as those which rocked its rivals – nobody went mad, nobody was deposed, there was no bloodbath and the fundamental basis of the constitution was not altered – the reverberations within Denmark were sufficiently serious to remove it forever as an effective force in the eastern Baltic. The Danish political system revolved round the relationship between the king and the Council, in which the monarch's position was ambiguous. Whereas in Sweden the achievement of independence and the requirements of maintaining it had allowed Gustav Vasa to secure recognition of the Swedish monarchy as hereditary in 1544, the Danish monarchy remained elective. The Council claimed a central role in the constitution as the bearer of sovereignty, and the king was obliged to consult it on matters of taxation, privilege and foreign policy. Yet the king was not the Council's prisoner, partly because of the considerable financial independence granted by the Sound Dues and partly because he controlled appointment to the Council.

The Council was not itself a unified body. This was clear at the start of the war, when Frederik enjoyed the support of at least a third of its members, many of them from the younger generation, to overcome the opposition of the majority to war with Sweden.[27] The acute financial problems consequent upon the failure to end the war at one blow threw him back on Council support. The political situation in 1565–6 was noticeably tense, with the return from exile of the disgraced councillor Peder Oxe, an old political adversary, and suggestions that Denmark should not elect another Oldenburg after Frederik's death. Yet if the relationship was certainly tense, with Frederik threatening abdication on at least one occasion, the Council played a large part alongside Frederik in introducing the sweeping financial and administrative reforms which helped Denmark to saddle the burden of war more effectively. In January 1566 a general excise was introduced to replace the old system in which different tolls had been set by different provinces. At the end of the year, a tax was introduced on the nobility, including the royal family; nobles were henceforth to pay twelve rigsdalers on every last of corn sold; this is often seen as Oxe's measure, but was in fact the result of close consultation between Frederik and noble representatives at several meetings from August 1566.[28]

There was considerable tension following Sweden's rejection of the abortive peace of Roskilde, negotiated in 1568 after Erik's fall. Frederik's financial situation was now desperate: he pointedly took Oxe and Hans Skovgaard to show them his empty treasure-chamber on one occasion. As Council opinion hardened, he called the only meeting of the *Rigsdag* between 1536 and 1627, writing a strongly-worded letter to the Council threatening to abdicate if he did not receive the funds he needed to end the war. The ploy was successful; after months of bargaining, Frederik persuaded both *Rigsdag* and Council that, following the Swedish rejection of peace, there was little alternative to agreeing new taxes, which were granted on condition that they should be used to end the war.[29] In the event, the taxes came in too slowly for Frederik to launch the great offensive he had planned for 1570, and peace came anyway in December. Nevertheless, the degree of acceptance by Danish society of the burden of war after 1565 was impressive. It was not so clear, however, that Danes would support further military adventures. As Christian IV (1588–1648) was soon to demonstrate, monarchs were far from prisoners of the Council after 1570; nevertheless Denmark abandoned its assertive policy in Livonia along with the ill-fated Magnus. This decision owed as much to Frederik as to the Council; he had learned his lesson.

The political upheavals of the late 1560s experienced by the other three major combatants in the Northern Wars were all more dramatic, but none resulted in disengagement from the Livonian War. In Sweden and Muscovy, the personality of the monarch lay at the centre of the crisis and the extent to which the misfortunes of war induced psychological reactions in the highly-strung personalities of both Erik XIV and Ivan IV has long provoked debate. In the light of the former's increasing tendency to violent denunciation of his subordinates for their incompetence, and his frequent dismissal of commanders after the failure of particular campaigns without regard for the problems they faced in pursuing his ambitious strategy, it does not seem unreasonable to accord a significant role in the breakdown of Erik's personality to the immense strain that the war placed upon his delicate psychological balance. Similarly, Ivan's increasing frustration with Muscovite military failures undoubtedly helped detonate the *Oprichnina*. Where Erik dismissed his unsuccessful commanders and struck out in a frenzy to murder the Stures in May 1567, Ivan conducted a more sweeping purge against those who had failed him. As early as 1560 he began to strike against those whose loyalty he suspected. The first victims, such as Aleksei Adashev, merely suffered disgrace and the confiscation of their estates; some, including I.D. Belskii, who was accused of plotting with the

Poles, suffered disgrace but were subsequently pardoned. From 1563, the temperature began to rise, as Muscovite armies suffered reverse after reverse. Daniil Adashev, together with other members of his clan, and the distinguished general N.V. Sheremetev, were executed in 1563–4.

The *Oprichnina* was relatively short-lived, however, and Muscovite engagement in the Livonian War resumed in the 1570s. Political change in Poland-Lithuania after 1569 was to have more immediate and far-reaching effects on the course of the Northern Wars. For war was an essential catalyst for the radical political transformation which took place between 1569 and 1572. While Poland and Lithuania had been growing together culturally, and while support for closer political union was strong in Poland, the powerful Lithuanian magnates had fiercely defended their autonomous political status and the Lithuanian political system, in which the hereditary Grand Duke enjoyed more power than he did as King of Poland, but in which the magnate-dominated Council was the central political institution. If Sigismund Augustus's lack of an heir gradually concentrated minds in both Poland and Lithuania on the possibility that the union would lapse with his death, it was the developing war which pushed both states towards the decisive act at Lublin in 1569.

For, despite protestations of their separate identity, and the proud defence of their traditional system, the Lithuanians could not ignore one fundamental change in the position since the fifteenth century, when Lithuania had for long periods been all but independent, with a Grand Duke who, though closely related to the king in Cracow, had been able to pursue his own policies. This, however, had been in the days before the emergence of a strong, united Muscovite state, whose rulers laid claim to all the Grand Duchy's Ruthenian territories. By 1533, the Muscovites had driven the border westward in a series of short but savage wars, and Lithuania was thrown back increasingly on the resources of its more populous, wealthier partner. The Poles were growing restless, however, at the one-sided relationship. While Lithuanians constantly demanded, and usually received, military and financial help from the Poles, the reverse was seldom the case. When the military crisis of the 1560s coincided with growing fears about the succession, the calls for closer union grew ever more powerful. With the king determined to involve Poland more closely in the war, he was forced in 1562 to abandon his previous hostility to the idea, which threatened to deprive him of the greater degree of power he enjoyed in Lithuania.

Over the next seven years, the Lithuanian magnates stubbornly resisted closer union, but the loss of royal support and the course of the war led to their increasing isolation, even within Lithuania. The fall of Połock in 1563 was a tremendous shock to Lithuanian opinion, since it removed a vital defensive bastion and rendered large areas of the Grand Duchy vulnerable.

Already there was substantial support for closer union among large sections of the Lithuanian *szlachta*, attracted by the greater privileges enjoyed by their Polish counterparts and burdened by the heavy taxation required for the prosecution of the war: by the 1560s, Lithuanian land-taxes were three times greater than in the 1540s and five times greater than in the 1550s. That union was delayed until 1569 was in large part due to the improved military situation after 1564, when the Lithuanian victories at Czasniki and on the Ula river stemmed the tide of Muscovite success, while the beginning of the *Oprichnina* in 1565 turned Muscovy in on itself. The movement towards union could not be stemmed. The first years of the *Oprichnina* might have relieved the direct pressure on Lithuania, but as accounts of Ivan's blood-soaked deeds filtered through, arguments for closer union became irresistible. Between 1562 and 1565, the Lithuanian treasury had spent nearly 2,000,000 złoties. Of the 626,000 złoties in taxation voted by Poland at the 1565 *Sejm*, the substantial sum of 483,000 złoties went to support Lithuania.[30] This was in addition to the significant contingents of Polish troops which bolstered the defence of the eastern borders. Already the floodgates were opened: during the 1560s, Lithuania's political institutions were brought into line with their Polish counterparts: in 1565 thirty-one *sejmiki* were established, and a bicameral Lithuanian *Sejm* came into being on the Polish model.

The magnate opposition could not prevent union, but its intemperate walkout from the 1569 *Sejm* as a protest against the terms on offer was to have momentous consequences. The move backfired disastrously. The Poles had by now lost patience. First Podlasie and Volhynia (to which Poland had a tenuous historical claim), and then the palatinate of Kiev (to which it had none) were incorporated directly into the kingdom of Poland, removing at a stroke over half the territory of the old Grand Duchy. This bold act succeeded triumphantly. When the great Lithuanian lords reappeared in Lublin there was little that they could do but accept the reasonably generous terms on offer for the union of the dramatically truncated Grand Duchy with Poland. There was to be a common *Sejm*, but Lithuania was to keep its own army, its own administration and its own laws. Resentment at the dramatic coup of 1569 was to fester long among magnate circles in Lithuania, but the Union was to prove successful, since it was founded on an act of consent by the majority of the Polish and Lithuanian *szlachta*, despite the stormy process by which it was achieved. It was the Ukrainian lands incorporated into Poland which were to prove a problem.

When Sigismund Augustus died in 1572, nothing had been agreed except for the principle that Poland and Lithuania would hold a common election to elect a successor. The young Commonwealth was plunged into a period of intense political uncertainty, in which it first had to agree a system for royal elections and then find a monarch capable of cementing the Union. Thanks to the initiative of the dynamic royal secretary Jan Zamoyski, the problem was solved with breathtaking radicalism. Seizing on the anti-magnate feeling which had united the middling Polish *szlachta* in the Movement for the Execution of the Laws in the 1560s, and which had provided much of the support for union in Lithuania, Zamoyski expounded a vision of noble equality which drew upon Polish tradition and the Roman republican ideal of citizenship, rallying *szlachta* opinion by calling for the right of all citizens of the new Commonwealth to participate in royal elections. The triumph of this vision over a more traditional form of election by Council or *Sejm* was to shape the Commonwealth's entire history.

The Union's strength was demonstrated by the political upheavals between 1573 and 1576 which accompanied the search for a successor to Sigismund Augustus. Out of a bewildering array of candidates, the *szlachta* settled upon Henry Valois, brother of Charles IX of France, in 1573. Henry was forced to swear at his Coronation *Sejm* to a series of conditions which explicitly laid down the terms of his election, and which sealed the political revolution by guaranteeing the changes of the last four years, including the right of free election of the monarch, and the stipulation that the *Sejm* must be called every two years at least. The delicate French flower did not take easily to the rich soil of east-central Europe, however; within a few months of arriving, he fled Cracow at dead of night to return to France and mount the throne after his brother's unexpected death. When he refused to return, he was held to be in breach of his coronation oath and deposed. A two-year interregnum then followed, to be ended in February 1576 with the election of Stefan Batory, a capable soldier.

The period of intensive warfare in northeastern Europe put immense strain on the political systems of all the combatants. In both Sweden and Muscovy, the pressures of conducting war helped provoke political crises. The crisis in Sweden was short-lived, however, and John III was able to secure his hold on power quickly and effectively. In Muscovy, despite the lurid drama of the *Oprichnina*, the great boyar families continued to dominate, shorn perhaps of one or two members, and the system of *mestnichestvo* continued undisturbed. In Denmark, despite the strain put on the relationship between king and Council, war did not mark a new departure. Even in Poland-Lithuania, where a much closer relationship can be detected between the demands of war and fundamental political change, it would be foolish to argue that war changed the course of political development. Rather it provided the final catalyst which acted decisively on a set of processes which had been steadily moving Poland and Lithuania together over a long period. As war resumed in the 1570s, it was by no means clear which of these very different political structures was best suited to carry the strain.

Over the next fifty years, however, Poland-Lithuania emerged as the most powerful and successful of the combatants.

Notes

1   A. Tuulse, *Die Burgen in Estland und Lettland* (Dorpat, 1942) pp. 15, 90, 235.
2   Kiek in de Kök was still of sufficient importance for it to be extensively re-modelled by Erik Dahlberg, the governor of Livonia, in his reconstruction of the Reval fortifications in the 1690s.
3   Tuulse, *Die Burgen* p. 173; *Dopolneniia k Nikonovskoi Letopisi sokhranivshiiasia v spiskakh Sinodal'nom, Levedevskim i Aleksandro-Nevskom* PSRL XIII (Moscow, 1965) pp. 303–4. According to Parker the angle-bastion did not cross the Alps until 1530; that it reached Narva by 1560 suggests that northeastern Europe was not as remote as is sometimes supposed: Parker, *Military Revolution* p. 12.
4   T. Esper, 'A 16th century anti-Russian arms embargo' *JGO* NF 15 (1967) pp. 180–96.
5   T. Nowak, 'Artyleria polska do końca XIV w. Problematyka i stan badań' *SMHW* 9 (1963) pp. 37, 39.
6   T. Esper, 'Military self-sufficiency and weapons technology in Muscovite Russia' *SR* 28 (1969) pp. 186–8; Hellie, *Enserfment* pp. 154–8.
7   A.A. Zimin, 'K istorii voennykh reform 50-kh godov XVI v.' *IZ* 55 (1956) pp. 354–5; A.V. Chernov, *Vooruzhennye sily russkogo gosudarstva v XV–XVII vv.* (Moscow, 1954) pp. 46–50 and 'Obrazovanie streletskogo voiska' *IZ* 38 (1951) pp. 281–90; Keep, *Soldiers* pp. 60–1; Hellie, *Enserfment* pp. 160–4.
8   Roberts, while by no means exculpating Erik, follows Swedish historiography in blaming Frederik: *Early Vasas* pp. 210–11. For a different view see Jensen, *Danmarks konflikt*, chapters 1–3.
9   U. Renner, 'Herzog Magnus von Holstein als Vasall des Zaren Ivan Groznyj' in N. Angermann (ed.), *Deutschland – Livland – Russland* (Lüneburg, 1988) pp. 137–58.
10 Rüssow, *Chronica* pp. 124–5.
11 F. Nyenstädt, *Livländische Chronik* G. Tielmann (ed.) (Riga, 1839) p. 77.
12 Rüssow, *Chronica* pp. 135–6. The joke only works in German.
13 Roberts, *Early Vasas* pp. 215, 400.
14 Viljanti, *Gustav Vasas* I pp. 112, 115–19, 240–1.
15 A point Roberts appreciates: *Early Vasas* p. 133; Viljanti, *Gustav Vasas* I pp. 229–30.
16 Tidander, *Nordiska Sjuårkrigets* p. 72; Jensen, *Danmarks konflikt* p. 75.
17 Ibid. p. 76.
18 Westling, *Nordiska Sjuårskrigets* VI p. 461; Jensen, *Danmarks konflikt* pp. 78–9; Tidander, *Nordiska Sjuårskrigets* pp. 87–91.
19 Jensen, *Danmarks konflikt* p. 75.
20 Ibid. pp. 76, 85–6.

21   Swedish accounts suggest 9,000, but this is based on a simple multiplication of the number of units involved; as Jensen shows, Danish units were seriously undermanned. Ibid. p. 151.

22   L.G.T. Tidander, *Daniel Rantzaus vinterfälttåg i Sverige 1567–8* (Stockholm, 1886) pp. 7–8.

23   This view was presented in the Swedish General Staff work on the wars of Gustav Adolf. Delbrück, Roberts and Corvisier all depict Sweden as the first state to establish a standing army based on the principle of universal military obligation: S.A. Nilsson, *På väg mot militärstaten* (Uppsala, 1989) pp. 4–9.

24   Glete, *Navies* p. 112.

25   Roberts, *Early Vasas* p. 217.

26   Arnell, *Bidrag* pp. 106–7.

27   Jensen convincingly attacks older views that blamed the war on Frederik's aggressive instincts, encouraged by his German mercenary captains. Without denying that there was considerable disagreement, he suggests that Frederik consulted the Council throughout, and did not declare war without its knowledge: *Danmarks konflikt* pp. 34–7, 66–7, 333.

28   The traditional view, which attributes the reform entirely to the genius of Oxe, is no longer sustainable; there is little evidence for his supposedly dominating role, and many of the reforms had little to do with him: ibid. chapter 11, especially pp. 194–6, 198.

29   Ibid. pp. 286–98. The taxes were heavy: every peasant landholder had to pay 7 dalers, with landless peasants paying half.

30   H.E. Dembkowski, *The Union of Lublin* (Boulder, Col., 1982) pp. 101–19.

CHAPTER THREE

The Ascendancy of Poland-Lithuania

The end of the First Northern War and the Time of Troubles

After the Muscovite defeat at Wenden (September 1578), Ivan proposed peace, but Batory was not interested. Already the military advantages of closer union were becoming apparent. The 1578 *Sejm* backed Batory's appeal to carry the fight into enemy territory, voting taxation at the unprecedented level of one złoty per *łan* to pay for it. Despite some opposition, this tax, voted for two years, brought in substantial sums – 800,000 złoties in 1578 – which provided a solid basis for military action.[1] Batory's strategy was bold. Although his main aim was to expel the Muscovites from Livonia, he decided that a direct strike at Livonia was unlikely to produce a quick victory. Instead he launched three great campaigns against Muscovy itself, retaking Połock (1579), capturing Velikie Luki and Kholm (1580) and besieging Pskov (1581–2). If Pskov fell, Muscovy could neither control Livonia nor hope to mount an effective campaign to recover it.

Pskov did not fall, despite a five-month siege. Batory's strategy, however, was successful; perhaps too successful, since the intense pressure on this vital nerve-centre of Muscovite power opened the way to a spectacular Swedish campaign led by Pontus de la Gardie which climaxed in the storming of Narva and Ivangorod. In January 1582 Ivan was forced to settle with Batory at Iam Zapolskii, abandoning all his Livonian conquests in order to preserve Pskov. A year later he signed a three-year truce with Sweden (later extended until 1590), which left Narva and Ivangorod in Swedish hands. Muscovy still had a narrow foothold on the Ingrian coast but Ivan's great dream was over, although after resuming war with Sweden in 1590, Muscovy retook Ivangorod and Kopor'e and regained Ingria and Kexholm at the peace of Teusino (1595).

This success took place against the background of a momentous change in Polish-Swedish relations. Batory died in 1586; a year later Sigismund Vasa, son of John III and Katarzyna Jagiellońka, was elected king of Poland-Lithuania. This attempt to seal the Polish-Swedish alliance was to miscarry badly, however. Ivan's defeat fulfilled the alliance's immediate purpose, and arguments over Estonia, which Sigismund swore to cede to the Common-wealth in his electoral charter, rapidly soured relations. Sigismund III (as he was known in the Commonwealth), succeeded to the Swedish throne in 1592, but he had been brought up a Catholic, which caused problems in Sweden from the outset, as his uncle, duke Charles of Södermanland, who acted as regent during Sigismund's lengthy stays in Poland, displayed all the ruthless ambition of his father, Gustav Vasa. By the late 1590s Charles had placed himself at the head of a powerful coalition of interests which saw Sigismund's Catholicism as a grave threat. Sigismund's brief stay in Sweden in 1593–4 failed to resolve the problems and revealed the strength of sup-port for Charles among the clergy and peasantry. Sigismund had substantial support in Finland, where the sense of a Swedish-Polish alliance had been confirmed by the loss of Ingria and Kexholm in 1595, and from leading councillors who distrusted Charles's authoritarian temper. In 1597, civil war broke out.

Sigismund led a small force, mostly Hungarian and German mercenaries, to Sweden in August 1598. Although Samuel Łaski took Stockholm castle and Sigismund's army – no more than 7,000, including the Swedes who joined him after his landing – defeated Charles's much larger force in a brief ecounter at Stegeborg (8/18 September), Sigismund displayed a lack of ruthlessness uncharacteristic of a Vasa in allowing Charles to escape with his army intact. It cost him his throne. In the decisive encounter at Stångebro on 25 September (OS), Charles seized the advantage by offering talks and then mounting an attack under cover of mist as Sigismund's forces were withdrawing to their camp. Although Sigismund's mercenaries gave a good account of themselves under unfavourable conditions, the battle was decided by the refusal of large numbers of Swedes in his army to fight their fellow countrymen. Sigismund was forced to surrender his Council supporters for trial by a supposedly impartial court of foreign princes. Although he still enjoyed significant support, his fate was sealed by his decision to return to Poland in late 1598.[2] In 1599, Charles persuaded the *Riksdag* to depose Sigismund, although he waited until 1604 before accepting the throne as Charles IX.

Sigismund's deposition was a profound shock. Although Poland-Lithuania was a richer and more powerful state than Sweden, the taciturn Sigismund had not taken kindly to its turbulent politics, and briefly considered abdicating in 1589. He maintained a substantial Swedish court in Poland, and for the rest of his long reign the recovery of his birthright was his primary aim, although it was one his subjects were reluctant to support: there were few Poles in the 1598 invasion force, despite Charles's lurid propaganda. Nevertheless, the junior branch of the Vasas long felt insecure on the Swedish throne, and Charles soon decided that attack was the best form of defence. In 1600, he invaded Livonia, starting a long series of Polish–Swedish wars which rapidly became entangled in the growing crisis in Muscovy.

For Muscovy was lurching into chaos. Ivan died in 1584; he was succeeded by his sickly son Fedor, whose success in the 1590–5 war was largely due to the energetic Boris Godunov, his chief minister. Yet the gathering internal crisis ensured that Godunov, acclaimed as tsar following the death of the childless Fedor in 1598, was unable to exploit his victory. He crushed initial resistance to his rule, but Muscovy was hit by catastrophic harvest failures in 1601–2 which spread famine across northeastern Europe. With peasant revolts flaring up from 1603, Godunov, lacking the sanction of legitimacy, was faced in August 1604 by the appearance of the first of three pretenders claiming to be Dmitry, Ivan's son, who had died in May 1591. Despite Godunov's propaganda, which maintained – probably accurately – that this first False Dmitry was Grishka Otrepev, an unfrocked monk, the pretender's following grew rapidly. Godunov's forces were able to block Dmitry's advance on Moscow, but before they could follow up their victory, Godunov died in April 1605. His young son Fedor failed to secure the throne as leading boyars defected to Dmitry, who declared himself tsar, taking Moscow in triumph in June.

Dmitry had entered Muscovy in August 1604 from Poland, where he had secretly converted to Catholicism; he was accompanied by a retinue of Polish adventurers and Jesuits. In May 1606 he married Marina, daughter of Jerzy Mniszech, palatine of Sandomierz, one of Dmitry's most powerful Polish supporters. This act brought to a head the festering discontent which the behaviour of Dmitry and his Polish supporters had provoked; a week later, he was murdered in a bloody popular rising, which claimed the lives of 2,000 of his supporters, many of them Poles. The boyar Vasilii Shuiskii was proclaimed tsar, but was unable to restore order. Like Godunov, he lacked legitimacy, and Dmitry's death had not destroyed popular belief that Ivan's son still lived. As a massive rebellion broke out, led by Ivan Bolotnikov, a second, then a third False Dmitry appeared, and Muscovy collapsed into anarchy. The massacre of so many Poles in May 1606 stimulated Polish intervention, first unofficial, and then sanctioned by Sigismund. As Sigismund besieged Smolensk in 1609, Swedish troops were sent to aid Shuiskii, but a crushing victory by the Polish Grand Hetman Stanisław Żółkiewski over a

Muscovite-Swedish army at Klushino in July 1610 opened the road to Moscow. With Shuiskii's forces scattered, Żółkiewski entered the capital in triumph. A group of boyars acclaimed Władysław, Sigismund's eldest son, as tsar; the Shuiskii brothers were dragged to Warsaw, to be humiliatingly paraded in front of Sigismund and the *Sejm*.

Władysław was never to claim his throne. Sigismund, always ambivalent about his son's candidature, was more interested in Smolensk, which fell in 1611. Although a Polish force garrisoned the Kremlin for two years from 1610, the Muscovite adventure was unpopular, and no substantial force could be raised to establish Władysław's rule. Anti-Polish feeling in Muscovy and the Swedish attempt to advance the candidature of Charles IX's younger son Charles Philip for the Muscovite throne, united opinion against foreign intervention. The Polish garrison in the Kremlin was starved out in 1612, and Michael Romanov, son of the Patriarch Filaret, was elected tsar in 1613. The new government restored a semblance of order, but the cost of the Time of Troubles was high. Smolensk had fallen, and although the Swedes were pushed out of Novgorod and failed to take Pskov, Gustav Adolf, who succeeded Charles IX in 1611, retook Ingria and Kexholm. At the peace of Stolbovo with Sweden (1617), Muscovy accepted the loss of territory which cut it off from the Baltic, as the necessary price for a peace which enabled it to concentrate on the Polish threat, as Władysław sought to claim his throne by mounting a great attack on Moscow in 1617–18. The Poles were beaten off, but the exhausted Muscovites had to sign a fourteen-and-a-half year truce at Deulino (January 1619), surrendering Smolensk, Seversk and Chernihiv. Having also expelled the Swedes from Livonia, the Commonwealth was triumphant.

A hostile environment

'*A different sword, a different bow, though he sat at home;*
A different kind of war in Italy, different again in Germany,
A different enemy, a different game,
So one must deal differently with Tatars and Italians.' (Krzysztof Ostrogski)[3]

In August 1581 Father Jan Piotrowski, on the Pskov campaign as a royal secretary, noted in his diary the case of a foreign mercenary company which complained that conditions were not as they had been promised. Piotrowski says nothing of the cause of their grumbling, concluding laconically: 'we are not fighting in France or the Netherlands'.[4] Indeed they were not. The Muscovite war was conducted in an environment very different to Flanders or Burgundy. It is necessary to take this into account when examining the reception in eastern Europe of techniques and tactics developed in the west.

For eastern Europe was no ignorant backwater. Piotrowski had no direct experience of warfare in France or the Netherlands but there were many in Batory's army who did. The rich humanist culture of Renaissance Poland was deeply permeated with western influences, particularly from Italy, where so many Poles studied, and writing on military matters reflected general European fascination with the Ancients. Stanisław Łaski (c. 1500–49) had travelled extensively in France, Germany, the Netherlands, Italy, Hungary, Palestine and Egypt. He fought in the French army at Pavia in 1525 and took part in the sieges of Naples (1528) and Buda (1531), drawing on his experiences for a posthumously-published treatise.[5] Grand Hetman Jan Tarnowski, author of *Consilium rationes bellicæ* (1558) had fought against the Moors in North Africa, and visited France, England, Germany and Bohemia. He was an avid collector of military literature, and was particularly influenced by Valtarius.[6]

Thus knowledge of western military science was not all theoretical. Poland had deployed substantial numbers of western mercenaries since the fifteenth century: over 11,000 from the Holy Roman Empire and Spain served in the Polish army between 1506 and 1572, not including 7,000 from Bohemia and Hungary. The army at Pozwol in 1557 contained 2,000 cavalry and 3,000 infantry raised in Germany, about a quarter of the force. Apart from substantial contingents of Hungarians, Batory's army at Pskov contained 838 reiters, including 504 Germans and 250 Livonians, and a foreign infantry regiment of 1,941 men, including 1,601 Germans and 248 Scots.[7] Krzysztof Rozrażewski, who raised a regiment of foreign infantry for the Połock campaign, and who was killed at Pskov, had fought at the 1567 battle of St Denis.[8] Prokop Pieniążek, who led hussar companies at Połock and Pskov, had fought at Lepanto and was a Knight of the Order of Jerusalem, recommended by none other than Don John of Austria. Many colonels had experience of war in France, Spain and Italy, including Jan Herburt, Andrzej Zborowski and the Livonians Georg Farensbach and Ernst Weiher; others had served the Habsburgs against the Turks, or had fought in the wars of the Schmalkaldic League.

Thus if Polish-Lithuanian armies were different it was not through ignorance. It is true that Muscovy's Orthodox culture and tradition represented a more serious barrier to western influences. Although the extent of Muscovite isolation is often exaggerated, Muscovites did not travel on anything like the scale of Poles and Lithuanians; nevertheless, Muscovy did not exist in a cocoon of ignorance. Foreign craftsmen had been imported from the late fifteenth century to teach the techniques of cannon manufacture, which were quickly mastered by Russians, while Poland-Lithuania was a significant conduit of western ideas and western techniques, as is shown by the large number of military loan-words entering Russian through Polish.[9] Muscovites did serve in Polish armies: in 1556 there were fifty Muscovite cavalrymen in one unit in Podolia; between 1569 and 1573 fifty were serving on the southern frontier. Some 200 Russians served in the Polish army under the last two Jagiellon rulers; there is, unfortunately, no similar analysis of the Lithuanian army, which might reveal more substantial numbers: 10 per cent of the 1581 register of Ukrainian Cossacks were Muscovites. Many Muscovite émigrés took refuge in Lithuania, such as Semen Federovich Belskii and Ivan Latskii, who defected with 400 men in 1534 and took part in Lithuanian attacks on Seversk in 1535; many Lithuanians also defected to Muscovite service.[10]

There was a great deal of military innovation in eastern Europe after 1550; much of it influenced by developments elsewhere. Nevertheless, military change took its own course in the specific geographic, social and economic circumstances of eastern Europe. One has to be careful, however, with arguments based on geography. It is frequently suggested that the principal reason for east European backwardness was the fact that both Poland-Lithuania and Muscovy had to defend themselves against non-European enemies in the south: thus Hellie argues that Muscovy's failure to make 'a full commitment to the gunpowder revolution' in the sixteenth century was because its 'basic orientation was still toward steppe warfare, with horse-men and bows and arrows'.[11] Yet if it is true that cavalry remained central to both Polish-Lithuanian and Muscovite efforts to provide defence against the constant threat of Tatar attacks, and was of great importance in opera-tions against the Turks, it is a fundamental misconception that steppe warfare stifled the development of infantry; in fact both Poland-Lithuania and Muscovy sought to increase the contribution of infantry and firepower to their wars against both enemies after 1500.

The military threat from the Ottomans and Tatars was considerable; the Tatars were far from mere 'raiders'.[12] Attacks on Poland-Lithuania and Muscovy were virtually annual affairs in the sixteenth century, and the Tatars were quite capable of striking far to the north: they reached Brest Litovsk in 1500, Mińsk in 1505 and Wilno itself in 1510.[13] Tatar armies avoided pitched battles where they could, seeking booty and prisoners to sell on the slave markets of Istanbul, but were perfectly capable of defeating Muscovite or Polish-Lithuanian forces. The Turks and the Muscovites were just beginning their long rivalry for the lands between the Black and Caspian seas, but the establishment of Ottoman power to the south of the Carpathians after 1526 represented a direct threat to Poland, and instituted a long battle for control of the Ottoman vassal states of Moldavia, Wallachia and Transylvania.

Infantry played a vital role on the southern front. Tarnowski's army on his successful 1531 Moldavian campaign contained 4,452 cavalry and 1,167 infantry – 26 per cent of the total; the firepower of his infantry, operating from a fortified camp, was central to his victory at Obertyn.[14] Supply problems made it impossible to support large numbers of infantry, but the tactics of the fortified tabor, in which wagons were linked together with chains and protected with elaborate earthworks, meant that a relatively small force of infantry, supported by cavalry, could beat off much larger armies, as at Obertyn. Cavalry was crucial to provide cover and reconnaissance for the ponderous columns of infantry, artillery and supplies which were vital on the thinly-populated steppe, where armies could not live off the land, but decisive victories could not be won with cavalry alone.

Tarnowski stressed the importance of deploying both light and heavy cavalry, 'because one without the other is useless', and called for the raising of infantry armed with firearms, 'good gunners' and sappers to dig trenches.[15] Infantry and firearms were also necessary to garrison fortified strongpoints which acted as focal points for defence, including Kamieniec Podolski, Bratslav and Kaniv. Firepower was also central to the tactics of the many Cossack bands which had begun to appear in the remote Ukrainian steppe. The popular image of the Cossack is of a cavalryman, but this derives from a later period; although Ukrainian Cossacks used cavalry, the core of their army remained infantry armed with firearms.[16] Cossack bands were based in fortified settlements, the most famous of which was the *Sich* below the rapids on the Dnieper, the headquarters of the Zaporozhian Cossacks. In their frequent battles with the Tatars, Cossacks employed firepower and the tabor to great effect.

Muscovite commanders also appreciated the importance of firepower for the southern front. The reforms of the 1550s owed much to Ivan Peresvetov, whose proposals of 1546–9 derived from experience gained in six years fighting the Turks in Hungary and Poland; to increase firepower he recommended the formation of an infantry force of 20,000. Clearly influenced by the tabor, he suggested the use of mobile fortifications to provide protection for the infantry, something the Muscovites developed in the shape of the *gulai gorod*, a prefabricated moving fortress whose wooden sections were carried on wagons and bolted together for action.[17] Firepower was the key to the conquest of Kazan and Astrakhan, possession of which opened up the lower Volga to Muscovite settlement, and enabled the construction of an elaborate defensive system, based on a combination of infantry, artillery and the *pomest'e* cavalry. These methods worked, as western interest in Polish methods shows: the text of a 1542 dialogue between Tarnowski and the Dutch humanist Jan Stratius, in which the former discussed the problems of fighting the Turk in the light of the failed siege of Buda in 1541, was published in Würzburg in 1595, with a second edition in 1595–6, and a third as late as 1664.[18] Expertise travelled west as well as east.

The Northern Wars were fought in a very different environment. Much of the fighting took place at a latitude of 55–60 degrees – roughly that of Scotland, without the benefits of the maritime climate which softens the Scottish winter, or of northern Canada. The climate is continental, with short, hot summers, long cold winters and heavy autumnal and spring rains which rendered the few and poor roads impassable. Although relatively flat, this theatre of war was difficult to cross, since much of it was either forest or bog, drained by an immense network of rivers and lakes. Of the major rivers, only the Dvina and the Niemen flow east to west; the north-south direction of the Dniester and the Dnieper reduced their value to commanders. Campaigning was easiest in the short summer – although this, too, could see heavy rain – and in the long winter, when the ground froze, transport of both men and bulky supplies became easier, and frozen rivers and lakes ceased to be a barrier.

Armies were used to fighting in winter. The Swedes deployed units of ski-troops, who were responsible for the spectacular victory at Joutselkä (March 1555), when Finnish ski-troops swept down from a ridge on the Muscovite advance guard, whose horses struggled in the deep snow; their panic-stricken withdrawal disordered the main force behind and started a rout in which 900 Russians perished.[19] Winter warfare was common in Livonia, although the Swedes were not always successful: they suffered heavy casualties when caught by a Polish force on the Wieck border in early February 1567; the Swedish infantry, floundering in the snow, was helpless.[20]

Foreign observers were amazed that war could be waged at all in such conditions: an astonished Ottoman envoy at Pskov during the savage winter of 1581–2 observed that the Sultan would never be able to persuade his troops into the field in such a bitter frost.[21] John of Nassau, commander of the Swedish forces in Livonia in 1601–2, was similarly impressed, and was particularly struck by the ski-troops. It was difficult, however, to conduct large-scale operations in winter, when problems of supply became acute and the intense cold hampered operations: Pontus de la Gardie blamed the failure of the siege of Wesenberg in March 1574 on the problems faced – especially by infantry – in fighting under such conditions.[22] Daniel Rantzau, at the end of his great trail of devastation through central Sweden in 1567–8, faced disaster as his small force, unable to return through country they had laid waste, turned east into a hilly, forested wilderness; progress was painfully slow as the horses pulling supply wagons suffered badly from lack of fodder. Escape only came when the weather snapped colder and Rantzau was able to lead his 2,000 men across a frozen lake to safety.[23] The Poles who crossed the ice on Lake Peipus during the siege of Pskov to plunder the islands were not so lucky: they were trapped by a sudden thaw.

Armies in northeastern Europe had to travel vast distances through sparsely-populated country. The distance between the main areas of concentration of the Lithuanian and Muscovite forces (Wilno and Smolensk) was 430 kilometres in a direct line; if Smolensk was in Lithuanian hands (as it was between 1611 and 1654) the Muscovites could concentrate at Velikie Luki, which was only 375 kilometres from Wilno, but across exceptionally difficult terrain, and a similar distance from Moscow. Other gathering-points were even further away: Viazma was 580 kilometres from Wilno; Briansk 625.[24] In Batory's Pskov campaign, Voronets, the point of concentration for the Commonwealth forces, was 410 kilometres from Wilno.[25] Considering that the many Poles in Batory's army had similar distances to travel before even reaching Wilno, and that Muscovy faced similar problems, it represented a considerable feat of organisation merely to put an army in the field, let alone supply it once it arrived.

The problems of distance were compounded by the terrain through which the armies had to pass. As late as 1750, half of Lithuania consisted of forest and marsh; in the borderlands with Muscovy, where most fighting took place, this rose to 70 per cent.[26] Once an army entered Muscovy it faced a wide belt of forest deliberately left to grow wild to hinder its advance. In 1580 it took four days to cross the 100 kilometres (over half of it through forest and bog) which separated Uświat from Velikie Luki; the acidic soil meant that nothing much grew on the forest floor, and horses had to eat fodder brought with the army, or bark and leaves.[27] In 1581, marching 100 kilometres from Połock to Zavoloche, Batory's men entered a vast, trackless forest wasteland which they crossed in five days in pouring rain. Piotrowski complained that 'we are in this dark wilderness, as if plunged in the deepest circle of Hell'. While it was possible to float the guns down rivers to near Zavoloche, they had to be dragged overland for 25 kilometres.[28]

These armies were not passing through the fat, well-populated lands of western Europe. Northwestern Lithuania round Wilno had a population of 750,000 in 1528, rising to 1,300,000 in the mid-seventeenth century, at a density of fifteen per square kilometre. The rest of the Grand Duchy was even more sparsely populated, with some 1,250,000 inhabitants in 1528, rising to 2,600,000 by 1650, spread over a much larger area.[29] The population was not evenly distributed, but concentrated in cultivated islands round the network of small market towns which were centres of civilisation amidst the echoing wilderness. Much of Livonia and Estonia, which formed a much smaller theatre of war, was covered in forest and marsh; apart from Riga, Reval and Narva on the coast, and Dorpat inland, settlements

were small and population density low: though about the size of the Netherlands, Livonia and Estonia lacked the human frontiers formed by the dense,
closely-linked network of relatively large urban settlements spread over a
small area which determined the nature of the fighting in the Spanish–
Dutch wars, when advances of a few kilometres represented a considerable
success.

This hostile environment shaped warfare in northeastern Europe. Despite
the common perception that, because of their large component of cavalry,
east European armies were better-suited to fighting battles than conducting
sieges, battles were relatively rare – though skirmishes were very frequent –
and most campaigns consisted of large-scale raiding and sieges, for although
there were comparatively few fortified strongpoints, the importance of
those that did exist was magnified greatly, since they often controlled vital
communication routes, and were besieged regularly.[30] Moreover, Muscovy's
efficiency in stockpiling munitions and other supplies ensured that Muscovite
towns were tempting targets for besiegers seeking food and weapons. The
major battles that did take place were almost invariably the result of attempts
to relieve besieged cities.[31] The reason was simple: supply problems made it
difficult to keep a large force together for any length of time, while the problems of distance meant that an opponent was unlikely to be able to respond
by raising a large army quickly enough for the set-piece battles beloved of
military historians. The impressive Muscovite supply system could sustain a
large force for a short campaign, but while raiding provided additional
supplies, it was not long before the law of diminishing returns set in.[32] Thus
Ivan pursued a dual strategy of devastating the countryside and assembling
short-term, large concentrations of troops to overwhelm the tiny garrisons
scattered through Livonia. It was not a systematic army of occupation,
however, and its strategy of devastation made it difficult for a large force to
maintain itself for long in Livonia, or for the Muscovites to win the war. It
was Batory's ability to sustain a large force through three consecutive campaigns which won the war, and it was the Commonwealth which initially
proved itself most capable of adapting to the problems of fighting in this
hostile environment.

Polonia triumphans

The Commonwealth's success owed much to the military structure it evolved
during the sixteenth century.[33] Non-Polish historians often suggest that its
supposed military backwardness was because it depended for its defence on
the noble levy:

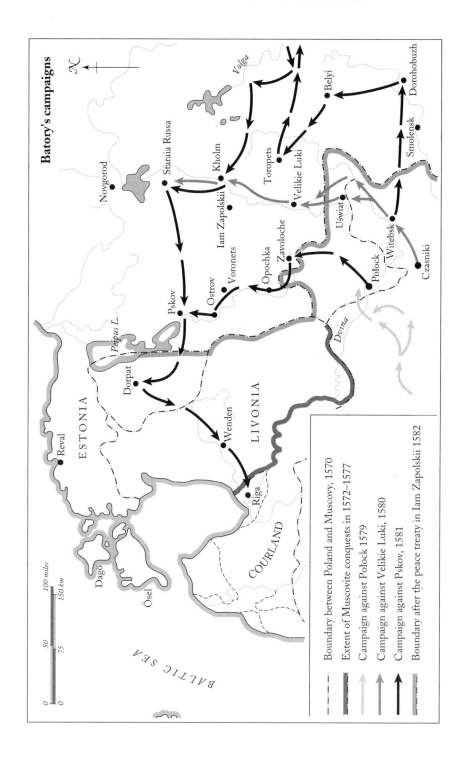

Batory's campaigns

Boundary between Poland and Muscovy, 1570

Extent of Muscovite conquests in 1572–1577

Campaign against Połock 1579

Campaign against Velikie Luki, 1580

Campaign against Pskov, 1581

Boundary after the peace treaty in Iam Zapolskii 1582

> *Szlachta* control of the polity meant control of the military . . . Poland
> entered the seventeenth and even the eighteenth century without a modern
> military structure. . . . From the earliest struggles in the medieval period
> until the eighteenth century, the Polish military was based on the levy of
> gentry knights.[34]

This is quite simply wrong. The noble levy (*pospolite ruszenie*) had not formed
the basis of Poland's defence since 1454, when the Wielkopolska levy had
been summoned by Casimir Jagiellończyk against the Teutonic Knights.
The levy first refused to fight until the king agreed that in future it should
not be called out without the agreement of the *sejmiki*, and then proved
useless in the battle of Chojnice (September 1454). Henceforth the king
could not oblige the levy to serve outside the borders of the state without
remuneration; he also had to accept the principle that defence should be
funded from the royal demesne.[35] If further funds were required, the king
was dependent upon extraordinary taxation voted by the *sejmiki*, or the *Sejm*.

After this sobering experience, Casimir Jagiellończyk initiated a process
of change. Ignoring the levy, which was called out only twice more in the
fifteenth century, he and his successors created a flexible system based on
professional troops which was well-adapted to the problems of defending a
vast state with few natural borders. It was based on a well-integrated combination of professional forces, both native and foreign, paid for by taxes
voted by the *Sejm*, royal forces maintained by the king, professional forces
raised and paid by *sejmiki*, and private forces raised by individuals, with the
levy only used as a supplementary force, usually on a local basis. The need
for a permanent military presence on the southern frontier had become
apparent in the light of regular Tatar raids: the hiring of troops in the
normal way simply took too long; by the time they reached the scene, the
Tatars had long since departed; this led to the development of a new force
at the end of the fifteenth century: the *obrona potoczna* (general defence). It
was placed on a legal basis in 1511 and 1520; henceforth, except for a few
years when money was tight, Poland maintained a permanent force of
3,000 cavalry and several hundred infantry along its southern frontier.[36]

Recruitment took place annually, and soldiers signed up for one or more
of the four service quarters into which the military year was divided. Of the
85 captains who served between 1548 and 1574, 26 (31 per cent) only
served for up to 1 year, and 16 (19 per cent) for 1–2 years; 26 (31 per cent)
served for 2–4 years; 8 (9 per cent) for 4–6 years, 2 (2 per cent) for 6–8
years and 7 (8 per cent) for over 10 years. In the same period, of 1,511
towarzysze (see below), 1,002 (66 per cent) served for up to 1 year (of which
63 only served one quarter), 260 (17 per cent) served for 1–2 years, 169
(11 per cent) for 2–4 years, 49 (3 per cent) for 4–6 years, 22 (1.4 per cent)

for 6–8 years and a mere 9 (0.6 per cent) for more than 8 years.[37] Thus, even allowing for the fact that the figures may underestimate those with longer service (lists were not compiled after 1566, and Plewczyński's study does not extend beyond 1574), his conclusion that this was not a regular, standing army is justified: it contained a core of men with five years' service or more, with the vast majority signing up for one or two campaigns.

Nevertheless, the *obrona potoczna* was a professional, paid force, costing 150,000 złoties per year: apart from receiving their wages, soldiers were paid compensation for the cost of their horse and equipment, which they had to provide themselves. By law, the king was responsible for paying for the defence of the realm from his income, which consisted of permanent taxes (the *poradlne*, a nominal tax on noble land), the income from royal lands (about 65,000 złoties per year), customs duties, profits from the salt mines, the minting of coins, the *Pfahlgeld* paid by Danzig and Elbing for the protection of their ports, and other minor sources of revenue. Royal income was insufficient, however, to cover the full cost of the *obrona potoczna*, which had to be met in part by extraordinary taxes, voted by the *Sejm*; when these were not forthcoming, the *obrona potoczna* was either reduced (as in 1544–52, when it was only 1,000-strong) or could not be deployed at all.[38] In 1562–3, there was an attempt to place its financing on a more regular footing, when the state took over responsibility; henceforth it was to be funded from a quarter of the annual revenues of the royal lands following the return to royal control of those lands illegally alienated since 1504, to be paid into a special quarter treasury at Rawa. After 1563, as a result of this legislation, the *obrona potoczna* became known as the *wojsko kwarciane* (the quarter army).[39] This provided a nucleus, 3–4,000 strong, for defence. In the event of attack, local *sejmiki* raised further units, paid for by taxes they voted themselves, by calling on local magnates to raise forces from their retainers, or by summoning the noble levy, which in Podolia and Ruthenia remained of substantial military value. As such, it suited Poland's decentralised political structure. It was also relatively cheap.

The quarter army may not have been a true standing force, but it provided an excellent training-ground in military skills. While many of its recruits came from areas most directly threatened by Tatar attack, especially Podolia and Ruthenia, many came from elsewhere, often from provinces with a large concentration of poor nobles such as Podlasie or Mazovia. Many of the short-term recruits were the sons of wealthier families, however, for whom a taste of the military life was seen as part of their education as a citizen: in the reign of Sigismund Augustus alone, 18,000 individuals served in the *obrona potoczna*. If contemporary commentators lamented the decline in *szlachta* willingness to leave their estates to serve the Commonwealth, and if Plewczyński is right to be cautious about the extent to which the *obrona potoczna* was responsible for militarising *szlachta* society, nevertheless it created a small nucleus of professional, career soldiers, from whom many commanders of later campaigns emerged, a larger number of semi-professionals and a substantial pool of reserves with some experience of war. Twenty-five of Batory's captains in the Livonian War had served in the *obrona potoczna*.[40]

This was a flexible system, well suited to the demands of warfare in eastern Europe; its structure, however, was fundamentally different from the west-European model. The basic unit was the *chorągiew* (company; literally 'banner'), recruited by a captain (*rotmistrz*) granted a commission by the king. The captain would not raise all the prescribed number of men himself, but would recruit a certain number of noblemen as *towarzysze* (comrades). Each of these would bring with him a retinue (*poczet*) of retainers, usually between 2 and 6 (the latter being the preferred number); the captain himself would maintain a retinue of 12–16. The members of the retinue were not mere servants, but fully-armed soldiers, who formed an integral part of the company's fighting strength. The size of the retinue depended upon the wealth of the *towarzysz*: he was paid by the captain according to a set scale, but had to pay and equip his retinue himself. The size of a company varied: it could contain as many as 500 men; usually, however, it was between 150 and 300.[41]

This structure is often dismissed as medieval. Such labels are unhelpful. It survived because it was excellently suited to its military environment. The fact that the state effectively subcontracted the business of recruiting and equipping the bulk of the troopers was efficient and passed on part of the cost to the *towarzysze*: although they received compensation for equipment costs, this was usually inadequate, and was abandoned altogether in 1563, when rates of pay were raised accordingly. In practice, a considerable part of the cost was born by individual *towarzysze*, although they could hope to recoup some of their outlay in the form of booty. It was a form of military organisation perfectly suited to a noble-dominated society, where the *szlachta* formed such a high proportion of the population. Although in theory all nobles were equal before the law, in practice there were vast differences in wealth between rich magnates and poor, often landless nobles. It was from among the wealthier nobles that the *towarzysze* were recruited; they in turn would enlist poorer nobles and commoners in their retinue.

The position of *towarzysz* was one of status. It clearly marked both wealth and position; as such it was important to appear with a well-armed and well turned-out retinue. It was this which created the magnificent appearance of the elite hussars. To raise a hussar company, or to serve in its ranks, was to demonstrate a certain position within society. The accoutrements of captain and *towarzysz* – the armour, the plumes, the leopard, lion and tiger skins – were extremely costly, and the magnificent horses were the dearest of all.[42]

Such a force could never have been raised by the state alone. Rates of pay did reflect the greater cost of raising hussar units, but inevitably a substantial portion of the cost was passed on to the captain and *towarzysze*. The muster-rolls of hussar units, which often detail the equipment carried, bear testimony to the ability of the system to provide well-armed, well-equipped soldiers. The contrast to the *pomest'e* cavalry in Muscovy is striking.

The military was an important route of social advancement. The ideal of the nobility as a martial class survived, and military service was recognised as a legitimate means for a commoner to enter the nobility. Troopers who distinguished themselves in battle, or managed to enrich themselves through booty, or catch the eye of a powerful patron, might themselves become *towarzysze*. The flexible cell-like structure of the *towarzysz* system, in which it was not uncommon for an individual to serve in different companies in different campaigns, and in which companies could be mixed, with retinues of cossack cavalry[43] or arquebusiers combined with hussars, allowed different tactical formations to be constructed according to the demands of the moment.

To depict this system in language derived from western armies is to distort it. There was no vertical chain of command, with hierarchical ranks and non-commissioned officers. It was a system which developed in a noble society with an ethos of equality, and a suspicion of hierarchy, but which was subject to great differences in wealth and status. All *towarzysze* were of equal status and had an equal voice in the circle (*koła*) which governed the affairs of the company under the captain. This was an important factor in the high degree of self-belief and morale displayed by Polish-Lithuanian cavalry. The cell-like structure was of great value on the battlefield: a 300-strong company might contain up to eighty *towarzysze*; this ensured that units were able to carry out the rapid manoeuvres and swift regrouping which was the key to battlefield success. It was a structure ideally suited to the requirements of warfare in eastern Europe, which consisted largely of scouting, raiding and minor actions by small, mobile units, often operating far from their bases.

Cavalry armies alone could not win wars, however. Batory was well aware of this fact, and introduced important organisational and tactical reforms, creating a force of peasant infantry, the *piechota wybraniecka* (chosen infantry), in which one infantryman was to be raised and equipped by every ten peasants on royal estates. The nominated soldier was to be exempt from taxes and feudal levies in recognition of his military service, and was to muster for training at set times in the year.[44] Tactically, Batory increased infantry firepower by cutting the number of troops armed with pikes, halberds or battleaxes. Henceforward, apart from units of foreign infantry, which still deployed pikes, Polish-Lithuanian infantry was characterised, like its Muscovite counterpart, by its high reliance on firepower.

By June 1579 the paper strength of the Commonwealth's armies reached 56,000, with 25,500 raised by Poland, and 30,500 by Lithuania, including 29,741 cavalry and 11,973 infantry (29 per cent).[45] The army on the Połock campaign was 41,814 strong, in which the proportion of infantry to cavalry was 2:1, but 1:1 among the regular troops, excluding the Lithuanian levy and private forces. After the fall of Połock, almost the entire complement of regular troops which survived the campaign – 17,568 men – were kept in service over the winter, to form the nucleus of the army for the 1580 campaign, in which 48,399 men were deployed in the main theatre of war, of which 34,475 (70 per cent) were cavalry. Then 22,417 were kept in service over the winter (of which 12,050 had to be recruited afresh to fill gaps in the ranks), and 47,000 were deployed in 1581–2, of which 16,500 were infantry.[46]

Batory's infantry reforms were important, but they were not the main reason for his success. Muscovy's defeat, insofar as it has been considered at all by historians of Muscovite military development, has usually been explained in terms of backwardness. Hellie, who does not mention the campaigns, suggests that failure in the Livonian War was due to the incomplete commitment to the gunpowder revolution. Yet the Muscovites enjoyed superiority in artillery during Batory's three campaigns, while with regard to infantry, both sides had followed largely similar paths of development. By 1600 there were 20–25,000 *strel'tsy*, including 2,800 in twenty-eight elite companies based in Moscow.[47] Like the Polish-Lithuanian infantry, the *strel'tsy* depended overwhelmingly on firepower; there was no attempt to arm them with pikes. As Polish accounts acknowledge, the *strel'tsy* and other infantry units demonstrated their worth by putting up fierce resistance in a series of sieges.

The main difference between the two armies was the quality of the Polish-Lithuanian cavalry. Western-style heavy cavalry was too slow and ponderous to match the swift-moving Tatars, and the hussars evolved as medium cavalry which was swift and manoeuvrable, yet which could mount shock attacks with considerable force. Batory completed this development, by dispensing with old-style lancers in full armour, who still constituted a third of hussar companies under Sigismund Augustus. The vast majority of Batory's regular cavalry consisted of hussar units, supplemented by cossack cavalry, Lithuanian Tatars, units of Hungarian horse, German reiters and the light cavalry of the noble levy.

This development was not paralleled in Muscovy. Although there seems to have been some improvement in the arming and equipping of the *pomest'e* cavalry after 1550, it remained essentially light horse in the Tatar style, armed with bows, short spears and, increasingly, sabres. As such, it fought like Tatars, excelling at swift raids and skirmishing rather than pitched battles, and was no match for the Polish-Lithuanian horse. The *pomeshchiki* were less willing to experiment and develop their tactics, and failed to match the cohesion and discipline of the hussars, fighting more as individuals.[48] In 1579–80, Muscovite cavalry mounted large-scale raids into Lithuania, but beyond devastating the countryside, they were unable to achieve anything, and were easily repulsed. Although the Muscovites had substantial forces available – Ivan was planning a major attack on Livonia in 1579 – they never made any concerted move to challenge the besieging forces. When, after the fall of Velikie Luki, it appeared that a Muscovite attack was imminent, Batory sent a detachment of 2,000 hussars, arquebusiers, Hungarian horse and infantry under Janusz Zbaraski towards Toropets, where 4,000 Muscovites, including a detachment of *strel'tsy*, were gathered. On 20 September 1580, Zbaraski's cavalry smashed into the Muscovites unhindered by the fire of the *strel'tsy* and swept it off the field, slaughtering many in the pursuit.[49] Toropets, the only major field encounter of the campaign, demonstrated the inability of the *pomest'e* cavalry to match the Polish-Lithuanian forces in open battle.

Yet the key contribution of Batory's cavalry was in the great siege operations on which his strategy was based. For in eastern Europe, cavalry was not a useless encumbrance in sieges, but played a central role. The requirements of siege warfare in eastern Europe were very different from the west, and the judgement that the east was primitive merely because of the relative (though by no means absolute) lack of fortifications built in the latest Italian style is unjustified. The pattern of settlement in the east, where most towns were small by western standards and built of the wood which was so plentiful, meant that communities were too small to afford elaborate fortifications of stone or brick, while the lack of local brickworks and the problems of quarrying and transporting stone represented a further obstacle. Furthermore, given the problems of gathering and supplying a large army, it was most unlikely that any but a handful of the most important strongpoints would face a large-scale siege; fortifications were mostly designed to keep out relatively small, cavalry-based armies. It was therefore appropriate to construct most strongpoints of wood and earth. Their military value was limited: when Roman Sanguszko suggested in 1567 that fortresses be built along the Muscovite frontier, Jan Chodkiewicz scornfully remarked that the army should not sit dispersed on hilltops, but should be with the king, seeking to destroy the Muscovite forces at one blow; the small Muscovite garrisons could be safely ignored: 'for if the Lord grants us victory over this enemy, then all these chicken-coops will have to surrender anyway.'[50] Batory was of the same opinion: in 1582, he proposed that most of Livonia's castles be destroyed, although local opposition prevented much being done.

The fact that Batory failed to take Pskov in 1581, or that it was only after a siege of nearly two years that Sigismund was able to take Smolensk in 1611, should not be taken to indicate incompetence or ignorance on the part of the attacking forces. Neither city was protected by the *trace italienne*, but both possessed massive stone walls: those of Smolensk, built between 1595 and 1602, were 6.5 kilometres in circumference, 13–19 metres high and 5–6 metres thick. Muscovite defensive strategy consisted in packing these powerful cities with supplies of food and ammunition, and enlisting the support of the burghers and peasants from the surrounding countryside, as a supplement to a large garrison: in 1581, Pskov possessed a garrison of 7,000 *strel'tsy* and 2,000 cavalry for mounting sorties, supplemented by 10,000 men from the local population. Neither Batory nor Gustav Adolf in 1615 was able to bring more than 20 heavy cannon to the walls of Pskov. Infantry was in short supply, but Batory's cavalrymen were perfectly capable of dismounting and entering the trenches or taking part in attacks alongside the infantry. When much of the German infantry left Pskov in December 1581, Jan Zamoyski ordered seven cavalrymen out of every company of 150 and five out of those with 100, to serve on foot. Batory specifically praised the willingness of the cavalry to serve on foot in a speech to the *Sejm* on his return.[51] Yet when the Poles breached the wall, they were thwarted by internal defensive systems and the ability of the defenders to fill the breach rapidly with temporary barriers of timber and earth; like the Swedes in 1615, they were suffering from a shortage of gunpowder.[52] In such circumstances, blockade was the only realistic strategy. If blockade failed to reduce Pskov, it did force Muscovy to settle on terms that were highly advantageous to the Commonwealth, and proved successful at Smolensk in 1609–11.

It was not, however, in its occasional role as infantry support that the cavalry's true importance lay. It was deployed to blockade besieged towns, which meant that elaborate circum- and countervallations did not have to be constructed and manned by the infantry. Nine hundred cavalry were permanently on duty at Pskov, keeping a watch on the fortress and acting immediately to counter attempts to mount a sortie; at Kokenhausen in 1601 Krzysztof Radziwiłł beat off a Swedish relief army with his cavalry while maintaining his direction of the siege. Cavalry also supplied a forward defence, disorganising and distracting relief operations. In 1581, Radziwiłł's 5,600 men covered the eastern flank of Batory's march from attack by the main Muscovite force which had entered Lithuania to devastate the palatinates of Mścisław and Witebsk. He expelled the Muscovites, forcing them to march on a wide arc northeast to Novgorod, far from the main direction of Batory's operations. Meanwhile, Filon Kmita took 2,000 men and raided Muscovy as far as the upper Volga.

Another vital function was to secure the supplies which ensured that Batory's army, despite serious problems, could maintain the siege for five months. The Poles had brought an enormous supply-train, but it was impossible to feed such a large body of men for long from what could be brought with them, while the distances involved and transport problems, especially in the autumn rainy season, were unlikely to tempt merchants to make the long journey with further supplies. Piotrowski was already complaining of shortages of bread and beer in late August; by the end of September, hay and oats had all but run out.[53] Yet there were few villages or roads, and Ivan had systematically devastated much of the border region; there was no point in establishing elaborate commissariats to milk the countryside on a systematic basis; in eastern Europe there was little scope for organised contribution systems: it was better to loot and burn.

The army had to forage far afield. This was done by teams of wagoners and servants escorted by cavalry to protect them and to enforce supply. In October 1581 Zamoyski ordered that every company should second a fifth of its strength to form parties of 120 horses. Despite the serious difficulties involved, these units succeeded in maintaining the army before the walls of Pskov for five months from an astonishingly wide area, as they ventured ever further afield to find supplies. In September 1581, they were travelling 40–70 kilometres in one direction: a round trip of 4–6 days. By December, these journeys had risen to 210–280 kilometres; by January, some units were travelling up to 350 kilometres in one direction: the round-trip took nearly a month. This took them as far as Pernau in the west, Narva and Kopor'e in the north, past Novgorod to the northeast, and Toropets and Połock in the south.[54] An infantry army would have starved.

East versus west

It was not just against the Muscovites that the Polish-Lithuanian forces were successful. The course of the war against Charles IX in Livonia after 1600 and of the fighting in Muscovy during the Time of Troubles demonstrated that Polish-Lithuanian methods were more than a match for western-trained troops. Roberts, who recognises the quality of the Polish cavalry, regards the rejection of Erik XIV's tactical reforms as the main reason for the series of Swedish defeats in Livonia, which culminated in the disaster at Kircholm (17/27 September 1605). After Erik's fall, the Swedish infantry abandoned the pike and John's attempts to reintroduce it on the Russian front were resisted. The only way to combat the Poles, according to Roberts, was to adopt the new Dutch tactics which combined firepower with the defensive rigidity of pikes.[55] This is indeed what Charles tried: after defeats at Wenden and Kokenhausen, he persuaded John of Nassau, brother of Maurice, the creator of the Dutch School, to enter his service in the summer of 1601. Nassau began to train the Swedes, pressing for the creation of heavy infantry, armed with pikes on the western pattern.

According to Roberts, he was only partially successful; returning home after one year: 'to spread reports of his experience which did no good to [Charles's] prestige abroad, he left behind him a force upon which he had imposed a reorganization which lacked the basic requirements for its proper functioning. The army had been half-reformed; and the last state of it was arguably worse than the first.'[56] Thus the disaster at Kircholm was the result of incompetent Swedish soldiers who did not know what they were doing. Yet Charles had long realised that pikes were important for defence against the Poles: before Nassau's arrival, he urgently requested 8,000 pikes to be shipped to Livonia. At Kokenhausen (13/23 June 1601), the Swedish foot based its defence on a *Wagenburg* (tabor) which they strengthened with Spanish riders: long, sharpened stakes driven into the ground to provide defence against cavalry.[57] Once the Swedish cavalry was routed in the first phase of the battle, however, the infantry was left completely exposed. As cossack and Tatar cavalry pursued the Swedish horse, the hussars and arquebusiers regrouped to deal with the helpless infantry with their own infantry and artillery. The Polish combination of firepower, manoeuvrability and shock attack also proved irresistable in June 1602, when Żółkiewski confronted a Swedish force outside Reval. Finding his way blocked by infantry, armed in part with pikes and occupying a favourable situation protected by Spanish riders, which his hussars were unable to break through, he entertained himself by keeping the enemy occupied with repeated charges, while his cossack cavalry went on a ten-mile trip round a lake to take the Swedes in the rear. The Swedish horse was chased to the walls of Reval; the foot was annihilated.[58]

Musketeers and pikemen, however skilful, were still vulnerable to a shock attack with lance and sabre. The effective range of the musket was too short to permit more than one or two salvos before cavalry, charging home at speed, could close on the infantry. Polish-Lithuanian cavalry always charged in waves: there were between three and five ranks which charged home in succession. Even if the intial salvo was effective in preventing the first rank from closing, it was unlikely to stop the second: the cavalry rode in extended formation until the enemy fired their volley, before closing up to mount attacks 'knee to knee'. The countermarch, by which ranks of infantry fired in turn before returning to the rear to reload, in an effort to keep up continuous fire, may have been effective against slow-moving or static infantry, or even cavalry wedded to the caracole – a manoeuvre developed by western cavalry, in which they trotted up to the enemy, with each rank discharging its pistols in turn before wheeling away to the rear – but it could not provide defence against lancers. Despite suggestions that the 'much-vaunted "shock" value of the cavalry charge was . . . near impossible to achieve in practice',[59] it is clear from contemporary accounts that Polish-Lithuanian cavalry did charge home at the gallop against infantry armed with pike and shot, as they did at Kircholm, to win their most famous victory.

The argument that the Swedish defeat at Kircholm was due to inferior pikemanship depends on the dogma that it was impossible for cavalry to break pike formations, and depends on circular reasoning: the pike in skilled hands was invincible against cavalry; at Kircholm, the Swedish infantry was broken by cavalry, therefore the Swedish infantry must have been lacking in skill. It is true that pikemanship was a highly skilled art, but the Swedish army at Kircholm did not consist of half-trained Swedish peasants. The 1604 *Riksdag* voted taxes for three years to enable Charles to hire 9,000 foreign mercenaries, substantial contingents of which were present at Kircholm: the 8,368 infantry formed fifty companies, of which eighteen (36 per cent) were foreign mercenaries, under two experienced western commanders, duke Frederick of Lüneburg and count Joachim Frederick of Mansfeld.[60] Together with the western mercenaries in the cavalry, they outnumbered Jan Karol Chodkiewicz's entire army, yet they suffered a spectacular defeat. Charles left 3,000 men besieging Riga and chased Chodkiewicz down the Dvina, drawing up in battle-order on the morning of 27 September 1605 with 10,868 men (8,368 infantry and 2,500 cavalry). Occupying the crest of a ridge in a narrow corridor between the Dvina and a heavily-wooded hill, which precluded the sort of enveloping movement of which his enemy was so fond, he was confident of victory against Chodkiewicz's much smaller force of 3,600 (2,600 cavalry and 1,000 infantry).[61] Charles drew up in four lines, with four infantry battalions in the first and six in the third, with cavalry forming the second and fourth lines. This formation was clearly informed by Swedish experience in previous encounters, when the cavalry had been driven off the flanks, leaving the infantry exposed in the centre; thus gaps were left between the infantry battalions to allow the cavalry to charge through and engage the enemy. The infantry battalions were drawn up in impeccable western style, in squares of thirty by thirty, formed of a nucleus of pikemen bordered by shot. At least 3,350 of the infantry were armed with pikes or halberds, virtually the size of the whole Lithuanian army.

Chodkiewicz, outnumbered nearly threefold, sought to lure the Swedes out of position, sending out light cavalry to skirmish between the two armies, and ordering his force to close ranks to make it appear even smaller than it was. After four hours waiting, Chodkiewicz pretended to withdraw, an old Tatar trick. It was the perfect moment psychologically. The Swedes had marched 10 kilometres overnight in pouring rain to confront the force which alone could threaten their siege of Riga, only to stand inactive for hours in roasting heat. Unwilling to let his enemy escape, Charles advanced onto the plain. The cavalry of the second line was deployed on the wings to provide flanking cover, while the infantry of the first line closed up and advanced to the bottom of the slope with nine field guns. Chodkiewicz timed his attack well. Wincenty Wojna, at the head of Chodkiewicz's own hussar regiment, smashed into one of the Swedish infantry squares. Twelve *towarsysze*, 12 troopers and 100 horses were killed, and 14 wounded, but the hussars, supported by the Kettlers' Courland arquebusiers, penetrated the square before withdrawing. This charge was not designed to break the infantry, but to disorder it. The main battle was to take place on the flanks, particularly on the Lithuanian left. Supported by steady infantry fire, 900–1,200 hussars and cossack horse charged home against Mansfeld's 720 reiters, who were shattered after the briefest of resistance; in their flight they seriously disordered the infantry of the third line. On the right, Chodkiewicz could not deploy so much weight, sending in 650 hussars and light horse under Jan Piotr Sapieha. This attack did not break through immediately, and Charles committed 700 cavalry from his reserve to hold the line. Chodkiewicz in turn committed his reserve. Within half an hour, the Swedish cavalry was in retreat on both flanks. With the light cavalry in full pursuit, the hussars could turn on the infantry in the centre. The Swedish foot was now separated into three groups, facing combined attack from the firepower of Chodkiewicz's foot and the shock attacks of the horse.[62]

The result was a massacre. Hyperbole is routinely employed in describing casualties, but in the case of Kircholm it is entirely justified. Relative to the size of the forces engaged, it was one of the bloodiest encounters ever fought. The infantry was largely butchered where it stood, among them Frederick of Lüneburg, who had seized a pike on being accused of cowardice by Charles when he questioned the decision to attack. The road to Riga was littered with the bodies of the Swedish cavalry; many drowned trying to cross the Dvina. Charles's drabant company lost 110 out of 150 men; the average losses of infantry units reached 75 per cent, most of them killed. Cavalry losses were less dramatic, 35 per cent on average. The burghers of Riga, who had to bury the dead, recorded the bodies which were thrown into mass graves. Two separate sources record 8,983 and 8,918 corpses, representing over 82 per cent of the Swedish forces.[63] The Lithuanians lost 100 men killed. If east European methods were backward, they were remarkably effective.

Kircholm was no fluke. It was merely the greatest of a series of victories, and was soon followed by another demonstration of the ability of Polish-Lithuanian troops to defeat western troops, when Żółkiewski led a small

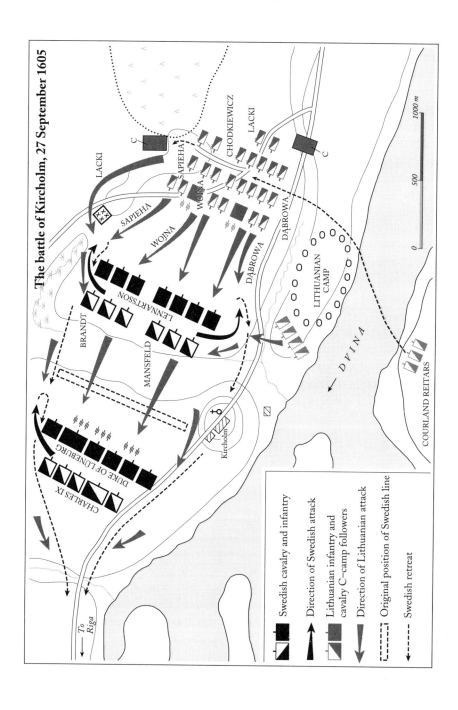

The battle of Kircholm, 27 September 1605

LACKI

CHODKIEWICZ

LACKI

SAPIEHA

WOJNA

DĄBROWA

DĄBROWA

SAPIEHA

WOJNA

LENNARTSSON

BRANDT

MANSFELD

Kircholm

DUKE OF LÜNEBURG

CHARLES IX

LITHUANIAN CAMP

D V I N A

COURLAND REITTARS

To Riga

1000 m

500

0

Swedish cavalry and infantry

Direction of Swedish attack

Lithuanian infantry and cavalry C–camp followers

Direction of Lithuanian attack

Original position of Swedish line

Swedish retreat

army of 5,556 hussars, 679 cossack horse, 290 *petyhorcy* (the Lithuanian equivalent), 200 infantry and two small field guns to victory at Klushino on 4 July 1610 against a combined Muscovite-Swedish army with a massive numerical advantage. Żółkiewski took his small army on a forced march at dead of night through difficult forested terrain to arrive just before dawn at the Muscovite-Swedish encampment. The Muscovites, led by Dmitrii Shuiskii, numbered some 30,000 if the numerous peasant auxiliaries are included; of this, perhaps 16,000 were *strel'tsy*, *pomest'e* cavalry and mounted arquebusiers. The Swedes, led by Christoph Horn and Jakob de la Gardie, who had spent two years in Holland learning the art of war from Maurice of Nassau himself, were largely composed of French, German and British mercenaries, some 5–7,000 in all: on their own they possibly outnumbered the Poles.[64]

Żółkiewski enjoyed the advantage of surprise, but his plan of an immediate attack on the two enemy camps before they awoke was thwarted. As the Poles emerged from the forest, they had to negotiate a palisade and a small village before reaching the enemy camps. At first light, as Żółkiewski's men smashed gaps in the palisade and set fire to the village, the Muscovites and Swedes began to deploy. The battle which followed was a dramatic demonstration of the effectiveness and endurance of the Polish cavalry. Żółkiewski directed his first assault against the Muscovite horse on his right. With no possibility of a flanking attack, he sent Zborowski's hussar regiment, no more than 2,000-strong, in a direct attack on the hordes of Muscovite horse. Samuel Maskiewicz, who took part, described how:

> The panic-stricken enemy . . . began to stream out of their encampments in disorder; . . . the Germans were first to form up, standing in their usual fieldworks, on boggy ground by the palisade. They did us some damage, by the numbers of their infantry armed with pikes and muskets. The Muscovite, not trusting himself, stationed reiters amidst his formation, and drew up the common folk, a numberless horde so great that it was terrifying to observe, considering the small number of our army.

Some units charged into the mass of Muscovite horse eight or ten times:

> for already our arms and armour were damaged and our strength ebbing from such frequent regrouping and charges against the enemy . . . our horses were almost fainting on the battlefield, for we fought from the dawn of a summer's day until dinner-time, at least five hours without rest . . . we could only trust in the mercy of God, in luck and in the strength of our arms.[65]

The hussars were seriously hampered by the palisade, which had only been partially demolished: the gaps were only large enough for ten horses to pass through in close order; this prevented them attacking in their usual extended formation and the steady fire of the foreign infantry, protected by the palisade, was causing heavy casualties. The Muscovite horse, however, was beginning to crack. Shuiskii asked de la Gardie to support it with his cavalry. As the reiters advanced, however, the hussars exposed the caracole as a useless parade-ground manoeuvre:

> they handed us the victory, for as they came at us, we were in some disorder, and immediately, having fired their carbines, they wheeled away to the rear in their normal fashion to reload, and the next rank advanced firing. We did not wait, but at the moment all had emptied their pieces, and seeing that they were starting to withdraw, we charged them with only our sabres in our hands; they, having failed to reload, while the next rank had not yet fired, took to their heels. We crashed into the whole Muscovite force, still drawn up in battle-order at the entrance to their camp, plunging them into disorder.[66]

As the Muscovite cavalry fled, Żółkiewski turned on the Swedes. His hussars, many of whose lances were shattered, had little chance of defeating the 'Germans' unsupported. At this point, however, Żółkiewski's small force of infantry and the two guns, which had become bogged down in the forest, arrived to rescue the situation. As the infantry and the cannon shot gaps in the palisade and inflicted casualties on the foreigners, Żółkiewski sent in Jędrzej Firlej's company, whose lances were still intact, against 'the whole foreign infantry ... standing in battle-order, protected by stakes, beside their camp ... Firlej broke this infantry, having attacked it with courage. We ... supported him; ... having broken our lances, we could only join the attack with our sabres in our hands.'[67] As the rest of the foreign cavalry was driven from the field, accompanied by de la Gardie and Horn, the infantry took refuge in their camp. Abandoned by their commanders and by the Muscovites, individuals and groups began to slip over to the Poles.[68] By the time Horn and de la Gardie returned to the battlefield, it was too late; they were forced to negotiate an honourable surrender. Many of the foreign mercenaries entered Polish service; de la Gardie led the Swedes and Finns to Novgorod.

Russian historians have frequently explained the outcome of Klushino as the result of foreign treachery.[69] This is a travesty of what happened. Polish and foreign accounts agree that it was the Muscovite horse which left the battlefield first, and it was the foreigners who felt abandoned.[70] If Klushino demonstrated anything, apart from the inadequacy of the *pomest'e* cavalry, it was that western methods were no magic elixir. Foreign mercenaries had been involved in Muscovy from the start of the Time of Troubles. De la Gardie had instructed Muscovite troops in western methods, especially pike tactics, and there were native Muscovite units of mounted western-style arquebusiers, officered by foreigners, at Klushino. Yet if western-style tactics certainly improved the defensive capacity of the Muscovite infantry, they could not win the war. For that, cavalry was still the decisive arm in eastern Europe. Pike and shot alone could not produce a military revolution in the east.

Notes

1   A *łan* was a unit of land measurement: there were two in use in Poland: the Culm *łan* (16–17.5 hectares) and the Franconian *łan* (22.6–25.36 hectares).
2   Roberts, *Early Vasas* pp. 369–84; *Kungl. Svea Livgardes Historia* II B.C. Barkman (ed.) (Stockholm 1938–9) p. 372; K. Tyszowski, 'Z dziejów wyprawy Zygmunta III do Szwecji w roku 1598' *RZNO* I (1927) pp. 25–48.
3   Ostrogski was commenting in 1512 on young noblemen who learned to fence in western Europe. Quoted by M. Plewczyński, *Żołnierz obrony potocznej za panowania Zygmunta Augusta* (Warsaw, 1985) p. 107.
4   J. Piotrowski, *Dziennik wyprawy Stefana Batorego pod Psków* A. Czuczyński (ed.) (Cracow, 1894) p. 69.
5   S. Łaski, *Spraw i postępków rycerskich i przewagi opisanie krótkie z naukami w tej zacnej zabawie potrzebie* (Lwów, 1599).
6   W. Dworzaczek, *Hetman Jan Tarnowski* (Warsaw, 1985) pp. 20–1. J. Sikorski, introduction to J. Tarnowski, *Consilium rationes bellicæ* (Warsaw, 1987) p. 6.
7   M. Plewczyński, *Armia koronna 1506–1572. Zagadnienia struktury narodowościowej* (Warsaw, 1991) pp. 86, 116; H. Kotarski, 'Wojsko polsko-litewskie podczas wojny inflanckiej 1576–1582' IV *SMHW* 18:1 (1972) pp. 79–80, 82.
8   Kotarski, 'Wojsko' II *SMHW* 17:1 (1971) p. 94; V *SMHW* 18:2 (1972) p. 55.
9   For example *zholdak* (paid soldier) from German *Soldner* via Polish *żołdak* or *mozhzher* (mortar) from German *Mörser* via Polish *moździerz*: M.-E. Sobik, *Polnisch-russische Beziehungen im Spiegel des russischen Wortschatzes des 17. und der ersten Hälfte des 18. Jahrhunderts* (Mannheim, 1969) pp. 122–44.
10 'Popis wojska kwarcianego w 1569 r.' Z. Spieralski and J. Wimmer (eds), *Wypisy źródłowe do historii polskiej sztuki wojennej* 5 (Warsaw, 1951) p. 37; Plewczyński, *Żołnierz* p. 50; idem, 'Liczebność wojska polskiego za ostatnich Jagiellonów (1506–1572)' *SMHW* 31 (1988) p. 37; idem, *Armia* p. 116; idem, *Ludzie wschodu w wojsku ostatnich Jagiellonów* (Warsaw, 1995) pp. 28–42.
11 Hellie, *Enserfment* pp. 165–6.
12 B. Downing, *The Military Revolution and Political Change* (Princeton, 1990) p. 149. Downing, whose account of the Polish military system is riddled with errors and misconceptions, suggests that Poland had only to contend with 'Tatar and Cossack raiding parties', thereby ignoring completely the Turkish threat.
13 J. Ochmański, 'Organizacja obrony w Wielkim Księstwie Litewskim przed napadami Tatarów krymskich w XV–XVI wieku' *SMHW* 5 (1960) p. 362.

14 Dworzaczek, *Jan Tarnowski* pp. 40–2.

15 Tarnowski, *Consilium* p. 47.

16 I. Krip'iakevich, *Istoriia ukrainsk'koho viis'ka* (L'viv, 1936) pp. 26–8. Cavalry constituted under a fifth of the Cossack forces at Berestechko in 1651: J. Wimmer, *Historia piechoty polskiej do roku 1864* (Warsaw, 1978) p. 219.

17 Hellie, *Enserfment* p. 165.

18 *Joannis comitis in Tarnovii in Poloniae Regno strategi nominatissmi de bello cum iuratissimis Christianae fidei hostibus Turcis gerendo, disputation sapientissima ad Invictissimum Imperatorem Carolum scriptore Joanne Strasio* (Würzburg, 1595). The second edition was published in Nikolas Rausner, *Selectissimarum orationum et consultationum de bello Turcico variorum et diversorum auctorum volumina quattuor* (Leipzig, 1595–6) and the third in *De bello contra Turcas prudenter gerendo libri varii selecti etc. uno volumine edita* (Helmstedt, 1664). Tarnowski was consulted frequently by Albrecht von Hohenzollern, whose extensive manuscript treatise on the art of war drew heavily on Polish experiences against the Turks.

19 Viljanti, *Gustav Vasas* II pp. 398–9. Muscovy also deployed ski-troops in the 1560s: 'Razriadnaia kniga Polotskago pokhoda tsaria Ivana Vasilevicha 1563 g.' A. Sapunov (ed.) *Vitebskaia Starina* IV (Vitebsk, 1885) p. 31.

20 Rüssow claimed 2,000 were killed: *Chronica* pp. 74–5.

21 Piotrowski, *Dziennik* p. 160.

22 J. Dow, *Ruthven's Army in Sweden and Esthonia* (Stockholm, 1965) p. 36.

23 *Dagbog over Daniel Rantzovs Vinterfelttog i Sverig fra den 20de Oktober 1567 til den 14de Februar 1568* MHD Række 2 Bd I (1868) pp. 103, 124, 126.

24 S. Alexandrowicz and K. Olejnik, 'Charakterystyka polskiego teatru działań wojennych' *SMHW* 26 (1983) p. 48.

25 Kotarski, 'Wojsko' V p. 99.

26 Alexandrowicz, Olejnik, 'Charakterystyka' p. 49.

27 Kotarski, 'Wojsko' III *SMHW* 17:2 (1971) p. 97.

28 Piotrowski, *Dziennik* p. 35; Kotarski, 'Wojsko' IV p. 18.

29 Alexandrowicz, Olejnik, 'Charakterystyka' p. 54.

30 B. Dybaś, *Fortece Rzeczypospolitej* (Toruń, 1998) pp. 74, 81. To mention only a few: Dorpat (1558, 1601, 1603, 1625, 1656, 1704), Narva (1558, 1581, 1700, 1704), Reval (1561, 1570–1, 1577, 1710), Riga (1605, 1621, 1656, 1700, 1710), Połock (1563, 1579, 1654), Pskov (1581, 1615), Smolensk (1609–11, 1632–4, 1654), Moscow (1610–12; 1618), Thorn (1658, 1704), Cracow (1655, 1657, 1703).

31 For example: Kokenhausen (1601), Kircholm (1605), Mitau (1622), Mewe (1626) and Smolensk (1633–4). Wisner, 'Polska sztuka wojenna pierwszej połowy XVII wieku. Wątpliwości i hipotezy' *KH* 84 (1977) pp. 410, 414.

32 D.L. Smith, 'Muscovite logistics, 1462–1598' *SEER* 71 (1993) pp. 35–65.

33 For a good introduction see R. Brzezinski, *Polish Armies 1569–1696* 2 vols (London, 1987).

34 Downing, *Military Revolution* p. 147.

35 J. Gerlach, 'Pospolite ruszenie i obrona za Zygmunta I' *Księga pamiątkowa ku czci Władysława Abrahama* (Lwów, 1931) II p. 401.

36 A force was maintained throughout the reign of Sigismund I, and for nineteen out of twenty-five years under Sigismund Augustus: Plewczyński, *Żołnierz* pp. 9, 154; Gerlach, 'Pospolite ruszenie' p. 404. The infantry garrisons were maintained even when the cavalry force was not raised.

37 Plewczyński, *Żołnierz* p. 133.

38 Ibid. p. 62.

39 In fact the treasury only received a fifth of the revenue net. This brought in 80–100,000 złoties per year, which only covered about half of the army's cost.

40 Plewczyński, *Żołnierz* pp. 12, 185–6. There is no detailed study of the quarter army after 1574, and the failure to keep detailed lists of *towarzysze* after 1566 means that it is quite possible that the number of professionals is larger than Plewczyński allows, since records of units that fought in the Northern Wars are not as complete as those of the *obrona potoczna*, so the figures he gives for those who served subsequently in the northeast are probably too low: ibid. p. 188. Others served in the royal guard, or in magnate retinues, for which muster-rolls are virtually non-existent. Large numbers of Poles also served in the Lithuanian army, whose records are sparse for this period.

41 Each unit was counted by the total number of horses it contained, not the number of *towarzysze*. I shall use the term 'trooper' for members of retinues. Units of Polish and Hungarian infantry were also recruited on the *towarzysz* system.

42 The quality of horses always impressed foreigners; see for example the memoirs of I. Massa, who saw hussars in Moscow in 1610: *A short history of the beginnings and origins of these present wars in Moscow under the reigns of various sovereigns down to the year 1610* G.E. Orchard (tr.) (Toronto, 1982) pp. 128–9.

43 In this context, 'cossack' merely refers to a particular formation of medium cavalry, armed with a sabre, a short spear and a bow, and has nothing to do with official or unofficial Cossack units. After 1648 the term *'pancerna'* (armoured) began to be used for these formations, to avoid the confusion with the Cossack rebels.

44 Batory intended the scheme to cover all peasants, but the *Sejm* restricted it to royal estates.

45 Kotarski, 'Wojsko' II p. 102. The Lithuanian figures contain 10,000 private troops and 11,000 from the Lithuanian noble levy, whose exact numbers cannot be determined. Not all units were up to strength, although the hussar company mentioned by Piotrowski which arrived in July 1581 with 150 men instead of the 300 for which the captain had drawn pay, was the exception, not the rule. Piotrowski, *Dziennik* p. 16. Kotarski exhaustively compares figures from muster-rolls with literary sources, whose estimates correspond closely with the official lists.

46 Kotarski, 'Wojsko' II pp. 104–5, 119; III p. 108; IV pp. 5, 39.

47 Hellie, *Enserfment* p. 162; Chernov *Vooruzhennye* p. 83.

48 M.M. Denisova, 'Pomestnaia konnitsa i ee vooruzhenie v XVI–XVII vv.' *VIS* 20 (1948) pp. 29–46; S.K. Bogoiavlenskii, 'Vooruzhenie russkikh voisk v XVI–XVII vv.' *IZ* 4 (1938) pp. 259–60.

49 Five Polish troopers who caught a Muscovite group of about seventy, remarked that the Muscovites 'fought like cattle, for they did not defend themselves.' Quoted by O. Laskowski, 'Wyprawa pod Toropiec. Ze studiów nad wojnami moskiewskimi Stefana Batorego' *PHW* 9 (1936–7) pp. 47, 79.

50 Quoted by K. Piwarski, 'Niedoszła wyprawa tzw. radoszkowicka Zygmunta Augusta na Moskwę w r. 1567–8' *AW* 4 (1927) p. 274.

51 Ł. Działyński, 'Diariusz oblężenia i zdobicia Wieliża, Wielkich Łuk i Zawołocia' *Sprawy wojenne króla Stefana Batorego* I. Połkowski (ed.) (Cracow, 1887) pp. 267, 288. The cavalry could prove touchy. In July 1610, at the siege of Smolensk, as the appointed moment for an attempted storm approached, the cavalry went into a collective huff, refusing to dismount and join the infantry because they had been ordered, not invited, to participate. Only when the palatine of Bratslav went from unit to unit to plead in person did they consent to participate. 'Wyprawa krola i.m. do Moskwy r. p. 1609' *Pamiatniki otnosiashchiesia k Smutnomu Vremeni* (St Petersburg, 1872) pp. 654–6.

52 Batory lost much of his powder in an accidental explosion en route; he sent to Riga for replacement supplies, but they were late and not substantial. The detonation of the main Swedish magazine by a lucky shot in 1615 led directly to Gustav Adolf's abandonment of his siege.

53 Piotrowski, *Dziennik* pp. 63–4, 97.

54 Kotarski, 'Wojsko' IV pp. 51–5.

55 Roberts, *Early Vasas* p. 401.

56 Ibid. p. 402; cf. *Livgardes Historia* II pp. 532–3.

57 'Warhaftige und grundtliche beschreibung des itzigen betriebten Liefflendischen kriegs . . .' *MGGLEK* 17 (Riga, 1900) p. 139.

58 J. Besala, *Stanisław Żółkiewski* (Warsaw, 1988) pp. 144–5.

59 F. Tallett, *War and Society in Early-Modern Europe 1495–1715* (London, 1992) p. 30; J. Keegan, *The Face of Battle: a Study of Agincourt, Waterloo and the Somme* (London, 1976) pp. 154–60. By 1815 musket technology and infantry tactics had changed fundamentally.

60 *Livgardes Historia* II pp. 524–5. Roberts does not mention the presence of the foreign units in his brief account of Kircholm: *Early Vasas* p. 403.

61 *Livgardes Historia* II p. 525. Figures for the Lithuanian army give between 3,600 and 4,350; the lower figure seems more probable. H. Wisner, *Kircholm, 1605* (Warsaw, 1987) p. 107.

62 T. Korzon, *Dzieje wojen i wojskowości w Polsce* II (2nd edn, Warsaw, 1923) p. 146; Wisner, *Kircholm* p. 112; *Livgardes Historia* II p. 538; J. Teodorczyk and Z. Żygulski jr. 'Dwugłos o bitwie pod Kircholmem. Historia i ikonografia' *RHS* 24 (1999) pp. 99–107.

63 *Livgardes Historia* II p. 544.

64 According to Żółkiewski the Swedes were drawing money for 10,000 men, but he estimated them at just over 8,000, adding that Skopin-Shuiskii, captured after the battle, claimed there were over 40,000 Muscovites present. S. Żółkiewski, *Expedition to Moscow* M.W. Stephen (tr.) (London, 1959) p. 79. Thomas Chamberlayne, an English eyewitness, whose estimate of the hussars was fairly

accurate (4,000) stated that there were at least 16,000 Muscovites: Chamberlayne to Robert Cecil, 'Relatio de servitio militari cum Moscovitis contra regem Poloniae, dein cum Polonis contra Moscoviam praestito' C.H. Talbot (ed.), *Res Poloniae Iacobi I Angliae Regnante Conscriptae ex Archivis Publicis Londiniarum* EFE VI (Rome, 1962) p. 118. The figure of 16,000 is also given by a Polish source: 'Historia Dmitra fałszywego' p. 195.

65 *Pamiętniki Samuela i Bogusława Kazimierza Maskiewiczów* A. Sajkowski (ed.) (Wrocław, 1961) pp. 128, 129.

66 Ibid. p. 130.

67 M.S. Marchocki, *Historya wojny moskiewskiej* (Poznań, 1841) p. 90.

68 Chamberlayne, as a good Englishman, naturally blamed the French: 'Relatio' p. 118.

69 Chernov, *Vooruzhennye* p. 115; Hellie, *Enserfment* pp. 169–70. For a more measured account, which uses Polish as well as Russian sources, see D. Buturlin, *Istoriia Smutnago Vremeni v Rossii v nachale XVII veka* III (St Petersburg, 1846) pp. 162–81.

70 Chamberlayne, 'Relatio' p. 118.

CHAPTER FOUR

A Time of Troubles:
the Impact of War, 1558–1619

Destruction

By 1619, northeastern Europe had experienced over sixty years of war, fought in a hostile environment by states with limited human and material resources. War was almost constant, campaigns were longer and more intensive than ever before, and armies were significantly larger. Both Muscovy and Poland-Lithuania had to face regular Tatar invasion on their southern frontiers, which frequently brought war on two fronts a thousand kilometres apart. Denmark and Sweden had to cope not only with the increased demands of land warfare, but also the construction and maintenance of large fleets in an age of rapid development in naval warfare. The reactions of each state to these demands differed fundamentally, even where – as in the case of Denmark and Sweden – there were broad similarities between their social and political structures. All the combatants were profoundly affected. Denmark might have avoided long-term engagement, but the political aftershock of its involvement in the 1560s was substantial. Poland-Lithuania, Sweden and Muscovy all experienced major political, social and economic dislocation between 1558 and 1619. While it would be foolish to see war as the sole cause of upheaval in what was a period of rapid social and political change, the demands of war, and the social dislocation caused by war, fundamentally shaped the development of all three powers, with important consequences for the outcome of the Northern Wars.

It is hard for the twentieth century – the age of the Somme, Hiroshima and Dresden – to take seriously the destructive capacity of early modern warfare. Yet for all its comparative lack of technological sophistication, early modern warfare could and did destroy on an impressive scale. If armies were considerably smaller than modern forces, and their weaponry far less destructive, the duration of wars, undeveloped transport networks and primitive medical techniques meant that war had profound economic, social and demographic consequences. Agricultural production and the market for agricultural produce were highly susceptible to disruption by adverse weather or military action; this was especially true of northeastern Europe, where much land was marginal, population density low, the growing season short and yield ratios poor. The slightest disruption of production, or of the local grain-market, could have devastating effects, a fact which was frequently exploited by commanders.

This was certainly recognised during the 1560s, when the Swedish and Danish governments experienced enormous difficulties in assembling and supplying their forces. Both armies had to live off the land, exacting contributions from the local population. Frederik II might have assured the population of the Swedish borderlands that he would respect their privileges, but his army was already harrying his own subjects before it even crossed into Sweden. In 1567 Daniel Rantzau issued proclamations claiming that his force did not wish to destroy, but only to seek out the Swedish army:

> and therefore wished to leave the poor peasants, who had little indeed to do with the war, in peace, if they only agreed to pay Contribution; where this happened, they wished to do them no harm, but leave them safe in their houses with their families, and protect them from all violence, and desire or take nothing from them apart from these Contributions, and necessary fodder and food.[1]

The price of such magnanimity was eight *lod* of silver per household.[2] Rantzau claimed that most paid willingly, although seventy-eight were hanged as traitors.

Such claims were disingenuous. Both sides recognised the importance of campaigning on enemy territory to avoid overburdening their own subjects, and of destroying the enemy's supply base. Erik ordered Nils Pedersen: 'to do damage to our enemy . . . with attacks over the border, roving and burning, so that he will have little opportunity to harm us and our subjects.' Frederik ordered Sten Rosensparre to take his men onto enemy soil: 'where [they] can do the enemy most harm, for it is ever difficult to have this mass of men lying in the King's own lands, where it impoverishes the people.'[3] These starkly realistic considerations destroyed any hope of winning over the local population. Both sides burnt and harried their way across enemy territory. Collart, sent to conquer Norway with 4,000 men in 1564, was ordered to kill all 'Jutes' (Danes), sparing only true Norwegians, and to secure Norway for Sweden by introducing Swedish colonists. This was an impossible aim with such a tiny force, but Collart did his best to implement Erik's wishes by executing all Danish prisoners. The savagery was catching.

Ronneby was razed and its population massacred after refusing to surrender in September 1564. Erik unrealistically ordered the round-up of the entire population of Blekinge province on the pretence of swearing oaths of loyalty, for deportation to Kalmar and Stockholm. When Varberg fell in 1565, its garrison was massacred, except for 150 Scottish, German and French mercenaries (including Pontus de la Gardie) who entered Swedish service.[4] The Danes were no different. For all his assurances, Rantzau blazed a trail of destruction across southern Sweden in late 1567. With their foragers coming under constant attack, the Danes showed no mercy to Swedes who fell into their hands. In November, the convent at Alvastra was burnt; two days later, the Brigittine convent at Vadstena was plundered. While the nuns were spared, all males found in the convent were slaughtered.[5] Vadstena, where the Danes found rich booty, was sacked twice more and the church was destroyed; in December, Söderköping was plundered and burnt.

The devastation of the border provinces was considerable, but the small size of the forces involved, and the war's comparatively short duration, ensured that recovery was relatively rapid after 1570. In Sweden 60–100 per cent of the farms received tax relief for having been destroyed, plundered or burnt completely or partially in the strip of land from the river Viskan to just south of lake Bolmen, and along the main river valleys; in 1570, 65 per cent of the farms in Mark and 49 per cent in Sunnerbo were receiving relief. Nevertheless, although many of them were designated as waste in the tax registers, this did not necessarily mean that they had been abandoned. In two hundreds the 1571 registers for the payment of the Älvsborg ransom indicate that only 102 (9.2 per cent) of the farms in Sunnerbo and 98 (10.1 per cent) in Mark were uninhabited. The policy of tax-relief represented a realistic attempt by the government to ensure as large an income as possible from the affected areas, in which its bailiffs (many of whom were local farmers) and the parish authorities were able to assess the extent of damage and grant relief in a relatively fair way. This conclusion is confirmed by the subsequent recovery of most of the affected areas: by 1584, only 6.5 per cent of farms in Mark were still receiving relief compared with 65.7 per cent in 1570; 3.9 per cent in Kind (50.7 per cent), and 1 per cent in Västbo (50 per cent). In the worst-affected areas along the border, recovery seems to have been rapid; although signs of the devastation were still apparent in a few areas in 1600, the affected farms were largely in the north, on marginal land.[6]

Thus the Nordic Seven Years War caused little long-term damage to the agricultural economies of Sweden and Denmark. This was mainly due to the short duration of the fighting, the relatively small armies involved and the fact that neither side was able to mount any sustained occupation of enemy territory. Although substantial numbers of homesteads were wholly or partially destroyed – of 970 listed in Mark in 1570, $356\frac{1}{6}$ were listed as ruined, 94 as burnt and 89 as plundered – population loss was limited and recovery relatively swift.[7] The war may have been nasty and brutal, but its effects were short-lived. It set a pattern for subsequent Swedish–Danish conflict: each of the wars in 1611–13, 1643–5, 1657–8, 1658–60 and 1674–9 was brief, if furious, and areas affected by what could be substantial short-term devastation were granted a long period of peace to recover.

The contrast with Livonia and Estonia is stark. Not only did they experience more sustained campaigning, but the armies that fought there were larger and, with both Poland-Lithuania and Muscovy employing cavalry-based forces, more skilled at the basic destructive arts. There were none better at raiding, destroying and plundering. Between 1558 and 1629, intensive fighting was concentrated in bursts – 1558–61, 1570–1, 1577–83, 1600–5, 1617, 1621–3 and 1625–9 – interspersed with periods of calm, or low-intensity warfare. Österberg suggests that it took up to fifteen years for Sweden's border areas to recover from the direct effects of war; Livonia and Estonia were hit by periods of intense fighting every ten to fifteen years over seven decades. Any recovery was halted abruptly by a new wave of destruction. The results were catastrophic. The population of Estonia dropped by about a half through death and emigration, from 250–270,000 in the mid-sixteenth century to 115–120,000 in the 1630s; only in the late seventeenth century did it return to pre-1558 levels.[8]

Moreover, the Livonian War was from the outset a civil war; as in all civil wars, divisions within estates and families compounded the general savagery. For Rüssow, as for many of the Livonian elites, the main enemy was Muscovy: Ivan made it clear that he regarded the Germans as interlopers and Muscovite commanders attempted to distinguish between the German elites and the local Estonian or Latvian population in their treatment of captured towns. This has led some to depict the war as a class struggle, in which the oppressed peasantry rose up against their German masters, counting on support from 'the Russian nation and the Russian army'.[9] This view is based on extremely selective use of sources. It is true that Muscovite commanders attempted to foment divisions between the largely German elites and the local population. It is also true that there were many examples of active help given by the local population to the Muscovites: Eilert Krause stressed in his report to the Archbishop of Riga on the surrender of Dorpat that one of the arguments used by burghers in favour of surrendering was the unreliability of the many '*Unteutsch*' (non-German) inhabitants;[10] it was a common story, as many nobles paid the price for the steady increase in the burdens placed on the enserfed peasantry in the early years of the century.[11] Peasant resistance to the nobility peaked in the rising in Harrien and Wieck in 1560–1, in which many nobles were attacked and their farms destroyed.

Nevertheless, attempts to present the Livonian War as a peasant revolution or war for national independence, with Ivan's armies improbably cast as liberators, are unconvincing. There is no reason to doubt that many peasants aided the Muscovites, or that there existed a great deal of hostility towards the German elites, yet care should be exercised before inferences are drawn: Krause, after all, was explaining to his superior why Dorpat surrendered to the Muscovites; the non-German population may well have been unreliable, but it was convenient to use them as scapegoats to deflect criticism of Dorpat's German defenders for their feeble resistance. Krause, who enjoyed a well-deserved reputation for duplicity, also claimed that Dorpat was badly supplied with artillery, although Muscovite sources stress the opposite. Renner, who describes many cases of peasants aiding the Muscovites, also reports peasant attacks on Dorpat's besiegers.[12] Henning's account of the capture of Salis in 1575 suggests that active help for Muscovite armies was not as common as is sometimes suggested: 'something took place which, thankfully, had never happened before: some people acted as guides for the Russians and showed them the approaches to the blockhouse.'[13]

There were many reasons why locals might cooperate with the Muscovites. They faced an unenviable choice: resistance against overwhelming odds, flight (which left property and livestock at the mercy of the invader), or cooperation. The issuing of manifestos by invading armies promising protection of the common people and claiming that war was being waged only on their rulers was universal practice; such documents were usually worthless, intended to justify the levying of contributions, and reveal little about actual behaviour. Peasants were caught between a rock and a hard place, liable to be punished by the enemy if they did not cooperate, or by their own rulers if they did: both sides executed those who aided the enemy.[14]

The peasantry inevitably bore the brunt of the attacks. If cooperation with the invader could provide temporary protection, there was no guarantee that the next unit to pass by would recognise or respect agreements made. Peasants frequently took revenge on small Muscovite units roving the countryside in search of plunder. In September 1558, Robert van Gilsenn, with 100 horses and other peasants from the Reval area, attacked a unit of forty Muscovites in Jerven, killing five and putting the rest to flight; the Russians retaliated by massacring 300 peasants and burning across Harrien. Reports of atrocities were legion; many were directed against the German elites, but the peasants were certainly not spared. In 1558, near Wittenstein, the Muscovites began by breaking Hans Bare on the wheel; they then baked a German woman alive, before massacring 105 people in the village of Cardinol. Near Randen in September 1558, 'The Germans who live there were killed, along with many peasants.'[15]

How reliable are the sources? In a stream of broadsheet accounts the atrocities of the Muscovite armies were catalogued in detail:

> the Muscovite came . . . and took Salisch, . . . several maidens were spitted and roasted; and what became of the little children: they were thrown into the snow, wretchedly impaled on fenceposts and murdered. . . . Reliable men tell how 1,000 men were driven away to Moscow; may God the Almighty protect them in their misery and poverty under the Cross. Old men and women were locked in a house, which was then set alight; they were horribly burned to death.[16]

According to such accounts the Muscovites tortured, murdered and raped their way across Livonia. The local population was stripped, robbed, plundered and impaled. Women had their children torn from them and murdered in front of their eyes; their breasts, ears and noses were hacked off, and they were subjected to mass rape.

Much of this was lurid exaggeration or crude propaganda designed to win financial and military support from the Empire, and later encouraged by Poland-Lithuania and Sweden to justify their war against Muscovy and block support for Ivan.[17] Nevertheless, despite the derivative and formulaic nature of many of the tales, accounts of Muscovite atrocities cannot be written off as mere literary constructs, or the result of Ivan's descent into madness during the 1560s. This is the position adopted by a number of historians of Russia, many of whom use the undoubted exaggeration of Ivan's excesses as an excuse to question or belittle their significance. Kirchner admits that Ivan's policies took a nasty turn after 1570, but argues that the behaviour of his armies was 'above reproach'.[18] Thaden argues that chronicle discussions of the conduct of Muscovite troops 'used the same, perhaps exaggerated language' as the broadsheets, but does not consider the extent of the exaggeration, merely remarking that 'the reports of terror, treason and arbitrary rule in Muscovy did not encourage voluntary submission to the will of Ivan IV in Livonia'.[19] Livonians had no need to pay much attention to reports from Muscovy, having a great deal of first-hand experience of Muscovite behaviour.

Attempts to play down the extent of Muscovite atrocities and to call in question every contemporary source smack too much of special pleading. The accounts by Rüssow, Henning, Renner, Nyenstädt and Hjärn were contemporary chronicles. Though they are certainly not objective histories, none of these authors indulged in the formulaic litanies of the broadsheets; all were specific in their accounts, often naming victims. Neither the numbers involved nor the bestial treatment to which they were subjected seem implausible. Renner told how, in September 1558:

> On this occasion, the Russians burnt everything round Tricaten and
> Harrien; they . . . killed a nobleman in Jerven called Clawes Maidel. In
> Harrien they sliced off the breasts of maidens and women, then cut off the
> hands and feet of the menfolk; in one village they threw fifty small children
> into a ditch and covered them with stones. In Jerven they took one man,
> named Wilm Wrede, cut open his side after whipping him, filled his side
> with gunpowder, lit it and blew him into pieces.[20]

When Ivan captured Połock in 1563, he separated out the Poles and the
Lithuanians; the former were released, the latter were led into captivity or
massacred and thrown into the Dvina along with Catholic priests and Jews.[21]

The picture which emerges is by no means merely a litany of Muscovite
crime. Henning, who certainly embellishes his account with rhetorical
flourishes, lists many incidents, but also stresses the occasions when, to his
surprise, nothing happened, and the invaders treated the local population
with consideration. Nyenstädt's account of the fall of Dorpat in 1558 indeed praised Shuiskii's behaviour.[22] Rüssow, while not sparing in his condemnation of Muscovite barbarity, did not overlook atrocities by others,
even when they were carried out by locals or the Swedes he supported.[23]
He stressed the good behaviour of the Muscovites on several occasions,
including the 1575 capture of Pernau.[24] Barbarity was not a Muscovite
monopoly. When the Swedes stormed Narva in 1581, they gave no quarter;
according to Rüssow, 7,000 Muscovites were killed.[25] Polish-Lithuanian
armies easily matched Ivan's troops in the destructive arts. This incident
was matched by the brutal sack of Velikie Luki in 1580, after Batory had
agreed terms with the garrison.[26] After retaking Kokenhausen in June 1601,
Chodkiewicz's Lithuanians embarked on a savage and pitiless massacre
which resulted in a panic-stricken stampede for safety: one source claims
2,000 men, women and children were killed or drowned in the Dvina.[27] Far
from being one-sided anti-Muscovite propaganda, these accounts give a
believable picture of a savage war, in which atrocities were followed by
reprisals in a pattern hideously familiar to anyone who has lived through
the twentieth century. While exaggeration was commonly employed, it should
not be equated with invention: it was a common literary device to heighten
the importance of the events described and its use suggests that contemporary observers were genuinely traumatised by what they had seen.[28] Its
use should not be taken as evidence that atrocities did not occur.

For the Commonwealth and Muscovy, however, the indirect consequences
of war were more important than actual physical destruction. Muscovy's
dramatic socio-political collapse in the Time of Troubles (*Smuta*) was caused
by more than the dynastic crisis following the death of Ivan's successor
Fedor in 1598 and the devastating famine, occasioned by the failure from
1601 of three successive harvests due to bad weather. These factors were

important, but the social turbulence experienced between 1605 and 1613 was in large part caused by a dramatic crisis within the Muscovite military and service state. Moreover, Muscovy's prolonged agony was part of a wider crisis of eastern Slavic society, in which the indirect impact of war upon both Muscovy and the lands of the pre-1569 Grand Duchy of Lithuania – whose social structures bore many similarities – produced immense strain at a time when the two states were diverging rapidly following the Union of Lublin and the establishment of the Uniate Church at the 1596 Union of Brest, in which the hierarchy of the Orthodox church in the Commonwealth agreed to accept papal supremacy in return for being allowed to keep their Orthodox rite. By these two acts, the Commonwealth's Lithuanian and Ruthenian ruling elites opted decisively for the Polish political model of noble republicanism. The process of adjustment to this dramatic change was long and painful, and if Lithuania and the Ukraine did not experience an internal crisis on the scale of Muscovy's Time of Troubles, they certainly underwent a period of great strain.

Smuta

The Muscovite military and political system was founded on the principle of service. The rise of the Grand Dukes of Muscovy to supremacy in north-eastern Russia had been based on a combination of military success and the ability to provide lucrative opportunities to their servitors. The two factors were mutually dependent. Servitors followed success, for that was where the greatest rewards were to be found. The salaries paid to military servitors on campaign and the *kormlenie* (feeding) system of local administration, by which a centrally-appointed governor drew a salary in cash or kind from the region assigned to his charge, drew men into government service.

The system depended on a symbiotic relationship between the ruler and his servitors. Between 1470 and 1558, the complex relations between the various categories within the elaborate hierarchy of service were established in a process of legislative dialogue between monarch and servitors. In a system short of labour, which relied on the ability of its middling and petty servitors to arm and equip themselves, rulers attempted to balance the needs of all levels of the landholding hierarchy, including the state and the great monasteries who were the most powerful landowners of all. Since wealthy boyars were able to offer more favourable terms to peasants than middling and lesser servitors, the government came under increasing pressure to strengthen legislative restrictions on peasant mobility to prevent the flight of the peasant labour necessary for *pomeshchiki* to equip themselves. In

the favourable climate for agricultural expansion after 1450, various concessions were made by Vasilii II and Ivan III to individual landowners
(mostly monasteries) limiting the right of peasants to move to a brief period
of two weeks after St George's Day (26 November). This limitation was
extended to all landholders in the codification of Muscovite law undertaken
in 1497. Although it does not seem that pressure from *pomeshchiki* played
any great part in this decision, since large-scale grants had only been instituted in the 1480s, they certainly benefited from it; over the next 150 years
pomeshchik pressure played a central role in the progressive enserfment of the
peasantry.

The *pomest'e* system was designed to produce the cavalry army essential
for success in eastern warfare. Until the 1550s, it functioned reasonably
well. Inevitably, however, there were pressures and inconsistencies. As the
system became fully established, it became increasingly difficult to guarantee sufficient profitable land to enable servitors to meet their obligations.
On a servitor's death, his land reverted to the state and was reassigned by
the *Pomestnyi Prikaz*. The problem was that the number of *pomeshchiki* tended
to increase with the passing of the generations, especially in the favourable
agrarian and demographic conditions of the first half of the sixteenth century. By the 1550s, the supply of land with the peasant labour-force which
alone made it economically viable was running short. For if individual
estates were not hereditary, government policy ensured that status and
economic position was, at least in theory: it was a recognised principle that,
on coming of age at fifteen, the sons of hereditary servitors would be granted
estates equal to those of their father. Since it was by no means unusual for
pomeshchiki to have two or more sons, demand for productive land grew
rapidly, and was increased by the 1556 decree on service, which extended
the obligation to serve to all landowners, thus undermining the distinction
between *votchina* and *pomest'e*, and stipulating that one horseman should be
provided from every 100 quarters of land.[29]

As Skrynnikov remarks, this was a grandiose utopia.[30] A system where
the state guaranteed to provide land and a career for its military servitors
on a level equal to that enjoyed by their fathers was highly attractive, since
it avoided the perennial problems of subdivision of holdings and provision
for younger sons which faced any contemporary landed elite. It was, however,
unsustainable without expansion, not so much of the stock of land, as of the
labour to work it. To an extent, the rising population of the first half of
the sixteenth century postponed the day of reckoning, as the area under
cultivation grew; inevitably, however, despite the best efforts of the *Pomestnyi
Prikaz*, the growing shortage of productive land meant that subdivision of
service estates was inevitable, which threatened to undermine the whole
principle of service-tenure, since any reduction in the size of an estate

threatened the ability of its holder to meet his obligations. By the 1550s, the internal pressures within the system made renewed attempts at territorial expansion highly likely, in order to avoid its collapse.

Expansion was initially successful. The capture of Kazan and Astrakhan, the annexation of Dorpat and eastern Livonia, and the seizure of Połock enabled Ivan to reward his servitors with extensive grants of *pomest'ia*. In the northwest, however, after initial deportations of thousands of Livonians and Estonians, *pomest'e* cavalry proved to be unsuitable for the systematic defence of occupied territory. Moreover, the conquest of the Tatar khanates, and above all the subjugation and defence of Livonian and Lithuanian territory, required substantial amounts of money. The *pomest'e* cavalry might provide its own horses, arms and equipment, but *pomeshchiki* were paid while in service, as were the non-hereditary servitors: the *strel'tsy*, service cossacks and *pishchal'niki*, who were armed and equipped at state expense.

The taxation required to keep the military system running placed a heavy burden on Muscovite society, not just on the peasantry, but on the servitors themselves, since *pomest'ia* were not exempt from taxation until the late sixteenth century. The tax burden rose steeply throughout the Livonian War, with much of the extra income generated by extraordinary taxes.[31] Already by the mid-1560s the strain was beginning to show. The division between boyars and ordinary servitors began to widen. For, although Ivan IV's reforms of the 1550s had sought to erode the distinction between *votchina* and *pomest'e*, in practice the boyar elite retained a large array of privileges, including important tax exemptions, which increased *pomeshchik* frustration.

The origins of the crisis of the service state lay in the simple fact that the Muscovite armies were unequal to the tasks set for them by Ivan. As with all aggressive military systems where expansion brings the rewards necessary to sustain economic and social status, danger threatens when that expansion can no longer be sustained. In Muscovy, Ivan's tortured personality meant that the initial phase of the crisis took a peculiarly savage form, yet if the anarchic brutality of the *Oprichnina* owed much to the tsar's personal demons, it was a symptom of problems within the Muscovite system much deeper than the cruel paranoia of a deranged tyrant. If frustration at the failure of the Muscovite armies to crush their enemies helped push Ivan into establishing the *Oprichnina*, nevertheless, its formation depended crucially on both the internal logic of the service state, and on the existence of widespread social tension within its upper levels. The *Oprichnina* was not a rational assault on the position of the princely and boyar elite.[32] Much of Ivan's anger, particularly in its first phase, was directed against individual boyars or whole families, but his victims were selected on an irrational and unsystematic basis. Confiscations and banishments were frequently reversed, and if lowly-born servitors were often prominent among the *oprichniki*, so were members of more exalted houses: an early leader of the *Oprichnina* was A.D. Basmanov, a distinguished commander from the Livonian War, while princes of illustrious lineage, including F.M. Trubetskoi, N.R. Odoevskii, A.P. Khovanskii and I.A. Shuiskii, who was president of the *Oprichnina* council in its closing period, all served the institution whose victims they had previously been. In the second phase of terror, which began in 1566, it was among lower levels of the service elite that victims were principally found, including many humble provincial servitors.[33]

Whatever the motives behind it, the *Oprichnina* substantially disrupted the service state. Ivan exalted many of humble background and cast down a few of high birth; the elaborate system of *mestnichestvo* by which the rigid and complex hierarchy of service was maintained, was shaken to the core. At a deeper level, the turbulent years between 1565 and 1572 had revealed the dangers of a service system predicated on reward. With the faltering of the rapid expansion which had enabled the government to meet the growing claims of the next generation of servitors in the 1550s, there was a risk that the system would turn in on itself: land and rewards would have to be sought from within, merely to sustain the growing body of servitors, if they could not be seized from others. Redistribution of land had begun already in 1550, when service lands round Moscow were reassigned to 1,000 selected servitors; postponed by the great annexations after 1552, it resumed in a more savage form in 1565. The division of Muscovite territory into *Oprichnina* and *Zemshchina* was followed by a wave of confiscations, as Ivan deprived all within the *Oprichnina* area whom he did not trust, reassigning their holdings to those he did.

The *Oprichnina* was relatively short-lived, but it only deepened the developing crisis of the service state. The status of servitors was ever unsure; that of their children even more so. As Giles Fletcher observed:

> the lands assigned to mainteine the army, are euer certein, annexed to this office without improuing, or detracting one foot. But that if the Emperour haue sufficient in wages, the roomes being full so farre as the lande doeth extend already, they are manie times deferred, and haue nothing allowed them, except some one portion of the land be deuided into two. Which is a cause of great disorder within that countrie: when a souldier that hath many children, shal haue sometimes but one intertained in the Emperours pay. So that the rest hauing nothing, are forced to liue by vniust and wicked shiftes, that tend to the hurt & oppression of the Mousick, or common sort of people. This inconuenience groweth by mainteining his forces in a continual succession.[34]

Sons of low-grade servitors competed for *pomest'e* estates with the offspring of boyar families whose patrimony had been ravaged by subdivision to the point where they could no longer sustain their status.[35] It was a competitive and unstable system, in which the tenuous and shifting links between individuals, families and service estates eroded horizontal links within the complex framework of *mestnichestvo*, and precluded the formation of locally-based alliances which might have provided a counterbalance to autocracy.

The *Oprichnina* was an irrational response to the growing crisis which merely exacerbated the problems without attacking the root cause. After 1572, Muscovy again enjoyed a brief period of military success, as Ivan took advantage of the temporary distraction of Sweden and Poland-Lithuania. The 1577 campaign succeeded because it was largely unopposed, while the refined savagery Ivan had learned in the charnel-houses of the *Oprichnina* merely united his enemies. When Batory and John III turned against Muscovy, it was in no condition to defend its gains. While *strel'tsy* units and garrison troops fiercely resisted Batory's invasion, the performance of the *pomest'e* cavalry was lamentable. As Polish-Lithuanian troops ravaged northwestern Muscovy, they met little resistance. After they departed, the thousands of villages they had burned were left desolate in a landscape that was already emptying before they came.

For peasants had already begun to seek relief in flight from the escalating tax demands imposed during the 1560s and 1570s, or from the devastation wrought during the *Oprichnina*. Many fled to the southern borderlands, or sought less demanding landlords. Northwestern Muscovy entered a period of catastrophic decline. As peasants departed in ever-increasing numbers, the agrarian economy's capacity to withstand the vagaries of climatic fluctuation was substantially reduced; as the *Oprichnina* reached its height, bad weather and harvest failures brought widespread famine. The cadastral surveys undertaken between 1585 and 1588 reveal depopulation on a massive scale. The population of the Novgorod district, which had reached some 500,000 by 1500, and held steady or rose slightly by 1550, was reduced fivefold. The Pskov area, which had a rural population of 110,000 in 1500, had a mere 18,000 left by the 1580s; the population of Pskov and other towns fell from 10,000 to 3,000, of which 1,000 were soldiers. Only the far north, which was spared the attentions of the enemy, apart from some Swedish activity in the 1590s, and where there were few *pomest'ia*, experienced a slight rise in population.[36]

The massive depopulation provoked a catastrophic collapse of the agrarian economy. By 1585, almost threequarters of settlements had been abandoned in the Moscow province; in the northwest, it was even worse: abandoned settlements in the Votskaia district rose from 7.1 per cent in 1568 to 78 per cent in 1582–3. In the Shelonskaia district, 66.4 per cent of settlements had been abandoned by 1576; in a mere 6–7 years this figure rose to 92.6 per cent.[37] While these figures are not entirely trustworthy, they cannot be explained away as the mere result of large-scale tax avoidance. The compilers of the cadastres were central officials, not local communities intent on minimising their tax burden, while travellers' accounts confirm massive depopulation. In the 1550s Richard Chancellor had found a flourishing agrarian economy; forty years later Fletcher found a desert.

It is difficult to escape the conclusion that war played a central role in this catastrophic decline. The service state's escalating demands dramatically reversed the steady economic expansion of the first half of the century. The attempt to create a military system based on service and the *pomest'e* system had proved a spectacular failure. This is clearly demonstrated by the fact that it was the lands of the *pomeshchiki* which suffered the greatest level of depopulation. Round Pskov, *pomest'ia* had been virtually destroyed as viable economic units by the 1580s; the Church, which held some 36.1 per cent of the land, was not so badly affected.[38] The *pomest'e* system in the Pskov area had only been established in the 1530s and 1540s; by the 1580s, 25 of the 300 *pomeshchiki* in the area held less than the 100 quarters of land specified in the 1555–6 reforms; a further 48 held only uninhabited land.[39]

Peasant flight destroyed the economic basis of the *pomest'e* system; although Fedor's reign (1584–98) saw a slight recovery, this did little more than halt the rate of decline, and the rural economy lacked the reserves to cope with the bad weather which destroyed three successive harvests (1601–3). Famine brought further devastation and stimulated the widespread disorder which opened the Time of Troubles. It was the service class which lay at the centre of the social crisis. Peasant flight had, by the 1580s, pushed the *pomeshchiki* to the brink of disaster. The state had created a hierarchy of privileged servitors between the boyar aristocracy and the mass of the peasantry, but had failed to provide either sustained success in war or a stable economic base for it. If Ivan's supposed assault on the boyars has attracted most attention, boyars were better able to survive the economic disasters of the 1570s and 1580s: the possession of *votchina*, on which tax and service burdens were lighter, meant that peasants frequently fled to boyar estates from *pomest'ia*. Unable to sustain their social position, or guarantee a secure career for their children, it was the *pomeshchiki* whose discontent and uncertain status ignited the Time of Troubles. Already in the 1590s, Fedor's fragile government was under growing pressure to limit peasant freedom of movement, to stem the haemorrhage of peasants from *pomest'ia*, and to prevent boyars and the Church from winning the increasingly desperate battle for peasant labour. The introduction of the 'Forbidden Years' at the end of the 1580s was an ad hoc attempt to stem the flood of departures by temporary suspensions of the traditional freedom of peasants to move in the two-week period round St George's Day in November, and to tie peasants and townspeople to the tax-registers to shore up the state's collapsing fiscal base.

Soviet historians long sought to prove that the social crisis of the Time of Troubles was a manifestation of class war, in which peasants rebelled under a series of leaders, from Khlopko in 1603 to Bolotnikov in 1606–7. It is true that peasants suffered greatly, and that the early attempts to tie peasants to the land from the late 1580s, followed by the devastating famine of 1601–3, stimulated substantial peasant participation, but it is clear that the social composition of the armies of insurgents was extremely mixed, and that their core was formed by impoverished servitors. The various measures taken under Godunov which, taken together, provided the legal basis for the enserfment of the Muscovite peasantry, were a response to the widespread flight of the peasantry, not its cause. Social banditry and rebellion was essentially the result of the implosion of the service state, not a reaction to the imposition of serfdom.

The heart of the problem was the incipient collapse of the middling and lower levels of the service state. The sheer scale of peasant flight from *pomest'ia* rendered many of them unworkable, while legal attempts to limit peasant mobility fashioned a bolt for the door of a long-empty stable.[40] Unable to support themselves, let alone equip themselves with the necessary means to perform service, large numbers of *pomeshchiki* and their children joined runaway peasants, slaves released by their masters because they could no longer afford to feed them, and other casualties of the subsistence crisis in the burgeoning Cossack bands roaming the southern borderlands. The Cossacks were a dangerous group: many had entered government service from the 1550s to profit from the opportunities offered by Ivan's wars, and there were some 5–6,000 service Cossacks by 1600, entitled to twenty quarters of land, raised to fifty in 1577, though the shortage of available land meant that few received their entitlement. Classed as non-hereditary servitors, Cossacks formed a dangerous social group poised between hereditary servitors and the mass of the tax-paying population. The freedom of the southeastern borderlands, where serfdom had not yet established itself, meant that they had long adopted a robust attitude to the central state. Moreover, there were thousands of Cossacks outside state service, whose numbers were swelled in the late sixteenth century by a great influx of fugitive serfs and *pomeshchiki* no longer able to support themselves, as *dvorianstvo* numbers dropped 20 per cent.[41]

Cossacks provided much of the organisation and independent spirit which animated the various risings after 1600, and it was middling and petty servitors, not peasants, who largely lay behind them, although thousands of peasants certainly participated. The tsars had created a successful service state; they were unable to sustain it. The result obeyed the logic of the service system: the shattered strata of servitors began to seek an alternative lord, who could guarantee them status and economic security. It was this which underlay the explosion of pretenders after 1605, many of whom were initially backed by Cossack bands who sought a good Cossack tsar to provide them with service and sustain their independent existence.[42] Only the first False Dmitry received sufficient backing from boyar groups to secure the throne, albeit briefly; it was not until a broad coalition of boyar and servitor groups coalesced round the unexceptional figure of Michael Romanov that stability was restored.

The price of victory

The heavy involvement of Poles and Lithuanians in Muscovy's Time of Troubles has often been depicted as the result of a deliberate attempt by the Commonwealth to exploit Muscovy's misfortune. The fact that the first False Dmitry had an audience with Sigismund before invading Muscovy, together with the close interest taken by the Catholic Church in his expedition, have led many historians of Russia to lay much of the blame for the turbulence of the period at the door of the Poles. Even those, like Platonov, who warns against seeing the Time of Troubles as the result of Polish intrigues, tend to suggest that the Commonwealth pursued a coherent policy.[43] Yet if Sigismund did not actively discourage Dmitry from his expedition, and later sought to profit from the growing chaos in Muscovy, the pretender was not foisted on Muscovy by a malign *diabolus ex machina*. The pretender phenomenon was a symptom of the crisis within the service state, not its cause, and Sigismund was sucked into the Muscovite political morass against his will: it distracted him from his main aim, the recovery of the Swedish throne. When Sweden invaded Livonia in 1600, Sigismund agreed a twenty-year truce with Godunov; with victory apparently within his grasp after Kircholm, he was little inclined to enter the Muscovite imbroglio. Moreover, he faced serious domestic problems of his own. For the Commonwealth was itself experiencing the social consequences of the burden it had borne for nearly half a century. Poland-Lithuania may have suffered less direct destruction than Muscovy – apart from the limited Muscovite campaigns in eastern Lithuania in 1563–4 and 1579–80 there had been little fighting within its borders – nevertheless, war fundamentally shaped the Commonwealth's development in the first decades of the Union. Between 1590 and 1620 it experienced the first rumbles of the socio-cultural earthquake which was to strike in 1648.

The Commonwealth's consensual political system was already seeing a struggle between concepts of *maiestas* and *libertas*. On the one hand, kings were bound by growing legal restrictions on their power, embodied in the

Henrician Articles and the *Pacta Conventa* (individual charters each new monarch swore to uphold at their coronation), supplemented by frequent legislation. On the other hand, the king still had considerable scope for manoeuvre. He was responsible for governing between the biennial sessions of the *Sejm*, and there was much scope for independent action. He enjoyed substantial patronage powers, appointing all government ministers and other members of the Senate, which as well as forming the upper house of the *Sejm*, acted as the royal council; although it was seen by the *szlachta* as the guardian of the constitution, meetings were usually attended only by ministers and royalist politicians, and the king enjoyed considerable latitude in the formation of policy. His judicious use of his powers to distribute leases on royal lands gave him an extremely useful political weapon. If Mączak has argued that the king should be seen 'not . . . as head of state so much as the head of his own faction, more or less equal to the others,' that was not how contemporaries saw matters.[44]

War gave the *szlachta* the opportunity to extend the legal checks on royal power. The *Sejm* voted impressive sums in taxation for Batory's campaigns, but the *szlachta* was only prepared to fund such adventures up to a point, and Batory paid a heavy price for *Sejm* support: the condition for voting supply for the 1579 campaign was the establishment of an independent Tribunal in Poland followed by a similar body in Lithuania in 1581, which ended royal appellate jurisdiction over the *szlachta* in a fundamental blow to royal power. Moreover, the *Sejm* was unwilling permanently to underwrite substantial expenditure for military purposes. In such a vast state, where much power was held at the local level, it was hard to persuade the nobility of southern or western Poland of the need for vast sums in taxation to pay for the defence of Pernau or Smolensk, as distant from them as Paris. While the *szlachta* enjoyed substantial tax privileges, they were by no means unaffected by taxation. The main extraordinary land tax – the *pobór łanowy*, based on registers drawn up in 1578 and covering livestock and artisan production as well as land – was levied on noble serfs as well as those of crown and church lands; it was paid directly by nobles without serfs.[45] From the outset, there was a tendency to call for the Commonwealth's defence to rest upon the quarter army, supplemented by local musterings of the noble levy, and for large-scale expeditions involving paid, regular troops to be limited. Batory's ambitious plans for war against the Turks, and Sigismund's plans to recover his Swedish throne, or to intervene in Muscovy, were regarded with deep suspicion, as being causes more in the interests of the monarch than the Commonwealth.[46]

Moreover, the monarch's control of foreign policy between meetings of the *Sejm* stimulated fears that he would use this power to encroach on *szlachta* liberties. Suspicion that Sigismund was seeking to introduce *absolutum dominium* was increased by his close contacts with the Habsburgs, whose conflicts with their estates in Bohemia, Moravia and Silesia were closely observed in Poland. Conflict came to a head in 1606–7, after Sigismund's second Habsburg marriage and his plans to elect his son Władysław *vivente rege* (in the king's lifetime) were revealed. The right of free election after the king's death was increasingly regarded as the fundamental guarantee of liberty, and a coalition of forces, in which Protestants were prominent, met at Sandomierz in 1606. Claiming the right of resistance in defence of the constitution, they launched what they argued was a legal rebellion which they called *rokosz*.[47] The Sandomierz *rokosz* produced a flood of anti-royalist pamphlets and sparked a brief civil war; although Sigismund defeated his opponents, he had to abandon his reform plans. It was more of an expression of the tensions already apparent in the new political system than a real threat to royal authority, and after 1607, Sigismund showed a greater willingness to work within the system to achieve his aims, with considerable success; nevertheless, the *rokosz* left a legacy of bitterness which was difficult to overcome.

The Commonwealth and Muscovy are usually portrayed as polar opposites. The contrast between the autocratic, highly-centralised Muscovite state and the decentralised *szlachta* republic is indeed striking. As Muscovy developed into a service state, in which landholding was directly linked to service performed, the liberties of the Polish-Lithuanian nobility were increasingly codified and extended. Poland-Lithuania in the sixteenth century saw no assault on the principle of hereditary landownership, and, despite much windy rhetoric attacking the monarchy's tyrannical leanings, saw nothing remotely comparable to the *Oprichnina*. In 1584, the year of Ivan's death, the outrage caused by the execution of one magnate – the contumacious Samuel Zborowski – was in stark contrast to the passive acceptance of Ivan's shambles in Muscovy.

Yet the deep differences in political culture should not disguise the fact that Poland-Lithuania, like Muscovy, was an unstable society in the second half of the sixteenth century, as it experienced a period of intense social and political change against the background of large-scale foreign war. Moreover, the Commonwealth was experiencing serious unrest in the very groups which lay at the heart of the Muscovite crisis. For if the Commonwealth's middling and petty nobility had acquired theoretical equality with the magnates after 1569, the vast majority were in the same position as the Muscovite servitors: poor or impoverished, they faced a relentless struggle to maintain an economic position which matched their social status. With partible inheritance the norm under Polish and Lithuanian law, only about half the nobility owned land at all; many, like the legion of noble tenant farmers, were impoverished smallholders, distinguishable from the peasantry only through their proud assertion of noble status.

Whereas Muscovy's expansion by conquest enabled its rulers to establish the *pomest'e* system, Poland-Lithuania expanded through consent, a process wherein the great privileges enjoyed by Polish nobles, including extensive legal protection for private landowners, played a central role. Thus the monarchy never acquired the vast reservoirs of land seized by Muscovy's rulers from conquered territories, while, in contrast to Muscovy, private ownership of land was increasingly protected by law. Only the wealthiest and most powerful nobles were able to mitigate the worst effects of subdivision through access to lucrative leaseholds on royal estates (starosties); for those further down the economic scale, there were fewer options. Many entered the service of wealthier nobles; others took up residence in towns and scratched a living as best they could. Under these circumstances, war could provide a perfectly respectable career for a noble, one which gave some prospect of economic gain and social advancement. Nevertheless, despite the fact that the Commonwealth was at war almost continuously for two decades after 1562, and then again from 1600 to 1629, and despite the substantial successes its armies met on the battlefield, it proved unable to place its military system on a stable footing.

At the heart of the problem lay the lands of the old Grand Duchy of Lithuania, divided in 1569. The Union was built on two fundamental pillars: the need of the Lithuanians for the military support of the wealthier and more numerous Poles, and the extension of the attractive privileged position of the mass of the Polish nobility to their Lithuanian counterparts. Despite the fact that Polish influence on Lithuania had strengthened steadily since 1385, in culture and social structure the Commonwealth's eastern lands were in many respects closer to their Muscovite enemies than their Polish compatriots. Although the Lithuanian nobility had converted to Catholicism in the 1380s, the Grand Duchy's Ruthenian majority had remained Orthodox and was, until the mid-fifteenth century, largely excluded from the privileges extended to Catholic nobles. Polish social – and especially legal – influences gradually increased their hold, but the three codifications of Lithuanian law in the statutes of 1529, 1566 and 1588 still owed much to traditional Ruthenian law. Until 1569, Lithuania continued to be ruled by the Grand Duke and a narrow aristocratic council; the power the Grand Duke enjoyed in Lithuania was much less circumscribed than that which he exercised as king of Poland, although his absence from Lithuania for most of the time following Alexander's election as king of Poland in 1501 meant that in practice much power devolved to the magnates who dominated the Lithuanian Council and monopolised public office.

One of the main differences between Muscovy and Lithuania was that in the latter the grand dukes had not acquired the outright control of service enjoyed by their Muscovite counterparts. In Lithuania, magnates still maintained their own servitors, to whom they distributed land in return for service in their armed retinues. These tenant nobles were required to provide military service directly to their landlords, either for private ends, or to fulfil their master's obligation to supply contingents for the *obrona zemskaia* – the Lithuanian noble levy. Some members of the independent nobility held land granted directly by the Grand Duke to their families, or purchased from those who had also performed military or administrative service for magnates.[48] When the growing military demands of the sixteenth century stimulated reform, government attempts to overhaul the basis of military service were complicated both by the partial refraction of service through the magnates, and by influences from Poland, which undermined the principle of service by promoting the concept of equal privileges to be enjoyed by all nobles.

The political and military changes in Lithuania after 1500 provoked a crisis of status in the servitor-noble groups, which became most acute in the lands transferred to Poland at the Union of Lublin. The problem was that the theoretical division of Lithuanian society into those who provided personal military service, and those who paid taxes, the *potiagli*, no longer matched economic or social reality, as partible inheritance brought the decline of many families once numbered among the elite and blurred distinctions between various social groups. Rapid subdivision of holdings among nobles and servitors of lower ranks not infrequently reduced them to an economic state worse than that of the tax-paying peasantry. By the early sixteenth century, there was a large mass of servitors of uncertain nomenclature and widely varying economic position. Whereas in Muscovy, rapid expansion from the late fifteenth century provided reservoirs of land for the poorest hereditary servitors who formed the basis of the *pomest'e* system, the lack of such opportunities in Lithuania meant that this group lived under constant threat of social degradation, especially since large territorial losses to Muscovy in the early sixteenth century reduced the available supply of land.

This problem was exacerbated by the military and agrarian reforms of the sixteenth century, in large part stimulated by the need to exert greater control over the chaotic servitor groups. Lithuanian law did distinguish between hereditary land (*otchina*) and service land (*imenie*), but the precise distinction was not always clear, and the latter were not the exact equivalent of Muscovite *pomest'e*. While the rights of magnate families and the independent nobility to own, bequeath, alienate or sell hereditary land without the ruler's permission were established in law in the fifteenth century, the position of those further down the social scale was unclear: as late as the reign of Alexander (1492/1501–1506) Dremlik Taliushkovich, classed as a nobleman, was deprived of his *otchina* for failing to perform service.[49] Under Sigismund I (1506–48) a determined effort was made to establish the legal foundation for a new service system. In 1528, in the face of a triple threat from Muscovy, the Ottoman Empire and the Tatars, the Lithuanian *Sejm* passed a law regulating the extent of service required from service lands for the next ten years, and a list of cavalry servitors was drawn up: it included 19,842 men from 13,060 families, nearly 30 per cent of whom were provided by the great magnate houses.[50] The First Lithuanian Statute of 1529 specified that service land could be confiscated if its holder failed to meet his service obligations, while in 1533 Sigismund I's wife Bona Sforza, who had been granted substantial estates, demanded documentary evidence of title from her servitor-tenants. Large numbers of them were unable to produce clear proof of their rights to the land, such as the boyar[51] Andrei Mafeevich, who held a plot of arable land and four gardens, and claimed his grandfather had served a previous holder of the estate, but whose father had died 'without letters', so that he leased the land with his stepmother.[52] The exercise revealed just how much servitors had suffered from subdivision of holdings. Those with documentary proof of their status had possession confirmed; the rest were not evicted, but had their leases confirmed for life only, and their service obligations established.

Further steps were taken on the eve of the Livonian War. In 1557, the grand ducal estates were subjected to a major survey, which provided the basis for an extensive land reform. This attempted to standardise the size of peasant holdings and the extent of peasant obligations on the basis of a standard unit of land-measurement, the *włoka* (21.3 hectares). This reform, by tying the peasants to the land, introduced a sharp juridical dividing-line between peasants and servitors. Thus a great incentive was created for poor boyars and petty nobles to demonstrate their clear separation from the mass of the peasantry through the performance of the military service which was their main claim to higher social status. Although statutes of 1563, 1566 and 1567 slightly reduced the service requirements, the number of cavalrymen who turned out for the 1567 muster was 27,776, 40 per cent higher than in 1528. Only 4,890 men (18 per cent) were supplied by magnates, compared with 30 per cent in 1528; the turnout of petty nobles was particularly high.[53] With Polish practice increasingly influencing Lithuanian law, and with the growing prospect of closer political union with Poland promising greatly extended privileges to those who could sustain a claim to noble status, the stakes were high, and the appearance of an ancestor's name in the 1528 and 1567 muster lists was long to remain a prime test of noble status.

Yet attempts to exercise tighter control over noble servitors proved abortive. Lithuania had no effective equivalent of the Muscovite *Pomestnyi Prikaz* to register and control the distribution of service land. Apart from the occasional mustering of the Lithuanian noble levy, as in 1528 and 1567, central review was a rarity. It was at the local level of the new districts established in the reforms of 1565–6 that the more regular musterings took place, but this left considerable control in magnate hands. Thus it proved difficult in practice to regulate service estates, which were frequently inherited or divided without royal confirmation. Finally, the granting of the full range of Polish legal privileges to the ordinary Lithuanian nobility in 1569 destroyed the legal underpinning of the eastern Slavic service system. Noble land now enjoyed full legal protection, and although landholders were bound to serve in the noble levy, participation levels fell, since this was no longer the primary means of demonstrating noble status.

By no means all of the old servitor groups were ushered into the Promised Land, however, and the position of those at the bottom of the hierarchy of service remained legally unclear. This was particularly so of the boyars, who formed an intermediary group between the unfree peasantry and the privileged nobility. Siekierski argues that the boyars failed as a group to establish their status; it is perhaps better to see them as individuals poised in a precarious limbo between the more heavily-burdened serfs and the more prosperous members of the nobility, with each generation facing a desperate struggle to secure its position.[54] It was a question not of juridical boundaries defining a whole group, but of the constant battle of individuals, in an age of rising population and subdivision of estates, to avoid being sucked down into the mass of tax-payers and serfs.[55] This was a complex process, and by no means uniform in its effects: there were at least three commoners listed in the noble levy registers for the Smolensk palatinate as late as 1633, all of whom were ennobled in 1638 for their contribution to the defence of the city during the 1632–4 Muscovite siege, while landless nobles living in Smolensk were still listed in the 1654 registers.[56]

For the petty nobility and those of indeterminate status, prospects were bleak. Given the reluctance of the *Sejm* and *sejmiki*, dominated by the prosperous *szlachta*, to fund large, permanent forces, the state could not provide stable military careers, while Lithuania did not even have a quarter army. Some entered magnate service, or became military-service tenants, receiving plots of land in return for joining magnate retinues when called out, but could not be regarded as full members of the nobility, since they were under the private jurisdiction of their lords, not the noble courts at district level.[57] It was such men who formed the so-called 'private armies' of Lithuania, which were more amateur militias than the professional forces as which they are often presented, and who fuelled the explosion of Cossackdom in the Ukraine in the late sixteenth century: 80 per cent of Cossacks on the 1581 register whose origins are known came from the Ruthenian lands of pre-1569 Lithuania.[58] There were certainly Poles among the Cossacks – 17 out of the 356 on the 1581 register – but although there were substantial numbers of petty and impoverished nobles in Poland, particularly in Mazovia and Podlasie, their legal status was not under such great threat, since these areas had no magnate families and local political institutions were dominated by poor nobles who placed a high premium on the ideal of noble equality.

The social dislocation was greatest in the Ukrainian palatinates detached from Lithuania in 1569 and opened up to colonisation from Poland, where the combination of increasing settlement by outsiders, and what Sysyn has called the 'gross inconsistencies' with which the new divide between noble and non-noble ran through the old elite groups, created dangerous tensions.[59] There had long been Cossack bands in the vast open spaces of the ill-defined marchlands along the southern borders of Poland-Lithuania and Muscovy from the Carpathians to the Caucasus. Here ran the frontiers between Christendom and Islam, Orthodox and Catholic, nomad and settler. The thinly-populated steppelands became home to a harsh frontier civilisation, where adventurers and refugees from the civilisations further north fought, raided and mingled with Tatars and other Asiatic peoples. As such, Cossacks are occasionally portrayed as a primitive survival of an older, nomadic stage of civilisation, bound eventually to succumb to the inexorable advance of the modern state. Yet the spectacular explosion of the Cossack phenomenon which plagued both Muscovy and the Commonwealth at the end of the sixteenth century was a creation of the modern age: the result of the rapid socio-political changes in both states after 1550 which were in large part caused by the dramatic increase in the burdens of war. The rapid development of the Cossack problem was the most visible symptom of the crisis of the agrarian-military state in eastern Europe.

In both states military service offered a means for the preservation of status at worst, or a channel of social advancement at best; in Muscovy, the over-extension of Muscovite military power rendered the state incapable for a generation of providing those opportunities; in Poland-Lithuania, the refusal of the *Sejm* to fund further military adventures after 1582 brought the opportunities for petty servitors to an abrupt halt, and the threat of social degradation became ever more real. For such men, the attraction of the Cossack bands of the southern frontier was great. Here they could live in militarised bands, whose egalitarian ethos echoed that of the *szlachta*, and whose lifestyle, in which raids on Tatar territory and general social banditry was combined with hunting and agricultural pursuits, was highly attractive. In the 1580s and 1590s, the Cossack population of the southern frontier exploded, causing serious concern in the Commonwealth.

Control was sought through a policy of divide and rule. By creating and paying a select number of registered Cossacks, the *Sejm* hoped to be able to separate a Cossack elite from the mass of those who styled themselves Cossacks or served in the Cossack ranks. It was not a satisfactory solution. The 580 registered Cossacks allowed by Batory in 1581 soon swelled to 3,000, as the government accorded them a role in controlling the much larger number of unregistered Cossacks – perhaps as many as 40–50,000 – for whom leadership was provided from the centre of non-registered Cossackdom in the Zaporozhian *Sich*. The status and wealth of registered Cossacks brought pressure to increase their number from those excluded; in periods when their services were required by the Commonwealth the registers expanded substantially, reaching 20,000 in 1620.

Yet the number of self-styled Cossacks in the Ukraine was always much higher. While proving useful recruits in moments of crisis, such as during the 1621 Chocim campaign against the Turks, in which up to 40,000 Cossacks participated, it was unlikely that the *Sejm* would agree to support a substantially larger number of registered Cossacks than they permitted in the quarter army, the Commonwealth's only other permanent body of troops. In peacetime, however, the Cossacks were a source of endless problems: increasingly frequent Cossack raids into Ottoman territory, which occasionally reached Istanbul itself, soured relations with the Turks and helped provoke the first Polish-Ottoman confrontation since the 1530s, in which the Polish army suffered a shattering defeat at Cecora in Moldavia in 1620, where Żółkiewski was killed. Attempts to subordinate the Cossacks to government authority had already provoked the first of a series of Cossack risings in 1595–6; although this was suppressed easily enough, serious tension remained. Its most obvious expression was in the hordes of Cossacks and petty servitors who flooded over the border in the entourage of the First False Dmitry; they were following the ancient eastern Slavic practice of seeking service with a new lord.

To this extent the *Smuta* was more than just a crisis of the Muscovite state: it was a crisis of the whole principle of service in the eastern Slavic world. For, despite the undoubtedly stark contrast between the political systems of Muscovy and Poland-Lithuania there were, beneath the surface, a number of striking similarities. Both states faced problems centring on the tension between the opportunities provided by an increasingly commercialised agrarian economy which provided the necessary economic base of state power, and the need to deploy military power to defend it, or secure a decisive advantage over political rivals. In both states, growing wealth and agrarian development opened the door to a substantial expansion of military capacity, but stimulated at the same time a rapidly growing social tension centred on the petty servitor groups who swelled the expanding armies. During the sixteenth century, both states sought to define and regulate the position of these groups. In Muscovy, this took the form of stipulating the service obligations of landholders in a drive against the principle of allodial landownerhip. In Poland-Lithuania – or more accurately, in the lands of the old Grand Duchy, divided in 1569 – the *szlachta* sought to define the attributes, and assert control over the membership, of what was an increasingly privileged and protected elite. Yet in neither case were the bare legal definitions and pious ideologies of the iron law of service on the one hand, and the equality of all noble-citizens on the other, adequate to the task. The Muscovite solution to the problem – to establish an all-embracing service ethic – created an immense demand for land which was unsustainable. The Lithuanian solution – to define more rigidly the boundaries of the noble elite in such a way as to cast into doubt the social status of substantial portions of the service groups – created problems of its own in a system which sought increasingly to limit the growth of an army that might have created the opportunities for these servitor groups to sustain the sort of lifestyle that was central to the very ideal of nobility.

The result in both states was political and social dislocation. It might seem that Muscovy suffered by far the most, since the Time of Troubles all but saw the collapse of the Muscovite state between 1605 and 1613. In the Commonwealth, the political struggles in the aftermath of the constitutional upheaval of 1569–74 seemed far less dramatic in their scope: the brief civil war with Danzig in 1577 ended in an agreement which was to keep Danzig one of the most loyal members of the Commonwealth into the eighteenth century, while the 1606–7 *rokosz* resulted in a wary standoff rather than the complete collapse seen in Muscovy. Yet the eastern lands of the Commonwealth, situated between two rapidly diverging political and legal systems, faced a more fundamental breakdown. The more that the middling and upper nobility was seduced by the ideals of the new noble Commonwealth and learned how to turn its system to their own advantage, the more uncertain became the situation of members of the old servitor groups lower down the scale. The growing social dislocation in Muscovy and the lands of pre-1569 Lithuania had in part expressed itself in the series of wars between them after 1562, and was in turn fed by the social consequences of war. Despite the growing political and cultural divergence between the two systems, however, this social dislocation expressed itself in essentially similar ways: in widespread peasant flight to the sparsely-populated southern frontier in order to escape the rapidly expanding tax burden imposed upon the tax-paying sector of the community, and a rapid increase in social banditry among the battered servitor groups struggling to maintain their economic well-being and their social status. Both phenomena fed and sustained the explosion of the Cossack problem which was the most obvious expression of the deep social crisis facing both Muscovy and the Lithuanian-Ruthenian lands. The different ways in which this problem – symptomatic of deeper cleavages in both societies – was resolved were to prove of crucial importance in the struggle between the Commonwealth and Muscovy. The resolution of eastern Europe's Time of Troubles was to prove the hinge of the whole conflict round the shores of the Baltic.

Notes

1 *Dagbog over Daniel Rantzovs Vinterfelttog* pp. 47–8.
2 One *lod* = 15.625 grammes.
3 Quoted by E. Österberg, *Gränsbygd under krig* (Lund, 1971) p. 14.
4 Westling, *Nordiska sjuårkrigets* VI pp. 492–3; I. Andersson, *Erik XIV* (Stockholm, 1963) p. 141; Tidander, *Nordiska sjuårkrigets* p. 196.
5 Tidander, *Rantzaus vinterfälttåg* pp. 13–14; *Dagbog over Daniel Rantzovs Vinterfelttog* p. 39.
6 Österberg, *Gränsbygd* pp. 259–63.
7 Ibid. tables 1, 5, pp. 273, 277.
8 R.K. Brambe and Kh.E. Palli, 'Dinamika chislennosti naseleniia Estonii i Latvii v XVII–XVIII vv.' *Materialy mezhrespublikanskoi nauchnoi konferentsii po istochnikovedeniiu i istoriografii narodov Pribaltiki: Istoriografiia* (Vilnius, 1978) p. 47. The figures are for Estonia's post-1945 borders.
9 V.D. Koroliuk, *Livonskaia Voina* (Moscow, 1954) pp. 38–9.
10 E. Krause, 'Bericht . . .' in K. von Busse, 'Die Einnahme der Stadt Dorpat im Jahre 1558 und die damit verbundenen Ereignisse' *MGGLEK* I (1840) p. 473.
11 For a catalogue of incidents, see E. Donnert, *Der livländische Ordensritterstaat und Rußland 1558–1583* (Berlin, 1963) pp. 63–101.
12 J. Renner, *Livländische Historien 1556–1561* (Lübeck, 1953) p. 17.
13 *Salomon Henning's Chronicle of Courland and Livonia* V. Zeps (ed.) (Dubuque, Ia, 1992) p. 117.
14 Rüssow, *Chronica* p. 142.
15 Renner, *Livländische Historien* pp. 38–41.
16 'Warhafftige vnd Erschreckliche Newzeitung von dem grausamen Feind vnnd Tyrannen des Muscowiters . . .' reprinted in *SAGP* 11 (1926–9) (Pernau, 1930), p. 4.
17 See A. Kappeler, *Ivan Groznyj im Spiegel der ausländischen Druckschriften seiner Zeit* (Bern, 1972).
18 Kirchner, *Baltic Question* p. 104.
19 E. Thaden, 'Ivan IV in Baltic German Historiography' *RH* 14 (1987) p. 381. Thaden lists four reasons for the failure of Ivan's policy in Livonia without considering the behaviour of Muscovite troops *within* the province; ibid. p. 379.
20 Renner, *Livländische Historien* p. 40.
21 H. von Staden, *The land and government of Muscovy* T. Esper (tr.) (Stanford, 1967) p. 61; Piwarski, 'Niedoszła' p. 262.
22 Nyenstädt, *Chronik* pp. 51ff.
23 For example the slaughter of over a hundred Swedes 'contrary to all human feeling or compassion' by local nobles on the fall of Pernau in 1565, or the massacre of many Russian men, women and children by the Swedes when they burned the suburbs of Dorpat in 1578: Rüssow, *Chronica* pp. 71, 134.
24 Ibid. p. 109.
25 Ibid. p. 147.

26 Działyński, 'Dyaryusz' p. 234.

27 'Warhaftige und grundtliche beschreibung des itzigen betriebten Liefflendischen kriegs . . .' *MGGLEK* 17 (Riga, 1900) p. 141; S. Herbst, 'Kampania letnia 1601' *PHW* 4, no. 2 (1931) p. 223.

28 See the excellent discussion in J. Theibault, 'The rhetoric of death and destruction in the Thirty Years War' *Social History* 27 (1993) pp. 272–90.

29 1 quarter (*chetvert'*) = 1.35 acres.

30 R.G. Skrynnikov, 'The civil war in Russia at the beginning of the seventeenth century (1603–1607): its character and motive forces' in L.J. Hughes (ed.), *New Perspectives on Muscovite History* (London, 1993) p. 72.

31 R.G. Skrynnikov, *Rossiia posle oprichniny* (Leningrad, 1975) pp. 77–9.

32 R. Crummey, 'The fate of boyar clans, 1565–1613' *FOG* 38 (1986) pp. 241–56.

33 R. Hellie, 'What happened? How did he get away with it? Ivan Groznyi's paranoia and the problem of institutional restraints' *RH* 14 (1987) p. 209; R.G. Skrynnikov, *Ivan the Terrible* H.F. Graham (tr.) (Gulf Breeze, Fl., 1981) p. 144.

34 G. Fletcher, *Of the Russe Commonwealth* R. Pipes (ed.) (Cambridge, Mass., 1966) pp. 53–4.

35 Godunov himself was from a junior line of a boyar family reduced to the level of provincial servitors, dependent upon *pomest'e* land, and no longer able to secure the lucrative Muscovite administrative and military appointments it had once enjoyed. R.G. Skrynnikov *Boris Godunov* H.F. Graham (tr.) (Gulf Breeze, Fl, 1982) p. 1.

36 A.L. Shapiro (ed.), *Agrarnaia Istoriia Severo-Zapada Rossii XVI veka* III (Leningrad, 1978) pp. 136–9.

37 C. Goehrke, *Die Wüstungen in der Moskauer Rus'* (Wiesbaden, 1968) pp. 109–10.

38 Only 4,982 quarters out of 62,696.9 held by *pomeshchiki* (7.95 per cent) were still under cultivation; the average *pomest'e* estate of 189.9 quarters had only 15 quarters of inhabited land. Shapiro, *Agrarnaia* III pp. 91, 94, 99.

39 Ibid. pp. 96–7.

40 Even in the devastated lands of the northwest, many *pomeshchiki* managed to scratch some sort of existence from their estates, often farming the land themselves, in the absence of peasants, or using slave labour: J. Martin, 'Economic survival in the Novgorod lands in the 1580s' in Hughes (ed.), *New Perspectives* pp. 101–28. Martin's criterion of viability, however, is merely the ability to feed the estate's inhabitants. Only one third of the estates in the three districts she studies had land under cultivation. Of these, some were not viable, while few of those classed as such could have provided a sufficient surplus for the *pomeshchik* to meet his service obligations.

41 A.L. Stanislavskii, *Grazhdanskaia voina v Rossii XVII v.* (Moscow, 1990) pp. 9–20, 45.

42 For an excellent discussion of the problem see M. Perrie, *Pretenders and Popular Monarchism in Early Modern Russia* (Cambridge, 1995).

43 S.F. Platonov, *Ocherki po istorii Smuty v Moskovskom gosudarstve XVI–XVII vv.* (Moscow, 1937) p. 93.

44 A. Mączak, 'The structure of power of the Commonwealth of the sixteenth and seventeenth centuries' in Fedorowicz (ed.) *Republic* p. 128.

45 A. Filipczak-Kocur, *Skarb koronny za Zygmunta III Wazy* (Opole, 1985) p. 33.

46 See J. Maciszewski, *Polska a Moskwa 1603–1618* (Warsaw, 1968).

47 The term derived from the town of Rakosz near Budapest, where the Hungarian nobility had gathered in 1526. It appealed to the idea that representatives gathered in the *Sejm* were open to corruption by the king, and that sovereignty rested with the *szlachta* nation, gathered en masse.

48 For these tenant-noble servitors, see M. Siekierski, 'Landed wealth in the Grand Duchy of Lithuania: the economic affairs of Prince Nicholas Christopher Radziwiłł (1549–1616)' II *ABS* 21 (1992) pp. 195–205.

49 I.I. Lappo, *Velikoe Kniazhestvo Litovskoe vo vtoroi polovine XVI stoletiia* (Iur'ev, 1911) p. 195. See also O.P. Backus, 'Mortgages, alienations and redemptions: the rights in land of the nobility in sixteenth century Lithuanian law and practice compared' *FOG* 18 (1973) pp. 139–67 and K. von Loewe, *The Lithuanian Statute of 1529* (Leiden, 1976) pp. 128–36.

50 Lappo, *Velikoe Kniazhestvo* p. 7; J. Ochmański, *Historia Litwy* 3rd edn (Wrocław, 1990) p. 100. Service was only required from the restricted category of holders of an *imenie*; holders of allodial land were not required to provide military service. K. von Loewe, 'Military service in early sixteenth-century Lithuania: a new interpretation and its implications' *SR* 30 (1971) pp. 249–56.

51 In Lithuania, in contrast to Muscovy, 'boyars' were poor servitors at the bottom of the service hierarchy.

52 V.I. Picheta, 'Poverka prav na zemliu vo vladeniiakh korolevy Bony' *Belorussiia i Litva XV–XVI vv.* (Moscow, 1961) p. 14.

53 Ochmański, *Historia Litwy* p. 124. H. Łowmiański, 'Popisy wojska Wielkiego Księstwa Litewskiego XVI wieku jako źródło do dziejów zaludnienia' in Łowmiański, *Studia nad dziejami Wielkiego Księstwa Litewskiego* (Poznań, 1983) p. 458.

54 Siekierski, 'Landed wealth' II pp. 204, 240, n. 97. Boyar smallholders in areas such as Samogitia, where magnate power was less entrenched, were more able to sustain their status. Von Loewe sees the boyars as constituting a group of 'non-noble military servitors', but this is to assert firm divisions between groups which did not exist. The increasingly sharp legal definition of nobility was matched by the fuzziness of divisions in practice, as Siekierski recognises: 'Landed wealth' II pp. 204, 290. See A.P. Gritskevich 'Formirovanie feodalnogo sosloviia v Velikom Kniazhestve Litovskom i ego pravovye osnovy (XV–XVI v.)' *Pervyi Litovskii Statut 1529 goda* (Vilnius, 1982) pp. 65–73.

55 For examples of boyars fighting to demonstrate that their ancestors rendered military service, and that they should not therefore be classed as taxpayers, see Lappo, *Velikie Kniazhestvo* pp. 175–8.

56 B. Ostrowski, 'Pospolite ruszenie szlachty smoleńskiej w XVII wieku' *ABS* 13 (1980) pp. 154–5.

57 Siekierski, 'Landed wealth' II p. 290. Siekierski estimates that 25 per cent of M.K. Radziwiłł's estates were inhabited by this group by the end of the sixteenth century.

58   S. Luber and P. Rostankowski, 'Die Herkunft der im Jahre 1581 registrierten Zaporoger Kosaken' *JGO* NF 28 (1980) p. 375.

59   F. Sysyn 'The problem of nobilities in the Ukrainian past: the Polish period, 1569–1648' in I.L. Rudnitsky (ed.), *Rethinking Ukrainian History* (Edmonton, 1981) pp. 48–9.

CHAPTER FIVE

The Rise of Sweden

A new dawn

On 17 August 1621, the young Gustav Adolf disembarked from his war-fleet at Pernau, which had been in Swedish hands for a mere four years. It was nearly a decade since his accession, a difficult decade which gave little indication of what was to follow. Gustav Adolf, it is true, had stabilised the turbulent political situation he inherited from his irascible father, but the price of appeasing the aristocratic families Charles had so alienated was the acceptance of an accession charter which extended the nobility's social and economic privileges and secured the Council's position at the heart of government. Sweden, still fighting in Muscovy, now faced a challenge from Denmark. Although Christian IV made little progress in the War of Kalmar (1611–13), he seized Älvsborg, for whose return Sweden was forced to pay one million riksdalers. Despite the capture of Novgorod by Jakob de la Gardie in 1611, the Swedish war effort in Muscovy faltered: the 1615 siege of Pskov was abandoned, and the Swedish gains at Stolbovo (1617) were due more to Muscovite exhaustion than Swedish strength.

For all these undoubted achievements, of which the successful payment of the Älvsborg ransom by 1619 was perhaps the most notable, it seemed that little had changed in Livonia. True, the capture of Pernau was a minor success, but Pernau had changed hands frequently since 1558; the fact that most other towns taken in 1617 were rapidly retaken by the Poles did not suggest that the pattern of the Livonian wars had altered. It seemed that once the Poles were free of the Turkish war in the south, where they were currently deploying 45,000 troops to defend Chocim, it would not be long before they retook Pernau. The 2,000-odd Swedes who had captured it seemed insignificant indeed.

The contrast with 1621 was striking. The fleet which anchored off Pernau contained 148 vessels, including 25 warships, 3 pinnaces, 7 galleys, 7 smaller warships and 106 transport ships. The army was 17,850 strong, including 14,700 foot and 3,150 horse, larger than any Swedish force yet brought to Livonia.[1] By 29 August, they were at the walls of Riga, held by a garrison of 300. Riga was well supplied with arms and ammunition and intensive work had been undertaken to improve the fortifications since 1617. Nevertheless, the garrison was too small to resist for long, even supported by the 3,700-strong citizen militia. Although the Lithuanian Field Hetman Krzysztof II Radziwiłł did his best to harry the Swedes, he had barely 1,500 men. The garrison put up a good fight, but Riga surrendered on 25 September, four days before the Poles and Turks opened talks to end the stalemate at Chocim. Gustav Adolf had won his first major victory.

Riga, with a population of some 30,000 – three times the size of Stockholm – was prosperous.[2] Its capture began the stunning series of victories which by 1648 had catapulted Sweden from relative obscurity on Europe's northern fringe into the heart of European politics. The Poles were swept imperiously out of much of Livonia before Gustav Adolf attacked Royal Prussia in 1626, seizing Elbing and threatening Poland's access to the Baltic. In 1629, under pressure from England, France and the Netherlands, the Poles signed the disadvantageous six-year truce of Altmark. The stage was set for the landing at Peenemünde in July 1630 which launched the Swedish intervention that so dramatically changed the course of the Thirty Years War.

Fifty-two months later Gustav Adolf lay dead on the field of Lützen, leaving his infant daughter Christina on the throne but his brilliant run of victories, beginning with Breitenfeld (September 1631), had transformed Sweden's international position. Axel Oxenstierna, Gustav Adolf's chancellor and political executor, faced enormous problems after Lützen, including the failure of the Swedish-backed Heilbronn League in the Empire, the crushing defeat at Nördlingen (September 1634), serious army mutinies and the renewal of Altmark on much less favourable terms at Stuhmsdorf in 1635, yet the Swedish system proved robust enough to survive. Oxenstierna steered through the 1634 Form of Government which provided Sweden with a firm framework for Christina's regency and strengthened the grip of the aristocratic Council, while after the victory at Wittstock (1636), Sweden's fortunes in the Thirty Years War improved dramatically. The Franco-Swedish alliance gradually won the upper hand, as Swedish armies, led by talented commanders such as Lennart Torstensson, Johan Banér and Hermann Wrangel, proved more than a match for their enemies. The Danes were overwhelmed in 'Torstensson's War' of 1643–5, ended by the treaty of Brömsebro (August 1645), in which Sweden deprived Denmark of Halland for thirty years, breaking the Danish stranglehold over Älvsborg; it also gained the Norwegian provinces of Jämtland and Härjedalen and the islands of Ösel and Gotland. Sweden's new status was recognised at the 1648 peace of Westphalia, in which it gained western Pomerania, Bremen and Verden, which enabled it to threaten Denmark from the south; under Charles X Gustav (1654–60) Sweden fought against Poland-Lithuania (1655–60), Muscovy (1656, 1658–61), Austria (1657–60), Brandenburg (1657–60) and Denmark (1657–8; 1658–60), yet managed to emerge victorious from the war with Denmark at least: by the 1660 treaty of Copenhagen Sweden secured Scania, Bohuslän and Blekinge. The Danish grip on the Sound was broken at last; it was a far cry indeed from Kircholm.

The battle for Prussia

Responsibility for the dramatic change in Swedish fortunes has traditionally been ascribed to Gustav Adolf. At the heart of the transformation, according to Roberts, lay the military reforms introduced after Stolbovo. Accepting the Dutch insistence on small, flexible units, Gustav Adolf made the squadron – at 408 men plus NCOs and officers, slightly smaller than the Dutch battalion – the key building-block of his army. Two squadrons, each of eight companies, were joined to form a regiment, which meant that for the first time the main organisational and tactical units were identical. Based on this flexible, well-articulated structure, Gustav Adolf developed the blend of defence and offence which lay at the heart of his tactics: increasing the proportion of pikemen to shot compared with Maurice of Nassau, he fought in linear formations, seeking to maximise the advantages of both pike and musket. To increase firepower, he experimented with field artillery, reducing its weight to increase mobility – his famous leather guns were but one means by which he sought to attain this end – and using the new invention of cannister. Finally, under the influence of his experience against the Poles, he revived cavalry as a shock weapon by encouraging it to charge home with the sabre.[3]

Gustav Adolf's methods certainly appeared to work. The 1620s saw a string of Swedish victories at Wallhof (17 January 1626), Mewe (22 September and 29 September – 1 October 1626), Dirschau (17–18 August 1627) and Górzno (4 February 1629). At Mewe, a charge by hussars on the first day (22 September 1626) was beaten back; on 29 September two general attacks also proved unsuccessful. By 1 October, the hussars were so demoralised that it was only with difficulty that Sigismund persuaded them to charge the Swedish foot; when they were halted by a salvo from a second line of infantry after sweeping the first line off the high ground, they were again forced to withdraw in disorder. At Dirschau, they suffered the indignity of being driven from the field by Swedish cavalry; on the second day of the battle, there was near panic among the Polish cavalry as the Swedish foot marched purposefully on the Polish camp, only stopping when a Polish marksman shot Gustav Adolf through the shoulder.[4]

The introduction of better muskets, which replaced arquebuses as the main Swedish firearm, certainly increased the effectiveness of the infantry. It was not so much the musket's greater range which mattered – although this proved an advantage against Polish- and Hungarian-style infantry armed with arquebuses[5] – but its increased penetration: the hussars faced Dutch muskets with a calibre of 18–22mm using a charge of 35 grammes, sufficient to pierce body armour. Applied in one or two mighty salvos fired by three ranks simultaneously this improved musket caused great consternation among the hussars, some of whom had fought on the killing-field at Kircholm.[6]

Yet the improvement in firepower should not be exaggerated. The muskets used at Mewe may have been more penetrative than those deployed at Kircholm, but they were slow to fire, prone to misfire, and apt to miss once fired. Experiments suggest that it is possible to fire a seventeenth-century musket once every two minutes, but this rate of fire is hardly to be expected in the stress and confusion of battle, especially since emphasis was laid on firing together; the fact that Montecuccoli later in the century believed that sixteen rounds per day was ample for a musketeer suggests that rates of fire were low. Their killing-power was still relatively limited, and the death-toll was far higher in horses than hussars: one observer was surprised at how few were killed (eighteen) in the three great Polish charges at Mewe on 29 September; he could only conclude that God was catching the bullets, so thick was the hail of fire.[7] Once they had loosed their salvo, musketeers were vulnerable: on the third day at Mewe the Swedes were swept off the high ground by Tomasz Zamoyski's hussars because they had already fired a salvo at the Polish infantry and had not yet reloaded. The failure of Polish charges at Mewe may have had as much to do with the relatively low quality of the troops deployed. Of 3,000 hussars, only three companies were professionals. The rest were novices: 1,500 experienced hussars of the quarter army were in the Ukraine with Field Hetman Stanisław Koniecpolski, facing a threatened Tatar attack.

The Swedes did not rely on firepower alone, however. Their strategy was based on avoiding any encounter with Polish cavalry except on terrain favourable to infantry. The Swedish infantry did everything in its power to protect itself from cavalry attack. They began digging at Riga, where an elaborate 3-kilometre circumvallation was constructed against a relief army, and did not stop digging until Altmark. Whenever they advanced, they immediately began digging in, as von Thurn's troops were doing at Mewe in the few minutes they enjoyed between seizing the high ground and being swept from it by Zamoyski's hussars. Apart from pikes, they deployed swinesfeathers – the Swedish equivalent of Spanish riders.

The selection of terrain was vital. At Wallhof in January 1626, Gustav Adolf mounted a surprise dawn attack on the Lithuanian camp, sited unwisely between two woods, which meant that outflanking moves by the cavalry were impossible and the Swedes could send infantry into the woods to provide enfilading fire as the Lithuanian cavalry charged home. On the first day at Mewe Gustav Adolf took advantage of wooded terrain along the Vistula and the shelter of an anti-flood embankment to reconnoitre and challenge the strong position Sigismund had established on the high ground to the west; when the Poles launched a charge against the Swedish left, it was over the only piece of open ground available to them; the hussars had to form up on the move after crossing the embankment, and charge 200 metres over soft, sandy ground; although they easily routed the Swedish reiters the charge faltered against the salvos of the Swedish foot. The two great charges on 29 September across the plain at the foot of the escarpment further to the north again swept the reiters from the field, but the Swedish foot was well dug in, protected by an embankment and the village of Grünhof; both attacks faltered.

Mewe was undoubtedly a great shock to the Poles. Sigismund had led a substantial army against the Swedes, had taken the strategic initiative, had forced the Swedes to fight on ground of his choosing, and had lost.[8] Gustav Adolf's tactical innovations undoubtedly worked, yet if they posed problems for the Poles, they did not surprise them, for they applied ideas long familiar in eastern Europe, where the use of field fortifications and firepower against cavalry had been a feature of warfare since the fifteenth century. Polish tactics had long relied on the combination of cavalry with infantry firepower: in 1621, as Gustav Adolf was advancing on Riga, 45,000 Poles, Lithuanians and Ukrainian Cossacks, with forty-eight guns, were successfully defending a fortified camp covering 8 square kilometres at Chocim against nearly twice that number of Turks and Tatars.[9] The Poles themselves were attempting to improve methods of constructing and defending field fortifications, and had already drawn on western expertise before 1621, experimenting in Livonia with the advice of the Dutchman, Wilhelm Appelman.

Thus it was frustration, not surprise, which occasioned Polish mutterings in the 1620s against the Swedish 'moles', who refused to come out and fight in the open. Prince Władysław was not, as Parker suggests, 'dispatched to the Netherlands to learn about these deceitful tactics at first hand'.[10] Władysław, who had led an army to the walls of Moscow in 1618, did visit the Spanish siegeworks at Breda in 1624 and took an interest in the latest developments in western military technology, but it was merely part of his Grand Tour. Krzysztof Radziwiłł, who raised the first Lithuanian dragoon company in 1617 and was well acquainted with western warfare – unlike Gustav Adolf he had actually seen the great Maurice of Nassau in action, at the 1603 siege of s'Hertogenbosch – knew exactly what was required. In 1622, he told Sigismund:

> Antiquity has its virtues; domestic methods have great value, but in military affairs less than in others: every century teaches soldiers some new trick; every campaign has its own discoveries; each school of war seeks its own remedies. Gustav's father Karolus, whenever he heard of the approach of our army, immediately abandoned his sieges and rushed into the field to fight a battle. . . . But [Gustav], mindful of his father's defeats, conducts war in a new way, not risking field engagements; therefore one must fight him by taking account of his stratagems.[11]

Radziwiłł argued that the Commonwealth should establish a ratio of infantry to cavalry of 1:1,[12] and although, as a Calvinist, he was Sigismund's bitter political opponent throughout the 1620s, his advice was not ignored. After 1626, the numbers of infantry rose rapidly, both absolutely and relatively. If the army in Prussia contained only 2,200 German-style foot, 1,000 dragoons and 2,000 Polish-style foot in 1626, by 1627 there were 11,609 German-style foot, 1,152 dragoons and 2,600 Polish-style foot. By 1628, Koniecpolski was planning for 13,000 German-style infantry and 2,000 Polish-style foot to only 5,000 cavalry.[13]

The Polish infantry, although outnumbered, performed well at Mewe, despite the fact that over half were Polish- or Hungarian-style foot armed with arquebuses and sabres rather than muskets. Several Swedish attacks were beaten off by resolute firepower. The key moment of the battle – the Swedish seizure of the high ground on 1 October, which Roberts explains in terms of superior Swedish fire-discipline and morale – was as much due to the fact that the Polish infantry holding the ridge did not open fire as the Swedes climbed the escarpment, believing in the smoke of battle that they were a Polish unit withdrawing from the intense fighting on the plain below, and were wholly unprepared when the Swedes loosed their salvo. Thus, it was not quite as dramatic or significant a victory as Swedish historians suggest. Once the Swedes had entrenched themselves on the hilltop as darkness fell, the Poles were unable to dislodge them, and had to abandon the siege of Mewe, since the Polish camp was now within range of the Swedish artillery.

The next major encounter was at Dirschau (17–18 August 1627), where Gustav Adolf confronted Koniecpolski, who took command after arriving from the Ukraine in November 1626. Dirschau is celebrated as the first occasion on which the Swedish cavalry worsted the Poles in open battle, charging home against the hussars with sabres, proving that they could now 'meet the Poles on more or less equal terms'.[14] This is to overstate the case. The first day of the battle showed that Koniecpolski, who was outnumbered,[15] was not going to be tempted, as Sigismund had been tempted at Mewe, by Gustav Adolf's tactics of sending out skirmishers to lure the Poles into charging his carefully-prepared infantry positions. Instead Koniecpolski himself tried to draw the Swedes out from behind their fieldworks. After two hours of fruitless waiting, the Poles began to withdraw along a narrow causeway through the marshy ground which lay between them and their camp. At this point Gustav Adolf launched his horse in a surprise attack, which caught the Poles unawares. In the resulting confusion, the two Polish columns were pushed into the marsh, before a powerful salvo from the Polish foot and a flank attack by Marcin Kazanowski's cavalry stopped the Swedes in their tracks. The Poles lost 80–100 men killed or drowned in the bog. It was dramatic, but it was no Kircholm.[16]

Dirschau merely confirmed Koniecpolski's inclination to avoid open battle. His strategy was simple. It was clear after Mewe and Dirschau that the Poles could no longer rely on one shattering victory to end the war. Gustav Adolf had turned battles into long, attritional affairs which the Swedes, with their superior firepower, were more likely to win. Despite the humiliating experience at Dirschau it was clear that Koniecpolski's cavalry was superior, both quantatively and qualitatively. If that was no longer sufficient to decide a battle, it could still play a decisive role in a campaign. For infantry was still highly vulnerable to cavalry outside prepared fieldworks. It was most exposed on the march, where its firepower was seriously blunted because of the shortcomings of matchlocks: since matches burned quickly – about 10–15 centimetres per hour – only every tenth soldier on the march kept their match alight. Since matches were slow to light, infantry on the march was a tempting target for cavalry, and Gustav Adolf had to recruit archers to provide protection.

Koniecpolski exploited this advantage to deny the Swedes the freedom of movement necessary for supplying and feeding their army. Despite his numerical superiority, Oxenstierna, left in charge by Gustav Adolf in the winter of 1626–7 when he returned to Sweden to raise reinforcements, was wary of Koniecpolski, reluctant to believe a reasonably accurate prisoner's report that he had only 6,800 men at his disposal.[17] Gustav Adolf hoped that the Swedes could harry the Poles with frequent sorties, but by the end of the year he recommended a more defensive strategy. Despite Oxenstierna's reports of Swedish reiters attacking Polish foragers, it was Koniecpolski who seized the initiative, helped by the stance of Danzig.[18] Although the city was deeply hostile to the Maritime Commission established by Sigismund in

November 1626 to oversee the small royal fleet which was stopping and boarding Swedish and other vessels, it had no intention of surrendering to the Swedes. The Danzigers recruited 5,000 German infantrymen and garrisoned every crossing on the Vistula between Dirschau and Weichselmünde, cutting the Swedes off from Putzig, their only foothold apart from Mewe on the left bank. Koniecpolski besieged Putzig, cut off from the sea by the stormy Baltic winter; it fell in early April 1627 in a great blow to Swedish hopes of taking Danzig.

Once the Vistula and Nogat rivers had frozen in December 1626, it was easy for Polish cavalry to slip across to raid deep into the rich agricultural lands of the Danziger Werder, driving off livestock, burning the villages from which the Swedes were seeking to support their forces, and attacking units in winter quarters. The Poles regularly raided and burned round Elbing itself, forcing peasants to flee the countryside and to take refuge in Elbing, which put further pressure on resources.[19] In December, Wrangel reported that there was not a single village in the Grosse Werder between Montauer Spitz and Ließau that the Poles had not 'visited', taking grain above all. The pattern continued into the spring: in one raid in April 1627 the Poles drove away 91 horses, 94 head of cattle, 132 sheep and 98 pigs from four farmsteads.[20]

The Swedes were helpless. Their inferior mounts were too slow to catch the raiders, and there was no indication as to where they would strike next. By early 1627, peasants were complaining vociferously about the shortage of grain, and Oxenstierna introduced an embargo on its export from Elbing, where the price of rye was over six times higher than in Thorn. The army suffered through hunger and disease: by the time Gustav Adolf returned in the spring, the cavalry had been reduced by 20 per cent, and the infantry by 13 per cent; although Oxenstierna could muster 14,000 foot and 2,600 horse, many were unfit for service.[21] Although the Poles also suffered from hunger and desertion of unpaid troops, Koniecpolski kept the initiative throughout the spring, using his superior mobility in April to surround 2,500 German mercenaries on their way to join the Swedes at Hammerstein, where some agreed to enter Polish service; those who refused were massacred by local peasants on their way back through Pomerania in retaliation for forced requisitioning on the outward march.[22]

Gustav Adolf returned to Prussia in May 1627 with 7,000 infantry, followed in June by 1,700 cavalry. Yet although the Swedish forces (now 22,600-strong) had a numerical advantage, many were scattered in garrisons, and Koniecpolski was able to roam at will. He seized Mewe in July, thus winning control of another vital crossing of the Vistula and forcing Gustav Adolf to march south for a showdown. Koniecpolski may have been embarassed by his reverse at Dirschau in August, and lucky that Gustav

Adolf's wound forced a period of recuperation which effectively ended Swedish activity for the summer, but he was heartened by receiving 3,000 reinforcements from the Empire immediately after Dirschau, the first sign that the conquest of Mecklenburg and Pomerania by the imperial commander Albrecht von Wallenstein might help break the deadlock in Prussia. Apart from the capture of Wormditt in October, Gustav Adolf had little to show for his activity. Danzig had completed its defences, while at the battle of Oliva (28 November) a Polish fleet of ten ships startled the Swedes by slipping out of Danzig to capture the Swedish flagship and sink another vessel.

The 1628 campaign was equally frustrating, although Gustav Adolf once more had a numerical advantage, and had significantly increased the proportion of cavalry in his army, fielding 8,873 foot and 6,085 horse at the start of the campaign.[23] If Gustav Horn was sustaining the Swedish position in Livonia, about which Gustav Adolf had been concerned in the winter of 1627–8,[24] the growing threat to Stralsund from Wallenstein distracted the Swedes. A summer of numbing rain and flooding made campaigning difficult and unpleasant, and Koniecpolski's attritional strategy exacerbated the problems. The Polish hetman had drawn his own conclusions from Mewe and Dirschau, and was content to avoid battle, sitting behind fieldworks of his own, buttressed by the growing proportion of infantry at his disposal, while using his cavalry to harry the Swedes and destroy their supply-base. Gustav Adolf advanced on Koniecpolski's fortified camp at Graudenz, but despite much huffing and puffing the Poles were not to be tempted into battle, and Gustav Adolf decided that the position was too powerful to risk a frontal attack. He contented himself therefore with the capture of Marienwerder in Ducal Prussia, which enabled the Swedes to extend their exiguous supply-base but did little to improve relations with his brother-in-law George William, elector of Brandenburg.

Koniecpolski's strategy was beginning to bite. In October, after the capture of Strasburg, Gustav Adolf had to bring a ravaged and demoralised army back through a devastated wasteland, in constant fear of cavalry attack. Illness and desertion were rampant: altogether the Swedes lost nearly 5,000 men on the Strasburg campaign. One Swede observed that officers with thirty years' service had never seen anything like it: Swedish soldiers were deserting in large numbers, while the foreign mercenaries were on the verge of mutiny.[25] It was little different in 1629. Theoretically the Swedes still had 23,000 men in Prussia (15,400 infantry and 7,650 cavalry), but they were constantly harried by the Poles. In February, Wrangel mounted a determined thrust to relieve pressure on the isolated Strasburg garrison, blockaded by Stanisław Potocki and on the point of surrender. His surprise attack on the inexperienced Potocki at Górzno in February was successful: Potocki tried to lure the Swedes into a frontal attack on his infantry and reiters, but was outmanoeuvred. Potocki, who was outnumbered, sustained almost 2,000 casualties – nearly half his army – substantially higher than the losses at Mewe and Dirschau.[26] Górzno demonstrated that the Swedes were learning to fight in the Polish style: Wrangel had 3,400 cavalry – over half his force – and won with a daring flanking manoeuvre. Potocki's self-serving account stressed that he had no time to prepare field fortifications to protect his infantry who, without pikes, were vulnerable against cavalry.[27]

Wrangel soon discovered the problems of fighting in the Polish style: he might have won a sharp victory, but he was unable to exploit it. He made a quick dash at Thorn, but with only 4 twelve-pounder and 2 six-pounder guns, plus 4 captured at Górzno, he could not hope to take the city, though he gave it a fright. He ran the risk of his small force being caught and destroyed, so he beat a hasty retreat northwards. He was right to be cautious, for, as Gustav Adolf himself was soon to find out, the Poles still had the edge in this war of movement, despite the improved performance of the Swedish cavalry. If the Poles were reinforced by imperial troops, Gustav Adolf, many of whose 23,000 men were scattered in garrisons, risked being seriously outnumbered by Koniecpolski, who had 7,942 cavalry and 10,800 infantry. In June, with 5,000 reinforcements from Wallenstein marching to join Koniecpolski under Hans Georg von Arnim, Gustav Adolf moved south with 5,450 horse and 1,900 foot hoping to defeat Arnim before he joined Koniecpolski.[28]

His boldness all but brought disaster. He was too late to prevent Arnim reaching Koniecpolski at Graudenz on 25 June, where they agreed to attack Marienwerder; two days later, Gustav Adolf decided to cut and run. Sending his infantry north towards Stuhm, he deployed his cavalry to the southeast to provide cover. Arnim wished to wait until the Polish and imperial infantry arrived, but Koniecpolski decided on immediate attack.[29] On 17/27 June a small party of dragoons beat the Swedes to a vital crossing of the river Leibe near Honigfelde. The Swedish rearguard – 2,000 horse and a small contingent of musketeers under Rheingraf Johann Wilhelm – deployed on the crest of a gentle slope. Koniecpolski stationed his cossack cavalry on the left and Arnim's reiters in the centre; when Johann Wilhelm turned his front to the southwest and moved to outflank the cossacks, Koniecpolski led his hussars through a valley, hidden from the Swedes, and caught them with a devastating attack in the left flank as they closed with the cossacks.[30] Driven from the field, the Swedes regrouped at Straszewo; stiffened by reinforcements they counterattacked against the pursuing cossacks, who were pushed back, but regrouped; the arrival of the slower reiters and hussars prompted the Swedes to turn tail. When Gustav Adolf rallied them with fresh troops and made a stand at Pulkowitz, the Poles were already tiring; the battle developed into fierce hand-to-hand combat, in which Arnim's fresher reiters, who had not taken part in the earlier clashes, played a notable part. Gustav Adolf, in the thick of the action, was almost killed or captured on two occasions, before the Swedes managed to disengage and retreat to join the infantry and baggage-train at Stuhm.

This was achieved at quite a cost. It is a measure of the success of Swedish propaganda that Honigfelde's significance has consistently been played down. Gustav Adolf claimed that the Swedes only lost 200 killed, but Polish sources suggest the figure was much higher: according to one witness 1,000 Swedish bodies were counted at Honigfelde, 300 at Straszewo and 167 at Pulkowitz. Thirty senior Swedish officers died, including the Rheingraf, and the Poles captured 200 Swedes, 10 standards, 10 leather guns and 5 other cannon; a harvest on this scale suggests the Polish casualty figures are nearer the mark.[31] Although Koniecpolski failed to destroy Gustav Adolf's expeditionary force, Honigfelde was just as significant as Mewe, Dirschau and Górzno, and perhaps more so, for it restored Polish morale and demonstrated that they could still match the Swedes in battle. After Honigfelde, Gustav Adolf withdrew behind his elaborate defences at Marienburg, where he successfully repulsed Koniecpolski's attacks while the diplomats talked peace.

The truce of Altmark (September 1629) was a recognition by both sides that neither was capable of outright military victory. Gustav Adolf's new tactics had not produced a military breakthrough, and the strategic advantage which he gained over the Commonwealth was achieved right at the start of the war when his armies faced no opposition: in 1621, the largest field army Sweden had yet brought to Livonia was faced by a small garrison and barely 1,500 cavalry. His arrival in Prussia in 1626 was also unopposed; by the time the Poles had scrambled together an inadequate force Gustav Adolf had occupied Elbing, Marienburg, Dirschau and the Danziger Haupt, which formed the powerful quadrilateral from which the Swedes were not shifted for the rest of the war. Yet when the Poles organised more substantial opposition, Swedish military achievements were less impressive. As Roberts recognises, by the late summer of 1629, the Swedes stood much where they had in 1626.[32]

Had the Poles but known it, the Swedes were stretched to breaking-point. The conscript levies of 1627 and 1628 had sparked widespread unrest, and in the winter of 1628–9 the Swedes had to import grain into the Vistula delta, which had once supplied the whole of Europe.[33] Oxenstierna had a miserable time trying to keep together a scarecrow army in a devastated landscape, only doing so by dint of moving into Ducal Prussia and levying contributions there, which did not endear him to George William. Gustav Adolf, with his superiority in infantry – although even that was

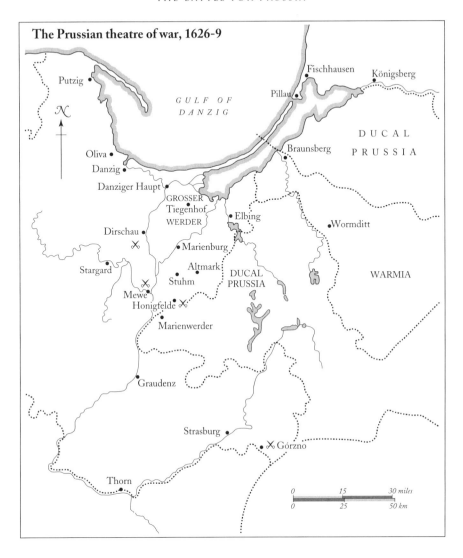

The Prussian theatre of war, 1626-9

substantially reduced by 1629 – could hold most of what he had taken; what he could not do was break out of the quadrilateral, or defeat Koniecpolski. Honigfelde demonstrated that Gustav Adolf could only realistically pursue a defensive strategy, but in country that had been devastated by three years of war, he risked seeing his army melt away. Altmark came at a very good moment for the sake of his reputation; there was to be no Prussian Breitenfeld and the war ended in strategic stalemate.

Yet the Swedes undoubtedly won it. Altmark left them in *de facto* control of Livonia north of the Dvina. Elbing was left in Swedish hands; in addition to the duties collected from the areas under its control, Sweden was also to receive the lion's share of the 5.5 per cent toll levied on the lucrative Danzig trade. Marienburg, Danziger Haupt and the Grosse Werder were not returned to Poland, but sequestered to Brandenburg for the duration of the truce, to be returned to Sweden if no peace were made on its expiry. With unusual generosity for a mediator, George William allowed Sweden to occupy – and draw the tolls from – his own cities of Pillau, Fischhausen, Lochstädt and Memel, as a pledge for the return of the sequestrated lands.[34]

These gains were out of all proportion to Sweden's actual achievement. Gustav Adolf was lucky. The Habsburg breakthrough to the Baltic after 1626 had dramatically altered the balance of power in northern Europe, and meant that powers worried at possible Habsburg control of the north German coastline – especially France, England and the United Provinces – were desperate to find someone to reverse the long series of Habsburg victories after the crushing defeat of Christian IV, who intervened in Germany in 1625, but was forced to make peace at Lübeck in 1629. The small Polish fleet which had won the battle of Oliva was sent by Sigismund to Wismar in 1628 to join the ships with which Wallenstein was hoping to construct an imperial navy, a prospect which even brought Denmark and Sweden briefly together in 1628 to help Stralsund resist Wallenstein's siege.

Thus the mediators at Altmark were hardly neutral, and the generous terms won by Sweden – which was also to receive French and Dutch subsidies as an incentive to intervene in the Empire – were the result of enormous pressure on the Poles. They were accepted because many among the *szlachta* blamed Sigismund for provoking the Swedish attack by refusing to compromise over the Swedish throne after Gustav Adolf hinted that he was willing to surrender Livonia in return for Sigismund resigning his claim. The Poles were weary of the high level of taxation required to fight the Prussian war and suspicious of Sigismund's intentions with regard to the war in the Empire.[35] Under domestic and international pressure, Sigismund was forced to accept the unpalatable terms, and Gustav Adolf's new army, on the point of disintegrating, could move to feed in pastures new.

The coming of the military state

'*Other powers wage war because they are rich. Sweden, in contrast, must wage them because it is poor, to improve its material condition.*'

(Johan Adler Salvius)[36]

Sweden's achievement between 1621 and 1629 was undoubtedly substantial. It had triumphantly reversed the pattern of the previous half-century in which, for all its limited military success against Muscovy, it had experienced a long run of reverses against the Danes and the Poles. It was Sweden's dramatic success in the Thirty Years War, however, which astonished contemporaries; historians ever since have sought to explain how it could be achieved on such a precarious economic base: Sweden had a population of barely 1,250,000, an underdeveloped economy with relatively low yield ratios, a short growing season and a government which raised a large proportion of its income in kind. For such a state to defeat within a few short years two of the leading powers in Catholic Europe would certainly seem to require explanation. It is, however, the successes of the 1620s rather than the achievements of the post-Altmark period which pose the greatest problems for the historian. For 1630 in many respects marked a lessening of the intense burden which Swedish society had borne in the previous decade, since it marked the beginning of a period in which the cost of warfare was overwhelmingly sustained by others: by the merchants forced to pay the new tolls at the Prussian ports, by the French and Dutch governments and – above all – by the German people who supplied contributions and recruits to feed the bloated Swedish armies. The decision to transfer the Polish war to Prussia in 1626 had been taken in large part because of the difficulties of supply which the Swedish armies faced in Livonia. The Swedish eruption into the wealthy Danziger Werder was thus the first attempt to pursue the aim of *bellum se ipse alet* – the idea that war could pay for itself – but Koniecpolski's marauding cavalry ensured that it was only in Germany after 1630 that the Swedes came close to realising this ideal. In the 1620s, although the inhabitants of Royal Prussia were bled of both cash and produce, it was Sweden itself which bore much of the burden of war, at a time when the abrupt Spanish decision to suspend the minting of its *vellón* coinage in May 1626 had knocked the bottom out of the lucrative copper market, which provided Sweden with vital foreign exchange.

The burden was considerable. Between 1625 and 1629, 50,000 men were shipped over from Sweden and Finland to fight. Since losses through death, disease and desertion were so high (35–40,000 in the 1620s alone), merely keeping the army up to strength required prodigious levels of recruitment.[37] The peasantry faced seven conscript levies in nine years, each of which took one man from a file of ten, drawn up from all crown peasants and peasant freeholders between the ages of fifteen and sixty, and one in twenty noble peasants until 1627. A range of new direct and indirect taxes were raised, payable in cash: in 1620 the Stock and Land Tax; in 1622 the Little Toll, a levy on all goods brought in for sale at town markets; in 1625 a tax on grain brought to the royal mills; and in 1628 the Three Marks' Aid. Not only did these replace older taxes in kind, the rates at which they were levied rose steadily. Yet although peasant protest grew substantially towards the end of the 1620s and although efforts at tax-evasion were common, enough men and money were raised to ensure that the Swedes were not dislodged from Prussia until peace was secured.

How was this done? Traditional accounts stress the importance of Gustav Adolf's accession in 1611, which represented a clean break with the past, as the death of the last of Gustav Vasa's talented but unstable sons opened the way to a new generation. Gustav Adolf and Axel Oxenstierna were undoubtedly brilliant administrators who, within a very short period, presided over Sweden's political, administrative, military and fiscal transformation; nevertheless, their talents are not in themselves sufficient to explain the scope or extent of the changes. The transformation is even more striking in traditional accounts, since great stress is usually laid on the desperate situation in which Sweden found itself in 1611, facing a determined attack from Denmark, still mired in the Muscovite imbroglio, and with only a short-term truce with Poland-Lithuania preserving it from the nightmare of war on three fronts. Sweden had been fighting almost without a break since 1555; it had experienced internal political upheaval which had seen two kings deposed and leading members of the greatest noble families exiled or executed. The burden of war had all but bankrupted the state and had led to peasant unrest of which the savage Finnish Club War in the 1590s had merely been the most violent. During the Kalmar War, after which Sweden had to pay the massive ransom for Älvsborg, law and order in parts of Sweden all but collapsed.

Yet in 1617, the very year that Sweden managed to extract itself from the war with Muscovy, Gustav Adolf was already attacking Livonia. It is true that the truce had expired in October 1616, and that the *Sejm* had passed a resolution condemning Sigismund's deposition and given a vague warning of military action, but the immediate resumption of war was far from what the Poles desired: in 1617, Władysław was preparing his great expedition to Moscow to claim the crown of the tsars. While the Poles sought an extension of the truce, the Swedes approached the Calvinist Krzysztof Radziwiłł in the name of Protestant solidarity, and tried to exploit the dispute between the two dukes of Courland, the brothers Frederick and William Kettler. Four years later, there could be no doubt who was the aggressor, as Gustav Adolf sailed into Riga bay, with the Poles otherwise engaged on their southern frontier. If Sweden was suffering from war-weariness, its neighbours might be pardoned for misdiagnosing the patient's affliction.

The debate about the reasons for Sweden's aggressive drive for imperial expansion has long focused on the issue of whether it was motivated by a desire for security, or by the urge to control the mouths of the major Baltic rivers in the interests of profit. Much of this debate has centred round questions of individual motivation, without too much attention paid to the vital question of why Swedish society was prepared to tolerate and pay for a further round of aggression after 1617. For the concentration on the plans and ideas of Gustav Adolf and Oxenstierna, and the discussion as to whether their justification of Sweden's actions as defensive hid deeper motives, cannot explain why the decision for an active policy was accepted, especially in a state where the Council had apparently just won a battle to reassert its control over the monarchy after the bloody confrontations with Charles IX.[38] In Denmark, whose political institutions and traditions bore more than a superficial resemblance to Sweden's, Christian IV was to start an aggressive war twice within fifteen years, but on both occasions the Council, mindful of the events of the 1560s, deeply disapproved of its monarch's actions, and if it was pulled reluctantly into the Kalmar War, it refused to sanction Christian's rash plunge into the Thirty Years War in 1625, a step he had to take in his capacity as duke of Holstein, and which he paid for himself, at least until Wallenstein's invasion of Jutland persuaded the *Rigsdag* to support a defensive war.

Part of the explanation lies in the different political situations of the two states. Christian found it difficult to convince the Council that the Catholic threat from the Habsburgs and their allies was sufficient to justify intervention in the Empire, and his concern with the Lower Saxon bishoprics was patently inspired by personal motives. In Sweden, however, the Catholic threat seemed much more real. Sigismund, after all, had been driven from the throne in part because he was a Catholic, and Poland remained a centre for Swedish Catholics and Jesuits. The government occasionally arrested the odd Catholic missionary to prove that the threat was real. Sigismund remained notoriously committed to reclaiming his throne, had invaded once already, and had even managed to seize Stockholm, which was most useful for subsequent attempts to represent the Poles as dangerous. Furthermore, he had sought both his wives in the Habsburg family and clearly hoped that a close relationship with the Habsburgs might bring about his restoration. The fact that his Polish subjects showed little interest in helping him was immaterial; enough Swedes had acquired land confiscated from Sigismund's supporters, or stood to lose in other ways, for the relentless government propaganda to strike a chord. Gustav Adolf lost no opportunity of emphasising the dangers of Polish attack, echoing the earthy rhetoric of his father and grandfather.

The existence of a plausible external threat, however, cannot in itself explain the remarkable aggression displayed by Sweden after 1617. Of greater significance were social forces. Sweden's poverty may have made it difficult to sustain the status of a great power, but it provided an essential impetus for aggression. The Kalmar War had confirmed the lessons of the

1560s: Sweden was unable to defend itself effectively in a war on its own territory, when poverty made a rapid surrender on disadvantageous terms very likely. The need to make war pay for itself was very early apparent: to achieve it, Sweden's armies had to fight on enemy soil where they could pass as much as possible of the burden of war onto the shoulders of others; it was this argument for entering the Thirty Years War which the *Riksdag* found most convincing in 1629.[39] When it proved impossible to sustain the Swedish army for more than one or two campaigns in Livonia, it had to be transferred to Prussia; when Prussia was exhausted, the Swedes had to go elsewhere.

Yet none of this explains why the army should reach Livonia in the first place. Christian's inclinations were as martial as Gustav Adolf's, yet it was only through using private funds that he was able to intervene in Germany in 1625, and he was certainly incapable of persuading his Danish subjects that such aggression was in any way necessary or justified. Sigismund's abiding obsession was to mount an invasion of Sweden to regain his throne, but after 1598 he failed utterly to win any backing from the *Sejm*, despite a propaganda campaign that was no whit less dedicated or effectively mounted than that of Gustav Adolf and Oxenstierna. Yet the success of propaganda depends substantially on the audience's willingness to listen and be persuaded; the Polish and Danish examples suggest that such a phenomenon could not be created by a simple act of will on the part of the ruler. Sweden's capacity for waging aggressive war was dependent on the tacit or open consent of important groups within Swedish society.

Sweden's aggressive, expansionist drive was fuelled as much from below as above, and it was the very poverty of the state which drove it. The foundations of Sweden's military state were already laid by 1611. Gustav Adolf and Oxenstierna certainly brought a new energy and ability to government, but they were working with the grain of Swedish historical development, not against it. Gustav Adolf's predecessors may not have been talented soldiers, as he undoubtedly was, but the long period of virtually unbroken warfare since 1554 had seen the slow development of a new relationship between the armed forces and society which was the essential precondition for his dramatic achievements.[40] Gustav Adolf's tactical reforms were masterly indeed, but they were only possible because he was working with a core of experienced professional soldiers, and especially officers, who had served in the long wars of John III and Charles IX, and who had a material interest in the further development of Sweden's armed forces.

By 1590, 20 out of 57 Swedish infantry captains (35 per cent) had been in service for over ten years; the brief respite in Sweden's wars in the 1590s, and Charles IX's policy of hiring foreign officers meant that in 1610, the percentage was smaller, even if the number remained the same (20 out of

70; 28.6 per cent). In each year, 4 captains had over twenty years' service.[41] The number of officers grew steadily. Between 1561 and 1568, Sweden employed 171 infantry captains, of whom 18 (11 per cent) were foreigners. Between 1569 and 1592, it employed 186, of which 38 (21 per cent) were foreign. The figures dropped in the 1590s, but between 1599 and 1610 it employed 319 infantry captains; if 87 (27 per cent) were foreigners, 232 were Swedes. Interestingly, considering the traditional emphasis on the importance of infantry, Charles employed a significantly larger proportion of foreign officers in the cavalry (90 out of 187; 48 per cent) between 1599 and 1610.[42]

Regardless of whether their armies performed competently or not, the Vasas had, through simply fighting for so long, created a steadily expanding demand for officers which was largely met from domestic sources.[43] Service as an army officer in this period was attractive as a career which offered prospects of economic security or social advance. Sweden, like other areas which produced large numbers of soldiers, was poor, underdeveloped and offered few opportunities for a comfortable living, especially for younger sons of nobles, peasant freeholders or burghers. It is true that Sweden had felt the effects of the general European rise in population which increased agriculatural profitability, but few were in a position to exploit these favour-able conditions on any substantial scale. If the long period of war brought heavy burdens for all groups of society, it also provided opportunities for individuals from every estate.

The nobility consisted in 1600 of 500–600 adult males; with the inclusion of their families, a maximum of 3,000 people.[44] Of these, the vast majority were impoverished; indeed the noble status of many was in doubt, since it was not until the establishment of the *Riddarhus* in 1626 that Sweden acquired a true nobility of birth. Hitherto, nobility depended upon the possession of land freed of fiscal burdens which required in return the provision of *rusttjänst* (knight service); such land, and the status derived from it, was termed *frälse*, from the word for deliverance. The vast majority of noble estates were small, with low levels of investment. In 1560, of 566 noble landholders, 228 held only one or two farms; 102 held between three and five, with 69 holding between six and ten. Thus just over 70 per cent of the nobility held ten farms or under.[45] At the other end of the scale, 21 held 51–100 farms, with 32 owning over 100.[46] If historians have concentrated on the small group of wealthy families at the top of the nobility, poor nobles formed by far the majority of the estate; in economic terms there was often little to distinguish them from peasant freeholders beyond tax-exemption.

The long cycle of wars forced the royal government to put great pressure on the nobility. It tried to ensure that nobles either provided the *rusttjänst* which their *frälse* status demanded; if a nobleman could not, it sought to downgrade him to the level of the tax-paying peasantry. The monarchy also attempted to regulate the number of horsemen provided according to income, and to introduce more rigorous control of noble incomes, instead of relying on the system of self-assessment by which it lost out. Until 1526, nobles were obliged to supply one horseman regardless of the size of their estates, which was very much to the advantage of the richer nobility, while poorer nobles had often secured exemptions in practice. Gustav Vasa negotiated several agreements between 1526 and 1559, but they were localised or temporary; it was not until the 1562 *Riksdag* that general agreement was reached on the provision of one horseman, supplied and equipped, for every 300 marks of rental income for allodial land, and 200 marks for income from fiefs, including income in kind; unfortunately, in order to secure a long-term agreement the government had to make various concessions compared with the rather harsher but short-term agreement of 1559; in particular it had to lower the tariffs at which produce in kind was assessed; thus the nobility gained from inflation after 1560.[47]

Despite its drive to produce more accurate assessments of noble income, the government failed to enforce compliance. Musterings of the *rusttjänst* produced only 25 per cent of those required in 1562, 12 per cent in 1563, 17 per cent in 1564 and 40–50 per cent in 1565.[48] Erik sought to deprive those nobles who failed to provide their quota of their *frälse* status and place their lands under tax, but this policy failed to survive his deposition: under the privileges agreed in 1569, the nobility gained further concessions, in that impoverished nobles were to be obliged to sell their *frälse* land to a relative if they could not supply their horseman, but were not to lose their status.[49] John was forced to make wide-ranging concessions: he fended off the Council demand for allodial land to be exempt from *rusttjänst*, but had to accept the exemption of fiefs, and the raising of the threshold at which a horseman was provided to every 400 marks of rental income, which suited the wealthier nobility. Furthermore, a nobleman's manor was to be exempt from assessment, and the period in which he had to support his horseman in a campaign outside Sweden's borders was reduced from three months to two weeks: thereafter the obligation fell upon the crown; this condition was to apply to Swedish nobles serving in Finland or Livonia, and to Finnish nobles serving in Sweden.[50]

This agreement held until 1612 despite constant bickering over its terms. Essentially, however, the monarchy had failed in its attempt to force the nobility to meet its obligations. The system of control which Erik had tried, with some success, to introduce did not long survive him; the failure to adjust the tariffs upwards meant that the government lost out through inflation, and the nobility was reluctant to serve in campaigns against Muscovy. The real problem was noble poverty. In 1607, when the *rusttjänst* tariff was set at one horse per 100 riksdalers of rental income, 70 per cent of the nobility fell under this level: the median income was only 60 riksdalers.[51] Despite the monarchy's energetic efforts, it was clearly impossible to raise anything like enough cavalry for war in the east through *rusttjänst*. Most nobles were able to supply one horseman at best; many of them not even that. Unlike Poland-Lithuania, the high nobility was neither wealthy enough nor large enough to raise substantial numbers on its own: in the 1562 muster-roll, only six noblemen provided over 10 horsemen: Gustaf Johansson Tre Rosor (21), Svante Sture (20), Gabriel Christiernsson Oxenstierna (18), Johan Persson Bååt (14), Per Brahe (12) and Johan Åkesson Natt och Dag (10). The top thirty-two nobles by rental income provided 179 cavalrymen.[52] It was hardly a force to keep the Poles awake at night.

Noble unwillingness or inability to provide the Crown with the cavalry it required did not, however, mean that nobles stayed at home to tend their livestock; far from it: nobles served as volunteers in large numbers in all branches of the armed forces during the long period of warfare. Throughout the second half of the sixteenth century, they provided substantial numbers of officers at all levels, particularly in the cavalry (see Table 1). Thus, if there were 500–600 adult males in the Swedish nobility between 1554 and 1610, in the two periods of greatest conflict (1561–8 and 1599–1610), 28–35 per cent of them were serving at the top levels of the military hierarchy; considering that nobles also served in lower ranks, the level of military engagement was even higher.

For if it was difficult to persuade nobles to serve out of obligation, they were perfectly happy to serve for reward. Moreover, thanks to a remarkable and successful shift in government policy, instituted under Gustav Vasa, developed rapidly under Erik as a direct response to the demands of war, and fully established under John, the rewards were attractive. The attention of historians outside Sweden has often been caught by the methods by which the state mobilised its ordinary soldiers, but the principal driving

Table 1 Nobles by birth in Swedish service, 1555–1610[53]

Period	Generals/ colonels No. (%)	Admirals No. (%)	Cavalry captains No. (%)	Infantry captains No. (%)	Naval captains No. (%)
1555–60	11 (85)	3 (67)	13 (81)	16 (27)	7 (25)
1561–8	43 (80)	22 (71)	33 (43)	21 (12)	57 (17)
1569–92	44 (66)	14 (61)	49 (48)	9 (5)	29 (12)
1593–8	23 (77)	8 (67)	19 (68)	9 (9)	9 (15)
1599–1610	38 (45)	20 (69)	75 (40)	18 (6)	20 (13)

force behind the creation of the Swedish military state was the development of the unique system by which it rewarded its officers: without it, Gustav Adolf's exploits would have been impossible.

Crown land was the basis of the system. It is impossible to conceive the creation of the Swedish military state without the Reformation, which had brought so much land into Crown possession. In 1523, it possessed 3,754 farms, the Church 14,340, the nobility 13,922 and the tax-peasants 35,239; by 1560, the Crown owned 18,936, the Church none, the nobility 14,175 and the peasants 33,130.[54] The expropriation of the Church gave the monarchy a resource which could easily have been sold off to pay for expensive foreign mercenaries as occurred elsewhere. It was unlikely, however, that the impoverished Swedish nobility could have purchased land on anything like the scale that would have been required.

These harsh realities ensured that the monarchy had to use royal land in a more creative fashion. While it was necessary for monarchs from Gustav Vasa to John III to grant large fiefs to members of the high nobility who offered them political support – under John, newly-created counts received fiefs of 450–600 farms, while barons received 40–60 – Charles IX's assault on the high nobility helped break the practice, which by 1611 had been discontinued. On the accession of Gustav Adolf, four counts and nineteen barons had been created but only seven barons had been granted fiefs.[55] By 1592, holdings of territorial fiefs had been greatly reduced while the number of individual farms granted as fiefs rose rapidly. The grant of such a fief (*förläning*) was increasingly linked to service performed: in 1568, there were 500 in the whole state; by 1572, this had more than doubled to 1,010, excluding the royal duchies.[56] If this kind of fief dropped in number thereafter, it was linked to the development of a new kind of grant, even more favourable to the interests of the Crown, the *beställning*. This was also a method of payment dependent upon the assigning of the revenues of particular crown farms, the enjoyment of which was closely defined and limited by contract to a fixed term, often of one or two years. Unlike *förläningarna*, which were attached to a given person, a *beställning* was tied to a specific function and lapsed when the contract expired.[57] Originally, *beställningarna* had been granted to commoners, with nobles receiving *förläningarna*, but by the start of John's reign, *beställningarna* were being granted to nobles at all levels, including admirals and provincial governors, although the number of serving noble officers holding *beställningarna* was still relatively small.

The advantages for the Crown were clear. In an impoverished, specie-starved economy, the combination of *förläningarna* and *beställningarna* offered the most effective means available for exploiting royal revenues. The key elements of the system were the existence of tight control, through the registers established under Erik, and the policy of distributing royal lands in small blocks. This was a far more efficient way of utilising royal land, since nobles had proved no more effective at exploiting territorial fiefs than the crown, but were more able to extract their dues from those based on individual farms: in 1593, although territorial fiefs (most of which by now were no larger than parishes) contained 3,850 farms and 1,300 *frälse* farms to only 1,117 farms and 17 *frälse* farms distributed individually, the rental income of the latter was 63 per cent of the former (9,256 to 15,441 riksdaler).[58] Finally, the relatively small size of *förläningarna* made it harder for great nobles to establish a territorial political base: the exception, of course, being the royal duchies, where it was the dukes who distributed fiefs. They were to cause trouble enough before their elimination in 1622.

The system would not have worked had it only suited the Crown. Roberts suggests that the nobility suffered from the changes,[59] and it is true that certain groups among the high nobility were adversely affected. Nevertheless, the call for maintenance (*underhåll*) when on royal service had been one of the nobility's central demands in the discussions which led to the privileges of 1569, and certain groups among the high nobility benefited, such as the faction centred round the Bielke, the Banér and Erik Sparre, whose combined income from *förläningarna* and *beställningarna* in 1587–8 reached 13,363 riksdalers.[60] Thus, although faction-struggles within the high nobility destabilised politics after 1560, the Crown could exploit the relatively small number of rich and powerful families through grants of fiefs and, in particular, of outright donations of royal land in hereditary possession which became increasingly common towards the end of the century. The high nobility also won concessions in partial compensation, such as the exemption of *förläningarna* from assessment for *rusttjänst* which was conceded in 1569. Nevertheless, the growing political unrest in Council circles by the end of the 1580s undoubtedly reflected the squeeze which the monarchy's policy had placed on the high nobility; the position was worsened by the aftermath of the confrontation at Reval in 1589, when John called in the fiefs of the Bielke-Banér-Sparre faction in revenge for their opposition.

The lesser nobility had most to gain. The reduction in territorial fiefs affected only a minority of the nobility: only 87 out of over 500 adult male nobles possessed one in 1571–2.[61] The grant of the income, even temporarily, from one or two farms could make a great difference to an impoverished noble struggling to maintain his *frälse* status; he might double his income or better. Furthermore, if pressure over the performance of *rusttjänst* was a stick with which the government sought to beat the lesser nobility, the payment system by *förläning* and *beställning* was a most tempting carrot.[62] In the case of the former, some sort of security was granted to those who enlisted in the forces: although fiefs were not hereditary, and could be called in by the Crown, nevertheless they represented a degree of security, in that they could provide a pension for those who had served the Crown well, or even support their widows: on average, a tenth of all *förläningarna* were held by women, who constituted a fifth of all holders of fiefs.[63]

That the system tended to benefit the poorer rather than the richer nobles is demonstrated by the fact that the group which derived most benefit from the changes was the numerous but impoverished Finnish nobility. Finland had the highest concentration of poor nobles: 40 per cent of the Finnish nobility lost its *frälse* status under Gustav Vasa, and there were only 1,133 *frälse* farms in Finland in 1560, compared with 15,425 in Sweden.[64] Finns were disproportionately represented in the armed forces, however. The number of Finnish companies grew dramatically after 1570, when there were two in service compared with thirty-one Swedish; by 1601 the ratio was 25:68; by 1618 it was 23:36.[65] Finnish commanders received lavish rewards: Klas Fleming, Henrik Klasson Horn, Klas Åkesson Tott, Jöran Boije, Hans Björnsson and many others received substantial donations of crown land. Finland was in the front line in the war against Muscovy after 1570, which may explain the willingness of Finns to fight, but the fact that the Finnish contribution to Sweden's military effort remained greatly disproportionate to the size of its population throughout the seventeenth century suggests that it was Finland's poverty which acted as the principal recruiter, not least among the nobility, who derived clear benefit: by 1600, the number of *frälse* farms in Finland had almost doubled, to 2,137.[66]

After 1560 the Swedish nobility was gradually turned into a service class. This change – by no means securely established by John's death in 1592 – was not achieved smoothly, and the disruption it caused was an important factor in the current of opposition among the high nobility which led, among other things, to Erik's deposition and to the Reval confrontation in 1589. Yet it cannot be said to have been imposed on the nobility: it could only work because so many stood to gain, if on a relatively small scale. State service was an important road to economic and social advancement for many poor nobles, not just in the ranks of the army, but also as local administrators and civil servants. In the circumstances, it represented an effective use of royal resources: *förläning* cast the onus of extracting royal revenues and rents upon the holder, who often proved more efficient at it than royal officials. There were more problems with *beställningarna*, where the crown still collected the dues and paid wages in kind or in cash; these were frequently in arrears, but the tying of payment to specific sources of revenue was considerably more efficient than the usual haphazard practice of contemporary governments, who were all better at promise than delivery. If the wages due to officers in the field were usually in arrears, the combination of *förläningarna* and *beställningarna* was for the most part able to deliver the *årslön*, the annual pay due to all soldiers.

Table 2 Native commoners in Swedish service, 1555–1610[67]

Period	Generals/ colonels No. (%)	Admirals No. (%)	Cavalry captains No. (%)	Infantry captains No. (%)	Naval captains No. (%)
1555–60	1 (8)	2 (33)	2 (33)	38 (63)	20 (71)
1561–8	4 (7)	5 (16)	5 (16)	131 (77)	250 (75)
1569–92	2 (3)	2 (9)	2 (9)	138 (74)	196 (78)
1593–8	1 (3)	0 (0)	0 (0)	73 (71)	37 (62)
1599–1610	4 (5)	2 (7)	2 (7)	212 (67)	85 (56)

The system provided rewards and opportunities for more than just the nobility. By 1600, nearly half a century of virtually uninterrupted warfare had created a substantial officer corps in which the majority were native-born commoners (see Table 2). These figures demonstrate that if nobles and immigrants dominated the higher ranks and the cavalry, the majority of infantry and naval captains were commoners. It was for commoners that *beställningarna* had originally been devised, and it was only gradually that they came to be extended to nobles as well. By 1600, the officer corps contained 400–500 commoners, who dominated it numerically.[68]

The rewards for such service could be substantial. Fifty-four men in the ranks reviewed in Tables 1 and 2 were new nobles, who began their military careers as commoners.[69] Tönne Olofsson till Kiula, a Finnish commoner, rose to command Erik's guard regiment. Ennobled in 1563, he was a general by 1567, leading the infantry in the 1567–8 campaign; he was shot for his part in resisting the 1568 coup. Samuel Nilsson till Hessle, a goldsmith's son from Stockholm rose, like his brother, in Charles's service. He received his military education in the Netherlands; on his return Charles appointed him to train the infantry during the civil war against Sigismund. He led half of Charles's army at Stångebro in 1598, and was ennobled in 1604 (his brother had been similarly elevated in 1590), before being killed outside Dorpat in 1607. Nilsson received large grants of *förläningarna*, and married into the high nobility.[70]

Men like these had a material stake in the developing military state, and a direct interest in the continuation of war, despite the relatively indifferent performance of the Swedish armies. Since so many of them were paid in the form of *beställning*, on the basis of limited contracts, the end of the war would bring economic uncertainty, and put paid to any hopes of advancement: war, on the other hand, created opportunities for promotion. Moreover, alongside the officers was a growing body of administrators which ran – and fed off – the military state. A new, politically influential group was emerging among the Swedish social elites with a direct interest in war. Such men played a central role in the political upheavals from the end of the 1580s. At the ill-tempered Reval meeting in 1589, when John tried to persuade Sigismund to renounce the Polish throne and return to Sweden, the army commanders present played an important part, alongside members of the Council, in frustrating his plans. Their discontent may well have been due to changes in policy over *förläningarna* which had squeezed their incomes.

Nevertheless, the extent of the common ground between army officers and members of the Council was limited; in the political crisis which followed Sigismund's accession in 1592, the officer corps was to play a central role. As the political struggle developed, with Sigismund, Charles and the Council manoeuvring for position, it at first seemed as if there was little political unity among the officer corps. Indeed, the ending of the war with Muscovy in 1595 created serious problems. Klas Fleming, Sigismund's leading supporter, billeted his troops in Finland, which was to remain a centre of opposition to Charles, who had done much to whip up the opposition to the presence of the troops in Finland which produced the Club War in 1596–7. The Finnish army stayed loyal to Sigismund even after Fleming's death in 1597, but in 1598 it appeared too late to affect the outcome of Sigismund's clash with Charles; after Sigismund abandoned his followers to return to Poland, Charles brought his own forces over to defeat the leaderless Finns in 1599.

Charles, as he turned against the Council nobles, deliberately sought support among the officer corps, and in particular from the non-noble officers, although many petty nobles were also ready to support his cause. As early as 1594, the army officers were mentioned as a separate estate of the realm; at the 1595 *Riksdag*, called by Charles in direct defiance of Sigismund as part of his struggle with the Council, they were named as an estate before the burghers; even ordinary soldiers were named as an estate before the peasantry, an order which was repeated in 1600 and 1611.[71] The 1600 Linköping tribunal which sent five of Sigismund's leading supporters to the scaffold included 36 nobles, 24 burghers, 24 peasants, 23 bailiffs and legal officials, and no fewer than 46 army officers; later tribunals in 1605 and 1607 contained an even higher proportion of officers.[72] Although army officers were never formally established as a separate estate, and although the split between noble and non-noble still caused internal divisions, the growing political importance of the officer corps was undoubtedly of great significance. Charles's tense relationship with the high nobility prevented the wholesale support of army officers, and his increasing reliance on foreign officers during his Livonian war caused much unease; on the whole, however, he was backed by his officers. The prospect of a Catholic monarch was not welcome to holders of *förläningarna* or *beställningarna* on property that had once belonged to the Church; indeed, many actually received tithe payments as part of their income. When forced to choose at Stångebro in 1598, Sigismund's Swedish officers refused to fight.

Thus the great wave of reforms instituted after Gustav Adolf's accession represented the climax of a long period of change. The partnership with Axel Oxenstierna did not institute a radical new direction in Swedish history; rather it restored order after a period of political upheaval. Many of the demands put forward by nobles and commoners alike under Charles could now be fulfilled. Peace was made with the high nobility, including many families which had fallen foul of Charles's reign of terror. More importantly, the demands of servants of the state – noble and commoner alike – could be met, such as the 1594 Council proposal for the recruitment of young nobles for service in the chancery, and for salaries to be tied to offices rather than individuals. The officer corps was most interested in excluding the foreigners on whom Charles had relied for such poor reward. The great administrative and judicial reforms, such as the revival of the five great offices of state – now specifically limited to members of the high nobility – the creation of the Supreme Court in 1614, and the establishment of a new cameral system of administration all created opportunities for Swedes from a wide variety of backgrounds; the educational reforms of the 1620s were designed to provide young Swedes with a training suitable for the service of the state. Finally, the *Riddarhus* Ordinance of 1626 at last established the Swedish nobility on the basis of birth and gave some security to the lesser nobility who formed its third class.

The principal factors in the development of this new military state were the price inflation which steadily undermined rentier incomes, the general poverty of the mass of the Swedish nobility, the poorly-monetarised economy, the existence of plausible external threats, and the Reformation land-settlement. Several structural features of the Swedish system made it possible. The small size of the Swedish nobility, combined with the poverty of most of its members, made state service both desirable for the nobility, yet manageable for the government: the growth of the military state was slow and measured until the reign of Gustav Adolf, and there was nothing in Sweden to match the uncontrolled explosion of would-be servitors that lay at the heart of the Cossack problem in Poland-Lithuania, where the political system proved both unable and unwilling to meet the demand. For the moment at least, the Swedish military state was able both to satisfy the general noble desire for the domination of birth at the summit of the political and administrative system, while allowing for a measured degree of advancement for talented non-nobles.

Nevertheless, despite the military state's slow evolution, it is not inappropriate to regard its emergence as a revolutionary development. The landing at Riga in 1621 announced the arrival not so much of a new military power, as of a new kind of warfare. Aggressive war was nothing new in Europe, but aggressive war sustained by a substantial native army over a long period beyond the borders of the country undoubtedly was. Monarchs had always been able to call on their subjects for the defence of their realm, and for limited service beyond their boundaries, but had always faced insurmountable problems in sustaining such efforts, as native forces tended to be overwhelmingly amateur, serving out of unenforceable obligation, and almost invariably returned home at the end of a campaign; professional mercenaries could be hired, but the resources of most contemporary governments were insufficient to sustain them over a long period. The early Vasas struggled with such attitudes and problems, but the very constraints imposed by Sweden's poverty and the demands of war stimulated the emergence of something new: a native professional army, whose troops were raised by *utskrivning*, serving for twenty years or more, and whose officers saw military service as a career, not as a social obligation. Those involved in this military state, and who profited from it, whether as officers or as administrators, were also aware that it could not be sustained by native resources. The military state must feed abroad. It was self-interest, not the quality of Gustav Adolf's rhetoric, which persuaded Sweden's elites to launch the Age of Greatness, the *Stormaktstid*.

Notes

1 *Livgardes Historia* III:1 pp. 331–3; Generalstaben, *Sveriges Krig 1611–1632* II *Polska Kriget* (Stockholm, 1936) pp. 75–6. Roberts's figure of 14,000 does not take account of units which came overland: *Gustavus Adolphus* (London, 1953, 1958) I pp. 203–5.

2 E. Zechs, 'Gustav Adolf und die Belagerung Rigas im Jahre 1621' *Pirmā Baltijas Vēsturnieku Konference, Riga, 16–20.VIII.1937* (Riga, 1938) p. 401.

3 The fullest exposition of Roberts's views is in *Gustavus Adolphus*, II pp. 169–271.

4 For full accounts see *Polska Kriget*, which suffers, however, from the virtual absence of Polish sources. The best account of Mewe is J. Teodorczyk, 'Bitwa pod Gniewem (22.IX–29.IX–1.X.1626). Pierwsza porażka husarii' *SMHW* 12 (1966) pp. 70–172; see also J. Seredyka, 'Nowe poglądy na bitwę ze Szwedami pod Gniewem w 1626 r.' *ZH* 34 (1969) pp. 82–95.

5 The Poles also deployed foreign-style infantry armed with muskets.

6 David Parrott has questioned not just the effectiveness of the salvo, but whether it was used at all: 'Strategy and tactics in the Thirty Years' War: the "Military Revolution"' in Rogers *Military Revolution Debate* p. 235. His doubts seem unfounded. The salvo was specifically designed for use against cavalry attack,

where two salvos in quick succession by two lines each three ranks deep was all that the defenders had time to deliver. Polish sources testify to its impressive effects.

7 Quoted by Teodorczyk, 'Bitwa' pp. 133–4; Roberts, *Gustavus Adolphus* II p. 177, n. 7. Killing horses was, it is true, an effective method of stopping a cavalry charge.

8 By 29 September Sigismund had 15,000 men, opposed to 12,200 Swedes; the Swedes, however, had 74 guns, not counting regimental three-pounders, to only 20 on the Polish side: Teodorczyk, 'Bitwa' pp. 95–6, 126–7.

9 L. Podhorodecki and N. Raszba, *Wojna chocimska 1621* (Cracow, 1979) pp. 167–76.

10 Parker, *Military Revolution* p. 37.

11 'Justyfikacya na list J.K.Mości Pana Mego Miłościwego, dnia 30 sierpnia 1622 roku, de cessatione armorum pisany' K. Radziwiłł, *Sprawy wojenne i polityczne 1621–1632* (Paris, 1859) p. 308.

12 K. Radziwiłł to P. Sapieha, 3.X.1625; ibid. p. 96.

13 W. Majewski, 'Wojny polsko-szwedzkie 1600–1629' in L. Sikorski (ed.), *Polskie tradycje wojskowe* I (Warsaw, 1990) p. 246.

14 Roberts, *Gustavus Adolphus* II p. 248.

15 The Poles had 7,800 men, including 1,000 Polish and 2,000 German infantry and 300 gunners, against 10,200 Swedes (6,194 foot and 4,000 horse): L. Podhorodecki, *Stanisław Koniecpolski ok. 1592–1646* (Warsaw, 1978) p. 216; *Polska Kriget* pp. 356–7; *Livgardes Historia* III.i p. 525.

16 A Polish eyewitness stated that 80 Poles were killed: K.W. Wójcicki, *Pamiętniki do panowania Zygmunta III, Władysława IV i Jana Kazimierza* (Warsaw, 1846) I p. 136. The Swedes claimed 'about 100 killed and a large number of wounded': *Polska Kriget* pp. 361–2. Hoppe, who was not present, reported that 80 hussars and 100 Cossacks were killed: I. Hoppe, *Geschichte des ersten schwedisch-polnischen Krieges in Preußen* M. Toeppen (ed.) (Leipzig, 1887), p. 196.

17 Other reports estimated 20,000: Oxenstierna to Gustav Adolf, Elbing, 4/14.XI.1626; *AOSB* I.i p. 390. Oxenstierna had about 12,000 foot and 2,500 horse at the start of the winter: J. Teodorczyk, 'Wyprawa szwedzka z Meklemburgii do Prus Królewskich wiosną 1627 r.' *SMHW* 6 (1960) p. 124.

18 For example, Oxenstierna's report of the skirmish at Neuteich on 7/17 January 1627, where he claimed that 300 Poles were killed; he also claimed that 20–30 were killed in skirmishes every day: Oxenstierna to Gustav Adolf, 10/20.I.1627, *AOSB* I.iii, pp. 434–6. Fuchs claimed 150 were killed at Neuteich: M.G. Fuchs, *Elbinger Chronik* I, APG, Rękopisy Elbląskie 444 f. 28.

19 Two villages were plundered on 1 and 2 December; when a Finnish company arrived, the Poles were gone. Wöklitz was burned on 9 December; on 17 December, five further villages suffered. Two days later, the Poles raided the suburbs of Elbing itself, burning several houses; ibid. f. 27ff. See also Hoppe, *Geschichte* pp. 119–21, 137–9 and passim.

20 K.-R. Böhme, *Die schwedische Besetzung des Weichseldeltas 1626–36* (Würzburg, 1963) pp. 42, 55.

21   Ibid. pp. 66, 73.
22   Böhme suggests that the loss of 2,500 'bad soldiers' was no great blow, citing a letter in which Oxenstierna was clearly trying to make the best of a bad situation: ibid. p. 63; Oxenstierna to Gustav Adolf, *AOSB* I.iii p. 310.
23   *Polska Kriget* pp. 414–15.
24   Although the Lithuanian threat was far less serious than Roberts suggests: *Gustavus Adolphus* II pp. 362–3; cf. H. Wisner 'Wojna inflancka 1625–1629' *SMHW* 16 (1970) pp. 89–93.
25   Quoted by Korzon, *Dzieje* II p. 250; *Polska Kriget* p. 427.
26   Potocki's force was 4,000 strong; Wrangel had 5,337. Korzon *Dzieje* p. 251; *Polska Kriget* p. 443.
27   'Od Pana Potockiego Kastellana Kamienieckiego o przegraney bitwie pod Gorznem do Krola JMci'; Czart. 354 ff. 1032–3.
28   Swedish accounts exaggerate the size of Arnim's force, presenting it as the 12,000 men that Wallenstein agreed to send, or the 10,000 which Sigismund agreed to accept. Barely 5,000 turned up: Janusz Staszewski, 'Bitwa pod Trzcianą' *PHW* 9 (1937) p. 403. Cf. Roberts, *Gustavus Adolphus* II p. 392.
29   Most secondary accounts, based on the number of companies involved, give the Polish strength as 1,300 hussars, 1,200 cossack cavalry and 2,000 reiters but Arnim himself suggests 700 hussars, 1,000 cossacks and 2,000 reiters: Hoppe, *Chronik* p. 414. Arnim magnifies considerably the part played by the imperial troops, so this may be an underestimate, but it would be unusual for Polish companies to be up to strength. The small size of the Polish force would explain the decision of the Rheingraf, Johann Wilhelm, to attempt his fatal flanking movement.
30   The General Staff wrongly suggest that the flanking attack was by Arnim's reiters: *Polska Kriget* p. 537.
31   'Fragmentum diarii belli Suecici 1626 Iul 1–31'; Czart. 540, f. 427; Hoppe, *Chronik* p. 414. Korzon, *Dzieje* II p. 254; Staszewski, 'Bitwa' pp. 413. The General Staff accept without question Gustav Adolf's figures, placing uncharacteristic trust in one source. Oxenstierna also played down Honigfelde's significance, describing it as a skirmish and hinting that the Poles had come off worse: Oxenstierna to Gustav Horn and Alexander Leslie, 29.VI.1629 OS. *AOSB* I.iv, nos 427–8, pp. 553–4.
32   Roberts, *Gustavus Adolphus* II p. 395.
33   K.-R. Böhme, 'Schwedische Finanzbürokratie und Kriegführung 1611 bis 1721' in G. Rystad (ed.), *Europe and Scandinavia* (Lund, 1983) p. 55.
34   The agreement with Brandenburg was guaranteed by the treaty of Fischhausen (16.XI.1629), while the separate treaties with Danzig (at Tiegenhof, 28.II.1630) and Courland (8.IV.1630) granted the Swedes the right to levy tolls at Danzig and the Courland ports of Libau and Windau.
35   See R. Frost, 'Poland-Lithuania and the Thirty Years War' in K. Bußmann and H. Schilling (eds) *War and Peace in Europe, 1618–1648* I (Münster Osnabrück, 1998) pp. 197–205.

36   Salvius's remark was made at the Polish-Swedish peace talks at Lübeck in 1652: Linage de Vauciennes, *Mémoires de ce qui c'est passé en Suède tirés des dépêches de Chanut* II (Cologne, 1677) pp. 304–5.

37   S.A. Nilsson, 'Hemlandet och de stora krigen under Gustav Adolfs tid' in Nilsson, *De stora krigens tid* (Uppsala, 1990) pp. 161–2.

38   For an elegant demolition of the 'New School', which argues the commercial line, see M. Roberts *The Swedish Imperial Experience, 1560–1715* (Cambridge, 1979) chapter 1. See also S. Troebst, 'Debating the mercantile background to early modern Swedish empire-building: Michael Roberts versus Artur Attman' *EHQ* 24 (1994) pp. 485–509 and Zernack, 'Schweden' p. 210.

39   E. Ringmar, *Identity, Interest and Action. A Cultural Explanation of Sweden's Intervention in the Thirty Years War* (Cambridge, 1996) p. 130. Cf. Oxenstierna to Gustav Adolf, 2.XII.1628; *AOSB* I.iv p. 282.

40   For a critique of the idea that Gustav Adolf built up Sweden's military organisation from next to nothing, see G. Artéus, *Till Militärstatens Förhistoria* (Stockholm, 1986) pp. 76–7.

41   Ibid. table 1, p. 36.

42   Ibid., tables 3, 4, pp. 47, 50.

43   The figures given by Artéus for foreign officers are slightly inflated, since it is impossible in many cases to distinguish between German officers and Baltic Germans.

44   The large number of nobles of uncertain status, in particular in Finland, makes it difficult to reach an accurate figure. Elmroth suggests 441 adult males, but Artéus and Samuelson point out that he omits the 50–100 excluded from the *Riddarhus* in 1626: I. Elmroth, *För kung und fosterland* (Lund, 1981) pp. 39, 42; Artéus, *Till Militärstatens* p. 120, n. 9; J. Samuelson, *Aristokrat eller föradlad bonde?* (Lund, 1993) pp. 47–8.

45   The list includes female landholders, mostly widows. Samuelson, *Aristokrat* table 3, p. 62; the median holding was four, the mean twenty-one; ibid. p. 61.

46   The largest landowners were Svante Sture (601), Gabriel Christiernsson Oxenstierna (536), Magdalena Gyllenstierna (499), Nils Ryning (308) and Ture Persson Bielke (285); ibid. table 8, p. 72.

47   The Crown also lost out by having to raise the threshold to 300 marks from the 100–150 that was usual under Gustav Vasa's agreements: S.A. Nilsson, *Krona och frälse i Sverige 1523–1594* (Lund, 1947) pp. 22–3.

48   Ibid. pp. 68–9.

49   Samuelson, *Aristokrat* p. 82. Roberts suggests that this marked the introduction of a nobility by birth; this may have been so by implication, but many poor nobles still faced the threat of degradation. Roberts, *Early Vasas* p. 244; Samuelson, *Aristokrat* pp. 167–96.

50   Nilsson, *Krona* pp. 76–7.

51   Samuelson, *Aristokrat* p. 69.

52   Ibid. table 8, p. 72.

53 Based on Artéus, *Till Militärstatens* tables 3 and 4, pp. 47, 50. The percentages denote nobles among all officers at this rank. Sigismund's foreign officers are excluded.

54 Roberts, *Early Vasas* pp. 178–9. The figures exclude Finland, where tax-paying peasants owned 96.4 per cent of the land; ibid. p. 38 n. 1. The Vasas' private estates contained some 5,000 farms by 1560; ibid. p. 183.

55 Samuelson, *Aristokrat* pp. 103–4.

56 Ibid. p. 152. The drop is slightly exaggerated, since the figures for Erik's reign include the royal duchies, excluded in the figures for his brother's reign.

57 Nilsson, *Krona* pp. 127–8.

58 Ibid. p. 147.

59 Roberts, *Early Vasas* p. 306.

60 Nilsson, *Krona* pp. 156, 164.

61 Samuelson, *Aristokrat* p. 93.

62 *Förläningarna* were not just the preserve of senior officers; they were also important for company commanders: Nilsson, *På väg* p. 52.

63 Samuelson, *Aristokrat* p. 98.

64 Ibid. pp. 54, 218.

65 R. Fagerlund, 'De finska fänikorna under äldre Vasatid. Forskningsläge och problem' *THA* 38 (1982) p. 99.

66 Samuelson, *Aristokrat* p. 67.

67 Based on figures in Artéus, *Till Militärstatens* tables 3, 4, pp. 47, 50. The percentages refer to commoners among all officers at this rank. Sigismund's foreign officers are excluded.

68 Ibid. p. 92.

69 Based on figures in ibid. tables 3, 4, pp. 47, 50.

70 For these and other similar examples see ibid. pp. 94ff.

71 'hertig Karl och Sveriges rikes råd, biskopar, ridderskap och adel, fri[ta]rna frälsemän, klerikeri, krigsbefällningsmän, borgerskap, meniga krigsfolk och allmogen.' Quoted in Nilsson, *På väg* p. 13.

72 100 out of 300 in 1605; a similar proportion in 1607; ibid. p. 30.

CHAPTER SIX

New Beginnings

Stormakt

Altmark ended seventy years of virtually continuous fighting in northeastern Europe. Together with Stolbovo and Deulino, it established a peace which, apart from the Smolensk War of 1632–4 and the Danish–Swedish war of 1643–5, lasted until 1654. The six-year truce agreed at Altmark was extended at Stuhmsdorf in 1635 for a further twenty-six, when Sweden, deeply embroiled in the Thirty Years War, was forced to surrender much of what it had gained in 1629 as the necessary price for ensuring that it could continue its German adventure undisturbed. Yet the peace was fragile. If Stolbovo was a peace treaty, Deulino, Altmark and Stuhmsdorf were all truces. Sooner or later, the substantive problems which these settlements of exhaustion had not tackled were bound to reemerge. Stability had not returned.

By 1654 the context had been transformed by Sweden's staggering successes in the Thirty Years War which established it as one of the greatest military powers in Europe and a guarantor of the 1648 Peace of Westphalia. The crushing of Denmark in Torstensson's War appeared to indicate a decisive shift in the balance of power in Scandinavia, and European powers had now to contemplate the real possibility of a Swedish *Dominium Maris Baltici*; by 1650, Sweden had a larger navy than Denmark, and the gap was growing.[1] Sweden had entered upon its *Stormaktstid*, yet it remained to be seen whether it had the resources to sustain its position. Whatever the reality, the implications of Swedish success for northeastern Europe were considerable.

Sweden's German triumphs owed much to its experiences in the Northern Wars. Johan Banér, Gustav Horn, Lennart Torstensson and Hermann Wrangel, the brilliant commanders who, under the sure political guidance of Axel Oxenstierna, ensured that Sweden did not collapse after Gustav Adolf's death at Lützen, had served long apprenticeships in the east. The disciplined, integrated tactics which so astonished contemporaries had been honed in the Muscovite and Polish wars, whence came many of the tactical ideas which proved so effective in the Empire: the use of field artillery, the revival of the cavalry charge, to which Gustav Adolf ascribed much of the responsibility for the victory at Breitenfeld, and the interspersing of musketeers with cavalry units to give greater defensive rigidity.[2] Swedish commanders, used to the long years of toil in the sparsely-populated lands of eastern Europe, found the wealthier German lands a much more satisfactory base for an army, helped as they were by a more favourable political situation. The prosperous villages of the Rhineland or Bavaria were a far cry from the scattered settlements of northeastern Europe, while the network of fortified towns, in easy reach of each other, provided the necessary infrastructure for a permanent, and profitable, military presence. The Swedes could concentrate on milking the local population to support their expanding forces, over half of which were composed of German and other foreign mercenaries, in particular Scots. Although the aim of war sustaining itself was unattainable, except locally for limited periods,[3] the cost of sustaining the Swedish armies was largely borne by the German population.

The profits were immense. The devastating campaigns against Bavaria and other Catholic regions in the early 1630s yielded massive booty, which enriched Swedish nobles and commanders. Magnificent aristocratic palaces sprang up in Stockholm on the proceeds of war. The Swedish armies raiding Prague in 1648, sensing that this might be their last chance to lay their hands on central European riches, devastated the collections built up by Rudolf II. The groaning carts which set off for the north contained 69 bronze figures, 26 of amber, 24 of coral, 660 ornamental agate vessels, 174 earthenware vessels, 403 Indian curios, 16 valuable clocks, 185 pieces of jewellery, 317 mathematical instruments and chests of jewels wrenched from their mountings, dozens of medals and coins, and paintings by Michelangelo, Leonardo, Raphael, Titian, Tintoretto, Veronese, Dürer, Bosch and Breughel. This was apart from the 12 barrels of ducats and 2.5 tonnes of silver removed from the palace of Colloredo, Prague's commandant, and the 30 large cases of books taken from Eggenberg's palace to enrich the libraries of Sweden's new universities and gymnasia, including the *Codex Argenteus*, the fifth-century Gothic bible now in Uppsala university library.[4]

The new Goths were reclaiming the past they were in the process of inventing. For the two decades spent in the imperial fatlands gave the Swedes more than a taste for Catholic property. The stunning victories over the Habsburgs seemed to confirm the manifest destiny of the Swedish people. The cult of the Goths, originally developed by the Catholic Magnus brothers in opposition to Gustav Vasa, was adopted with enthusiasm by Erik and especially Gustav Adolf to celebrate the martial qualities of the Swedish people, supposedly descended from the ancient Goths. Gustav Adolf appeared dressed as king Berik at the tournament to mark his coronation in 1617; in his famous farewell to the *Riksdag* before leaving for Pomerania in 1630, he reminded his audience that they were descended from the ancient Goths 'who . . . conquered almost the whole earth, and brought many kingdoms into subjection.'[5]

Sweden's victories after 1621 seemed to confirm this exalted lineage. The descendants of Alaric had once more confronted and conquered the forces of Rome, and the cult of Gothicism, mingled with providential Lutheran triumphalism, seized hold of the Swedish imagination. Whereas the long years of war in the east had been a bitter, protracted fight for survival, the glittering successes in the Thirty Years War suggested that war might be more than a grim necessity; war was profitable, both financially, and in the heightened sense of personal esteem it gave to Sweden's elites. There were thus cultural as well as social forces behind the development of the Swedish military state. The triumphs of the Thirty Years War cemented the psychological revolution which changed Swedish political culture and secured the basis of the *Stormaktstid*. The gains of 1617–48 granted Sweden unprecedented influence in European politics, and the combination of military success and artful political propaganda created a level of support for the Swedish imperial adventure which was to sustain successive governments through the stormy days which lay ahead. Northeastern Europe was to encounter a new Sweden after 1648.

Denmark: the battle for control

Sweden's achievement is the more remarkable when it is contrasted with the experience of its rivals. The support received by Gustav Adolf for his aggressive, expansionist foreign policy was entirely absent in Denmark, where the substantial financial independence enjoyed by Christian IV enabled him to pursue an adventurous foreign policy. Since 1570, the Council had sought to avoid war with Sweden, not least through the periodic meetings with representatives of its Swedish counterpart established by the peace of Stettin. Christian was already urging a preemptive war in 1604, when he was dissuaded, but in 1611 he bludgeoned a reluctant Council into accepting an attack on Sweden by threatening to declare war as Duke of Holstein. The war, provoked largely by the mutual suspicion and ambition of Charles and Christian in the Arctic wastes of Finnmark, was little more than a brief rerun of the Nordic Seven Years War. Despite his seizure of Kalmar in 1611, Christian experienced the same problems that had bedevilled Frederik II. Although Denmark's superior navy secured control of the seas and enabled the capture of Öland, and although Sweden's involvement in Muscovy meant that it had to rely on rapidly-assembled forces of native conscripts, Christian made little headway. His mercenary army was professional enough, but too small to carry out his ambitious plans: the force which took Kalmar comprised a mere 4,580 infantry, of which 1,330 were native conscripts, and 645–700 cavalry.[6] As in the 1560s, it was held up in the difficult terrain of southern Sweden, and although Älvsborg was seized in June 1612, Christian decided to negotiate after a grim war of mutual devastation.

The Kalmar War brought limited military success, but resulted in the favourable peace settlement which saw Christian's coffers swelled notably by the Älvsborg ransom, paid directly to the king; with an annual surplus of 250,000 rigsdalers by 1608, and assets Christian himself valued at 1,000,000 rigsdalers by 1618, he appeared to be in a good position to exploit the new possibilities afforded by the outbreak of the Thirty Years War.[7] The Council was determined to avoid war, however. In the early 1620s, Christian energetically pursued his expansive policy in north Germany, exploiting the growing unease in the Lower Saxon Circle, of which he was a member as Duke of Holstein. In 1621 he succeeded in having his twelve-year-old second son Frederik elected as coadjutor to the bishoprics of Bremen and Verden. This buttressed his position with regard to Hamburg, which had been bullied into accepting Danish suzerainty in 1603 pending a judgment from the Imperial Cameral Tribunal, which decided in the city's favour in 1618, causing Christian to threaten war in defence of his rights. In 1622, his third son Ulrik became coadjutor of the bishopric of Schwerin; in 1623–4, when Frederik succeeded to the bishopric of Verden and became administrator of Halberstadt, the way seemed open for Christian to extend his control over the vital Elbe trade, something the Dutch had long resisted, but were now prepared to countenance as their war with Spain made them desperate for allies. In 1625, with the Catholic League army under Tilly approaching Lower Saxony, and with promises of military and financial support from England and the Dutch, Christian struck. Despite Council opposition, he orchestrated the meeting of the estates of the Lower Saxon Circle at which he was elected commander of the Circle forces in March 1625, and prepared to move troops into the Empire.

The outcome was disaster. Christian proved unlucky in his timing: he intervened in 1625, when the eruption of Wallenstein's army into north Germany meant that he faced two hostile armies, rather than the one he had anticipated. Furthermore, the coalition of anti-Habsburg powers which seemed to be emerging in 1624–5 had rapidly fallen apart, after the Spanish onslaught which culminated in the fall of Breda in 1625 reduced Dutch capacity to offer financial and military support, while England failed to provide the financial support Christian expected, and French backing also failed to materialise: by 1627 France was allied with Spain and at war with England.

The failure of the anti-Habsburg coalition left Christian dangerously exposed, reliant on his own resources to pay his expensive mercenaries. The crushing defeats at Dessau Bridge and Lutter (April and August 1626) left Denmark exposed. Although Christian rapidly restored his forces, now with support from the Council, which recognised the danger to Denmark itself, he could not sustain his position against the 50,000-strong force which invaded in September 1627, driving the Danish army out of Holstein and Jutland. Christian's German policy lay in ruins. Although the changing international situation in the wake of the astonishing Habsburg victories enabled Christian to achieve a remarkably favourable peace at Lübeck in 1629, the war had consumed his financial reserves and he was thrown back on the Council. Already, in the aftermath of Lutter, it had acted to bring the military under its control by reviving the office of Marshal as a commander responsible to it, appointing Jørgen Skeel, one of Christian's main critics. In April 1628, a four-man General War Commissariat was established to oversee wartime taxation and its payment to the General War Treasury Official: all five officials were Council members, most of whom opposed Christian's foreign policy.[8]

As Sweden's position grew ever stronger, Christian sought to reestablish his finances without foreign subsidies, and to revive his international position. Unfortunately, many of the means he used served only to alienate his potential supporters: by steadily raising the Sound Dues and patrolling the Elbe from his new stronghold of Glückstadt near Hamburg, he upset the English and Dutch, while his attempts to rebuild his position in northern Germany alienated the Council, itself concerned at the dramatic rise in Swedish power. As Christian flirted with the emperor, sending prince Ulrik and other young Danes to serve in the Habsburg armies, thereby risking the wrath of the Habsburgs' enemies, his refusal to commit himself to the Habsburg side, and attempt to establish himself as a mediator, merely infuriated Emperor Ferdinand III.

In 1643, despite the successful rebuilding of much of his position in north Germany, Christian's pursuit of his private interests brought catastrophe. Enraged by his aggressive policy with regard to Hamburg and the Elbe, and his overtures to Spain, the Dutch were on the point of war, while Sweden, hit as badly as the Dutch by Christian's tariff policy, had long abandoned the brief period of cooperation after the 1628 siege of Stralsund, when it had sanctioned the return of Bremen and Verden to Danish control. The

Swedish Council, accepting Oxenstierna's contention that Denmark was a real threat, sanctioned war; in December, Torstensson concluded a truce with the Habsburg forces and launched a devastating attack without even the courtesy of a formal declaration of war, while Gustav Horn attacked Scania in early 1644. The Danes were completely unprepared: Jutland was swiftly overrun, and although the navy initially performed well, winning the battle of Kolberger Heide in July 1644, a smaller Danish fleet was crushed at Femern in October. Luckily for Denmark, Sweden's continuing involvement in the Empire, and French concern at its ally's distraction in the north, ensured that the war was brief, and it did not lose as much at Brömsebro as it might have done, although the Dutch withdrew as mediators in May 1645, sending a fleet of forty-seven ships into the Baltic which flagrantly refused to pay the Sound Dues. Swedish ships were also blatantly sailing through Danish waters without paying. Given the military advantage that the Danes had held over the Swedes as recently as 1613, it was a sobering shock.

Christian's plans lay in ruins. Excluded from the Westphalian negotiations, Denmark saw Sweden acquire Bremen, Verden and western Pomerania, a firm base from which Danish ambitions in northern Germany could be held firmly in check. This, plus the acquisition of Halland and the freeing of Sweden from the Sound Dues, effectively ended Denmark's long claim to *Dominium Maris Baltici*. The marked shift in the balance of power within Scandinavia was to produce renewed tension after 1648; in the short term, however, the reaction of the Danish Council to Christian's aggression was more significant. Christian died in early 1648, shortly after his eldest son, also called Christian. Denmark was an elective monarchy, but it was customary for the monarch's eldest son to be elected Crown Prince in his father's lifetime; Christian was so designated in 1608 at the age of five. When Christian IV died, the Council exploited the fact that his second son Frederik had not been formally designated Crown Prince to impose an electoral charter which seriously curtailed his freedom of action. If in Sweden the pursuit of aggressive war after 1560 had seen the development of an effective military state, in Denmark it apparently had the opposite effect. Frederik III (1648–70) was to be prevented from waging aggressive war, and significant restrictions were placed on his power. Such was Christian's legacy.

Despite the contrast between Gustav Adolf's dazzling success and Christian's apparent failure, Christian's reign did see the establishment of a permanent military force in Denmark, the core of the national army which was to play a significant role in Danish social and political life after 1648. The need for such a force was clear not just to Christian. Despite the Council's stubborn resistance to what it saw as his reckless policies, it was aware that the rapidly shifting international situation had serious implications for

Denmark's security. Thus when Christian proposed military reforms in the wake of the difficulties experienced by his mercenary army in the Kalmar War, the Council was not as uncooperative as its dogged opposition to his foreign policy might suggest.

It is often contended that Christian, like his father, placed greater faith in foreign, professional mercenary soldiers than he did in the native levies who were cheaper but often proved next to useless on campaign. It is true that in one famous letter, written in 1611, Christian remarked that the 1,000 native troops deployed in the first attack on Kalmar in 1612 were 'worse than beasts', and that the army he marched into the Empire in 1625 consisted largely of professional mercenaries.[9] Nevertheless, in the wake of the Kalmar War, Christian laid the foundations of a trained, semi-professional force of native troops, led by a full-time native officer corps. He had already established a system of training and periodic mustering for Zealand burghers in 1599, and for the peasants of the Sound provinces in 1600 and 1602; in 1603, he conscripted an infantry company from royal lands in Schleswig and Holstein, while a mustering of peasants produced forces of 4,000 in Malmo district and 4,700 in Landskröne. In Norway, where the threat from Sweden was greatest, where there was less noble resistance, and where Christian was personally popular, a law was passed in 1604 decreeing that peasants should arm themselves according to the size of their holdings and muster regularly to be drilled. In 1609 he felt confident enough to call a universal muster of the peasant militia (*bøndekarle*) alongside the noble knight service (*rostjeneste*) across the whole state, while the new division of the knight service into geographically-based companies, each with a captain, lieutenant and ensign, gave it a permanent structure in peacetime as well as war; the *Rostjeneste* Ordinance of 1625 changed the basis of assessment from income to size of landholding.[10]

The peasant units, though undoubtedly poorly-equipped and only semi-trained, did provide useful garrison service during the Kalmar War. Despite his doubts as to their quality, Christian sought to ensure that in future native units would be better prepared. In this, he had some hope of support: always suspicious of foreign mercenaries, the Council was more favourably inclined towards the development of a national militia which might fall more readily under aristocratic control, while the international situation was growing ever more threatening.[11] Thus the royal instructions of September 1614 and Christian's 1620 proposals led directly to the military ordinances of 1615 and 1621, agreed by the Council, which sought to provide the basis for Denmark's first truly national army.

To establish the new system required time. Denmark lacked a reservoir of experienced native officers to provide the backbone of a permanent force: it had been at peace between 1570 and 1611, and few of the officers who fought in the Kalmar War were Danish; most were Holsteiners or foreigners, although many Danes, with royal encouragement, had served in the Dutch army against Spain.[12] The initial plan was to raise two regiments in Scania and Jutland; a plan to establish a Norwegian regiment initially foundered owing to the different structure of the Norwegian peasantry, which made the application of the Danish pattern difficult. Four thousand royal farms were designated as the basis for the new force; in return for exemptions from all ordinary and extraordinary taxes, each was to support a soldier, who was to live and work on the farm outside the designated periods in the year when he was to serve in the ranks and receive training. In practice, most peasants did not serve themselves, but they were responsible for finding a replacement. Each regiment had a permanent structure, with companies under a captain who was responsible for recruitment and training. Much of the cost of maintaining the army in peacetime – some 40,000 rigsdalers per year – were met by a special toll levied with Council agreement.[13]

At first, this new force was used largely to build fortifications at Kristianstad, Copenhagen and the new fortress at Glückstadt, for the construction of dykes in Schleswig, and for ceremonial duties during state visits. In the light of difficulties in mustering and paying the troops, both Christian and the Council were dissatisfied with the early performance of the new system, and sought to reform it in the early 1620s, as the stormclouds gathered to the south and Sweden's successes in Livonia altered the Baltic balance of power. Although Christian's proposal for a standing army of 24,000 was curtly rejected by the Council, concerned about the uses to which he might put such a force, nevertheless, after serious debate in 1620–1, a new structure was devised. The system of designated 'soldier-farms' was scrapped, except for 400, which were to support officers; instead all royal and clerical farms were to support the army, and for the first time a system of conscription (*udskrivning*), with a three-year period of service, was introduced to replace the volunteer system of 1614, a change which was to produce a slightly larger force of 5,000, increased to 5,400 on Council initiatve in 1624. It was to be composed of fifty-six companies, each with a professional captain, a sergeant and ten experienced soldiers to provide a solid basis of expertise.[14]

With the use of both *inddelning* (the assignation of individual soldiers to designated farms for support) and *udskrivning*, there were distinct similarities to the system which was developing in Sweden, although Danish *udskrivning* differed from the Swedish *utskrivning* in that conscription was based not on a set ratio of troops to the male population, but on a quota system based on Denmark's administrative divisions.[15] The new system of recruitment and payment, wherein it was the king, and not the peasant, who had the primary responsibility to pay the soldier, and it was the individual soldier's duty to serve and not that of the peasant in the 'soldier-farm', worked reasonably well, and remained the basis of the Danish army throughout the seventeenth century.

These were but small beginnings. An army of 5,000 was simply insufficient to resist the imperial forces. Moreover, the Council saw it as entirely defensive, and when Danish troops crossed into Holstein in 1619–20 to work on the Glückstadt fortifications, the desertion rate increased rapidly and Christian was faced with a general refusal to serve. He had little choice but to base his intervention on the troops provided by the Lower Saxon Circle and on foreign mercenaries funded from his own resources. Christian was well aware of the fact that native troops – paid $2\frac{1}{2}$ dalers per month as opposed to 4 dalers for mercenaries – were far cheaper, but there was little he could do; the Danish army was too small and too recently established to provide a suitable instrument for his aggressive foreign policy.[16] Having been at peace for so long, Denmark lacked the solid body of experienced native soldiers – and especially officers – that Gustav Adolf had at his disposal. The consequences were only too apparent. During the invasion of Jutland in 1627 the Danish forces – supplemented by the *opbud*, the Danish equivalent of the Swedish *uppbåd*, in which one man in five was called up from the peasantry – fought bravely but were no match for the imperial forces.

Nevertheless, the experience of war did stimulate improvement. Christian had funnelled men from the two Danish regiments into his mercenary army from the start of the war, thus ensuring that they gained vital military experience, while many of the captains who recruited mercenaries were natives either of Denmark or of the duchies. By 1629, 22,000 men had been raised in Denmark, a further 6,000 in Norway and 19,000 in Schleswig. Three new regiments were created in Fyn, Zealand and Lolland-Falster, with another in Norway. Although these were dissolved in 1629, the changing situation in Germany, where the war often drew near to Holstein's borders, and where Sweden's dramatic gains had profound implications for Danish security, provoked an increase in the military establishment in 1633–4. The Jutland regiment, which had almost ceased to exist by 1629, was brought back up to strength, and the Zealand regiment was restored, thus bringing the army up to a nominal 9–10,000 in Denmark, including the *rostjeneste* and 1,500 regulars on permanent garrison duty, plus units in Norway.[17]

This force was increased again between 1637 and 1641, when the threat of war brought an appeal for support from the Holstein Estates which resulted in the defensive union of 1636. The result was the creation of the first recruited army that Denmark had seen in peacetime, with three regiments of foot and two squadrons of horse raised among the union partners to produce a field army, stationed in Holstein and regularly fed with conscripts from Denmark. Furthermore, the principle of noble contribution to Denmark's military was established, with the conscription of 850 men (doubled in 1641) from among noble peasants. Although there was a shortage of officers and therefore these new units were not necessarily as good as the established army, with the new conscripts kept largely as a reserve and no new regiments being created, by 1641 the Danish army had doubled to some 16,000 men, plus 6,500 raised in Norway, where six new regiments were established in 1641, and some 11,000 mercenaries in Holstein; together with the *rostjeneste* this created a peacetime force of some 35–40,000 by 1642, by no means negligible in European terms.[18]

It was a mixed force, supported by various means, including an extraordinary 'union tax' agreed by the *Rigsdag* and paid mostly by the peasantry. Unfortunately, when Torstensson invaded in December 1643, the moment was well chosen: the conscripts were demobilised for the winter, and the mercenaries were in winter quarters. Nevertheless, the Danish army gave a reasonable account of itself considering the circumstances. A further fourteen infantry regiments and fourteen cavalry squadrons were raised, plus volunteer companies, to create an army whose maximum strength was 40,000 (33,000 in 1644), with a field army of some 14,000.[19] This army might not have been able to prevent the humiliating peace of Brömsebro, but it held up the Swedes long enough to ensure that France put pressure on them to make peace without demanding the other provinces across the Sound. Although the army was again reduced between 1648 and 1652, it remained at a strength of 17–18,000 men, comprising 7,100 in the three Danish land regiments, 7,000 in three Norwegian regiments (Bohus, Akershus and Trondheim), 2,000 or so *rostjeneste* and at least 1,000 regulars in Denmark and the duchies.[20] As the situation in the Baltic deteriorated this was increased to 20,000 by 1656, as *udskrivning* from noble lands, suspended in 1648, was reactivated, and a new system of raising cavalry, based on the parish, was introduced. A peacetime force of this size represented 1.5–2 per cent of the population. Denmark had entered a new military age.

The Smolensk War, 1632–4

Denmark was not the only state where royal foreign policy was viewed with suspicion. If Poland-Lithuania had been in the ascendant until 1620, it had suffered a serious reverse in 1629. After Sigismund's death in April 1632 and the uncontested election of his eldest son Władysław IV (1632–48) in November, it seemed, however, that a new age might be dawning. Władysław was popular, with a warmer personality than his reserved father; he had long adopted a more tolerant attitude towards religious dissidents and had high hopes that following the succession of the infant Christina he might reclaim the Swedish throne he regarded as his birthright.

Before he could advance his plans, however, Władysław had first to deal with Muscovy. Despite the traditional emphasis on trade as a motivating factor in the Northern Wars, it was not the loss of Muscovy's access to the Baltic which most exercised its government after 1619, but the lands ceded at Deulino. Hostility to Poland-Lithuania, not Sweden, dominated Muscovite policy for the next half century. The bitter legacy of the Time of Troubles was compounded by religious antagonism deriving from Orthodox fears of a Catholic offensive following the creation of the Uniate Church in 1596. The Jesuits were active in Połock and Smolensk from the moment they were returned to Lithuanian rule, and although Władysław lifted the ban on Orthodoxy in 1632, religious animosities remained deep.

None was more hostile to the Commonwealth than Michael's father, Patriarch Filaret, who dominated the government after his return from Polish captivity in 1619, until his death in October 1633. Captivity turned Filaret into a bigoted Polonophobe, and Muscovy soon began preparations for war on Deulino's expiry in 1633. Muscovy had signed away Kexholm in 1609 to win Swedish aid against the Commonwealth; after Gustav Adolf attacked Royal Prussia in 1626, contacts grew more animated. The Swedes encouraged Muscovy to invade Lithuania after 1630, and Gustav Adolf's agents talked of an invasion of Poland from Silesia by an army of 10,000, to coincide with a Muscovite thrust on Smolensk.

It is unlikely that Gustav Adolf seriously intended to relaunch the Polish war at a time when the Swedish position in the Empire, despite Breitenfeld, was by no means secure; nevertheless, his encouragement of Muscovite bellicosity soon bore fruit. When Sigismund died in April 1632, Filaret seized the opportunity to launch an attack before Deulino expired, calculating that the interregnum would delay the Polish response and hoping that Smolensk would fall before relief could be organised. By late September the army was on the move; it took Dorohobuzh and a number of small fortresses before arriving at Smolensk on 28 October.

This army was different from anything the Muscovites had yet put in the field. The experience gained by 1619 had convinced the government that sheer weight of numbers was insufficient to defeat Polish or Swedish armies. The size of the Muscovite military establishment was impressive by any standard: in 1630, after a period of recovery following the Time of Troubles, it was calculated at 92,555 men, of whom just under 30 per cent (27,433) were hereditary servitors. There were 28,130 *strel'tsy* (30 per cent), 11,192 Cossacks (12 per cent), 10,208 Tatars (11 per cent) and 4,316 gunners (4.5 per cent), with the rest made up of foreigners, Ukrainian Cossacks and Mordvinian and Chuvash auxiliaries. Of these 92,555 men, some 20,000 were in permanent service in peacetime.[21] Yet although infantry – principally the *strel'tsy* – constituted 40 per cent of these forces, it was recognised that their performance against Muscovy's western enemies had not been impressive, except in the dogged defence of fortified strongpoints. If Muscovy were to recapture the lands it had lost, it would have to develop a greater offensive capacity. To this end, foreign expertise was sought on a scale hitherto unknown. Despite doubts about the reliability of foreign mercenaries, reinforced during the Time of Troubles, it was recognised that there was much to learn from abroad.

In January 1630, the Scotsman Alexander Leslie, who had fought for the Poles and the Swedes, arrived in Moscow as a military adviser.[22] He was among the first of a wave of experienced foreigners engaged to train and lead the new-formation regiments which were now established. Petty hereditary servitors without *pomest'ia* were ordered to Moscow for training in one of two new regiments, each planned at a strength of 1,000. It proved impossible, however, to form the regiments entirely from such men: by September, only sixty had turned up, and recruitment was thrown open to Tatars, Cossacks and other 'free people'. By December 1631, the two regiments had a combined strength of 3,323, with 190 foreign officers acting as instructors.[23] In early 1632, the number of projected regiments was increased to six. Altogether 17,000 men were recruited by 1634, in ten new-style regiments.

Sigismund inconsiderately died before the training programme was complete. The opportunity, however, proved too tempting. Thus the army was not as well-prepared as it might have been had Filaret waited until Deulino's expiry in 1633. Nevertheless, it was an impressive force, numbering 34,500 effectives, including 9,000 in six new-formation regiments, not counting the large numbers of slaves and auxiliaries.[24] It began a systematic siege, led by Mikhail Borisovich Shein, who knew the fortifications intimately, having been the commandant during the siege of 1609–11. Smolensk was surrounded by an impressive system of entrenchments and earthworks. Although the heavy artillery did not arrive until December, and the nineteen heaviest siege guns not until March,[25] the siege proceeded methodically until the late summer of 1633, when the garrison had been reduced to a desperate state. Already in March, it was running low on provisions: there was no wheat left, only $276\frac{3}{4}$ of the $1,501\frac{1}{2}$ barrels of rye in store at the start of the siege, and $1,218\frac{3}{4}$ out of $2,336\frac{1}{2}$ barrels of oats.[26] The ceaseless Muscovite bombardment seriously damaged the walls and the fall of Smolensk seemed only a matter of time.

Time, however, was the one commodity Shein did not have at his disposal. He reached Smolensk in October 1632, a month before Władysław's election. The new king immediately began organising a substantial relief army to support the 2–3,000-strong force with which Krzysztof Radziwiłł had launched thirty raids between late January and March 1633, in which scores of Muscovites were killed or captured for the loss of only four of his own men; in early March, he succeeded in smuggling 294 men into Smolensk, each carrying four pounds of gunpowder and other supplies.[27] In February the Coronation *Sejm* approved an army of 23,427 which, given that there were already 8,000 under arms, meant that a further 15,000 had to be raised. In early September 1633, Władysław reached Smolensk with 14,000 men; his forces grew steadily as others followed, including 15,000 Ukrainian Cossacks.[28]

This force proved more than adequate to defeat Shein. In a series of bold operations, Władysław broke the siege and forced the Muscovites back to Shein's main camp on the south bank of the Dnieper to the east of Smolensk. The first exploratory attack, on 7 September, after a night march through the forest, was on Mattison's powerfully-fortified position on Pokrowska hill to the north of Smolensk. After fierce fighting, in which Mattison's forces were subjected to a surprise attack in their rear from the besieged city on the other bank of the river, Władysław withdrew. The more coordinated operations of 21–22 September, after the Cossacks had arrived, forced Mattison off the Pokrowska hill to take refuge in Shein's camp. On 28 September, a series of concerted attacks on Muscovite positions to the west of the city forced a similar withdrawal. By 3 October, the Muscovites had abandoned their last positions around Smolensk.

The next task was to destroy or drive off Shein's main army. A bold raid by Aleksander Piaseczyński on Dorohobuzh, ninety kilometres away, resulted in the complete destruction of the huge supplies of food and ammunition stockpiled there. Władysław now launched a carefully-prepared envelopment, skirting the Muscovite camp to the north to mount a surprise attack on Żaworonkowe hill, overlooking Shein's position to the east. By midday on 19 October, he had secured positions on Żaworonkowe hill, and to the south at Bogdanowa. Once Shein realised the danger, he attacked across the Dnieper, in an attempt to dislodge the Poles before they had dug themselves in. Despite fierce fighting, which saw the Commonwealth troops under serious pressure at various points, the line held. By 23 October, the Poles were established on Żaworonkowe hill, whence they could easily bombard the Muscovite positions without reply, since the Muscovite guns could not achieve sufficient elevation. By the end of the month, the Cossacks had crossed the Dnieper to block Shein's retreat to the south. Blockaded on all sides, he could only wait for relief which failed to arrive. On 1 March, the Muscovites filed out of their camp; Shein and his fellow commanders had to dismount and prostrate themselves at Władysław's feet until commanded to rise, before being escorted on the road back to Moscow.[29]

The war petered out shortly after Shein's ignominious surrender. A desultory siege of Belyi by the Poles was cut short in May by the conclusion of the Eternal Peace of Polianovka, in which Władysław, in return for Muscovite recognition of the Polish conquests at Deulino and a large war indemnity, agreed to surrender his claim to the Muscovite throne. It was a price he was willing to pay as he turned his eyes to the west, where Altmark was due to expire. Flushed with the success of his first military campaign, he had other plans to implement.

Although the Muscovite government, which lost much of its drive on Filaret's death in October 1633, had abandoned Shein to his fate, he became the scapegoat for the Smolensk disaster. Tried on charges of having been a Polish agent, he was executed, along with Izmaelov, his second-in-command; their families, along with lesser officers, were dishonoured and exiled. The new-style regiments raised for the war were disbanded and, apart from a few officers who converted to Orthodoxy, foreign soldiers were ordered to leave Muscovy. Such was the price of failure.

Why did Shein fail? Hellie approvingly quotes Porshnev's view that his forces were 'vastly superior in numbers, armaments and the military art to the Polish forces' and can only conclude that if Shein had been left alone by the government he would have taken the city 'without difficulty'; the only other explanation he offers is that the Muscovites did not yet trust foreign mercenaries.[30] Fuller, who provides a more thoughtful analysis, concludes that the siege operations were perfectly well conducted; defeat was not due to Shein's incompetence, but to the quality of the Polish troops and the transport difficulties which ensured that his heavy guns were late in arriving.[31] Yet the Poles, who did not arrive in force until nearly a year after the siege began, faced similar problems. Eyewitnesses testify that they were astonished by the quantities of gunpowder, ammunition and artillery that the Muscovites had assembled, which they compared unfavourably with their own supplies.[32]

It would be easy to conclude that the defeat was due to the lack of time allowed the new-formation units to absorb their training in western methods of warfare. Yet western methods were not entirely new to Muscovites, having been applied during the Time of Troubles, and since the establishment of the *strel'tsy* in the mid-sixteenth century, Muscovite troops had long shown themselves to be tenacious in siege warfare and fully aware of the importance of firepower. The *strel'tsy* might be ill-disciplined, but they were not ineffective, as they had demonstrated at Pskov in 1581. Thus foreign instructors were improving technique and introducing new ideas rather than starting from scratch. The Poles, many of whom had fought Gustav Adolf, testified that the Muscovite infantry performed very effectively, marvelling at the scale of the Muscovite fieldworks: Jan Moskorzowski felt that they were so huge and constructed with such labour that it would take the Poles as long to capture them as it would take the Muscovites to reduce Smolensk itself.[33] He expressed admiration for Muscovite firepower and discipline during the struggle for Żaworonkowe hill:

for the fire was so intense that all experienced soldiers stated unanimously that they had never been under such fire in various encounters in Prussia, Livonia or Muscovy. Over several hours the enemy guns fired at least a hundred times, for fire was maintained without break from three batteries; sometimes from ten guns at once; and from muskets fire was so heavy that it seemed that Hell itself had opened up.[34]

Yet firepower was insufficient in itself to defeat the Poles. The greatest problem facing Shein was that, owing to the inferiority of his cavalry, he was effectively trapped in his field fortifications once the Poles arrived. Władysław was able to manoeuvre his infantry into position under the cover of his cavalry, leaving Shein helpless, despite his advantage in men and materials, to send relief to his isolated outposts round Smolensk. All he could do was sit tight. At first the Muscovites were confident:

> in no way do they wish to give battle, but only stand behind their fortifications, from which it is impossible to lure them except under cover of their guns. One can only fight them in the Dutch style, constructing approach trenches, digging and tunnelling like Gustav [Adolf]. And are we disposed to this, although we have invested so heavily in Polish-German infantry . . . ? They do not think of withdrawing from this fortress, but they are very scornful of us, mocking us as traitors.[35]

Yet sitting tight invited disaster. If the Polish cavalry suffered serious casualties from Muscovite firepower, it played a critical supporting role: in the battle for Żaworonkowe hill the cavalry occupying the valley held off the Muscovite infantry despite heavy losses, giving the Polish infantry time to establish their position on the slopes above.[36] It was in its control of the surrounding territory, however, that the cavalry played its most vital role. Polish superiority in cavalry enabled the raid on Dorohobuzh and ensured that Shein remained bottled up in his camp from October until February. As in Batory's campaigns, the Muscovites were unwilling to risk battle in the open, and no relief army arrived despite frequent promises to the beleagured Shein. One foreign officer who fell into Polish hands:

> seeing the cavalry force was much surprised, saying that the Muscovites feared nothing more than . . . the hussars, . . . saying that they could easily deal with other forces; when he was told that this was not all the cavalry . . . he said that with such an army we could take the enemy and chase him back to his capital.[37]

Shein may have paid the ultimate price for his failure as a political gesture to direct attention away from the performance of the new-style units; it was the inadequacy of his cavalry which was the true cause of his defeat.

Poland-Lithuania and military reform

The triumphant scenes outside Smolensk in March 1634 were a splendid start to what promised to be a glittering reign. Władysław had been raised in Poland, unlike his father, and had inherited the vigorous Vasa genes so apparent in his cousin, Gustav Adolf. His popularity ensured the first uncontested election since 1572 and was increased by the restless energy with which he organised the Smolensk campaign. Moreover, while he conducted operations in the north, a serious threat was repelled in the south, where a Polish army of 11,300 under Koniecpolski used its superior firepower to defeat a Turkish and Tatar force of 24,500 at Kamieniec (October 1633).[38] In the positive atmosphere created by these successes, the 1635 *Sejm*, angered by Swedish encouragement of the Muscovite attack, agreed to an offensive war against Sweden on the expiry of Altmark, due later that year, voting considerable sums of money to support an army of 9,170 cavalry and 11,800 infantry and dragoons.[39] Although the question of a fleet was only raised by individual senators, Władysław continued his energetic efforts to establish one, creating a Maritime Commission and buying ten ships and a galley.[40]

The honeymoon was soon over. Ironically, Władysław's very success in raising this force ensured that it would not be used. The Swedes were facing serious difficulties in Germany after their defeat at Nördlingen (September 1634), widespread mutinies in the Swedish armies in the summer of 1635, and the peace of Prague (May 1635), which reconciled Saxony and Brandenburg with the emperor. Although Oxenstierna wished to take a hard line with the Poles, the Regents in Stockholm were more concerned at the Polish build-up, and proved willing to make concessions. Thus, although the vexed questions of Livonia and the claims of the Polish Vasas to the Swedish throne proved insoluble, the Swedes agreed to evacuate Royal Prussia and surrender the revenues from the Prussian tolls to achieve agreement at Stuhmsdorf in September. Władysław was enraged by the Commonwealth's unwillingness to support him; for his subjects the Swedish evacuation of Prussia was sufficient. Although the *sejmiki* had agreed taxes to keep the army in service until 1 December 1635, many decided to collect them in two instalments. If an acceptable settlement were reached, they would not collect the second instalment; it was, and they did not.[41] Władysław had no choice but to accept.

Nevertheless, the Commonwealth's achievements by 1635 were considerable. Often dismissed as an anarchic and chaotic political system which failed to respond to the challenges of the seventeenth century, in fact there had been a considerable amount of development as a result of the enormous military burden, which had grown steadily throughout a period of almost constant warfare. It is true that during the first half of Sigismund's reign, the consensual political system had come under intense strain. The *Sejm*, which controlled the taxation necessary for defence, was not a representative body, but an assembly of delegates from local *sejmiki*, which received royal proposals for taxation and legislation, instructed their envoys as to their response, and scrutinised the legislation passed to see whether it accorded with their instructions; if it did not, they frequently refused to implement it. Legislation was decided not by majority voting, but by a process of bargaining between 160–170 envoys and the Senate to produce consensus. When political differences were acute, it was not uncommon for the *Sejm* to break up without achieving anything; this had occured on no fewer than six occasions (1576, 1582, 1585, 1597, 1600, 1606) by the time that opposition to Sigismund culminated in the 1606–7 *rokosz*.[42]

The situation improved in the second half of Sigismund's reign, however, when only the 1615 *Sejm* failed to reach a conclusion. Between 1613 and 1635, the *Sejm* approved a steadily-increasing tax burden to meet the spiralling costs of war, at a time when the Commonwealth's economic situation was worsening as the international grain market slumped and the Prussian war disrupted trade. The Crown treasury collected 1,239,720 złoties between 1 January 1581 and 31 December 1582, during the last period of the war against Muscovy; 777,063 złoties in 1583–4, after the making of peace.[43] By 1613, at the height of the war against Muscovy, it was clear that the traditional sources of revenue were not generating enough to cover the mounting costs of war. Despite the considerable hostility which the official intervention in Muscovy had generated, the *Sejm* agreed to a radical boosting of direct taxes, by sanctioning the first multiple levying of the land-tax, which had been collected at a rate of 1 złoty per *łan* of cultivated land since 1578.[44] The March *Sejm* of 1613 agreed a threefold rate; by December, the land-tax, together with the *czopowe*, a tax on alcohol, had already raised 1,176,907 of the projected 1,410,078 złoties, a shortfall of 16.5 per cent; including other taxes, 1,670,290 złoties had been raised of a projected 1,948,078, a shortfall of 14.3 per cent. In addition, the Lithuanian treasury raised 833,253 złoties.[45] This was sufficient to liquidate the confederations formed by soldiers who had fought in the freelance mercenary units in Muscovy, but the army's continuing financial needs saw the voting of a sixfold rate of the land-tax by the December *Sejm*.

From 1613, multiple rates of the land-tax became the norm; the peak was reached with an eightfold rate in 1620 for the Turkish war, and a twelvefold rate in 1628.[46] Although *sejmiki* regularly refused to accept the multiple rate agreed at the *Sejm* if it conflicted with their instructions, it was not unknown for *sejmiki* in areas that felt particularly threatened to agree a higher rate than the *Sejm*: a convocation of Lithuanian envoys in Wilno in

October 1614, for example, agreed to an additional rate of the land-tax on top of the six agreed at the *Sejm*, among other measures designed to raise money for the defence of Smolensk, while in Wielkopolska an extra rate above the six accepted at the Thorn *Sejm* of 1626 was collected for 'domestic defence'.[47]

Serious efforts were made to reform the taxation system. One of the problems with the land-tax was that it continued to be based on the tariffs agreed in 1578; its potential yield was undermined both by inflation and by the fact that a considerable amount of new land had since come under cultivation. Although efforts to administer oaths concerning the amount of cultivated land on which tax was paid proved impossible to enforce, the problem was recognised as serious; since proposals to conduct a definitive land-survey were opposed vociferously (though opposition was by no means universal), the introduction of multiple rates after 1613 was an attempt to circumvent this problem. The 1629 *Sejm*, which agreed a fourfold land-tax, also introduced a hearth-tax, which became standard under Władysław, and was frequently voted at multiple rates, as in 1635, when a sixfold rate was agreed. Although the hearth-tax was recognised as somewhat unfair, since it burdened all households equally regardless of economic position, it was easier to assess than the land-tax, and was levied on the basic economic unit, the household. Finally, at the start of Władysław's reign, a second, or 'new' *kwarta*, which had been raised occasionally under Sigismund, was introduced permanently, to raise the treasury's income from the royal lands; from 1632, the *kwarta* was also levied in Lithuania, which had previously only happened occasionally.

The Polish-Lithuanian system is often condemned for not being what it never tried to be. Judged on its own terms, however, its achievement by 1635 was considerable. Despite the inevitable problems, a confederal, consensual, decentralised, multi-ethnic state had waged almost constant warfare for nearly eight decades. It had coped with the constant threat of Tatar raids, and had significantly extended its border. Between 1620 and 1635, it beat off serious attacks by the Ottoman Empire (twice), by Sweden and by Muscovy, all of them substantial military powers, for the loss of Riga and most, but not all, of Livonia, occupied when it was fighting on two fronts. It had mobilised significant resources during an economic recession: the Swedish war of 1626–9 cost 12,000,000 złoties, of which the Polish treasury contributed over 10,426,363 złoties. The Smolensk War cost 6,450,000 złoties.[48]

The Commonwealth had substantially increased the burden on its citizens. Prices had risen 21 per cent between 1591 and 1630, while the official value of the currency had fallen threefold; the tax burden had risen nearly sevenfold. These efforts enabled it to raise armies which were substantial on a European scale: some 86,000 troops were mobilised during 1621, most of them deployed against the Turks; 35,400 were mobilised in 1629 and 53,000 in 1634. Even during the peaceful years after 1635, the Commonwealth maintained 12,250 men: 4,045 in the quarter army, 2,000 in the Lithuanian army and 6,000 registered Cossacks.[49] Moreover, the Commonwealth had shown considerable flexibility, adjusting the composition of its forces according to the nature of the enemy it faced. The 1620 *Sejm* had projected an army of 45,000 cavalry and 15,000 infantry to meet the Turkish threat, a ratio of three to one in favour of cavalry, but this does not take account of the 20,000 Cossacks, most of whom fought on foot. The army at Chocim had a paper strength of 33,180 (25,000 actual soldiers), with 19,130 cavalry (58 per cent) and 14,050 infantry (42 per cent).[50] The *Sejm* voted an état of 12,000 cavalry (44 per cent) to 15,000 foot (56 per cent) in November 1626, while the army in the Smolensk War contained 8,880 cavalry (37 per cent), 2,450 dragoons (10 per cent) and 12,850 infantry (53 per cent).[51] From 1633, as a direct result of the experiences in the Swedish war, it was decided to institutionalise the practice of raising troops armed and trained in the western style through the division of the army into two parts: the native contingent (*autorament narodowy*) and the foreign contingent (*autorament cudzoziemski*); the latter which, despite its name, was largely recruited within the Commonwealth, played a central role in the Smolensk War, and was a permanent feature of the Commonwealth's armies thereafter.

All this was achieved largely from taxation revenue, without burdening the Commonwealth with long-term debt. The operation of the Commonwealth's fiscal machinery was by no means as chaotic as it is frequently painted, at least before 1648. The Crown and Lithuanian treasurers were responsible to the *Sejm*, and had to account for the expenditure voted by previous diets. The Treasury Tribunal, first summoned in 1591, which met in Radom from 1613, was designed to ensure the smooth functioning of the system. Although not a permanent body, it was regularly summoned by the *Sejm* according to the pattern established in 1613. The commissioners, appointed from among senators and *Sejm* envoys, were responsible for examining treasury receipts, chasing tax arrears and auditing expenditure.[52] Arrears were not forgotten: in 1628, the sum of 300 złoties was paid in respect of taxes due from 1598 and 1602, in a total of 478,631 złoties arrears paid that year.[53]

The *Sejm*-appointed commissions dealt reasonably efficiently with the problem of paying the army, and no less so than many contemporary powers. Although army pay was regularly in arrears, and army confederations were frequently threatened, debts to the troops were settled reasonably efficiently. If in time of war arrears of pay immediately began to accumulate, and the gaps had to be filled by commanders from their own pockets to be repaid later by the *Sejm*, apart from the chaotic first period of the intervention in the Muscovite wars, when opposition to royal policy caused serious problems, the Commonwealth managed just about to keep afloat. Despite constant problems with unpaid units roaming the country, and regular complaints from *sejmiki*, in comparison with contemporary parliamentary systems, the Commowealth performed well: despite lacking the sophisticated financial systems and commercial wealth of the United Provinces, it managed to sustain a considerable military effort over eight decades; its performance was unquestionably superior to that of Britain under the early Stuarts.

It appeared in 1635 that the Commonwealth had weathered the storm. Despite Altmark, it had emerged victorious alongside Sweden from the first phase of the Northern Wars, with Muscovy as the decided loser. Denmark had failed to exploit its opportunities, and was shortly to suffer its first major setback in Torstensson's War. Yet little did Władysław know it as Shein grovelled before him outside Smolensk that this was to be his last triumph, and the Commonwealth's last act as a great power. To his frustration, the *szlachta* decided that they were not prepared to support the expansive foreign policy he now intended to pursue. His ambitious plans to exploit the Thirty Years War to further his interests in Silesia, and his scheme for a great anti-Turkish crusade in the late 1640s, foundered on the rock of *szlachta* opposition. In 1635, the Commonwealth settled down to peace with relish. Polish commentators praised their political system, which kept a tight control on the martial ambitions of their monarchs, and reflected with more than a touch of *Schadenfreude* on the unfortunate events in the Empire.

They soon received a rude shock. On 16 May 1648 at Zhovti Vody in the Ukraine, four days before the unexpected death of the bloated and gout-ridden Władysław, a small Polish army was destroyed after a grim two-week defensive battle by a force of Cossack rebels and their Tatar allies, led by the Zaporozhian hetman Bohdan Khmelnytsky. Ten days later the core of the regular army, 5,000 strong, was destroyed at Korsun; both hetmans, Mikołaj Potocki and Marcin Kalinowski, fell into Tatar hands. Within weeks the Ukraine was engulfed by a massive Cossack and peasant revolt. Once more, an interregnum had begun amidst a crisis; on this occasion, however, the Commonwealth proved wholly unable to cope. A new phase of the Northern Wars was about to open, which was to shake the Commonwealth to its very foundations and present unexpected opportunities to its neighbours.

Notes

1 In 1650, Sweden's advantage in large ships was 28 to 25; in 1655, it was 28 to 21: Glete, *Navies* I p. 186.

2 For an admiring assessment by one who served Gustav Adolf, see *Robert Monro. His expedition with the worthy Scots Regiment (called Mac-Keyes Regiment)* (London, 1637) II pp. 66, 68.

3   Torsten Stålhandske, commander of the Swedish forces in Silesia, claimed in 1641 that he had sustained his troops for two years without drawing any food or money from outside the province: K.-R. Böhme, 'Geld für die schwedischen Armeen nach 1640' *Scandia* 33 (1967) p. 64.

4   Englund, *Ofredsår* pp. 473–4.

5   M. Roberts (ed.) *Sweden as a Great Power, 1611–1697* (London, 1968), p. 15; K. Johannesson, *The Renaissance of the Goths in Sixteenth-century Sweden* J. Larson (tr.) (Berkeley, 1991) p. 221; G. Barudio, *Gustav Adolf – der Große* (Frankfurt, 1985) pp. 26–34. Ringmar, *Identity* pp. 156–64.

6   *Livgardes Historia* II p. 562.

7   E. Ladewig Petersen, 'The Danish Intermezzo' in G. Parker (ed.), *The Thirty Years War* (London, 1984) p. 72.

8   P. Lockhart, 'Denmark and the Empire. A reassessment of the foreign policy of king Christian IV, 1596–1648' *SS* 62 (1992) p. 233.

9   Letter of 15.V.1611, *Kong Christian den Fjerdes egenhændige Breve* C.F. Bricka and J.A. Fridericia (eds) (Copenhagen, 1887) p. 59; G. Lind, *Hæren og magten i Danmark 1614–1662* (Odense, 1994) p. 35.

10 Lockhart, *Denmark* p. 65; Lind, *Hæren* p. 31.

11 It used to be argued that the measures taken after the Kalmar War were a Council initiative forced upon an unwilling king. In the light of recent research, this view is no longer sustainable: E. Ladewig Petersen, 'Christian IV's skånske og norske fæstningsanlæg, 1596–1622' *HTD* (1995) pp. 338–9.

12 Lind, *Hæren* p. 32; Lockhart, *Denmark* p. 66.

13 Indeed, it was only in June 1615 that it was decided to establish the two regiments; originally the army was to be based on the companies. The fact that the colonels of the regiments were not the main contractors was to prove important. Lind, *Hæren* pp. 40–1.

14 Ibid. pp. 44–5.

15 The Council proposed a system of dividing peasant households into groups of nine, which would be responsible for supplying and equipping one soldier; Christian originally opposed the idea, but adopted it in April 1621. Lockhart, 'Denmark' p. 336.

16 Lind, *Hæren* p. 42. For a comparison of Danish and Swedish war costs see K. Krüger, 'Dänische und schwedische Kriegsfinanzierung im Dreißigjährigen Krieg bis 1635' in K. Repgen (ed.), *Krieg und Politik 1618–1648* (Munich, 1988) pp. 275–98.

17 Lind, *Hæren* pp. 60–4.

18 Ibid. pp. 68–74.

19 Ibid. p. 78.

20 Ibid. p. 87.

21 Chernov, *Vooruzhennye* pp. 130–1.

22 P. Dukes, 'The Leslie family in the Swedish period (1630–5) of the Thirty Years War' *ESR* 12 (1982) pp. 401–24.

23 Chernov, *Vooruzhennye* pp. 134–5; Hellie, *Enserfment* pp. 170–1.

24 Chernov, *Vooruzhennye* pp. 136–7. Hellie suggests that new-formation regiments constituted half the army, but his figure of 17,400 is the total number of

new-formation troops raised during the war; it is unclear how many reached Smolensk; Hellie, *Enserfment* p. 172. The figure of 9,000 accords with the 'no more than 7–8,000 infantry' given by a 'well-informed' French officer captured by the Poles in September 1633; the wastage is what one might expect after a year's campaigning: 'Dyaryusz expedycyej J.K.M. przeciwko nieprzyiacielowi moskiewskiemu ktory 14 8bris in anno 1632 Smolensk obleg y onego potężnie dobywał 25 augusti ro. 1633' in O. Tselevich,'Uchast' kozakiv v Smolenskii viini 1633–4 rr.' *ZNTS* 28 (1899) p. 33.

25 W.C. Fuller, *Strategy and Power in Russia 1600–1914* (New York, 1992) p. 11.

26 'Copia z listu cyframi pisanego z oblężenia Smoleńskiego de data 7 Martii, a przyniesionego 20 Martii do Krasnego' *Dyariusz Wojny Moskiewskiej 1633 roku* A. Rembowski (ed.) (Warsaw, 1895) p. 14.

27 Ibid. pp. 4, 13.

28 W. Lipiński, 'Organizacja odsieczy i działania wrześniowe pod Smoleńskiem w r. 1633' *PHW* 6 (1933) pp. 175, 177–8, 197.

29 Idem, 'Bój o Żaworonkowe Wzgórza i osaczenie Szeina pod Smoleńskiem (16–30 październik 1633 r.)' *PHW* 7 (1934) pp. 39–74; Jan Moskorzowki to Andrzej Moskorzowski, 3.III.1634, *Dyariusz* pp. 110–12.

30 Hellie, *Enserfment* pp. 172–3, 187; B. Porshnev, 'Sotsial'no-politicheskaia obstanovka v Rossii vo vremia Smolenskoi voiny' *Isoriia SSSR* 1:5 (1957) p. 113.

31 Fuller, *Strategy* pp. 21–34.

32 Jan Moskorzowski to Andrzej Moskorzowski, September 1633; *Dyariusz* p. 17.

33 Jan Moskorzowski to Andrzej Moskorzowski, October 1633; ibid. pp. 42–3.

34 Jan Moskorzowski to Andrzej Moskorzowski, 31 October 1633; ibid. p. 59.

35 Jan Moskorzowski to Andrzej Moskorzowski, September 1633; ibid. p. 18.

36 Lipiński, 'Bój' p. 62.

37 'Dyaryusz' p. 60.

38 Podhorodecki, *Stanisław Koniecpolski* pp. 285–300.

39 J. Wimmer, 'Wojsko i skarb Rzeczypospolitej u schyłku XVI i w pierwszej połowie XVII wieku' *SMHW* 14:1 (1968) p. 65. The Polish treasury paid out 3,143,664 złoties for its support, with a further 250,000 from Lithuania, though this latter figure only represented half of what Lithuania had agreed. A. Filipczak-Kocur, *Skarb koronny za Władysława IV 1632–1648* (Opole, 1991) p. 44; idem, *Skarb litewski za pierwszych dwu Wazów 1587–1648* (Wrocław, 1994) p. 91.

40 W. Czapliński, *Polska a Bałtyk w latach 1632–1648* (Wrocław, 1952) pp. 41–52.

41 W. Czapliński, 'Na marginesie rokowań w Sztumsdorfie w 1635 r.' *PW* 17 (1938) p. 117.

42 The diet of 1605 also failed to agree any taxes, which prevented Sigismund from exploiting the victory at Kircholm. Filipczak-Kocur, *Skarb koronny za Zygmunta III* pp. 87–8.

43 Ibid. p. 47.

44 Although noble manors were exempt, nobles without serfs paid at a rate of $\frac{1}{2}$ złoty.

45 Part of the shortfall was due to the destruction wrought in parts of the Commonwealth by war; ibid. pp. 106–7.

46 For a complete list, see the tables in Wimmer, 'Wojsko i skarb' pp. 82–8. Filipczak-Kocur's figures for the tax-yields are based on fuller data than Wimmer's.

47 S. Ochmann, *Sejmy z lat 1615–1616* (Wrocław, 1970) p. 41; J. Seredyka, *Sejm zawiedzionych nadziei (1627 r.)* (Opole, 1981) p. 12.

48 Filipczak-Kocur, *Skarb koronny za Zygmunta III* p. 145, idem, *Skarb koronny za Władysława IV* p. 31. Filipczak-Kocur does not give a breakdown of her aggregated figures of 6,420,716 złoties spent by the Lithuanian treasury on the war in Livonia from 1600 to 1629: idem, *Skarb litewski* p. 88.

49 Wimmer, 'Wojsko' pp. 79, 90–1.

50 Ibid. pp. 35, 38–9. The presence of 20,000 Cossacks tilted the balance in favour of infantry.

51 Ibid. pp. 61–2. Unless otherwise indicated, the figures refer only to the Polish army, and give paper strengths; 10–15 per cent should be subtracted for the real strength. The actual strength of the 1633 army, including Lithuanian units, was 21,800.

52 L. Babiński, *Trybunał skarbowy radomski* (Warsaw, 1923); J. Rafacz, 'Trybunał skarbowy koronny' *KH* 38 (1924) pp. 413–55.

53 Filipczak-Kocur, *Skarb koronny za Zygmunta III* p. 141.

CHAPTER SEVEN

The Thirteen Years War and the Second Northern War

Crisis

It was no accident that Khmelnytsky's revolt began at the end of the longest period of peace the Commonwealth had known since 1558. Although it had adapted effectively to the rapidly-changing circumstances of contemporary warfare, there were serious shortcomings in the Commonwealth's military structure which were exposed after 1648. The principal problem was the failure to develop a permanent framework within which its semi-professional forces could develop. This was in part a consequence of the way in which its armies were sustained. The Commonwealth had fought its wars largely on the proceeds of taxation, yet its *szlachta* citizens remained deeply attached to the ideal of the domain state. For them, taxation was extraordinary: it was to be under the tight control of the citizens, without whose consent it could not be voted, and it was temporary, voted for limited periods, from one *Sejm* to the next, to cover necessary expenses. Otherwise, the infrastructure of defence was to be provided out of the royal domain. As the 1615 *Sejm* reminded Sigismund, he had promised in his electoral charter to build and maintain a fleet, and to sustain 'the apparatus of war' at his own expense; proposals, such as that made at the Sieradz *sejmik* in 1632, suggesting that a set number of royal estates be set aside to support the construction of a fleet, were common.[1]

There is no reason to dismiss such proposals as anachronistic. As the case of Sweden demonstrates, imaginative use of the royal domain could provide the basis for an effective military system; a suggestion from the Środa *sejmik* in 1627 that all leases on royal lands which became vacant in the first three months of every year should automatically be assigned to soldiers indicates that some among the *szlachta* were thinking along similar lines.[2] Indeed, if the Commonwealth's laws had been strictly applied, the government would have had substantially greater revenues to fund the military infrastructure. In the 1560s the anti-magnate Movement for the Execution of the Laws had attacked the alienation of royal land, expressly forbidden by the *Sejm* in 1504, but a common royal expedient to raise money, particularly between 1548 and 1561. As an increasing amount of royal land fell into magnate hands, the protests of the middling *szlachta* crystallised into a powerful movement. Their cause was helped by Sigismund Augustus's adoption of the call for execution of the laws, which opened the way to the political revolution of 1569–72, when the middling *szlachta* forced through their vision of the Commonwealth as an egalitarian state of noble citizens.

Legislation passed in 1562–3 and 1565 annulled all alienations since 1504, and ordered audits of royal estates in 1564–5 and 1569–70. The original plan, in which a quarter of the income from all royal estates (the *kwarta*) would be paid directly to a new, permanent treasury at Rawa, was modified in 1567, when the *Sejm* agreed that the 'quarter' would be set at a fifth of the gross income; this would go to the Rawa treasury, with leaseholders receiving a further fifth, and the remaining three-fifths paid to the Crown. Although Henry of Valois, under pressure from senators who held most of the leaseholds, issued a decree in 1574 increasing the share of leaseholders to 50 per cent of the proceeds in judicial starosties, whose holders performed judicial functions, and to 40 per cent in the rest, this was never recognised by the *Sejm*; thus the *szlachta* continued to assume that the king enjoyed three-fifths of the revenue from all royal estates.[3]

Had monarchs received the three-fifths to which they were entitled, they might have been able to build a fleet, maintain and improve fortifications and fill the royal armouries, as required by their electoral charters: the audits of 1565–74 established revenues of 550,000 złoties per annum for the lands of pre-Lublin Poland alone, of which 60 per cent would have constituted the considerable sum of 315,000 złoties.[4] Unfortunately, they were never in a position to enjoy what was legally theirs. After 1574, it became increasingly common for the royal demesne to be regarded as the property of the Commonwealth, not the monarchy, and income from royal estates came to be seen as legitimate reward for service. A succession of foreign monarchs was thrown back on the political support of their ministers and members of the senatorial elite; the distribution of starosties proved to be both a useful reward for services rendered and a means of winning over opponents of royal policy. Under the Vasas, who lacked substantial private holdings of their own after losing the Swedish throne, control of access to royal land proved a powerful political weapon.

Already in the 1574 Treasury register it emerged that a quarter of royal lands was assigned illegally on lifelong leases without any payments due; a further 57 per cent were held on various types of contract. Only 18 per cent remained under direct Treasury control; by 1580, the proportion assigned for the lifetime of the holder had risen to half.[5] Furthermore, the fact that the Execution legislation was passed before 1569 ensured that it did not apply to Lithuania, where royal estates were not subject to the *kwarta*. Exemption from its provisions was the necessary price for the acceptance by Lithuanian magnates of Poland's 1569 annexation of the Ukraine.

Thus the Execution Movement's triumph had the opposite effect to what was intended. The Rawa treasury kept reasonable control over the payment of the *kwarta*, and constant pressure from *sejmiki* for audits of royal estates at five-year intervals did secure a partial audit between 1615 and 1620, which boosted its income substantially. Further progress was made with the successful extension of the *kwarta* to Lithuania and the establishment of the second *kwarta* in Poland after 1632; nevertheless, despite widespread pressure from *sejmiki* to ensure payment of the 'three-fifths' to the royal treasury, and the regular auditing of the royal lands, the fact that so many of the envoys sent by *sejmiki* to the central *Sejm* themselves held, or hoped to hold, starosties, ensured that the *Sejm* itself did not always press the complaints of the ordinary *szlachta* too enthusiastically. Thus wars were principally funded from taxation, while the vast income of the royal lands was largely directed into private hands. Even in the relatively favourable years between 1632 and 1655, when the introduction of the second *kwarta* meant that 40 per cent of the income from royal estates should have reached the Rawa treasury, the actual sum was 10–15 per cent.[6] Meanwhile, the small elite with access to royal land waxed rich on the proceeds: Jan Zamoyski held two judicial starosties and ten other starosties; six of them were exempt from the *kwarta*, and he paid barely a ninth of the real income from the others to Rawa. Over half his income came from royal land. It was a familiar tale.[7]

It is easy to attack the *szlachta* for selfish short-sightedness and to condemn those such as Jan Karol Chodkiewicz, who complained at the lack of money which so hindered his campaigns, yet reacted with outrage when the 1613 *Sejm* agreed that the *kwarta* should be collected in Lithuania for the first time, observing that he had never paid it and did not intend to begin now.[8] Yet his position was not unreasonable: he had served the Commonwealth long and loyally and had spent large sums of his own money to keep his armies together. Although he could claim repayment from the *Sejm*, and although he held a substantial number of starosties, he constantly faced financial problems. Many magnates did build colossal fortunes on the proceeds from royal land; for others, however, the concept of 'bread well earned' (*panis bene merentium*) was not entirely a pious myth.

Whatever the justification for such thinking, its prevalence meant that in practice there was no alternative but to fund war from extraordinary taxation.

While this was largely successful down to 1635, all the Commonwealth's wars since 1558 had been fought outside its borders, or on its periphery. The apparent ease which which its enemies had been defeated seemed to demonstrate that it had little to fear from its neighbours. Moreover, suspicion of royal motives and the enormous expense of contemporary warfare ensured that the *szlachta* was increasingly reluctant to sanction aggressive war, and the ambitious plans of Batory and Władysław for Turkish wars, or of Sigismund and Władysław for intervention in the Thirty Years War, were met with indifference or hostility. The Vasa obsession with recovering the Swedish throne, and their willingness to conduct their own foreign policy in secret, sowed the seeds of distrust. If the monarchy could not be trusted to preserve the peace which the *szlachta* desired, it must be deprived of the means of waging war. The *szlachta* would defend the Commonwealth if attacked; they would not indulge in power politics.

Such attitudes were dangerous, however. The Commonwealth, unlike Sweden, Denmark or Britain, was not protected by sea; indeed, the *szlachta* opposed plans to build a Baltic fleet. Danzig, fearing that a navy would be used to levy tolls upon its trade, was even more hostile. Without a large, permanent army, the Commonwealth invited attack. It had beaten off the Swedes in the 1620s and the Muscovites in the 1630s, but if forced to wage a long war on its own soil, when the yield from taxes was bound to suffer, it might not find it so easy to repel the invaders. Moreover, the Commonwealth's failure to establish a permanent military force had important social consequences, and played a central role in igniting the Cossack Revolt which was to usher in a new and darker phase in its history.

The Commonwealth's relationship to the various categories of Cossacks, and the broader strata of ill-defined servitors and petty nobles from which they were drawn, had long been ambivalent. If Cossacks were skilled and dogged infantrymen, Cossack indiscipline ensured that their employment outside the southeastern borderlands was often resisted, as it was by Krzysztof Radziwiłł in the 1622 Livonian campaign.[9] In its hours of greatest need – during the 1618 Moscow campaign, the 1621 Chocim campaign and the Smolensk War – the ability of Cossack hetmans to raise substantial forces had proved useful; nevertheless, the *szlachta* was unwilling to meet the substantial cost of paying thousands of Cossacks in peacetime. The *Sejm* always sought to keep strict control over Cossack numbers, and the peacetime register, established at 8,000 in 1630, was cut to 6,000 in 1638.

The relationship was characterised by periods of cooperation punctuated from the 1590s by Cossack risings of an increasing level of violence. The regular army always proved capable of crushing revolts before 1648, although the savagery with which this was conducted created festering resentment. The democratic traditions of the Cossack host, in which power was vested in the elected hetman and his officers, ensured that even the registered Cossacks could prove anything but an obedient instrument of the Commonwealth; the Zaporozhians and others excluded from the register were a law unto themselves. The Commonwealth may have been grateful for the substantial Cossack force which fought at Chocim in 1621, but it did not forget that the Cossacks had done much to provoke the war.

The decade of peace after the crushing of the 1637–8 revolt, while calm on the surface, saw much hidden tension, as the extension not of state, but of noble, power represented a growing threat to the status of thousands of non-registered cossacks and petty servitors. In the palatinates of Volhynia, Bratslav and Kiev magnate families, many of Ruthenian origin, such as the Wiśniowieckis and the Ostrożskis, dominated noble society. The hearth-tax registers of 1629 reveal that leading magnate families owned or leased 68.3 per cent of hearths in the Kiev palatinate, 79.8 per cent in Volhynia and 89.5 per cent in Bratslav, with the ten leading families controlling 38.3 per cent in Kiev, 61.5 per cent in Volhynia and 63.7 per cent in Bratslav.[10] The growing dominance of this small group of families gradually transformed social and political relations. In particular, the large group of petty nobles or boyar-servitors was left stranded: as petty landowners, leaseholders, or landless servitors, they inhabited a broad twilight world between commoners and nobles. *Sejm* control of public finance rendered the state merely an intermittent and unreliable provider of service, and therefore status. Some could be accommodated in magnate entourages, but though men like Jarema Wiśniowiecki, the greatest landowner in the Commonwealth, who controlled 616 hearths in 1630, 7,603 in 1640 and 38,000 in 1645,[11] could raise substantial forces for short campaigns, he could not offer permanent service to large numbers: if Wiśniowiecki kept a permanent entourage of 1,500–2,000 men, and could perhaps raise up to 6,000 in an emergency,[12] these forces were largely composed of part-time or amateur soldiers, and he could not support them for long without passing them on to the state's budget. Those who did not find a position which conferred some status were faced with the serious prospect of social degradation: magnates were more interested in labour for their rapidly growing estates than they were in maintaining large retinues of servitors. The Cossack lifestyle had always proved attractive for these groups, but after the 1637–8 rising, opportunities declined, as the government drastically curbed Cossack autonomy, even for the registered elite. The 1638 *Sejm* abolished the previous privileges and rules governing the register, together with the position of hetman, replacing him with a commissioner who would have the responsibility of overseeing the force and ensuring order. All officers were to be appointed by the commissioner from among the local *szlachta*; Cossack settlements were to be strictly controlled and it was made a capital offence to travel to the *Sich* without official sanction.

The 1638 measures were a bold attempt to bring the registered Cossacks firmly within the structures of the Commonwealth.[13] To succeed, however, it would be necessary to secure their loyalty, not least through regular and efficient payment of their wages. This, however, proved beyond the government's powers. Without such loyalty, the situation was dangerous indeed. For *szlachta* determination to remain at peace, combined with the stricter control exerted by the new Cossack Commissioner, removed all hope of employment for the large body of town Cossacks, ex-Cossacks, petty nobles, and the remnants of the old boyar-servitor military class. Opportunities for these sectors of Ukrainian society had closed up rapidly: many had served in the Lisowczyk formations which had fought for the Habsburgs between 1618 and 1622, but their destructive talents, honed in the east, brought constant complaints, and the Habsburgs were less eager to recruit such units thereafter. The Lisowczyks – named after their original leader, Aleksander Lisowski († 1616) – were raised largely in the Commonwealth's southeastern territories and were composed of units of cossack cavalry; the attempt to portray them as patriotic Ukrainian freedom fighters officered by a few 'noble Poles' is fancifully anachronistic.[14] The reality was far more complex: there were no rigid divisions between 'noble Poles' and 'Ukrainian Cossacks' at this stage, although the social crisis of the old service class was certainly stimulating the formation of identities; it was only after 1648 that choices had to be made.[15]

The deceptive peace in the Ukraine was disrupted by Władysław himself, through his secret contacts with non-official Cossack leaders, including Khmelnytsky, himself of petty noble origins, with a view to raising a large force of Cossacks in connection with his plans for a Turkish war in the mid-1640s. When the 1646 *Sejm* rejected the idea, the Cossacks were left deeply resentful. Moreover, the Commonwealth had left itself fundamentally vulnerable, for the haste with which it had disarmed after 1635 had left it virtually unprotected. The quarter army, already a mere 4,300 strong, was reduced further to a real strength of only 3,780. With the reduction of the royal guard to 1,200 during the controversy over the Turkish war plans, this meant that at the start of the Cossack rising, the Commonwealth's forces had a paper strength of 11,800, of which no fewer than 6,000 were registered Cossacks. The rest represented an effective strength of no more than 5,300.[16] Although reinforcements could be raised reasonably quickly, the situation was dangerous, especially in the light of rumours of military preparations among wide sectors of Ukrainian society: one alarmist report claimed there were 60,000 concealed firearms among Wiśniowiecki's serfs alone.[17]

When the explosion came in 1648, the rebels attracted followers from all sectors of society. Their increasing identification with the cause of Ruthenian patriotism and the Orthodox Church against a largely Catholic, Polish-speaking elite provided a cultural and ideological basis for the revolt, which attracted support from peasants, Cossacks and all whose status was under threat. Of the 40,000 names entered in the Cossack register after the short-lived peace of Zborów in 1649, Lipiński estimates that 1,500 were nobles, with many more of doubtful status; one Polish source estimated that there were 7,000 nobles in the Cossack force which reached Zamość in 1648.[18] The Commonwealth was paying the price for failing to usher these groups unequivocally into the noble paradise.

The government forces were engulfed, as registered Cossacks deserted en masse. After Korsun, where Cossacks and Tatars took 8,000 prisoners, the Commonwealth was all but defenceless. Wiśniowiecki, at the head of 2–3,000 troops, blazed a bloody trail as he withdrew northwest from his estates, mounting savage reprisals en route which only inflamed the local population.[19] Facing disaster and deprived of royal leadership during the interregnum, the *sejmiki* assembled to improvise defence. Only one fifty-strong company of cossack cavalry from the quarter army remained intact; together with private forces, whose numbers were not great, this formed the sum total of the Commonwealth's defences.

The problems were exacerbated by poor leadership. The extensive powers enjoyed by the four hetmans ensured that the position was highly-desired and of enormous political significance. From the late sixteenth century, hetmans were regarded as subject to the normal Commonwealth principle of life-tenure, which meant that monarchs, unable to dismiss them, proved reluctant to appoint men who might use the office to further their own political agenda; thus hetmans were often appointed for political rather than military reasons. The problems were already clear under Sigismund, who was lucky to be served by three outstanding commanders in Żółkiewski, Chodkiewicz and Koniecpolski. In Lithuania, the domination of politics by magnate families who were bitter rivals meant that the situation was particularly difficult. Chodkiewicz was appointed grand hetman after Kircholm; on his death in 1621 Sigismund was reluctant to promote the first permanent Lithuanian field hetman (from 1615), the Calvinist Krzysztof Radziwiłł. To general consternation, he appointed the seventy-year-old ex-chancellor Lew Sapieha, who had no military experience. Sapieha kept the baton until his death in 1633, but his appointment inflamed Sapieha–Radziwiłł relations, while his inexperience seriously compromised the army's performance.

The dangers of this situation were vividly exposed during the Cossack Revolt. The 1648 campaign was marked by bitter arguments between the incompetent and inebriate grand hetman Mikołaj Potocki and the equally incompetent field hetman Marcin Kalinowski; their decision to divide the army helped produce the disasters at Zhovti Vody and Korsun. The situation after their capture was even worse. In the chaos of an interregnum, Grand Chancellor Jerzy Ossoliński was unwilling to give command to the blood-thirsty Jarema Wiśniowiecki. He therefore summoned a gathering of Mazovian nobles to Warsaw, where he forced through the appointment of three temporary commanders: Mikołaj Ostroróg and Dominik Zasławski, who had minimal military experience, and Aleksander Koniecpolski, who was nineteen. They were accompanied by a thirty-two man commission appointed by the *Sejm* to monitor their performance. It was no way to run a war.

The army scraped together by the *sejmiki* was far from impressive: although it was not, as is frequently asserted, composed of the noble levy, it was barely 14,000-strong, of which a mere 1,800 were infantry or dragoons; the *szlachta* were reluctant to mobilise peasant infantry to fight what they saw as a peasant revolt.[20] This ill-assorted force, in which the different pay-levels agreed by different *sejmiki* caused endless bickering in the ranks, was swelled to perhaps 30,000 by private contingents, including two infantry regiments; it marched into rebel territory where it fell apart at Pyliavtsi on 23 September when it heard that the Tatars were about to join the numerically-superior Cossacks. The result was a scandalous rout. Within two weeks Khmelnytsky was at the walls of Lwów, defended by a skeleton garrison; with Poland lying unprotected before him he allowed himself to be bought off, withdrawing to await the result of the November election which placed Władysław's brother John Casimir (1648–68) on the throne.

The government now recovered some of its nerve but no clear advantage was gained by either side. In 1651, John Casimir, a competent soldier, won a comprehensive victory at Berestechko, but was unable to follow it up; a year later, the professional core of the Polish army, rashly led by the incompetent Kalinowski into Moldavia, was ambushed and destroyed by Khmelnytsky at Batoh. Yet it was by no means clear what the rebels were fighting for, and the numerous divisions between registered and non-registered Cossacks, between Zaporozhians and other Cossacks, between the elite of Cossack officers, who were willing to negotiate, and were by no means averse to the principles of landownership and serfdom, and the mass of their followers, ensured that victory was an elusive prospect. Meanwhile, the failure to crush the revolt sparked off a political crisis in the Common-wealth. By 1654, the deep divisions between the king and malcontent mag-nates, especially the Calvinist Lithuanian field hetman Janusz Radziwiłł, had virtually paralysed political life. In 1652 the notorious principle of the *liberum veto* was first recognised by the *Sejm*; never before had the veto of one envoy been regarded as sufficient. It was a baleful precedent, for the breaking of a *Sejm* ensured the failure of all legislation, including the taxes necessary for the conduct of the war. Although the disaster of Batoh concentrated minds at the second *Sejm* of 1652, the *liberum veto* was cast again in 1654.[21]

Collapse

As the Commonwealth's crisis deepened, its neighbours watched. The failure to crush the Cossacks stimulated increasing interest on the part of Michael Romanov's son Alexis (1645–76). Khmelnytsky appealed several times to Alexis for help, whose initial response was cautious. He was wary of possible cooperation between Ukrainian and Don Cossacks, as had occurred during the Time of Troubles, especially since the 1648 Moscow rising, in which discontented elements among the *strel'tsy* had played a central role, brought uncomfortable reminders of 1606. In 1653, however, Alexis decided that the Commonwealth's plight was too good an opportunity to miss. At Pereiaslav in January 1654 Khmelnytsky signed an agreement with Muscovy the exact nature of which has long been a matter of bitter controversy between Ukrainian and Russian historians, but whose immediate effect was to establish an anti-Polish alliance.

Preparations were already well advanced. The immediate result of the 1648 Moscow rising was the calling of a *Zemskii Sobor*, in which discontented *pomeshchiki* were heavily represented. This produced the 1649 *Ulozhenie* which, by abolishing the time-limit on the recovery of fugitive peasants, met a central *pomeshchik* demand and completed the legal foundations of serfdom. Henceforth, peasants who fled from *pomest'ia* could be returned to their original masters without limit of time. In the long term, the *Ulozhenie* provided the basis for the new system of taxation and service which was to develop after 1650; in the short term, the ending of a long-held grievance was the climax of the reconstitution of the service state after 1613.

The army was ready. Although the new-style regiments which had fought the Smolensk War were disbanded after 1634, the government had been impressed with their performance. New-formation infantry, reiter and dragoon regiments were raised in December 1637 during preparations for war against the Tatars. By late 1638, 5,055 dragoons and 8,658 infantry had been recruited; although they were then disbanded, further new-formation units were raised in subsequent years and between 1642 and 1648, peasants on the southern frontier were drafted as part-time dragoons exempted from taxation, a model later followed in the northwest. In stark contrast to the Commonwealth, the government encouraged servitors who had dropped out of the service class during the Time of Troubles to enrol in the new-formation units, giving them an incentive to regain their status and avoid social degradation.[22] In 1651, 7 per cent of the 133,210 men in the Muscovite military establishment were in new-formation units; by 1663, they constituted 79 per cent of the army.[23] Efforts were made to ensure that the army was well supplied and equipped: new arms factories, the most famous of which was established by Dutch specialists at Tula in 1632, manufactured 10,172 matchlocks, 26,609 flintlocks and carbines between 1647 and 1653; a further 20,000 muskets were bought from the Dutch in 1653 alone; further supplies were purchased from the Swedes and other western sources. Meanwhile, the end of the Thirty Years War had created a buyer's market for mercenaries. Since the Muscovite government was known to pay high wages a steady stream of foreigners arrived to take up commissions and train the new-formation units.[24]

After the experiences of 1632–4, preparations were more carefully laid, with the heavy artillery sent down to Viazma ahead of the main force, and a different strategy was adopted: instead of one great strike against Smolensk, which had exposed Shein to envelopment and destruction, the campaign was launched on several fronts. A force of 7,000 guarded the southern frontier against Tatar attack, a real threat after the hostile Tatar reaction to Pereiaslav. The main army, 41,000 strong under Ia. K. Cherkasskii, headed for Smolensk, protected by V.B. Sheremetev's 15,000-strong force on its right, which was to advance along the Dvina through Połock and Witebsk. On the left, 15,000 men under Aleksei Trubetskoi secured the southern flank by occupying Roslavl, Mścisław and Borisov. Finally, in agreement with Khmelnytsky, a Zaporozhian force of 20,000 under Ivan Zolotarenko entered Lithuania from the south.[25] The advance guard left Moscow in late May, followed by Alexis at the head of his own regiment three days later, after a glittering parade through the city which made clear the nature of the war: this was no less than a holy crusade to bring the Commonwealth's Orthodox subjects under Muscovite rule.

The contrast with the Commonwealth was stark. By the time the June *Sejm* agreed a Lithuanian army of 18,000, a Polish army of 35,000 and the appointment as Grand Hetman of the sixty-six-year-old Stanisław Potocki, nearly 100,000 Muscovites and Cossacks were on the move. Lithuania was in no position to defend itself. Radziwiłł's army had a nominal strength of 11,261, but he may have had only 4,000 men, supplemented by 2,000 from the noble levy.[26] Although he inflicted a painful reverse on Cherkasskii at Shklov on 12 August, he was defeated with considerable losses at Shepeleviche twelve days later. Retiring to Minsk to lick his wounds, he abandoned Smolensk to its fate.

The Muscovites, in contrast to 1632, picked off a series of barely-defended towns and cities, systematically extending control over the Smolensk area and gradually isolating the main prize. Smolensk was in a terrible condition. Little more than cosmetic repairs had been made to the damage inflicted in 1633; the mortar used was so poor that it crumbled at the very sound of cannon-fire, while only ten of thirty-two towers were in a reasonable state.[27] Short of arms and ammunition, the garrison numbered barely 3,500, a substantial portion of which was drawn from the burgher militia. Shein's earthworks were still largely intact, and the aged Alexander Leslie took up position in trenches he had occupied twenty years earlier. Nevertheless, Smolensk defended itself tenaciously, but its position was hopeless after Shepeleviche: with the Polish army heading for the Ukraine, there was no hope of rescue this time, and it surrendered on 3 October. It was the crowning moment of a successful campaign which left the Muscovites secure on the Dvina and the Berezina, and controlling the upper reaches of the Dnieper from Dorohobuzh to Mohylew.

Although most of the Muscovite army returned home at the end of the campaigning season, and a devastating plague epidemic forced Alexis to hurry back to Moscow, the Commonwealth was in no position to recover its losses. A meeting between John Casimir, Radziwiłł and other dignitaries in Grodno in October produced more recriminations over the fall of Smolensk than positive suggestions for the future. Radziwiłł, with barely 6,000 men, began a campaign of harassment to exploit the reduced Muscovite military presence. Reinforced by his bitter rival, field hetman Wincenty Gosiewski, which brought the army up to 12,000, he shut 6,000 of Zolotarenko's Cossacks in Nowy Bychów in January, but an attempt to take Witebsk and an extended siege of Mohylew came to nothing in weather so cold that wine froze in the bottle.[28]

Another threat loomed to the north. It had not gone unremarked in Stockholm that although Alexis had offered Khmelnytsky protection, he had sent only 4,000 to support him, while the main army attacked Lithuania. Further Muscovite advances would threaten Polish Livonia, Courland and Prussia, which would have serious implications for Sweden. By December 1654 it was clear that neutrality was out of the question. Charles X Gustav who succeeded to the throne in July 1654 on the abdication of his cousin Christina, brought a new dynamism to the government. Commander-in-chief of the Swedish forces in Germany in the closing phases of the Thirty Years War, he was a soldier of great ability whose impatient temperament saw in the crisis in the east an opportunity for Sweden to complete unfinished business and escape from the domestic problems which had followed the end of the Thirty Years War. In a series of Council meetings in December 1654 it was agreed that serious military preparations be undertaken.

The engagement of expensive mercenaries meant that a rapid entry to the war was inevitable: Sweden could not afford to keep a large army together without exporting it to be supported at someone else's expense. The problem was where to send it. Although in the short term Muscovy represented the greatest direct threat to Swedish interests, to attack Muscovy would be risky: it might provoke a rapid Muscovite-Polish settlement and an anti-Swedish alliance, with the added danger of a stab in the back by Denmark. If Sweden were to fight Muscovy, it could only be in alliance with the Commonwealth. Yet there was little prospect of a rapid settlement of Swedish-Polish differences. Although many Poles had convinced themselves that Sweden would support the Commonwealth in return for Livonia and the final abandonment of John Casimir's claim to the Swedish throne, it was certain that the Swedes would demand more, including territorial concessions and financial compensation. John Casimir, however, refused to surrender his hereditary rights without territorial compensation from the Swedes or political concessions from the Commonwealth. This stalemate left Charles little room for manoeuvre. An attack on Muscovy without a Polish alliance would be dangerous; in the light of the increasingly pessimistic reports from the Commonwealth, neutrality might be even more so. In March 1655 he opted for an attack on the Commonwealth to preempt further Muscovite gains. That this policy ran the risk of provoking war against Muscovy was clearly understood, although Charles ordered that every precaution be taken to avoid it.

The Commonwealth's situation was hopeless. While the siege of Mohylew continued until April, Radziwiłł had at his disposal only a fraction of the 18,000-strong Lithuanian army agreed by the 1654 *Sejm*. Meanwhile the Polish hetmans Stanisław Potocki and Stanisław Lanckoroński were fully engaged in the Ukraine, where they won a partial victory at Okhmativ in January 1655 with an army of 22–23,000 supported by a Tatar force.[29] There was no hope of increasing the army substantially before the deluge. As the Swedish armies crossed the borders, the Polish army numbered a mere 18,300, since five regiments of foot, one of dragoons and several companies of Tatars had gone to reinforce the Lithuanians; barely 7,500 were infantry or dragoons.

The odds were overwhelming. Alexis reached Smolensk at the end of March to organise the campaign. Bad weather, the need to expel Lithuanian forces operating in areas taken the previous year and the fact that assembly-points for the campaign were now further west, meant that the start was delayed, and no muster-lists were drawn up for the main force to save time; it is therefore difficult to establish the size of the army. It is unlikely, however, that it was substantially different from the previous year.[30] Once again, it moved west in three main groups; progress on all fronts was inexorable. Although Radziwiłł and Gosiewski fought doggedly they were heavily outnumbered, having only 10–12,000 men at their disposal. The noble levy produced a mere 2,825 men, and the Lithuanians withdrew towards Wilno, which fell on 8 August; the next day, Alexis made a triumphal entry to the city which had so long challenged Moscow for leadership of the eastern Slavic world.[31]

The Swedes were already on the march. Although Charles's primary aim was to secure Royal Prussia, he decided against a risky landing on the Prussian coast, opting instead for a two-pronged attack from Livonia, led by Magnus de la Gardie, and from the new Swedish possession of Western Pomerania. De la Gardie seized Dünaburg on 12 July with a force of 7,200, in a preemptive strike to keep it out of Muscovite hands. The main blow came from the west. After a rapid march across Brandenburg territory, Arvid Wittenberg crossed the Polish frontier on 21 July with 13,650 men and seventy-two guns.[32] When Charles left Pomerania at the end of the month with a further 12,700 men, Wittenberg had won his first victory with hardly a shot fired. The Poles were in no state to resist. Most of the regular army – 9,385 men – was still in the Ukraine, where it was stretched to the limit to hold a new advance by Khmelnytsky, supported by a Muscovite force of 12,000 under F.V. Buturlin.[33] Although 8,735 regulars were to be deployed against the Swedes, there were problems assembling them in time. Wittenberg's path was barred by the 13,000-strong Wielkopolska levy, supplemented by 1,400 peasant infantry, hurriedly called up on the eve of the invasion. Thoroughly demoralised, the *szlachta* showed little inclination to fight the Swedish professionals. At Ujście on 25 July the palatinates of Poznań and Kalisz surrendered, accepting Charles's protection and promising him the loyalty and obedience due to the king of Poland. By the time Charles joined Wittenberg on 24 August there was a Swedish garrison in Poznań, and all Poland lay open before him.

For Janusz Radziwiłł, locked since 1648 in bitter conflict with John Casimir, Ujście provided the perfect justification for a move long under consideration. Furious at the lack of support Lithuania had received against Muscovy, Radziwiłł had long been in contact with Sweden. Presenting Ujście as the ultimate betrayal of Lithuania by the Poles, he signed the treaty of Kiejdany with Sweden on 17 August, which protested at the lack of help received from the Poles and accepted Swedish protection. Although the treaty respected the Union and it was explicitly stated that Lithuanians would not fight the Poles, the possibility of a new relationship of Lithuania with Sweden was implicit; on 20 October Radziwiłł signed a second treaty recognising Charles as Grand Duke of Lithuania and proclaiming the union of Lithuania with Sweden.

Ujście and Kiejdany provoked disbelief, disorientation, panic and collapse. As John Casimir tried to rally support, the Senate Council offered the throne to the Habsburgs, in the desperate hope of attracting support. With Khmelnytsky and Buturlin advancing on Lwów, the king abandoned Warsaw in August, heading west in a brave effort to confront the Swedes with Lanckoroński's regulars and units from the levy. After clashes with the Swedish advance guard, John Casimir retreated south towards Cracow.

Charles entered Warsaw on 8 September and turned south in pursuit. With the noble levy threatening to disperse, John Casimir stood at Żarnów on 16 September. A cavalry charge was repulsed by Swedish firepower, and the Poles withdrew after heavy rain interrupted hostilities. A desperate effort by Lanckoroński and Koniecpolski to relieve Cracow was repulsed near Wojnicz on 3 October; with John Casimier heading for exile in Silesia, Stefan Czarniecki surrendered Poland's ancient capital on 19 October. As de la Gardie occupied Courland and crossed the Niemen, heading for Royal Prussia, the regular army gave up the struggle. Koniecpolski surrendered near Cracow with 5,385 men on 26 October; two days later Lanckoroński and Potocki followed suit with 10,000 men. On 31 October, after a clash at Nowy Dwór near Warsaw, the Mazovian levy signed an act of subjugation to the Swedes. With Lublin already in the hands of Muscovite and Cossack forces, and only Lwów holding out, the collapse was all but complete.

Recovery

The Commonwealth's sudden implosion, which brought Swedish armies to the Hungarian border and Muscovite troops to the Vistula, reverberated far beyond northeastern Europe. For the Habsburgs, the Swedish victories represented a real threat to the fragile peace achieved in 1648 since the Habsburg patrimonial lands were intensely vulnerable to attack from Poland. France, ironically, feared the opposite: that the resumption of the Swedish–Polish wars would scupper Mazarin's hopes of involving Sweden directly in the Empire to prevent the resumption of the alliance between the Austrian and Spanish Habsburgs broken in 1648. For the Dutch, already involved in an unresolved conflict with England, a Swedish conquest of Royal Prussia and Danzig would complete Swedish domination of the Baltic coastline. For Denmark, Sweden's success in 1655 threatened complete eclipse and ultimate encirclement. To the south, concern at the shift in power from the Commonwealth to Muscovy had already provoked the Crimean Tatars to change sides, and the ambitious George II Rákóczi, prince of Transylvania, was in close contact with a number of Polish magnates, especially the ambitious Grand Marshal, Jerzy Sebastian Lubomirski.

The attitude of foreign powers would depend upon political and military developments within the Commonwealth. As yet, neither Muscovy nor Sweden had faced a real military test. The *szlachta* were rapidly to discover, however, that their much-vaunted liberties could not safely be entrusted to conquering foreign monarchs. Although the Swedes entered Poland under strict military discipline – Patrick Gordon claimed that on the month-long march from Stettin to Konin 470 men were executed, mostly for trivial offences – there was little hope that trouble could be avoided. Charles had an expensive army of foreign mercenaries to feed and pay, even without the Polish regulars who joined him in October hoping that he would pay their arrears; his own men were already complaining that plundering was due to the failure to pay their wages.[34] In order to meet these pressing needs, the Swedes sought substantial contributions: Cracow had to pay 300,000 złoties; 240,000 were demanded from Warsaw, a sum many times larger than its annual tax revenues.[35] In the countryside, Swedish promises to respect *szlachta* privileges were soon broken. Although efforts were made to limit looting to the lands of those still resisting, it proved impossible to police.

Perhaps most influential in turning opinion against the invaders was their behaviour towards the Church. For the veteran champions of the Protestant Cause, the wealthy Catholic Church was a natural target for looters. The tone was set by Charles himself. On arriving in Cracow, he demanded 300,000 złoties from the city's churches; when told this sum could not be raised, he ordered churches to be stripped of valuables to the required sum.[36] His soldiers quickly followed suit. In September in the Cracow suburb of Kazimierz, a group of drunken Swedes murdered subdeacon Jakub Mrowiński. The Swedes occupied the monastery; while in residence, they devastated the library, stealing books and ripping out the pages to light fires. On their departure two years later a hundred carts of horse manure had to be removed.[37] It was a story repeated in churches, monasteries and Jesuit colleges across Poland. Jan Branecki, suffragan bishop of Poznań, was murdered in his own house in August 1655; Wojciech Gowarczewski, archdeacon of Poznań, had his arm cut off before being flung in a river; one contemporary claimed that twenty Franciscans alone were killed by the Swedes.[38]

Discontent spread rapidly. Resistance began in Lithuania, where Radziwiłł's pro-Swedish policy failed to win wide support, and much of the Lithuanian army, under Paweł Sapieha, opposed him, forming a confederation at Wierzbołów in August. In the autumn, mixed bands of noble and peasant partisans began operating across Poland. In October, one such band surprised the small Swedish garrison at Kościan with a classic ruse, shooting dead Charles's brother-in-law Frederick of Hesse in an incident which gave the resistance movement all the publicity it could desire.[39] It was the start of a long campaign which was to cause the Swedes serious problems until Czarniecki's regulars entered Wielkopolska in May 1656. Similar activity in the uplands of Małopolska saw the capture of Nowy Sącz in December by a peasant force, while the defence of the Pauline monastery of Jasna Góra in Częstochowa against a half-hearted Swedish siege was later to become a symbol of heroic resistance to the heretical invader.

Against this background, John Casimir's political position improved dramatically. Now that Swedish duplicity had been exposed, his refusal to cooperate was retrospectively vindicated. On 20 November, a manifesto was issued in Oppeln, proclaiming his return, and calling for Poles of all estates to rise up against the invader; by 1 January 1656 John Casimir was back on Polish soil. Three days earlier, the Confederation of Tyszowce condemned the nation for having allowed the false promises of a deceiver to seduce it from its loyalty to its legally-elected monarch, and called it to arms in the name of the Commonwealth and Catholicism. The signatures of Potocki and Lanckoroński marked the return to loyalty of a substantial portion of the army. After the king's arrival in Łańcut in mid January, the Tyszowce confederates were joined by Lubomirski, who had long opposed John Casimir, and Stefan Czarniecki; by February, most of the regular army had abandoned Swedish service. The patriotic fervour reached a peak in April at Lwów, when John Casimir dedicated the Commonwealth to the Virgin Mary, whom he proclaimed Queen of Poland, and swore to lighten the burdens on the peasantry once peace was restored.

The return of the will to fight was of crucial importance, but the task that faced the Commonwealth was immense. The Ukraine and most of Lithuania were under Muscovite or Cossack control, while Charles had moved into Royal Prussia, which was defended by 3,600 regulars, 600 infantry raised by the Prussian estates, 3–4,000 from the noble levy, and mercenaries raised by the cities.[40] John Casimir had urged the Prussians to reach a settlement with elector Frederick William of Brandenburg, who, as Duke of Prussia, was a Polish vassal, and who had an army of 14,000. A treaty was signed between Frederick William and the Royal Prussian *szlachta* at Rinsk on 2/12 November, although Danzig, Elbing and Thorn refused to accept Brandenburg garrisons. Against the background of the surrender of Cracow and John Casimir's exile, Charles persuaded Thorn and Elbing to surrender, although Marienburg held out until March. Danzig, however, continued to resist behind its impressive fortifications. Frederick William, ignoring the promises he had made at Rinsk, hastily withdrew his garrisons and signed the treaty of Königsberg (7/17 January 1656), in which the link between Ducal Prussia and Poland was sundered, with Frederick William accepting Charles as his feudal superior.

The military situation was unpromising. Apart from Danzig and Lwów, every major city in the Commonwealth was in enemy hands. John Casimir's operational base was limited to a small area of southeast Poland. The Swedes controlled the Vistula, occupying Cracow, Warsaw and Thorn, enabling them to cut off Danzig's trading lifeblood. With so much of the Commonwealth under occupation, raising taxes on a scale sufficient to pay regular troops would be difficult indeed, and the army was woefully short of infantry, artillery and ammunition: in early 1656, it consisted of 7,200 regulars under Potocki and Lanckoroński, 2,500 Lithuanians under Paweł Sapieha, 3,500 foot scattered in garrisons, and Lubomirski's units, 13,500 strong.[41] Despite these problems the Commonwealth mounted a spirited campaign. By March, 2,597 regular cavalry had been raised, while a start had been made on the reconstruction of the foreign contingent, with the recruitment of three new infantry regiments, the reconstruction of one dragoon regiment and the raising of two new companies. Together with Koniecpolski's units and the noble levy of several southeastern palatinates, the army reached nearly 30,000 men.[42] Although command was nominally held by the hetmans, Czarniecki and Lubomirski largely took control of operations.

Despite the quality of the Swedish army, Charles was actually rather vulnerable. When he turned north at the end of October, he left Wittenberg in Cracow to control southern Poland with only 3,000 men, apart from those scattered in garrisons across a wide area, supplemented by 2,000 Poles of dubious loyalty. When they abandoned him, Wittenberg was left dangerously exposed. The substantial garrisons in the main cities may have been safe enough, given Polish shortcomings in infantry and artillery, but even here the Swedes were handicapped by the frequently poor fortifications, which meant that towns were easy to take but difficult to hold. The situation was worse in the countryside. In small towns and villages, Swedish garrisons huddled in crumbling medieval castles or did without serious protection altogether. Foragers were vulnerable to ambush by peasants or marauding cavalry. The experience of Hieronymus Christian von Holsten in Lanckorona with 150 men, including only 16 horse, was typical: the town had no defences, so the Swedes withdrew to the protection of the medieval castle at night, but were forced to call for reinforcements in the shape of 50 horse after their vulnerability was underlined when they came across several Swedes in a noble manor who had been murdered 'in dastardly fashion'.[43] As the bitterness provoked by Swedish looting and contributions grew, the war escalated into a savage cycle of slaughter and retribution.

The Poles were fighting an enemy who had learned much since the 1620s. The importance of cavalry was fully recognised: the Swedish invading force in July 1655, contained 14,000 horse (40 per cent) to 1,250 dragoons and 20,050 foot. Recruitment subsequently concentrated on cavalry, with the raising of thirty-eight cavalry regiments (13,888 men), six dragoon regiments (3,264) and only seven of foot (6,048), increasing cavalry units by 75 per cent compared to 35 per cent for infantry units.[44] With such an army Charles was able to fight a mobile war, though such a strategy was fraught with danger. In early 1656 Charles set off in pursuit of Czarniecki's force of 2,400 with about 11,000 horse, defeating him at Gołąb before advancing on Lwów.[45] He received a sharp lesson in the realities of eastern warfare. Zamość's modern fortifications enabled Jan Zamoyski politely to decline an invitation to surrender, and although Charles had been joined by 3,000 infantry and numerous guns, he had left part of his infantry in Lublin and a siege was out of the question. Harried constantly by Czarniecki and abandoned by Koniecpolski, Charles faced encirclement, as John Casimir's army swelled to 30,000 by March. With Sapieha's Lithuanians on the eastern bank of the San, and Czarniecki rapidly approaching from the south, Charles retreated north but was trapped in the confluence of the Vistula and the San and facing disaster with 5,500 men against over 20,000.

As the Poles waited for their artillery and infantry, Charles escaped with characteristic bravado before the trap snapped shut. Forcing his way over the San under cover of darkness on 5–6 April he broke through the Lithuanians, who had no infantry or guns. It cost him most of his artillery and much of his baggage, together with a relief force of some 4,500 cavalry and dragoons which had set off from Warsaw under Margrave Frederick of Baden, turning back when Frederick heard that Czarniecki and Lubomirski were approaching. The slower-moving Swedish force was caught at Warka on 7 April and destroyed. Frederick had performed his function, however: by drawing Czarniecki away from Sandomierz, he had prevented him reinforcing Sapieha's Lithuanians as had been intended, which would have seriously reduced Charles's chances of escape.[46]

The tide had turned with a vengeance. It was clear that the forces at Sweden's disposal were insufficient to force a quick end to the war. The dash to the south had meant that Charles had to abandon any hopes of a quick capture of Danzig, while the Poles had cleared the Vistula between Cracow and Warsaw. John Casimir arrived at the capital in June with 28,500 regulars and 18–20,000 from the noble levy. On 29 June a force of peasant infantry stormed the city. In these circumstances, Charles could only turn to diplomacy. At Marienburg on 25 June 1656, Frederick William signed a military alliance with Sweden, in return for the grant of hereditary sovereignty over Wielkopolska, although he was to remain a Swedish vassal in Ducal Prussia.

The result was the battle of Warsaw (28–30 July 1656), in which Charles demonstrated just how much the Swedes had learned from the Poles: while the allied infantry played its part, it was the cavalry on which victory depended. It was the Poles who, despite the composition of their army, tried to fight a western-style battle: the forces at John Casimir's disposal consisted of 24–25,000 regulars, 2,000 Tatars and 10–13,000 from the noble levy – about 40,000 men, of which a mere 4,500 were infantry.[47] After a disagreement with Czarniecki, who argued that the Poles should avoid open battle in the light of Swedish firepower, John Casimir ferried his army across the Vistula, intending to march up the right bank to attack the Swedish camp; Czarniecki was sent with 2,000 horse up the left bank to prevent a Swedish attack on that side of the river.

Charles now seized the initiative. The allied army was a mere 18,000 strong, but its composition is striking: it contained sixty cavalry squadrons (12,500 men) and a mere fifteen infantry brigades (5,500 men), only 1,000 more than the Poles.[48] With this mobile force, Charles marched down the right bank of the Vistula on 28 July to mount a frontal assault on the Poles, most of whose infantry was dug in across a narrow corridor of open land beside the river. The next day, unable to dislodge them, Charles carried out a bold and highly risky manoeuvre which was only possible with a largely cavalry army. Wheeling left through the Białołęcki forest, with his infantry shielded by the cavalry, he moved his entire force onto the narrow plain which opened up on the Polish right. By the time the Poles launched Połubiński's hussars at the allies they had consolidated their position.

The charge was launched not against the allied infantry in the centre, but against the reiter units that flanked it. Although they suffered from infantry flanking fire, the hussars smashed into the reiters, with the brunt of the impact absorbed by the Uppland and Småland regiments. The hussars performed their primary task, breaking through the first line and penetrating into the second, where they were brought to a halt and forced back. The failure of the attack was due to the deployment of the allied cavalry in three lines, which gave the necessary depth to the defence, and by their numbers. For the Poles, the main problem was that the initial attack was not followed up; John Casimir simply had too few hussars, the most expensive formation in the army. A maximum of 800 took part in Połubiński's charge; it was not enough, and the *pancerna* cavalry in reserve did not press home the attack.[49] The allies held their ground; deciding that the battle was lost, John Casimir began to withdraw across the single bridge over the Vistula. The next day the allies rolled forward across the open plain; as the Polish-Lithuanian cavalry escaped north and south along the Vistula, John Casimir abandoned his capital for the second time in twelve months. The Poles had been beaten at their own game; the ghost of Kircholm had finally been laid to rest.

Warsaw was a famous victory, but the Swedes derived little benefit. The allies set off in pursuit, occupying Radom on 10 August, but Frederick William had no intention of supporting further Swedish gains. With Brandenburg garrisons having replaced the Swedes in Wielkopolska, the elector refused further military cooperation. Since the Brandenburg contingent of 8,500 had constituted nearly half the allied army at Warsaw, Charles's own forces were inadequate for any sustained campaign. Withdrawing his isolated garrisons from the Sandomierz palatinate, he strengthened the Cracow garrison and withdrew north to Royal Prussia, where Danzig was still resisting.

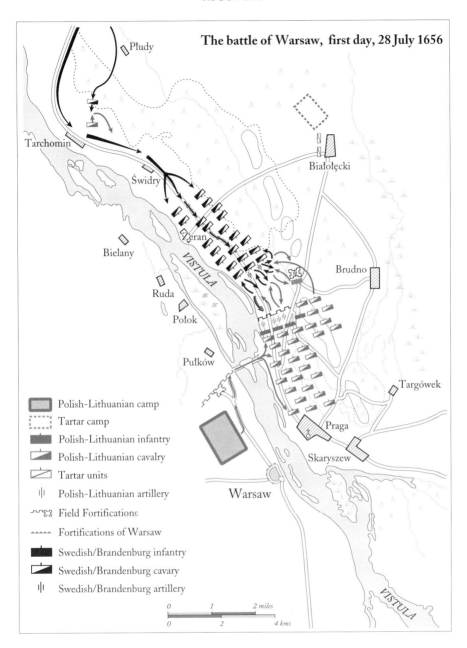

The battle of Warsaw, first day, 28 July 1656

Płudy

Tarchomin

Świdry

Białołęcki

Bielany

Żeran

Brudno

Ruda

Połok

Pułków

Targówek

Polish-Lithuanian camp
Tartar camp
Polish-Lithuanian infantry
Polish-Lithuanian cavalry
Tartar units
Polish-Lithuanian artillery
Field Fortifications
Fortifications of Warsaw
Swedish/Brandenburg infantry
Swedish/Brandenburg cavary
Swedish/Brandenburg artillery

Praga

Skaryszew

Warsaw

VISTULA

VISTULA

0   1   2 miles
0   2   4 kms

There was little hope that it would fall, or that the Swedes would be able to bring the war to a rapid and successful conclusion as the international situation shifted against them. In late July thirty Dutch warships arrived off Danzig, supported by a small Danish fleet, to break the Swedish blockade

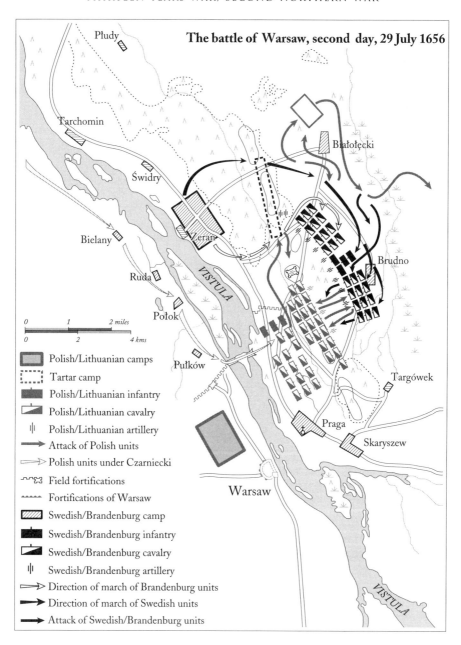

The battle of Warsaw, second day, 29 July 1656

Płudy

Tarchomin

Białołęcki

Świdry

Bielany

Żerań

Brudno

Ruda

Połok

Targówek

Pułków

0   1   2 miles
0   2   4 kms

Polish/Lithuanian camps
Tartar camp
Polish/Lithuanian infantry
Polish/Lithuanian cavalry
Polish/Lithuanian artillery
Attack of Polish units
Polish units under Czarniecki
Field fortifications
Fortifications of Warsaw
Swedish/Brandenburg camp
Swedish/Brandenburg infantry
Swedish/Brandenburg cavalry
Swedish/Brandenburg artillery
Direction of march of Brandenburg units
Direction of march of Swedish units
Attack of Swedish/Brandenburg units

Praga

Skaryszew

Warsaw

VISTULA

VISTULA

and ensure free trade; the Dutch also brought 1,300 men to strengthen the garrison.[50] More worryingly, Sweden was now fighting a war on two fronts. In May Alexis declared war; in November he signed an alliance with the Commonwealth near Wilno which promised him the Polish throne after

176

John Casimir's death. With de la Gardie's 7,000-strong army in Prussia, the Baltic provinces were dangerously exposed. The Livonian field army comprised a mere 2,200 men and 400 dragoons, with 6,933 men spread in garrisons round Livonia, Estonia and Ingria. Estonia was protected by the 142-strong Reval garrison.[51] This was wholly insufficient to contain the three-pronged Muscovite assault launched in July and August. The 35,000-strong main army took Dünaburg in July and Kokenhausen in August, before besieging Riga; Dorpat was invested by 15,000 men and smaller forces raided Estonia, Ingria and Kexholm.

Unfortunately for Alexis, Riga's fortifications were more sophisticated than anything his army had yet faced, while attempts to utilise cossack naval skills to blockade the city from the sea were unsuccessful. His campaign began too late to take the city before the onset of winter; despite heavy bombardment from the Muscovite guns, the garrison of 5,335 effectives held out until the Muscovite withdrawal in October.[52] Alexis had more success elsewhere: the Dorpat fortifications had suffered from such neglect that in 1653 it was no longer possible to walk right round the medieval walls, while its garrison was only 520 strong.[53] By 22 October, with its effective strength reduced to 150 surrender was inevitable. Ninety-eight years after they had first captured Dorpat, the Muscovites again had a foothold in Livonia.

Luckily for Sweden, the 1656 campaign was the last major effort made by the Muscovites, themselves suffering from the strain of mounting three major campaigns in as many years. So long as they were only able to operate on a large scale during the campaigning season, whose start was always delayed by the problems of assembling the army, they were unlikely to threaten either Riga or Reval. Having signed a truce with the Commonwealth, and with the Cossacks chafing at Muscovy's authoritarian rule, Alexis was content to observe events, and 1657 saw no repeat of the attack on Riga; although substantial Muscovite forces were sent into Livonia, the Swedes defeated an 8,000-strong army at Walk on 18 June, wounding and capturing its commander, M.V. Sheremetev.[54] It was Gosiewski's Lithuanians who attacked Pernau and blockaded Riga in the autumn of 1657. In early 1658, the Swedes and Muscovites agreed an uneasy truce.

Charles was lucky that the Muscovites did not mount a more determined challenge, for elsewhere the war was going badly. Polish-Lithuanian losses at Warsaw were insignificant, and John Casimir swiftly regrouped at Lublin.[55] As Charles retreated northwards to Royal Prussia in August, Gosiewski led a Lithuanian force of 12–13,000 cavalry, including a substantial force of Crimean Tatars, to punish Frederick William for his treachery.[56] On 8 October 1656, at Prostken in Ducal Prussia, Gosiewski destroyed a smaller Swedish-Brandenburg force by luring it out from a prepared defensive position through a feigned retreat. The allies were overrun, sustaining perhaps up to 5,000 casualties, half their army and substantially more than the Poles had lost at Warsaw.[57] Although Gosiewski, weakened by the departure of the Tatars, was defeated by 9,000 Swedes at Philipowo on 22 October and withdrew north into Lithuania, he had already spread devastation, burning thirteen towns and 250 villages. Although exaggerated figures are often given for the numbers killed and taken as captives to the Crimea, the impact of the campaign was substantial, with folk-memories of the Tatar attack lasting into the twentieth century.[58] Meanwhile, John Casimir advanced into Wielkopolska, storming Łęczyca on 4 October. Reinforced by 2,000 men under Jakub Wejher, he marched into Royal Prussia, taking Bromberg and Konitz and heading for Danzig, where he was rapturously received on 15 November, and where he stayed until late February. After taking Kalisz, Polish units raided Brandenburg itself, before signing a truce in December. The initiative lay firmly with the Poles.

Charles, encamped near Elbing, was in a difficult situation. Although by the summer of 1656 Sweden had raised 26,400 new recruits, the net increase was only 14,975, since losses totalled 11,425 in the same period.[59] Since the defection of most of the Poles in the spring, he had been unable to raise more than a handful of recruits in the Commonwealth, and his forces were thinly spread, especially after the Muscovite attack on Livonia. Although Polish shortages in infantry and artillery made the larger Swedish garrisons in Cracow and Prussia relatively safe, military control was impossible; Charles could only break the deadlock by diplomatic means. In the treaty of Labiau (20 November 1656), he sought to persuade Frederick William to resume a more active role by recognising his sovereignty over Ducal Prussia. Shortly afterwards, he secured a new ally, signing the treaty of Radnot (6 December) with Transylvania, promising to recognise Rákóczi as king of Poland and grand duke of Lithuania, and to grant him most of Małopolska in return for military assistance. Rákóczi invaded in January with an army of 25,000, forcing Lubomirski to break the siege of Cracow. Charles moved south to meet his new ally, supported by four Brandenburg regiments. There followed an intensely mobile campaign, as Charles chased Czarniecki, Lubomirski and Sapieha round Poland, without being able to force a general engagement, although he succeeded in taking Brest Litovsk in May, despite its modern fortifications and a garrison of 2,000; on 17 June, Warsaw surrendered to Rákóczi, supported by a Swedish force under Stenbock.

The treaties of Radnot, Marienburg and Labiau taken together envisaged a partition of the Commonwealth between Sweden, Brandenburg, Transylvania and the Zaporozhians. The plan had little chance of success, however: having gained Swedish recognition for his sovereignty in Ducal Prussia, Frederick William had no interest in furthering the extension of Swedish power into Royal Prussia, while the Transylvanian army, although numerous, was not of high quality. Moreover, Charles was not the only one who could play the diplomatic game: since 1655, John Casimir had been urgently seeking foreign allies, not least to provide the infantry he so desperately needed. By the treaty of Vienna (1 December 1656) Ferdinand III agreed to support the Commonwealth with 4,000 men. The Poles, however, were not satisfied with the terms, urging Ferdinand to make a greater commitment; his death in April 1657, three days after ratifying the treaty was a great blow, since his successor, Leopold, faced the prospect of a difficult Imperial election, the first since Westphalia. With France keen to cause trouble and Brandenburg in alliance with Sweden, Leopold was understandably cautious. Nevertheless, the involvement of Rákóczi, whose ambitious aims in both Poland and Hungary represented a threat to the Habsburg patrimonial lands, helped persuade Leopold to risk intervention. By the second treaty of Vienna (27 May 1657) he promised to provide 12,000 men, although the cost was to be borne by the Poles, while the Austrians were to garrison Cracow and Poznań as security. As Austrian troops entered Poland in June, Charles faced a more direct and dangerous challenge. Frederik III was keen for revenge after Brömsebro; in June, as soon as he received news of the Vienna treaty, he declared war on Sweden, signing an alliance with the Commonwealth in July. Already a Danish army from Holstein had taken most of Bremen; in mid-July, Danish forces invaded Jämtland and Västergötland.

Charles immediately abandoned Rákóczi to his fate. Leaving a small force of 8,600 men in Prussia to defend it as best they could, Charles marched rapidly across Pomerania and Mecklenburg with an army of only 12,750 men, including 9,950 horse, and only 2,800 foot, to attack Denmark through Holstein and Jutland.[60] Within a month, the hapless Rákóczi was pursued across Poland into the Ukraine, surrounded and forced to capitulate; the rest of the Transylvanian army was annihilated by the Tatars. With Cracow surrendering to a combined Polish and Austrian force in August, and Frederick William, having obtained all he wanted from Sweden, taking the opportunity of Charles's absence to change sides at the treaties of Wehlau (19 September) and Bromberg (6 November) in return for Polish recognition of his sovereignty in Ducal Prussia, the Swedish position in the Commonwealth had all but collapsed.

In Denmark, Charles found a war more to his taste. He despatched Karl Gustav Wrangel to clear the Danes out of Bremen, before swinging north into Jutland. He rapidly swept the defenders out of his path, but the key to a rapid victory was occupation of the island of Fyn, which would provide a launch-pad for an attack on Zealand and Copenhagen. This would require possession of the powerful new Danish fortress at Fredriksodde and a degree of naval control. Charles, establishing himself at Wismar, ordered the forty-strong Swedish fleet out in September. It fought an inconclusive battle off Møn, after which it anchored off Wismar. An attempted Danish blockade had to be abandoned due to bad weather, and the Danish fleet was forced back to Copenhagen in early December. With the storming of Fredriksodde in November, the way was open for an invasion of Fyn, but it seemed too late in the year.

As the Danes settled down for the winter, however, Charles sprang to life. On the night of 9 February 1658, having waited impatiently for the right conditions, he led his army across the frozen waters of the Little Belt at its narrowest point. Sweeping aside a small, extremely startled Danish force, the Swedes rapidly secured Fyn, then waited anxiously while they reconnoitred the state of the Great Belt, the much broader stretch of water between Fyn and Zealand. Despite the doubts of Wrangel, who warned that several men had drowned when the ice cracked under a reconnaissance party, Charles accepted Erik Dahlberg's favourable report of the condition of the ice on the less direct route which used the islands of Langeland, Lolland and Falster as stepping-stones to Zealand.[61] Although only 5,000 men came over the Belts, the unexpected appearance of Swedish units in the Copenhagen suburbs on 25 February was too much for Frederik. Caught completely unawares, he hurriedly signed the humiliating peace of Roskilde (8 March), which stripped Denmark of Scania, Bohuslän, Blekinge, Bornholm and Trondheim, breaking the Danish grip on the Sound and driving a wedge of Swedish territory through the middle of Norway.

The lightning victory stunned Europe, as Charles made sure that his strategic coup was widely publicised.[62] Yet his brilliant success did little to improve Sweden's position, despite serious strains within the anti-Swedish alliance. Both Austria and Brandenburg proved reluctant to support John Casimir's desire for an attack on Swedish Pomerania, which ran the risk of reigniting the Thirty Years War in the run-up to the Imperial election in July, while Alexis's increasing impatience over the Commonwealth's failure to confirm him as John Casimir's successor threatened a renewal of war, especially since elements in the Cossack leadership under Ivan Vykhovsky were moving closer to the Commonwealth following Khmelnytsky's death in 1657. It was by no means clear, however, what Charles should do next. While he maintained that Royal Prussia remained his chief goal, his military position in the Commonwealth was precarious following Brandenburg's defection, Rákóczi's defeat and the fall of Cracow. Although Elbing and Marienburg were still in Swedish hands, a Polish and Austrian force began the siege of Thorn in July. There was little hope of international support for a new attack on Prussia. France was urging Sweden to settle, to release Swedish forces for a possible attack on Austria through the patrimonial lands, while the Dutch were certain to oppose any Swedish move against Prussia, especially since Roskilde sought to ban foreign fleets from the Baltic.

Charles had to decide swiftly. Under the terms of Roskilde, the Danes were to supply him with 2,000 men, and maintain the Swedish army until it withdrew in May. Charles knew that it was impossible for him to support his army in Sweden for long, and unthinkable to disband it when the Poles were thirsting for revenge, prepared to support an aggressive war beyond the Commonwealth's borders for the first time since 1635. Yet where could he go? Experience suggested that sustaining a large field army in Livonia and Estonia would be difficult, while, given the increasing tension between Muscovy and the Commonwealth, the Muscovites were unlikely to mount a substantial attack in the short term. If a return to Prussia was attractive, not least because the temptation to punish Frederick William was strong, to effect a landing would be far more difficult than in 1626, with the Poles prepared for it and the Dutch hostile, while the move overland through the Empire when both Austria and Brandenburg were allied against him, would be fraught with danger, especially since Mazarin stressed that France would offer no military aid.[63]

Charles's resolution of this dilemma shocked Europe. On 16 August, he embarked from Kiel with 10,000 men. Instead of heading for Prussia, as everyone expected, he disembarked a day later at Korsør in Zealand; within a week he was back at the walls of Copenhagen. Charles had decided to attack Denmark again, seeking to establish Swedish domination in Scandinavia once and for all. While the move was certainly surprising – and, for Brandenburg and the Commonwealth, most welcome – there were, as far as Charles was concerned, good reasons for it. As soon as Roskilde was signed, he expressed regret that he had been forced to abandon such a favourable position, adding that if Austria and Poland had shown themselves willing to treat seriously for peace he would never have settled. The prospect of resuming the war in Poland was unattractive; Charles was well aware that the conditions of war in the Commonwealth made it deeply unpopular with his men.[64] An attack on the Habsburgs, however, would violate Westphalia, of which Sweden was a guarantor, and provoke widespread opposition from the German princes. Other plans, including partitioning Poland with Austria, Brandenburg, Muscovy and the Cossacks, were mere fantasy.[65] Meanwhile, relations with Denmark remained extremely tense. The Danes haggled over the payment of Swedish troops; 1,064 of the promised 2,000 Danish reinforcements deserted rather than serve the Swedes, and the Danes, with Dutch encouragement, showed no interest in enforcing the clause of Roskilde excluding foreign fleets from the Baltic. In July, Charles took the easy option. The Polish quagmire was not enticing; he preferred a war he might win.

This time, however, Sweden was the aggressor and the Dutch were therefore obliged to intervene by the terms of their 1649 treaty with Denmark. In November, a Dutch fleet of forty-five ships and 1,838 guns brushed aside a Swedish attempt to block its entry to the Baltic and broke the blockade of Copenhagen from the sea, despite the fact that, after the fall of Kronborg in September, the Swedes controlled both sides of the Sound.[66] Meanwhile, 10,600 Austrians under Montecuccoli, 14,500 Brandenburgers under Frederick William, and 4,500 Poles under Czarniecki reached Hamburg before heading through Schleswig into Jutland. The allies took the island of Als and the fortress of Kolding; by January, the Swedes had abandoned Fredriksodde, concentrating on the siege of Copenhagen, where a Danish garrison of 10,650, including 2,000 Dutch foot, put up dogged resistance. The Swedes found it hard to bring their heavy artillery to bear on the walls of the city, which were protected by natural and man-made water defences and elaborate modern fortifications. An attempt to storm the city over the ice on the night of 21–22 February by 6,250 infantry, 2,800 horse and 1,800 sappers, was beaten back despite meticulous planning, which included the dressing of sappers in white to camouflage them against the snow.[67]

Charles had won his first Danish war with a dramatic coup; once his attempt to achieve the same result with the same strategy had failed, he lacked the means to force a conclusion against a coalition of powers. Trapped in the Danish islands by Dutch and Danish naval supremacy, it was difficult to feed and supply his army. Prospects seemed bleak, especially after France joined England and the Dutch in the first Concert of the Hague to urge peace with Denmark on the basis of Roskilde. Yet the coalition of Sweden's enemies was fragile from the outset. Public opinion in Poland swung strongly against Austria, as the Habsburg army demanded ever-larger sums of money to support it, while pursuing the war in a distinctly half-hearted manner. Since much of the Polish army had been sent into the Ukraine, it was not until December 1658 that Thorn fell, and the Swedes held out in Elbing and Marienburg throughout 1659. The Austrians did prove more enthusiastic about operations in Pomerania, where an army of 17,000 joined 13,000 Brandenburgers to besiege Stettin, and in Jutland, but Philip of Sulzbach put up a dogged defence of Fyn and Langeland in the autumn, although the defeat of a largely-cavalry Swedish army at Nyborg on 24 November forced their evacuation.[68] With the allies preparing an invasion of Zealand and Mitau falling to Połubiński in January 1660, the Swedes were in retreat on all fronts.

Charles returned home for a meeting of the *Riksdag*. His unexpected death on 23 February could not have come at a better time for Sweden. Peace talks under French mediation continued throughout 1659, as war-weariness affected all the combatants. Peace was signed at Oliva on 3 May between Sweden, the Commonwealth, Austria and Brandenburg, from which Sweden gained nothing it had not held *de facto* in 1655. Its possession of Livonia was finally recognised. John Casimir resigned his claim to the Swedish throne, though he was allowed to keep the title of hereditary king of Sweden for life. Sweden's possessions in the Empire were left undisturbed. The most significant clause was the confirmation of the treaties of Wehlau-Bromberg, by which Hohenzollern sovereignty over Ducal Prussia was confirmed. Oliva was followed by a separate treaty between Sweden and Denmark, signed at Copenhagen on 6 June, which stripped Sweden of Bornholm and Trondheim, but otherwise left its 1658 gains intact. The final settlement came in 1661 at Kardis between Muscovy and Sweden, in which Sweden benefited from Muscovy's continuing engagement with the Commonwealth: the areas occupied by Muscovite troops, including Dorpat, were handed back to Sweden, and there was a return to the 1656 status quo. It was a long way from the glory days of 1655, but taken together, the treaties of 1660–1 represented a lucky escape for Sweden.

The end of the Thirteen Years War

The Commonwealth's long agony was not yet over, however, as the Polish–Muscovite war resumed in 1658. With Sapieha moving towards Nowogródek and Gosiewski stationed near Wilno, Alexis sent an army of 30,000 into Lithuania. In October at Werki the Muscovites launched a surprise attack on Gosiewski, scattering his force and taking Gosiewski prisoner. The situation, however, was much less favourable for Alexis than in 1654–5. The most serious problem was the gradual disintegration of the Muscovite–Cossack alliance. In part this was due to the increasingly authoritarian air with which Moscow conducted its relations with what it now regarded as its subjects, but it was also connected with the changes in the international situation. The Cossacks were angered not least by the 1656 Wilno treaty, which was agreed without consultation. Khmelnytsky had long seen the Swedes as potential allies, and his decision to send Cossack troops to support Rákóczi's invasion in 1657 was a clear indication that he might abandon the Muscovite alliance and attempt to establish a genuinely independent Cossack state.

The collapse of the Swedish-led coalition, however, and Khmelnytsky's unexpected death in August 1657 saw the emergence of divisions long latent within Cossack ranks. The youth and unassertive character of his sixteen-year-old son Iurii rendered him unfit for power as yet, so Ivan Vyhovsky, one of Khmelnytsky's closest associates, was elected hetman until Iurii should come of age. Vyhovsky was of noble origin and had originally fought against the rebels, only changing sides after his capture in 1649. He represented an anti-Muscovite group which wished to settle with the Commonwealth: for many Cossack leaders, brought up in the Commonwealth's egalitarian ethos, it was hard to accept the subordinate position of their Muscovite counterparts. After tortuous negotiations, an agreement between the Commonwealth and the Cossack leadership was signed at Hadiach in September 1658, which envisaged the establishment of a Grand Duchy of Ruthenia from the palatinates of Kiev, Bratslav and Chernihiv, thus creating a tripartite confederation. The Cossack hetman was to be subject to the king alone, Orthodox bishops were to be admitted to the Senate, and the Uniate church was to be abolished. The Cossack host was fixed at a peacetime strength of 30,000. With the majority of the Cossack rank-and-file regarding any agreement with the Commonwealth as anathema, however, and the *szlachta* still deeply suspicious of the Cossacks, Hadiach's prospects were not good. It was rejected by the 1659 *Sejm*, and never came into effect; its failure did not, however, heal the rifts within Cossackdom. The Zaporozhians were not powerful enough to sustain an autonomous Cossack state, and as different parties looked to the Commonwealth and Muscovy for support, rivalry rapidly turned into civil war. Hadiach opened the period of Ukrainian history known as *Ruina*.

These shifts in Cossack politics fundamentally affected the course of the Polish–Muscovite war. The help given to Muscovite armies by Cossack forces in the campaigns of 1654–5 had been considerable; after 1660 Muscovy faced a resurgent Commonwealth at last able to concentrate on the eastern front. The deteriorating Cossack situation persuaded Alexis to send a large army under Aleksei Trubetskoi into the Ukraine. Tempted into besieging a small Cossack garrison at Konotop, Trubetskoi fell into a trap. Attacked on 8 July 1659 by a small Cossack force, he was drawn into pursuit, but he stumbled across Vyhovsky's Cossack and Tatar army and was destroyed; as Cossack firepower cut down the Muscovite cavalry, five thousand Muscovites were captured, and many were killed. Although Vyhovsky was soon forced to stand down in favour of Iurii Khmelnytsky, Konotop was a great blow to Alexis. The Muscovites sought to exploit growing unease about Vyhovsky's pro-Commonwealth policy, but a new agreement at Pereiaslav gave far more control to Muscovite officials. Once the significance of the changes was recognised, the pro-Commonwealth group of Cossacks was only strengthened.

The Muscovite position in Lithuania was, if anything, more precarious than in the Ukraine, where at least Muscovy still enjoyed support from a substantial group among the Cossacks, led by Ivan Briukhovetsky, the power behind the ineffectual Iurii Khmelnytsky. Unable to maintain a large force permanently in Lithuania, Muscovy failed to generate support for its rule. The question of attitudes to the Muscovite invasion on the part of the local population has long been controversial. Whatever the competing claims of historians from the modern nations of Russia, Poland, Lithuania, Belarus and Ukraine, it is clear that the situation from the outset was more complex than is often allowed, and that the simple categories of 'nobles', 'peasants' 'Catholics' or 'Orthodox' do not explain the reaction of Lithuanians to the Muscovite invasion. Soviet historians depicted the war as one of 'national liberation for reunification with Russia', and there was indeed some initial support for the Muscovite invaders. Although many nobles fled westwards, the invaders promised to respect local privileges, and many others, keen to stay on their estates, swore loyalty to Alexis. Some entered his service with enthusiasm, like the Orthodox noblemen Konstanty Pokłoński, who raised a regiment of 6,000 Cossacks from the petty nobility, boyars and peasants, for which he was handsomely rewarded.

Muscovite behaviour quickly undermined this support, however. The fate of towns which fell into Muscovite hands was often cruel. Mścisław, where many nobles had gathered with their families because of its relatively powerful fortifications, resisted for several days before being overrun in July 1654; describing the massacre which followed its fall, even Muscovite sources claimed that 10–15,000 people died.[69] The capture of Wilno in August was followed by a similar massacre, as the magnificent stone city burned for seventeen days; as many as 8,000 people may have perished.[70] While contemporary reports of killings and atrocities are certainly exaggerated, Muscovite rule was undoubtedly harsh. Alexis might have sworn to uphold the liberties of all social groups, but his armies paid scant attention. The liberties of non-Orthodox peoples were ignored. Particular hostility was directed towards Uniates and Jews, but Catholics also came under sustained attack. Large numbers of Jews – many of whom fought against the Muscovite armies – were massacred or forcibly baptised.[71] Catholic churches and monasteries were particular targets, but Orthodox churches also suffered, since many priests opposed the supremacy of the Patriarch of Moscow, which the Lithuanian Orthodox Church had long rejected. Outside the cities, the invading forces cut a swathe of destruction, with constant reports of burnings, murders and rape. Thousands of people of all classes were forcibly deported to Muscovy. Already in 1655, Patriarch Nikon fancifully claimed to have 300,000 Belorusians on his estates; if some were undoubtedly refugees from the fighting rather than forced migrants, the glut of captives on the market drove down the price of slaves.[72]

Such behaviour was counterproductive. Despite generous grants of land, Pokłoński had abandoned Muscovite service by early 1655, handing over

Mohylew to Radziwiłł, and joining the fight against Alexis. For nobles, even if they were Orthodox, experience of the extensive privileges they enjoyed in the Commonwealth made the demands of loyalty to the tsar particularly irksome: Pokłoński, while still in Muscovite service, stated that he would address the tsar as his subject (*poddany*) and not his slave (*kholop*).[73] It was not just nobles who objected. Peasants, burghers and petty nobles took to the forests and attacked Muscovite forces seeking supplies or raising taxes. In the autumn of 1655, a group of 3,000 peasants and nobles was operating in the Oszmiana region; round Mścisław, peasant bands attacked nobles who had entered Muscovite service.[74] The occupying forces took savage revenge; by 1658, increasing *szlachta* involvement ensured that partisan bands were more dangerous than ever.

As soon as Oliva was signed, John Casimir launched twin offensives. Sapieha, with 9,000 Lithuanians and Czarniecki, with 4,000 Poles, mostly cavalry and dragoons, drove into the heart of Lithuania, where, on 27 June, they destroyed a larger Muscovite force under Khovanskii at Połonka. The battle was another demonstration of the virtues of the Polish style of fighting: Polish dragoons hussars and *pancerna* cavalry, supported by two field guns, drove the Muscovite foot out of prepared positions on an embankment, while the cavalry on the right attacked in the Muscovite rear. The hussars drove off the Muscovite horse, leaving Khovanskii's infantry completely exposed. Surrounded by the Polish infantry and artillery in a small wood, they were butchered; one eyewitness remarked how 'hard it was to look upon so much human blood as there was in that throng, the soldiers being packed close together and so to perish corpse upon corpse; the blood poured down from there in streams . . . just like water after a heavy rain.'[75] Khovanskii escaped, but much of his army perished or was captured.[76]

Sapieha and Czarniecki pushed on into the heart of Lithuania, taking a string of lesser fortresses, although an attempt to recapture Mohylew failed. The main effort was, however, directed towards the Ukraine, where Potocki and Lubomirski with 28,800 men, including 9,800 foot and 4,600 dragoons, supported by 15,000 Tatars, caught V.B. Sheremetev in open country near Lubar in September with an army of 33–34,000, of which 19,200 were regulars, including 6,100 foreign-style cavalry, 3,000 foreign-style infantry and 4,000 dragoons, supported by 20,000 Cossacks. Aware that Iurii Khmelnytsky was approaching from Kiev with 40,000 men and nearly 30 guns, Sheremetev formed a tabor; after twice moving position in his mobile fortress, pursued by the watchful Polish army, he dug in near Chudnovo. In a daring raid, Lubomirski took half the Polish army and attacked Khmelnytsky at Slobodyshche; although he failed to storm the Cossack tabor, his determined assault persuaded them to sign an agreement on 17 October, whereupon he withdrew leaving Sheremetev to his fate. With no hope of relief, and subject to constant bombardment and assault, Sheremetev surrendered on 2 November; 20,000 Muscovites were taken prisoner. Sheremetev was to spend two decades in Tatar captivity, since Alexis refused to pay his ransom. At least he was spared Shein's fate.[77]

The Commonwealth was, however, unable to follow up these victories, fortunately for Muscovy which was under great strain, as inflation caused by Alexis's large-scale minting of copper coins to fund his wars brought widespread hardship. As for the Commonwealth, after twelve years of debilitating warfare fought on its own territory, exhaustion set in. Widespread devastation had seriously undermined the Commonwealth's ability to raise enough money to pay its regular armies. From 1659, troops began to form confederations, refusing to fight unless they were paid. Although the 1659 confederations were liquidated with the help of taxes voted by the *Sejm*, thus opening the way to the triumphs of 1660, new confederations formed in the Lithuanian and Polish armies in 1661, and the question of pay was linked to the wider political situation, as John Casimir tried to force through his plans for an election *vivente rege* in 1661 and 1662.[78] The failure of those plans reduced the political tension enough for the confederations to be successfully wound up in 1663, thus allowing new campaigns in 1664, which, although not as successful as in 1660, did succeed in beating off a renewed Muscovite attack, with the defeat of Khovanskii at Witebsk in 1664, and for the first time, conducting operations on Muscovite territory, round Pskov, Novgorod and Voronezh.

Overall, however, the 1664 campaigns were a disappointment. Although the Muscovites were expelled from central and western Lithuania, the Ukrainian campaign, from which much had been expected, proved a fiasco, as the increasing complexity of Cossack politics rendered any long-term political solution impossible. With both sides exhausted, talks were now the only viable option, especially after the outbreak of civil war in the Commonwealth in 1665–6, as the political fallout from the failed election campaign saw John Casimir's successful impeachment of Lubomirski, one of his leading opponents at the 1664 *Sejm*, and then a *rokosz* led by the disgraced marshal. Although the civil war was ended in 1666, the political situation remained extremely tense; in these circumstances, further offensives against Muscovy were impossible. On 30 January 1667, a thirteen-and-a-half-year truce was signed at Andrusovo. Muscovy retained Smolensk, Chernihiv and part of the palatinate of Witebsk. The intractable Cossack problem was solved by partition: Muscovy took the Ukraine on the left bank of the Dnieper, together with Kiev for a period of two years, while the Commonwealth was to keep the right-bank Ukraine.

Notes

1   Ochmann, *Sejmy* p. 35; Filipczak-Kocur, *Skarb koronny za Władysława IV* pp. 9–10.

2   Seredyka, *Sejm* p. 39.

3   W. Pałucki, *Drogi i bezdroża skarbowości polskiej XVI i pierwszej połowy XVII wieku* (2nd edn, Wrocław, 1974) pp. 34–9; A. Sucheni-Grabowska, 'Losy egzekucji dóbr w Koronie w latach 1574–1650' *KH* 80 (1973) p. 4.

4   Ibid. pp. 4–5.

5   Ibid. p. 6; Sucheni-Grabowska, 'Walka o wymiar i przeznaczenie kwarty w końcu XVI i na początku XVII wieku' *PH* 54 (1965) p. 28 n. 16.

6   Sucheni-Grabowska, 'Losy' p. 17.

7   Pałucki, *Drogi* p. 152; the same was true of Mikołaj Krzysztof Radziwiłł: Siekierski, 'Landed wealth' II p. 263.

8   Filipczak-Kocur, *Skarb litewski* p. 42,

9   Radziwiłł to the bishop of Wilno, 5.III.1622, *Sprawy* p. 174.

10   N.M. Iakovenko, *Ukrains'ka shliakhta z kintsia XIV do seredini XVII st* (Kiev, 1993) pp. 196–7, table 17. The top fourteen families in the Bratslav palatinate controlled 85.7 per cent of the hearths: Z. Anusik, 'Struktura społeczna szlachty bracławskiej w świetle taryfy podymnego z 1629 roku' *PH* 76 (1985) p. 243.

11   Z. Wójcik, *Dzikie pola w ogniu* (3rd edn, Warsaw, 1968) p. 140.

12   J. Wimmer, *Wojsko polskie w drugiej połowie XVII wieku* (Warsaw, 1965) p. 35.

13   C. Kumke, 'Die Reform der Registerkosaken im Jahre 1638' *FOG* 48 (1993) pp. 105–24.

14   G. Gajecky and A. Baran, *The Cossacks in the Thirty Years War* 2 vols (Rome, 1969, 1983) print some useful documents, but their arguments are tendentious and wholly unconvincing. For a sceptical and informed consideration of the legend that Khmelnytsky and the Zaporozhians served the French at the siege of Dunkirk, see Z. Wójcik, 'Czy Kozacy Zaporoscy byli na służbie Mazarina?' *PH* 64 (1973) pp. 575–85.

15   See the excellent discussion in C. Kumke, *Führer und Geführte bei den Zaporoger Kosaken* (Berlin, 1993), pp. 56–8.

16   Wimmer, *Wojsko polskie* pp. 32–3, 35.

17   Wójcik, *Dzikie* p. 157.

18   Lipiński estimates that there were 663 noble names in the register, representing 1,324 individuals; he classes another 550 names (660 individuals) as of doubtful status. W. Lipiński, 'Stanisław Michał Krajewski. Z dziejów walki szlachty ukraińskiej w szeregach powstańczych pod wodzą Bohdana Chmielnickiego' in idem (ed.) *Z dziejów Ukrainy* (Kiev, Crakow, 1912) pp. 160, 486–90.

19   The size of Wiśniowiecki's force is usually cited as 6,000. Wimmer argues that the reason only 2–3,000 arrived was due to heavy desertion: *Wojsko polskie* p. 40. It may have been because Wiśnioweicki's 'private army' was smaller than is frequently maintained.

20   Based on ibid. p. 49.

21 For the political crisis, see R.I. Frost, *After the Deluge. Poland-Lithuania and the Second Northern War* (Cambridge, 1993) chapter 1.

22 Chernov, *Vooruzhenye* pp. 137–8; Hellie, *Enserfment* pp. 186, 192; B. Davies, 'Village into garrison: the militarized peasant communities of southern Muscovy' *RR* 51 (1992) pp. 481–501.

23 Hellie, *Enserfment* p. 269.

24 Ibid. p. 183.

25 Sahanovich, *Neviadomaia* p. 10; A.N. Mal'tsev, *Rossiia i Belorussiia v seredine XVII veka* (Moscow, 1974) pp. 29, 34.

26 H. Wisner, 'Działalność wojskowa Janusza Radziwiłła, 1648–1655' *RB* 13 (1976) p. 93.

27 L. Kubala, *Wojna moskiewska* (Warsaw, 1910) p. 229; Sahanovich, *Neviadomaia* pp. 12, 21.

28 Wisner, 'Działalność' pp. 96–7; Sahanovich, *Neviadomaia* pp. 34–9; Kubala, *Wojna moskiewska* p. 274.

29 Wimmer, *Wojsko polskie* p. 83.

30 Mal'tsev, *Rossiia* p. 88.

31 Sahanovich, *Neviadomaia* pp. 44–5.

32 J. Wimmer, 'Przegląd operacji w wojnie polsko-szwedzkie 1655–1660' in idem (ed.) *Wojna polsko-szwedska 1655–1660* (Warsaw, 1973) pp. 137–8; L. Tersmeden, 'Carl X Gustafs Armé 1654–1657. Styrka och dislokation' in A. Stade (ed.), *Carl X Gustafs Armé* (Stockholm, 1979) p. 192.

33 Wimmer, *Wojsko polskie* p. 94; D. Mal'tsev, 'Voennye deistviia russkikh voisk v Belorussii i Litve letom 1655 g.' *ISKS* 13 (1954) p. 54.

34 P. Gordon, *Tagebuch des Generals Patrick Gordon während seiner Kriegsdienste unter den Schweden und Polen* M.A. Obolenksi and M.C. Posselt (eds) (Moscow, 1869) I pp. 17–18.

35 J. Wegner, 'Warszawa w czasie najazdu szwedzkiego 1655–1657' *PODWP* II pp. 239–40.

36 W. Tomkiewicz, 'Zniszczenie wojenne w dziedzinie kultury' *PODWP* II p. 444.

37 S. Ranatowicz, *Opisanie inkursji Szwedów do Polski i do Krakowa (1655–1657)* J. Mitkowski (ed.) (Cracow, 1958) pp. 15, 21.

38 W. Kochowski, *Annalium Poloniae* (Cracow, 1688) pp. 91–2.

39 W. Sauter, *Krzysztof Żegocki, pierwszy partyzant Rzeczypospolitej 1618–1673* (Poznań, 1981) pp. 51–67.

40 Wimmer, 'Przegląd' p. 151.

41 Wimmer, *Wojsko polskie* pp. 100–1.

42 Ibid. pp. 101–2.

43 More of his comrades were slaughtered shortly afterwards. Christian von Holsten, *Kriegsabenteuer . . . 1655–1666* H. Lahrkamp (ed.) (Wiesbaden, 1971) pp. 11–12.

44 Tersmeden, 'Carl X Gustafs Armé' pp. 192, 198.

45 J. Teodorczyk, 'Wyprawa zimowa Czarnieckiego 1–20.II.1656 r. Bitwa pod Gołębiem' in Wimmer (ed.), *Wojna* pp. 268, 277–9.

46 L. Podhorodecki, 'Bitwa pod Warką (7.IV.1656)' *SMHSW* 2 (1956) pp. 300–23.

47 S. Herbst, 'Trzydniowa bitwa pod Warszawą 28–30 VII 1656 r.' in Wimmer (ed.), *Wojna* pp. 303–4; M. Nagielski, *Warszawa 1656* (Warsaw, 1990) pp. 112–13.

48 Ibid. p. 120.

49 After 1648, 'cossack' cavalry was increasingly referred to as '*pancerna*' (armoured).

50 E. Cieślak, 'Wojskowo-politycne i gospodarcze znaczenie Gdańska w wojnie polsko-szwedzkiej 1655–1660' in Wimmer (ed.), *Wojna* p. 366.

51 R. Fagerlund, *Kriget i Östersjöprovinserna 1655–1661* (Stockholm, 1979) pp. 77, 224.

52 Ibid. pp. 89–91.

53 F. Bienemann (ed.) 'Briefe und Aktenstücke zur Geschichte der Verteidigung und Kapitulation Dorpats 1656' *MGGLEK* 16 (1896) p. 519.

54 Fagerlund, *Kriget* pp. 109–10.

55 The Poles lost 1,600 men, despite the inflated claims of the allies. Patrick Gordon, who fought in the Polish ranks, estimated losses at 2,000. Most damaging were the significant infantry casualties of 600 killed, wounded or captured. Allied losses were about 700. Gordon, *Tagebuch* p. 66; Nagielski, *Warszawa* p. 211.

56 Frederick William estimated the Tatars at 6,000; Baranowski suggests 2,000. B. Baranowski, 'Tatarszczyzna wobec wojny polsko-szwedzkiej w latach 1655–1660' *PODWP* I p. 479.

57 The allies lost forty-one standards and six guns. W. Majewski, 'Bitwa pod Prostkami (8 X 1656 r.)' *SMHSW* 2 (1956) p. 338. Wimmer suggests that the allied force was only 6,000 strong, but accepts the figure of 5,000 casualties; 'Przegląd' p. 175.

58 Piwarski suggests 23,000 dead and 34,000 taken captive, an undoubted exaggeration: K. Piwarski, 'Stosunki szwedzko-brandenburskie a sprawa polska w czasie pierwszej wojny północnej' *PODWP* I p. 445. Contemporary figures, however, give a total of 871 males and 1,306 females taken from Johannisburg Amt alone: R. Seeberg-Elverfeldt, 'Der Tatareinfall in das Amt Johannisburg im Oktober 1656 und 1657' *MVGOWP* 8 (1933–4) p. 64. Lick Amt lost 2,563 captive and 211 killed: G.C. Pisański, 'Nachricht von dem im Jahre 1656 geschehenen Einfalle der Tataren in Preußen. Aus zuverlässigen Urkunden zusammen getragen' *MLGM* 7 (1901) p. 100.

59 Tersmeden, 'Carl X Gustafs Armé' pp. 199–200.

60 Ibid. p. 208.

61 A. Stade, 'Natten före natten före tåget över Bält. Ett rekonstruktionsförsök' idem (ed.), *Carl X Gustaf och Danmark* (Stockholm, 1965) pp. 159–84.

62 A. Stade, 'Krigsrelationen om Tåget över Bält. Den samtida svenska propagandalitteraturen i källkritisk belysning' *Carl X Gustaf och Danmark* pp. 67–139.

63 F. Askgaard, 'Den korte fred. Mellemkrigstiden 26/2–7/8.1658' p. 259.

64 Charles X to Biörenklou, Roskilde, 2/12 March 1658. 'Bref från Konung Carl X till Presidenten Biörenklou' *HS* V (Stockholm, 1822) pp. 177–8, 184.

65 Charles X to Biörenklou, Gothenburg, 5/15 April 1658 ibid. p. 201.

66 R.C. Anderson, *Naval Wars in the Baltic* (London, 1919) pp. 82–3.

67   L. Tersmeden, '"Stormen för Köpenhamn" Planen för det svenska anfallet natten till den 11 Februari 1659 och orsakerna till dess misslyckande' in A. Stade (ed.) *Carl X Gustaf och Danmark* pp. 313–61.

68   L. Tersmeden, 'Strategisk defensiv. Carl X Gustaf, Philip av Sulzbach och slaget om Fyn hösten 1659' in A. Stade (ed.), *Carl X Gustaf och Danmark.* pp. 363–97.

69   'Zapiska o voennykh deistviiakh vo vremia Pol'skago pokhoda 1655 goda, s rospis'iu pokorennykh Russkimi voiskami gorodov' *ASBARIAEIAN* IV no. 89 p. 128; Sahanovich, *Neviadomaia* p. 17.

70   'Zapiska' p. 129; Sahanovich, *Neviadomaia* pp. 45–6.

71   In 1654, a complete Jewish company of 130 well-armed volunteers fought in Radziwiłł's army; ten companies of Jews fought in the defence of Dubrowna; 1,000 Jews helped defend Stary Bychów: Wisner, 'Działalność' p. 93; Sahanovich, *Neviadomaia* pp. 25, 27.

72   Mal'tsev, *Rossiia* p. 185; Sahanovich, *Neviadomaia* p. 74.

73   *AOIIuZR* XIV p. 330.

74   Sahanovich, *Neviadomaia* pp. 76–7.

75   J.C. Pasek, *Memoirs of the Polish Baroque* C.S. Leach (tr.) (Berkeley, 1976) pp. 72–3.

76   It was claimed that Czarniecki's division alone received the colossal sum of 2,000,000 złoties in ransom for their prisoners. A. Kersten, *Stefan Czarniecki, 1599–1665* (Warsaw, 1963) pp. 423–5.

77   Wimmer, *Wojsko polskie* p. 130; A. Hniłko, *Wyprawa cudnowska w 1660r.* (Warsaw, 1931) pp. 86–169; R. Romański, *Cudnów 1660* (Warsaw, 1996).

78   See Frost, *After the Deluge* chapter 7.

CHAPTER EIGHT

Northern Europe and the Military Revolution

An uneasy peace

The treaties of 1660–7 ended the second phase of the Northern Wars. Although the foundations of peace were hardly firm, and the bitter hostility engendered by decades of war was by no means assuaged, a combination of exhaustion and distraction ensured that peace held until 1700, apart from the Scanian War (1674–9). The Cossack problem, which Andrusovo could not solve, involved the Commonwealth in a protracted series of wars on its southern frontier, as the new hetman Petro Doroshenko, disillusioned with both Muscovy and Poland, looked to the Sultan for protection which might allow the Cossacks the autonomy they craved. War between Poland and the Tatars had broken out as soon as the ink was dry on Andrusovo; in 1672 the Turks seized the southern palatinate of Podolia, and it was not until the 1680s, when the Ottoman resurgence prompted the formation of a Holy League of the Commonwealth, Venice and Austria, that the pressure began to ease. John III Sobieski (1674–96), elected after his victory over the Turks at the second battle of Chocim, led a Polish army to relieve Vienna in 1683, in what turned out to be the Commonwealth's last great military triumph. Muscovy, intermittently at war with Turkey since 1677, joined the League after Andrusovo was converted into a permanent peace in 1686, by which the Commonwealth recognised Muscovite possession of Kiev. During the 1690s the Holy League pushed back the Ottoman armies, with the Commonwealth regaining Podolia at the Peace of Carlowitz in 1699.

Peace allowed the combatants to adjust after what had been a devastating experience. All the powers involved had been changed profoundly. The demands of raising, equipping and sustaining armies over long periods had everywhere altered the nature of the armed forces and their relationship to state and society. The political, cultural, social and economic effects of prolonged and sustained warfare over the previous century were substantial, while the cumulative effects of military change created serious pressures within states whose political culture was deeply resistant to change. The emergence of new social groups – especially army officers, but also bureaucrats – with an interest in sustaining a system which promised professional and social advancement placed strains upon existing political institutions, while the enormously increased financial burden on societies and the colossal demand for soldiers, brought political and social turmoil. All the states involved in the Northern Wars experienced periods of political crisis in the seventeenth century; the particular form in which they were resolved depended upon the very different structures and political cultures of the societies involved. While the resolution of these crises differed widely, in most cases there was a revolutionary shift in political culture, which, while reflecting the long-term, gradual changes which preceded it, nevertheless radically altered the direction of socio-political development. None of these societies would ever be the same again.

The Danish revolution

In September 1660, four months after peace was signed, Frederik III summoned the *Rigsdag* to deal with a disastrous financial situation which threatened to overwhelm the government. The cost of fighting two wars in such a short time had been substantial. The army had risen from 20,000 in 1655 to 40–50,000 at its peak in October 1657; required to disarm by Roskilde, by the summer of 1658 it had dropped to 229 companies (just over 20,000 men), compared with 530 in October 1657. Since the increase had favoured the more expensive cavalry units, which had risen sixfold compared with the three-and-a-half-fold rise in infantry units, and since the Danes had to bear the costs of the Swedish occupation from February until May, the state was already heavily burdened when Charles launched his second invasion. With Jutland and the duchies rapidly occupied by Swedish forces, recruiting a new army was both difficult and expensive, but Frederik managed to field 30,000 men, raising eight additional regiments of foot and fourteen of horse.[1] Now he faced the substantial costs of demobilisation for the second time in two years, at a point when his debts had risen to over 5 million rigsdalers.[2]

Although Frederik's election charter gave substantial power to the Council, his aristocratic ministers reverted to the standard procedure of calling the *Rigsdag* in a crisis. On this occasion, however, it did more than settle the government's debts. During protracted negotiations over taxation, the nobility's robust defence of its traditional exemptions was met by fierce opposition from the clergy and particularly the burghers. When stubborn noble resistance brought deadlock, the leaders of the other estates, Hans Svane, the bishop of Zealand and Hans Nansen, senior burgomaster of Copenhagen, introduced on 14/24 October a revolutionary proposal for a fundamental restructuring of the Danish state, based on the introduction of a hereditary monarchy through the annulment of Frederik's election charter and the abolition of noble privileges. Although the nobility rejected this radical document, Frederik backed the non-noble estates in what amounted to a military coup. On the evening of 20/30 October, he made it unofficially known that he was prepared to accept the offer without noble agreement and placed Copenhagen under martial law, having already tightened military control across the country. The Council was comprehensively outmanoeuvred and had to yield. Three days later, Council representatives and delegates from the *Rigsdag* unanimously offered the hereditary throne to Frederik and his successors. A Commission was established, in which nobles were heavily outnumbered, to consider the constitutional implications, and on 27 October (OS), Frederik's coronation charter was ceremoniously returned to him. Twelve years after the most radical curtailment of royal power in Danish history the king was given absolute power by his subjects to establish a new constitution.

The break was decisive. On 20/30 January 1661 Frederik issued the Act Concerning Absolute and Hereditary Government which was circulated and signed by 183 nobles, 987 clerics and 381 burghers from fifty-seven towns, and which constituted one of the most radical claims to unlimited royal power by any contemporary state. Although there was something of a retreat from this extreme position in the 1665 Royal Law, the power it gave the Crown was substantial: the 'absolute and hereditary' monarch was explicitly stated to be above all human laws and – apart from upholding Lutheranism as laid down in the Augsburg Confession, and maintaining Denmark's territorial integrity and the hereditary succession – the king was explicitly freed from all constraints on his power.[3]

The Danish Revolution was a stunning defeat for the narrow group of high noble families which had dominated politics for so long. It did not, however, mark quite such a radical break with the past as was once believed.[4] The foundations of noble power in Denmark had long been crumbling. Partly this was due to socio-economic factors unconnected with the changing military situation, but the gradual transformation of Denmark's military establishment after 1614 and Denmark's involvement in the wars of 1625–9, 1643–5, 1657–8 and above all 1658–60, played a decisive part in this process, and in provoking the political crisis.

The Danish nobility was not numerous, comprising a mere 181 families in 1600, or some 1,850 individuals, of whom 4–500 were adult males.[5] Although there was no titled nobility, and all nobles were legally equal, between the revolution of 1536 which established the Council's extensive powers, and 1648, noble solidarity was seriously undermined. The restricted membership of the Council, which consisted of twenty-three members by 1650, concentrated power in the hands of a narrow elite, while economic trends since 1600 had opened up a growing gap between a small group of wealthy families and the rest: if the nobility's share of cultivated land remained relatively steady at about 44 per cent, the richest 10 per cent of the nobility held 27.5 per cent of noble land in the 1550s, but 42 per cent by 1625.[6] As the Council nobility distanced itself from the rest of the estate, the lesser nobility, which had suffered badly from inflation, challenged Council authority, using the 1648 debates over Frederik's election charter to demand greater political decentralisation.

The strains within the nobility emerged after Torstensson's War. Hitherto, the Council had pursued a policy of neutrality, which had enabled Denmark to remain a domain state, in which the Crown, which owned 52 per cent of Denmark's cultivated land, was expected to live off its own, with extraordinary taxation only agreed in an emergency. This policy had been reasonably successful until the 1640s, and the government's debts at the end of the wars in 1570 and 1629 had been paid. Although the Council's opposition to Christian IV's wars protected it from attack over the increased taxation burden, its domination of the government left it vulnerable in the very different climate after 1643. Already the creation of the small permanent army after 1614 had brought a new charge upon the government which represented a constant drain on resources, especially after the destruction of Christian's healthy financial position after 1625. The 1630s saw a growing debate over the increasingly difficult position of the national finances, as the domain state demonstrated its inability to meet the new demands placed upon it. The annual deficit was running at 425,000 rigsdalers in 1646, and 344,700 rigsdalers in 1651; in 1650 treasurer Oluf Daa estimated the national debt at 4,850,000 rigsdalers.[7] Thus the inelasticity of the domain state was already causing problems before the disasters of the 1650s; indeed, the Council was already moving towards the collegial principles of government which were adopted after 1660 in an attempt to solve some of the problems. The dramatic increase of the tax burden by 500–600 per cent between 1600 and 1640 had already created serious discontent even before the three wars fought on Danish territory in the space of seventeen years brought devastation.[8]

It was the 1658–60 war which hit Denmark hardest, as it suffered the depredations not only of the Swedes, but also of its own allies. The Poles in particular were demanding guests, and there were frequent complaints that the allies extracted far higher rates of contributions than the Swedes.[9] In February 1659 the allies took from the 400–500 inhabitants of the parishes of Grindsted and Grene 2,292 rigsdalers, 246 horses, 887 cattle and 3,762 smaller animals: on average the war years cost each homestead 2 horses, 6 cows and 30–35 smaller animals, 16–17 rigsdalers and 2–3 barrels of grain. By 1662, twenty-eight of sixty-four homesteads were deserted. No wonder Pasek praised Denmark as a land flowing with milk and honey. The devastation was heightened by the arrival of typhus in 1658. Death rates rose alarmingly: in six parishes in Varde, Åbenrå and Velje, which normally saw 6 deaths per month, the figure reached 133 in August, 134 in September, and 100 per month until the end of the year; the death rate from August to November, usually about 25, passed 450, an eighteenfold rise. In 1662, some parishes claimed over 75 per cent deserted homesteads.[10] Even if one acccepts a degree of exaggeration, it is incontestable that the experience was devastating.

It was against this background of distress that the *Rigsdag* assembled in September 1660. Although peasants were not directly represented, the clergy were well aware of their problems and adopted a hard line. Neither were the burghers in any mood to listen to noble pleas. The war of 1658–60 had destroyed any military justification that the nobility might have for its privileged position. This was partly a matter of perception: although *rostjeneste* had provided hardly any troops for the Swedish wars, nobles did serve in relatively large numbers. The officer corps of the new army was dominated by the native nobility between 1614 and 1658, with six out of seven infantry regiments still commanded by native nobles in 1656, while noble domination among cavalry officers was even greater; in all, 200 out of 400 nobles of military age served in the Swedish wars. Moreover, the nobles bore much of the cost of mobilisation in 1657–8 when the contribution of Danish and Holstein nobles was not much short of that of the state – 83,000 rigsdalers compared with 100,000.[11]

Other estates had also contributed, however. The summoning of the *opbud*, even if its military contribution was negligible, underlined the fact that all had a responsibility to defend the fatherland, yet only nobles used their service to justify fiscal privileges. Moreover, between 1658 and 1660 war, noble domination of the officer corps was decisively undermined, as its size doubled in under a year, and officers were recruited regardless of social background. Fourteen of the new regiments had hardly a nobleman above subaltern rank, eight had none at all, and eleven had only one.[12] In 1659, it was the Copenhagen burghers who defied the Swedes, for which Frederik granted the city as a corporate body full noble privileges. Satires questioning the military worth of the nobility, which had circulated since Torstensson's War, became more frequent, while the fact that many nobles owned property across the

Sound, in territory seized by Sweden, often made them reluctant to fight and the object of popular suspicion.

The Danish nobility was simply too small and most of its members were too poor to perform the functions which might justify the extensive claims they made for social privilege, while the loss of the provinces across the Sound further reduced the number of nobles able or willing to serve. In the chaos of 1658–9, wealthier nobles found it impossible to fulfil their traditional role of military entrepreneur, and the state took over. From 1614, the king had maintained control of commissions: captains and subalterns were appointed by him, not by regimental commanders. By 1657 the noble-dominated provincial commissions which ran the army were consolidated into a newly established central War College. Officers were thus dependent for their careers on the king, and Frederik had built up a loyal core of support, both noble and non-noble.

With firmer central control of the military, and an officer-corps in which commoners, foreigners and new nobles had, by 1660, swamped the old nobility, the army was unlikely to oppose moves to strengthen royal power. Military change since 1614 had helped undermine noble rule. The policy of neutrality had been wrecked by Christian's ambition and Swedish aggression, while the domain state had crumbled: in effect Denmark was a tax state long before the massive sales of royal land after the establishment of absolutism sealed the fate of the old fiscal order. Finally, the increasing divisions within the nobility rendered the Council helpless in the face of its opponents; by 1660 it represented only itself.

If the 1660 reforms were the culmination of a series of long-term developments, their revolutionary nature must be recognised. The *Rigsdag* deliberately destroyed the old order and placed the destiny of the state in the monarchy's hands. The publication of the new estates privileges in June 1661 demonstrated that the old nobility's status as a distinct social group was no more, as the king suspended for ten years – in practice forever – the requirement to perform military service; in consequence, the nobility was stripped of its tax-exemption and its monopoly on many offices. By 1700, the number of top political advisers from the old nobility had dropped from 95 to 20; in the local administration from 93 to 19.[13] Nobles began to pay the new land-tax, introduced in 1662; in 1688, the compilation of a comprehensive land-register provided a proper basis for the new tax-state.

Yet the reforms were more a redefinition of nobility than an attack upon it. The emphasis on birth and the equality of the nobility was downplayed; in its place, the new system stressed the concept of service and constructed a new social hierarchy based largely on merit. In May 1671, the government promulgated a table of ranks for members of the administration, with the monarchy at the top, which undermined traditional concepts of the social order: the emphasis was on the kind of service performed, not social background; commoners with important posts were ranked above well-born but more lowly servants of the state, while the creation of ranks of count and baron stressed that the concept of nobility itself was not under attack. In 1679, public servants of non-noble origin were given a series of privileges; in 1693 the process was completed with the grading of the nobility into a hierarchy of ranks and the automatic ennoblement of commoners in the three highest ranks of the administration.

Denmark's experience of war had demonstrated that traditional government structures and social roles no longer adequately provided for the defence of the realm. By 1660, the demands of war had forced the Danish Council into a series of ad hoc measures which widened the gap between theory and practice. The disaster of 1658–60 created a coalition of forces which succeeded in pushing through the absolutist coup that placed the destiny of the state in the monarchy's hands and completed in a more systematic manner the reforms begun in an uncoordinated fashion under Christian. The new, cameral system was to survive in its essentials until 1849 by integrating the old elite of birth with the new elite of service. After the hiatus of 1658–60, old nobles flocked back into the officer corps; the number of foreign officers was reduced and the noble presence increased absolutely and relatively in all positions, although the small size of the Danish nobility ensured that, unlike other contemporary states, nobles only ever constituted between a fifth and a quarter of all army officers.[14] The way was open for a new assertiveness in Danish foreign policy and a war of revenge on Sweden. In Denmark the Military Revolution was over.

Brandenburg-Prussia: shaky beginnings

The Second Northern War marked the arrival of a new force in northeastern Europe, albeit one whose position remained fragile. In 1640, Frederick William succeeded to a fragmented and devastated inheritance. Although the Hohenzollerns enjoyed a prominent position in Imperial politics, their impoverished and scattered lands rendered them less significant than their fellow-electors of Saxony and the Palatinate. Until 1640, the Thirty Years War proved disastrous for Brandenburg, as George William manoeuvred ineffectually between Sweden and the Habsburgs; after he signed the 1635 peace of Prague, most of his lands were occupied by the Swedes. The Hohenzollern possessions, scattered across the north European plain from the Rhine to the Niemen, were difficult to defend, while political fragmentation ensured that efforts to create a coherent government faced enormous obstacles.

Despite the unpromising circumstances of his accession, between 1640 and 1648 Frederick William displayed the first signs of what – until 1918 – was to prove a noted Hohenzollern talent: the ability to end up on the right side at the end of wars, thereby securing rewards that were scarcely justified by their contribution to the common cause. In 1641, Frederick William signed a truce with Sweden, despite his obligations under the peace of Prague, and manoeuvred effectively in the closing years of the Thirty Years War to win important territorial concessions at Westphalia. French concern at the implications of Sweden's new status as an Imperial power ensured that Mazarin was prepared to back Brandenburg as a counterweight in north Germany: consequently Frederick William was able to win part of the duchy of Pomerania, over which Brandenburg had been in dispute with Sweden since 1637, and the secularised bishoprics of Cammin, Halberstadt, Minden and Magdeburg.

Yet Frederick William's position was still precarious. The end of the war brought pressure from the estates of his devastated lands for the demobilisa-tion of his 8,000-strong army. Renewed tension after the breakdown of the Polish-Swedish talks at Lübeck in 1652, however, provided a new oppor-tunity. Experience of occupation by foreign armies had led to some support in the 1640s for the maintenance of an army which might prevent foreign occupation; Frederick William played on this in the 1652 meeting of the Brandenburg Estates. Negotiations were protracted and difficult, but finally resulted in 1653 in an agreement by which the Estates voted taxes worth 530,000 thalers, to be collected over six years, in return for confirmation of extensive noble privileges. The Recess, as this agreement was known, opened the way to the establishment of a force of 5,000, which Frederick William was able to increase after the outbreak of the Polish-Swedish war: by June 1656 he had 22,000 men under arms, which made him a desirable ally for both sides and led to the achievement of sovereignty in Ducal Prussia.

Nevertheless, he was lucky. The change of sides in 1657, hailed by his admirers as a masterstroke, was nearly a disaster, as Sweden unexpectedly routed the Danes; Frederick William's panic-stricken letters after Roskilde indicate how much he feared a Swedish revenge attack which might deprive him of Ducal Prussia. Moreover, his domestic situation remained precarious. Despite complaints from the Estates, he levied taxes without consent to sup-port his new army, which also raised contributions to feed itself. Although he reduced the army to between 7,000 and 12,000 in the 1660s, he did not disband it. Exploiting the lack of any central forum for opposition in his fragmented inheritance, Frederick William won agreement to new taxes for the support of what was now a standing army, breaking promises he had made in 1653, and stirring up nobles against cities, and the popular elements in cities against the patrician elites, as in the long-running dispute over the excise in the 1660s and 1670s. Taxation revenues rose steadily, from 264,000 thalers per annum in 1662 to 324,000 in 1666, though they fell to 288,000 by 1674.[15]

In Ducal Prussia, he used force. Despite the treaties of 1657 and 1660, his position was by no means secure. The Prussian Estates refused to accept the Polish concession of sovereignty without their consent, and although the 1661 *Sejm* confirmed Wehlau-Bromberg, disputes between Warsaw and Berlin over unfulfilled clauses provoked tension, especially since the Prussian opposition looked to Poland to support them in their fight against the Hohenzollerns, which led to difficulties for Frederick William when he sought confirmation of the treaty from the new Polish king Michael Korybut Wiśniowiecki (1669–74). The Commonwealth's continued involvement in war after 1660, however, meant that the Poles failed to support the Prussian opposition, although Polish troops did occupy Elbing – which had been assigned to Frederick William as temporary security for the payment of 400,000 thalers pledged to him by the Commonwealth – when the Swedes withdrew in 1660. In October 1662, Frederick William brought 2,000 troops to Königsberg to crush resistance from the Prussian Estates, which had refused to swear homage to him as their sovereign. The leader of the burgher opposition, Hieronymus Roth, was arrested and incarcerated for the rest of his life; in 1671, Christian von Kalckstein, the leader of the noble opposition, was kidnapped in Warsaw, smuggled back to Memel and executed.

The foundations of Hohenzollern power were far from secure. Whereas in Sweden and Denmark the creation of substantial military establishments by the early 1660s rested on the emergence of a growing native officer corps and rational systems for recruitment and training, the Brandenburg army was still very much a mercenary force. Although the fragmented nature of the opposition had enabled Frederick William to establish and maintain his army, the Privy Council and administration which sustained it at the centre were largely divorced from the local communities and political institutions which paid for it. It was – as Frederick William well knew – a dangerous situation and one he laboured hard to overcome. He was lucky that neither Poland-Lithuania nor Sweden sought to overturn the 1660 settlement; although Sobieski devised a plan to seize Ducal Prussia in the 1670s, it foundered on *Sejm* opposition. Brandenburg-Prussia was too insignificant as yet to cause serious concern.

Sweden: war cannot feed itself

By 1660, Charles X's martial dash had shown he was a worthy successor to the great Gustav Adolf, and Sweden's military reputation had never been higher. The exalted position it had achieved by 1648 had been maintained in difficult circumstances, against a coalition of the greatest powers in central and eastern Europe. The spectacular conquest of Poland in 1655, the repulse of Muscovy's attack on Riga and Denmark's humiliation had impressed all Europe, yet the campaigns of the 1650s demonstrate that the extraordinary set of circumstances which had encouraged the rapid expansion of the Swedish war-machine no longer applied.

Acquiring an empire was one matter; defending it quite another. Sweden's success in Germany was achieved by a force in which the Swedish contingent remained fairly constant, at about 38,000, many of whom were assigned to less costly garrison duties, and the proportion of foreign mercenaries – mostly Scots and Germans – grew steadily, to 50,000 – well over half – by the late 1630s; the proportion was higher in the field armies: Swedes constituted only a fifth of the Swedish armies at Breitenfeld and Lützen.[16] The problem with foreign mercenaries was that they had to be paid in cash, not kind; the Swedish system of *förläning*, which enabled it to sustain an effective native force was unsuitable for the support of mercenaries. Despite the efforts of Gustav Adolf and Oxenstierna to develop trade and industry to provide a cash income, it was impossible for Sweden to meet the costs out of its own resources. Foreigners would have to pay.

The parasitic nature of the Swedish system was well understood. War could only be sustained if it could be made to pay for itself, and that was only conceivable if war was fought abroad; as Gustav Adolf remarked: 'Nowhere are we weaker than within our own borders.'[17] Yet the ideal of *bellum se ipse alet* was never attainable, even in the favourable conditions in the Empire after 1636. Much of the day-to-day running of the system required loans to raise the money required to pay the troops and to fill the ranks. This could be sustained during the war; after 1648, the bill came in. Creditors had invested in the continuing success of the Swedish forces; once the war was over, their loans had to be repaid without the ability to draw funds from outside Sweden, while the huge costs of paying off the Swedish army had to be met in an unfavourable international economic situation, in which Sweden was badly affected by the collapse of copper prices in the early 1650s.

There was also a political price for Swedish success. The insistent demands of Swedish negotiators at Westphalia for compensation and satisfaction were not well received by those who had suffered the rapacious demands of Swedish armies. Even those who had cause to be thankful to the Swedes were alienated by the high price Sweden exacted: the dukes of Mecklenburg might owe their restoration to Swedish arms, but were deprived of Wismar in consequence. Although Sweden received the archbishopric of Bremen in 1648, the city of Bremen maintained its claim to independence, which led to a brief war in 1654, called off when the Polish crisis pulled Sweden in a different direction, but which demonstrated unexpectedly united support within the Empire for Bremen.

Aggression did not win friends, yet the very success it had brought by 1648 suggested that Sweden might need them, as the problems of defending its Baltic empire became increasingly apparent. Sweden now controlled a long, vulnerable border in the east and a series of exposed enclaves in northern Germany, all of which required massive expenditure on men and fortifications: Charles X claimed in 1658 that Pomerania required an army of 8,000 men to garrison it in peacetime, and 17,000 in wartime, but gave no indication of how it was to be paid.[18] Sweden itself could not maintain forces on this scale, while its new acquisitions were unlikely to accept the substantial burden of their own defence. Such expenditure required money in quantities that Sweden simply did not possess. Under Gustav Adolf and Oxenstierna, the urgent need for cash forced substantial alienations of royal land in the form of outright donations to the nobility, which increased greatly after Christina came of age.[19] In part this was due to problems experienced after the rapid expansion of *förläning* under Charles IX. The embryonic central bureaucracy was neither large nor efficient enough to keep track of all the fiefs, and revenues supposed to support individual officers or civil servants often proved fictional: many farms, especially in Finland, were abandoned or unproductive. Nevertheless, Gustav Adolf did not abandon the policy of *förläning*, directing his efforts towards ensuring that the system was kept under control, so that farms were in the possession of those actually rendering service and were able to provide a suitable income. In the 1620s, the peacetime support of the cavalry was reformed by the establishment of the first true allotment (*indelning*) system in Sweden, whereby both officers and ordinary soldiers were assigned to individual farms which provided their pay and equipment; usually these were crown farms: if a cavalryman was assigned to a tax-farm, the cost of his upkeep was deducted from the farmer's tax obligation. Yet Gustav Adolf also sought to increase the government's cash income, which could only be achieved by tapping noble revenues and curtailing noble privileges. The price for this was extensive donations, in particular to members of the high nobility. It was hoped that nobles would farm the land more effectively than the Crown, and that the exchequer could cream off part of the increased revenues in loans or taxes: noble privileges were extensive, but nobles were liable to contributions outside the *frihetsmil* – the privileged area within the mile surrounding noble manors – and were certainly affected by the indirect taxes and tolls introduced by Oxenstierna.[20]

By 1654, after the massive increase in donations during Christina's reign, 66 per cent of Swedish land was in noble hands, and the Crown's income had dropped from 6,360,000 rigsdalers in 1644 to 3,790,000 in 1653.[21] Already by 1632, 2,264 farms had been given away, compared to 2,998 leased as *förläningarna*: the figures for 1611 had been 799 and 4,970 respectively.[22] Alienations and donations on this scale might suggest that Sweden, like Denmark, was moving from being a domain state to a tax state. Yet such a development was unsustainable in Sweden. Although the burden on Sweden lessened considerably between 1636 and 1648, the demands for new taxes – in particular the indirect taxes which the government increasingly favoured – proved highly unpopular. The widespread alienations of royal land cast into doubt the legal position of the peasants who had passed under noble control, forming a new class of *skattefrälsebönderna* (tax-noble-peasants). Although detailed study of the fate of this group suggests that the change brought no substantial deterioration in their position, there was fierce opposition from tax and crown peasants, since the burden of taxation and conscription fell most heavily on the reduced number which remained.[23]

Thus the 1650 *Riksdag*, called to confront the financial crisis, saw a determined attack on alienations of crown land, led by the burghers who were especially hard hit by the new indirect taxes, and by the peasants, who saw the new system as a direct assault on their position; the lesser clergy, responsible for compiling the conscription and taxation registers, sided with the peasants. The opposition had a good constitutional case, since Magnus Eriksson's Land Law banned alienations of the royal domain, while the 1604 Norrköping *Riksdag* had declared that donations could only be made under 'feudal' conditions, which meant that confirmation had to be sought from all new rulers, and that rights of disposal were limited. The call for a *reduktion*, as the resumption of royal lands was termed, was popular, and resumed in 1654 on Charles's accession. The alternative, suggested by the peasants in 1634, 1638 and 1644, was for the abolition of noble tax privileges. For this there was some precedent: the Älvsborg ransom after the Kalmar War had been paid by noble peasants at the same rate as crown and tax peasants, as had the new taxes introduced in the 1620s – the three marks aid of 1628 being payable even within the *frihetsmil*; finally, conscription had been levied at the same rate after 1627, and even nobles had contributed to the Älvsborg ransom and the 1629 ship tax.[24]

Many of these concessions were subsequently reversed. The lower rate of conscription for noble peasants was restored in 1635, although the exemption within the *frihetsmil* was not, while the payment of one-off taxes by noble peasants did not invalidate the general principle by which they were exempt or paid lower rates than non-noble peasants on other taxes. In 1654 the Crown was in no position radically to restructure the fiscal system. The chosen alternative was to drive through a partial *reduktion* in 1655, reclaiming a quarter of the alienated lands, together with a three-year tax on noble peasants, which went some way towards satisfying the non-noble estates. This plan was viable because the issue divided the nobility and won support among army officers and administrators, for whom the shrinking of the royal domain had fundamentally threatened the system of payment based on *förläning* and *beställning*. The effects of the alienations had been disguised during the long years of war, but the return of peace meant that many on the lower rungs of the military and administrative hierarchy who did not have large estates and were therefore dependent on the state, found that their wages could no longer be paid. Thus fierce Council opposition to a *reduktion*, led by Magnus Gabriel de la Gardie, Christina's erstwhile favourite, was insufficient to block it.

There was a further option for improving the Crown's financial situation. If Sweden could not afford peace, it might be better to go back to war. Yet the Polish War merely demonstrated that war could not always be made to pay for itself. It began promisingly enough. The importance of Sweden's new military reputation was clearly demonstrated, as a substantial mercenary army was raised despite Sweden's chronic lack of specie. Swedish agents in Germany succeeded in raising sufficient capital to fill the ranks, and recruitment was brisk. Much of the credit came from the officers themselves, both foreigners and servants of the Swedish crown such as Hans Christoffer von Königsmarck, the governer of Bremen, and Salvius's ninety-five-year-old widow, who, as a result of her husband's former position as the Swedish agent in Hamburg, had excellent contacts in the city which had become the financial capital of northern Germany during the Thirty Years War.[25]

Recruitment was only possible because Sweden's performance in the Thirty Years War persuaded creditors that they would receive a return on their investment. Despite the stunning victories of 1655, however, Swedish hopes were soon dashed. Deprived of Polish support by the spring of 1656, the Swedish forces were simply too small to dominate the sprawling Commonwealth, and Swedish garrisons remained isolated and unable to control the countryside. Even in Royal Prussia, where the Swedes instituted a regime of admirable efficiency it proved impossible to make war feed itself. Income was drawn from the local starosties and rates of the local land and hearth taxes were increased. Altogether, 425,085 thalers were collected in 1656, of which the largest elements included 97,189 thalers in contribution from the Marienburg palatinate, 55,535 from the land and hearth taxes, and 20,000 each in contributions from Elbing and Thorn: the two cities also paid 14,441 and 7,914 respectively in excise and further contributions.[26]

The deficit run by the Prussian administration at the end of 1656 was a mere 50,592 thalers. The large ransoms raised from towns and cities after their surrender were one-off payments, and although substantial sums were raised in tolls, overall levels of income dropped in 1657 to just over 281,600 thalers, while the deficit reached 87,213 thalers.[27] The real collapse came in 1658, however. Although total expenditure shot up to 515,487 thalers, while income remained on the surface steady at 280,543, which left a deficit of 253,713 thalers. The revenues, however, included 10,000 thalers raised in loans in Hamburg, a further 15,000 from Vincent Möller, the Swedish resident in Hamburg, and 2,710 from the Stockholm tolls.[28] Far from war paying for itself, it was being subsidised by the fatherland.

Sweden itself had to bear the burden at levels last seen in the 1620s. The crippling conscription rate of 1 in 10 for both noble and crown peasants, first introduced in 1627, was abandoned in 1635, when it was reduced to 1 in 30 for noble peasants, and 1 in 15 for the rest. Although the quotas were increased to 1 in 10 and 1 in 20 in 1636, Sweden's strong position after 1641 brought a further relaxation: the quotas were left at the same level, but there was a popular move towards calculating not by head (*bondetal*), but by farmstead (*gårdetal*) which allowed greater flexibility to those required to meet the quotas without reducing the total number raised. The failure to recruit in the Commonwealth after early 1656 ensured that the ranks could only be filled with a return to conscription on a large scale. Already in 1653–4, the quotas had been increased to 1 in 8 and 1 in 16; eased back in the successful year of 1655, the urgent demand for manpower saw the increase of the noble quota to 1 in 10 in 1656, and a switch to selection by *bondetal* in 1657, although selection by *gårdetal* and the 1655 rates were reintroduced in 1658 after the victories over Denmark.[29]

The burden was immense: altogether conscription was levied in forty-five years in the six decades before 1679.[30] The steady drain of scarce manpower resources had profound implications for economy and society: between 1626 and 1630, Sweden and Finland provided 51,367 conscripts, an average of 10,273 men per year.[31] Since Swedish and Finnish losses for the 1620s were 35–40,000, the new recruits did little more than plug the gaps in the ranks, and the high death rates experienced in the army, especially from disease, ensured that the demand for replacements was unrelenting. The effect on local communities could be dramatic, as Lindegren's famous study of Bygdeå showed: 236 men were conscripted from the parish in sixteen levies between 1620 and 1639, of whom 215 died during the war, which radically altered the demographic profile of the parish, whose population fell from 1,900 in 1620 to 1,700 in 1640, with a sharp reduction in males between fifteen and sixty from 468 in 1621 to 288 in 1639.[32]

Lindegren presents the role of the state in enforcing conscription in terms of 'oppression' and 'exploitation', stressing the role of force. Yet the striking feature of Sweden in this period is the extent to which local communities were themselves involved in the process, and influenced its implementation. While there was a considerable amount of indirect protest and avoidance of government demands through flight, sabotage or simple avoidance, it is misleading to see the relationship between peasant community and central government merely in terms of exploitation and the exercise of state power. *Utskrivning* was organised by the local community, through its own institutions, with the twelve-man jury composed of local peasants playing a central role; this fact above all others ensured that conscription, though undoubtedly unpopular, was implemented over a long and difficult period with minimal use of force.

The consensual nature of the Swedish political system, and above all the regular involvement of peasant representatives in the *Riksdag*, underpinned the system. Although Gustav Adolf's illegitimate half-brother Carl Carlsson Gyllenhielm claimed in 1627 that the king was entitled to call an *utskrivning* as often as he wished without recourse to the *Riksdag*, as occurred in 1626, 1629 and 1637, the Council was reluctant to do so, with Jakob de la Gardie arguing in 1633 that although the king did not need *Riksdag* consent, it would be unwise not to obtain it, since the failure to do so might well provoke unrest among the lesser nobility and the clergy, who were mainly responsible for implementing conscription and who provided the essential link between the central government and the provinces. Although these comments suggest that the legal basis was unclear, it was generally accepted that *Riksdag* consent was required before an *utskrivning* was legal; until 1680 it was certainly normal practice to obtain it.[33]

This mediation was vital to the success of *utskrivning*, for it was close attention to the protests and complaints of those responsible for supplying the levies which enabled the system to be adapted or moderated to take account of differing local conditions, or peasant concerns about its implementation. Thus in 1629 the peasants of Norrland were granted a reduced quota of 1 in 20 after serious protests; while both the temporary equalisation of noble and peasant quotas in the 1620s and 1656, and the shift from calculation by *bondetal* in favour of *gårdetal* were direct responses to peasant concerns. In general, although crown officials drove a hard bargain, it was clear that there was flexibility within the system; they did also listen.[34] Despite the more efficient inspection of local claims for tax relief by provincial governors in the 1620s, and widespread complaints about the increasing burdens, Sweden never experienced anything like the massive peasant revolts which shook France on its entry to the Thirty Years War.[35]

Moreover, despite the apparently dramatic effects of conscription on Bygdeå, one should be careful about extrapolating from this one example. Bygdeå was in remote and sparsely-populated Västerbotten, not far short of the Arctic Circle; as such, it was far from typical of the rest of Sweden, and while Lundmark suggests that Lindegren's figures are plausible for the rest of Västerbotten, they are probably misleading for Sweden as a whole.[36] Bygdeå was unusual, in that there was no noble land in the parish: this meant that it was hit harder by conscription than areas with concentrations of noble land, where the lower quotas for noble peasants and the *frihetsmil* provided a degree of protection. Furthermore, the experience of comparable areas in seventeenth-century Europe suggests that regions where a harsh climate ensured that the agricultural economy remained marginal often saw a major exodus of adult males seeking employment in the armed forces, even where conscription was unknown. Perhaps 10 per cent of the adult male population of Scotland embarked for service in central and northern Europe between 1626 and 1632,[37] while within the Swedish empire, Finland supplied troops at a level far above its relative share of the population: of 30,000 Swedish infantry in 1630, 12,000 (40 per cent) were from Finland, with a similar proportion among the cavalry – 3,250 (38 per cent) out of 8,500; 15 per cent of the adult male population in Finland was in the army.[38]

As Lindegren shows, despite the undoubtedly critical situation faced by Bygdeå in the 1630s, in the long run the haemorrhage of adult males from the parish, far from threatening the fragile agricultural economy, was actually followed by a rise in production and a rapidly-increasing surplus. The structure of the local economy changed, as peripheral activities were abandoned in favour of a concentration on basic agriculture.[39] This suggests that opportunities in Bygdeå, as in Finland, were limited for a population which tended to outstrip the capacity of the local economy to satisfy more than its basic needs. While the burden of conscription was undoubtedly substantial, it did not threaten the parish's economic viability: for a community on the margin with more mouths to feed than work available, it may not have been as inconvenient as it might at first appear to establish a regular mechanism for exporting young males.

For the fact that selection of recruits was in local hands ensured that *utskrivning* could perform a useful social role for local communities. As the case of Bygdeå suggests, there was often a surplus of labour in areas where productive land was scarce, and the grumbling about the burden of conscription should not obscure the extent to which communities might be glad to be rid of certain elements, in particular youths who might be experiencing difficulty in establishing their economic independence, and whose nuisance value and ever-open mouths might encourage the idea that military service a thousand miles away could be socially useful not just to the king. Initially, the government had viewed askance the practice of paying substitutes to fulfil one's military duty, but by the 1640s, it had come to realise that there were advantages in allowing it. Wealthier farmers increasingly anticipated the conscription board by hiring substitutes in advance, and it was increasingly common for the better-off farmers to contract with a poor family to take one of their sons into their household, feeding and clothing him as he grew up, and preparing for him eventually to fulfil his role before the conscription board.[40] Such an arrangement was beneficial for all: the government got its soldier, the farmer did not have to go to war, and children from poor households received a more comfortable upbringing than they otherwise might have enjoyed. Even their families benefited: they did not have to feed an extra mouth, while there is evidence that families who entered into such contracts were looked after better in old age or illness.

Thus while the burdens of Sweden's long years of war were considerable, and many undoubtedly suffered, their effects were not all negative. The constant demand for soldiers led to the creation of new social arrangements and hastened the process of social differentiation, as – especially in Finland – the division between a group of prosperous yeoman farmers and a growing landless rural proletariat widened. It was from this latter group that the military state drew its cannon-fodder, with soldiers' families emerging as a new feature of rural society after 1650. It was not just elites who benefited from the military state. Within the increasingly stratified hierarchies of Swedish rural society, the constant demand for soldiers enabled the creation of a more stable order, in which not only did property-holders win greater security, but landless labourers could find a respected place as military servitors. The system was only secured, however, after a new war had demonstrated the fragility of Sweden's defences.

The Scanian War, 1674–9

The coming of peace in 1660 saw a return of the problems which had haunted Sweden between 1648 and 1655. The poorly-monetarised economy was again faced with a burden of debt without sufficient means to service it, let alone repay it. The acquisition of new territories in 1648 and 1658–60 merely added to the load. Although the 1660 absolutist coup ensured that most nobles in the conquered provinces accommodated themselves more readily to Swedish rule than might otherwise have been the case in return for guarantees of their privileges, the need to billet troops on Halland and Scania and the introduction of Swedish administrative practices caused discontent among the local peasantry which might prove dangerous in any future Danish war. Finally, the need to fortify and defend the German provinces demanded substantial resources and the maintenance of fragile lines of naval communication.

The problems were exacerbated under the regency for Charles XI, led by Chancellor Magnus Gabriel de la Gardie, which did not enjoy the authority of its predecessor after 1634. The 1660 modification to the 1634 Form of Government ensured that its actions were subject to scrutiny by regular meetings of the *Riksdag*; nevertheless, political control was again effectively in the hands of a narrow aristocratic group. The tentative *reduktion* launched in 1655 was abandoned with little achieved of what even that limited programme had envisaged. The treasurer, Gustav Bonde, initiated radical cutbacks in government spending which made few inroads into the debt but compromised Sweden's security as arrears of army pay grew and investment in fortifications and the navy was curtailed. The purse-strings were loosened somewhat on Bonde's death in 1666, but that merely aggravated the financial crisis. Moreover, changes in the international situation since 1660 brought new threats. If Sweden's new position had made it a desirable ally, it had also won it the hostility of many, most conspicuously Denmark and Brandenburg-Prussia. The favourable conjuncture which had aided Swedish expansion from 1617 had passed.

The 1650s might have shown that Sweden could not afford war; it appeared that it could not afford peace either. The search began for the chimæra of subsidy without commitment. In April 1668, de la Gardie's opponents on the Council, who saw friendship with the Maritime Powers (England and the United Provinces) as less likely to end in war, were behind Sweden's entrance into the anti-French Triple Alliance, but the end of the War of Devolution three days before Sweden signed the subsidy treaty ended hope of payments. In 1670, the alliance was broken when Charles II shifted to friendship with France, and de la Gardie was able to explore the more lucrative option of a French alliance. In April 1672, Sweden signed a treaty with Louis XIV that guaranteed subsidies of 400,000 riksdalers per year to maintain 16,000 men in Germany, to be raised to 600,000 riksdalers in the event of Sweden entering the war.

De la Gardie has often been blamed for recklessness. He was not wholly irresponsible, however: subsidies were not the only consideration behind the French alliance. Hostility to Sweden had led Denmark into a series of anti-Swedish alliances: with England in 1661, with France in 1663, and with the Dutch in 1666. Relations with Denmark were not helped by Sweden's cultivation of the house of Holstein-Gottorp, which had inherited various appanage duchies created for younger sons of the kings of Denmark, and which had come into increasingly bitter disputes with the Oldenburgs over the complex scattering of ducal, royal and jointly-administered lands in Schleswig and Holstein. By marrying the redoubtable Hedvig Eleanora of Holstein-Gottorp, Charles X formed a dynastic alliance which was to bedevil relations with Denmark for decades. The threat of Danish attack was ever-present; in the intricate diplomatic manoeuvres of the 1660s and early 1670s, Sweden could not risk isolation, especially given the shaky state of its defences. In September 1672, Denmark joined Leopold I, Brandenburg, Brunswick-Celle, Brunswick-Wolfenbüttel and Hesse-Cassel in a defensive alliance, which was to maintain an allied force of 10,500 horse and 21,000 foot; in May 1673, it signed a treaty with the Dutch who agreed to subsidise a warfleet of twenty vessels and an army of 12,000.[41]

It briefly appeared as if de la Gardie's balancing-act might succeed: when war began in 1672, Sweden managed to keep out of it, and – while drawing French subsidies – acted as mediator in the successful 1673 peace talks between Brandenburg and France. It was not enough, however. Although England withdrew from the war in early 1674, the anti-French alliance strengthened. In May 1674, the Imperial Diet formally declared war on France; in June, Denmark was locked into the anti-French alliance by the Hague treaty, under which the Dutch promised to pay annual subsidies of 168,000 rigsdalers in return for the maintenance of a Danish army of 16,000. With the return of Brandenburg to the anti-French alliance in June 1674 the jigsaw was complete.

Sweden could not ignore a conflict in which Bremen and Verden were likely to be in the front line. A coalition containing both Denmark and Brandenburg was highly dangerous for Sweden, and neutrality was perhaps riskier than commitment, even if commitment inevitably had a price. With France pressed on all sides, it was unlikely that Sweden could continue to pocket subsidies without giving Louis any return on his investment. By the end of 1673, Sweden was maintaining an army of 15,000 on the continent; France promised to raise its subsidies to 900,000 riksdalers if it was increased to 22,000, which was achieved by September 1674. Although the Council tried to keep out of the war, Sweden could not feed such a large army in Swedish Pomerania; when Louis tugged his golden string it had to respond. The French threat to withold subsidies if the Swedes failed to attack, and growing difficulties with supply forced the invasion of Brandenburg in December 1674; this time, however, Sweden's heart was not really in it.

The usual verdict on the Scanian War is that it exposed Sweden's weakness and revealed a precipitous decline in the quality of the Swedish army. The course of the war was certainly different to what Swedes had come to expect. The tentative push by Karl Gustav Wrangel into Brandenburg in late 1674 was in stark contrast to Gustav Adolf's confident thrust into the heart of the Empire in 1631. Wrangel had only 13,000 men under his command; the rest of the 25–26,000 Swedes under arms in Germany were scattered in garrisons: 4–5,000 in Bremen, 2–3,000 in Wismar and 6–7,000 in Pomerania.[42] Scrabbling for supplies in the barren Uckermark, Wrangel planned a move westward once the weather improved to rendezvous with the 12,000-strong Hanoverian army, but before this could be effected, Frederick William had returned from the Rhine front against the advice of those who still feared Swedish military prowess. On 18/28 June 1675, he defeated the Swedes near Fehrbellin, shattering their aura of invincibility.

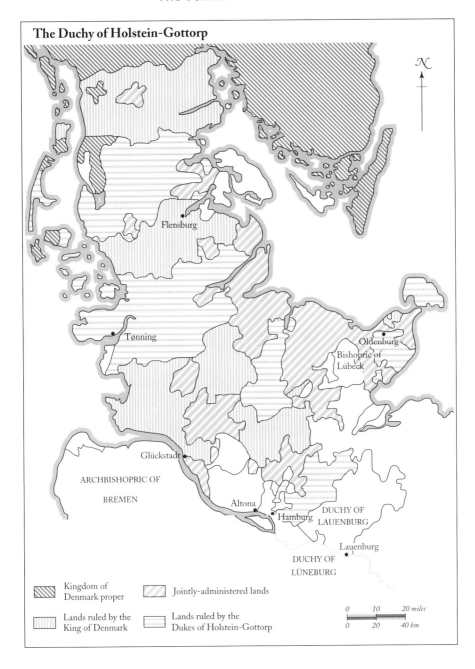

The Duchy of Holstein-Gottorp

Flensburg

Tønning

Oldenburg
Bishopric of
Lübeck

Glückstadt

ARCHBISHOPRIC OF

BREMEN

Altona
Hamburg
DUCHY OF
LAUENBURG

Lauenburg

DUCHY OF
LÜNEBURG

Kingdom of
Denmark proper

Jointly-administered lands

Lands ruled by the
King of Denmark

Lands ruled by the
Dukes of Holstein-Gottorp

0   10   20 miles
0   20   40 km

The consequences were dramatic, as Sweden's many enemies hurried to join the war, including Leopold I, the United Provinces and Christoph Bernhard von Galen, the ambitious bishop of Münster. In August, as the morale of the unpaid Swedish troops began to collapse, Christian V of

Denmark (1670–99) decided to curb his inclination for an immediate invasion of Sweden for the sake of his allies; pausing only to imprison his brother-in-law Christian Albert of Holstein-Gottorp, he hurried with 9,600 foot, 5,500 horse, 1,200 dragoons and 312 guns to help Frederick William drive the Swedes out of north Germany and secure Denmark's southern frontier before launching his bid to reconquer Denmark's lost provinces.[43]

Since Louis could only offer money and encouragement, there was little Sweden could do in the face of this coordinated onslaught. Christian attacked Wismar and Bremen, while Frederick William concentrated on subduing Swedish Pomerania. Wismar fell at the end of 1675; the Swedes were pushed out of Bremen despite support from Hamburg and England, while Brandenburg took Stralsund and Stettin. With the fall of Greifswald in November 1678, the Swedes lost their last toehold on the German coast and succeeded in scrambling only a small part of their German army back to Sweden. It had taken Sweden twenty years to acquire their German lands; they were lost in under three.

The key to the allied victory lay at sea. The Swedes had largely dominated the Baltic since the 1620s, yet as on land, they were unable to sustain their position. After the introduction of absolutism, the Danes strengthened their navy considerably, building twenty-four ships of about 18,000 tons between 1661 and 1670; in the same period Sweden constructed fifteen ships of 17,000 tons.[44] It was not enough; moreover, Denmark obtained Dutch support, while Sweden was still deploying converted merchantmen which were no longer effective in an age of rapidly-advancing naval technology. A Swedish fleet under Gustaf Otto Stenbock was defeated in October 1675; in May 1676, the Danish admiral Niels Juel opened the way to a landing on Gotland with a victory between Bornholm and Rügen, thereby providing the allies with a good point from which to mount a blockade of the Swedish coast. At Öland in June 1676, an allied fleet under the Dutch admiral Cornelis Tromp won another victory, before a crushing reverse at Köge Bay in July 1677 definitively ended Swedish control of the seas: the Swedes lost twelve large and ten smaller ships, 1,200 dead and wounded, and 3,000 prisoners.[45] Sweden could only watch helplessly as its German strongholds fell one by one.

The loss of naval control threatened more than the loss of an empire. On 29 June 1676 (OS), the Danes landed 14,000 men at Rå in Scania to establish a bridgehead for the reconquest of the lost provinces. The days when Swedish armies had taken Munich, Prague and Cracow seemed distant indeed. Although the Swedes, led by Charles himself, fought the Danes to a standstill in Scania, Halland and Bohuslän, the coming in 1679 of what was undoubtedly a favourable peace settlement for Sweden was less the result of Sweden's efforts, than of French diplomatic manoeuvrings at the peace talks in Nijmegen and divisions among Sweden's enemies – such as Denmark's quarrel with Lüneburg over possession of Bremen-Verden – which led to the collapse of the common front and the negotiation of separate settlements in which French pressure forced Brandenburg, Sweden's most intractable opponent, to settle at St Germain in June 1679. Apart from the loss of two insignificant Pomeranian districts to Brandenburg, Sweden recovered all its German possessions. French pressure on Denmark, which included the invasion of Oldenburg, ensured that Danish hopes of extending control over Holstein-Gottorp were disappointed in the peace of Fontainebleau (August 1679); despite the dominance of the Danish-Dutch fleet, the Danes failed to recover the provinces lost between 1643 and 1660. At the peace of Lund (September 1679) Sweden kept its conquests and its exemption from the Sound Dues in what amounted to a crushing defeat for Danish hopes.

This outcome was not the result of French diplomatic pressure alone. Despite frequent assertions that the Swedish army was in terminal decline by the 1670s, it did enough to ensure that the Danes had little with which to bargain. Much is often made of the failed thrust into Brandenburg in 1675–6, but Frederick William's rousing propaganda after his self-proclaimed triumph at Fehrbellin, sustained by generations of German historians, should not obscure the fact that the Swedes undertook the campaign in deeply unfavourable circumstances. Ill-prepared, forced into a war they did not wish to fight against a gathering coalition, the Swedes were deprived at the outset of their experienced commander Karl Gustaf Wrangel, who was largely incapacitated by illness and was unable to take direct control until after Fehrbellin. With Helmfelt, his second-in-command, also indisposed, control passed to Mardefelt, who was a fortifications expert, not an experienced field officer.

Frederick William had learned from Brandenburg's experiences during the Thirty Years War. He ordered his subjects to retreat in the face of the Swedish army, hiding or removing food supplies. The Swedes passed through areas denuded of people and supplies: in May 1675 Mardefelt gloomily noted reports that there was nothing to eat for twenty miles, admitting that his men were complaining bitterly at the lack of bread.[46] With a mere 13,000 men, the Swedish army was too small to have any realistic chance of controlling Brandenburg, or of mounting effective opposition to a retaliatory thrust by Frederick William.

Fehrbellin itself was far from the crushing triumph as which it is often portrayed. Wrangel had ordered the bulk of his army, including the infantry, to take up position at Alt-Brandenburg, on the Havel river west of Berlin, aiming to march further west to join up with Sweden's Hanoverian ally. Partly to ease supply problems, his half-brother Volmar was stationed further north at Havelsberg. Poor reconnaissance enabled Frederick William to thrust between the two Swedish forces and capture the bridge at Rathenow, whereupon Wrangel ordered his brother to cross at Fehrbellin. Volmar, however, found that the Brandenburgers had destroyed the bridge; while the Swedes hastened to repair it, they were caught on unsuitable terrain by Frederick William, and battered by the Brandenburg artillery, stationed on high ground. Although pressed by a much larger Brandenburg force, the Swedish right succeeded in covering the withdrawal of the rest of the army over the improvised bridge, before retreating itself. If the battle was undoubtedly a Brandenburg victory, it was far from shattering: Swedish losses were a mere 600 and the determined rearguard action meant that Frederick William was unable to press home his advantage.[47]

Subsequent military failures in Germany owed more to the loss of naval control and overwhelming odds than military incompetence. They were balanced by the determined defence of Sweden itself, in which the young king played a central role. The Danes used their powerful, well-equipped army to seize Helsingborg, Landskröna and Kristianstad by mid-August. Charles, however, was determined to avoid the unpalatable prospect of a long war on Swedish soil by seeking decisive victory on the battlefield. This strategy brought an early Swedish success at Halmstadt (August 1676), when a Danish force, sent on a speculative mission into Halland, was crushed by a bold strike in which the threefold Swedish advantage in cavalry proved decisive.[48]

It was the Swedish victory in the battle of Lund, however, on 4/14 December 1676 which prevented the Danes from securing Scania, and demonstrated that the Swedish army had not lost its edge. The outcome should have been a foregone conclusion. The Danish army, including substantial contingents of experienced German mercenaries, was well-equipped, rested and fed, having been sent into winter quarters in October. With 5,000 horse, 1,300 dragoons and 6,000 foot, it was 50 per cent larger than the Swedish army, which may have been only 7,500 strong and was ravaged by disease and hunger; moreover, the Danes enjoyed a threefold advantage in infantry and artillery. The Swedes had entered Scania in October with 11–12,000 men; on the eve of Lund their effective force was 1,750 foot and 4,700 horse.[49]

Exploiting a cold snap which froze the Lödde river, Charles launched a daring night attack; when this failed, he found himself in a bitter, eight-hour attritional struggle fought across difficult ground criss-crossed by stone walls and ditches. Under such conditions the Danish advantages should have proved decisive, especially when the impetuous Charles, together with his entire right wing and senior command, were swept up in headlong pursuit of the cavalry on the Danish left, broken in the first stage of the battle. The chase did not stop until the Swedes reached the Lödde, having shot through and looted the Danish camp; it took a further hour and a half to rally the scattered Swedish horse before returning to the main battlefield, where the exhausted Swedish centre and left was pinned back against Lund after a grim struggle in which the Danes exploited their substantial advantages in infantry and artillery. Just as the Danes threatened to overwhelm their opponents in the gathering dusk, Charles swept up at the head of nine squadrons in the Danish rear. Bursting through the Danish lines, the rein-forcements tipped the balance. The Danish horse was outflanked and driven off; the helpless infantry was abandoned to its fate. Just south of Vallkärra church, where the Danish foot made its bloody last stand, the slaughter did not stop until Helmfelt ordered quarter for all who laid down their arms. Between 2,300 and 3,000 Swedes and perhaps as many as 6,000 Danes – nearly half their army – were buried on the field of the bloodiest battle in the Danish–Swedish wars.[50]

Lund demonstrated the virtues of the aggressive Swedish style of fighting. It was the superior Swedish cavalry which decided the battle, despite the undoubted shortcomings in command which almost cost them victory after the madcap pursuit of the Danish left. Before the battle, in the light of their experiences at Halmstad, Rutger von Ascheberg, the experienced German commander in Swedish service, issued new orders for the cavalry at Charles's request, in which the last remnant of western cavalry tactics was abandoned. Gustav Adolf had urged his cavalry to charge home with the sword, but only after discharging their firearms. Convinced that this merely wasted time, Charles and Ascheberg commanded their cavalrymen to abandon this practice. Henceforward, Section Four of Swedish military regulations decreed that as soon as the cavalry saw the whites of their enemy's eyes, they were to press home their attack '*med gevalt*' (with force), and on no account to discharge their firearms. The aggressive tactics, learnt originally from the Poles, had finally been fully absorbed; the basis was laid at Lund for a philosophy of attack which was to reach its bloody heights under Charles XII. By the end of the war, the Danish horse had also been ordered to abandon the sterile caracole, but they lacked the training and skill to adopt the Swedish tactics. The Swedes remained masters of the battlefield.

It was hardly surprising, therefore, that the Danes henceforth sought to avoid battle, relying on the slow, grinding siege warfare so popular in western Europe, supported by the odd raid across the Norwegian border. As in 1563–70 and 1611–13, however, this strategy was incapable of bring-ing victory, despite considerable Danish advantages, including control of the seas. Before Lund, Christian only held Helsingborg, Landskröna and Kristianstad after a whole season of campaigning; after Lund, the Swedes retook Helsingborg. In 1677, the Danes failed in two attempts to retake Helsingborg, were beaten back from the walls of Malmo and were defeated outside Landskröna in July, having declined to give battle at Rönneberg in May when Charles rashly led 5,000 men and twenty-five guns into the field 400 metres from Christian's force of 12,000 and fifty guns. In the summer of 1678, a Danish force of 12,000 failed to prevent the recapture of Kristianstad. By late 1678, the Danes, despite outnumbering the Swedes, were reduced to clinging on to Helsingborg, which they had recaptured, and Landskröna. They were not sufficiently strong bargaining-counters to force the Swedes into concessions.

Absolutum dominium

If from the military point of view the Scanian War was not the disaster as which it is frequently portrayed, it starkly revealed the precariousness of Sweden's position. Above all, it demonstrated that the attempt to base Sweden's military power on a cash economy had seriously compromised its defences. Despite the successful expansion which had brought control of some of the most important trading cities in the Baltic, the substantial development of Sweden's commercial and industrial base, and extensive new taxes, Sweden could only afford to maintain a large professional army at somebody else's expense. That was possible only in the unique circumstances of the Thirty Years War. The subsidies provided by France after 1667 were wholly inadequate, and were in any case only offered to entice Sweden into a damaging war in pursuit of French interests. The arbiter of Europe had become a French marionette, barely able to defend its own territory and in possession of much of its empire after 1679 only by the grace of Louis XIV.

Denmark's invasion threw Sweden back on its own resources and revealed the price paid by the Swedish monarchy since Gustav Adolf began large-scale alienations of royal land. For the Swedish core of the army in the Scanian War was still based on *förläning*, *utskrivning* and *indelning*. By the 1670s, some two-thirds of Swedish land was in noble hands, and the Crown's share had fallen accordingly. With the dramatic reduction in the number of crown farms available to support the military state, the quality of both troops and equipment dropped alarmingly: the contrast between the well-armed, well-equipped Danish forces and the ragged, hungry troops who opposed them was shattering for Swedes who remembered the glory days of the 1640s and 1650s. A much-reduced royal domain was attempting to support a similar-sized army to that of the 1630s; it was an impossible task.

The response of the king and the *Riksdag* was radical. In an atmosphere of hostility towards the regency government, which had dragged Sweden into the Scanian War, the 1680 *Riksdag* put its faith in the young monarch who had won his spurs so dramatically at Lund. In December 1680, in response to a direct question from Charles, delegates of the four estates of the *Riksdag* asserted unanimously that the king was not bound by the 1634 Form of Government, but only by the law; furthermore, he was not required to seek the advice of the Council in forming policy since, as a hereditary adult king, he was responsible to God alone. The *Riksdag* further undermined aristocratic power with a sweeping *reduktion*, which went far beyond the cautious measure of 1655, in returning three-quarters of alienated farms to royal hands, and reducing the proportion of land in noble hands to a third.[51] Sweden had become an absolute monarchy.

Or rather Sweden had been declared to be an absolute monarchy by the *Riksdag*. For, unlike Denmark in 1660, what happened in Sweden was a reinterpretation of existing law; there was no rewriting of the constitution. The 1680 *Riksdag* and the 1693 Declaration of Sovereignty merely stated that the hereditary Christian monarchs of Sweden were answerable for their actions to God alone, not to any human agency. While the practical implications of this vanquishing of the long tradition of aristocratic constitutionalism were not to become fully apparent until the next reign, it was the *reduktion* rather than the declaration of an absolute monarchy which was the central achievement of the 1680 *Riksdag*. For the resources which thereby accrued to the monarchy underpinned the astonishing rebirth of the Swedish army that was again to dazzle Europe under Charles XII.

The events of 1680 were no military coup, but the culmination of a long political struggle; whatever else occurred in 1680, the *Riksdag* was not overawed by a display of royal power.[52] The dramatic political changes were generated from within the system, for the cumulative effects of a series of developments since the 1620s had ensured that even before the Scanian War the military state was facing a profound crisis. The resolution of that crisis took the form that it did because the growth of the military state had given substantial groups within Swedish society a direct interest in its efficient functioning.

Swedish society, at least at its upper level, had been transformed beyond recognition since 1611. The establishment of the military state had seen the creation of a new elite of army officers and civil servants, whose rapid growth threatened the grip of the small coterie of families which had dominated the Council since Gustav Adolf's reign: of forty-seven Council members between 1602 and 1632, thirty-four were related to each other, with a group of seven interlocked families at the heart of the oligarchy. Yet by 1650 this cosy clique was by no means representative even within its own estate. The nobility had expanded rapidly, as was recognised in the establishment of the *Riddarhus* in 1626; by the 1650s, half the nobility consisted of new creations.[53]

This was accompanied by a clear shift in its nature. The new nobles were state servitors, and the old ideal of the noble as above all a landowner had been comprehensively undermined: by 1680, only a third of new nobles owned allodial land, and there was little chance of them ever acquiring it.[54] It was this group which was most affected by the massive alienations of royal land. A large part of the donations comprised farms in Sweden's richest agricultural areas; the poor land that was left was therefore even less suited to sustaining the military state than the bare figures might suggest.

The coming of peace in 1648 revealed the extent of the problem. The royal domain was no longer capable of supporting the lower levels of the military state. Charles X postponed the day of reckoning by launching his Polish war, but it was impossible to disguise the extent of the problems after 1660, when the government reduced the army from 93,000 to 46,000; although most of those laid off were mercenaries, many Swedish officers found their career prospects sharply reduced. They were also left with few means of support, as the state increasingly proved unable to pay their wages or provide a living in kind. The regency government, whose members were visibly waxing fat on the proceeds of the alienated royal lands, initiated a sharp retrenchment in government finances, but demonstrated their priorities with their virtual abandonment of the 1655 *reduktion*: despite Charles X's express wish, and loud protests from the non-noble estates, Herman Fleming – a strong supporter of *reduktion* – was dismissed as treasurer in favour of Gustav Bonde, a member of the old guard.

The long political struggle which climaxed in 1680 was not simply a battle between the noble estate and the commoners, or a struggle between old and new nobles. The regents and Council-members were well aware of the problems; as state officials themselves they were also affected by the state's increasing inability to reward its servants, even if their personal financial loss was cushioned by the income they received from alienated royal lands. For all that its consequences were disastrous, de la Gardie's subsidy policy was a genuine attempt to solve the acute problems of public finance. Moreover, as those responsible for the direction of government during the regency, they were concerned directly with the efficient functioning of the state machine: de la Gardie himself had argued as long ago as 1655 that while service should be provided at a suitable level for those of good birth, there was a pressing need for competence, and had attacked the harmful effects of clientage.[55] There were always powerful dissentient voices within the high nobility itself: two of the leading critics were Johan Gyllenstierna and Clas Rålamb, both of impeccable aristocratic background. Gyllenstierna led attacks on the Council at the 1660 and 1664 *Riksdag*s, and emerged as a forceful opponent of de la Gardie when the chancellor pushed through his pro-French policy in 1667–8. Elected to the Council in 1668, Gyllenstierna continued his vociferous criticisms alongside Rålamb, who was already a member.[56]

Gyllenstierna, with support from other Council-members, urged an energetic completion of the 1655 *reduktion*. In the 1672 *Riksdag* he strongly backed the campaign by the lesser nobility for the institution of a more carefully-delineated hierarchy than had been provided for by the crude division of the nobility into three classes in 1626. This battle, which brought the establishment of a table of ranks in 1672, was one of the earliest signs of a cultural revolution within the nobility. The influx of new men had provoked the questioning of old assumptions about the nature of nobility. As an increasing number of nobles derived their income from sources other than landowning, and most particularly from state service, there was an increasing tolerance of commercial and industrial pursuits which would have made Axel Oxenstierna blanch. Lesser nobles attacked the traditional insistence on birth and lineage as the fundamental determining features of nobility, and the sources of noble virtue. It was increasingly argued that virtue derived from meritorious service to state and community rather than blueness of blood. The call for a table of ranks was a reflection of this cultural shift within the nobility: although the 1672 version fell short of what was envisaged by its proponents since it had a mere nine levels and only covered the top fourteen offices, it was amended in 1696 and 1714, and was an important statement of the principle that virtue was earned, and that birth played a small part in determining one's value to society.

Thus the assault on the Council came not just from the non-noble estates, but from within the ranks of the nobility – and even of the Council itself – and was flourishing before the mishandling of the Scanian War further compromised the narrow clique of aristocrats at the top. Baulked in their attempts to delay Charles's majority, which he attained in 1672, and to tie his hands by making him subject to the provisions of the Form of Government, the regents were strongly criticised for the state of the Swedish armed forces as revealed in the war, in which Charles's bravery and leadership qualities stimulated the growth of a significant royalist party, with Gyllenstierna playing a central role until his untimely death in the summer of 1680.

The die was already cast. With Charles now of age, the attack on the regents began at the 1675 *Riksdag*, which appointed a commission to examine the conduct of the regency government. Although its work proceeded slowly it prepared the ground for 1680. The stark question faced when the *Riksdag* assembled in October was how to cope with the desparate financial situation left after the Scanian War. There were but two alternatives: either to increase contributions from all estates, or to carry through a *reduktion* which would far exceed the relatively moderate measure of 1655. The mood of the lower estates and the lesser nobility was summed up by Gyllenstierna's brother

Krystoffer, who asked pointedly whether everyone should pay contributions for the sake of a few families who controlled 'the whole realm'.[57] In the light of the burdens born during the Scanian War, when *utskrivning* had reached its highest levels since the 1620s, there was little sympathy for holders of alienated crown lands. In a masterly tactical stroke Hans Wachtmeister, who piloted the *reduktion* through the *Riksdag*, ensured enthusiastic support from the lesser nobility by protecting them from its worst effects through a proposal to exempt all those whose total income from alienated Nörrköping-resolution estates did not exceed 600 dalers.

The high nobles were defenceless. The attack on alienations rested on solid legal foundations: the 1604 Norrköping resolution was quite clear on their illegality: in the 1680 debate over royal power it was stressed that the monarch, though absolute, must obey the law. The *Riksdag* passed a sweeping measure which far exceeded the 1655 *reduktion*, and the process of resumption of royal land began. Moreover, the royal government did not content itself with its overwhelming victory. With its powers confirmed, it surprised the nobility by demanding a contribution in addition to the *reduktion* – revealing that these were complementary, not alternative, solutions to the state's financial problems – and conducting a new wave of *reduktion* in 1682, which resumed many of the estates spared in 1680 by abandoning the 600-daler criterion.

The *reduktion* represented a remarkable success not just for the new royal government but for the service nobility as a whole – which included many of those most severely affected by it. Despite the rigour with which Charles insisted it be applied, it was a negotiated process. He was well aware that he depended on the service nobility to lead his new army, and nobles who had carried out improvements on their farms could petition for concessions. It was by no means Charles's aim to impoverish the nobility, and cases of genuine hardship were dealt with leniently.[58] It was, however, the use to which the Crown put its windfall which ensured its ultimate success. The *reduktion* returned revenues of 4 million riksdalers to the Crown and the national debt, which had bedevilled every Swedish government since 1648, fell from 40 to 50 million riksdalers in 1681 to 10 million by 1697.[59] More importantly, the *reduktion* was used to estabish for the first time a firm basis for the civil service and armed forces.

For it was the *indelningsverk*, which took the rest of Charles's reign to implement, rather than the *reduktion* which represents the true measure of his achievement. As Charles noted in 1688, the scheme was to establish the military on a 'certain and secure basis', above all to ensure that the system would be able to produce a continuous stream of recruits to fill the ranks when losses occurred, as it had failed to during the Scanian War.[60] The key to its success was the move away from the arbitrary recruitment which had characterised *utskrivning*. Building on a precedent established in Dalarna as long ago as 1611–12, later extended to Jämtland and Härjedalen, the government abandoned the emphasis on periodic conscriptions in which it sought to raise whatever number of troops it thought necessary, towards a system in which individual provinces contracted to raise and maintain regiments of a set size in both peace and war: 1,200 men in the case of the infantry. To support them, it extended and improved the system of allotment (*indelning*) used to support the cavalry since the 1620s. To spread the load of recruiting and maintaining a soldier, farms were grouped together in pairs, to form a file (*rota*), which was the basic unit of the system which supported the infantry. The basic unit supporting the cavalry was the *Rusthåll*: one or more prosperous farms which individually or collectively supported one or more cavalrymen. The farmers did not have to serve themselves, but recruited a soldier whom they provided with a house and his pay; in return he would help with farmwork when not on military service. It was the province's responsibility to maintain its regiment at the agreed size. Commissioners ensured that, in the event of losses, a rota system spread the load of finding and equipping replacements; this avoided the problems of the older allotment system, under which a *rusthåll* did not always feel obliged to replace a cavalryman killed in action, or keep his uniform and equipment up to standard. Thus the burdens were spread far more evenly than before, when the load of *utskrivning* had largely been carried by the dwindling number of crown peasants. The *indelningsverk* was extended to tax-peasants, and, although there were still some exemptions for nobles, the extent of their privileges was greatly reduced.[61]

The *indelningsverk* succeeded because it was a well-thought-out plan, designed on the basis of experience, which corrected some of the problems of the earlier version, and passed the ultimate test of satisfying the social groups which supported the political revolution of 1680. It established an arrangement which was mutually beneficial to the state, which required an army, and the propertied peasantry, which was responsible for providing it. The key elements of the new scheme were the definitive move away from the previous tendency to insist that service should be performed by the actual holder of the allotted farm, and the establishment of fixed norms, so that all parties involved knew what was expected of them, thereby removing the uncertainty of *utskrivning*, under which requirements varied greatly from year to year. Its establishment was based on long negotiation with local communities before the provincial contracts were agreed, and the system was administered locally.

The peasant farmer had much to gain. He was now exempt from service in perpetuity, as were his family and his servants, and the burden remained predictable. Thus there were extensive profits to be made, since increases in production were not matched by significant increases in the tax burden.[62]

Wealthy farmers involved in a *rusthåll* were completely exempt from taxation, although this was not the case for those supporting infantrymen. What appears at first sight to be a return to more traditional forms of military recruitment was therefore to play an important part in the social differentiation of the Swedish countryside, and provide a stimulus to agricultural development. It was not difficult to find recruits from among the poorer elements of rural society, since soldiers, who served until the age of forty, were provided with accommodation – usually a small cottage – and wages in return for military service and, in peacetime at least, a certain amount of agricultural labour. Although the end of his period of service threatened social degradation, with eviction from his billet, soldiers were often able to live on in their cottages if they had a son who could take their place in the ranks.[63] Peasants in the richer areas of Sweden often recruited far afield, in the poorer areas of the north, where opportunities in agriculture were not so lucrative.

Although there were enormous problems posed by the introduction of the *indelningsverk*, most notably with regard to the recruitment and maintenance of cavalry, the system succeeded in establishing by Charles's death in 1697 a permanent, native, professional army with a constant size of eleven cavalry and twenty-three infantry regiments, a total of 11,000 horse and 30,000 foot. It was well trained and well equipped, while the formation of provincial regiments meant that local patriotism helped strengthen morale. The funds released by the *indelningsverk* also permitted the maintenance of a further 25,000 mercenaries to garrison the overseas provinces, and a major reconstruction of the navy, with the establishment of a new naval base at Karlskrona, south of Kalmar, which was free of ice earlier in the year than Stockholm; by 1700, the Swedes possessed a fleet of 53,000 tons, compared to Denmark's 46,000 tons.[64] The transformation wrought in Swedish society was significant: some 16 per cent of the units of land assessment (*mantal*) in Sweden were devoted to the maintenance of the cavalry alone, while in some areas, agricultural life was dominated by the needs of the army. In Fellingsbro parish in central Sweden, ninety-three farmsteads (31.1 per cent) were already supporting a cavalryman in 1684. When other forms of *indelning* are added to this figure, such as farms supporting officers, farms providing horses for the cavalry, and those providing the extra revenues (*augmentatshemman*) assigned to the cavalry, a total of 130 of the 297 farmsteads in the parish were directly involved in supporting the new military state. By 1700, this figure had risen to 202 – over two-thirds.[65]

The new system was successful because it rested on consent. The assertion of the absolute nature of the monarchy and the construction of the new military system was neither an act of arbitrary state power nor a victory of one class over another. Both developments represented the response of a consensual political system to an urgent dilemma: military success had by 1660 brought benefits to wide sectors of Swedish society, but had led to an unequal spread of the burdens. Too many people, however, had an important interest in the better functioning of the new state machine. Its creation had stimulated substantial changes in Swedish society and culture since 1560. Those changes had been most widespread among the nobility, but many sectors of society had benefited from the enhanced opportunities it had brought. Between 1680 and 1697, Charles XI presided over the refoundation of the military state. Sweden's military revolution was secured and the survival of his system for over two centuries bears eloquent testimony to its aptness for Swedish conditions. Within three years, however, it was to face its greatest test, in a conflict whose origins were, at least in part, bound up with its formation.

Notes

1　Lind, *Hæren* pp. 92–105.
2　E. Ladewig Petersen and K.J.V. Jespersen, 'Two revolutions in early modern Denmark' in E. Kouri and T. Scott (eds), *Politics and Society in Reformation Europe* (London, 1987) p. 488.
3　S. Olden-Jørgensen, 'Enevoldsarveregeringsakten og Kongeloven. Forfatnings-spørgsmålet i Danmark fra Oktober 1660 til November 1665' *HTD* 93 (1993) pp. 295–321. For an English translation of selections from the Royal Law, see E. Ekman, 'The Danish Royal Law of 1665' *JMH* 29 (1959) pp. 102–7.
4　K.J.V. Jespersen, 'Absolute monarchy in Denmark: change and continuity' *SJH* 12 (1987) pp. 307–16; L. Jespersen, 'The *Machtstaat* in seventeenth-century Denmark' *SJH* 10 (1985) pp. 271–304; idem. '1648 – Magtstat eller minimumsstat? Begreber og udviklingslinier' in L. Jespersen and A. Svane-Knudsen, *Stænder og magtstat* (Odense, 1989).
5　K.J.V. Jespersen, 'The rise and fall of the Danish nobility, 1600–1800' in H.M. Scott (ed.), *The European Nobilities in the Seventeenth and Eighteenth Centuries* II (London, 1995) p. 41; Ladewig Petersen and Jespersen, 'Two revolutions' p. 478.
6　Jespersen, 'The rise' pp. 45, 48.
7　E. Ladewig Petersen, 'From domain state to tax state. Synthesis and interpretation' *SEHR* 23 (1975) p. 137.
8　Jespersen, 'Absolute monarchy' p. 310, n. 7.
9　The Poles demanded 55 rigsdalers contribution per month from one parish where the Swedes had levied 16. A. Lassen, *1659 da landet blev øde* (Copenhagen, 1965) p. 17.
10　Pasek, *Memoirs* p. 9; Lassen, *1659* pp. 38–40, 68, 96–7.
11　Lind, *Hæren* pp. 208–12, 236–7.
12　Ibid. p. 229.
13　Jespersen, 'The rise' pp. 55–7.

14 Lind, *Hæren* p. 249; idem., 'Military and absolutism: the army officers of Denmark-Norway as a social group and political factor, 1660–1848' *SJH* 12 (1987) p. 228.

15 F.L. Carsten, *The Origins of Prussia* (Oxford, 1954) pp. 192–201.

16 A. Åberg, 'The Swedish army, from Lützen to Narva' in M. Roberts (ed.), *Sweden's Age of Greatness 1632–1718* (London, 1973) p. 267; Böhme, 'Geld' p. 55.

17 Quoted by Zernack, 'Schweden' p. 212.

18 Roberts, *Swedish Imperial Experience* p. 126.

19 S.A. Nilsson, 'Från förläning till donation. Godspolitik och statshushållning under Gustav II Adolf' *HTS* (1968) pp. 401–38.

20 Since a Swedish mile measured ten kilometres, the importance of this exemption should not be underestimated.

21 S. Dahlgren, *Karl X Gustav och Reduktionen* (Uppsala, 1964) p. 3; M. Roberts, 'Queen Christina and the General Crisis of the seventeenth century' in idem, *Essays* p. 115. Although Christina's lavish donations meant that 62 per cent of the alienations occurred in peacetime, as Roberts points out, this does not mean that they had nothing to do with the war. It was precisely after the war's end that the clamour for rewards from officers and nobles was at its peak.

22 Nilsson, 'Från förläning' p. 403, table 1.

23 See K. Ågren, *Adelns bönder och kronans* (Uppsala, 1964).

24 S.A. Nilsson, 'Reduktion eller kontribution. Alternativ inom 1600-talets svenska finanspolitik' *Scandia* 24 (1958) pp. 73–83.

25 H. Landberg, 'Krig på kredit. Svensk rustningsfinansiering våren 1655' in H. Landberg, L. Ekholm, R. Nordlund and S.A. Nilsson (eds), *Det kontinentalna krigets ekonomi* (Uppsala, 1971) pp. 18, 29, 77, 89.

26 RA, Kamm. PR: 1656 1 Preussen: Huvudbok ff. 1–3.

27 RA, Kamm. PR: 1657 1 Preussen: Huvudbok ff. 1–4.

28 RA, Kamm. PR: 1658 1 Preussen: Huvudbok ff. 1–3.

29 B. Fredriksson, *Försvarets finansiering* (Uppsala, 1976) p. 27.

30 N.-E. Villstrand, *Anpassning eller protest* (Åbo, 1992) p. 163.

31 Based on figures in Nilsson, 'Hemlandet' p. 157.

32 J. Lindegren, *Utskrivning och utsugning* (Uppsala, 1980) pp. 144–77.

33 Villstrand, *Anpassning* p. 59.

34 S. Lundkvist, 'Resurser, skattetryck och fattigdom i 1610-talets Sverige' in M. Revera and R. Torstendahl (eds), *Bördor, bönder, börd i 1600-talets Sverige* (Motala, 1979) p. 144. For a critique of those who see Sweden's institutions in this period as instruments of control and exploitation by the central government and a 'feudal' class, see E. Österberg, 'Local political culture versus the state. Patterns of interaction in pre-industrial Sweden' in idem, *Mentalities and other Realities* (Lund, 1991).

35 Österberg's findings with regard to tax-relief after the First Northern War are largely applicable to Småland in the 1620s: L.-O. Larsson, 'Lokalsamhälle och centralmakt i Sverige under 1500- och 1600-talen' in N.-E. Villstrand (ed.), *Kustbygd och centralmakt 1560–1721* (Helsingfors, 1987) pp. 194–5.

36   For a discussion of the problem, see Villstrand, *Anpassning* pp. 53–8.

37   Parker, *Military Revolution* pp. 49, 196, n. 18; there were 13,400 Scots in Danish service alone in the 1620s: S. Murdoch, 'Scotland, Denmark-Norway and the House of Stuart. A diplomatic and military analysis' unpublished Aberdeen University Ph.D. thesis (1998) p. 247.

38   Viirankoski, 'Impact' pp. 118–19. Finns formed nothing like 40 per cent of the empire's population.

39   Lindegren, *Utskrivning* pp. 256–60.

40   Viirankoski, 'Impact' pp. 123–4.

41   F. Askgaard, 'Nordisk udenrigspolitik 1660–1675' in F. Askgaard and A. Stade (eds), *Kampen om Skåne* (Copenhagen, 1983) pp. 23–9, 34–6.

42   'Handlingar rörande sommarfälttåget i Brandenburg 1675 och striden vid Fehrbellin' J. Mankell (ed.), *HB* III (Stockholm, 1877) p. 240.

43   E. Gyllenstierna, 'Kampen i Tyskland' *Kampen om Skåne* p. 269.

44   Glete, *Navies* p. 192.

45   C.E. Almgren, 'Svensk strategi och krigsledning' *Kampen om Skåne* p. 146.

46   'Fältmarskalken Mardefelts diarium' in Mankell (ed.), 'Handlingar' no. 1 p. 245.

47   Gyllenstierna, 'Kampen' pp. 268–9.

48   A. Stade, 'Fältslagen under Skånska Kriget' *Kampen om Skåne* pp. 183–9.

49   Ibid. pp. 206–9.

50   Ibid. p. 233.

51   A.F. Upton, 'The *Riksdag* of 1680 and the establishment of royal absolutism in Sweden' *EHR* 403 (1987) pp. 305–6; idem *Charles XI and Swedish Absolutism* (Cambridge, 1998) pp. 31–50; K. Ågren, 'The *Reduktion*' in Roberts (ed.), *Sweden's Age of Greatness* pp. 246–7.

52   B. Asker, *Officerarna och det svenska samhället 1650–1700* (Uppsala, 1983) pp. 137–43.

53   P. Englund *Det hotade huset* (Stockholm, 1989) p. 13; A.F. Upton, 'The Swedish nobility, 1600–1772' in Scott (ed.), *European Nobilities* II pp. 11–28.

54   Englund, *Det hotade huset* p. 129.

55   Asker, *Officerarna* p. 106, n. 3.

56   G. Rystad, *Johan Gyllenstierna, rådet och kungamakten* (Lund, 1955) pp. 6–11; 37–47.

57   Quoted by Nilsson, 'Reduktion' p. 68.

58   Upton, *Charles XI* pp. 62–4.

59   A. Åberg, *Karl XI* (Stockholm, 1958) p. 119; Ågren, 'The *reduktion*' p. 247.

60   S. Ågren, *Karl XI:s Indelningsverk för Armén* (Uppsala, 1922) p. 27.

61   Upton, *Charles XI* pp. 71–89.

62   J. Backlund, *Rusthållarna i Fellingsbro 1648–1748* (Uppsala, 1993) p. 9.

63   Åberg, 'The Swedish army' p. 243.

64   Upton, *Charles XI* pp. 83–4; Glete, *Navies* p 233.

65   Backlund, *Rusthållarna* p. 46, table 1.

CHAPTER NINE

The Start of the Great Northern War

The outbreak of war

In the hands of his gifted son, Charles XI's army was to prove a formidable force. It was, however, an army built for peace, not for war, designed to provide a powerful deterrent sustained by Sweden's own resources, thus avoiding the need for foreign subsidy which had proved so disastrous in the 1670s. After 1680 Charles sought peace. He married Christian V's daughter Ulrika Eleanora in 1680, hoping to promote rapprochement with Denmark, and if Swedish contingents did fight against Louis XIV in the Nine Years War, Charles was careful to keep Sweden out of direct involvement in the quarrels of western Europe.

The stormclouds were already gathering, however, when Charles died prematurely in April 1697. The treaties of the 1660s had left much unsettled, while the Scanian War had revealed Sweden's vulnerability. The long period of peace was more due to the distraction of Poland-Lithuania and Russia by Turk and Tatar than the emergence of stability in northeastern Europe. Denmark was smarting from losing control of the Sound, and the English were mounting a serious challenge to Dutch commercial hegemony in the Baltic. Brandenburg-Prussia and Russia were increasingly concerned about their lack of a major Baltic port, especially since Sweden's endemic financial weakness ensured that it sought to maximise its income from customs duties. Despite Charles's reconstruction of the army and navy – restored to 34 ships of the line and 11 frigates by 1697 – Sweden's grip on its empire remained fragile.

An age was passing. Charles XI's death was one of a series which saw the departure from the scene of a generation of monarchs who had experienced the last round of the Northern Wars. The first to go, in June 1696, was

John Sobieski, who was followed into the grave by Christian V in August 1699. Alexis was long dead, but two decades of uncertainty in Russian politics were ended by the death of his invalid son Ivan V in February 1696, which left Ivan's energetic half-brother Peter (1682–1725) in sole charge of a state whose new military potential was demonstrated by the capture of Azov from the Turks in July of that year. Charles was succeeded by his precocious fourteen-year-old son, Charles XII, whose military talents were to prove greatly superior to those of Frederik IV of Denmark (1699–1730) and the new king of Poland-Lithuania, Frederick Augustus, elector of Saxony, who took the name Augustus II on his election in 1697. Finally, Frederick William's successor in Brandenburg, Frederick III (1688–1713) transformed his status in 1701 by securing Leopold I's permission for his coronation as Frederick I, king in Prussia.[1]

European politics had changed substantially since 1667. Statesmen in western Europe were increasingly obsessed with Spain as the childless Carlos II shuffled towards his grave. It also affected eastern Europe, where the long series of Turkish wars was winding down as Leopold I prepared to contest the Spanish succession with Louis XIV. The ageing Sobieski had lost the fire which had animated him during the 1683 Vienna campaign and his subjects forced him to withdraw from the Holy League in 1696. Augustus, who had led the imperial forces against the Turks in 1695–6, was keen enough, but the Commonwealth hastened to make peace. Only Peter was still enthusiastic, planning to extend Russian power along the shores of the Black and Caspian seas. His diplomacy on his famous embassy to western Europe in 1697–8 was largely devoted to reviving the anti-Turkish coalition, but he was unwilling to fight alone. When Austria, Poland-Lithuania and Venice settled with the Ottomans at Carlowitz (January 1699), Peter opened negotiations, securing a twenty-year truce in June 1700.

A new Northern War had already begun. For Sweden's perceived weakness under its adolescent monarch had roused those with scores to settle. Chief among these was Denmark. Despite Charles XI's efforts at détente, neither Christian nor Frederik accepted the losses of 1645–60. Moreover, despite Ulrika Eleonora's mollifying presence at court, the Holstein-Gottorp party remained strong, led by Hedvig Eleonora, Charles X's widow. The principal bone of contention remained the question of whether the duchy's sovereign rights, confirmed in all Swedish-Danish treaties after 1645, included the *jus armorum*, which for Denmark represented a permanent provocation, since the duchies provided easy access to its vulnerable southern frontier. Ulrika Eleonora died in 1693, and although the dying Charles XI seems to have recommended that his son marry Christian's daughter Sophia, Hedvig Eleonora and Frederick IV of Holstein-Gottorp scotched the plan. Barely a month after Charles's death, Denmark exploited the annoyance of the

Maritime Powers with Sweden on account of its neutral stance in the Nine Years War by razing the fortresses built by Holstein-Gottorp in Schleswig in breach of the 1689 Altona agreement, in which the Maritime Powers upheld the rights of Holstein-Gottorp in the hope of securing Swedish support against Louis XIV.[2]

This was merely a shot across the bows; past experience had shown the folly of attacking Sweden without international support. The Maritime Powers had long sought to maintain the balance between the Scandinavian kingdoms and, as the Spanish succession crisis built up, opposed any war in the north which might interrupt the flow of naval supplies from the Baltic and prevent Sweden or Denmark joining an anti-French alliance. Christian therefore looked east for allies. The first to respond was Augustus, who sought to strengthen his position in the Commonwealth through an active foreign policy, coveting Livonia, which he saw as a potential hereditary duchy for the Wettin dynasty that would improve its prospects of retaining the Polish throne.

In March 1698 the Danes and Saxons signed a defensive alliance. Five months later Augustus met Peter at Rawa near Lwów where, between colossal drinking bouts, they held private discussions at which an anti-Swedish alliance was discussed. It is unlikely that any concrete plans were made; for Augustus, Livonia was still only one of a number of possible hereditary principalities he coveted, including Moldavia, Wallachia and Ducal Prussia: indeed, the seizure of Elbing by Frederick III in November 1698 on the pretext of the Commonwealth's failure to pay its debts to Brandenburg after the Second Northern War provoked outrage in Poland which might stimulate support for a war.[3] Gradually, however, an anti-Swedish alliance formed: in April 1699, Peter signed a defensive agreement with Denmark, to come into effect after Russia had made peace with Turkey; in September, he put flesh on the bones of his informal pact with Augustus by signing an agreement at Preobrazhenskoe committing Russia to an attack on Ingria in 1700. Danish enthusiasm was not dulled by Frederik IV's accession in August: four days after the Preobrazhenskoe treaty a new Saxon–Danish defensive-offensive treaty was signed in Dresden. The coalition was complete.

By the time the Russo-Ottoman peace was signed in June, the war was well under way. The Danish army moved into Schleswig and Holstein in late 1699 to await Augustus's attack on Livonia. After an attempt to take Riga by surprise in December was thwarted, a Saxon force of three infantry and four dragoon regiments – 5,000 men – crossed the Dvina in February, and seized Dünamunde (23 March), as Frederik moved into Holstein-Gottorp to besiege Tønning.[4] In late August, within days of hearing of the peace with Turkey, Peter's armies were on the move. For Sweden, the nightmare of a three-front war had become reality.

A surprise beginning

The allies did not expect a long war. The military odds seemed entirely in their favour, while they hoped to exploit anti-Swedish feelings in the Baltic provinces. For if the *reduktion* succeeded in Sweden without provoking major opposition, it was a different story across the Gulf of Finland. Livonia's tangled history made it extremely difficult to determine just what should be regarded as royal land, and the *reduktion* in Livonia, after a comprehensive land-survey, affected 80.8 per cent of the land and 74.2 per cent of peasant households, leaving the Crown with 72.3 per cent of the land, compared with only 1.25 per cent in 1680. The situation was slightly better in Estonia; nevertheless, 53 per cent of estates were affected.[5] Although efforts were made to compromise with the lesser nobility, opposition was fierce. Two delegations led by the choleric Johann Reinhold von Patkul to Stockholm attacked the *reduktion*; by late 1694, it was largely complete, but talks had reached deadlock, which the government sought to break by trying Patkul for *lèse majesté*. After delivering a passionate defence of Livonian liberties, he slipped into exile, where he fomented anti-Swedish feeling, assuring all who would listen that the Baltic nobility was on the point of rebellion. All was apparently set fair for a rapid victory

Nobody expected what followed. By the time Peter declared war on 9/20 August as the Saxons began the siege of Riga in earnest following the arrival of their artillery, Denmark was already out of the war. Sweden, having promised in January to back the Maritime Powers in upholding the treaty of Rijswick against Louis XIV, was able to call on their support as guarantors of the Altona agreement. On 13–14 July (OS), the Swedish fleet evaded a slightly larger Danish force with a daring manoeuvre along the Swedish coast, and joined up with an Anglo-Dutch fleet before landing a 10,000-strong army on Zealand and marching on Copenhagen. Faced by a blockade of his capital and under pressure from the Maritime Powers, Frederik caved in, signing the treaty of Travendal on 7/18 August. By the time the Russian army left Moscow, the last Swedish troops had left Danish soil.

Travendal was a serious blow. Livonia was still recovering from the devastating effects of the great famine of 1695–6, in which some 50,000 had died, and despite Patkul's promises, the Livonian nobility showed little enthusiasm for the Saxons. Augustus's siege of Riga was chaotic; without naval support he had no means of cutting off supply from the sea, and an administrative oversight meant that the Saxon ammunition was mostly of the wrong calibre for the heavy siege guns.[6] Having achieved nothing but the capture of Dünamünde, optimistically rechristened Augustusburg, he raised the siege on 29 September. By the time that the Russian army, at least 35,000-strong, began its bombardment of Narva on 31 October, the Saxons were entering winter quarters south of the Dvina. As the Russians laboriously constructed their elaborate siegeworks, Charles was already heading for Estonia. In the battle of Narva (19/30 November), the Swedes hurled themselves at the Russian defences under cover of a fortuitous snowstorm. Outnumbered nearly three to one, they broke through at two points, smashing the Russian line into three parts before rolling it up. The Russians were routed; including those drowned in a desperate stampede across the river they lost 8,000 men and 145 guns. The Swedish empire was not as vulnerable as it looked.

Far from it: for the next six years, Charles swept all before him. He first attacked Augustus. Deterred from invading Saxony by the Maritime Powers, who wished to prevent diversions in Germany which Louis XIV might exploit, Charles forced his way across the Dvina into Courland in July 1701 then invaded Lithuania in January 1702, before destroying a Saxon-Polish army at Kliszów (July 1702). Warsaw, Cracow, Poznań, Thorn and Elbing were occupied and in July 1704 Charles presided over the election of his own candidate, Stanisław Leszczyński, as king of Poland-Lithuania. Two years later, following a crushing victory by Karl Gustaf Rehnskiöld over a Saxon-Russian army at Fraustadt (February 1706), Charles invaded Saxony where, in Augustus's absence, he forced the treaty of Altranstädt (September 1706) on the Saxon Estates, by which Augustus was to abdicate his Polish throne. Augustus – who had already secretly ratified the treaty – led a Saxon-Russian army to victory at Kalisz a month later, but Charles's publication of Altranstädt exposed his duplicity and forced his compliance: in November he returned to Saxony.

Charles's long sojourn in the Commonwealth, however, left the Baltic provinces open. In 1703 Peter seized Ingria, where he began to build his new capital of St Petersburg; in 1704, he took Dorpat, Narva and Ivangorod, while Russian troops streamed into the Commonwealth to support the anti-Swedish forces who were not reconciled to Leszczyński by Augustus's abdication. In 1707, with three of his enemies out of the war, Charles turned east for the showdown with Peter. With his army rested and replenished, he rejected Peter's offer of peace in return for the cession of Ingria, and marched east. Peter, however, had prepared his strategy well: his armies withdrew into Russia, devastating the country as they went. For most of the summer of 1708, Charles sat in Lithuania waiting for Adam Ludvig Lewenhaupt to gather supplies for the attack on Russia. In September, without waiting for Lewenhaupt, Charles decided to turn south to winter in the Ukraine, where he hoped for support from the rebel Cossack hetman Ivan Mazepa. The risky strategy proved disastrous. Peter pounced on Lewenhaupt at Lesnaia (28 September 1708 OS), defeating him and seizing the supply train.

Lewenhaupt joined Charles in October, but the Swedish army suffered dreadfully in the bitter winter of 1709: constantly harried by the Russians, soldiers died in their thousands from cold and disease. With Polish and Russian forces blocking Leszczyński from coming to his aid, Charles was trapped. By the time Peter was ready to give battle outside Poltava, which Charles had been besieging since early April, the Swedes were running low on ammunition and morale. On 27 June 1709 OS, the army built by Charles XI and perfected by his son was shattered on the narrow plain north of Poltava. Three days later, as Charles crossed the Dnieper into Turkish exile, 17,000 demoralised Swedes surrendered at Perevolochna. The war was to last another twelve years, but the *Stormaktstid* was over.

Transformation

The Swedish victory at Narva surprised nobody: spectacular victories over large Russian armies were nothing new. Ever since, Narva has been central to accounts of Peter's transformation of the Russian army. Most begin, as Voltaire began, by stressing Russian backwardness:

> The Russians are sturdy, tireless, and perhaps as brave as the Swedes, but it takes time to harden troops to war, and discipline to make them invincible. The only regiments from which something might be expected were commanded by German officers, but they were few in number. The rest were barbarians, dragged away from their forests, dressed in the skins of wild animals, some armed with bows and arrows, others with clubs. Few possessed firearms and none . . . had witnessed a regular siege; there was not a single competent gunner in the entire army. One hundred and fifty cannon, which should have reduced . . . Narva to ashes, had scarcely made a breach in it, whereas the town's artillery was constantly slaughtering entire files of men in the trenches. Narva was practically without fortifications, and . . . Horn . . . had less than a thousand regular troops; nevertheless, an immense host had been unable to reduce the town in six weeks.[7]

Clausewitz discounted Narva as an example of a small army conquering a larger force because the Russians were 'hardly European', while Frederick II of Prussia claimed that Peter's army was 'a horde of badly-armed and undisciplined barbarians without good commanders', comparing Narva to Spanish triumphs over South American Indians.[8] Peter himself stressed that defeat was only to be expected, since there was only one veteran regiment (the Lefortvskii) and the two guard regiments had only experienced two attacks at Azov; apart from 'a few colonels, officers and ordinary soldiers' the rest of the army were inexperienced recruits.[9] It was the shock of Narva that caused Peter to launch his indefatigable efforts to transform this motley force into the army that destroyed the Swedes at Poltava.

It is a beguiling story, beguilingly told; like many historical myths, there is some truth behind it. Yet Peter's description of the Russian army, let alone Voltaire's, is colourful hyperbole. General Ludwig Nikolaus von Hallart, an experienced fortifications expert sent by Augustus to help the Russians during the siege, and by no means an uncritical admirer of the Russian army, had a rather different opinion. In October he described the arrival of nineteen battalions 'of fine infantry . . . all the infantry were not only well-dressed and particularly well drilled, but also well-armed; each regiment had its own uniform.' He also had good things to say of later arrivals, including 2,000 'Poles' from Smolensk, whose mounts and armaments 'were of the best'. He did complain that during the battle the Russians behaved 'more like a flock of sheep than a regular army', but blamed the defeat on the flight of Sheremetev's old-style cavalry which, if it had attacked the Swedish flank, would have secured victory.[10] According to Adlerfelt, the Russian camp was 'advantageously fortified', with several batteries 'placed in the most advantageous manner, and with a strong line of countervallation', an opinion shared by an engineer in the Swedish army.[11]

Whatever the reasons for its defeat, the Russian army was hardly Voltaire's bunch of hide-clad savages. It was certainly new: the expansion of Peter's new army from its original core of the two Guards regiments (Preobrazhenskii and Semenovskii) and the veteran Lefortovskii and Butyrskii regiments had only begun in earnest in November 1699. Early projections of sixty new regiments proved optimistic, and the shortage of recruits and officers meant that it was only after the amalgamation of under-strength formations in the summer of 1700 that an army of 32,000 was assembled, comprising two dragoon and twenty-seven infantry regiments, each 1,200–1,300 strong. Twenty-five regiments were sent against the Swedes, with a paper strength of 29,543.[12] The size of the Russian army at Narva is difficult to establish with any degree of accuracy, although the contention that the regiments were seriously under strength is open to question: this was true of those raised initially, but mergers brought the numbers much closer to the 1,200–1,300 projections. The new regiments, reinforced by units of *strel'tsy*, old-style cavalry and Cossacks, formed an army of at least 35,000 men,[13] of which only 26,000 were able to cram into the 7-kilometre countervallation to face the Swedish attack. Even if the odds were not as heavily stacked against the Swedes as is sometimes suggested, they were still outnumbered by more than three to one without taking into account the substantial Russian reserves; nevertheless, the assumption that the Swedish victory against such odds merely confirms that the Russians

were an inexperienced rabble deserves a more critical consideration than it
has frequently received.

It suited Peter to depict his army at Narva in such terms. For it was basic
to the myth, launched by Peter himself, of Peter the Great, Pushkin's far-
sighted bronze horseman who opened the window on the west and dragged
Russia into the modern world. Yet if Peter's achievement was indeed
considerable – and his central role in Russia's military transformation is
beyond doubt – Narva's spectacular outcome should not obscure the important military continuities between his reign and those of his predecessors,
continuties which Peter himself recognised. It is true that the army had
been hastily thrown together in under a year. Nevertheless, although their
opponents were certainly well-trained and well-drilled, the Swedes were no
more experienced in battle than the Russians. The great Swedish armies of
Gustav Adolf and Charles X were distant memories. Since 1660, Sweden
had fought one brief, unhappy war, and even that was nearly a generation
ago. The few surviving veterans of Charles X's wars were too old for active
service; men like Karl Gustaf Rehnskiöld who had served in the Scanian
War had done so as junior officers. It is true that many Swedes served in the
long wars against Louis XIV – Lewenhaupt had fought with the Bavarians
against the Turks, subsequently rising to the rank of lieutenant-colonel in
Dutch service – nevertheless, most ordinary soldiers had little or no direct
experience of battle before 1700. They were part-time soldiers who, in
peacetime, spent much of the year at home; one report of Narva suggests
that the Finnish cavalry did more harm than good, once charging their own
men rather than the enemy.[14]

Even if one accepts Peter's contention that only the Lefortovskii regiment
was composed of veterans, and that the Guards had only limited experience
of actual warfare, these three regiments on their own were not substantially
outnumbered by the entire Swedish infantry. Furthermore, it is open to
question whether the rest of the Russian army was composed entirely of raw
recruits. Unlike Sweden, Russia had done a considerable amount of fighting
since 1660. Apart from the need for constant readiness against Tatar attack,
the end of the war with Poland-Lithuania in 1667 had brought little respite.
Ottoman aggression and the continuing chaos in the Ukraine ensured that
for much of the 1670s Russia was engaged in the southwest. After 1680, it
was fully committed against Turkey in a war which saw the abortive Crimean
campaigns of 1687 and 1689, and the Azov sieges of 1695 and 1696.

The army with which Russia fought these wars had already been transformed. Far from being a period of stagnation, the seventeenth century had
seen rapid and comprehensive change not just in the nature and composition
of the army, but in the administrative system which supported it: this was a
period in which Russia's territory expanded threefold and its administrative

personnel grew tenfold.[15] Much of this administrative expansion was due to changes which occurred long before Peter began playing soldiers at Preobrazhenskoe. The decisive shift away from the old-style Muscovite forces – the *strel'tsy* and the *dvorianstvo* cavalry – had taken place during the Thirteen Years War. Already by 1663, new-formation units constituted 79 per cent of an army of 98,150 (excluding *strel'tsy*); by 1667–8 old-style units were a minority even among the cavalry: 19,000 out of 42,500. Golitsyn's army on the 1689 Crimean campaign was 110,000 strong; it included a mere 17,206 *dvorianstvo* cavalry and *strel'tsy*, alongside nearly 30,000 new-style cavalry and 50,000 new-style infantry.[16]

It is true that this new army hardly covered itself in glory during the Thirteen Years War, while the two disastrous Crimean campaigns, the abortive attempt to take Azov in 1695 and even the successful siege of 1696, have often been used as proof of Russian military incompetence. Yet to argue that Narva showed that the Russian forces 'were totally inadequate', is too harsh.[17] Inadequate they may have been on the day, but the army's performance over the next few years suggests that Peter's predecessors had laid more of a solid foundation than legend allows. Already in 1696, the Russian army contained 47 foreign cavalry colonels, with a further 77 in the infantry; there were 27 foreign majors in the cavalry, 79 in the infantry, 41 foreign cavalry and 130 infantry captains; 18 foreign cavalry and 140 infantry lieutenants. Many were highly experienced officers: one colonel had thirty-six years service in that rank; another had served twenty-eight years, 3 had twenty-two years' service, another 3 had seventeen years and there were 4 with sixteen years' service.[18]

It was not the large number of foreign officers which was the most significant feature of the Russian army, however, but the growing number of Russian officers with experience of new-formation regiments. Initially, it is true, there had been great problems with Russians serving under foreign officers, especially with hereditary servitors forced against their will into infantry regiments. When Patrick Gordon, who entered Russian service in 1661, was put in charge of a regiment recently converted to infantry, he was ordered to instruct its colonel 'the exercise of foot, he haveing never served to foot befor, neither knew any thing what belonged to the command of a regiment'.[19] There were numerous clashes between foreign officers and the reluctant Russians they were supposed to train, and the relationship was never easy. Nevertheless, it is clear that by the 1690s, the greatest barriers to the creation of the new army had been overcome. Foreign officers had been training and drilling Russians for over fifty years. In arms and equipment, the Russians were abreast of contemporary European developments; indeed, with regard to the large-scale manufacture and deployment of flintlocks, and in techniques of cannon-founding, they were ahead of some:

between 1647 and 1653, the Armaments Chancery supplied 26,606 flintlocks and carbines, while the cannon factories of Tula and Kashira replaced clay moulds with more effective iron ones for casting guns around 1690, in advance of the French.[20]

The key shift, however, was not technological but cultural. The seventeenth century had seen substantial change for the hereditary servitors who formed the old-style cavalry. The 1649 *Ulozhenie* at last guaranteed *pomeshchiki* the control of their serfs that they had sought for so long at precisely the point when their military role was called seriously into question, as the government moved away from the old-style cavalry, which formed 34 per cent of Shein's army in 1632, but only 8 per cent of Golitsyn's in 1680.[21] Solov'ev's famous depiction of the flower of the Muscovite horse being cut down at Konotop in 1659 may be overdrawn, but it remains true that the old-style cavalry was shattered as a fighting force in the disastrous campaigns of the early 1660s. There were a mere 5,000 present at Narva in 1700; they turned tail and fled at the first Swedish attack, which was hardly sensible, since there was a river behind them, in whose icy waters many perished.

The problem with the old-style cavalry was not that cavalry was obsolete, which it was not, but that its members were amateurs. Contemporary warfare was dominated by professionals, and the major problem facing the Russian government after 1650 was the professionalisation of Russia's military elite. It is difficult, given the current state of scholarship, to give any definitive answer on the extent to which it was successful. Nevertheless, it is clear that much progress had already been made by 1700.[22] Despite the continuing high status attached to service in the old-style cavalry, a growing proportion of hereditary servitors had joined new-formation regiments, either through government coercion or, increasingly, because they had little option.

Russia's elites, from the greatest boyar to the humblest *pomeshchik*, needed to serve, and accepted the service ethic in a way which was entirely alien to Polish noble culture. Service, and the *pomest'ia* it brought, were essential to the maintenance of status and economic position of Muscovy's hereditary elites. The end of the Time of Troubles, and the resumption of Russian expansion to the south and east in the seventeenth century, which greatly increased the availability of land, had stimulated a revival, yet the great *pomest'e* experiment had failed. The attempt to ground Russia's defences on the obligation of hereditary servitors to supply and equip themselves for war from the revenues of lands assigned by the central administration could not produce an adequate army. Large numbers of hereditary servitors neither possessed, nor had any hope of possessing, sufficient land to enable them to fulfil their obligations: the law stipulated that a holding of fifteen peasant households was the minimum necessary to support and equip a member of the old-style cavalry, yet in many areas the majority of servitors failed to reach that level.[23] Many possessed no peasant households at all; there were even boyars of Duma rank who had neither hereditary nor service land.[24] Most provincial servitors had between one and ten peasant households; the average holding in the Vladimir-Suzdal' region was 7.6, almost exactly half of what was required.[25]

It was no wonder that the *pomest'e* cavalry failed to live up to expectations. Nevertheless, it was to the government's advantage that there was a large pool of hereditary servitors incapable of performing the service on which their status depended. There was little choice for such men but to accept whatever was offered; thus recruitment for new-formation regiments was expanded from the bottom up. The first to be enrolled in the 1630s were non-hereditary servitors and landless *deti boiarskie*, soon to be followed by hereditary servitors with small estates. From 1678, the government began to pressurise richer servitors: henceforth nobody with under twenty-four peasant households was to be allowed to serve in the old-style cavalry; there were further requirements of status and lineage. This decree was part of a series of reforms between 1678 and 1682 which sought to standardise requirements for service in infantry and cavalry regiments, and to secure the future of the new-formation regiments as the basis of the Russian army. The strategy was cunning: by restricting access to the old-style cavalry to those at the top of the service hierarchy the government recognised its social cachet, yet ensured that it would survive only as a small part of the army. The long-term intention was made quite clear in 1682 when the abolition of *mestnichestvo* was accompanied by a stipulation that male children of court rank would begin their service as junior officers in new-formation regiments before being permitted to transfer to the *dvorianstvo* cavalry, thus ensuring their exposure to modern military techniques.[26]

The foundations of Russia's new system were therefore laid gradually, and the crucial reforms were implemented before Peter came to the throne. By 1699, Russia already had a large pool of men with experience of service in new-formation units. It is true that, with the exception of the Butyrskii and Lefortovskii regiments, there was no continuity of such units in the pre-Petrine army, although increasingly units were disbanded at the end of wars rather than the end of campaigns; moreover, at the end of the Thirteen Years War, during which the number of new-formation infantry regiments reached fifty-five, with 50–60,000 men, 20–25 regiments were retained in service, containing 25–30,000 men.[27] Yet even if regiments were disbanded, this does not mean that the training soldiers had received was forgotten. Given the amount of fighting in which Russia had engaged since 1667, and the large numbers of men, and especially officers, who had served in new-formation units, one should not read too much into such breaks in continuity.

The men who filled Peter's officer corps after 1700 had received their training in the 1680s and 1690s. For, despite the frequent concentration by historians on the large numbers of foreigners in Russian service, it is clear that Russian officers were already playing a significant part in the new army long before 1700. As early as 1651 4.5 per cent of the *dvorianstvo* – 1,700 men – were serving in new-formation units,[28] a proportion which rose steadily. It is true that foreigners dominated positions of command – in 1681, there were 34 foreigners and only 3 Russians among the colonels of new-formation units[29] – nevertheless, despite Ustrialov's oft-repeated contention that foreigners also dominated the lower ranks, Russians were already playing a much greater role as junior officers than is frequently allowed.[30] Already by 1639 there were 316 foreign and 428 Russian officers, mostly *deti boiarskie*, in units serving in southern towns. New-formation cavalry units attracted nobles of higher social status: 200 were serving as officers in reiter regiments in 1649, a year when Muscovy was at peace. By 1662–3, the majority of officers in new-formation regiments in the rank of captain and below were Russians; by 1682, foreigners constituted only 10–15 per cent of the officers in such units.[31] Already by 1657, 43 out of 44 officers of the elite Butyrskii infantry regiment were Russians; the only exception was the colonel, M. Krovkov, a russified Dane who led the regiment until 1682, when he was briefly succeeded by a Russian, Rodion Zhdanov.[32] By 1675, less than half of the 491 officers of units in the Belgorod region were classed as foreigners; there were only 249 foreigners out of the 525 listed in 1684, although 149 of the remainder were recent converts to Orthodoxy from territories recently absorbed into Russia. Foreigners signing in a language other than Russian were concentrated in ranks above captain; even here, they only held 44 per cent of the positions with only 25 per cent of those below this rank.[33] Foreigners might still dominate the higher ranks, but already in the 1670s, Russians were emerging to high position: in 1678 A.A. Shepelev, who had commanded the elite infantry regiment later known as the Lefortovskii since 1657, was promoted major general; by 1680, he was a full general.[34]

This gradual increase in the proportion and competence of Russian officers within the new-formation regiments lay at the heart of the cultural transformation of the Russian military elite which was by no means complete by 1696, but which was the essential precondition for Peter's reforms. For, once initial opposition to innovation was overcome, service in the new-formation regiments had much to offer *pomeshchiki*. One advantage was that soldiers in new-formation infantry regiments were – at least theoretically – not required to supply and equip themselves, a task which was increasingly beyond middling and lesser servitors. Moreover, these regiments were not subject to the constraints of *mestnichestvo* – which was another reason why the government favoured them – and promotion on merit was possible, although the tendency to place men of good birth in the higher ranks long survived. By 1670, nearly a quarter of officers in the Belgorod region were literate in Russian, which is perhaps an indication that Russians were beginning to master the requirements of the trade in an effort to improve their prospects of promotion. From the military point of view, the abolition of *mestnichestvo* in 1682 was merely the culmination of a long process.[35]

The battle over the future shape of the Russian army had been won long before Peter began to learn the rudiments of military science; the revolt of the Moscow *strel'tsy* in 1698 demonstrated that there was still hostility to reform among old-style units, but was not indicative of wider hostility to change among the service elite. Nevertheless, it remains true that an enormous amount needed to be done, and any stress on the continuities between Peter's reforms and those of his predecessors must be balanced by a recognition of the serious shortcomings of the army he inherited. Peter's predecessors had presided over the gradual dismantling of the old system, and had gone a long way towards laying the foundations of the new; nevertheless, it remained chaotic and incomplete. It was still an uneasy amalgam of the old and the new, and too great a distinction should not be drawn between old and new-style formations: for a long time, particularly in the cavalry, noble servitors in new-formation units were still expected to supply and equip themselves.[36]

Apart from organisational chaos, the greatest problems were the lack of continuity in new-formation regiments, and the lack of firm direction from the top. Neither Michael nor Alexis had been soldiers, although Alexis liked to accompay his armies on campaign; moreover, since the highest-status servitors, from whom Muscovy's military leaders had traditionally been selected, were now the only people still allowed to serve in the old-style cavalry, many of the highest commanders had failed to receive the training which might equip them to lead new-formation regiments. The abolition of *mestnichestvo* in 1682 had removed one obstacle to the opening up of command at the highest level to those best fitted for it, but there was little indication in the 1690s that the problems had been solved.

Peter's reforms were devoted to rectifying these shortcomings. From 1687, when he established his famous play regiments, he gradually built up a circle of dedicated followers committed to the transformation of the Russian army and, most importantly, a growing core of permanent regiments to provide continuity of service for their officers. Although Peter insisted on promotion being earned by merit, famously advancing through the ranks himself, starting as a not-so-humble bombardier, and although some of his closest collaborators were of low birth, such as his favourite Aleksander Menshikov, most were drawn from Russia's traditional elite, of Peter's generation or slightly older, including Boris Sheremetev (1652–1719),

F.M. Apraksin (1661–1728), I.I. Buturlin (1661–1738), who was promoted major-general at the start of the war and commanded the guards at Narva, or A.I. Repnin (1668–1721), who was already a full colonel by 1687, and who led a division during the Narva campaign. These men provided the nucleus of Peter's new Russian high command and indicated that, for all the talk of promotion by merit, Russia's traditional elite was to play the central role in Peter's transformation of the army, with the guards, as in Sweden, functioning as a training-ground for young Russian officers who would later lead line regiments.

With their help, Peter's restless energy transformed virtually every aspect of the Russian military. In place of the confusing jumble of *prikazy* with their tangled undergrowth of conflicting jurisdictions, he sought to establish a rational, uniform system of administration. In 1680 the government had already established the organisation of the new-formation regiments on a territorial basis and placed control of the army largely in two chanceries: the *Razriadnyi Prikaz* and the Foreigners' and Reiter *Prikaz* which, despite its name, had extensive control over new-formation units manned by Russians. Peter streamlined this structure. Since he wished as far as possible that the new army should be supplied by the state he established a Provisions Chancery under Ia. F. Dolgorukii to provide everything from food to uniforms and weapons. Recruitment, along with control of the new-formation regiments, the development of the officer corps, and general discipline, was assigned to a new body, the *Voennyi Prikaz* (War Ministry).[37]

These bodies were primarily responsible for the transformation of the Russian army after Narva. It was decided to increase the army to forty-seven infantry and five grenadier regiments, the latter formed from grenadier companies in existing regiments. The cavalry was subjected to a more radical overhaul: a survey of all who had served in new-formation cavalry units and young members of the *dvorianstvo* who had not yet entered service produced a force of 27,326 men (18,547 reiters and lancers, and 8,779 new servitors), from which nine dragoon regiments were formed in 1702. As under the old system, servitors were to supply their own horses, although when many of those mustered turned out to be of poor quality, 100,000 rubles was assigned to purchasing replacements.[38] Recruitment was intensive. From 1699, all male members of the service class over fifteen were to be registered for service.

If the *dvorianstvo* were to fill the new officer corps, the ranks were increasingly filled with non-hereditary servitors and, as the army grew rapidly, with peasant conscripts. After a series of ad hoc measures, a decree of February 1705 finally introduced the recruitment system which was to supply the infantry for the rest of the war and was to survive in its essence until 1874. Henceforth, one recruit was to be provided by every twenty households, and supplied with bread, clothes and footware; if he was killed, wounded or deserted, another was to be supplied in his place.[39] This system, which also supplied the growing needs of the new navy, was a return to methods first introduced under Alexis, but was pursued with a new sense of purpose. The areas called upon, and the ratio of recruits to households, varied from year to year, but henceforth the recruiting levy was a permanent feature of Russian rural life. It supplied a steady stream of recruits: two levies in 1705 raised 44,539 men; in 1706, there were another two, producing 12,579 men, and three cavalry levies. In 1710, the government, which had been relying on registers of households drawn up in 1678, carried out a new survey. Unsurprisingly, the number of households had fallen dramatically, from 812,131 to 606,404, as peasants responded to the new demands by creating large, extended households. Neverthless, recruits were found: in 1711, three separate levies produced a total of 51,912 men.[40]

It was not until 1710 that the projected forty-seven infantry regiments were complete; even then, in the aftermath of Poltava, the size of the army was reduced to forty-two infantry regiments, including two guards regiments, five of grenadiers and thirty-five of fusiliers, a total of 52,164 combatants and 10,290 non-combatants. From 1708, regiments consisted of eight companies in two battalions, a total strength of 1,487 men including officers and non-combatants, except in the Guards and Ingermannland regiments, which had twelve companies in three battalions. The infantry remained at this strength more or less throughout the rest of the war: in 1720, it numbered 54,560 men and NCOs and 3,396 non-combatants. The greatest growth came in the cavalry, which expanded to an état of thirty-three regiments containing 34,320 combatants and 9,504 non-combatants established in 1711 which, as with the infantry, remained at this level until the end of the war. This field army, backed by field artillery which varied between 108 and 157 guns, and 40–45,000 Cossack and Kalmuk irregulars, was supplemented by a garrison army, composed of veterans, retrained units of strel'tsy and others not considered fit for field service, which reached 68,139 men in 1720.[41]

There were problems, however. For all Peter's organisational talent, his reforms were not carried out in a systematic manner, with a stream of edicts creating a network of overlapping institutions charged with running the army. Resistance was strong among non-hereditary servitors, such as the strel'tsy and Cossacks, who saw their privileges and status threatened. The Moscow strel'tsy had caused trouble in 1682, and their rising in 1698 was punished with savage cruelty. The Astrakhan rebellion of 1705, Bulavin's rising and the Cossack betrayals of 1708–9 were serious threats. Recruitment was often chaotic, and desertion-rates were high: of 2,500 recruits sent from Moscow to Sheremetev in May 1708, 703 (28.2 per cent) deserted, 8 died and 43 fell ill en route. Only 1,746 arrived.[42] If the Russians could mobilise some 175,000 men from 1710, over a third were low-quality garrison troops and over a fifth were irregulars. In 1706, Hallart complained that his infantry units had muskets of six different calibres, and that provisioning was chaotic.[43] One of the most pressing problems was the constant shortage of competent officers:

> the soldiers desert in very great numbers; seven hundred are run away from one regiment of dragons . . . and of the eleven foot-regiments now here, scarce one has lost less than two hundred men, though they were delivered compleat about two months ago. The want of competent officers (few regiments in this town having above two captains and three lieutenants to command twelve hundred men) to keep the soldiers to their duty and their not duly providing for their subsistance has increased these disorders.[44]

Do these shortcomings support Fuller's contention that 'Peter did not win the Great Northern War by creating a regular Russian army for the simple reason that he never succeeded in creating a regular Russian army at all'? This seems unduly harsh; as Fuller admits, it rather depends on what is meant by 'regular'.[45] Much of the chaos is explained by the fact that Peter's reforms were of necessity conducted in haste, as a response to the demands of a longer, more intensive war than Russia had ever fought. The problems faced were common to all contemporary armies and, for all the shortage of competent officers, there were sufficient to ensure that even foreigners, always prone to scepticism, began to recognise the new qualities of the Russian forces:

> The foot are generally very well exercised, and the officers tell me, they cannot enough admire what application the common soldiers use till they have learned their duty. The two regiments of guards, and that of Ingermanland are well armed and cloathed, though most of the rest are but indifferently provided with habits and fire-arms; nor can they be looked upon otherwise than as new levies, several of the regiments not being above two years standing.[46]

Thus Whitworth, like other commentators, distinguished between regular and irregular or new troops,[47] and for all its shortcomings, the nucleus of Peter's army does deserve the name 'regular': even Fuller mysteriously concludes that although Peter failed to create a regular army, a regular army was 'one of the most important legacies he left his successors'.[48] Peter took the semi-professional, disorganised forces bequeathed to him by his predecessors and, however haphazardly, gave them the permanent regimental and administrative structures which not only enabled him to win the war, but to develop an ethos and culture which, though much was derived from foreign models, was essentially Petrine and peculiarly Russian. At its heart lay the small but growing body of Russian officers who, even in the immediate aftermath of Narva, were already demonstrating that they could give a good account of themselves. Foreign officers may well have written patronising accounts, but Narva has for too long overshadowed other less trumpeted encounters, many of which were won by Russian commanders. If Peter insisted throughout the war that at least a third of his officers should be foreigners, his main aim remained the creation of a Russian army, led by Russian officers. The numerous successes they achieved in the early years of the war demonstrates that Russian military culture had already changed.

The first victories were won over the Swedish forces charged with the defence of the Baltic provinces after Charles moved south in 1701–2, leaving an army of 24,700, plus 8,000 militia.[49] Peter sent Boris Sheremetev against this force with ten infantry and nine new dragoon regiments. With characteristically blunt encouragement from Peter, Sheremetev gradually took the initiative, fighting a series of small encounters in late 1701 with mixed results, before he led a force of 8,000 horse, 5,000 foot and 15–20 guns in a surprise attack which caught Schlippenbach, the Swedish commander in Estonia and Livonia, with 3,800 men at Erastfer on 29 December 1701 (OS). Erastfer demonstrated that the Russians were no longer brittle in a field engagement: after Schlippenbach had attacked and repulsed Sheremetev's advance guard, the main Russian force caught him attempting to withdraw to the shelter of a fortified camp; once the Swedish cavalry, much of it from the local militia, had scattered in panic, the infantry was exposed and the encounter turned into a massacre.[50]

Erastfer was a notable boost to Russian morale, and was followed by further successes, as Schlippenbach's overstretched forces were ground down by Sheremetev, before the remnants of his field army was destroyed at Hummelshof (18/29 July 1702), where 7,000 Swedes were overwhelmed by 16–17,000 Russians.[51] Hummelshof destroyed Swedish control of Livonia and Estonia outside the main cities; the Russians swept across both provinces with fire and sword. To the northwest, F.M. Apraksin, with five infantry and two dragoon regiments, attacked Swedish forces in Ingria and on lake Ladoga. In October Peter combined with Apraksin and Sheremetev to seize Nöteborg, where the Neva flowed out of lake Ladoga. In May 1703, he took Nyenskans, at the mouth of the Neva, where he decided to construct his new capital of St Petersburg. In June 1704, Dorpat fell, followed by Narva in August. The Swedish grip on Livonia and Estonia was prised open.

A nation once illustrious

Peter's achievement can best be appreciated if it is compared with developments in Poland-Lithuania. Charles's decision to turn south in 1702, which gave Peter the vital breathing-space he needed after Narva, has long provoked debate. With the wisdom of hindsight, many have condemned it, arguing that if he had turned against Russia after forcing the Dvina, Charles would have faced Peter when he still had a chance of defeating him. By 1707, when he launched his Russian campaign, it was already too late. Peter's modernising policies had born fruit, and the army that the Swedes faced at Poltava was very different from the one they routed at Narva. Once Russia, with its enormous human and natural resources had cast off its backward ways and embraced western technology and western methods, so the argument goes, the days of Swedish hegemony were numbered. It was therefore dangerous to ignore the real enemy in order to embark on a fool's errand in the Commonwealth.[52]

Many of Charles's advisers certainly agreed, although when Chancellor Bengt Oxenstierna, who had served in the Swedish administration in Poland in the 1650s, prepared a famous memorandum attacking the decision to invade the Commonwealth, he drew on his knowledge of the past, not the future.[53] Observing that Gustav Adolf had negotiated a truce with Poland to enable him to devote his full attention to forcing Muscovy to accept peace at Stolbovo, Oxenstierna argued that it was possible to seize more Russian territory to protect Sweden's Baltic possessions and to secure its eastern flank against attack during any campaign in the Commonwealth.[54] In the summer of 1701, detailed plans were drawn up by Oxenstierna and Quartermaster-General Carl Magnus Stuart for an invasion, in which three Swedish armies would thrust south of lake Peipus, aiming to seize Pskov and its surrounding territory, to deny the Russians their main base for attacks on Livonia.[55]

Oxenstierna's memorandum was written when Charles had already committed himself. His reservations, however, were based on fear not of Russia, but of Poland-Lithuania. Hindsight makes it easy to laugh at his concerns, but at the time, they seemed well-founded. He argued that Charles X had failed, despite being secure on his Russian flank, despite invading with three powerful armies and despite having useful allies. In all respects, Charles XII's position was weaker. The Poles were in a far better position than in 1655, since Augustus possessed in Saxony that external power-base that the Polish Vasas had sought for sixty years; thus he had at his disposal a considerable army 'of good German soldiers', and in particular, of infantry, of which the Poles were always short. Although it was easy to chase the Poles from the field, Oxenstierna argued, they were hard to defeat; able to call on Saxon reinforcements, they would be formidable indeed.[56]

Oxenstierna was wrong, however. The Saxon army in 1697 was indeed a well-trained, disciplined and experienced force of 26,000, which had seen extensive action against the Turks and in the Nine Years War. Yet although it fought bravely enough, it was to prove spectacularly unsuccessful against the Swedes. More significantly, there was to be no repetition of the dogged resistance put up by the Poles after 1656. When Grand Hetman Hieronim Lubomirski led his 6,000 men from the field at the height of the battle of Kliszów in July 1702, abandoning Augustus to crushing defeat, he set a pattern which was to become familiar. To the astonishment of observers, both native and foreign, the Commonwealth all but collapsed as a military power: in a series of battles, including Warsaw (1705), Fraustadt (1706) and Kalisz (1706), Polish troops proved more of a liability than useful allies. Even to their enemies, it was a sad spectacle. Nordberg wrote that it was impossible not to observe events without commiserating with 'a Nation once so illustrious' and observers often remarked upon the lack of spirit shown by Commonwealth troops. Their former subjects were more direct; one Cossack colonel taunted his Polish prisoners: 'You . . . were once our lords, and we your serfs. But then you had courage; now you have as much as an old woman, and are worthy only of our scorn, for you cannot even defend yourselves.'[57]

What caused this sad decline? Historians have routinely ascribed the Commonwealth's military failure to backwardness and rejection of modern technology and techniques, in stark contrast to Peter's Russia. Yet Poles remained fully abreast of modern military developments. In Adam Freytag (1608–1650) from Thorn, the Commonwealth produced one of the leading theorists on fortifications of his day: his *Architectura militaris nova et aucta*, published in Leiden in 1631, went through ten editions, including three in French.[58] Kazimierz Siemienowicz, who served for many years in the Dutch army and was later Władysław IV's deputy captain-general of artillery, published an important work on artillery, translated into French (1651), German (1676) and English (as late as 1729), and was a leading pioneer of rocket technology.[59] The unpublished *Architectura militaris* of Józef Naronowicz-Naroński (†1678) was an extensive work which sought to establish a Polish vocabulary for the science of fortifications. Krzysztof Arciszewski, captain-general of the Polish artillery from 1646 to 1650, studied military engineering and gunnery in the Netherlands and fought at Breda and la Rochelle before he took service with the Dutch West India Company, playing a significant role in the conquest of Brazil. His successor Zygmunt Przyjemski, killed at Batoh in 1652, had served under Saxe-Weimar and Condé; Marcin Kątski (1636–1710), general of artillery from 1667 until his death, was sent at royal expense to Padua for military training and served under Condé from 1653 to 1657 as a dragoon colonel.

There were many others; the lessons they learned reinforced those taught by the large numbers of foreigners who fought in the Polish armies, including the Saxon Christoph Houwaldt, a major-general in Polish service between 1649 and 1655, who had fought throughout the Thirty Years War, the experienced Milanese Giovanni Paulo Cellari, promoted major-general in 1658 after ten years service, or Johann Dönnemark, who passed from Brandenburg service on his capture in 1657, rising to major-general in 1665 and presidency of the Military Court in 1681. Foreigners constituted 10–15 per cent of foreign-contingent officers after 1648, and many served in the ranks: in 1652, Denhoff's dragoon regiment was composed largely of Swedes.[60] Poles fought with as well as against the Swedes in the 1650s; in the 1680s, they fought alongside western forces in the Turkish wars, while Augustus's election opened the way to cooperation and mutual influence between the Polish and Saxon armies. Many served in western armies after 1667 especially that of Brandenburg; by 1714, some 200 young Polish noblemen had been educated at the military academy in Dresden; 100 had taken up commissions in the Saxon army; others studied at the new Habsburg military academy in Liegnitz.[61] They were merely following a long tradition.

Long exposure to western military theory and practice ensured that Poles were well aware of the need for change. Hetmans from Krzysztof Radziwiłł in the 1620s to Hieronim Lubomirski after 1700 stressed the need to increase the proportion of infantry to cavalry, while theorists like Andrzej Maksymilian Fredro (†1679) devoted much attention to schemes for producing a regular supply of footsoldiers. This concern was behind the creation of the foreign contingent in the 1630s, and was recognised by the *Sejm* in determining the size of forces to be raised. There was a steady increase in the proportion of infantry and dragoons, which were raised in large numbers from the 1620s, and maintained their original character of mounted infantry rather than fighting more as cavalry, which was increasingly the case elsewhere. Ratios of cavalry to infantry in the 1640s and 1650s varied according to the nature of the enemy, but the underlying trend in favour of infantry and dragoons is clear. If the état established after the November 1650 *Sejm* comprised 22,410 cavalry (64 per cent) 2,000 dragoons (6 per cent) and 10,400 infantry (36 per cent) to face Khmelnytsky's Cossacks and their Tatar allies, to meet the Swedish threat, the 1655 *Sejm* agreed an état of 12,641 cavalry (just under 50 per cent), 3,661 dragoons (14 per cent) and 9,275 infantry (36 per cent).[62] For the 1673–4 Chocim campaign, the army consisted of 17,960 cavalry (43 per cent), 7,312 dragoons (18 per cent) and 16,403 infantry (39 per cent). If the état agreed by the 1683 *Sejm* for the Vienna campaign had a large preponderance of cavalry (two-thirds of an army of 36,000), this was at the request of the Commonwealth's allies, and 10,000 peasant infantry were raised outside the official état.[63] Polish armies underwent significant tactical and technological change, particularly under Sobieski, a commander of real talent, and the Commonwealth was not significantly behind the rest of Europe in the application of new methods and new technology: Sobieski reduced the proportion of pikemen to 15 per cent in foreign-style regiments, while flintlocks were introduced to the guards around 1695; thereafter they were systematically introduced to the rest of the infantry; by 1708, flintlocks with bayonets were standard issue.[64]

If the proportion of cavalry remained substantially higher than elsewhere, this was due to the nature of warfare in eastern Europe: the ratio of cavalry to infantry in the Swedish forces in 1655 was roughly comparable. The problem was more one of the quality of the infantry which could actually be raised. The Cossack revolt had a serious impact: until 1648 the assumption that the Cossacks would provide substantial infantry reinforcements was reflected in the balance between infantry and cavalry in the états agreed by the *Sejm*. Thereafter, the Commonwealth faced serious problems in recruiting the infantry for which its commanders were desperate, and which was required for the war against the Cossacks, who based their strategy on dogged defence of fortified encampments: as one Pole remarked in 1648, 'we shall have a long and difficult Dutch war with them'.[65] In part, this was met by raising substantial quantities of foreign-style infantry in the regular army. There was a determined effort to revive the *wybraniecka* infantry which had raised 2,306 men in 1590, and regularly provided up to 1,500 men until the Smolensk War.[66] In March 1655, as the threat of war with Sweden loomed, John Casimir, in ordering the *szlachta* to prepare for the noble levy, also called for the raising of an infantry force through the provision of one man for every 10 *łan* of cultivated land, and from every 20 households in large towns, and every 30 in smaller towns. The idea was approved by almost all *sejmiki*; in May the *Sejm* settled the terms at one man from every 15 *łan* and one from every 20 households in large towns, 35 in smaller towns and 50 in the smallest towns.[67]

Although the *łanowa* infantry never produced the numbers envisaged, realising 4,680 men in 1655 instead of the desired 10,000, in conception it was similar to the Russian decree of 1705; moreover, it marked the concession of an important principle. The *wybraniecka* infantry had been raised exclusively from royal lands, but the *łanowa* infantry was to be drawn from noble and ecclesiastical estates as well, thereby vastly increasing its potential size. The acceptance of this principle was due to the fact that it was no mere royal command, but was based on similar schemes already introduced by individual *sejmiki* in 1649 and 1653.[68] The acceptance of this measure was significant, for it demonstrates that despite frequent accusations of *szlachta* 'selfishness', noble institutions were prepared to suspend noble privileges to meet pressing military needs.

Attention was also paid to fortifications. It is an oft-repeated myth that Poland-Lithuania had no modern fortifications. It is true that many cities, including Warsaw, Cracow, Poznań, Lwów and Wilno, were surrounded by outmoded medieval walls, and that the fortifications faced by the invaders in 1654–5 were hastily improvised and utterly inadequate. All of these cities, however, lay in the Commonwealth's interior, or along borders which had long been peaceful, and there had been no indication before 1648 that any were under serious threat, although a hastily-improvised set of bastions was thrown up round Warsaw in 1620 during the Turkish war. Although the city of Cracow was poorly fortified, the defences of the royal castle at Wawel were strengthened significantly by Władysław IV.[69] Along its most vulnerable borders, the Commonwealth did possess cities, fortresses and other strongpoints protected by modern fortifications. The most impressive were in Royal Prussia (Danzig, Elbing, Thorn and several others) but many private towns such as Zamość, Słuck, Brody or Birże, or even monasteries, such as Jasna Góra, were also fortified using modern methods. Hetmans from Krzysztof Radziwiłł to Stanisław Koniecpolski urged the importance of further construction, and often took the initiative themselves.[70] If concern was frequently expressed at the political implications of fortresses as an aid to the imposition of absolute power, the military disasters of the 1650s promoted a sober mood at the 1658 and 1659 diets, where resolutions were passed for the fortification of Cracow, Poznań, Brest, Lwów and Warsaw, with garrisons to be maintained at the state's expense in Cracow, Warsaw, Poznań, Lwów, Kamieniec and Lubowla; another resolution in 1658 urged every palatinate to establish one well-defended fortress as a place of refuge and resistance in time of war.[71]

These were not the only reforms introduced after 1648. Following the destruction of virtually the entire quarter army along with substantial contingents of experienced infantry at Batoh in 1652, the whole basis of the Commonwealth's armed forces was reorganised. The second *Sejm* of 1652 abolished the old distinction between the quarter army and the 'supplementary army' – the additional contingents raised in an emergency. Henceforth there was to be one force, known as the *komputowe* army (from '*komput*', meaning 'état'), whose size was to be set by the *Sejm*. The old distinction, in which the quarter army had been administered and paid centrally, while the suplementary units were supported locally, was abolished in favour of a system in which the whole army was to be supported locally. The responsibilities of each palatinate for providing taxes to support the army were established; as the *komput* was raised or lowered, so was the proportional load on individual palatinates.

It is easy to write off this development as merely another example of the Commonwealth's wilful rejection of the 'modern' process of centralisation. It is undoubtedly true that there were serious problems with the new system, but in many ways it was a rational and sensible reform which took account of the nature of the political system. Moreover, the Swedish example shows that substantial local involvement in military administration could be both effective and important for securing support for the military state. The most important result of the 1652 reforms was a substantial increase in the size of the Commonwealth's permanent forces. For the first time, Lithuania, which had no quarter army, was to have a standing army, with a separate *komput*. Despite the devastating effects of war, the *komput* stood at 40,305 for Poland and 20,000 for Lithuania in 1659, a combined strength of 54,000: the largest professional army yet fielded by the Commonwealth. In 1667 the peacetime *komput* was established at 15,990 in Poland and 7,271 in Lithuania, for a real strength of 20,400, of which over half (11,960) were infantry and dragoons, although 3,100 of these were only to be maintained while the Ukrainian situation remained disturbed.[72] In the brief peace with the Ottoman Empire between 1676 and 1683, the army's paper strength was kept at 17,500–18,000, of which 6,000 were Lithuanian; in 1699, following the peace of Carlowitz, the Polish army alone was established at a paper strength of 18,000.

It is true that a regular army of 18–24,000 in peacetime was comparatively small by contemporary standards. One should be careful, however, to compare like with like. In 1699, the Commonwealth had just made peace and the *szlachta* had no intention of going back to war. It is pointless to compare this figure to maximum paper strengths in wartime. If the French army reached a paper strength of 420,000 during the 1690s, the actual strength was nearer 340,000, while the peacetime strength between 1698 and 1700 was 140–145,000.[73] This is still considerably higher than the Commonwealth, but the gathering crisis over the Spanish Succession meant that the circumstances were rather different. The Commonwealth's military establishment should be compared not to that of the largest and most populous state in western Europe, but to its neighbours and potential enemies. There was no reason to suppose that an army of 18–24,000, which could be supplemented quickly in the event of war, was inadequate in 1699, especially if reinforced by the 26,000-strong Saxon army.[74] It is true that the Swedish army numbered 61,000, but a good half was tied up in garrisons and Charles's invasion army in 1702 barely reached 21,000.[75] Peter's new army numbered little over 30,000 in 1700; even if he planned to expand it dramatically, and could mobilise substantial forces of irregulars, experience suggested that there was little to fear from large Russian armies. The Brandenburg army in peacetime, stripped of lucrative subsidies, was the same size or slightly smaller than the

Saxon army, as was the Danish army. The only major difference between the Commonwealth and its neighbours in 1699 was that it was planning for peace, not war.

Yet all was not right beneath the surface. In other states, military disaster or experience of foreign invasion had proved the crucial spur to military reform. Yet, despite the establishment of the *komputowe* army and the numerous measures passed by the *Sejm* to improve the Commonwealth's fortifications and military preparation, there was no decisive break with the past, and the Commonwealth's noble society failed after 1660 to establish an effective working relationship with its armed forces. Whereas in Russia the new-formation regiments gradually eclipsed the old-style Muscovite army, to which Peter administered the *coup de grâce* after Narva, the foreign contingent in the Commonwealth did not. The introduction of foreign-style infantry and dragoon regiments had, it is true, led to the virtual disappearance of infantry units of the national contingent by the 1650s: if in 1652, Polish and Hungarian infantry, organised on the *towarzysz* principle, still formed 18 per cent of infantry and dragoon units, this figure dropped to 5.5 per cent in 1659 and 3 per cent in 1683, although it stabilised at about 5 per cent in the 1690s.[76] Nevertheless, despite general recognition of the foreign contingent's military importance, the cavalry units of the national contingent remained dominant within the army, and were the most socially prestigious. The army high command was almost exclusively drawn from men whose military experience was limited to the cavalry: for all that talented hetmans such as Czarniecki, Jerzy Sebastian Lubomirski or Sobieski recognised the importance of infantry, their military careers had been moulded in large-scale cavalry operations. Talented officers who had served in the infantry or artillery might reach the position of general of artillery, but were rarely given wider command.

Moreover, if the *komputowe* army was a standing force, manned by professionals, it was not a regular army in the true sense of the word. There was, it is true, a small core of regular soldiers and officers, with long years, if not decades, of service, but men like Stefan Stanisław Czarniecki, who served for fifty-two years, forty of them as an officer, were the exception rather than the rule. Most officers of the national contingent served for under ten years. Of 359 lieutenants in the cavalry, 335 (84.9 per cent) served for under ten years, 38 (9.6 per cent) for 10–20 years, 15 (4.2 per cent) for 20–30 years, and 7 (1.7 per cent) for over thirty years. The proportion was rather higher among lieutenant-colonels in the infantry, where 38 out of 60 officers (63.3 per cent) served up to twenty years, and 22 (36.7 per cent) served for over twenty years, but the numbers were hardly large, and lieutenant colonels were in any case selected from among the most experienced officers.[77] For hussars, service as a *towarzysz* was overwhelmingly a short-term matter:

even during the long period of war between 1648 and 1667, in the prestigious company of Grand Hetman Stanisław Potocki, 19.1 per cent of *towarzysze* served for only one year; 55.3 per cent served for 1–5 years; 20.8 per cent for 5–10 years, and only 4.8 per cent for over 10 years; in Władysław Myszkowski's company, 37 per cent of the *towarzysze* served for only one year, with 50.3 per cent serving for 1–5 years: thus a mere 12.7 per cent of its *towarszysze* can be regarded as professional soldiers.[78] Thus the core of long-term professionals in the Commonwealth's armies was tiny, despite the long years of war. As in the sixteenth century, there was a large reservoir of ex-soldiers with military experience capable of joining improvised defence in an emergency, but in the new military world after 1650 this was no longer sufficient. The Swedes had shown that discipline, drill and professionalism were more than a match for the inspirational semi-professional improvisation which had served the Commonwealth so well for so long. Yet despite the reforms of 1652, it did not create a truly regular army; this was to cost it dear after 1700.

The explanation of this failure is primarily political and cultural. The Commonwealth succeeded better than anywhere else in Europe in realising the Renaissance ideal of a citizen army, whose virtues had been preached by Machiavelli, Justus Lipsius and a legion of contemporary theorists. Elsewhere, this ideal proved impossible to realise, and the new standing armies which emerged after 1648 were mixed forces of foreign mercenaries and native units, usually led by an officer corps in which native nobilities played a dominant role, while the ranks were filled with the lower orders who served as volunteers, conscripts or pressed men, but who were emphatically subjects, not citizens. In Poland-Lithuania, however, the ideal of a citizen army remained very much alive.

This was deliberate. The *szlachta* was well aware of what was occurring elsewhere in Europe, where the liberties of citizens appeared to be trampled in one state after another by monarchs claiming absolute power and possessing a loyal army with which to implement it. Historians have recently attempted to explode the 'myth' of absolutism, and emphasise the extent of tacit consent involved in the emergence of new systems of royal government after 1600, but to contemporary observers in the Commonwealth, absolute monarchy seemed a very real threat. The *szlachta* was already convinced that Russia was a tyrannical despotism beyond salvation, but the fate of Bohemia during the Thirty Years War, the military coup in Denmark in 1660, the shattering of Estates liberties in Ducal Prussia in the 1660s and the introduction of absolute monarchy in Sweden in 1680 seemed to demonstrate the real dangers to the constitution from rulers backed by a standing army.

Thus, far from embracing the new military world with enthusiasm, Andrzej Maksymilian Fredro argued passionately for the firmer grounding of the principle of the citizen army. Fredro was no soldier, but he had organised the *łanowa* infantry in the palatinate of Ruthenia during the 1650s and took a close interest in military matters. He was well aware of contemporary military developments, and of the need for change: his earliest intervention on military affairs came in 1648 after the disaster at Pyliavtsi, when he urged the recruitment of cheaper and more effective dragoons rather than costly hussars; later he argued that the main reason for the problems faced against the Swedes was the shortage of infantry, and was behind the publication of the first Polish manual of infantry tactics in 1660. Nevertheless, he was a firm opponent of the increase of the *komputowe* army in general, and the foreign contingent in particular. In 1666, he proposed the limitation of the army to a few thousand, to be supplemented in an emergency by the noble levy; he also urged a radical reorganisation of the foreign contingent, involving the complete Polonisation of the officer corps, the breaking up of the regimental structure in favour of the system of small companies of the national contingent, and the introduction of Polish-style uniforms and Polish as the language of command.[79] He was by no means a naive idealist – his vision of the new role of the noble levy included the introduction of regular training and the establishment of substantial contingents of infantry organised under noble officers – nevertheless, his military speeches and writings demonstrate a struggle to reconcile his appreciation of the military importance of infantry with a conviction that cavalry was the military basis of the aristocratic form of government he preferred, while infantry was associated with royal despotism.[80]

Fredro's ideas were popular because they confronted the *szlachta*'s central dilemma – how to reconcile the need for defence with the maintenance of noble liberties and privileges – and the related issue of the place of the army within a society of noble citizens. For, despite the dominance of the cavalry units of the national contingent within the army, and despite the fact that the army in general and the national contingent in particular reflected the institutions and the ethos of the noble Commonwealth, the relationship between the army and *szlachta* society remained difficult throughout the seventeenth century; it was the failure to reconcile these differences which lay at the heart of the Commonwealth's military crisis after 1700.

In Russia the gradual eclipse of the *dvorianstvo* cavalry was not achieved without difficulty; nevertheless, service in it was a burden as well as an opportunity, and its replacement by new-formation units merely provided a different form of the service Muscovy's elites needed, which in many ways was more appropriate to their circumstances, as the state increasingly provided not just the opportunity of service, but the means to fulfil it. In the Commonwealth, the ideal of the noble levy survived for three centuries after its military usefulness was at an end because of its political not its military significance. For the noble levy was associated with the institution of a horseback *Sejm* (*sejm konny*), in which the *szlachta* turned up en masse to decide great matters of state. It was the ultimate expression of direct citizen democracy, and although it was essentially a myth by the seventeenth century, it survived as a potent political ideal whose practical expression came in the numerous confederations formed at local or national level, whose authority was derived directly from the sovereignty of the *szlachta* nation. Any attempt to dispense with the noble levy was therefore seen as a threat to the very essence of the noble Commonwealth.

The ideal of direct, participative noble democracy suffused the Commonwealth's armies. For most *szlachta* soldiers, military service marked but a brief interlude in their lives, while noble egalitarianism and the non-hierarchical structure of the *towarzystwo* system encouraged the extension into the army of institutions, in particular the *koło* (circle), which echoed those of the wider Commonwealth and introduced the consensual ideals of *szlachta* culture into the heart of the army. Originally, the *koło* was merely a council of war formed by the hetmans and their captains: on Batory's Pskov campaign, such assemblies took place every few days and were given official status in the 1580 Articles of War; their membership was frequently widened to include *towarzysze* as well as captains, officers of the foreign contingent were drawn in, and it was not unknown for members of retinues to attend.

The inevitable problems over pay and conditions of service and the deep legalism and love of consensus ingrained within Polish political culture, however, ensured that these meetings rapidly acquired broader significance, especially when they ocurred without the sanction of the hetman, or in direct opposition to his authority, as happened increasingly. Such gatherings claimed a legal right to consider pay and conditions of service, and disciplinary issues (including the powers of the hetmans); even the right to express or withold agreement to the continuation of a campaign, especially if their legal term of service, fixed in four quarters ending on St Martin's Day (11 November), had expired, and if, as was normal, their pay was in arrears.

The *koło* came to be regarded as a natural and legal institution in what was a citizen army composed of volunteers who contracted their services to the state of which they were a part. Since equipment, arms and armour was supplied by the soldiers themselves, an expense which was considerable, particularly for hussars, they might refuse to participate in a campaign in which they ran the risk of damaging or losing their costly investment; they might even ask for compensation from their commander for lost or damaged equipment. For all the attempts of monarchs and hetmans to control or prevent such gatherings, it was difficult, given the permanent problems over arrears of pay, to prevent troops refusing to fight, such as happened in 1674, when Sobieski could not stop part of the Lithuanian army leaving camp, despite declaring them deserters and fugitives.[81] Although a hetman's edicts had the force of laws passed by the *Sejm*, and a hetman could not be bound to accept decisions passed by a *koło*, it was difficult in practice to resist.

Yet although the army was so clearly a reflection of wider *szlachta* society, and a repository of noble values, it came to be regarded with suspicion. The constant problems over pay provoked soldiers into forming assemblies without the permission of the hetman which technically made them legal, claiming the right as citizens of the Commonwealth to form confederations, thus meeting accusations that they were undermining military discipline with an appeal to the *szlachta* liberties they were supposed to protect. Military confederations, an increasing feature of the seventeenth century, were drawn up with great formality, complete with the publication of articles of confederation, strict disciplinary codes, elected officials and elaborate oaths. This appropriation of the forms of *szlachta* democracy was not always welcome, and often brought conflict and bitterness; after Pasek was accused of being a spy from the confederated Polish army, he mounted a bold defence of his fellow soldiers:

> I have wasted already half my father's substance . . . more than once have I shed blood copiously for my country; I would have consented to find my name closing the list of *bene meritorum* [men of merit; i.e. those granted position and reward by the king] but neither I nor many others more deserving . . . happened to taste that recompense.[82]

He attacked the rewards given to those who had not served their country, but whose obstruction of the *Sejm* and *sejmiki* for their private concerns had 'torn the bread from the mouths of the deserving, using it for factions, intrigues, for graft and the furtherance of their own interests; they grope blindly toward the treasury of the Commonwealth like a kitten for its milk.' He ended with a ringing declaration of his rights: 'I shall know how to seek redress from everyone who is my equal by birth. I have the regional dietines, I have the tribunals, I have the general assembly [*koło*]; I am doubly a citizen, for I am both a [nobleman] and a soldier.'[83]

Such claims were controversial. When an envoy to the 1672 *Sejm* claimed to speak 'as a deputy and a soldier' he was sharply rebuked: 'Sir, you cannot speak as a soldier, for we have no Fourth Estate here.'[84] Concern was justified, for in the early 1660s, military confederations showed an increasing willingness to interfere in politics, and became the natural targets of politicians who wished to exploit them for their own ends. The radical 'Fraternal Union' of the Lithuanian army demanded that *sejmiki* should send deputies to military confederations to debate matters of state. Furthermore, for all the opposition to John Casimir's election plans, the army, overwhelmingly drawn from the middling and lesser *szlachta*, displayed a general regalism which disturbed many politicians.[85]

The politicisation of the army reached its peak in the 1650s and 1660s. The Commonwealth's collapse in 1655 was partly brought about by a political act: the acceptance of Swedish overlordship by the Polish army, and resistance to the Swedes was begun with the Confederation of Wierzbołów (August 1655), in which part of the Lithuanian army withdrew its loyalty from Janusz Radziwiłł after the treaty of Kiejdany, and the Confederation of Tyszowce, in which much of the Polish army returned to loyalty to John Casimir. Yet such acts were technically illegal, as the rapid subsuming of the Tyszowce Confederation into the civilian-led Łancut Confederation demonstrated. Four years later, however, the Commonwealth's inability to pay the army provoked further confederations in both Polish and Lithuanian armies which soon became highly politicised, as both John Casimir and his opponents looked to them for support in the battle over political reform.

Despite the Court's hopes that a disgruntled, unpaid army might look to the monarchy for support, and help implement its plans after their categorical rejection by the 1661–2 *Sejm*, the citizen army refused to cooperate and stood out for the cause of *szlachta* liberty. It was a decisive moment; despite the fact that there were no further military confederations between 1672 and 1696, perhaps because of the esteem in which Sobieski was held by the army, the best chance the monarchy ever had of initiating a Danish-style military coup was gone. Since most were not career soldiers, it was their identity as citizens, not soldiers, which ultimately triumphed. Military confederations might have had political demands, but they had no political programme beyond the defence of the very *szlachta* liberties which made it so difficult for the Commonwealth to raise the taxes by which they might have been paid.

The greatest fears, however, were raised by the foreign, not the national contingent. Despite the fact that the foreign contingent was overwhelmingly manned and officered by subjects of the Commonwealth – on average only 5–15 per cent of its officers were foreigners – its character as a citizen force was much less clear.[86] For the ranks were composed almost entirely of commoners; moreover, given that the *towarzysz* system of recruitment was not practised, there was a much greater proportion of them within individual units. As for the officers, many were drawn not from the Commonwealth's Polish and Lithuanian heartlands, but from the German-speaking borderlands, especially Royal Prussia and Livonia, who were more likely to possess the relevant skills and education.[87] This was a policy deliberately followed by the Vasas, in particular in their guard units which were a training-ground for officers in the rest of the foreign contingent. Poles preferred service in the more prestigious national contingent, and the large numbers of Poles within the foreign contingent and the royal guard were often drawn from the poorer nobility, particularly from Mazovia and Podlasie, who could not afford service in the national contingent. Concern at this situation was expressed as early as 1646, when the royal guard was limited by law to 1,200 and placed under the control of the Grand Marshal in a direct response to Władysław's attempts to use it as the core of the army he was attempting to raise to implement his Turkish war plans. In the 1650s John Casimir made a determined effort to build a royal power-base within the foreign contingent. Against the background of a growing crisis in royal finances, the royal guard proper was run down to a level far below the 1,200 allowed by law; in 1653, it was under 500 strong.[88] In compensation, several units were transferred to the new *komput* after 1652, where they were paid by the state treasury; regiments which were part of this '*komputowa*' royal guard bore the appellation 'royal', as did the king's own companies of hussars and *pancerna* cavalry.[89] By early 1659, the *komputowa* guard consisted of three regiments of foot and two of horse (dragoons and reiters), totalling just over 3,500 men, dropping to just over 3,000 in 1660.[90]

Such numbers may seem insignificant, but these units formed 10–30 per cent of the foreign contingent, and in practice were under John Casimir's direct control after the defection of both hetmans to the Swedes in 1655. He had already nominated Bogusław Radziwiłł as general of the royal guard, a new position which attracted much criticism as it became clear that he intended to extend Radziwiłł's powers over the whole foreign contingent and build up a rival to the hetmans more subject to his control.[91] Although Radziwiłł's treason in 1655 and the inactivity of his successor, Jan Zamoyski, meant that little came of this plan, nevertheless royal control of the foreign contingent by 1660 was extensive, as John Casimir played an increasing military role. In sharp distinction to the national contingent, the foreign contingent was reluctant to form or join confederations, and remained loyal to the king throughout the political struggles of the 1660s, when very few of its units – and none of the *komputowa* guard – joined the anti-royalist side during Lubomirski's *rokosz*.

Fear that the monarchy might use the army to overthrow the constitution also helped undermine the measures taken in the 1650s to modernise the Commonwealth's fortresses. Although Fredro was well aware of the import-ance of fortifications in modern warfare, he expressed the widely-held fear that they represented a threat to liberty, arguing that the *szlachta* should not permit the construction of too many or too powerful fortresses. Since the Poles were more accustomed to fighting on horse than foot, the large garrisons required by modern fortresses were often composed of foreign mercenaries, who were prone to go over to the enemy and were useful tools in the hands of those planning to implement absolute power. Thus Fredro suggested in

1670 that fortresses should be built and maintained by *sejmiki*; an idea which had actually been proposed by John Casimir in 1652. Such fears were strongly expressed from the early 1660s, when the king's desire to put the garrisons of the Royal Prussian fortresses under the command of the Frenchman Andrault de Buy provoked angry protests from those who feared that he wished to establish a Prussian bridgehead to secure by force the election of Condé, the French candidate for the Polish throne, and Fredro's call for all garrisons to be commanded by Polish noblemen met with wide approval.[92]

Thus the growing opposition among the *szlachta* to the foreign contingent was not due to obscurantism, or a lack of understanding of the importance of modern technology and the role of infantry in warfare. All of these played a part, but the essential motivation was political. Given the monarchy's tendency to conduct a private foreign policy, from Sigismund's attempts to reclaim the Swedish throne, through Władysław's Turkish war plans, to Sobieski's schemes for the annexation of Ducal Prussia, it was seen as vital to limit royal control of the army. Moreover, the loyalty of the foreign contingent to the king and the political role played by the royal guard, which was responsible for keeping order in Warsaw during sessions of the *Sejm*, meant that there was ample reason for *szlachta* suspicion. John Casimir had demonstrated his willingness to use the army to further his political aims in open defiance of the *Sejm*; if the national contingent refused to cooperate, the position of the foreign contingent was seen as dangerous. If *szlachta* liberty were to be preserved, it seemed that the *komput* must be kept as low as possible, the Commonwealth must stay at peace and avoid aggressive war, and the foreign contingent must be kept at a bare minimum. To many it seemed that the greatest danger to the Commonwealth came from within, not without.

After the failure of John Casimir's attempts at political reform, the Commonwealth became locked in struggles between magnate factions which were exacerbated during the reigns of Michael Korybut Wiśniowiecki (1669–74) and John Sobieski, who himself had been a leading malcontent during Wiśniowiecki's reign, shamelessly exploiting his position as Grand Hetman and the regard in which he was held by the army for political ends, forming the military confederation of Szczebrzeszyn in 1672 to oppose Wiśniowiecki. John Casimir, aware of the dangers of magnate power, made a determined attempt in the early 1650s to curb the excessive powers of the hetmans, but, despite the disgrace of Janusz Radziwiłł in 1655, and of Jerzy Sebastian Lubomirski in 1664, he failed. Hetmans continued to utilise their power-base in the army for their own political ends, turning up at the *Sejm* with large military retinues, building their own patronage networks in the army and frequently frustrating the royal government. Attempts by the monarchy to appoint a rival as field hetman, as John Casimir did with Gosiewski in

Lithuania in 1654, or Sobieski did with Kazimierz Jan Sapieha in 1681, caused more problems than they solved: Gosiewski's rivalry with Janusz Radziwiłł all but crippled Lithuanian resistance in 1654–5, while Sapieha's appointment, meant to provide a counterbalance to Grand Hetman Michał Kazimierz Pac, had baleful consequences. Benedykt Sapieha, Kazimierz's brother, had bought the office of Lithuanian treasurer in 1676; the brothers ostentatiously moved into opposition, establishing a tyrannical domination of Lithuania which eclipsed anything that Radziwiłł or Pac had enjoyed. Control of the treasury and the army was the basis of their power. With scant regard for the law, they turned Lithuania into a virtual fiefdom, carrying on their own foreign policy and raising illicit levies to support the army, which devastated the lands of any who opposed them. The failure of the Crown to establish firm control of the army, and the failure of the *Sejm* to provide a solid financial basis for a standing army it might have been able to control had opened the door to arbitrary rule not by the king, but by the supposed servants of the state and guardians of its laws.

The backlash to the Sapieha hegemony in Lithuania, led by the Radziwiłłs, the Ogińskis and Ludwik Pociej created the unprecedented political situation which greeted Charles when he invaded Lithuania in 1702. The key factor was the intense opposition of the ordinary Lithuanian *szlachta*, who sought to curb magnate power by demanding the harmonisation of Lithuanian law with that of Poland. This was a radical proposal: since 1569, Lithuanian law had provided fewer restraints on office-holders than was the case in Poland. At the 1697 election *Sejm*, the campaign was successful: Lithuanian officials were brought firmly under the jurisdiction of the Tribunal on the same basis as the ordinary *szlachta* and chancery Ruthenian was abandoned as the Grand Duchy's official language in favour of Polish, by now the first language of the Lithuanian *szlachta*.[93]

The partial harmonisation of the laws was a major blow to the Sapiehas, as was their complete failure in the 1697 election, when Augustus II triumphed over the Prince de Conti, the Sapieha's favoured candidate. Yet their power was by no means broken, and a rather wary truce patched up in July 1698 proved short-lived. The Sapiehas' rivals had no intention of letting matters rest, while the ordinary *szlachta* put increasing pressure on Augustus to mount a decisive blow against the hated brothers. As Augustus hesitated over whom to support, hoping to persuade the Sapiehas to back his Livonian campaign, their Lithuanian opponents acted decisively. At Olkieniki in November 1700, the Sapieha forces were comprehensively routed by the Lithuanian noble levy. Michał Sapieha, Kazimierz's son, was captured; handed over to the *szlachta*, he was butchered in cold blood.

Olkieniki sent shockwaves around the Commonwealth. The victorious republicans, as they called themselves, declared Sapieha offices and lands confiscated, and turned to Augustus to confirm their decisions. This put him in a difficult position. The Sapiehas received strong support in Poland, which had not experienced the horrors of Sapieha domination, and their treatment in 1700 stimulated widespread fear, in particular among senators, who suspected that Augustus had whipped up the Lithuanians in order to justify bringing Saxon troops into the Commowealth to strengthen royal power. With the republicans energetically pursuing the Sapiehas, Augustus's attempts to broker a settlement were unavailing, and he was unable or unwilling to protect Sapieha estates from Grzegorz Ogiński's troops. Despite the Pacification *Sejm* of 1699, which had formally reconciled Augustus with those who had opposed his election, his policies still aroused fierce opposition and fears for the constitution. His possession of an external power-base in Saxony and a modern standing army gave him an independence the Vasas had never enjoyed. Augustus's use of the Saxon bureaucracy and diplomatic service to conduct Commonwealth business circumvented the numerous legal controls on his power; with his own army, he could pursue his own foreign policy, as the attack on Riga in 1700 demonstrated. With the crushing of the Sapiehas, the spectre of royal absolutism enforced at bayonet-point returned to haunt the Commonwealth. There was no large officer corps or body of government officials within the nobility who might benefit from increased royal power; the army reflected the political attitudes of the citizens who composed it. Despite its troubles since 1648, the Commonwealth had apparently seen off its enemies: the Swedes had been expelled, the Muscovites pushed back, and Podolia recovered from the Turks, while Sobieski's triumph at Vienna had restored the military reputation of the Polish army. Unfortunately for the Commonwealth, the next war was to be different.

Notes

1 The inhabitants of Royal Prussia opposed this act, successfully preventing the Hohenzollerns calling themselves officially kings 'of' Prussia; henceforth they called their province 'Royal Polish Prussia' or 'Polish Prussia'.

2 G. Jonasson, *Karl XII och hans rådgivare* (Uppsala, 1960) pp. 3–4, 20–7.

3 'Sobstvennoruchnyia popravki Petra Velikago v gistorii voiny sveiskoi, pre-dstavlennoi kabinet-sekretarem Makarovym v 1722 godu' in N.G. Ustrialov, *Istoriia tsarstvovaniia Petra Velikago* (St Petersburg, 1858–64) IV:ii p. 451; Jacek Staszewski, *August II Mocny* (Wrocław, 1998) pp. 90–1.

4 J. Wimmer, *Wojsko Rzeczypospolitej w dobie wojny północnej* (Warsaw, 1956) pp. 49–50; O. Schuster and F.U. Francke, *Geschichte der Sächsischen Armee von deren Errichtung bis auf die neueste Zeit* (Leipzig, 1885), I pp. 145–6. Hatton gives a figure of 14,000 for the Saxon army, but the main force of five infantry and

four cavalry regiments did not leave Saxony until early May: R. Hatton, *Charles XII* (London, 1968), p. 117.

5 E. Dunsdorfs, *Der Grosse Schwedische Kataster in Livland 1681–1710* (Stockholm, 1950), pp. 105, 190; J. Vasar, *Die grosse Livländische Güterreduktion* (Tartu, 1930), pp. 111–12.

6 Staszewski, *August II* pp. 110, 115–16.

7 Voltaire, *Lion of the North, Charles XII of Sweden* M. Jenkins (tr.) (London, 1981) p. 50.

8 C. von Clausewitz, *Vom Kriege* (Frankfurt, 1994) p. 170; Frederick II, 'Betrachtungen über die militärischen Talente und den Charakter Karls XII' *Die Wercke Friedrichs des Großen* G.B. Volz (ed.) VI (Berlin, 1913) pp. 370, 378.

9 *Zhurnal, ili Podennaia Zapiska, Blazhennyia i vechnodostoinyia pamiati Gosudaria Imperatora Petra Velikago s 1698 goda, dazhe do zaliucheniia Neishtatskago mira* (St Petersburg, 1770–1), I p. 27.

10 *Das Tagebuch des Generals von Hallart über die Belagerung und Schlacht von Narva 1700* F. Bienemann (ed.) (Reval, 1894) pp. 25, 37–8, 57–8; Hallart to Augustus II, 25.X.1700 (OS), Ustrialov, *Istoriia* IV:ii, no. 44, p. 170.

11 G. Adlerfelt, *The Military History of Charles XII* (London, 1740) I p. 50; 'Dagbok af en Inginiör-Officer antagligen L. Wisocki-Hochmuth 1700–1708' *KKD* II (Lund, 1903) p. 119.

12 M.D. Rabinovich, 'Formirovanie reguliarnoi Russkoi armii nakanune Severnoi Voiny' in V.I. Shunkov (ed.), *Voprosy Voennoi Istorii Rossii XVIII i pervaia polovina XIX vekov* (Moscow, 1969) pp. 223–8.

13 E.V. Tarle, *Severnaia Voina i shvedskoe nashestvie na Rossiiu* (Moscow, 1958), p. 50.

14 Charles Wrede, Narva, 24.XI.1700; Ustrialov, *Istoriia* IV:ii, no. 50, p. 180.

15 Kivelson, *Autocracy* p. 19.

16 Hellie, *Enserfment* pp. 218, 269; idem., 'The Petrine army: continuity, change and impact' *CASS* 8 (1974) p. 239.

17 Hellie, 'Warfare' p. 94.

18 A.Z. Myshlaevskii, 'Ofitserskii vopros v XVII veke. Ocherki iz istorii voennago dela v Rossii' *VS* 247 (1899) pp. 295, 298–9.

19 P. Gordon, *Passages from the diary of General Patrick Gordon of Auchleuchries. A.D. 1635–A.D. 1699* (Aberdeen, 1859) p. 53.

20 Hellie, *Enserfment* p. 185; Esper, 'Military self-sufficiency', p. 201; Fuller, *Strategy* p. 25.

21 Hellie, *Enserfment* pp. 271–2.

22 C.B. Stevens, 'Evaluating Peter's military forces' in A. Cross (ed.), *Russia in the Reign of Peter the Great: Old and New Perspectives* SGECRN II (1998) pp. 90–1.

23 Kivelson, *Autocracy* pp. 50–1.

24 For example, in 1670 the *stol'niki* prince M.Iu. Dolgorukii and prince P.V. Prozorovskii: R. Rexheuser, 'Adelsbesitz und Heeresverfassung im Moskauer Staat des 17. Jahrhunderts' *JGO* NF 21 (1973), p. 2.

25 Ibid. p. 7; Kivelson, *Autocracy* p. 50.

26 Rexheuser, 'Adelsbesitz' p. 17; Stevens, *Soldiers* pp. 77–8.

27 Chernov, *Vooruzhennye* p. 145.

28 Hellie, *Enserfment* p. 214.
29 Ibid. p. 360, n. 136, based on Ustrialov, *Istoriia* I p. 302.
30 Ibid. p. 184. Hellie suggests that less than 20 per cent of officers were Russians. From the context, it appears he is talking of the 1650s; he fails to consider if the percentage rose thereafter: *Enserfment* p. 192.
31 Chernov, *Vooruzhenye* p. 150.
32 P.O. Bobrovskii, *Istoriia 13-go Leib-Grenaderskago Erivanskago ego Velichestva Polka za 250 let 1642–1892* I (St Petersburg, 1892) pp. 13, 28.
33 C.B. Stevens, 'Belgorod: notes on literacy and language in the seventeenth-century Russian army' *RH* 7 (1980) p. 120.
34 Chernov, *Vooruzhennye* p. 150.
35 Stevens, 'Belgorod' p. 119; Myshlaevskii, 'Ofitserskii' pp. 305–7.
36 Whitworth to Harley, Moscow, 14/25.III.1705; *SIRIO* 39 (St Petersburg, 1882) no. 12, p. 56; V.N. Avtokratov, 'Pervye komissariatskie organy russkoi reguliarnoi armii (1700–1710)' *IZ* 68 (1961) p. 163.
37 Avtokratov, 'Pervye' pp. 164–5.
38 L.G. Beskrovnyi, *Russkaia Armiia i Flot v XVIII veke* (Moscow, 1958) pp. 40–2.
39 Ibid. pp. 25–6; E.V. Anisimov, *The Reforms of Peter the Great: Progress through Coercion in Russia* J.T. Alexander (tr.) (Armonk, NY, 1993) p. 61.
40 Beskrovnyi, *Russkaia Armiia* pp. 26–7.
41 Ibid. pp. 40–9.
42 Sheremetev to Peter I, Vitebsk, 3.VI.1708 (OS) *PiB* VII:ii, no. 2439, p. 894.
43 Hallart to Peter I, Smolensk, 12.IX.1706; Ustrialov, *Istoriia* IV:ii, no. 422, p. 429.
44 Whitworth to Harley, Moscow, 24.XII.1707/4.I.1708; *SIRIO* 39, no. 135, p. 441.
45 Fuller, *Strategy* p. 44. Chernov identifies the emergence of a regular army with the reforms of the 1630s, which is surely premature; for Ustrialov, it was Peter's creation. Beskrovnyi sees Peter's reforms bringing a shift from a 'standing' (*postannaia*) to a 'regular' (*reguliarnaia*) army, though he does not explain the difference. Chernov, *Vooruzhennye* p. 133; Ustrialov, *Istoriia* I pp. 187–8; Beskrovnyi, *Russkaia Armiia* p. 19.
46 Whitworth to Harley, Moscow, 14/25.III.1705; *SIRIO*, 39 no. 12, p. 55.
47 Cf. Whitworth to Harley, Moscow 14/25.III.1705 and 6/17.III.1706; ibid. nos 12, 60, pp. 54, 252–3.
48 Fuller, *Strategy* p. 84.
49 Generalstaben *Karl XII på slagfältet* (Stockholm, 1918–19) II pp. 397, 403.
50 Kh. Palli, *Mezhdu dvumia boiami za Narvu* (Tallinn, 1966) pp. 147–59. Schlippenbach's account is printed by Adlerfelt, I pp. 105–11.
51 Palli, *Mezhdu* pp. 176–85.
52 See G. Rystad, 'Ryssland eller Polen? Karl XII:s planer efter Dünaövergången. Några synpunkter' *Scandia* 27 (1961) pp. 298–333.
53 Printed in G. Nordberg, *Konung Carl XII:tes historia* (Stockholm, 1740) I, pp. 215–23; A. Stille, 'Bengt Oxenstiernas memorial af den 5 Mars 1702' *KFÅ* (1914) pp. 23–52; G. Jonasson, *Karl XII:s polska politik* (Stockholm, 1968) pp. 19–25.

54   Nordberg, I p. 222.

55   G. Jonasson, 'Planläggningen av ryska fälttåget år 1701' *KFÅ* (1965) pp. 63–72.

56   Nordberg, I pp. 216–17.

57   Ibid. II p. 847; N. Kostomarov, *Mazepa i Mazepintsy* (2nd edn, St Petersburg, 1885) p. 321. Cf. Whitworth to Harley, Moscow, 13/24.VI.1705, *SIRIO* 39, no. 26 p. 126.

58   T. Nowak, 'Przegląd polskiego piśmiennictwa z dziedziny fortyfikacji i inżynierii wojskowej w XVI–XVIII w.' *SMHW* 11 (1965) pp. 127–8, 139.

59   K. Siemienowicz, *Ars Magnæ Artilleriæ Pars Prima* (Amsterdam, 1650).

60   M. Wagner, *Kadra oficerska armii koronnej w drugiej połowie XVII wieku* (Toruń, 1992) table 29, p. 167; p. 25; Wimmer, *Historia piechoty* p. 224.

61   J.A. Gierowski, *W cieniu Ligi Północnej* (Wrocław, 1971) p. 117.

62   Wimmer, *Wojsko polskie* pp. 69–70,

63   Ibid. p. 203.

64   J. Wimmer, 'Polskie wojsko i sztuka wojenna w czasie Wielkiej Wojny Północnej' *SMHW* 21 (1978) p. 361; M. Wagner, *Kliszów 1702* (Warsaw, 1994) p. 67.

65   Łukasz Miaskowski to unknown, Bar, 3 April 1648. *Jakuba Michałowskiego Księga Pamiętnicza* L. Morsztyn (ed.) (Cracow, 1864) no. 6, p. 10.

66   Wimmer, 'Wojsko i skarb' pp. 88, 90.

67   Wimmer, *Historia piechoty* p. 226; J. Gerlach, *Chłopi w obronie Rzeczypospolitej* (Lwów, 1938) p. 134.

68   Wimmer, *Historia piechoty* pp. 225–6.

69   Dybaś, *Fortece* p. 157.

70   Ibid. pp. 85, 103–4.

71   *VL* IV, pp. 256, 262, 289–92; Dybaś, *Fortece* pp. 127–8.

72   Figures based on Wimmer, *Wojsko polskie* pp. 122, 152–3.

73   J.A. Lynn, 'Recalculating French army growth during the *Grand Siècle*, 1610–1715' in Rogers (ed.) *Military Revolution Debate* p. 125.

74   20,000 infantry and 6,000 horse; calculations based on Schuster and Francke, *Geschichte* pp. 130, 142.

75   J. Cavallie *Från fred till krig* (Uppsala, 1975) p. 35; Generalstaben, *Karl XII* II p. 403.

76   Wimmer, *Wojsko polskie* p. 285.

77   Wagner, *Kadra*, pp. 100, 141.

78   E. Janasz and L. Wasilewski, 'Społeczne aspekty rozwoju husarii w latach 1648–1667 na przykładzie chorągwi hetmani wielkiego koronnego Stanisława Potockiego i wojewody sandomierskiego Władysława Myszkowskiego' *SMHW* 23 (1981) p. 96.

79   J. Wimmer, 'Andrzej Maksymilian Fredro jako projektodawca reform woyskowych' in J. Gierowski, (ed.), *O naprawę Rzeczypospolitej XVII–XVIII w.* (Warsaw, 1965) pp. 110–14.

80   A.M. Fredro, *Militarium, seu axiomatum belli ad harmoniam togae accomodatorum libri duo* (Amsterdam, 1668) pp. 180–1.

81   J. Urwanowicz, *Wojskowe 'sejmiki'. Koła w wojsku Rzeczypospolitej XVI–XVIII wieku* (Białystok, 1996) pp. 47, 50.

82 Pasek, *Memoirs* p. 105.

83 Ibid. pp. 105, 108.

84 Quoted by Urwanowicz, *Wojskowe 'sejmiki'* p. 141.

85 Ibid. pp. 161–2.

86 Wagner, *Kadra* p. 22.

87 M. Nagielski, 'Społeczny i narodowy skład gwardii królewskiej za dwóch ostatnich Wazów (1632–1668)' *SMHW* 30 (1988) pp. 61–102.

88 M. Nagielski, *Liczebność i organizacja gwardii przybocznej i komputowej za ostatniego Wazy (1648–1668)* (Warsaw, 1989) p. 30.

89 Ibid. p. 31.

90 Ibid., table 2, pp. 82–3, 174.

91 Nagielski, 'Opinia szlachecka o gwardii królewskiej w latach 1632–1668' *KH* 92 (1985) p. 553.

92 Dybaś, *Fortece* pp. 96–7, 110–12, 138–9.

93 J. Malec, 'Coequatio Iurium stanów Wielkiego Księstwa Litewskiego z Koroną Polską z 1697 roku' *ABS* 12 (1979) pp. 203–15.

CHAPTER TEN

Russia's Triumph

The war in the Commonwealth

When Augustus II invaded Livonia in 1700 he had reason to hope for Polish support. His coronation charter included a promise to reconquer the lands lost to the Commonwealth since 1620 and his planned seizure of Riga was intended to present his new subjects with a *fait accompli*. He had discussed the plan with a small group of senators, including the primate, cardinal Michał Radziejowski, and Polish treasurer Hieronim Lubomirski. Believing that he had their permission for his Livonian policy, he summoned the Senate Council in May 1700 to approve war against Sweden.[1] The Council, however, with Radziejowski's encouragement, opposed the Commonwealth's involvement in the war. Only in Lithuania were the anti-Sapieha forces prepared to back Augustus in return for protection against the Sapiehas, and there were Lithuanian troops in Flemming's invading force.

The failure to take Riga and the startling Swedish victories over Denmark and Russia left Augustus in a delicate position as the Sapiehas, facing complete destruction, turned to Sweden for protection. For Charles, this seemed a golden opportunity. He was aware of the support for the Sapiehas in Poland, and of concern about Augustus's political aims, demonstrated when the *Sejm* broke up in bitterness in late 1701 after agreeing to offer mediation between Charles and Augustus. Charles found this ridiculous: how could the Commonwealth mediate between its own king and his enemy? The crumbling of Augustus's position in Poland seemed too good an opportunity to waste: Augustus had failed to establish a strong regalist party, and the circle of Polish malcontents was extensive, led by a group of Wielkopolska magnates, including Rafał Leszczyński, his son Stanisław, and Jan Pieniążek. This group had close links to the Sobieskis, who were still smarting from the failure of

Sobieski's maladroit eldest son Jakub to secure the throne in 1697. In Małopolska the Lubomirskis and Potockis, who were closely linked with Radziejowski, led a broad faction of magnates with extensive Ukrainian estates who had little interest in Livonia, but were attracted by the idea of an alliance with Sweden against Russia to recover the lands lost in 1667. For them, war with Sweden was particularly inconvenient.

When Charles invaded, the Swedes met little resistance outside Lithuania. The Commonwealth was all but defenceless: the Polish army numbered barely 13,000, 5,000 short of its agreed état; the situation was even worse in Lithuania, where Augustus had deliberately run down the army, an important Sapieha power-base, to under 4,000. Most of the Polish army was in the Ukraine, where the outbreak of Semen Palii's revolt threatened a return to the savagery of the 1650s. As far as the Commonwealth was concerned, it was still neutral, and politicians awaited Sweden's response to its mediation offer. The Swedes enjoyed a guardedly favourable reception: Quartermaster-General Axel Gyllenkrook, sent ahead to establish magazines for the march on Warsaw, found Mazovian nobles happy enough to supply the necessary provisions.[2] Augustus's attempt to buy off the opposition by appointing Rafał Leszczyński Treasurer and bestowing the Grand Hetmanship on Feliks Potocki and then – after Potocki's death – on Hieronim Lubomirski, merely strengthened his enemies. Leszczyński remained in obdurate opposition, and if Lubomirski did fight at Kliszów in July, he remained in close contact with the Sapiehas. His presence was largely due to a fear that if, as expected, Augustus defeated Charles with the Saxon army alone, his position would be immeasurably strengthened.[3]

Yet Oxenstierna was right to warn Charles of the pitfalls of Polish politics. The Great Northern War was largely won and lost in the Commonwealth long before 1709; for, despite the fact that Charles won every battle that mattered until Lesnaia in 1708, he was comprehensively outmanoeuvred by Peter, who showed a far surer grasp of Polish politics than Charles or, indeed, any of Peter's predecessors. For the Great Northern War was as much a Polish civil war as a Swedish-Russian conflict. Despite the fact that it was largely fought in the Commonwealth until Poltava, the Poles and Lithuanians raised substantial numbers of troops: by 1708 its armies may well have surpassed the 48,000 *komput* agreed by the 1703 Lublin *Sejm*; at the peak of the fighting perhaps 100,000 Poles and Lithuanians were mobilised on both sides, although their performance was often lamentable, with contemporaries observing that they displayed more enthusiasm for fighting each other than Swedes or Russians.

The struggle for control of the Commonwealth between 1702 and 1708 was decisive. Not only was Peter given time to construct his new army and push back the Swedes in the Baltic provinces, he was able to fight for six years outside Russian territory; for all the Russian subsidies given to Peter's Polish supporters, the benefits greatly outweighed the expense. The increasing Russian demands caused problems, and there were bitter complaints even from the Lithuanian lesser nobility, who were among their most loyal supporters;[4] nevertheless, Peter proved to have a much more subtle understanding of the dynamics of Polish politics than did Charles, whose Polish policy focused on his demand for Augustus's deposition, an idea long floated by his opponents, in particular the Sobieskis, with whom Radziejowski was linked. Deposition seemed to offer the sort of quick, painless solution which Charles had achieved in Denmark, but it proved a dangerous policy. Instead of isolating Augustus by accepting the Commonwealth's neutrality, Charles insisted on regarding it as a combatant, while the demand for deposition was a clear interference in its internal politics: Augustus might be widely unpopular, but he enjoyed substantial support in Lithuania and was the legally-elected king, whose title to the throne had been confirmed in 1699. Charles, like many historians, overestimated the power of magnate coteries. His association with the Sapiehas was particularly ill-considered: this odious family was universally hated in Lithuania, and Charles's support for them ensured that his armies met fierce resistance. More ominously, when Augustus proved unable to protect Lithuania from the Swedes, the Lithuanian *szlachta* turned to Russia. In April 1702, a Lithuanian–Russian treaty guaranteed Russian military support and 40,000 roubles in aid, in return for revenues from Sapieha land.

Lithuanian support for the Russian alliance was of incalculable importance for Peter, since it cut off the Swedish army in the Baltic provinces and provided him with a firm base in the Commonwealth. Matters did not look so good in Poland, where there was substantial opposition to the Russian alliance. Yet Charles's obstinate refusal to accept anything less than Augustus's deposition as the price for evacuating the Commonwealth played into Peter's hands by violating the Poles' innately legalist sensibilities. Radziejowski, whose cardinal's hat had gone to his head, tried to use Charles to weaken Augustus's position in favour of his own, but his exalted views of the powers of the primate were not widely shared, and he was reduced to what Charles understandably regarded as duplicitous manoeuvres, refusing publicly to support deposition. Most *sejmiki* were in favour of a show of strength to persuade the Swedes to leave, petitioning Augustus in June 1702 to issue the final summons to the noble levy, and the palatinate of Sandomierz formed a confederation to organise defence. Even in the Leszczyński heartland of Wielkopolska, the general *sejmik* at Środa agreed to summon the levy and petitioned Lubomirski to support them with troops from the foreign contingent.

Augustus patiently built his support, as it became clear that most of the *szlachta* regarded magnate intrigues with Sweden with hostility: in August

1702, Feliks Lipski, member of a delegation to Charles, who had actually been accused by his fellow envoys of being too favourable to Augustus, was lynched at a gathering of the noble levy on suspicion of conspiring with the Swedes. By March 1703 Augustus was supported by the majority of the Senate, by both Polish hetmans, and by four confederations on the model of that drawn up in Sandomierz, including a general confederation of Wielkopolska, where Leszczyński's death in January had weakened the opposition. Only a handful of senators turned up to a rival meeting called by Radziejowski in Warsaw, and there was widespread condemnation of the primate's presumption.[5]

The strength of Augustus's position was demonstrated at the Lublin *Sejm* of June–July 1703, which provided the legal basis for his defence of his throne. By calling it, Augustus made it clear that he, unlike the opposition, was basing his actions on the Commonwealth's legal institutions. He agreed to uphold *szlachta* liberties and promised not to begin any wars, either as elector of Saxony, or as king of Poland-Lithuania. The Swedish demand for deposition was categorically rejected. There were to be no territorial concessions, and peace was to be on the basis of the *status quo ante bellum*. Charles's supporters were declared enemies of the fatherland; those who did not abandon him within six weeks were to lose their offices, lands and honour. The *Sejm* agreed to raise an army of 36,000 in Poland, and 12,000 in Lithuania, to be supplemented by 12,000 Saxons, 21,000 from the noble levy (15,000 in Poland and 6,000 in Lithuania), 10,200 private troops, and Brandt's corps of 600. Taxes were agreed to support these forces, and the fiscal autonomy of *sejmiki* was substantially trimmed to the advantage of the central treasury. Considering the weakness of Augustus's position in 1701, it was a triumph.[6]

The *Sejm* did not, however, declare war; the show of strength was merely to persuade the Swedes to leave. Yet Charles still held the military advantage; despite his exasperation with the slippery Radziejowski – who attended the Lublin *Sejm* – and the Polish malcontents, he continued to insist on dethronement. Gradually his position improved, as Augustus squandered much of his accumulated political capital. There had been some opposition in Lublin to royal proposals, and envoys from Poznań and Kalisz had been excluded from its debates; this provoked the formation of a confederation which became a focus for opposition. Augustus's blatant bid to align the monarchy with patriotic *szlachta* opinion was worrying for many magnates, while there was resistance to the Lublin decisions from some *sejmiki*, alarmed at limitations on their autonomy, while the difficult economic situation ensured opposition to the new taxes. The most explosive issue, however, was that of relations with Russia. The *Sejm* had confirmed Augustus's powers to make alliances; when his hopes of international intervention to force Sweden to accept a reasonable settlement failed, and as it became clear that the *Sejm*'s military decisions would only be implemented slowly and in part, Augustus drew closer to Russia. Peter, anxious to ensure that the Commonwealth continued as the main theatre of war for as long as possible, tempted him with offers of financial and military support.

The need for aid was pressing. The Swedes occupied Poznań in September to secure their position in Wielkopolska, while delays in implementing *Sejm* decisions meant that Augustus was unable to save the 6,000-strong Saxon garrison in Thorn, which surrendered in October. In November, Saxon envoys signed a treaty in Moscow in which Peter promised financial and military support with the clear aim of drawing the Commonwealth into open war against Sweden; this was followed in December by the 'triple alliance' signed at Jaworów, in which Augustus drew on the strong Lithuanian support for the Russian alliance. Peter agreed to send 12,000 infantry and pay subsidies of 300,000 roubles annually; the treaty was ratified by the Lithuanians who, in return for raising 14,000 men, would be supported by 10,000 Russian infantry, 5,000 cavalry and subsidies of 60,000 roubles per annum.[7]

Despite Charles's refusal to compromise, this was a dangerous step. Opposition to closer ties with Russia grew among senators, including Lubomirski, who lodged a formal protest. Meanwhile, the anti-Augustus confederates were gathering support. The behaviour of Saxon troops in Polish Prussia from November 1702 alienated opinion in a province in which Augustus had never been popular, and which would be in the front line in any war against Sweden. There were no Prussian envoys at the Lublin *Sejm*, which meant that its decisions were of doubtful validity in Prussia. The Swedish siege of Thorn in 1703 provoked hostility to Swedish demands for contributions, but Augustus's failure to relieve the city enabled his opponents to gain the upper hand. In October, a confederation was formed at Stargard; although it was not initially opposed to Augustus, it soon drifted towards an alliance with the Środa confederates.[8] Now Radziejowski openly declared for Sweden, humiliated by his hostile reception at Lublin where he was accused of treason and forced to swear oaths of loyalty to Augustus and the Commonwealth. He told Charles in December that the Polish army would abandon Augustus if it was paid, and agreed to call the *szlachta* to Warsaw to effect a dethronement. On 14 February 1704, Radziejowski declared an interregnum; two days later, a general confederation was called to rally Augustus's supporters.

Initially, this bold move seemed to work. In March Lubomirski, who had long harboured hopes of the throne for himself, abandoned Augustus and joined the Warsaw Confederation, after the daring kidnap of Jakub and Konstanty Sobieski by Augustus's agents in Silesia in February which deprived

Charles of his leading candidate for the throne. In June he unexpectedly proposed the candidature of Rafał Leszczyński's son Stanisław, after Aleksander Sobieski's refusal to accept what he felt was his elder brother's due. With Leszczyński's formal election in July, Charles had achieved the aim for which he had entered the Commonwealth two years earlier, yet it hardly solved his problems. For two years, his armies had seen little serious fighting; if he wished to consolidate Leszczyński's position he could not abandon the Commonwealth. In May, Augustus's supporters established their own general confederation at Sandomierz, where the Commonwealth – or at least that portion of it which supported Augustus – finally declared war on Sweden. In August, the Russian alliance was formalised at Narva. The phoney war was over.

Despite holding the military advantage for the next five years, Charles proved unable to secure victory. Although Leszczyński attracted consider-able support, particularly in Polish Prussia and Wielkopolska, Charles was unable to conciliate or crush his enemies. Individual magnates were enticed over from the Sandomierz camp, including Lithuanian Grand Hetman Michał Wiśniowiecki, but factional intrigues merely divided Augustus's enemies. Radziejowski opposed Leszczyński's election, absenting himself from the formal proclamation of the new king. Lubomirski was similarly disappointed, while his defection had destroyed his control of the crown army, threequarters of which remained loyal to Augustus. Together with Radziejowski, whose actions were condemned by the Pope after lobbying from Augustus, he had already begun secret negotiations with Augustus in August 1704; in November he openly abandoned Leszczyński. Radziejowski withdrew to Danzig, where he met Leszczyński in January 1705, but refused to call a general assembly to confirm the election. By 1706, death had re-moved Radziejowski and Lubomirski from the scene.

Even the invasion of Saxony and the treaty of Altranstädt did little to improve Leszczyński's position. Despite Augustus's abdication, Leszczyński failed to win over his enemies, and his tenure of the throne was too obviously dependent upon Swedish arms. An awareness of what was to come has meant that for some Polish historians, the Commonwealth's failure to rally round Leszczyński represented the loss of a great opportunity to prevent the 200-year Russian domination of Polish politics. Leszczyński, it is suggested, offered the prospect of a return to the Polish-Swedish alliance which had defeated Ivan IV, and which might have prevented the humiliations of the eighteenth century. Yet for contemporaries, there was more reason to see Sweden as the greatest danger to the Commonwealth: Narva had seemed to confirm the superiority of Swedish arms, while Turkish and Tatar threats and news of the 1705 Astrakhan rising suggested that Peter might be in danger of a major defeat, or even the loss of his throne.[9]

The bankruptcy of Charles's Polish policy was starkly demonstrated after Altranstädt. Since Leszczyński's election, several influential figures had defected to him, including Lithuanian Grand Chancellor Karol Radziwiłł, Lithuanian Vice-Chancellor Stanisław Szczuka and the Jabłonowskis. The bitter rivalry between Ogiński and Wiśniowiecki lay behind the latter's defection, while naked ambition led many to support Leszczyński when he began distributing offices and starosties. Nevertheless, many defectors maintained links with the Sandomierz confederates, and their loyalty was always suspect. Altranstädt might have knocked Saxony out of the war and deprived them of their king, but it did not win over the majority of the *szlachta*, who had little hope of such reward.

The manner of Leszczyński's election and the nature of his rule were a travesty of Polish law. With Radziejowski sulking in his palace, the election took place under the protection of Swedish bayonets, in the presence of a handful of senators and *szlachta*. There was no reading of the *Pacta Conventa*, the formal agreement made by every new king with the Commonwealth, and contemporary opinion was dismissive of a monarch chosen by a foreign ruler and elected at his insistence. The alliance Leszczyński signed with Sweden in November 1705 was too obviously drawn up to suit the Swedes, who were given the right to occupy Polish cities and fortresses. The Commonwealth was to annul all alliances deemed contrary to Swedish interests, Sweden was to be allowed unrestricted recruitment rights in the Commonwealth, whose trade was to be strictly subordinated to Swedish interests: all goods from Lithuania, Ruthenia, Courland and Polish Prussia were to be exported through Riga, while the Polish port of Połęga in Courland was to be abandoned.[10] In the war against Russia, Smolensk and Kiev were to be returned to the Commonwealth, but Courland and Polish Livonia were to be ceded to Sweden.

Peter's treatment of his Polish allies was a stark contrast. Despite anger at the behaviour of Russian troops in the Commonwealth, and growing fears of Russian annexations in Lithuania and the Ukraine, which played a part in Wiśniowiecki's defection, the alliance held firm. Peter dealt with Augustus and the Sandomierz confederates in a manner very different from Charles's peremptory contempt for the Commonwealth's legal norms. Although he clearly had no intention of surrendering his conquests in the Baltic, until after Poltava he maintained the polite fiction that Livonia would be returned to the Commonwealth once it had been taken from the Swedes. Russian armies crushed Palii's revolt and Peter promised to return the right-bank Ukraine to Polish control.

For all the undoubted tensions, and endless bickering over Peter's failure to fulfil the terms of the Narva treaty, his cautious approach paid dividends. When Charles launched his Russian campaign in late 1707 and the Russian armies withdrew towards the Russian border, the Sandomierz confederates remained largely loyal. Although they still demonstrated considerable independence in rejecting Peter's proposals on a number of important issues, including candidates for a new election, there was no mass defection. Many of those who changed sides were disappointed at their reception. Charles constantly interfered in the crucial question of appointments to office and honour – a highly sensitive issue, given that many of these appointments were to positions still held by his enemies. He favoured certain groups among Leszczyński's followers, in particular the Sapiehas, which did little to help Leszczyński. His insistence on offering the Lithuanian grand hetmanship to Jan Sapieha after browbeating Kazimierz Sapieha into resigning outraged Wiśniowiecki, who expected promotion to the post he had abandoned on defecting to Charles.

Charles's strategy assumed that Leszczyński and the Swedish general Krassau, who was left with a small Swedish corps in Poland, would lead a substantial force into the Ukraine in support of the main Swedish army. Yet to achieve this, Leszczyński would have to break through the confederate and Russian forces occupying Małopolska, Podolia and Volhynia. As he prepared to launch his campaign in March 1708, Wiśniowiecki withdrew to Lithuania to consider changing sides again. A significant number of other important figures, disillusioned by their reception, were already doing so, including the Lubomirskis and Michał Potocki. Throughout 1708, the two sides engaged in a vicious war of raids and counter-raids. In November, a pro-Leszczyński force of 10,000 was defeated by a confederate force of roughly the same size in a bloody encounter at Koniecpol.

Koniecpol made a great impression on *szlachta* opinion. Małopolska, which had been leaning towards Leszczyński, now lost all enthusiasm. Few would commit themselves until the outcome of the Russian campaign was known. Augustus, aware that many Poles did not recognise his abdication, gathered troops on Saxony's eastern borders, but was content to play a waiting game. After Koniecpol, neither Leszczyński nor Krassau could stop a Confederate thrust into Polish Prussia while Ogiński and the Confederate Grand Hetman Adam Sieniawski blocked the route eastwards. In the spring of 1709, with Charles waiting impatiently outside the walls of Poltava, Leszczyński made a half-hearted attempt to break through, but news of the approach of Russian reinforcements soon forced him back. Charles was about to face the consequences of the failure of his Polish policy. He had been unable to impose his will on the Commonwealth, and the Sandomierz confederates had shown that, even deprived of a king, the Commonwealth's decentralised military and political system was robust enough to thwart its enemies, if not defeat them. Winning battles was not

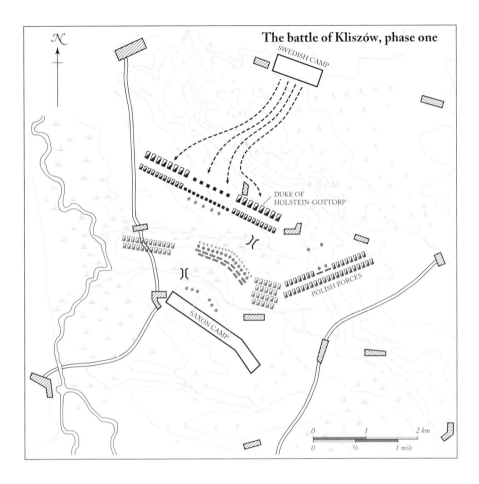

The battle of Kliszów, phase one

enough. Charles had failed to win the Polish war; his army paid the price at Poltava.

Nemesis

At 11.00 on the hot summer's morning of 8/19 July 1702 a surprised Augustus II was informed at his headquarters in Kliszów, south of Kielce, that the Swedish army which he had understood to be encamped five kilometres to the north had appeared unexpectedly out of woods near the village of Borczyn. After hurrying forward to confirm the report, he ordered the Saxon army to deploy in a strong position on a small rise to the north of their encampment. The Swedes were also surprised. Charles had persuaded his reluctant advisers to march on the Saxons at nine o'clock having spent two hours drawn up in battle order waiting for an attack which never materialised. He had not, however, expected the Saxon position to be so strong: protected by an impassible swamp it could not be outflanked on its left, while the stream which ran through the boggy valley between the armies made a frontal assault a risky proposition. Moreover, Charles was substantially outnumbered: the Swedish army consisted of 8,000 foot, and 4,000 horse; with most of its artillery struggling far to the rear on the dreadful roads it was supported by only four three-pounder guns. It faced 9,000 Saxon cavalry, 7,500 Saxon foot, 6,000 Polish cavalry and forty-six guns. With no fortuitous snowstorms to be expected from the clear July heavens, it looked as if the impetuous Charles would at last receive his comeuppance. The startled Saxon officers, forced to abandon their leisurely picnic, certainly thought so: as they dashed to take up their positions, they ordered their servants to keep lunch warm. They would soon be back.

If the servants heeded their masters, it was to no avail. After a brief survey of the terrain, Charles ordered a daring manoeuvre which decided the battle. Since the major weakness of the Saxon position lay on its right, where Lubomirski's Poles had just squeezed into line, he changed his battle order, strengthening his left wing to mount a bold enveloping move. After a Swedish charge was beaten back, the Swedes withstood two great onslaughts by Lubomirski's cavalry while the weakened centre and right beat back a Saxon thrust across the marshy valley which now offered them a measure of protection. When Lubomirski withdrew from the battlefield after his failed assaults, the main Swedish force turned in on the exposed Saxon flank as the Swedish right and centre advanced. The Saxons, hemmed in by the marshland to their left and rear, fought with great determination, but were slowly crushed between the Swedish pincers. By half past four, Charles was mounting a triumphal entry to the Saxon camp as Augustus and the remnants of his army squelched their way to safety through the evil-smelling bog. For the loss of some 300 dead, including Charles's brother-in-law Frederick of Holstein-Gottorp – sliced in two by a Polish cannon-ball – and 500–800 wounded, the Swedes killed some 2,000 Saxons and captured 1,000. Lunch would have to wait.[11]

It is important to consider Narva in the context of what happened at Kliszów. For it was not just Russian armies which were unable to deal with

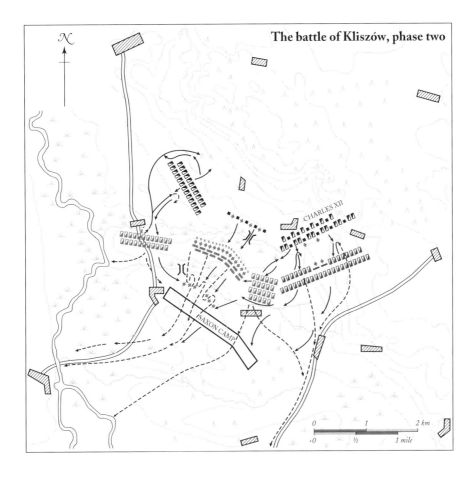

The battle of Kliszów, phase two

the Swedes. At Kliszów Charles routed a regular, numerically-superior and experienced western army drawn up in a strong defensive position with a substantial advantage in artillery. The Swedish army is often regarded as western, and many of its officers had considerable experience of warfare in the west, yet it did not fight as western armies were supposed to fight. Throughout the seventeenth century, European armies had built their strategy and tactics round firepower and fortifications. The improvements in firearms technology in the second half of the seventeenth century, which saw the replacement of the matchlock by the flintlock, the introduction of the bayonet, which enabled armies to dispense with pikemen, and the increased discipline which could be instilled into the new regular armies, ensured that gun-powder's role was more important than ever. The increased rate of fire made possible by flintlocks meant that experienced infantry who had time to form up could no longer be broken by cavalry, as Lubomirski's hussars discovered at Kliszów, and were less vulnerable on the march. The battlefield in the age of Marlborough and Eugene was increasingly obscured by the acrid black smoke of gunpowder, as the intricate geometrical patterns of Vauban's fortifications twirled their way round European cities.

Yet Charles obstinately refused to follow fashion. Even though flintlock and bayonet were standard issue in Swedish armies – indeed the Swedish bayonet was better fixed and hence superior to many western versions – the pike was retained, not because Sweden was backward, but because pikemen, who constituted about a third of each battalion, still had a role to play. Charles had a healthy contempt for firepower, placing far greater trust in cold steel. Each Swedish infantryman was armed with a sword, the design of which was of great concern to Charles. Swedish infantry regulations, from those drawn up by Magnus Stenbock at Lais in the winter of 1700–1, played down the role of firepower and stressed the importance of infantry attack at the double. Salvos were to be delivered as close as possible to the enemy, and attacks were to be pressed home with maximum vigour: eye-witness accounts describe how the Swedish foot charged at the run; even during its doomed attack against overwhelming odds at Poltava, the weary infantry was running so fast it was 'almost leaping'.[12] At Fraustadt (2/13 February 1706), most of the Swedish foot did not even bother to fire a salvo as it attacked in one line, five ranks deep, with pikemen between the second and third ranks; only the right wing loosed its muskets. Elsewhere, the infantry pressed forward across the last hundred yards through three artillery salvos and one musket volley, brushed aside the bristling Spanish riders chained together in front of the Saxon ranks, and plunged in at the run with sword, pike and bayonet.[13] At Hołowczyn (July 1708), which Charles considered the best of his battles, 'the King himself went from one battalion to another, . . . ordering them above all things, instead of firing, to use their pikes, their bayonets and their swords.'[14]

It was not that Charles failed to appreciate the importance of firepower: Swedish artillery and musket technology remained the equal of any in Europe and he was perfectly capable of using artillery effectively where he felt it appropriate, as at the forcing of the Dvina in July 1701, or to cover his surprise crossing of the Vabich at Hołowczyn which, despite Charles's urgings, was largely a bitter firefight. Yet Charles judged weapons in terms of effectiveness not fashion. Although technology had certainly improved, the profound limitations of contemporary firearms still shaped tactics. Flint-locks might be better than matchlocks, but their rate of fire was still slow and their reliability uncertain, especially in damp weather; battleplans consequently tended to emphasise the defensive over the offensive. Charles, however, believed in speed of movement and the seizure of the initiative; this led him to downplay the role of the musket and of field artillery. For, if cavalry was no longer capable of breaking ordered formations of infantry, a disciplined, aggressive charge by well-drilled, motivated infantry with high morale could achieve what cavalry could not. Even troops experienced in the handling of firearms were vulnerable to a coordinated and rapid infantry assault. At Fraustadt, where much of the Saxon army was composed of French, Bavarian and Swiss mercenaries, each infantry platoon, firing in turn, should in theory have been capable of unleashing five or six salvos in the time it took the Swedes to approach. In practice they only managed one or two, since they were ordered to wait until the Swedes were eighty paces away. If, as one source suggests, some of the Saxons fired high, the damage inflicted would have been minimal.[15]

Swedish success was not dependent upon infantry alone. Cavalry still played a central role on the battlefield, protecting the flanks and preventing envelopment by the enemy. With the division of the Commonwealth's forces in what became a civil war, the Swedish cavalry were able to play a more central role than had been possible in the 1650s. Backed by substantial quantites of Polish medium and light cavalry, either recruited directly into the Swedish army as Vallacker (Wallachian) regiments, or as part of the pro-Leszczyński forces, Swedish cavalry enjoyed the freedom to roam widely. On the battlefield, mounted on robust, powerful horses, they were direct and devastating. According to Stenbock's 1710 regulations, a cavalryman was to charge 'with sword in hand', and never to 'caracolle or use his carbine or pistol' in preference to his sword. The cavalry charged in closed wedge formation, with knees locked together. It is a matter of some controversy as to whether it was possible to maintain an attack in such close formation at high speed; in part it depended on the terrain, but eyewitness reports make it clear that Charles's cavalry charged home at the gallop, even if they did not always maintain close formation.[16]

The superior Swedish cavalry proved decisive in several battles, including Pułtusk (June 1703) and Ponitz (September 1704). At Fraustadt, where Rehnskiöld was outnumbered nearly two to one (and nearly three to one in infantry), he used his cavalry on both wings in a double envelopment of Schulenburg's force which was deliberately deployed in a position thought to be impregnable to cavalry attack, with each wing resting on a village, and battalions turned at right angles to offer flanking cover. The Swedish cavalry, attacking at the gallop, drove off the Saxon horse on the wings and pressed in on the allied centre as the infantry mounted a frontal assault against the allied foot. The result was a massacre. Of some 18,000 Saxons and Russians,

7–8,000 were killed, including the Russians cut down in cold blood after surrendering. Four-fifths of the allied army was killed or captured.[17]

The spectacular results of these aggressive tactics themselves played an important part in their success, since they ensured that morale remained high. Faith in Charles's powers as a general and a feeling of superiority towards other armies took root. Belief in the king, trust in the providential protection of a Lutheran God and the confidence which stemmed from an unbroken run of success drove Sweden's armies forward. Charles's oft-criticised insistence on leading from the front and exposing himself to danger helped strengthen this belief: his preservation from harm, especially given the mounting toll of men killed or wounded at his side, seemed to confirm that he enjoyed divine protection.

Charles's bravura tactics have endeared him to military historians with a romantic streak; in the early twentieth century, when the doctrine of attack *à l'outrance* was again fashionable, a team of historians in the Swedish General Staff under Carl Bennedich sought to rescue Charles's military reputation from charges of impetuous rashness, for which he had been condemned since his death. Bennedich saw in Charles's generalship the embodiment of the supreme military virtues. According to the General Staff, he perfected the Swedish school of Erik XIV, Gustav Adolf, Charles X and Charles XI. Throughout the work he is compared to Alexander the Great and Napoleon.[18]

The General Staff had nothing but contempt for the linear tactics of contemporary European armies. These led, it argued, to timid, defensive battles in which the initiative was handed to the enemy. This distinction between linear tactics and the war of movement and attack favoured by Charles led them to blame the Poltava disaster on a group of officers, in particular Lewenhaupt and Magnus Stenbock, who had served their apprenticeships in western Europe, and who were allegedly proponents of the western school. Lewenhaupt is criticised for his defensive posture at Gemauerthof (1705), which was at least a Swedish victory, and Lesnaia (1708), when his lack of initiative was supposedly to blame for his defeat and loss of the vital supply train. At Poltava the bitter disagreements between generals of the Swedish school, principally Rehnskiöld – who was in overall command – and those of the western school – in particular Lewenhaupt, who led the infantry – were blamed for fatally compromising Charles's brilliant battle plan.[19]

The General Staff account is tendentious and one-sided, relying too much on over-interpretation of the self-serving exculpations of Swedish generals granted too much time to ponder and quarrel over responsibility for the Poltava debacle in their long years of Russian captivity. The distinctions between linear and Caroline tactics are overdrawn, relying too much on a theoretical approach to the study of war which rests on questionable foundations. In their own way, Bennedich and his supporters were the Swedish equivalent of Soviet historians who claimed that western methods had little influence on the Russian military art, and explained Russian success by a chauvinist, wholly mystical and utterly unscientific belief in the invincibility of the Russian people.[20] Nevertheless, despite the obvious weaknesses in the General Staff's account of Charles's wars, it would be unwise to reject their arguments entirely.

For all that west European tactics in the age of Marlborough and Eugene were by no means as defensive as they were depicted by the General Staff, Wernstedt goes too far in asserting that there were no substantial differences between Swedish and western methods of waging war.[21] There is an abundance of contemporary evidence that western observers were nonplussed by Swedish tactics. De Croy, who commanded the Russian army at Narva, told the French envoy Guiscard that when the Swedish army approached the Russian countervallation he assumed it was merely the advance guard, unable to believe that Charles 'would have dared to attack an army so well intrenched, and so infinitely superior to his own'.[22] Guiscard himself was so surprised that he claimed to be unable to speak for several days, a condition as rare as it was excruciating for a French diplomat, as Bengtsson drily observed.[23] While Wrede, serving with the Swedes, dismissed reports that the Russian army numbered 80,000, he still found it astonishing for 8,000 men to attack 40,000, protected by extensive fieldworks, armed with 130 good artillery pieces and with such copious supplies of ammunition.[24] Magnus Stenbock, who had learned his trade in Dutch and Imperial service, wrote that he had now seen war waged 'in a completely different way from that which I understand or have learnt.'[25] In 1701, the Saxons defending the line of the Dvina were astonished when the Swedish infantry charged at them through a hail of bullets with pike, bayonet and sword.[26]

Charles's aggressive instincts and his relative neglect of firepower were quite distinctive. Yet the employment of such methods was not due to quirks of character or inspirational genius, as is often alleged, although Charles's powerful and unusual temperament played a part. He was nurtured in a military tradition which was already distinctive long before his birth. His principal instructors, Magnus Stuart and Rehnskiöld, had fought under Charles XI, and had themselves been instructed by those who had served Charles X, including Erik Dahlberg and Rutger von Ascheberg. Stuart insisted that his pupil study in depth the wars of Gustav Adolf and Charles X; as an adult, Charles was able to recall their campaigns in detail, and made a special tour of the site of the 1656 battle of Warsaw in 1702. Sweden's famous 'gå på' (have at them) tactics may have reached their apotheosis under Charles XII; he did not create them.

If even those hostile to Charles recognise his tactical ability, he is widely accused of having little strategic grasp. The aggression which, on the tactical level, brought such spectacular victories, it is argued, was his greatest strategic weakness; some have even seen it as indicative of mental imbalance: '[Charles's] motives were largely aggressive. . . . Here was a monarch . . . whose dedication to the practice of the martial arts and sciences at times bordered on the near-insane.'[27] Russian historians have been particularly critical. Leer argues that Charles was 'no strategist' and Tarle considers that his Russian campaign was based on wholly unrealistic premises, claiming that Charles's own generals by 1708–9 were horrified by his strategic decisions. Such arguments have been echoed by foreign historians of Russia, with Fuller claiming that Charles was 'deeply inferior' to Peter as a strategist.[28] Above all he is criticised for the decision not to follow up Narva by pushing into Russia to defeat Peter once and for all while he still had the chance; thereafter an attack on Russia would be more difficult since the loss of Ingria, Kexholm, Narva and Dorpat destroyed the land bridge between Finland and Livonia and ensured that Peter could disrupt Swedish communications by land and, with his new navy, by sea.

The Russian campaign of 1708–9 is usually presented as definitive proof of Charles's hubristic failure to take account of military reality. Ignoring Peter's peace offers and willingness to restore most of Russia's conquests in return for being allowed to keep St Petersburg, Charles launched his attack. Instead of attempting to reconquer the lost territories, or to invade via Pskov, so remaining close to his supply lines, he chose a direct thrust at Moscow through Lithuania. Even worse, it is argued, was the decision to turn south into the Ukraine without waiting for the provisions being brought laboriously from Livonia by Lewenhaupt, which ensured their loss at Lesnaia in September 1708 and condemned the Swedes to starve in the hideous winter of 1708–9. By May 1709, the proud force of 33–36,000 Charles had led into Russia had been reduced by at least a third, and it was short of food, ammunition and gunpowder.[29] Trapped at Poltava, it faced its nemesis 225 kilometres east of Kiev and over a thousand from Riga. The disaster, it seems, was eminently avoidable.

There is no shortage of contemporary accounts to substantiate such arguments. As early as the autumn of 1708, Whitworth's cogent summary of the situation anticipated many subsequent criticisms. He praised the qualities of the Swedish armies, but suggested that Charles 'seems to undervalue all subordinate means of proceeding with success and to rely wholly on the goodness of his army and justice of his cause, by which he has hitherto carried on a prosperous war, contrary to all ordinary rules of acting'. He concluded that if Charles had invaded Russia after Narva, Peter would probably have been forced to make peace on any terms; once that opportunity was missed, however, Peter was given the chance to train and discipline his new forces and, 'by acting with whole armies against small detachments the soldiers became inured to fire, and easily begun to taste the sweets of conquest'.[30] In their accounts of the campaign, several Swedish officers, in particular Gyllenkrook and Lewenhaupt, stressed that they had disagreed with Charles over many of his strategic decisions: Gyllenkrook, who had prepared the plan for a strike through Livonia at Pskov, claimed that he 'never advised' an attack on Moscow, but always sought to hinder it.[31] Lewenhaupt criticised Charles for failing to wait for the supply train when it was only a day's ride away by courier; over the siege of Poltava; and for the decision not to deploy artillery during the battle.[32] James Jeffreyes, an English agent attached to Charles's army, wrote immediately after Poltava:

> Thus . . . you see a victorious and numerous army destroy'd in less than two years time, much because of the little regard they had for their enemy; but chiefly because the King would not hearken to any advice that was given him by his Councillors, who I can assure you were for carrying on this war after another method.[33]

When Peter asked the captured Swedish generals after Poltava to explain certain of Charles's decisions which he found hard to comprehend, Lewenhaupt remarked that the only reply they could make was that they did not know.[34]

While it would be foolish to deny that the headstrong, intense Charles made mistakes, or bore a great deal of responsibility for what happened at Poltava, hindsight has overly coloured judgments of his strategic abilities. Concentration on the ill-fated Russian campaign unbalances many accounts,[35] while contemporary assessments cannot be regarded as objective: the desire of Gyllenkrook and Lewenhaupt to clear themselves of responsibility for Poltava and the shameful surrender at Perevolochna casts more than a shadow of doubt over their accounts.[36] One need not adopt the fervid hyperbole of the Swedish General Staff to acknowledge that the Charles who lost Poltava was also the Charles whose strategic grasp at the age of eighteen was sure enough for him to play a significant role in planning the spectacular victory over three powerful enemies in 1700. The brilliant campaigns of 1702–6 and the marshalling of exiguous forces in defence of Sweden against the most powerful coalition it ever faced between 1714 and 1718 suggest that those who dismiss his strategic abilities as negligible are the ones whose judgment is clouded.

The invasion of Russia was undoubtedly a gamble, yet the fact that it ended in disaster should not blind the historian to the reasons for adopting it, nor to the misfortunes which played a part in its failure. Russian historians frequently condemn Charles for his aggression, comparing him to Napoleon and Hitler, whose presumption also brought their downfall. It was the Russians, however, not the Swedes, who were the aggressors in the Great Northern War, which Peter launched on the flimsiest of pretexts. Moreover, Charles had good reason for rejecting Peter's peace overtures. In 1706–8, Peter's reforms were by no means secure, the regular core of his army was still small, and the Swedes were aware of the great upsurge in opposition to Peter which had begun with the Astrakhan rising in 1705, and the widespread Cossack discontent, which was to see Bulavin's rising in 1707–8 and the defection of Mazepa and significant numbers of Zaporozhians in late 1708. As Whitworth remarked:

> should this army come to any considerable miscarriage, it would probably draw after it the ruin of the whole empire, since I do not know where the Czar would be able to get another; for the new raised regiments in Ingria and much more those, who are now mustering up here and in the several garrisons on the frontiers, cannot deserve the name of regular forces, not to mention the usual despondency of the russians after any misfortunes, and their general discontent and inclinations to a revolt.[37]

Thus Charles is criticised for not invading Russia in 1700–1, and for invading in 1708–9. Yet conditions were far more favourable in 1708. Following the pleasant interlude in Saxony, the Swedish field army was larger, more experienced and better-equipped than at any point since 1700. The political situation in Poland-Lithuania was more favourable, and Saxony was out of the war. Even if the Russian army had improved substantially since Narva, the Swedes had good reason to believe that they were capable of defeating it if they could force it to battle. Why should Charles make peace, and permit the continued existence of a Russian bridgehead on the Gulf of Finland, thus giving Peter time to stifle dissent at home and build up his navy and army? Charles would have been naive to believe that Peter would be content with the cession of St Petersburg alone; it was the Russians who would benefit most from a suspension of hostilities. The only way to secure a lasting peace and long-term security for the Baltic provinces was to destroy the Russian army and force Peter to settle on Swedish terms. An invasion of Russia was the only way to achieve that end.

Charles's reign demonstrated once more the harsh realities of Sweden's strategic position, for all that it was better in 1700 than in 1655 or 1675. Sweden had a large, well-trained army which could be mobilised rapidly and effectively; it had to be supplemented by further recruitment, but the costs involved were not crippling. Although government income was largely static in the years before the war, it had been possible to build up a small reserve fund, amounting to roughly 1 million silver dalers in 1696, while regimental cash reserves were nearly as great, at 900,000 silver dalers. Yet although Sweden was better prepared for war than ever before, and was able to raise new funds from extraordinary taxes, such as the tenth penny levied between November 1699 and February 1700, and various expedients, the harsh realities of its chronic shortage of specie soon became apparent: the costs of mobilisation were reckoned in January 1700 at 6,374,141 silver dalers, while extraordinary sources were estimated to be capable of producing only 1,514,001. Hopes of raising loans in Holland and England at a maximum of 5 per cent interest, were dashed, since Sweden could offer little as security apart from customs tolls at Riga, Narva, Reval and Nyen. With Saxon and Russian armies heading for Livonia, the Dutch and English were understandably reluctant to risk their money, although a Dutch loan of 300,000 riksdalers was secured at 5 per cent in 1702. Sweden's reserves underpinned the mobilisation of 1700, and made possible Travendal and Narva, but they were rapidly exhausted, and were utterly incapable of sustaining a long war: government credit was poor, and loans from private individuals were difficult to raise, while the outbreak of war brought a serious liquidity crisis for the new Bank of Sweden.[38]

Thus Sweden, for all that Charles XI's reforms had transformed its military capacity, faced a familiar set of problems. It could not long fight a defensive war. As had been the case in 1655, once it mobilised its army, it was forced to carry the war into enemy territory, and the war could only be sustained by fighting abroad. The *indelningsverk* performed well in filling gaps in the ranks, but for all the meticulous preparations of the excellent commissariat, once the troops were detached from the farms which supported them in peacetime, the problems multiplied. They were already evident when the army gathered in Scania, Sweden's richest province; once it reached Livonia, they only worsened. In the winter of 1700–1 it rapidly became clear that if the army were to stay together it would have to leave the Baltic provinces. One of the most important arguments against an attack on Pskov was that even without taking into account the political problems following the *reduktion*, Livonia, devastated by famine in the 1690s, was exhausted: to strike at Pskov the army would have to retrace its steps northward across territories which had already paid substantial contributions.[39] The move south into Courland in July 1701 was thus partly motivated by supply considerations. Courland was small, however; by early 1702 it was exhausted, and the army was suffering: after it entered Poland one observer noted the contrast between the half-naked Swedish soldiers and the regiment of Sapieha foot which accompanied them, smartly clad in green uniforms.[40] Merely to support itself, the army had to move. It was difficult to imagine that an invasion of Russia could be sustained from an exhausted and politically unreliable supply-base, while the area round Pskov was not known to flow with milk and honey.

The decision to move south was eminently sensible. For the next six years, the Swedes supplied themselves without major difficulty. Charles did not face the concerted resistance that had frustrated his grandfather, he enjoyed substantial political support, and his army was manifestly superior to all its opponents. Small Swedish detachments were still vulnerable to attack, but the fact that they had significant support from Augustus's enemies meant that they could deploy Polish light cavalry of their own to counter the threat and provide reconnaissance; Charles placed great store on the recruitment of these Vallacker units, and there was an entire regiment in the army which left Saxony in 1707.[41] Swedish military dominance ensured that Magnus Stenbock, director of the General War Commissariat, could raise contributions from a wide area in a way which had not been possible in the 1650s: when the palatinates of Ruthenia and Volhynia were the object of a special expedition in the winter of 1702–3, he returned with six barrels of gold and a considerable haul of supplies in kind at a cost of 68 killed or missing and 36 horses.[42] After the fall of Thorn in October 1703 there were for the moment no Saxon troops in the Commonwealth. With the army stationed in Warmia and Polish Prussia in the first half of 1704, the supply situation was remarkably good. It remained so when the Swedes moved their headquarters to Rawicz after the 1704 campaign, or when Volhynia was placed under contribution in 1705.[43]

There was a price to be paid, however, for the very efficiency of the Swedish operation. Although marauding and looting were punished severely by the military authorities, who made conspicuous efforts to investigate Polish complaints against Swedish soldiers, there is reason to doubt Hatton's indulgent assessment of their behaviour.[44] Even in pro-Swedish areas, the very efficiency with which they collected contributions provoked hostile reactions from those subject to constant requisitions. Given that this was a civil war, and that Swedish control was never absolute, communities could be faced by successive demands from Swedish, Saxon and Polish forces: in December 1705 the villagers of Ilewo wrote to Thorn Council, their landlords, that, having been forced to pay contributions in cash and kind to support the Saxon garrison in 1703, they had then been placed under contributions by the Swedes, and had since faced Sapieha exactions.[45] In such circumstances, the demands of even the best-behaved troops were resented, and local officials were deluged with requests for the waiving of rent payments to take account of the demands of the military, which were often heavy: of 217 rams inventoried in the village of Gremboczyn in 1703, the Swedes took 100; by the end of the year, after deaths, other exactions and wastage, there were only 44 left.[46]

Such demands did little for Leszczyński's hopes of winning support; furthermore, if they had the advantage over Gustav Adolf and Charles X that they were not bottled up in one corner of the Commonwealth, but could occupy new areas when their supply-base became exhausted, this meant that they spread their unpopularity over a steadily widening area. Their exactions inevitably provoked resistance; where they met it, they behaved with striking ruthlessness. Hatton's picture of the Swedish soldier 'of peasant stock and a smallholder himself in peacetime' cheerfully chopping wood and helping round the farms on which he was billeted is not a complete fantasy, but it scarcely characterises the normal relationship between the Swedes and the local population. Charles believed it was good practice to deal 'harshly and brusquely' with Poles.[47] When Wojnicz failed to pay its allotted contributions in October 1702, he ordered its division into quarters, each of which was plundered by a detachment of 100 men, before the town was burnt. The properties of Augustus's supporters were treated with startling ruthlessness: Charles ordered Stenbock to ruin the estates of general Brandt, one of Augustus's commanders, 'as best thou can'.[48] On Charles's direct orders villages were burned, fields were laid waste, cattle were driven off to feed the army and any who objected were put to the sword. The harsh behaviour of the Swedes towards the local population during the Russian campaign of 1707–9 had its clear antecedents in Poland. At the very least, it ensured that potential supporters would think twice before abandoning the Sandomierz Confederation.

Swedish strategy was not entirely driven by considerations of supply. There were good military reasons for Charles's desire for a war of movement. Confident of the superiority of his army, he sought battle, as had Chodkiewicz or Żółkiewski before him. Charles's forces were too small to scatter around in garrisons, and he pursued Batory's policy of demolishing fortifications instead of manning them. After the fall of Thorn in 1703, Charles ordered the razing of its walls, behind which a Saxon garrison of 6,000 had mouldered away.[49] Charles could not afford to be so profligate with his army or waste too much time on irrelevant siege operations: when the Swedes captured Lwów in 1704, they spent five days on Charles's orders blowing up the best of the 160 'fine large guns' which had fallen into their hands.[50] Charles had no use for them; Swedish military dominance was not dependent upon control of fortresses.

Between 1700 and 1708, success bred success. The defeats inflicted on Schlippenbach in the Baltic provinces could be dismissed as of minor significance so long as the main army was victorious; once it could be turned against the Russians, Sweden's losses could be recovered. Yet the very confidence which flowed from the long run of victories could itself be a source of danger. For the threat from the Russian army was growing. Buoyed by their victories in the Baltic, Peter and his commanders were becoming more confident, while intensive drill was improving the quality of the ordinary soldiers. Despite the continuing shortage of talented officers, even foreign observers were beginning to recognise the good effects of Peter's work. In July 1705, the Austrian ambassador Otto Pleyer remarked after the mustering of the army in Moscow that 'the newly-arrived officers avowed they had seen no German army that was better clad, exercised or armed.'[51] In reporting Sheremetev's defeat at Gemauerthof (July 1705), Whitworth noted approvingly how firmly the Russians had stood their ground. For all his reports on Russian problems over desertion and the quality of officers, he described in 1708 how the army was 'composed of leesty, well made fellows' and recognised that 'the exercise [is] good, their air quite altered since their campaigns in Poland, and many of their regiments will doubtless fight well.'[52] The Russians themselves were increasingly confident of the quality of their troops: Peter, the harshest of critics, wrote in March 1707 that the army was 'in good shape'; in April 1708, Sheremetev wrote of the 'good state' of his infantry.[53] Most tellingly, if Charles is often accused of underestimating the fighting qualities of the Russians, there is much evidence to suggest that his army did not. After Hołowczyn, Jeffreyes remarked that:

> The Svedes must now own the Muscovites have learnt their lesson much better than they had either at the battles of Narva or Fraustadt, and that they equall if not exceed the Saxons both in discipline and valour, 'tis true their cavalry is not able to cope with owrs, but their infantry stand their ground obstinately, and 'tis a difficult matter to separate them or bring them in a confusion if they be not attacked sword in hand.[54]

Posse claimed that 'all those who saw and heard that action, must confess that they had never seen or heard such great fire from salvos, which we had to endure'. Lyth acknowledged the proficiency of Russian musketry and commented on the skill with which the Russians had chosen their positions. In the past, Swedes had felt that although the Russians had always fought sturdily enough they tended to take flight if the battle began to turn against them, but Lewenhaupt's grudging praise of their fighting qualities at Lesnaia included a recognition that they were now capable of rallying after being forced back.[55]

Most significantly, the Russian army was developing its own style of fighting, as Peter and his commanders gained experience of Swedish methods of waging war and realised that for all the technical help brought by westerners, western methods were not always effective. There were already signs of this at Narva, when it was Boris Sheremetev who suggested that the army should emerge from the protection of the countervallation to confront the Swedes in the open field, where its superior numbers could be made to tell.[56] As the Saxon army went down to defeat after defeat, the spell of western competence was broken, and Peter's reliance on western officers at the top level of service diminished steadily. The frequent military councils – twenty-two were held in 1708 alone – at which high-ranking officers, foreign and Russian, discussed strategy and tactics with government ministers were important for developing the fusion of western and eastern principles which increasingly characterised Petrine warfare. Papers were submitted by participants, debate was strongly encouraged, and decisions were only taken after full consideration of the situation.[57]

As Russian confidence grew, so arguments over strategy with western commanders became more frequent. The most significant such dispute came at Grodno in early 1706, where Peter had deputed Menshikov to keep an eye on the Scottish field-marshal Ogilvy who, following the departure of Augustus, was in sole command of forty-five infantry battalions and six dragoon regiments, some 35,000 men.[58] All correspondance with Ogilvy was conducted via Repnin, the senior Russian officer present, who received a copy of every order Peter sent Ogilvy.[59] As Charles advanced on Grodno, Peter, fearing the loss of much of his precious army, ordered Ogilvy to abandon the city and withdraw towards the Russian frontier. Ogilvy, despite the fact that supplies were running short, and against the advice of Repnin, Menshikov, Hallart and Wenediger, argued that it was impossible to evacuate Grodno, expressing his wish that Charles would attack, adding that: 'I do not doubt that it will bring complete victory in a few hours.' He objected that he would be forced to destroy the heavy artillery because he did not have enough horses to transport it.[60] Peter's reply, sent after he received news of the disaster at Fraustadt, was sharp: he ordered Ogilvy to abandon Grodno forthwith, to take only regimental artillery with him, and to destroy the heavy guns. Once he had left the city, Ogilvy was to divide his forces and send them eastwards by separate routes. This might expose individual sections to destruction, but Peter wished at all costs to avoid a general battle which might wipe out the whole army. Ogilvy finally began the evacuation on 11/22 March, but not before he had once more risked Peter's wrath by bluntly contesting his order, stating that it would be better to stay in Grodno until the summer, despite the shortage of provisions; as he admitted, the Swedish light cavalry was picking off foraging parties sent out from the city. Even when he was on the point of abandoning Grodno, he urged Peter to retake it.[61]

The dispute with Ogilvy demonstrated the extent to which Peter and his Russian commanders had begun to liberate themselves from the assumptions of their western advisers. Defence must be based on mobility, not fortresses, which could be death-traps for armies, something which Peter could not risk. The different philosophies were revealed in a further argument over the composition of the army, when Peter rejected Ogilvy's recommendation of a force of thirty regiments of foot and only sixteen of horse, deciding on a ratio of forty-seven infantry to thirty-three cavalry regiments; as Sheremetev recognised, cavalry was vitally important even in siege warfare in the east.[62] The parting of the ways was not long delayed. In April, Ogilvy requested his release from Russian service; in September, he was finally allowed to leave.[63] Henceforth, the Russian army was largely commanded by Russians. The long apprenticeship was over, and the new maturity of Russian strategic thinking was apparent in the council which met in Żółkiew in April 1707. Here the decision was taken not to join battle in Poland-Lithuania, despite Polish pressure, or to garrison fortresses in the Commonweath, but to withdraw through Lithuania into Russia itself, and organise a flexible defence against possible Swedish lines of attack.[64] Although Peter is often credited as the creator of this plan, it is clear that Russian commanders, especially Sheremetev, played an important part in its formulation. It was dangerous, since it risked alienating the Sandomierz confederates, who wished to adopt an offensive strategy and force Charles to a decisive battle in the Commonwealth.[65]

As the Swedes marched east, the Russians melted away before them, destroying everything in their path. The Swedes faced similar problems to those experienced by Batory 130 years earlier. Lyth's description of marching through deep forest in the autumn of 1708 could have been lifted from Piotrowski's diary:

> we lost many men and many horses, which died of hunger, so that our misery grew ever greater; we had to watch as both men and horses alike, exhausted by hunger, dropped to the ground and died there miserably; so it remained for us doubly worse.[66]

A month later the army emerged into a wilderness of deserted and smoking villages, whence everything had been carried away, in which they were constantly harried by enemy raids, so that they were not safe from attack 'for a single hour', as the great cry went up from the army 'what shall we eat?' Like Batory's army at Pskov, units had to forage for miles in all directions to obtain supplies. There was one major difference, however. When Batory laid siege to Pskov he was facing an exhausted and disorganised enemy, and his cavalry dominated the theatre of operations. Charles, for all the formidable qualities of his army, was facing a very different opponent. Peter might be cautious about exposing his precious new army in open battle, but his forces, augmented by large numbers of Cossack and Kalmuk irregulars, were more than capable of subjecting the Swedes to the high-level harrassment Charles X's armies had experienced in Poland in the 1650s. This ensured that Swedish supply problems steadily increased: forage parties were easy targets for roaming Russian units, and the constant skirmishes hit morale badly.[67] The Swedish cavalry may have been superior on the battlefield, but the Russians were numerically stronger and well-suited to a campaign of harassment.

For all the sense of tragic inevitability which pervades accounts of Charles's Russian campaign, he had little choice but to attempt what he recognised was a risky operation, and his conduct of it was by no means as strategically inept as it is often portrayed. There were good reasons for the decision to turn south in the autumn of 1708. The move into the Ukraine would open easier lines of communication through Volhynia, Podolia and Ruthenia to Leszczyński, and bring the Swedes closer to the Turks and Tatars, whom Charles had good reason to believe might be persuaded to join the war against Russia. Whether or not Charles wished to force Peter to a decisive battle after crossing the Dnieper, or, as Stille believes, he was attempting an ambitious flanking move, he had failed by mid September.[68] The Swedes did catch the Russian cavalry at Tatarsk (10/21 September), but the ground was unfavourable and Charles was unwilling to risk an attack. A march north was now impossible. The Russians were laying waste the countryside – the Swedes counted the flames of twenty-four burning villages from their encampment – while Lewenhaupt and Rehnskiöld agreed that the roads from Smolensk to Moscow would be impassable.[69] The supply situation was becoming serious, morale was suffering, and the army greeted the decision to turn south with relief:

> we have been in a very desolate country . . . half a mile from the boarders of Muscovy, where we found nothing but what was burnt and destroyd, and of large villages little left but the bare names, we had allso news of the like destruction as farr as Smolensko, which has had this happy effect on His Maj:ty that he has desisted from pursuing the ennemy, and turnd his march to the right, with intention as is suppos'd to make an incursion into Ukrain, this is a country . . . wery plentifull of all necessaryes and where no army as yet has been.[70]

It was undoubtedly an error to turn south without waiting for Lewenhaupt, or turning back towards the Dnieper to meet him, as Piper urged; it is clear that Charles, despite optimistic reports that Lewenhaupt was across the Dnieper, was aware that he was not.[71] Charles was confident that Lewenhaupt would be capable of beating off any attack, but underestimated the Russian ability to seize the opportunity. Peter sent Sheremetev to shadow the main Swedish army, while detaching a force of 6,795 dragoons and 4,830 infantry, mounted on horses to ensure rapidity of movement.[72] This *korvolant* (*corps volant*) moved swiftly on Lewenhaupt's force, whose speed was reduced by the need to maintain full battle order on the march to protect the cumbersome wagon train. The Swedes gave a good account of themselves at Lesnaia, but although they slightly outnumbered the Russians, they were unable to save the vital supply-train, losing nearly half their strength into the bargain. The Russian horse might be inferior to the Swedish cavalry, but Lesnaia underlined the usefulness of dragoons in the eastern theatre of war.

Charles had paid the price of not waiting for Lewenhaupt, and it is unlikely that Peter would have risked an attack if the main Swedish army had not turned south. Nevertheless, if the loss of the supply train was a blow, it was by no means fatal. Initially it seemed that the move south was justified. On crossing into the Ukraine in early November, Lyth reported that it was rich in grain, fruit, tobacco and cattle, with few forests and extensive fields. There was an abundance of honey, flax and hemp, which could be bought very cheaply; although the Russians had made some effort at destruction, the Swedes were able to excavate buried supplies, and bread, beer, spirits, wines, mead, honey, cattle and fodder for the horses were plentiful.[73] By December, however, the situation had deteriorated sharply; although the Swedes found ample supplies of tobacco, food and fodder began to be a problem, while the growing shortages were exacerbated by a sudden and vicious turn in the weather in what was to prove one of the fiercest winters of the century. In the coldest snap, in late December, men froze to death in the saddle overnight; on Christmas Eve, 25–26 men from Lyth's company succumbed and Lewenhaupt calculated that 4,000 men fell victim to the cold.[74] This seriously weakened the army and had a severe effect on morale, but Charles cannot be blamed for the exceptional severity of the winter. The period of extreme cold was relatively brief, and although conditions thereafter were far from comfortable, they were bearable, and if the Swedes suffered, so did the Russians.[75] The Russians were far better able to replace their losses, however, and it remains true that the Swedish losses helped shift the balance of advantage towards Peter.

If Charles's strategy was undoubtedly risky, it was not the work of a madman or an aggressive psychopath. Nevertheless, the Swedes were always fighting at a disadvantage in country familiar to their enemies. Further reverses were to follow. After the loss of Lewenhaupt's baggage train it was essential that an alternative store of supplies be secured, but the Swedes lost by a whisker the race for Baturyn, Mazepa's headquarters. After the Cossack hetman had finally declared for Charles, on 24 October (OS), Menshikov sacked Baturyn (2/13 November), cruelly massacring the population and destroying or carrying off the precious reserves of arms, ammunition and food with which Charles had hoped to augment his rapidly-diminishing supplies.[76]

Although Mazepa's defection was a considerable boost for Charles, especially when it was followed in March 1709 by that of the Zaporozhians, it was not to prove decisive. The 1650s, when the Cossacks had briefly promised to emerge as a significant political force in the southeast, were long gone. The Ukrainian *Ruina* had shattered Cossack unity. By looking to the Swedes Mazepa and the Zaporozhian hetman Kost' Hordiienko were merely continuing the politics of the last half century, in which Cossack leaders had manoeuvred between Poland, Russia and the Ottomans, seeking a basis for the autonomy they had enjoyed under Khmelnytsky. The Cossacks, although still extremely useful as sharpshooters and irregular troops, were not the military force they had once been. Indeed, the heavy casualties which Mazepa's Cossacks had incurred when forced by Peter to fight in the north against the Swedes, where they had proved no match for regular troops, had played a significant role in alienating them. Moreover, the Zaporozhians were strongly hostile to the Poles, and Charles's ill-disguised scheming with Mazepa to eliminate the Commonwealth once and for all from the Ukraine not only ensured the continuing hostility of the Sandomierz confederates, it also threatened his relations with Leszczyński, the Ottomans and the Tatars.[77] In March 1709, Wiśniowiecki, who had extensive Ukrainian estates, abandoned Leszczyński and rejoined the Sandomierz Confederation. The destruction of the Zaporozhian *Sich* by a Russian force in May 1709 merely demonstrated that Charles's hopes for a widespread Ukrainian rebellion against Russia were ill-founded, and that the mobile and much larger Russian forces were in control of the wider theatre of campaign.

Thus when Charles's diminishing army finally launched the general battle he had sought for so long at Poltava on 27 June 1709 (OS) it was not under the favourable circumstances for which he had hoped. Indeed, although it was characteristically the Swedes who took the initiative with an ambitious plan to assault the Russian camp, it was the Russians who had issued the challenge by crossing the Vorskla to the north of Poltava on 20 June (OS), three days after Charles's luck ran out when he received a bad wound in his foot from a stray bullet while observing the Russian positions. Two days later, he received final confirmation that neither Leszczyński nor Krassau would be joining him. Although he accompanied his army into battle borne on a litter, Rehnskiöld took operational command. Unable to provide the inspirational leadership for which he was famous, Charles was condemned to follow the battle from a distance, while the morale of his troops was undoubtedly affected. Nevertheless, a battle was necessary. A Swedish victory, while it might not destroy the Russian army, would relieve the pressing supply problems, would help Leszczyński, and might tempt the Ottomans and Tatars to commit themselves. The only viable alternatives were to withdraw across the Dnieper, southwards to the Crimea or back towards Poland; both would be hazardous with the Russians across the Vorskla.

Yet for all that Peter's crossing of the Vorskla threw down the gauntlet, he was thinking above all of fighting a defensive encounter, albeit one in which the painful lessons of Narva, Fraustadt and Hołowczyn had been absorbed. The ramparts of the large fortified camp constructed on the Vorskla, some 4 kilometres north of Poltava, contained gaps to enable the Russians to leave its shelter easily, to avoid being bottled up inside and destroyed, as happened at Narva. In a move which the Maréchal de Saxe, Augustus II's illegitimate son, regarded as decisive, Peter ordered the construction of a T-shaped system of redoubts in the gap between the woods to the southwest of the Russian camp, which was the most convenient route for any attacker to take. The projecting arm of the system was designed to act as a breakwater, providing flanking fire as the Swedes swept past. According to Saxe, it would have been impossible to attack the Russian camp without first taking these redoubts, since they were too dangerous to leave in the rear.[78]

Nevertheless, this is precisely what the Swedes planned to do, although the extent to which they were aware of the redoubts' existence is unclear: they certainly did not appreciate the full dimensions of the system as they formed up before dawn on 27 June (OS), since the original order for the infantry to deploy into line from the four columns in which they had approached had to be rescinded amid much confusion. As the Swedes launched their attack, the redoubts performed their function: the original orders issued to the leaders of the infantry columns, and to Lewenhaupt, who had overall command of the foot, did not take account of them, and the hastily-prepared orders sent out when they were discovered were ambiguous. While the principal objective was the Russian camp, many officers were left with the impression that they should first attack the redoubts. Thus although most of the infantry swept past, a substantial proportion wasted valuable time and resources, both human and material, in attempting to reduce them. When Major-General Roos, who found himself at the head of six battalions attacking the redoubts one by one, finally decided to break off the attack and seek the main army, he had no idea where it had gone. With 1,500 men, all that were left of the 2,600 he had led into the fray, he began a retreat south, away from the main Swedish force, harried by a large detachment of Russian infantry and cavalry, which pursued him until he was forced to surrender with the remnants of his men after his attempt to reach the security of the siegeworks round Poltava failed.[79]

Roos's misfortune was the decisive moment of the battle, for the rest of the Swedish army had succeeded in smashing through the line of redoubts and had wheeled left onto the narrow plain to the front of the Russian camp, while the Swedish cavalry had swept the Russian horse from the field, only halting their pursuit on the edge of a small, marshy valley to the north. The

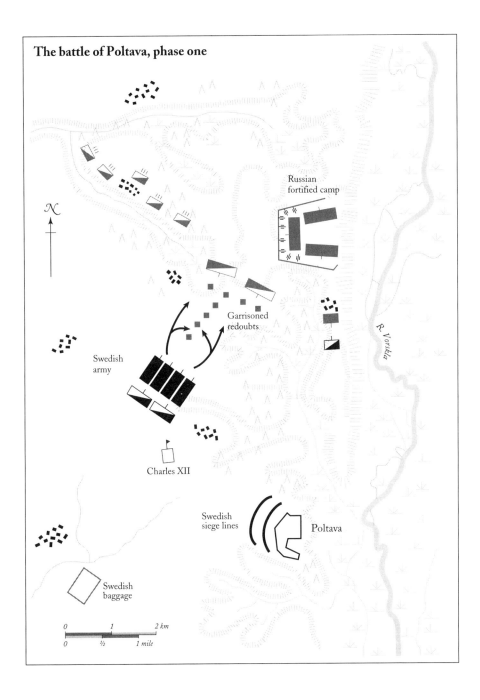

The battle of Poltava, phase one

Russian fortified camp

𝒩

Garrisoned redoubts

Swedish army

Charles XII

Swedish siege lines

Poltava

R. Vorskla

Swedish baggage

| 0 | | 1 | | 2 km |
| 0 | ½ | | 1 mile | |

Swedes began to form up for an assault on the camp, but as it became clear that Roos was missing with a third of the infantry, it was decided to wait until he arrived. Apart from Roos's absence, the circumstances were by no means unpropitious. The bulk of the Russian army, some 25,000 men, was crammed into the narrow confines of its camp, and much of its cavalry cover had been routed. The camp itself was by no means impregnable: indeed, Lewenhaupt, who had approached it from the south after leading the right wing of the infantry through the redoubts, considered that the Russian ramparts were not well manned, and thought of attacking immediately, although he was hindered by a narrow, deep ravine, and by his realisation that Roos's column to his left had failed to pass through the redoubts.[80] Swedish reconnaissance before the battle had revealed the weaknesses of the Russian position: the camp was surrounded with ramparts on three sides, but it was constructed on the edge of the precipitous, 60-metre embankment of the Vorskla, with the only escape-route to the north, which could be easily blocked by the Swedish horse. If the Swedes could press home an attack with vigour, it might turn into another Narva: confined in their camp the Russians would not be able to bring their superior numbers to bear, while any attempt to retreat down the embankment across the river would, in the absence of any bridge, risk disaster and a panic-stricken massacre. Indeed, Lewenhaupt observed signs of frantic preparations for a withdrawal as he approached.

For two hours, the Swedes waited for Roos with mounting frustration; the moment was lost. The delay, and the substantial boost to Russian morale which followed news of Roos's surrender, swung the balance decisively towards the Russians, who now threw off the defensive mentality which had long marked their encounters with the Swedes. Leaving the security of its ramparts, the Russian army filed out of its camp to maximise its over-whelming numerical superiority, as Sheremetev had recommended at Narva. Twenty-two thousand Russian infantry drew up in two lines, supported by sixty-eight field guns, to face the remnants of the Swedish foot, some 4,000 strong.[81] The Swedes stood for three-quarters of an hour under bombardment, before launching a hopeless attack. Outflanked on both sides, and with no cavalry support, the exhausted blue-clad attackers were swallowed up by the first Russian line, which outnumbered them over two to one on its own. Although Lewenhaupt, leading the Life Guards on the extreme right, managed to break and push back the first line, he lacked cavalry support and had drawn away from the units to his left. The impetus was not sustained and gradually all momentum was lost. The Russians buckled, but did not break; as they stood their ground, then pushed forward, the exhausted Swedish infantry broke and began to flee.

The aggressive Swedish style had failed at last; for all the General Staff criticisms of the conduct of the battle, it was inevitable that some day it

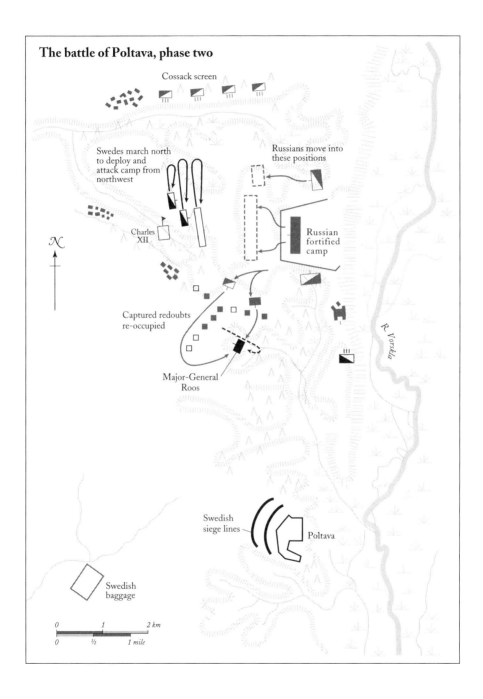

The battle of Poltava, phase two

Cossack screen

Swedes march north to deploy and attack camp from northwest

Russians move into these positions

Charles XII

Russian fortified camp

Captured redoubts re-occupied

Major-General Roos

R. Vorskla

N

Swedish siege lines

Poltava

Swedish baggage

| 0 | 1 | 2 km |
| 0 | ½ | 1 mile |

would. By disrupting the Swedish attack through the construction of the system of redoubts, the Russians broke the continuity of the Swedish attack. Massively outnumbered, disorientated and deprived of a third of their infantry after Roos became detached from the main force, the Swedes lost the element of surprise and could not deliver their attack with the necessary shock effect. Three days later 17,000 ragged and disheartened survivors of the proud army Charles had led out of Saxony surrendered at Perevolochna. Stripped of uniforms and weapons, they were forced to watch the grisly execution of those Cossacks who had failed to escape across the Dnieper, before being marched back across the field of Poltava, still scattered with the rotting remains of their comrades, on their way to long years of captivity in Russia.

Victory

The annihilation of the main Swedish army transformed the course of the war. With Charles kicking his heels in an increasingly frustrated exile at Bender in Moldavia, from which he did not return until late 1714, the coalition he had destroyed so effectively between 1700 and 1706 sprang back into life. Within a month of Poltava, Augustus was back in Poland at the head of 11,000 Saxons; in October he made a new agreement with Peter at Thorn. In November, Danish troops landed in Scania and Peter launched the siege of Riga by personally firing the first shells at the city he still detested for supposedly slighting him on his visit during his great embassy in 1697. Although Magnus Stenbock, charged with the defence of Sweden, succeeded in defeating the Danes at Hälsingborg in February 1710, it was impossible to save the Baltic provinces, where plague was ravaging the population and the destruction of the Swedish field army ensured that there was no hope of relief. Viborg surrendered in April, Riga in July, Pernau in August. In September, with the capture of Ösel and Reval, Peter's conquest of Livonia and Estonia was complete.

Charles's strategy now rested on persuading the Ottoman Empire to wage war on Russia. Although he was successful, the results did not match his hopes, despite the stunning victory of the Turkish army on the Prut river in July 1711, which took advantage of Peter's over-confidence and succeeded in surrounding him and threatening him with the annihilation of his army. Despite Charles's exhortations, however, this was to be no Poltava. By sacrificing Azov and the border fortresses, and promising to evacuate his forces from Poland-Lithuania, Peter escaped with his precious army intact. Azov was duly handed over, and the fortresses razed in early 1712, but although Peter ignored much of the rest of the treaty, three further Ottoman declarations of war were not followed up with any extensive military action, and the signature of the twenty-five-year peace of Adrianople in July 1713 marked the end of Charles's hopes that the Ottomans would fight his battles for him.

By the time he rode into Stralsund in November 1714, after a dramatic journey through Hungary and the Empire, the situation looked black indeed. Despite another victory over the Danes at Gadebusch (December 1712), Stenbock's army had been forced to surrender at Tønning in May 1713 after a four-month siege. The Russian galley-fleet provided the ideal plat-form for a series of attacks on the vulnerable Finnish coastal cities: in May 1713, the Swedes were forced to abandon Helsingfors and set it on fire; Åbo surrendered at the end of August. Meanwhile, Sweden's position in its German possessions had all but collapsed, and the Saxon-Danish-Russian coalition was joined by others anxious to join the carve-up. Prussia, which had hitherto resisted all blandishments, but which had been occupying Stettin since November 1713, signed a treaty with Russia in June 1714, in which it was promised Pomerania up to the Peene river in return for recognising Russia's Baltic conquests. The accession to the British throne of George I in August 1714 was another blow to Sweden: as elector of Hanover, George had designs on Bremen and Verden; in November 1714 he signed an agreement with Frederick William I of Prussia to oppose any German state – in particular Sweden's old ally Hesse-Cassel – which supported Charles. In May 1715, Prussia declared war on Sweden, taking Wolgast in July and Peenemünde in August; in October, Hanover seized Bremen and Verden. With Rügen falling in November, and Stralsund capitulating in December, Sweden had lost the last vestiges of its German empire by the time Charles finally returned to Sweden in December 1715.

With typical bravado, Charles refused to contemplate peace and in February 1716 began the first of two Norwegian campaigns in an attempt to force Denmark out of the war. By the time the second of these was brought to an abrupt end by the missile which smashed his skull at the siege of Frederiksten on 30 November 1718 (OS), Sweden's prospects had improved. This owed as much to the mutual suspicion of its enemies, however, as to Charles's military efforts. For the anti-Swedish coalition began to fall apart almost as soon as it was completed with the 1717 declaration of war on Sweden by Britain, angered by Swedish attempts to block Baltic trade and by Charles's flirtation with the Jacobites. There were bitter disagreements over the division of the spoils, but the central factor was the realisation of the possible consequences of the complete collapse of Swedish power. The growing shadow of Russia, whose armies by 1717 were spread out along the southern Baltic from St Petersburg to Jutland, loomed over the future. In particular, Russian designs on Mecklenburg, where Peter hoped to secure a naval base in the southern Baltic, directly conflicted with George's desire to establish Hanover as the leading north German power. By now, Augustus was a spent force: restored in Poland-Lithuania in 1710, he had neverthe-less faced serious opposition to his desire for an active foreign policy, and had come increasingly to resent Russian power, especially once Frederick William of Prussia – who blatantly coveted Royal Prussia – joined the anti-Swedish coalition. Britain, Austria and Saxony agreed to reduce Russia to its old borders at the treaty of Vienna (January 1719). With the succession of Charles's sister Ulrika Eleanora to the Swedish throne, Swedish policy was increasingly shaped by her husband, Frederick of Hesse, to whom she voluntarily transferred power in 1720. As a German prince, Frederick was quite prepared to accept Sweden's eclipse as a German power and to sacrifice the interests of the duke of Holstein-Gottorp, his rival for the Swedish throne. This shift in policy opened the way for the peace of Stock-holm (February 1720) in which Hanover, Britain and Prussia settled with Sweden. Hanover received Bremen-Verden and Prussia gained most of western Pomerania, including Stettin, although the desire of the French mediators to prevent Sweden's total collapse ensured that it kept Wismar, Rügen and Stralsund as its last foothold in Germany. Abandoned by its allies, and suspicious of Russian designs on Mecklenburg, Denmark paid the price of having again proved unable to exert real military pressure on Sweden: in the peace of Frederiksborg (June 1720) it was forced to accept Swedish possession of its one-time provinces across the Sound, and to abandon its claims to Wismar and Rügen. In return, Sweden surrendered its exemption from the Sound tolls, and abandoned its support for Holstein-Gottorp, whose lands in Schleswig were annexed by Denmark.

In making peace Sweden had been led to believe that it would receive sup-port from a coalition of Britain, France, Prussia, Saxony, Poland-Lithuania and even Denmark in a war to wrest Estonia and Livonia at least from Russia. Although Britain and France were wary of Russian power, domestic problems ensured that there was little hope of extensive aid. With Russian naval supremacy opening the coast of Sweden itself to frequent and devas-tating raids by galley-borne amphibious forces, which the Swedish navy was powerless to prevent, Frederick and the *Riksdag* had little choice. On 30 August 1721 (OS) Sweden and Russia signed the peace of Nystad, by which Russia agreed to evacuate Finland in return for the cession of Estonia, Livonia, Ingria, Kexholm and most of Karelia. The Northern Wars were not yet finally over: Sweden made several attempts to reverse the losses of 1721 over the next century, but all ended in failure. It took the loss of Finland in 1809 – somewhat compensated by the gain of Norway from Denmark in 1815 – before Sweden finally accepted the verdict of 1721. Nevertheless, the treaty of Nystad made clear who had won.

Notes

1 Staszewski suggested in 1973 that only a tiny circle knew of the plans, and that Radziejowski and Lubomirski had only agreed to support Augustus's proposal for a trading company, but has since argued that he had the approval of Radziejowski and several leading senators: J. Staszewski, *O miejsce w Europie* (Warsaw, 1973) p. 174; idem, 'Z listy najczęściej spotykanych błędnych mniemań na temat czasów saskich' *PHum* 1 (1996) p. 159; idem. *August II* pp. 110–12.

2 A. Gyllenkrook, *Relationer från Karl XII:s Krig* N. Sjöberg (ed.) (Stockholm, 1913) p. 13.

3 K. Piwarski, *Hieronim Lubomirski, hetman wielki koronny* (Cracow, 1929) p. 90.

4 Whitworth to Harley, 30.I.1705, *SIRIO* 39 no. 7 pp. 21–2.

5 J. Poraziński, 'Malborska rada senatu w 1703 roku' *ZH* 44 (1979) pp. 209–32.

6 Idem, *Sejm lubelski w 1703 roku i jego miejsce w konfliktach wewnętrznych na początku XVIII wieku* (Toruń, 1988) pp. 96–101, 119–22.

7 Wimmer, *Wojsko Rzeczypospolitej* p. 267.

8 S. Achremczyk, 'Konfederacja szlachty Prus Królewskich w latach 1703–1709' *ZH* 45 (1980) pp. 31–6.

9 A.S. Kamiński, *Konfederacja Sandomierska wobec Rosji w okresie poaltransztadzkim 1706–1709* (Wrocław, 1969) pp. 5–10.

10 Ibid. p. 11.

11 Generalstaben, *Karl XII* II pp. 412–22, 438; P. Stok, 'Bitwa pod Kliszowem w r. 1702' *SMHW* 6 (1960) pp. 194–214, 228–32, 239; Wagner, *Kliszów* pp. 122–35. Polish losses were minimal: some eighty killed, although a substantial number were wounded: ibid. pp. 188–9.

12 G. Artéus, *Karolinsk och europeisk stridstaktik 1700–1712* (Gothenburg, 1972) pp. 29–30, 36–7.

13 Generalstaben, *Karl XII* II pp. 459, 466–7; Lyth describes advancing on the Saxons 'without firing a single gun', although in his sector, one 'mighty salvo' was unleashed as the infantry reached the Spanish riders. *Löjtnant Joachim Matthiæ Lyths Dagbok 1703–1722*, KKD II (Lund, 1903) pp. 30–1.

14 Adlerfelt, III, p. 26.

15 H. Zechlin, 'Die Schlacht bei Fraustadt. Eine militärgeschichtliche Studie' *ZHGPP* 11 (1896) p. 43, n. 1.

16 Artéus, *Karolinsk* pp. 39–41.

17 Zechlin, 'Fraustadt' pp. 1–52, 207–74; Generalstaben, *Karl XII* II pp. 444–76.

18 See also A. Stille, *Carl XII:s fälttågsplaner 1707–1709* (Lund, 1908). For older, more critical views, see E. Carlson, 'Slaget vid Poltava och dess krigshistoriska förutsättningar enligt samtida källor' in *Historiska studier. Festskrift tillägnad C.G. Malmström* (Stockholm, 1897) and C. Hallendorff, 'Karl XII och Lewenhaupt år 1708' *UUÅ* (1902).

19 Generalstaben, *Karl XII* II, pp. 501–13; III, pp. 792, 823, 877–8.

20 For useful critiques of the Swedish and Soviet debates see G. Artéus, *Krigsteori och historisk förklaring. I. Kring Karl XII:s ryska fälttåg* (Uppsala, 1970) and J.-P.

Findeisen, 'Poltava – Mythos und Wirklichkeit. Einige kritische Anmerkungen zur bisherigen Darstellung dieser welthistorischen Schlacht durch die sowjetische Militärhistoriographie' *MM* 51 (1992) pp. 1–21.

21 F. Wernstedt, 'Lineartaktik och Karolinsk taktik. Några reflexioner med anledning av framställningen i "Karl XII på slagfältet"' *KFÅ* (1957) pp. 153–64 and *Livgardes historia* IV pp. 133ff, 150ff, 162ff, 265ff. For a more balanced assessment, see Artéus, *Karolinsk* pp. 111–17.

22 Adlerfelt, I p. 57.

23 F.G. Bengtsson, *Karl XII*. T. Baur (tr.) (Stuttgart, 1957) p. 111.

24 Charles Wrede, Narva, 24.XI.1700, Ustrialov, *Istoriia* IV:ii, no. 50, p. 181.

25 Quoted in Generalstaben, *Karl XII* I, p. 207.

26 Hatton, *Charles XII* p. 165.

27 D. Chandler, *The Art of Warfare in the Age of Marlborough* (London, 1976) p. 22.

28 G. Leer, 'Petr Velikii kak polkovodets' *VS* 3 (1865) p. 9; Tarle, *Severnaia Voina* pp. 164–5, 317; Fuller, *Strategy* p. 71

29 The commonly-cited figure of 44,000 was the inflated tally given to foreign ambassadors: Hatton, *Charles XII* p. 233; Englund, *Poltava* p. 42. Charles had led 26,000 men out of Saxony in 1707, but the numbers had been swelled by new levies from Sweden and local recruitment: S.M. Waller, 'Den svenska huvudarméns styrka år 1707' *KFÅ* (1957) p. 113.

30 Whitworth to Boyle, Moscow, 17/22.IX.1708, *SIRIO* 50 no. 26, pp. 59–60.

31 Gyllenkrook, *Relationer* pp. 35–8.

32 *Adam Ludvig Lewenhaupts berättelse* S.E. Bring (ed.) *HH* 34:2 (Stockholm, 1952) pp. 175–8, 220, 237.

33 Jeffreyes to Whitworth, from the Muscovite camp by Pultava, 9/20.VII.1709, version printed in R. Hatton (ed.), *Captain James Jeffreyes's letters to the Secretary of State, Whitehall, from the Swedish Army, 1707–1709* HH 35:1 (Stockholm, 1954) p. 78, n. 1; also printed in Whitworth to Boyle, Moscow 27.VII/7.VIII.1709, *SIRIO* 50 no. 79, p. 217.

34 Lewenhaupt, *Berättelse* p. 349.

35 Tarle's *Severnaia voina*, which supposedly covers the whole war, devotes 293 of 468 pages to the 1708–9 campaign; the twelve years that remained are covered in a mere 31.

36 For a demolition of the claims of Gyllenkrook and Lewenhaupt to have opposed many of Charles's decisions, and to have known little of the Poltava battle plan, see H. Villius, *Karl XII:s ryska fälttåg. Källstudier* (Lund, 1951) pp. 160–225. Englund's brilliant evocation of the battle is based substantially on the accounts of these two men, although he is well aware of their shortcomings.

37 Whitworth to Harley, Moscow, 6/17.III.1706, *SIRIO* 39, no. 60, pp. 252–3.

38 Cavallie, *Från fred* pp. 41, 43, 53–4, 65–6, 71–2, 94–6, 100–2.

39 S. Grauers, 'Den Karolinska feldhärens underhåll 1700–1703' *KFÅ* (1968) pp. 116, 118, 124–5.

40 E. Otwinowski, *Dzieje Polski pod panowaniem Augusta II od roku 1696–1728* J. Moraczewski (ed.) (Cracow, 1849) p. 32.

41 Charles XII to Rehnskiöld, 26 August and December 1705; *Konung Karl XII:s egenhändiga bref* E. Carlson (ed.) (Stockholm, 1893) pp. 272, 274; Waller, 'Den svenska' p. 111.

42 Z. Łakoczyński, *Magnus Stenbock w Polsce* (Wrocław, 1967) p. 65.

43 Grauers, 'Den Karolinska fälthärens underhåll 1700–1703' pp. 132–45; idem 'Den Karolinska fälthärens underhåll 1704–1707' *KFÅ* (1969) pp. 109–24.

44 Hatton, *Charles XII* pp. 188, 524. Otwinowski does comment on the sensitivity with which the Swedes collected the hearth-tax in 1702–3, but this was written two decades later by a notorious critic of Augustus: Otwinowski, *Dzieje* p. 35.

45 The inhabitants of Ilewo to the Thorn council, 18.XII.1705, APT, Listy do rady miasta Torunia 3457, ff. 55–55v.

46 Revision des Hofes Gremboczyn Ao 1703 nach dem Schwedischen Kriege. Der noch kein Endte hat, APT, Dobra i wsie miejskie 3524, f. 56.

47 Charles XII to Arvid Bernhard Horn, Heilsberg, 13.II.1704, *Egenhändige bref* no. 223, p. 319.

48 Charles XII to Magnus Stenbock, Thorn, VIII.1703, ibid. no. 209, p. 304.

49 Only 1,863 fit soldiers were left by the time Thorn surrendered, with a further 2,992 sick or wounded: B. Dybaś, 'Dzieje wojskowe Torunia w latach 1548–1660' in M. Biskup (ed.), *Historia Torunia* II (Toruń, 1996) p. 144.

50 Lyth, *Dagbok* pp. 14–15.

51 Otto Pleyer, Moscow 15/26.VII. and 12/23.IX.1705, Ustrialov *Istoriia* IV:ii nos. 39, 40, pp. 644–5.

52 Whitworth to Boyle, Moscow, 17/22.IX.1708, *SIRIO* 50 no. 26, pp. 62–3.

53 G. Iu. Gerbil'skii, 'Russko-pol'skii soiuz i zholkovskii strategicheskii plan' in *Poltava. K 250-letiiu Poltavskogo srazheniia* (Moscow, 1959) p. 83. Sheremetev to Peter, 11/22.IV.1708, *PiB* VII:ii p. 803.

54 Jeffreyes, Wolownika, 1/12.IX.1708; *Letters* no. 20, p. 59.

55 *C.M. Posses Dagbok 1707–1709* KKD I (Lund, 1901) pp. 310ff; Lyth, *Dagbok* pp. 55–6; Lewenhaupt, *Berättelse* p. 184.

56 Beskrovnyi, *Russkaia armiia* p. 186. Anisimov criticises the Russians for not doing this, without noticing that it was a Russian who suggested it: *Reforms* pp. 62–3.

57 E.P. Pod"iapol'skaia, 'Voennye sovety 1708–1709 gg.' *Poltava* pp. 112–36; Fuller, *Strategy* p. 72.

58 Tarle, *Severnaia voina* pp. 94–5.

59 A.S. Kamiński, 'Przeciwko Szwedom i Leszczyńskiemu. Działania wojsk rosyjskich na terenie Polski w 1705–1706 roku' *SMHW* 12 (1966) p. 244.

60 Ogilvy to Peter, Grodno 6/17.II.1706, Ustrialov, *Historiia* IV:ii, no. 369, pp. 397–8; cf. Whitworth to Harley, Moscow, 20.II.1706 OS, *SIRIO* 39, no. 58, pp. 244–5. Kamiński, 'Przeciwko' pp. 240–1.

61 Ogilvy to Peter, Grodno, 24.III.1706 OS, Ustrialov, *Historiia* IV:ii,. no. 384, p. 408.

62 L.G. Beskrovnyi, 'Strategiia i taktika russkoi armii v poltavskii period Severnoi Voiny' *Poltava* p. 23; Fuller, *Strategy* p. 73.

63 Ogilvy to Peter, Kovel, 13/24.IV.1706, Ustrialov, *Istoriia* IV:ii, no. 394, p. 412.

64 Gerbil'skii, 'Russko-pol'skii' pp. 63–90.

65 For a refutation of Gerbil'skii's claim that the Poles were fully involved in devising the plan, see Kamiński, 'Piotr I a wojsko koronne w przededniu szwedzkiego uderzenia na Rosję w 1707 r.' *SMHW* 15 (1969), pp. 48–53.

66 Lyth, *Dagbok* pp. 60–1.

67 Nordberg, I p. 922.

68 Stille, *Carl XII:s* pp. 71, 73.

69 Lyth, *Dagbok* p. 59; Stille, *Carl XII:s* p. 79.

70 Jeffreyes to Boyle, near Kruiczow, 18.IX.1708 OS, *Letters* no. 22, p. 62.

71 Stille, *Carl XII:s* p. 73; the reports were leaked to improve morale: Hatton, *Charles XII* pp. 267–8.

72 Tarle, *Severnaia voina* p. 202. The official Russian account gave the size of the force as three regiments and one battalion of foot, and ten regiments of dragoons, some 10–12,000 men. 'Reliatsiia o bitve pri derevne Lesnoi, 16.X.1708', *PiB* VIII:i no. 2731, p. 210.

73 Lyth, *Dagbok* pp. 63–4; Adlerfelt, III p. 214.

74 Lyth, *Dagbok* p. 66; Lewenhaupt, *Berättelse* p. 215. Lewenhaupt talks of casualties, not deaths, from the spell of cold weather as a whole. Tarle's claim that 3–4,000 Swedes froze to death in one night is substantially exaggerated: Tarle, *Severnaia voina* p. 290.

75 Though Hatton's claim that the Russian army lost a third of its strength while the Swedes only lost a fifth is dubious: Hatton, *Charles XII* p. 287.

76 B. Kentrschynskyj, *Mazepa* (Stockholm, 1962) p. 343.

77 Ibid. p. 339.

78 Maurice, Comte de Saxe, *Les Rêveries ou Mémoires sur l'Art de la Guerre* (The Hague, 1756) pp. 199–200.

79 Englund, *Poltava* pp. 113–15, 131–2.

80 Lewenhaupt, *Berättelse* p. 239

81 Englund, *Poltava* pp. 143, 147; E.E. Kolosov, 'Artilleriia v poltavskom srazhenii' *Poltava* p. 107. Pavlenko and Artamonov, like many Russian historians, argue that there were 10,000 Swedish foot, but their calculations are open to serious doubt: N. Pavlenko and V. Artamonov, *27 iunia 1709* (Moscow, 1989) pp. 231–2.

CHAPTER ELEVEN

Conclusion

Dorpat

Shortly before midnight on Pentecost Eve (4/15 June) 1704 a cannon-shot from the walls of Dorpat gave warning of the arrival of Russian troops outside the city. Over the next few days, they methodically constructed their siege-works and established the powerful batteries which were soon pounding Dorpat's hastily-repaired defences. On this occasion, in contrast to 1558 when the city had surrendered without a fight, Dorpat's burghers had little choice: the Swedish commandant, Carl Gustaf Skytte, ensured that resistance was maintained for over a month, until the besiegers smashed a breach in the wall near the Russian Gate and 5,000 Russians began a storm which drove the defenders back step by step and ended with the garrison's capitulation on 14/25 July. For the third time in 150 years, the Russians had taken Dorpat; this time it was to remain in their hands until 1918.

Throughout the siege, the city council kept a diary of the daily toll in lives and property exacted by the Russian bombardments, methodically noting every death, every injury and every shattered roof or splintered door. As the daily pounding continued, house after house was '*gäntzlich ruiniert*' (completely destroyed) or damaged. War was a great social leveller: the enemy guns were no respecters of status or wealth, and the rich were as likely to be hit as the poor. Neither was war a respecter of religion. Churches, with their high towers, were an attractive target for bored gunners: between 14 and 28 June, over fifty cannonballs struck the Marienkirche, destroying the roof, the vaulting, the pulpit and the pews; the Johanneskirche was hit by only fifteen, but its roof and vaulting was also destroyed; both churches were further damaged in July. Altogether, 70 burghers and inhabitants of Dorpat were killed and 48 wounded, two of them mortally, not including the 35 per cent casualties sustained by the 4,000-strong garrison. Hardly a house escaped undamaged; fifty were totally destroyed.[1]

Dorpat's experience in 1704 was not unusual; indeed the losses it suffered were relatively slight. The outbreak of plague in Reval during the siege of 1710, which prevented people from fleeing as they would normally have done, had a catastrophic impact: the inner city's population fell from 5,122 in 1708 to only 1,732 in October 1711; altogether 5,687 people died there, including members of the garrison and refugees. The population of the suburbs, from which many did flee, was reduced from 4,679 in 1708 to only 423 in February 1711.[2] Yet for all its relatively insignificant losses in 1704, Dorpat's experience between 1558 and 1704 was probably more typical of the small urban communities of northeastern Europe than that of Reval, which remained under unbroken Swedish rule between 1561 and 1710, and which had not experienced a siege since 1577. Dorpat was besieged and captured in 1558, 1601, 1603, 1625, 1656 and 1704; altogether it changed hands eight times. On each occasion, its conquerors signed agreements upholding its privileges, and its inhabitants adjusted their lives to the demands of their new rulers. Yet the regular destruction and disruption to the city's economic life took their toll. Piotrowski, visiting Dorpat in 1582 as Polish rule began, was impressed by what he recognised had been a properous city before the Muscovite occupation: he estimated that it was slightly smaller than 'our Thorn', but that there were no wooden houses, only fine stone buildings 'although what does it matter when no buildings at all are left?' In the late 1660s, more than a decade after the successful Muscovite siege of 1656, Hans Moritz Ayrmann could only discern the outlines of Dorpat's former prosperity: what the Muscovites had not ruined before handing the city back to Sweden in 1661 had been destroyed in the fire of 1667, and Dorpat's once-proud burghers were living in misery.[3]

In the eight decades between these two visits, Dorpat's recovery had regularly been disrupted by war: in the 1600s, the 1620s and the 1650s. It was over two decades after Swedish rule was restored in 1661 before it even began to revive. The city was heavily in debt, its accounts were in chaos, and its inhabitants riven by internal strife before the arrival in 1681 of a dynamic new town secretary, the Stralsunder Johann Remmin, elected bürgomeister in 1693. The period of recovery was all too brief, however, before the siege of 1704 opened a grim new chapter in the city's history. Although 3,000 serfs were requisitioned by Peter to repair the fortifications after it fell, most of the ruined buildings remained untouched to the end of the war. The population had fallen to a mere 1,427, of whom barely 350 were adult males capable of bearing arms; nevertheless Sheremetev, fearing a rising, introduced a garrison of 2,700 men, whose presence placed a huge burden on the city.[4]

By March 1708 there was nobody left at all. Despite Peter's promise at a council banquet given in his honour that the city would enjoy ten times more privileges than under the Swedes, life under Russian military control was harsh. Burghers were forbidden to leave the city without permission; they were banned from sending or receiving letters and were forbidden to assemble under pain of death; all weapons were to be surrendered, and a strict curfew was enforced after dark, when no fires or lights were to be lit. These draconian regulations profoundly shocked the burghers: they rendered business and trade all but impossible, and the ban on fires and light after dark during the long, cold northern winter was a threat to comfort, health, and life itself. Although the regulations were softened somewhat after strenuous appeals, for the next three years Dorpat lived under martial law. Punishments for the smallest infractions of the rules were fierce. Prices rose rapidly as the city was cut off from much of its normal economic activity and economic life was subject to ever-increasing regulation.

It was dealt a further blow in May 1707, when 279 people were deported, including all the former Swedish soldiers still living in the town, and 56 merchants, artisans and apprentices, including 3 goldsmiths, 2 cabinetmakers, 3 saddlers, 2 wigmakers, 5 hatters, 7 cobblers and all the town's linen-weavers.[5] It was but a foretaste of what was to come. On the bitter morning of Ash Wednesday (18 February OS) 1708 all 824 of Dorpat's remaining German inhabitants were assembled for deportation. Ordered to leave all the property they could not carry with them, and to supply their own horses and sleighs, the burghers finally embarked on their long journey in the evening twilight, accompanied by an armed escort and a thunderous salute from the Russian guns. No exception was made for the elderly, or for pregnant women: the sad procession included the seventy-four-year-old *Majorin* Helene Müller, née Wrangel, blind and bedridden for three years, and the seventy-seven-year-old Anna Hagedorn, widow of a *Ratsherr*, who was shortly to die from the rigours of the journey. As they laboriously made their way into exile, the city was stripped of all its valuables, including the church bells and organ from the Johanneskirche. In July, just after Hołowczyn, Dorpat was systematically destroyed: the fortifications were blown up and it was set on fire. After burning for several days, all that was left of the once flourishing city was a heap of smoking ruins. A mere 400 Estonian inhabitants remained in the ruined suburbs. Only after six long years in Vologda, Ustiug and Kazan were some of the deportees allowed to return. Many were destitute, like the eighty-year-old *Ratsherr* Jürgen Schlütter, once the proud owner of two houses and three gardens in Dorpat, who had to appeal for charity to the Riga council in February 1715 from Narva – whose inhabitants had also been deported – where he was living in desperate straits. Dorpat was eventually to flourish once more under Russian rule, but the old city had all but vanished. The road back to prosperity was to be long and hard.[6]

Brave new world

Dorpat's fate in 1704–8 was extreme, but much of its experience was shared by communities across northeastern Europe after 1648. A new military age had dawned, in which the relationship between governments, communities and the military had altered fundamentally. It is this change which Michael Roberts saw as lying at the heart of the Military Revolution; it was a shift which was more cultural than technological:

> The armies of Maximilian II . . . belong to a world of ideas which would have seemed quite foreign to Benedek and Radetzky. The armies of the Great Elector are linked infrangibly with those of Moltke and Schlieffen. By 1660 the modern art of war had come to birth. Mass armies, strict discipline, the control of the state, the submergence of the individual had already arrived; the conjoint ascendancy of financial power and applied science was already established in all its malignity; the use of propaganda, psychological warfare, and terrorism as military weapons was already familiar to theorists, as well as to commanders in the field. The last remaining qualms as to the religious and ethical legitimacy of war seemed to have been stilled. The road lay open, broad and straight, to the abyss of the twentieth century.[7]

It is hard not to discern in Dorpat's fate the stark outlines of this new world. It is not that destruction was anything new: as Piotrowski's account demonstrates, Dorpat had suffered greatly during the First Northern War, and deportations of artisans and merchants to Russia, which had long sought western technological and entrepreneurial expertise, had taken place during the occupations of 1558–82 and 1656–61. Yet none of its past experiences had prepared Dorpat for the arbitrary harshness of its military rulers after 1704. It is impossible to read the protocols of the council, or its copious correspondence with the Russian military authorities, without sensing the bewilderment at Dorpat's treatment by its new masters. Between 1700 and 1704, the city had loyally obeyed its Swedish overlords, and the burgher militia had defended the city alongside the Swedish garrison. If the burghers had been free to choose, they would probably have surrendered without a fight, as their forebears had done in 1558, but they had sworn an oath of loyalty which bound them to obey the Swedish commandant until he was no longer in a position to protect them. Sweden had treated the city well, with Gustav Adolf founding Dorpat University in 1632, but if Swedish rule was at an end, the burghers must now serve their new masters as loyally. It was the only way to survive.

Yet Peter suspected Dorpat of pro-Swedish sentiment; this was the principal rationale behind the harsh regulations imposed by the Russian authorities. All the council's patient attempts to convince him of its loyalty, and to point out that the ordinances were self-defeating, since it was barely possible for Dorpat's burghers to survive, let alone prosper, were to no avail. They were powerless; all they could do was carry on, upholding their values as best they could in the harsh new world. In 1709–10 Matthias Lyth, captured at Poltava, found communities of Dorpat burghers in the foreign suburb of Moscow, in Vologda and Ustiug, living reasonably well, conducting their trades and worshipping their Lutheran God. At least Peter had not denied them that solace.[8]

In the fifteenth century, prosperous cities like Dorpat, Reval or Riga had regularly defied princes and archbishops, secure behind their stone walls and protected by the wealth and power of the Hanseatic League. Since 1558, however, the balance of advantage had shifted decisively towards the territorial state and away from the self-governing urban communities of northeastern Europe; only Danzig managed to keep full control of its own defensive arrangements throughout the seventeenth century. The burghers of Reval, Dorpat and Riga, once largely in command of their own destiny, had gradually seen their autonomy whittled away as they ceased to be able to defend themselves. By 1700, even Danzig was unable to resist. It could not prevent the stationing of Saxon troops in its landed estates, and although it was not occupied by Charles, the threat of attack was sufficient: in 1703 Danzig was bullied into paying 100,000 reichsthalers contribution; its hopes of preserving its neutrality were soon dashed, however, as Charles forced it to abjure Augustus and accept Leszczyński as its king. In 1716–17, Danzig came under sustained Russian pressure to break off trade with Sweden and to build a privateering fleet to attack Swedish shipping. It was forced to sign an agreement with Peter in 1717, agreeing to pay him 140,000 thalers in cash, accepting a Russian commissar in the city and granting the Russian fleet the right to use its harbour.[9] Danzig was no longer its own master.

It was not just urban communities which were affected. Across north-eastern Europe, the emergence of standing armies and the vastly increased demand for recruits, supplies and above all money fundamentally altered the relationship between civil society and the military. Where the armies which devastated Livonia in the 1560s and 1570s had swept through in brief campaigns, and the destruction they wrought had often been aimless, armies after 1648 were increasingly present as permanent elements in city life in peacetime, and as bloated, demanding guests in time of war. The organised, systematic and regular collection of contributions from civilian populations did help bring an end to the random destruction of the sixteenth century, since armies were increasingly aware of the need to sustain the economies of the areas in which they were quartered, but while this meant that relations between civilians and military authorities in time of peace – or in quiet periods far from the front in time of war – could be reasonably harmonious, regions directly affected by hostile action were often subjected to more systematic and organised destruction as retreating armies sought to deny their enemy a supply-base and ruin the strongpoints he might use as bases: it was this consideration which lay behind Dorpat's systematic destruction in 1708.

Even in peacetime the burdens were extensive, and the ability of local communities to resist military demands was limited. Most burdensome of all was the cost of the increasingly elaborate fortifications surrounding contemporary cities, much of which was born by the community they were meant to defend. These fortifications were more extensive, more complex and vastly more expensive than medieval town walls; moreover, the rapidly changing demands of early modern warfare ensured that they rapidly became obsolete, and constant efforts had to be made to update and maintain them, all of which demanded labour and money. In 1622, Gustav Adolf told Reval council that the city's fortifications were outmoded and all but useless; in 1623 the council duly began repairs. Work continued through the 1630s. Nevertheless, despite further bursts of construction in the 1640s and 1650s, the Swedes ordered the complete reconstruction of the fortifications in the 1690s. Since much of Reval's land had originally been royal, it had been badly hit by the *reduktion,* and the council was forced to introduce a special tax, the *Wallgeld,* and substantially raise other taxes, from the excise to the *Bürgergeld.* Yet even though the Swedish government also spent half a million rigsdalers on the Reval fortifications, only two of the projected eleven bastions had been built by 1700, with one more under construction; the Scania bastion, finished in 1703, took two decades to build; four of the projected bastions, not yet begun, were in the east, whence the attack was most likely to come. Swedish money dried up once the war began, and the burghers had to bear the whole cost themselves, as well as supply the labour to construct the massive system. It was all to no avail. By 1710, the fortifications were still incomplete: the counterscarp was unfinished and only three bastions and one ravelin on the south side were ready for occupation. Reval's artillery was inadequate and it was short of supplies – in 1706 the council estimated they only had enough for fourteen days – and its ability to resist was shattered in 1710 by the outbreak of plague. All that twenty years of effort had accomplished was to ensure that the Russians would have less work to do, although Peter decided that Reval's defences needed strengthening on the seaward side, so he ordered a further series of works which were only completed in 1719.[10]

This shift in the relationship between communities, territorial states and the armed forces lay at the heart of the Military Revolution. Technology was central to military change in the early modern period, but the Military Revolution was not a technological revolution, and attempts to discern several military revolutions from the Middle Ages to the French Revolution and beyond based round individual advances in weapons technology are inherently futile. No single technological development could in itself transform warfare, and the question of whether or not particular weapons or fortifications systems were decisive in military terms is largely irrelevant. The association drawn by Roberts and others between the decline of heavy cavalry and the supposed eclipse of the nobility is too crude to carry conviction, and ignores the extent to which the military changes of the sixteenth and seventeenth centuries actually revitalised nobilities across Europe as a martial class.[11] What is striking about military technology in the early modern period is not that there was a revolutionary breakthrough, but the sheer pace of military innovation. The very limitations of gunpowder technology placed a premium on technological improvement, stimulating the immensely fertile attempts to devise better firearms which brought experimentation with bronze guns, cast-iron guns, breech-loaders, wheel-locks, matchlocks, flintlocks, multi-barrelled guns, rifled barrels, canister and cartridges. They also stimulated fertile experimentation to discover the best formations to maximise the effectiveness of firearms while minimising the vulnerability of the troops using them. Linear tactics, Spanish riders, the salvo, the countermarch and the caracole were all attempts to minimise the shortcomings of firearms. They all had one thing in common: to be effective, they required training, discipline, professionalism and a high level of corporate morale.

Initially at least, such attributes were to be found principally by hiring mercenaries. By 1550, the international mercenary market was highly sensitive to fluctuations in warfare, and soldiers crossed the continent to find employment: in 1581, four Englishmen joined Batory's army at Połock complaining that they had not been paid in the Netherlands and France because there was peace.[12] Mercenaries were the vectors of change, bringing new ideas and new methods to the armies in which they served, and learning from their employers: it was Scottish officers in Swedish service who developed the famous leather guns in the 1620s, while Robert Monro credited Stefan Batory with the invention of effective firebombs, which were particularly useful in sieges in eastern Europe where so many buildings were constructed of wood.[13]

Given the speed at which military technology was transferred, no state could ignore it, yet the cost of acquiring it, and of hiring the professional soldiers who knew how to apply it most effectively, was immense, and the challenge for states was enormous. Critics of the idea of a Military Revolution have suggested that states failed to rise to the challenge, pointing to the shortcomings of early modern military administration and the many examples of incompetence, poor planning or inability to fulfil over-ambitious strategies. David Parrott has claimed that the early modern state, far from being created as a result of military change, was increasingly pushed towards an 'all-pervasive inadequacy' by its demands, suggesting that one of the central features of the Military Revolution as envisaged by Parker and Roberts – the great increase in army size – has been greatly exaggerated.[14] Others have suggested that far from playing a central role in creating the modern state, the emergence of standing armies was only possible after the creation of the modern, absolutist state, and was its consequence, not its cause, or have denied the existence of any direct relationship.[15]

Yet if the failure to complete the Reval fortifications in time for the Great Northern War might be cited as an example of the inadequacy of the Swedish state to its task, the colossal nature of the undertaking should be recognised. For if early modern states were not always adequate to the challenges posed by the rapid development of military technology and military techniques after 1550, their achievements were often impressive. They were certainly more adequate to the task than noble warlords or isolated urban communities. The Livonian Confederation had a high level of knowledge of the latest military technology, but was no longer able to mobilise the resources to confront its enemies by 1558.

Many of the undoubted shortfalls and administrative shortcomings are only evident because of the vastly increased volume of paper generated by armies after 1600, itself compelling evidence for the emergence of the new military world: the account books for the Swedish army's administration of Royal Prussia between 1655 and 1659 run to 137 large folio volumes. The meticulousness with which these accounts were kept is often startling: the bakery accounts of the Swedish army besieging Thorn in 1703 contain minutely-detailed receipts for the grain, flour and other materials brought into the magazine, plus extensive lists of the regiments to which it was delivered. By the early eighteenth century such punctilious record-keeping was increasingly the norm, and makes possible a much more detailed picture of contemporary armies and their relationship with civil society.[16] If it is easy to exaggerate the increase in army size by uncritically presenting maximum paper strengths in wartime as if they were normal or accurate, the muster lists for the seventeenth and early eighteenth century do give a much more accurate picture of army size than the often wild literary exaggerations of earlier periods. Paper strengths often diverged – sometimes dramatically – from actual strengths, especially towards the end of a campaign, but given the colossal wastage rates of early modern armies this was hardly surprising. What was significant was not so much the size of individual field armies, but the fact that, despite the steady intensification of warfare, the ranks were filled year after year. They may only have been 80 per cent full, but they were 80 per cent full every spring; that in itself was an enormous achievement, especially by thinly-populated states like Sweden, which by 1708 had 110,000 men under arms – equivalent to 10 per cent of its adult male population. As late as the 1680s the great effort of putting a large army in the field could not be sustained for more than two or three years in a row by Russia, all of whose wars before 1700 were characterised by short periods of intensive campaigning, followed by long periods of inertia.[17] If Russia's enemies weathered the storm, they were usually able to make good many of their losses, as the Poles did in the 1660s. After 1700, however, Russia sustained a level of military activity unprecedented in its history, and despite huge desertion rates, fielded substantial armies year after year.

Quality, however, mattered more than quantity. At the heart of the Military Revolution lay the professionalisation of the armed forces and the emergence everywhere between 1600 and 1720 of permanent, regular, armies composed of career soldiers and career officers. These new forces possessed a permanent regimental and administrative structure, a clear hierarchy of rank, and the modern division into officers, non-commissioned officers and private soldiers. These new institutions spawned a new military culture which, as Roberts argues, is recognisably modern. With the emergence of permanent regiments came the development and strengthening of communal identity, especially amongst officers, as regiments acquired a history, invented their traditions and distinguished themselves through uniforms, insignia and modes of behaviour. Although Roberts, writing only a decade after 1945, emphasised the negative side of the growth of this military culture and of the militarism which has been widely blamed for causing two world wars in the twentieth century, it also had its positive side. Early modern commanders increasingly devoted their attention towards controlling and disciplining their forces, in order to regulate and civilise the interaction of civilian and military.

The growth of discipline, based on elaborate codes drawn up in all armies in the late sixteenth and seventeenth centuries, which often drew on the ideas of Grotius and other theorists seeking to develop concepts of legality and illegality in war, did have a noticeable effect on the conduct of war: for all the frequent breakdowns, and for all the harshness of military demands, especially in wartime, commanders did increasingly endeavour to maintain a relationship with civilian society based on enforced codes of behaviour. The burghers of Reval may have had to pay huge sums of money towards the construction of their new fortifications, but the Swedish authorities did pay compensation to those whose property was sequestered to provide land on which to construct the massive new bastions; the city archives contain a register, 337 folios long, of submissions from burghers seeking compensation from the 1630s to the 1680s. *Ratsherr* Hans von Schoten and another burgher, von Brekel, even engaged an artist, Heinrich Julien Woltematen, to paint elaborate watercolour plans of their gardens, which were to be swallowed up in 1683 by the new bastion outside the *Strandpforte*, to persuade the authorities of the value of the property they were surrendering.[18] It was the breach of such norms which the burghers of Dorpat found so shocking after 1704.

The new armies were sufficently similar to justify Roberts's concept of a Military Revolution, but there were significant differences between them, and it is impossible to fit them into too rigid a pattern. Some – such as those of Saxony and Prussia – continued to draw a substantial proportion of their recruits and even their officer corps from outside the state, while others – such as the Swedish or Russian armies – increasingly recruited from within. Above all the historian has to be cautious with applying the term 'modern'; if the modern army had been born, its growth would take a long time. The key elements of the revolution were permanence and professionalism, but the success of the revolution depended upon the blending of traditional noble ideas with newer concepts of service and merit. The states which deployed these armies were neither capable of destroying ideals of nobility based on birth, nor did they try to; instead they harnessed these ideals. Tables of ranks in Denmark, Sweden, Russia and Prussia represented a compromise between ideals of birth and merit, while regiments in many European armies remained for long the property of their aristocratic commanders, as commissions were bought and sold on the open market. The Military Revolution was certainly not achieved by the substitution of meritocracy for aristocracy.

The Military Revolution in northeastern Europe

It is important to stress the different paths of military development in early modern Europe, for it makes possible a proper evaluation of the relationship between military change and wider developments in northeastern Europe, which experienced warfare on a hitherto unprecedented scale between 1558 and 1721. Military change was rapid and extensive, and the burdens placed on society grew exponentially. By 1721, the relationship between governments, armed forces and society had changed fundamentally in every state involved, a process which in each case brought a greater or lesser degree of social and political upheaval; in Sweden, Russia, Denmark and Brandenburg-Prussia it is not inappropriate to term this process a Military Revolution.

Yet an examination of the relationship between war, state and society in northeastern Europe between 1558 and 1721 suggests that what took place was a series of individual military revolutions, not one Military Revolution. For in each case, the course and timing of change depended fundamentally on the very different economic, social and political structures of the powers involved, and the temptation to apply a single model of state-building, usually based on the experiences of England or France, should be resisted. Although the process of change was essentially evolutionary, in every case there was a critical point which can be seen as the definitive breakthrough of a new military system: in Sweden in the 1620s; in Brandenburg-Prussia in the 1650s; in Denmark in the 1660s and in Russia in the 1700s. The nature of these crises differed, but in each case these very different societies – or at least a substantial enough group among their social and political elites – accepted the new arrangements, usually as a result of the emergence of new groups within those elites who had benefited from the opportunities afforded by the growth of the military, and who had much to gain from the establishment of a permanent structure. Once that acceptance was achieved, the new military culture could develop and its values spread within society.

The Northern Wars confirm, however, that historians should be cautious about adopting crude technological determinism. For the effectiveness of technology depended fundamentally on the nature of the physical and social environment in which it was applied. Thus while cavalry may well have been all but useless in the siege warfare which played such a central role in the Eighty Years War between Spain and the Dutch rebels, it remained central to operations in eastern Europe throughout the period. Poland-Lithuania's success in the first phase of the wars was primarily due to the fact that the Commonwealth, instead of abandoning or downgrading cavalry, developed new ways of using it to take account of the new military technology; success depended on the successful integration of cavalry with infantry firepower, and control of the theatre of operations depended upon cavalry. If the Commonwealth's cavalry was increasingly ineffective after 1648, this was not because cavalry was obsolete, or was eclipsed by new technology, it was because of the Commonwealth's increasing inablity to raise sufficient infantry to give it the necessary support. Instead, other armies benefited: the highly effective Swedish cavalry tactics after 1621 were based on Polish examples, although it was not until the eighteenth century that most western armies replaced their straight cavalry swords – little more than pointed clubs – with the curved Polish sabres which were far more effective as cavalry weapons. The Polish hussars were the direct lineal ancestors of the lancers and uhlans of eighteenth- and nineteenth century armies, as is reflected in the stylised Polish uniforms they adopted. If its effectiveness on the battlefield undoubtedly declined, cavalry was still important for its mobility, and played a central role in reconnaissance, skirmishing and harrying the enemy. Despite widespread mockery of First World War generals for their attachment to cavalry, it remained important into the twentieth century: if it was indeed useless against trench and machine-gun on the Western Front, it was employed to notable effect in the east, during the Russian Civil War, the Polish-Soviet War, and by the Red Army during the Second World War, where its mobility was still important. As the *Wehrmacht* discovered after 1941, one doesn't have to put petrol in a horse.

The importance of cavalry in eastern Europe was a reflection of the fact that western military methods were not always appropriate in the different conditions of the east. Western commanders and western armies – such as the Saxon army in the Great Northern War – were often spectacularly unsuccessful in the east. Success was dependent upon adapting, rather than adopting, western methods and ideas to the conditions found in the east, something which was achieved with notable effect by the Poles down to 1648, the Swedes from the 1620s and the Russians after 1700. Thus northeastern Europe participated fully in the striking experimentation and interchange of technological and technical expertise and exploited the rapid development of the international mercenary market after 1500. Although few Muscovites served abroad, Poles, Swedes and Danes all travelled and fought in other European armies, and all states, including Muscovy, employed mercenaries.

Relying on the expertise of foreign mercenaries alone did not, however, guarantee success, as Denmark discovered during the 1560s. Mercenaries were expensive and difficult to handle. After 1570 the Danish Council, while willing to support the navy on which Denmark's security and trade so obviously depended, successfully opposed further involvement in the Northern Wars, until Christian IV was able to exploit the monarchy's relative financial independence thanks to its control of the Sound Dues to involve Denmark in two wars within fifteen years, again fought largely with foreign mercenaries, which Christian could afford to raise from his own pocket, but could not maintain. While the Council agreed to the establishment of a small native army after 1614, it remained reluctant to support Christian's adventurous policies. The *Rigsdag* was called in time of danger, and proved willing to provide the means for Denmark to resist the Imperial invasion of the late 1620s and the mid-century Swedish invasions, but it only played an occasional role in the Danish political system. Nevertheless, despite Denmark's relatively limited engagement in the Northern Wars, it did undergo a military revolution. If Christian's disastrous intervention in the Thirty Years War provoked the strengthening of Council power in 1648, the catastrophes of the 1650s opened the way to the establishment of the absolute monarchy in 1660. The emergence of the professional army after 1614, and the complete failure of the high nobility to perform its function as defenders of the realm in the crisis of the late 1650s opened the way to the constitutional revolution, in which old noble privileges were swept away and a new system of military service was instituted. The old nobility rapidly adjusted itself to the new situation, but Denmark moved decisively from being a domain-state to being a tax-state, and a socio-political system was established after 1660 which was to last for nearly two centuries.

Even after the introduction of the absolute monarchy, however, Denmark did not play a central role in the Northern Wars. Its resignation after 1570 from the contest in the eastern Baltic meant that, unlike Sweden, its elites lacked a direct material or security interest in the fate of Livonia and Estonia. The two serious attempts made to recover the lost provinces across the Sound, in the 1670s and 1700, came up against determined Swedish opposition, and in neither case was the Danish will strong enough to sustain the fight. Denmark's geographical position meant that the monarchy remained as interested in the conflicts of northern Germany and the North Sea littoral as it did in the Baltic, and Denmark's role in coalition politics during the wars of Louis XIV was a constant distraction. The concern of western European powers to prevent Swedish domination of the Baltic after 1648 ensured that at moments of crisis, the Maritime Powers would come to Denmark's aid, as in 1658–9, but even in the favourable conditions after Poltava, when Sweden was on the defensive on all fronts, Denmark proved unable to restore the advantage it had enjoyed before 1620. A Danish army invaded Scania in November 1709, but it was defeated by Magnus Stenbock at Hälsingborg (February 1710), and although they made better headway in northern Germany, the defeat of a joint Danish-Saxon army at Gadebusch (December 1712) demonstrated that Sweden still enjoyed military superiority; it took Russian support to repulse another Swedish invasion of Jutland in 1713, although the surrender of Stenbock's army after the siege of Tønning on 26 May 1713 (OS) was a notable success. Despite being part of a powerful anti-Swedish coalition, however, Denmark's rewards were ultimately minimal: the coveted prize of Bremen-Verden was snapped up by Hanover in 1719, while at the treaty of Frederiksborg (June 1720) British hostility to Danish gains in Scandinavia meant it was forced to abandon all its conquests except Royal Holstein. It won control of Holstein-Gottorp lands in Schleswig and Sweden lost its exemption from the Sound Dues, but it was poor reward for over a decade of fighting. Military Revolution did not guarantee military success.

It is Sweden which provides the clearest example of a military revolution in this period. This revolution was largely complete by the death of Gustav Adolf in 1632, although the emergence of the military state was not the result of a simple process of state-building on his part, but of a complex set of social, political and cultural developments, in which the impact of war on

Swedish politics and Swedish society was central. The nature of the Swedish political system, in which the four-chamber *Riksdag* played a far more
important role in balancing the power of the aristocratic council than its
Danish counterpart, enabled the Vasas to play on Swedish senses of vulnerability to build up the navy and to develop an increasingly effective army.
Sweden's weak strategic position, situated between three powerful states in
the shape of Denmark-Norway, Poland-Lithuania and Muscovy ensured
that the Vasas were able from the outset to exploit fears of outside threats.
The memory of the tyranny of Christian II was kept alive long after 1523 to
warn of the dangers of a return to Danish rule, while the weakness of
Sweden's strategic position with regard to Denmark, in which Norway,
Halland, Scania and Blekinge provided convenient springboards for invasion, and in which Denmark's powerful navy and control of the Sound
constituted a very real threat to Sweden's trading interests, was only too
obvious, and was confirmed in dramatic style by the wars of 1563–70 and
1611–13. The acquisition of Reval and Estonia after 1561 brought Sweden
into more direct contact with Muscovite military power, whose destructive
capacity was clearly demonstrated in the 1560s and 1570s, while many
members of the Swedish political elite acquired property interests in the
vulnerable Baltic provinces. Finally, the unfortunate outcome of John III's
ambitious religious and dynastic schemes ensured that the threat from
Poland-Lithuania after 1598 seemed all too real; as Gustav Adolf constantly
stressed, Sigismund and the Swedish exiles in Poland represented a threat
to religion and liberty.

The key to Swedish military success was that the system was built largely
on consent – albeit grudging at times. Sweden's poverty ensured that the
hiring of foreign mercenaries on a large scale was initially impossible, and
Sweden had to rely largely on native troops and native officers. During the
almost permanent wars between 1558 and 1620, the imaginative use of the
royal domain to create a means of support for this army, and in particular
the growing officer corps, attracted increasing numbers of impoverished
Swedish nobles and commoners alike into the officer corps and gave them
a direct stake in the developing military state. If it was undoubtedly a harsh
system, it was not as arbitrary as some. Its administration was to a large extent
a matter of negotiation between central crown officials and local bodies of
communal self-government, with the church playing a prominent role, and
people at all levels of society benefited as well as suffered from its operation.
Gustav Adolf's massive propaganda campaign after his accession depended
crucially on the Church, whose Lutheran authorities were happy to support
the government: in 1621, against the background of unrest following the
introduction of *utskrivning*, Archbishop Petrus Kenicius's exhortation to the
Swedish clergy emphasised the teaching of St Peter and St Paul on obedience

to secular authority and urged pastors to guard against disorder.[19] In a more secular vein, the goverment strongly encouraged the vision of the Swedes as a uniquely martial people: the title of '*Rex Gothorum et Vandalorum*' used by the Vasas and their successors was no empty phrase. At the 1630 *Riksdag*, after the burden of Sweden's war effort had provoked unrest in several parts of the kingdom, Gustav Adolf, addressing each estate in turn, stressed to the nobles the courage of their Gothic forebears and the benefits they drew from the military state; the appeals to the burghers and peasantry, however, promised that prosperity would result from success in the war.[20]

Thus Sweden's growing military state was intimately linked to the emergence of a new communal identity, both religious and political, in what Ringmar has termed a 'formative moment' in Swedish history.[21] Moreover, this emerging identity, and the skilful playing of royal propaganda on the foreign threat helped produce what was highly significant in the contemporary context: the full support of Swedish institutions for aggressive war waged abroad. If at the 1621 *Riksdag* Gustav Adolf had merely argued that it was good to hold the enemy far from Sweden's borders, a year later he was bolder, suggesting that the longer war was waged abroad, the better; in 1629, his emotional appeal to the *Riksdag* over the need to intervene in Germany was successful: the assembled estates fully endorsed his view that it 'was better that we tether our horse in the enemy's homestead than he in ours'.[22]

The consensual basis of the system was the key to its regeneration in the difficult years after 1660, when the end of the favourable conjuncture for the conduct of the aggressive wars abroad which largely funded the dramatic growth in the size of the Swedish army after 1620 revealed the great problems faced in defending the new empire and sustaining the military state on Sweden's slender economic resources. The brilliant solution to the problem institutionalised after 1680 demonstrates that military revolution did not necessarily produce the modern administrative tax state. The *indelningsverk*, established initially on the basis largely of revenues in kind, represented the institutionalisation of a domain state, for which it was harshly criticised by the great Swedish economic historian Eli Heckscher. Taxation certainly played an important part, but it was impossible to support an adequate army or meet the expectations of Sweden's new administrative-military elites on the basis of taxation alone. The *indelningsverk*, however, secured the basis of the military state and enabled the construction of an army which, for nearly a decade under Charles XII, proved itself the most effective in Europe.

Yet Charles's wars demonstrated one simple fact. Although his father's reforms had solved the problem of maintaining a powerful army in peacetime, to sustain and win a war Sweden must be aggressive. Just as the

engagement of mercenaries in late 1654 had predetermined Sweden's intervention in the Second Northern War, so the coming of war in 1700 forced
the Swedish military machine to find pastures in which to feed itself: although
the military revolution in Sweden had brought a great increase in the size
of the professional Swedish army to 60,000 in 1699, much of its strength was
dissipated in garrisons and the army Charles led into the Commonwealth in
1702 was the same size as that with which Gustav Adolf attacked Riga in
1621, and substantially smaller than Charles X's in 1655. Nevertheless, for
the next nine years, it appeared that Sweden was returning to the glory days
of the 1630s and 1640s: in contrast to Charles X, Charles XII secured and
maintained the support of a substantial party in the Commonwealth, and
was able to place Poland-Lithuania under contribution far more effectively
than his predecessors. The long stay in Saxony in 1706–7 brought a flood
of recruits from Germany and elsewhere, just as in the Thirty Years War,
although Charles was concerned to keep the core of the army Swedish, and
was particularly suspicious of the fighting quality of the Saxons.[23]

After Poltava Sweden's vulnerability was starkly revealed. Charles XI's
system was excellently suited to maintaining a large, powerful, well-trained
army in peacetime, but although the *indelningsverk* was able to fill many of
the gaps that appeared in the ranks during the war, the strain was already
beginning to show before 1709. Immediately the war began, Charles ordered
that files responsible for recruitment were to be grouped together to produce
an extra man; these recruits formed the so-called 'third-man regiments'.
Later, fourth- and even fifth-man regiments were raised. Such methods
were effective in the short term, and the Swedish army rose to a strength of
110,000 men by 1709, but the quality of recruits and equipment supplied by
the *indelningsverk* constantly declined. Already in November 1700, Colonel
Carl Gustaf Kruse rejected 3 men and 9 horses out of 15 presented in
Uppland; in February, he rejected 2 out of 12 men and 19 out of 25 horses
as unsuitable; much of the equipment and uniforms produced were un-
usable.[24] The situation only degenerated with time, and although Swedish
officials, acting in the spirit of the system which had emerged since 1620,
did what they could to mediate between the demands of the military machine
and the needs of local communities, the consequences of the introduction of
absolute monarchy rapidly became clear. No longer did Swedish monarchs
beguile the *Riksdag* with appeals to Gothic ideals; Charles never summoned
one. He issued his orders and expected them to be obeyed; appeals by the
Stockholm government to persuade him to make peace or soften his demands
fell on deaf ears.

This was particularly clear in the period after Poltava, when Charles
refused absolutely to make peace. As the war turned against Sweden, there
were continual levies to fill the ever-increasing gaps in the army, while in

1712 Charles issued a decree instituting a new property tax based on equality which amounted to 2 per cent on the value of property and ignored the privileges of the nobility, whom it hit relatively hard.[25] Yet Sweden, for all the quality of its army, could not long sustain a war fought on home soil. The military state was robust enough to fight on with no significant foreign support for twelve more years, for most of the time against a coalition of all Sweden's most powerful neighbours, and Sweden emerged in 1721 with its territory intact and some at least of its Baltic empire. Nevertheless it proved wholly unable to match the growing might of Russia or retake the Baltic provinces which had been the cornerstone of its Baltic hegemony, and which now provided Peter with a base for his new navy, whose rapid growth constituted the most serious threat Sweden had faced since 1558. After the Russian naval victory at Hangö (27 July 1714 OS), Sweden, and particularly Finland, were defenceless. The large Russian galley fleet was able to sail in close to the coast and land substantial units of troops, while the Swedish galleons had to stand helplessly offshore and watch. After the destruction of Helsingfors and the capture of Åbo in 1713, Finland was effectively lost, to be used as a vital Russian bargaining counter in peace negotiations, while devastating Russian raids on Sweden itself undermined Swedish resistance: the damage inflicted on Finland alone has been estimated at 1.5 million silver dalers, 30 per cent of its wealth according to the contribution tariffs of 1713.[26]

Despite the defeat in the Great Northern War, however, the Swedish military state survived. Moreover, the extent to which Sweden's elites were dominated by the military-administrative machine was demonstrated in the constitutional revolution following Charles XII's death in November 1718. Absolutism had been introduced in 1680 as a solution to the problems which had plagued the military state since 1648. Now it was dismantled because Charles's unchecked authority had, in the opinion of many, brought Sweden to the brink of catastrophe. The influence of the army as a corporate body, which believed its interests to be threatened, was of central importance in the radical stripping of the monarchy of much of its power during 1718–19. By 1700, the Swedish military-administrative elite had already established itself after the dramatic growth of the seventeenth century. The table of ranks, drawn up in 1680, amended in 1696 and 1714, was thereafter to survive unchanged until 1909. Between 1611 and 1699, the success of the military state had seen some 1,700 ennoblements, which expanded the nobility dramatically from the 500 families it had contained in 1600. As the nobility grew, so the influx of commoners into the officer corps slowed: by 1700, only 40 per cent of new officers were of common birth, compared with 70 per cent in 1653. High army officers dominated the 40 levels of the table of ranks: field-marshals, generals of artillery, generals and lieutenant-generals filled ranks 1, 2, 4 and 5, as their only members; colonels, in rank 11, were more prestigious than state secretaries (rank 16) or members of the Council of War (rank 18).[27] This was no modern meritocracy. The system provided the perfect framework for a service nobility, in which, although merit was important for the trajectory of a career, birth was of increasing importance, particularly in peacetime: Creutz, who commanded a guards regiment at Poltava, had been enrolled as a lieutenant at the age of two. In 1656, the young baron Gabriel Kurck was given the prestigious command of Prince Charles's regiment of horseguards despite his lack of experience: he had spent one year trailing a pike in Habsburg service, having been told by Archduke Leopold Wilhelm that all cavalrymen, whether aristocrats or not, had to serve their apprenticeship in the infantry.[28]

Such rapid promotion was less common in peacetime, and most officers worked their way up from lower ranks: commoners of talent usually began as privates or NCOs, while nobles entered as ensigns or lieutenants, although members of the aristocracy often started their careers as captains or privates in the guards. As the pool of educated young men grew, it became more difficult for commoners to rise high, in peacetime at least: between 1621 and 1660, fifteen commoners made the rank of captain in the Uppland, Södermanland and Västmanland regiments having begun as privates; between 1661 and 1674, there was not a single such case.[29] It was a comfortable system, especially in peacetime. Between 1735 and 1771, it consumed no less than a third of the government's annual revenue.[30] It is hardly surprising that it was to last for nearly two centuries, or that 1718–19 was only the first of three occasions in which the military corporations acted to overthrow the government when their interests were threatened: in 1772 the Age of Liberty was ended and absolute monarchy reestablished under Gustav III; in 1809, the hapless Gustav IV was driven from the throne. Yet the Great Northern War had been a salutory experience: Swedish history after 1721 demonstrates that a bloated military establishment and a militarised social elite does not necessarily produce aggressive militarism. Since 1813, Sweden has not fought a single war.[31]

Muscovy in the mid-sixteenth century was an aggressive power long before it acquired a modern military establishment. In contrast to Sweden, where the creation of a service nobility was a long, slow process after 1558, Muscovy already possessed a service-based system, regulated by the complex rules of *mestnichestvo*. The need to provide service and land for the growing service class turned Muscovy into an aggressive power. Its expansive urges were first directed towards the south, but it turned to the north as the developing crisis in Livonia provided both opportunity and danger for the Muscovite state. Yet although it could assemble large armies for short campaigns, they were largely amateur and unable to defeat the superior forces of Sweden and in particular Poland-Lithuania. As the tide of war turned in the late 1580s, and Muscovy began to lose territory, the strains within the service system played an important part in the detonation of the socio-political crisis of the Time of Troubles, in which the middling and lesser servitors, whose status and economic survival were directly threatened, played a central role.

Recovery from the Time of Troubles was a long process, and it was not until Peter I's reign that Russia's Military Revolution was complete. As in Sweden, where Gustav Adolf's reign saw the definitive breakthrough, the period of social and military development which made the revolution possible was a long one. Western military technology had been adopted on a large scale under Ivan IV, and western military experts played an increasing role in Muscovy after the Time of Troubles, but the Polish-Lithuanian victories at Klushino in 1610, Smolensk in 1633–4, and during the campaigns of the early 1660s, demonstrated that the application of western technology and western methods in themselves was no panacea, while deep-rooted Muscovite hostility to non-Orthodox foreigners ensured that resistance to westernisation remained strong.

Nevertheless, the gradual reconstitution of the service state under the first two Romanovs provided a firm basis for future development. The middling and petty servitors whose status had been threatened were reintegrated into the system; the price was that they increasingly had to serve in new-formation units. In return, the government secured their position and status by com-pleting the legal framework of serfdom and establishing the machinery to return runaway serfs to their masters, thus securing the economic basis of the mass of petty and middling servitors. By the 1650s, Muscovy could once more field substantial armies, now largely comprising new-style units. Even if their performance on the battlefield was often disappointing, Muscovy emerged in 1667 with substantial territorial gains, and the new system was not significantly threatened. Most importantly, a growing proportion of the service class, including the aristocrats at the top of the system, was gaining experience of the new military methods.

The process was by no means complete, however, as the unrest of the 1680s and 1690s demonstrated. The reigns of Michael and Alexis had seen substantial upheaval among the service elite, and the requirements of the new military hierarchy of western-style regiments seriously strained the trad-itional service framework provided by *mestsnichestvo*. The military reforms of 1678–82 and the abolition of *mestnichestvo* were important steps, but many of the problems remained unsolved, in particular the question of a clear framework of status. Despite the army reforms, in which foreigners had played such a central role, Russia was still not a full player on the European stage: suspicion of foreigners remained strong in wide sectors of society, and

Russia's peculiar diplomatic traditions ensured that it was isolated from many of the diplomatic manoeuvres which played such an increasing role in international relations after 1648.

Peter's great achievement was to provide a secure institutional and social framework within which the Russian military state was to operate down to its disastrous collapse in 1917. Drawing much inspiration from the Swedish example, he created a truly regular, permanent professional army commanded by a largely Russian officer corps and manned by peasant conscripts. To military power he added naval power, the lack of which had constantly frustrated his predecessors' attempts to take Reval and Riga. By 1724 the Russian fleet consisted of thirty-two ships of the line and sixteen frigates, enabling him to secure control of the eastern Baltic and force Sweden to make peace. He did not force the Russian elites to serve – Russia had long been a service state – but he laid down new conditions of service and tried to ensure that the reconstituted service elite would be educated to the required standard. Most importantly, he provided in the 1722 table of ranks a clear framework of status which – as in Sweden – made clear the domination of the military within the service system and allowed the possibility of promotion through merit without threatening the existing social hierarchy based on birth. The overwhelming acceptance of the new framework by the service class constituted Russia's military revolution.

The Russian example demonstrates, however, that military revolution cannot simply be equated with social or political modernisation. Peter's success was dependent as much on what he did not change as on the reforms he introduced. Russia was a highly centralised system long before he came to power, and much of what he achieved was only possible because of this fact. Although he attempted far-reaching administrative reform, much of it failed, in particular his attempt to establish efficiently functioning local institutions which might, on the Swedish example, secure the smoother running of the military state. In Russia, unlike Sweden, however, consent of the peasants was not important; the tsars could count on the support of the service elites to crush peasant resistance. Thus although he recognised its inefficiency, Peter realised that serfdom was the fundamental basis of the Russian service system, and therefore left it alone. Petrine Russia was an early demonstration of the fact, all too clear in the twentieth century, that modern military technology enables a small, militarised social elite to secure and maintain great power status on the basis of a backward and undeveloped rural economy. It was not until 1917 that Russia was to pay the price.

Peter's triumph was by no means inevitable. There was substantial opposition from wide sectors of Russian society to his reforms, both active and passive; many of them, such as the attempt to replace partible inheritance among the servitor elite with primogeniture, were to fail. Some of the most serious resistance came from non-hereditary servitors such as the *strel'tsy* and the various groups of Cossacks whose awkward relationship with the Russian state produced a string of risings and defections in the years before Poltava. While the Russian system did provide service, the constant inroads made into their autonomy ensured that Cossacks remained a volatile and dangerous force. Nevertheless, the abandonment of the Cossacks by the hereditary servitors after Michael Romanov's election allowed the government to crush those, led by Balovnev, who failed to accept the new terms on offer in 1615. Henceforth Russian Cossacks caused innmerable problems, but without the backing of hereditary servitors they were never again the political threat they had been between 1605 and 1613. The Ukrainian Cossacks absorbed with the acquisition of the Left Bank Ukraine in 1667 posed a different kind of problem, but the period of the *Ruina* in the Ukraine, and continuing sharp divisions within Ukrainian Cossackdom ensured that they were not the autonomous political force they had threatened to become under Bohdan Khmelnytsky, and Russia could always count on strong anti-Polish groups among them. Cossacks could still pose a serious threat, as the Astrakhan rising of 1705, and the defection of Mazepa and the Zaporozhians in 1708–9 demonstrated, but without wider support within the service elite there was little chance that they could reverse the tide of reform.

Defeat, however, might well have done. For the ultimate triumph of Peter's reforms was only sealed by victory in the Great Northern War, a success hitherto unparalleled in Russian history. It is no accident that Poltava was celebrated with such gusto, for Poltava was the ultimate justification of Peter's westernising policies. While it was twelve long years before Sweden was forced to concede defeat, and while Peter was fortunate that the Ottomans let him escape relatively unscathed from the disaster on the Prut in 1711, the destruction of the immediate Swedish threat in 1709 relieved the pressure enormously. Until Poltava, Peter was aware that his precious new army might cease to exist after one major defeat – as his intense agitation over Charles's threat to Grodno in 1706 demonstrates. After Poltava, he was able to build on the formidable foundations he had laid. By Peter's death the regular army was 130,000 strong; with the large numbers of Cossacks and other irregulars Russia could put in the field, it substantially outnumbered anything its neighbours could raise. Russia's position was secure: like Sweden, its noble-service elite was firmly based; unlike Sweden, its further development could be based once more on an expansive and aggressive foreign policy. War offered opportunities for the Russian service elite, not danger.

Yet the idea that Russia's vast human and natural resources ensured that the outcome of the Northern Wars was inevitable should be resisted. For the key to Russia's triumph was the defeat of Poland-Lithuania, the one major combatant in the Northern Wars which did not experience a military revolution. It is important to consider the reasons for this failure, for it casts light on the processes by which the new military system and the new military culture emerged in early modern Europe, and the barriers which had to be overcome before a revolutionary transformation could take place. Moreover, the trajectory of miliary development in Poland-Lithuania underlines the fact that it is futile to apply one simple model of 'state-building' to the complex process by which modern military establishments emerged. The experience of each state was radically different, even where such processes were successful, as the cases of Denmark, Sweden and Russia demonstrate. The Commonwealth's fate suggests that extensive military change was not in itself sufficient to secure the new relationship between the army, the state and society which determined the contours of the new military world.

For the Commonwealth experienced all the forces which elsewhere produced the Military Revolution; moreover, down to the 1650s and even beyond, significant military reforms were undertaken which could have produced in the long run the sort of transformation seen elsewhere. The Commonwealth's elites were fully conversant with developments elsewhere in Europe, more so than their Muscovite counterparts, for whom the Commonwealth was long a conduit of western military ideas. Until 1648, Poland-Lithuania enjoyed substantial military success, and seemed perfectly capable of defending itself against threats in both north and south. In its numerous petty and middling nobility it possessed in abundance that class which both respected soldiering as one of the few professions fit for noblemen, and which elsewhere was to benefit so greatly from the opportunities afforded by the growth of standing armies after 1648; indeed, as the Commonwealth's armies atrophied in the eighteenth century, many members of the *szlachta* were to take service in the armies of foreign powers.

Poland-Lithuania's failure to develop a powerful army and a powerful state structure is usually seen as a failure to engage with the forces of modernisation, and the price that it paid at the end of the eighteenth century is presented as the result of backwardness. It is easy to look at the chaotic politics of the eighteenth-century Commonwealth and compare them with those of the well-ordered police states which partitioned it, but the sight of twentieth-century historians working in comfortable modern democracies lauding the 'modernisation' of Frederick II's Prussia or Petrine Russia and contrasting them with the Commonwealth's supposed backwardness is ironic. For in many respects the central problem which the Commonwealth failed to solve was peculiarly modern: how to reconcile the protection of the state with the preservation of the liberties of the citizen. The Commonwealth's political theorists, in particular Andrzej Maksymilian Fredro, were well aware of the requirements of modern warfare, but they also lived in a Europe where the dangers of placing military power in the hands of the monarch seemed all too clear: a host of contemporary examples, from the crushing of the liberties of the Habsburg patrimonial lands in the 1620s to the vindictive military browbeating of the Ducal Prussian estates by the 'Great' Elector in the 1660s, within a decade of their losing the Commonwealth's protection, and the introduction of absolutism in Denmark and Sweden.

The Commonwealth is by no means the only consensually-based political system to fail to solve this problem in modern times. Throughout the Vasa period, royal control of the army was one of the most burning political issues, and the political struggles of the Vasa monarchs with the hetmans were fierce – in particular those of Sigismund with Jan Zamoyski and Krzysztof II Radziwiłł, and John Casimir with Janusz Radziwiłł and Jerzy Sebastian Lubomirski. Moreover, at two points during the period, the fears seemed entirely justified. John Casimir's attempt to build up his control of the foreign contingent in the 1650s and 1660s, and his attempt to win the army's support for the campaign for an election *vivente rege* after its rejection by the *Sejm* in 1661–2, which led ultimately to civil war, gave due warning of the dangers. Half a century later, Augustus II's control of the Saxon army and his clear intention to strengthen royal power brought a new threat.

The Commonwealth's response was to attempt to restrict royal control of the army – which led to the increasingly irresponsible and unhampered control of the hetmans – and to pursue a pacific foreign policy. If Poland-Lithuania had been an expansive and aggressive power in the sixteenth century, with the *Sejm* approving campaigns in Livonia and against Muscovy, the Vasa obsession with recovering the Swedish crown began a process in which the *szlachta* became increasingly reluctant to sanction aggressive war, especially after Władysław IV's abortive plans for a Turkish war in the 1640s, which involved him in talks with the Zaporozhian Cossacks whose political undercurrents were deeply suspect. The *szlachta* would defend the Commonwealth; they would not attack their neighbours. Despite the considerable royalist sentiment within the army, the continuing importance of the national contingent, based upon the *towarzysz* system, ensured that there was no equivalent of the loyal officer corps which had such a stake in the successful military revolutions in Sweden, Denmark and Russia. Forced to choose in the 1660s, most of the army asserted its identity as citizens, rather than soldiers.

In the new military world such sentiments were dangerous. Until 1648, it seemed that the Commonwealth could deal with external threats; thereafter the consequences of pacifism became clear. Already in the early seventeenth century, the problems of unpaid units of soldiers wandering the Commonwealth and living off what amounted to banditry was a problem. Groups like the Lisowczyks, who terrorised much of southern Małopolska after returning from Muscovy in 1617 and before entering Imperial service in 1619, were the inevitable result of the Commonwealth's refusal to support large-scale permanent forces, and were a perennial source of complaints in the *Sejm*. Most of these *kupy swawolne* (licentious bands) as they were known, were composed of impoverished nobles, precisely the social groups which elsewhere were recruited in ever larger numbers into the new military states. Whereas in Muscovy such bands were crushed or reintegrated into the service state after 1613, in the Commonwealth they were never satisfactorily dealt with. In the Ukraine, where they were increasingly excluded not just from military service, but from the noble status which might have reconciled them to the Commonwealth's rule, these groups proved highly dangerous. Deprived by the pacifism of the *Sejm* of the service which war would have brought and faced with the threat of social degradation, thousands joined the Zaporozhians, who began their revolt in the immediate aftermath of the definitive rejection of Władysław IV's Turkish war plans. Where the Commonwealth had dealt relatively effectively with external invasion before 1648, it failed utterly to crush internal revolt, which devastated wide areas of its territory, deprived it of much of its army and provoked foreign intervention.

This was the crucial turning-point. Between 1562 and 1648, the Commonwealth had been at war for some 34 out of 86 years, but war had been fought for much of that time abroad. Between 1648 and 1721, it was at war for some 67 out of 73 years, for over half the time on its own territory. This must be taken into account when its supposedly lamentable military performance is discussed. No contemporary European power fought for so long or so intensively on its own territory, or suffered such repeated devastation by the armies of both friend and foe. The demographic and economic consequences were catastrophic. The number of families living on royal estates in Wielkopolska dropped on average by 48.9 per cent between the audits of 1616 and 1661; in the palatinate of Kalisz, the figure was 60.1 per cent. In the Gniezno district, 69 per cent of land belonging to *szlachta* villages was abandoned in 1658–9; the figure for Church villages was 72 per cent and for royal villages 83 per cent. Although agricultural decline had set in before the war, most of the damage was war-related.[32] The population of Mazovia dropped 43 per cent, with the urban population dropping 70 per cent.[33] Unlike the Empire during the Thirty Years War, few regions escaped destruction, with Lithuania and the Ukraine suffering particularly badly: Lithuania's population fell from 3,800,000 in 1648 to 1,994,000, a drop of 48 per cent.[34] Moreover, although the burden of war lifted significantly after 1667, the long years of the Turkish war, during which frequent Tatar raids devastated southern areas of the Commonwealth, meant that military expenditure remained high, in a period when the Polish currency all but collapsed after the ill-advised reforms of the 1660s. Thus there was little chance of recovery before the Commonwealth became the main battleground in the Great Northern War between 1702 and 1709. Even when the fighting moved elsewhere after Poltava, the continuation of the civil war and the frequent presence of foreign troops in the Commonwealth ensured that contributions remained high.

The Commonwealth, in the circumstances, did remarkably well during the 1650s and 1660s to raise and maintain an army which was capable by 1659 of matching the Swedes and defeating the Muscovites. Yet a professional army cost money; given the levels of destruction experienced, taxes were increasingly difficult to raise and increasingly resisted by local *sejmiki* trying to protect their devastated communities from further exactions, especially as the unpaid army increasingly had to support itself through contributions or simple appropriation of the necessary resources. Thus resistance to more taxation and further military expenditure by *sejmiki* was not entirely due to suspicion about royal intentions, but reflected the genuine concern of locally-based politicians to protect their local area from further exactions. It was increasingly difficult to raise units of professional, trained infantry, while the quality of the cavalry suffered, as increasing numbers of nobles were not in a position to afford the costly equipment and high-quality mounts which had played an important part in its success before 1648. Moreover, the problem of *kupy swawolne* grew to hitherto unprecedented levels after 1648 as the state's ability to pay its soldiers declined drastically, and exactions by ill-disciplined units grew all too common, poisoning relations between noble society and its own army. Local court records abound with complaints by local inhabitants of illegal exactions by Commonwealth troops, and by military commanders of the refusal of billets or payment of contributions which were perfectly legal. Ironically, the increasingly well-disciplined armies of foreign invaders were by the Great Northern War often less arbitrary and destructive in their demands than Polish-Lithuanian troops.

If after 1656 the *szlachta* had rallied remarkably well to expel the invaders, it was a different story after 1700. Economic recovery from the mid-century wars had been slow, and had been undermined by the rapid inflation which resulted from John Casimir's unfortunate currency reforms of the 1660s. Augustus had launched his attack on Livonia despite the Commonwealth's clear desire for peace after the end of the long Turkish war, and although he did secure the support of the majority of the political nation after Charles's invasion, he was opposed by a substantial minority, and the resultant civil war destroyed all hope of a military revival. Although the Lublin *Sejm* in 1703 agreed a regular army of 48,000, the agreed quotas of infantry were impossible to raise, and the Commonwealth's forces could play no decisive role in the outcome of the war, although the defeat of Leszczyński's attempt to break through to support Charles in the Ukraine in 1709 by the Sandomierz confederates played an important part in Charles's ultimate defeat. Augustus's failure to win over many of Leszczyński's supporters after his return, and his clear intention of mounting a coup d'état with the help of Saxon troops, only provoked the 1715 Confederation of Tarnogród which successfully blocked his plans. His further participation in the war was based entirely on the Saxon army, which was not powerful enough for him to exert any influence on the course of events, especially once he had fallen out with Peter, and he was increasingly disregarded. The insignificance of the Commonwealth – and of Saxony – was made blatantly clear between 1719 and 1721, when they were completely ignored in the peace negotiations: Saxony only formally made peace with Sweden in 1728; the Commonwealth had to wait until 1732.

Yet the picture was not one of unrelieved blackness. If the enormous burden of war fought at home had shattered the Commonwealth as a major military power, changes had been made which, in different circumstances, might well have enabled it to develop in a more positive direction. The institutionalisation of the foreign contingent by Władysław IV and the introduction of the *komputowe* army in 1652 were sensible reforms which could have provided a basis for further development. Moreover, the reduction of the Commonwealth's politics to an oversimplified picture of a struggle between royal absolutism and *szlachta* licence underestimates the extent to which both monarchs and reformers took account of the nature of the Commonwealth's political system in promoting reform. The delegation of power to the *sejmiki* to organise the army in 1652 is frequently condemned as stimulating the decentralisation of the political system which is seen as fatal to the Commonwealth's chances of survival, but it at least recognised the nature of its political system and sought to avoid the endless disputes over the dangers of allowing the king too much control; indeed it was John Casimir who first proposed in 1652 that the *sejmiki* should take on responsibility for fortifying one major town in their district or palatinate. During the wars of the mid-seventeenth century, *sejmiki* did do much to raise and pay units, although this is an area which requires much more research before firm judgments can be made. It is worth noting, however, that Fredro's intelligent proposals for military reform were based on his experiences in organising defence in the palatinate of Ruthenia during the 1650s. Finally, although the military reforms secured in the peace agreement between Augustus II and the Tarnogród Confederation in 1716, and enshrined in the decisions of the 'Silent *Sejm*' of 1717 are often ridiculed for only establishing an army of 24,000 men, they at last supplied the army with a guaranteed income, funded from permanent taxation. At last a basis for a standing army had been established, even if it was too small to count in European politics.

It was certainly not allowed to grow by its neighbours, who took care after 1717 that the new system of power in northeastern Europe should not be disturbed. After Augustus signed the 1719 treaty of Vienna with Emperor Charles VI, Peter organised a system directed against all thoughts of reform in the Commonwealth. In 1719 he signed the treaty of Potsdam with Frederick William I of Prussia, in which both rulers agreed to block any political change in Poland-Lithuania. Similar treaties were signed with Sweden in 1724 and Austria in 1726. All the Commonwealth's neighbours had an interest in preventing a military revolution in Poland-Lithuania, and continued to use every method they could to persuade the Poles that the greatest threat to their liberties came from within, not without. Throughout the eighteenth century, Russia and Prussia, aware of the extent to which their international position depended on Polish weakness, cynically used every method at their disposal to corrupt the Commonwealth's political life. At the end of the century, when wide-ranging reform, including the increase of the army to 100,000 was agreed by the Four Year *Sejm* (1788–92), the Commonwealth's neighbours acted quickly to destroy it. The Russian and Prussian empires were built on the ruins of the Commonwealth, which paid dearly for drawing back from its Military Revolution.

Notes

1   'Kurtz Nachricht wegen belegerung der Stadt Dorpat und denen übergabe' Dorpater Magistrat, Protokollen, 1704; ESAT, Fond 995, Nimistu 1, 287, ff. 163–74.; F. Bienemann *Die Katastrophe der Stadt Dorpat während des Nordischen Krieges* (Reval, 1902) pp. 8, 15–16.

2   S. Hartmann *Reval im Nordischen Krieg* (Bonn, 1973) pp. 84–5.

3   Piotrowski to Andrzej Opaliński, 23.II.1582, *Sprawy wojenne* pp. 33–5.

4   Bienemann, *Die Katastrophe* pp. 11, 17–18, 22–3.

5   Ibid. I pp. 109–13; Dorpater Magistrat, Protokollen, 1707–8; ESAT, Fond 995, Nimistu 1, 290 ff. 91v–96v.

6   Bienemann, *Die Katastrophe* pp. 122–6; 146, 168–76; 181–93.

7   Roberts, 'Military Revolution' pp. 217–18.

8   Lyth, *Dagbok* pp. 81–2. Peter's treatment of Catholics and especially Uniates was less magnanimous.

9   H. Saarinen, *Bürgerstadt und absoluter Kriegsherr. Danzig und Karl XII. im Nordische Krieg* (Helsinki, 1996) pp. 17, 59–62, 137, 150, 324.

10 E. Gierlich, *Reval 1621 bis 1645* (Bonn, 1991) pp. 87, 263–70; A. Weinmann, *Reval 1646 bis 1672* (Bonn, 1991) pp. 50–8; Hartmann *Reval* pp. 2–3, 26–31.

11   See C. Storrs and H.M. Scott, 'The Military Revolution and the European Nobility, c. 1600–1800' *WH* 3 (1996) pp. 1–41.

12   Piotrowski, *Dziennik* pp. 22–3.

13   Murdoch, 'Scotland' p. 232; Monro, *His expedition* II p. 213.

14   D. Parrott, 'The Administration of the French Army during the Ministry of Cardinal Richelieu' unpublished Ph.D. thesis, Oxford University, 1985, p. i.

15   J. Black, *A Military Revolution?* (London, 1991) p. ix; J.R. Hale, *War and Society in Renaissance Europe, 1450–1620* (London, 1985) p. 201; M. Anderson, *War and Society in Europe of the Old Regime, 1620–1789* (London, 1988) pp. 28, 100.

16   Krigsarkivet, Stockholm, Stora Nordiska Kriget, Avdelning 2 Huvudarmén vol. 22: Rechnung von die Backerey vor Thorn waß einigekomen und außgeliefert ist worden Ae. 1703 d. 9 Juny.

17   There were bursts of activity in 1558–61; 1570–1; 1575; 1577–8; 1632–4; 1654–6; 1687–9.

18   TCA, B.e Kriegswesen 14. Suppliken der bei den neuen Fortifikationsbauten geschädigten Besitzer 1642–1703, ff. 124–5. It was different for the burghers of Thorn, who sent a delegation to Stockholm as late as 1700 in the vain hope of persuading the Swedish government to settle its debts from 1658: J. Buława, 'Toruń w okresie potopu szwedzkiego w latach 1655–1660' Unpublished MA dissertation, Nicholas Copernicus University, Toruń (1957–8) p. 67.

19   L. Gustafsson, *Virtus politica. Politisk etik och nationellt svärmeri i den tidigare Stormaktstidens litteratur* (Uppsala, 1956) pp. 90–1.

20   K. Johanesson, 'Gustav II Adolf som retoriker' in *Gustav II Adolf – 350 år efter Lützen* (Stockholm, 1982) pp. 19, 23–4.

21   Ringmar, *Identity* pp. 88–9.

22   Quoted by Englund, *Ofredsår* p. 73. A. Norberg, *Polen i svensk politik 1617–26* (Stockholm, 1974) p. 135.

23   A. Günther, 'Das schwedische Heer in Sachsen 1706–1707' *NASGA* 25 (1904) pp. 256–60.

24   R. Persson *Rustningar i Sverige under det Stora Nordiska Kriget* (Lund, 1975) pp. 58–64.

25   Å. Karlsson, *Den jämlike undersåten* (Uppsala, 1994).

26   V. Ahonen, 'Städernas återhämtning i Finland efter stora ofredan' *HTS* (1989) p. 162.

27   J. Cavallie, *De höga officerarna. Studier i den svenska militära hierarkien under 1600-talets senare del* Militärhistoriska Studier IV (Lund, 1981) pp. 14–15, 25; Asker, *Officerarna* p. 53.

28   Englund, *Poltava* p. 128; *Landshöfdingen Friherre Gabriel Kurcks lefnadsminnen upptecknade af honom själf* R. Hausen (ed.) (Helsingfors, 1906) pp. 34, 87–9.

29   K.-R. Böhme 'Officersrekryteringen vid tre landskapsregementen 1626–1682' in M. Revera and R. Torstendahl (eds), *Bördor, bönder, börd i 1600-talets Sverige* (Motala, 1979) pp. 233, 236.

30   G. Artéus, U. Olsson and K. Strömberg-Back 'The influence of the armed forces on the transformations of society in Sweden, 1600–1945' *MT* 185 (Bihäfte) (1981) p. 136.

31 For the debate on the extent to which eighteenth-century Swedish society was militarised see G. Artéus, *Krigsmakt och samhälle i frihetstidens Sverige* (Stockholm, 1982), B. Asker, 'Militärstat eller militariserat samhälle. Synpunkter på det karolinska Sverige med anledning av en aktuel debatt' *HTS* (1987) and 'Åter om det karolinska samhällets "militarisering".' *HTS* (1988) pp. 70–4.

32 W. Rusiński, 'Straty i zniszczenia w czasie wojny szwedzkie (1655–1660) oraz jej skutki na obszarze Wielkoposki' *PODWP* II pp. 276, 293.

33 I. Gieysztorowa, 'Zniszczenia i straty wojenne oraz ich skutki na Mazowszu' *PODWP* II p. 326.

34 J. Morzy, *Kryzys demograficzny na Litwie i Białorusi w drugiej połowie XVII wieku* (Poznań, 1965) tables 17, 20, pp. 134–47.

CHRONOLOGY

During the period covered by this book, four different calendars were in operation: the Gregorian Calendar (New Style) was used by all Catholic powers after 1582 (and Saxony, reluctantly, from 1697); Protestant Europe used the Julian Calendar (Old Style), ten days behind until 1700; thereafter eleven days behind. The Russians only adopted the Julian Calendar in 1700; previously they had dated their calendar from the creation of the world, not the birth of Christ. Between 1700, when the Swedes decided that the Catholics had a point, even if they could not admit they were right, and 1712, when they tired of the complications and reverted to Old Style, Sweden followed Swedish Style, which was ten days behind New Style, but one day ahead of Old Style. Thus the battle of Poltava has three different dates: 27 June Old Style, 28 June Swedish Style and 8 July New Style 1709. Since contemporaries were often careless about dates themselves, and historians usually follow their own national tradition, many inconsistencies of dating have entered the literature. I have tried to ensure that all dates given are New Style unless otherwise indicated. Where I have made mistakes, I hope readers will forgive me.

1554–7	**Swedish/Muscovite War**
14.IX.1557	Treaty of Pozwol between Poland-Lithuania and the Livonian Order (ratification of agreement negotiated in August)
1558–83	**First Northern War**
I.1558	Muscovite invasion of Livonia
2.VIII.1560	Battle of Ermes
28.XI.1561	Secularisation of the Livonian Order; Gotthard Kettler becomes first duke of Courland as a Polish-Lithuanian vassal
15.II.1563	Muscovites take Połock
VIII.1570–III.1571	Siege of Reval by Muscovite force, led by duke Magnus of Holstein
I–III.1577	Siege of Reval

21/22.X.1577	Battle of Wenden: Muscovites defeated by joint Polish-Swedish force
30.VIII.1579	Stefan Batory captures Połock
15.IX.1580	Stefan Batory captures Velikie Luki
VIII.1581–I.1582	Siege of Pskov
15.I.1582	Peace of Iam Zapolskii: Muscovy cedes its Livonian conquests to Poland-Lithuania

1563–70   **The Nordic Seven Years War**

1563	Danes capture Älvsborg
9.XI.1564	Battle of Mared: Danes defeat Swedes
28.VIII.1565	Swedes capture Varberg
20.X.1565	Battle of Axtorna: Danes defeat Swedes
13.XII.1570	Peace of Stettin between Denmark, Sweden, Poland-Lithuania and Lübeck

1590–5   **Swedish–Muscovite War**

V.1595	Peace of Teusino: Sweden secures Ingria and Kexholm
1598	Civil war in Sweden; battles of Stegeborg and Stångebro (September)
1599	Sigismund Vasa deposed as king of Sweden

1600–29   **Polish-Swedish War**

1600	Swedes invade Livonia
27.IX.1605	Battle of Kircholm: Chodkiewicz defeats Charles IX
12.IX.1621	Riga surrenders to Gustav Adolf
21.IX–9.X.1621	Battle of Chocim: Polish defensive battle against Ottoman/Tatar army
1626	Gustav Adolf invades Royal Prussia
22.IX–1.X.1626	Battle of Mewe: Swedes defeat Poles
17–18.VIII.1627	Battle of Dirschau: Swedes defeat Poles
28.XI.1627	Battle of Oliva: small Polish fleet defeats Swedish fleet off Danzig
27.VI.1629	Battle of Honigfelde: Gustav Adolf defeated by Koniecpolski
26.XI.1629	Truce of Altmark (Poland-Lithuania and Sweden)
12.IX.1635	Truce of Stuhmsdorf. Polish-Swedish truce extended for twenty-five years

1611–13   **Kalmar War (Denmark and Sweden)**

1609–19   **Polish–Muscovite War**

1609–11	Polish siege of Smolensk
4.VII.1610	Battle of Klushino: Polish victory over Muscovite/Swedish army
1610–12	Polish garrison in Kremlin

II.1617	Peace of Stolbovo (Sweden and Muscovy). Sweden retains Ingria and Kexholm, but returns Novgorod
1618	Polish attack on Moscow, led by prince Władysław
I.1619	Truce of Deulino. Fourteen-and-a-half year truce between the Commonwealth and Muscovy. Muscovy cedes Smolensk, Seversk and Chernihiv
1632–4	**Smolensk War** (Poland-Lithuania and Muscovy)
1643–5	**'Torstensson's War' (Sweden and Denmark)**
VIII.1645	Peace of Brömsebro. Sweden gains from Denmark Jämtland, Härjedalen, Ösel and Gotland, and Halland for 30 years
1648	Start of Khmelnytsky's Revolt in the Ukraine
2–3.VI.1652	Battle of Batoh: Polish quarter army wiped out by Cossacks
I.1654	Treaty of Pereiaslav: Cossacks accept protection of tsar
1654–67	**The Thirteen Years War (Poland-Lithuania and Muscovy)**
1654–5	Muscovite invasions of Lithuania; much of Grand Duchy conquered
8.VIII.1655	Muscovites take Wilno
27.VI.1660	Battle of Połonka: Poles defeat Muscovites
2.XI.1660	Surrender of Sheremetev and Muscovite army at Chudnovo
30.I.1667	Truce of Andrusovo: Muscovites gain Kiev (formally for 2 years) and the Ukraine on the left bank of the Dnieper
1655–60	**The Second Northern War**
25.VII.1655	Surrender of Wielkopolska noble levy to Charles X at Ujście
17.VIII.1655	Treaty of Kiejdany: Janusz Radziwiłł surrenders to Sweden
X.1655	Surrender of Cracow to Swedes
XII.1655	Confederation of Tyszowce: formal resistance to Swedes begins
28–30.VII.1656	Battle of Warsaw: Swedish/Brandenburg army defeats Commonwealth forces
I.1657	Invasion of Poland by George II Rákóczi of Transylvania
27.V.1657	2nd treaty of Vienna: Austria agrees to send 12,000 troops to help the Commonwealth
VI.1657	Denmark declares war on Sweden

IX/XI.1657	Treaty of Wehlau-Bromberg: Frederick William of Brandenburg acquires full sovereignty over Ducal Prussia
II.1658	Charles X crosses the frozen Belts to attack Copenhagen
8.III.1658	Treaty of Roskilde: Denmark loses Scania, Bohuslän, Blekinge, Bornholm and Trondheim
VIII.1658	Charles X attacks Denmark
3.V.1660	Treaty of Oliva: peace between Poland-Lithuania, Austria, Brandenburg and Sweden
6.VI.1660	Treaty of Copenhagen: Sweden and Denmark make peace; Sweden returns Bornholm and Trondheim
1674–9	**Scanian War**
18/28.VI.1675	Battle of Fehrbellin: Brandenburg defeats Sweden
4/14.XII.1676	Battle of Lund: Swedes defeat Danes
V.1686	'Eternal Peace' signed between Poland-Lithuania and Russia. Russia keeps Kiev and the left-bank Ukraine
1700–21	**The Great Northern War**
7/18.VIII.1700	Peace of Travendal: Denmark makes peace with Sweden
19.XI.1700	Battle of Olkieniki: defeat of Sapiehas by Lithuanian *szlachta*
19/30.XI.1700	Battle of Narva: Russians defeated by Charles XII
19.VIII.1701	Swedes force their way across the Dvina into Courland
I.1702	Swedes invade Poland-Lithuania
19.VII.1702	Battle of Kliszów: Swedes defeat Saxon-Polish army
V.1703	Peter begins construction of St Petersburg
14.II.1704	Cardinal Michał Radziejowski declares an Interregnum in the Commonwealth
27.V.1704	Sandomierz Confederation declares war on Sweden
12.VII.1704	Election of Stanisław Leszczyński as king of Poland by Swedish supporters
13.II.1706	Battle of Fraustadt. Rehnskiöld defeats a Saxon-Russian army under Schulenburg
23.III.1706 (OS)	Ogilvy withdraws from Grodno
16.IX.1706	Charles XII invades Saxony
24.IX.1706	Treaty of Altranstädt: Augustus to abdicate Polish throne; Saxony to withdraw from war
X.1706	Battle of Kalisz: Saxon-Russian army under Augustus defeats Swedes

14.VII.1708	Battle of Hołowczyn. Swedish victory over Russians
28.IX/9.X.1708	Battle of Lesnaia: Lewenhaupt loses supply train
13.XI.1708	Menshikov sacks Mazepa's headquarters at Baturyn
21.XI.1708	Battle of Koniecpol: defeat for pro-Leszczyński forces prevents breakthrough into the Ukraine to aid Charles XII
27.VI.1709 (OS)	Battle of Poltava
30.VI.1709 (OS)	Swedish army surrenders at Perevolochna
XI.1709	Danes land in Scania
20.XII.1712	Battle of Gadebusch: Swedes defeat joint Danish-Saxon army
26.V.1713	Stenbock's army capitulates to Danes at Tønning
VIII.1714	Battle of Hangö: Swedish navy defeated by Russian fleet
V.1715	Prussia declares war on Sweden
5.I.1719	Treaty of Vienna: Charles VI, George I and Augustus II agree to relegate Russia to its previous borders
20.XI.1719 (NS)	Sweden and Hanover make peace: Hanover gains Bremen and Verden
1.II.1720 (NS)	Peace of Stockholm. Britain and Prussia sign peace with Sweden. Sweden retains Wismar, Stralsund and part of Pomerania; cedes rest of western Pomerania with Stettin to Prussia
14.VI.1720	Peace of Frederiksborg. Denmark abandons all conquests except Royal Holstein; Sweden retains Scandinavian provinces, loses immunity from Sound Dues
30.VIII.1721 (OS)	Peace of Nystad. Sweden cedes Estonia, Livonia, Ingria, Kexholm to Russia; Russia returns Finland, except for Viborg and part of Karelia

LIST OF RULERS

Denmark

Christian II	1513–23
Frederik I	1523–33
Christian III	1534–59
Frederik II	1559–88
Christian IV	1588–1648
Frederik III	1648–70
Christian V	1670–99
Frederik IV	1699–1730

Brandenburg-Prussia

George William	1619–40
Frederick William	1640–88
Frederick III (from 1701 Frederick I, king in Prussia)	1688–1713
Frederick William I	1713–40
Frederick II	1740–86

Sweden
House of Vasa

Gustav Vasa	1523–60
Erik XIV	1560–8
	(† 1577)
John III	1568–92
Sigismund	1592–99
	(† 1632)
Charles IX	1604–11
Gustav Adolf	1611–32
Christina	1632–54
	(† 1689)

House of Pfalz-Zweibrücken

Charles X Gustav	1654–60

Charles XI	1660–97
Charles XII	1697–1718
Ulrika Eleanora	1719–20
Frederick I	1720–51

Russia

Ivan IV	1533–84
Fedor I	1584–98
Boris Godunov	1598–1605
Vasilii Shuiskii	1606–10
Michael Romanov	1613–45
Alexis Mikhailovich	1645–76
Fedor II Alekseevich	1676–82
Ivan V	1682–96
Peter I	1682–1725

Poland-Lithuania
The Jagiellonian Dynasty

Alexander	1492/1501–6
Sigismund I 'the Old'	1506–48
Sigismund Augustus	1548–72

The Elective Monarchy

Henry of Valois	1573–4
	(† 1589)
Stefan Batory	1576–86
Sigismund III	1587–1632
Władysław IV	1632–48
John Casimir	1648–68
	(† 1672)
Michael Korybut Wiśniowiecki	1669–73
John III Sobieski	1674–96
Augustus II	1697–1732

GAZETTEER

The form used in the book is given in bold; the form in current use is given in italics. The names are arranged in alphabetical order of the form used in the book. BR = Belarus'ian; Ukr. = Ukrainian.

German/ English	Polish	Russian	Swedish/ Danish	Estonian/ Finnish	Lithuanian Latvian
			Åbo	*Turku* (F)	
Birsen	**Birże**	Birzhai			*Biržai* (Li)
	Brześć	**Brest**			
	Cecora	Tsetsora			
	Chocim	*Khotyn* (Ukr)			
	Cudnów	**Chudnovo**			
Danzig	*Gdańsk*				
Dirschau	*Tczew*				
Dorpat	Derpt/Dorpat/ Dorpt	Iur'ev		*Tartu*	
Düna (River)	Dwina	**Dvina**		Väina	Daugava (La)
Dünaburg	Dwińsk	Nevgin or Dvinsk' or Borisoglebsk (named by Alexis)			*Daugavpils* (La)
Dünamünde	Diament/ Dwinaujście				*Daugavgrīva* (La)
Elbing	Elbląg				
Erastfer		Erestfer		*Erastvere*	
Ermes				Härgmäe	Ērgeme (La)
Fellin		Fellin/Vil'iandi		*Viljandi*	
Fraustadt	*Wschowa*	Fraushtadt			
Gemauerthof	Murmiza	Mur-Miza*			
Gorzno	**Górzno**				
Graudenz	*Grudziądz*				
	Grodno	*Hrodna* (BR)			
Hammerstein	Ammersztyn/ Czarne				
		Gangut	**Hangö**	*Hankoniemi*	
			Helsingfors	*Helsinki* (F)	

German/ English	Polish	Russian	Swedish/ Danish	Estonian/ Finnish	Lithuanian Latvian
	Hołowczyn	Golovchin *Holovchin* (BR)			
Honigfelde	*Trzciana*				
Hummelshof		Gummel'sgof		*Hummuli*	
		Ivangorod		Jaanilinn	
	Kamieniec Poldolski	*Kam"ianets' Podil'skyi* (Ukr)			
Karkus				*Karksi*	
Kecksholm		Keksgol'm	**Kexholm**	Käkisalmi (F)	
	Kiejdany				
Kokenhausen		Kukeinos Kokengauzen	Kokenhusen		*Kĕdainiaï* (Li) *Koknese* (La)
Königsberg	Królewiec	*Kaliningrad* (Since 1945)			
Koporje		**Kopor'e**		Kaprio	
Lais		Laiuze/Laius'		*Laiuse*	
Lemburg	**Lwów**	L'vov *Lv'iv* (Ukr)			
Marienburg	*Malbork*				
Marienwerder	*Kwidzyń*				
Masovien **Mazovia** (Eng)	*Mazowsze*				
Memel	Kłajpeda				*Klaipēda* (Li)
Mewe	*Gniew*				
Mitau	**Mitawa**				Jelgava (La)
	Mohylew	*Mahiloŭ* (BR)			
	Mścisław	*Mstislaŭ* (BR)			
Narva		Rugodiv/Narva			
Memel (River)	**Niemen**				Nemunas (Li)
Nöteburg		Oreshek/ Schlusselburg/ Petrokrepost'	Nöteborg	Pähkinälinna	
Neustad			**Nystad**	Uuisikaupunki (F)	
	Nowy Bychów	**Novy Bykhov**			
Nyenschanz			Nyenskans	Nevanlinna	
Oberpahlen		Polchev		*Põltsamaa*	
Obertyn	Kołomija				
Oppeln	*Opole*				
	Orsza	*Orsha* (BR)			
Ösel			Ösel	*Saaremaa*	
Peipus (lake)		*Chudskoe Ozero*			
Pernau	Parnawa	Pernov		Pärnu	Pērnava (La) Piarnu (Li)
Pleskau	Psków	**Pskov**		Pihkva	Pleskava (La) Pskovas (Li)

German/ English	Polish	Russian	Swedish/ Danish	Estonian/ Finnish	Lithuanian Latvian
Podolia (E)	Podole	*Podilia* (Ukr)			
Polangen	**Połęga**				*Palanga* (Li)
	Połock	*Polatsk* (BR)			
Punitz	*Poniec*				
Reval	Rewal	Kolyvan'/Revel'		*Tallinn*	
Rinsk	*Ryńsk*				
Schemaiten	Żmudż				*Žemaitija* (Li)
Samogitia (Eng)					
Serica		**Seritsa**			
Smolina		**Smolino**			
Stettin	Szczecin				
Strasburg	*Brodnica*				
Tannenberg	**Grunwald**				
Thorn	*Toruń*				
Traken	**Troki**				*Trakai* (Li)
Viborg			**Viborg**	Viipuri	
Vistula (E)	*Wisła*				
Weichsel					
Volhynia (E)	Wołyń	Volyń (Ukr)			
Walk				*Valga*	
Wallhof	*Walmojza*				
Ermland	**Warmia**				
Wenden		Kes'		Cēsis	*Võnnu* (La)
	Werki				*Verkiai* (Li)
Wesenberg		Vesenberg/ Rakobor/ Rakvere		*Rakvere*	
Wiek				*Läänemaa*	
Wierland				*Virumaa*	
	Wilno	Vil'na			*Vilnius* (Li)
	Witebsk	*Vitsebsk* (BR)			
Wolmar		Volodimirets		Volmari	*Valmiera* (Li)
Wormditt	*Orneta*				

* The Swedes and the Russians chose different names for the same battle, from two different places.

Adelsvælden (Danish)	'Noble Rule'; the system of noble power in Denmark before 1660.
Autorament Narodowy; *Autorament Cudzoziemski* (Polish)	See 'Foreign Contingent'.
Bellum se ipse alet (Latin)	'Let war pay for itself'; the idea that armies could sustain themselves in time of war.
Beställning (Swedish; pl. *beställningarna*)	In Sweden, the grant of revenues from a crown farm for a specified service, military or administrative. Unlike a *förläning*, a *beställning* was a contractual relationship, often for a set period, and the revenues might vary from year to year.
Bondetal (Swedish)	From 'Bonde' (peasant): the calculation of conscription levies by head, rather than by homestead (*gårdetal*).
Boyar (1) (Russian)	A member of the elite group at the top of the Muscovite hierarchy of status; a member of the Boyar Duma. See 'Boyar' (2).
Boyar (2) (Ruthenian)	In Lithuania, unlike Muscovy, a boyar was a petty servitor of uncertain status. See 'Boyar' (1).
Deti Boiarskie (Russian) (singular: *syn boiarskii*)	Members of the lowest level of hereditary servitors in Muscovite Russia (literally 'sons of the boyars').
Dominium Maris Baltici (Latin)	'Control of the Baltic Sea'. A claim, originally made by the Danish monarchy as a justification for levying the Sound Dues, it is used by historians in a looser sense to mean the hegemony of one power within the Baltic.
Dvorianstvo (Russian)	The middling ranks of the hereditary servitor class in Muscovy.
Execution Movement	The Movement for the Execution of the Laws was a political alliance of the Polish *szlachta* in the 1560s aimed against magnate domination.

One of its main aims was to execute laws banning the alienation of royal estates.

Förläning (Swedish; plural *förläningarna*)   In Sweden, the assignation of a crown farm to an individual to provide the revenues for a state servant.

Foreign Contingent   From the early 1630s, the Commonwealth's armies were divided into the National Contingent (*autorament narodowy*) and the Foreign Contingent (*autorament cudzoziemski*). The former was organised on the *towarzysz* system (q.v.); the latter was organised and fought on western lines, although it was recruited overwhelmingly within the Commonwealth.

Frihetsmil (Swedish)   The privilege by which Swedish nobles were exempt from state dues within a mile of their manor. Since a Swedish mile measured 10 kilometres, this was worth more than it might at first seem. The government fought to uphold the legal principle that each nobleman was allowed only one manor.

Gårdetal (Swedish)   The calculation of conscription levies by homestead, instead of by head (*bondetal*).

Henrician Articles   The conditions sworn by Henry of Valois in 1573 before his coronation, and by all subsequent Polish-Lithuanian kings, in addition to individual election agreements (see *Pacta Conventa*)

Hetman (Polish)   The Commonwealth's forces were commanded by the hetmans. Poland and Lithuania each had a Grand Hetman and a Field Hetman. The former was nominally superior, but Field Hetmans often operated entirely independently. The office was held for life and had wide powers.

Indelning (*Indelningsverk*) (Swedish)   Allotment. The system by which soldiers were assigned to individual farms which would support them. Officers were assigned farms on which they were the tenants and lived in peacetime; soldiers were assigned to peasant farms on which they lived and worked in peacetime. A broadly comparable system of *inddelning* operated in Denmark.

Komput (Polish)   État. From the establishment of the *komputowe* army in 1652, the *Sejm* set the size of the

340

Commonwealth's army; the system replaced the previous arrangements based on the permanent quarter army, supplemented in time of need.

Kwarta (Polish) Literally 'quarter'. A quarter (in fact a fifth net) of the revenue from royal estates in Poland from the 1560s for the upkeep of the quarter army (*wojsko kwarciane*, q.v.).

Łan (Polish) A measurement of land. Two different types existed: the Chełmno *łan* (16–17.5 hectares) and the Franconian *łan* (22.6–25.36 hectares).

Łanowa infantry (*piechota łanowa*) (Polish) Infantry raised from 1652 to replace the *wybraniecka* infantry (q.v.). It was originally to be raised at the rate of one man from every fifteen *łan* and one from every twenty households in large towns, thirty-five in smaller towns and fifty in the smallest towns. It applied to church and noble lands as well as royal lands.

Liberum Veto (Latin) 'Free Veto'. First accepted as valid in 1652, the *liberum veto* was the logical extension of the principle of consensus by which the Polish-Lithuanian *Sejm* operated. In practice it meant that one envoy could block the proceedings and break the *Sejm* before it was formally concluded.

Lisowczyks (Polish *Lisowczycy*) Units of Polish cavalry named after Aleksander Lisowski (†1617), formed during the Time of Troubles, which subsequently fought in the Thirty Years War.

Mestnichestvo (Russian) The Muscovite system of place abolished in 1682.

Obrona potoczna (Polish) 'General Defence'; the small force set up in the early sixteenth century to provide permanent defence against Tatar attack; from 1566 known as the *wojsko kwarciane* (quarter army).

Oprichnina (Russian) Literally 'government apart'. In 1565, Ivan IV divided Muscovy into two parts, the *Oprichnina*, which he ruled, and the *Zemshchina* (the Land). Each had its own administration and army. The *Oprichnina* was liquidated in 1572, and the term is used more widely to refer to the period of terror which its establishment initiated.

Pacta Conventa (Latin) Individual election charters drawn up for every Polish-Lithuanian monarch in addition to the Henrician Articles (q.v.).

Pancerna cavalry (Polish, *jazda pancerna*)	Medium cavalry, armed with a sabre, a bow and a short spear. Until 1648 this form of cavalry was known as cossack cavalry (*jazda kozacka*).
Piechota Wybraniecka (*Wybrańcy*) (Polish)	'The chosen infantry'; created by Stefan Batory; one infantryman was raised from every ten peasants on royal estates.
Pomest'e (Russian) (plural *pomest'ia*)	In Muscovy, conditional grant of land received from the tsar in return for lifelong military service, held by a *pomeshchik* (military servitor).
Pospolite ruszenie (Polish)	The general levy of all the *szlachta* called out by the king or the *Sejm* to defend the state. *Sejmiki* also called out the levy on a local basis. It survived more as a political than a military phenomenon.
Prikaz (Russian)	Chancery: the main administrative organ of the Muscovite state.
Quarter Army	See *wojsko kwarciane*.
Reduktion (Swedish)	The resumption of royal estates alienated illegally according to Magnus Eriksson's Land Law and the resolutions of the Nörrköping *Riksdag* of 1604. There was a partial *reduktion* in 1655 and a comprehensive one in the 1680s.
Riddarhus (Swedish)	(Literally the House of the Knights). Gustav Adolf's Riddarhus Ordinance of 1626 marked the full establishment of the Swedish nobility as a corporate estate, divided into three classes.
Rigsdag (Danish)	Meetings of the Danish Estates took place much less frequently in Denmark than in Sweden. Although the peasants were recognised as a separate estate, they ceased to be summoned to meetings of the *Rigsdag* after the reign of Frederik II.
Riksdag (Swedish)	The Swedish *Riksdag* was composed of four estates: the clergy, the nobility, the burghers and the peasants.
Rokosz (Polish)	A rebellion, claimed by those who launched it to be legal, since it was in defence of the constitution.
Rostjeneste (Danish) *Rusttjänst* (Swedish)	The obligation by Danish and Swedish nobles to provide cavalry service in respect of their privileged status.

Rusthåll (Swedish)	Under the *indelning* (allotment) system from the 1620s, one or more prosperous farms which individually or collectively supported one or more cavalrymen in return for tax-exemptions.
Sejm (Polish)	The Commonwealth's Diet, composed of two chambers, the Senate and the Chamber of Envoys.
Sejmik (Polish) (plural *sejmiki*)	The provincial assemblies in Poland-Lithuania which sent envoys to the *Sejm*, scrutinised *Sejm* legislation and carried out an increasing number of administrative and fiscal tasks.
Sich (Ukrainian)	The island headquarters of the Zaporozhian Cossacks, below the rapids (*za porohe*) on the Dnieper to the south of Kiev.
Sound Dues	The tolls levied by the Danish monarchy until 1857 on vessels passing the Sound, the narrow strip of water between the Scandinavian peninsula and Denmark.
Smuta (Russian)	(literally 'trouble'). The Russian name for the Time of Troubles in Muscovy in the early seventeenth century.
Spanish riders	Sharpened stakes dug into the ground in front of infantry formations to impede attackers.
Starosty (Polish *starostwo*)	A *starosta* (literally 'elder') was originally a royal official, who presided over courts at the local level, for which he received reward in the shape of the assignation of a lease on a royal estate. With time, the term 'starosty' came to be applied to royal estates leased to individuals on a wide variety of terms. The distinction continued to be drawn between 'judicial starosties' whose holders had functions to perform, and 'non-judicial starosties'.
Stormaktstid (Swedish)	Sweden's 'Age of Greatness' (literally 'Great Power Period'); usually dated by Swedish historians 1621–1721. It was followed the *Frihetstid* (Age of Liberty) (1721–72).
Strel'tsy (Russian)	The musketeer corps established by the 1550s military reforms, composed of non-hereditary servitors.
Swinesfeathers	The Swedish version of Spanish riders (q.v.).
Szlachta	The Polish-Lithuanian nobility.

Towarzysz (Polish; plural: *towarzysze*)	Literally 'comrade'; soldier in Polish units of the national contingent; served with a retinue (*poczet*) of two to six troopers.
Ulozhenie (Russian)	Muscovite statute of 1649, which completed the legal framework for serfdom.
Uppbåd (Swedish) *Opbud* (Danish)	The right of Swedish and Danish monarchs to call up their subjects to defend the realm against attack (usually one man in every five).
Utskrivning (Swedish)	The conscription system by which peasants were recruited into the Swedish army (literally 'Registration'); the Danish equivalent was *uddskrivning*.
Vivente rege (Latin)	'In the king's lifetime'. In elective monarchies such as Denmark-Norway or Poland-Lithuania, the succession could be decided *vivente rege*, as it was in the former, or after the king's death, as it was in the latter.
Votchina (Russian)	Hereditary, allodial land, as opposed to *pomest'e* (q.v.).
Włoka (Polish)	A Lithuanian unit of land-measurement, equivalent to 21.3 hectares.
Wojsko kwarciane (Polish)	The quarter army, as the *obrona potoczna* (q.v.) was known from the 1560s; so called because it was maintained by a quarter of the revenues from royal estates.
Wybraniecka infantry (Polish)	Established under Stefan Batory in 1578: one well-clad infantryman equipped with musket, sabre and axe to be supplied by every twenty households in royal towns and villages. The chosen infantryman (*wybraniec*) was freed from all labour service owed to the *starosta* or leaseholder.
Zemshchina (Russian)	See *Oprichnina*.
Zemskii Sobor (Russian)	Assembly of the Land. A periodic assembly of representatives of various groups within Muscovite society in the sixteenth and seventeenth centuries.

BIBLIOGRAPHY

Given the paucity of English-language material on the Northern Wars, there is no bibliographical essay in this volume in the series. This bibliography is by no means an exhaustive guide to the topic, but includes full bibliographical details of the works cited in the footnotes and others that I found particularly helpful.

Primary

Adlerfelt, G. *The Military History of Charles XII* 3 vols (London, 1740).

Akty otnosiashiesia k Istorii Iuzhnoi i Zapadnoi Rossii XIV (St Petersburg, 1863).

Ayrmann, H.M. *Hans Moritz Ayrmanns Reisen durch Livland und Russland in den Jahren 1666–1670* K. Schreinert (ed.) (Tartu, 1937).

Bienemann, F. jr (ed.) 'Briefe und Aktenstücke zur Geschichte der Verteidigung und Kapitulation Dorpats 1656' *Mittheilungen aus dem Gebiete der Geschichte Liv-, Est- und Kurland* 16 (1896).

Bienemann, F. jr *Die Katastrophe der Stadt Dorpat während des Nordischen Krieges nebst zeitgenössischen Aufzeichnungen* Bibliothek Livländischer Geschichte III (Reval, 1902).

'Bref från Konung Carl X till Presidenten Biörenklou' *Historiska Samlingar* V (Stockholm, 1822).

Charles XII, *Konung Karl XII:s egenhändiga bref* E. Carlson (ed.) (Stockholm, 1893).

Christian IV, *Kong Christian den Fjerdes egenhændige Breve* C.F. Bricka and J.A. Fridericia (eds) (Copenhagen, 1887).

Clausewitz, C. von *Vom Kriege* (Frankfurt/Main, 1994).

Dagbog over Daniel Rantzovs Vinterfelttog i Sverig fra den 20de Oktober 1567 til den 14de Februar 1568 Monumenta Historiae Danicae Række 2 Bd I (1868).

'Dagbok af en Inginiör-Officer antagligen L. Wisocki-Hochmuth 1700–1708' *Karolinska Krigares Dagböcker* II A. Quennerstad (ed.) (Lund, 1903).

Das Tagebuch des Generals von Hallart über die Belagerung und Schlacht von Narva 1700 F. Bienemann jr (ed.) (Reval, 1894).

Dopolneniia k Nikonovskoi Letopisi sokhranivshiiasia v spiskakh Sinodal'nom, Levedevskim i Aleksandro-Nevskom Polnoe Sobranie Russkikh Letopisei XIII (Moscow, 1965).

Dyariusz Wojny Moskiewskiej 1633 roku A. Rembowski (ed.) Biblioteka Ordynacji Krasińskich 13 (Warsaw, 1895).

'Dyaryusz expedycyej J.K.M. przeciwko nieprzyiacielowi moskiewskiemu ktory 14 8bris in anno 1632 Smolensk obleg y onego potężnie dobywał 25 augusti ro. 1633' in O. Tselevich 'Uchast' kozakiv v Smolenskii viini 1633–4 rr.' *Zapiski Naukovoho Tovaristva imeni Shevchenka* 28 (1899).

Działyński, Ł. 'Diariusz oblężenia i zdobycia Wieliża, Wielkich Łuk i Zawołocia' *Sprawy wojenne króla Stefana Batorego* I. Połkowski (ed.) (Cracow, 1887).

Fletcher, G. *Of the Russe Commonwealth* R. Pipes (ed.) (Cambridge, Mass., 1966).

Frederick II, 'Betrachtungen über die militärischen Talente und den Charakter Karls XII' in *Die Wercke Friedrichs des Großen* G.B. Volz (ed.) VI (Berlin, 1913).

Fredro, A.M. *Militarium, seu axiomatum belli ad harmoniam togae accomodatorum libri duo* (Amsterdam, 1668).

Gordon, P. *Passages from the diary of General Patrick Gordon of Auchleuchries. A.D. 1635– A.D. 1699* (Aberdeen, 1859).

Gordon, P. *Tagebuch des Generals Patrick Gordon während seiner Kriegsdienste unter den Schweden und Polen* M.A. Obolenksi and M.C. Posselt (eds) (Moscow, 1869).

Gyllenkrook, A. *Relationer från Karl XII:s Krig* N. Sjöberg (ed.) (Stockholm, 1913).

'Handlingar rörande sommarfälttåget i Brandenburg 1675 och striden vid Fehrbellin' J. Mankell (ed.) *Historiskt Bibliotek* III (Stockholm, 1877).

Henning, S. *Salomon Henning's Chronicle of Courland and Livonia* V. Zeps (ed.) (Dubuque, Ia, 1992).

'Historia Dmitra fałszywego' *Pamiatniki otnosiashchiesia k Smutnomu Vremeni izvlecheny iz rukopisei Imperatorskoi Publichnoi Biblioteki i Glavnago Shtaba* Russkaia Istoricheskaia Biblioteka izdaemaia Archeograficheskogo Kommissieiu I (St Petersburg, 1872).

Holsten, Christian von *Kriegsabenteuer des Rittmeisters Hieronymus Christian von Holsten 1655–1666* H. Lahrkamp (ed.) (Wiesbaden, 1971).

Hoppe, I. *Geschichte des ersten schwedisch-polnischen Krieges in Preußen* M. Toeppen (ed.) (Leipzig, 1887).

Jeffreyes, J. *Captain James Jeffreyes's letters to the Secretary of State, Whitehall, from the Swedish Army, 1707–1709* R. Hatton (ed.) *Historiska Handlingar* 35:1 (Stockholm, 1954).

Kochowski, W. *Annalium Poloniae Climacter Secundus. Bella Sueticum, Transylvanicum, Moschoviticam, aliasq. res gestas ab anno 1655 ad annum 1661 inclusive continens* (Cracow, 1688).

Krause, E. 'Des Dörptschen Stiftvoigts Eilert Krause Bericht an den Erzbischof Wilhelm zu Riga, von den Ursachen und Bedingungen der am 18ten Juli Uebergabe der Stadt Dörpt an die Moskowiter, d.d. im Hofe Erkull den 5.. August 1558 . . .' K. von Busse, 'Die Einnahme der Stadt Dorpat im Jahre 1558 und die damit verbundenen Ereignisse' *Mittheilungen aus dem Gebiete der Geschichte Liv-, Est- und Kurlands* I (1840).

Kurck, G. *Landshöfdingen Friherre Gabriel Kurcks lefnadsminnen upptecknade af honom själf* R. Hausen (ed.) (Helsingfors, 1906).

Łaski, S. *Spraw i postępków rycerskich i przewagi opisanie krótkie z naukami w tej zacnej zabawie potrzebie* (Lwów, 1599).

Lewenhaupt, A.L. *Adam Ludvig Lewenhaupts berättelse* S.E. Bring (ed.) *Historiska Handlingar* 34:2 (Stockholm, 1952).

Lyth, J.M. *Löjtnant Joachim Matthiæ Lyths Dagbok 1703–1722*, Karolinska Krigares Dagböcker II A. Quennerstad (ed.) (Lund, 1903).

Marchocki, M.S. *Historya wojny moskiewskiej* (Poznań, 1841).

Massa, I. *A short history of the beginnings and origins of these present wars in Moscow under the reigns of various sovereigns down to the year 1610* G.E. Orchard (tr.) (Toronto, 1982).

Maurice, Comte de Saxe, *Les Rêveries ou Mémoires sur l'Art de la Guerre* (The Hague, 1756).

Michałowski, J. *Księga Pamiętnicza* L. Morsztyn (ed.) (Cracow, 1864).

Monro, R. *Robert Monro. His expedition with the worthy Scots Regiment (called Mac-Keyes Regiment)* (London, 1637).

Nordberg, G. *Konung Carl XII:tes historia* 2 vols (Stockholm, 1740).

Nyenstädt, F. *Franz Nyenstädt's Livländische Chronik* G. Tielmann (ed.) Monumenta Livoniae Antiquae II (Riga, 1839).

Otwinowski, E. *Dzieje Polski pod panowaniem Augusta II od roku 1696–1728* J. Moraczewski (ed.) (Cracow, 1849).

Oxenstierna, A. *Rikskansleren Axel Oxenstiernas skrifter och brefväxling* Series I–II (Stockholm, 1888–1978).

Pamiętniki Samuela i Bogusława Kazimierza Maskiewiczów A. Sajkowski (ed.) (Wrocław, 1961).

Pasek, J.C. *Memoirs of the Polish Baroque* C.S. Leach (tr.) (Berkeley, 1976).

Piotrowski, J. *Dziennik wyprawy Stefana Batorego pod Psków* A. Czuczyński (ed.) (Cracow, 1894).

Pis'ma i Bumagi Imperatora Petra Velikogo 13 vols (St Petersburg, Moscow, 1887–1992).

'Popis wojska kwarcianego w 1569 r.' Z. Spieralski and J. Wimmer (eds) *Wypisy źródłowe do historii polskiej sztuki wojennej* 5 (Warsaw, 1951).

Posse, C.M. *C.M. Posses Dagbok 1707–1709* A. Quennerstad (ed.) Karolinska Krigares Dagböcker I (Lund, 1901).

Quellen zur Geschichte des Untergangs livländischer Selbständigkeit aus dem schwedischen Reichsarchive zu Stockholm C. Schirren (ed.) Archiv für die Geschichte Liv-, Est- und Curlands NF I–VIII (Reval, 1861–81).

Radziwiłł, K. *Księcia Krzysztofa Radziwiłła Hetmana Polnego Wielkiego Litewskiego Sprawy wojenne i polityczne 1621–1632* (Paris, 1859).

Ranatowicz, S. *Opisanie inkursji Szwedów do Polski i do Krakowa (1655–1657)* J. Mitkowski (ed.) (Cracow, 1958).

'Razriadnaia kniga Polotskago pokhoda tsaria Ivana Vasilevicha 1563 g.' A. Sapunov (ed.) *Vitebskaia Starina* IV (Vitebsk, 1885).

'Relatio de servitio militari cum Moscovitis contra regem Poloniae, dein cum Polonis contra Moscoviam praestito', C.H. Talbot (ed.) *Res Poloniae Iacobi I Angliae Regnante Conscriptae ex Archivis Publicis Londiniarum* Elementa ad Fontium Editiones VI (Rome, 1962).

Renner, J. *Livländische Historien 1556–1561* Veröffentlichen der Stadtbibliothek Lübeck, Neue Reihe II (Lübeck, 1953).

Rüssow, B. *Chronica der Provintz Lyfflandt* Scriptores Rerum Livonicarum II (Riga, Leipzig, 1853).

Sbornik Imperatorskogo Russkogo Istoricheskogo Obshchestva vol. 39 (St Petersburg, 1882), vol. 50 (St Petersburg, 1886).

Siemienowicz, K. *Ars Magnæ Artilleriæ Pars Prima* (Amsterdam, 1650).

Sprawy wojenne króla Stefana Batorego I. Polkowski (ed.) (Cracow, 1887).

Staden, H. von *The land and government of Muscovy. A sixteenth-century account* T. Esper (tr.) (Stanford, Cal., 1967).

Tarnowski, J. *Consilium rationes bellicæ* J. Sikorski (ed.) (Warsaw, 1987).

Vauciennes, L. de *Mémoires de ce qui c'est passé en Suède tirés des dépêches de Chanut* 2 vols (Cologne, 1677).

Voltaire, *Lion of the North, Charles XII of Sweden* M. Jenkins (tr.) (London, 1981).

Volumina Legum vols 2–5 (St Petersburg, 1859–60).

'Warhafftige vnd Erschreckliche Newzeitung von dem grausamen Feind vnnd Tyrannen des Muscowiters wie er so erbärmlich vnd jemmerlich viel Volcks vmbs Leben im Liefland hat bringen lassen, auch wie er ist vor Parnaw gezogen, dieselbige den 9 Julij dieses 75. Jars eingenommen hat' reprinted in *Sitzungsberichte der Altertumforschenden Gesellschaft zu Pernau* 11 (1926–9) (Pernau, 1930).

'Warhaftige und grundtliche beschreibung des itzigen betriebten Liefflendischen kriegs zwischen hertzog Carl und Kon. Mtt. zu Polen, darinnen mit vleiss die vornembsten geschicht, so sich im lande von Anno 99 bis auff den 29. Januarii entlaufenden jahres [begeben] zu finden' *Mittheilungen aus dem Gebiete der Geschichte Liv-, Est – und Kurlands* 17 (Riga, 1900).

Wójcicki, K.W. *Pamiętniki do panowania Zygmunta III, Władysława IV i Jana Kazimierza* 2 vols (Warsaw, 1846).

'Wyprawa krola i.m. do Moskwy r. p. 1609' *Pamiatniki otnosiashchiecia k Smutnomu Vremeni izvlecheny iz rukopisei Imperatorskoi Publichnoi Biblioteki i Glavnago Shtaba* Russkaia Istoricheskaia Biblioteka izdaemaia Archeograficheskogo Kommissieiu I (St Petersburg, 1872).

'Zapiska o voennykh deistviiakh vo vremia Pol'skago pokhoda 1655 goda, s rospis'iu pokorennykh Russkimi voiskami gorodov' *Akty istoricheskie sobrannye v bibliotekakh i arkhivakh Rossiiskoi Imperii Arkheograficheskoiu ekspeditsieiu Imperatorskoi Akademii Nauk* IV (St Petersburg, 1841–2).

Zhurnal, ili Podennaia Zapiska, Blazhennyia i vechnodostoinyia pamiati Gosudaria Imperatora Petra Velikago s 1698 goda, dazhe do zaliucheniia Neishtatskago mira 2 vols (St Petersburg, 1770–1).

Żółkiewski, S. *Expedition to Moscow* M.W. Stephen (tr.) (London, 1959).

Secondary

Åberg, A. *Karl XI* (Stockholm, 1958).

Åberg, A. 'The Swedish army, from Lützen to Narva' in M. Roberts (ed.) *Sweden's Age of Greatness 1632–1718* (London, 1973).

Achremczyk, S. 'Konfederacja szlachty Prus Królewskich w latach 1703–1709' *Zapiski Historyczne* 45 (1980).

Ågren, K. *Adelns bönder och kronans. Skatter och besvär i Uppland 1650–1680* Studia Historica Upsaliensia 11 (Uppsala, 1964).

Ågren, K. 'The *Reduktion*' in M. Roberts (ed.) *Sweden's Age of Greatness 1632–1718* (London, 1973).

Ågren, K. 'Rise and decline of an aristocracy. The Swedish social and political elite in the 17th Century' *Scandinavian Journal of History* 1 (1976).

Ågren, S. *Karl XI:s Indelningsverk för Armén. Bidrag till dess historia åren 1679–1697* (Uppsala, 1922).

Ahonen, V. 'Städernas återhämtning: Finland efter storer ofreden' *Historisk Tidskrift* (1989).

Alef, G. 'Muscovite military reforms in the second half of the fifteenth century' *Forschungen zur Osteuropäischen Geschichte* 18 (1973).

Alexandrowicz, S. and Olejnik, K. 'Charakterystyka polskiego teatru działań wojennych' *Studia i Materiały do Historia Wojskowości* 26 (1983).

Almgren, C.E. 'Svensk strategi och krigsledning' in F. Askgaard and A. Stade (eds) *Kampen om Skåne* (Copenhagen, 1983).

Anderson, M. *War and Society in Europe of the Old Regime, 1620–1789* (London, 1988).

Anderson, R.C. *Naval Wars in the Baltic* (London, 1919).

Andersson, I. *Erik XIV* (Stockholm, 1963).

Anisimov, E.V. *The Reforms of Peter the Great: Progress through Coercion in Russia* J.T. Alexander (tr.) (Armonk, NY, 1993).

Anusik, Z. 'Struktura społeczna szlachty bracławskiej w świetle taryfy podymnego z 1629 roku' *Przegląd Historyczny* 76 (1985).

Arnell, S. *Bidrag till belysning av den baltiska fronten under det nordiska sjuårskriget 1563–1570* Kungl. Vitterhets Historie och antikivets akadamiens Handlingar: Historiska Serien 19 (Stockholm, 1977).

Artéus, G. *Krigsteori och historisk förklaring. I. Kring Karl XII:s ryska fälttåg* (Uppsala, 1970).

Artéus, G. *Karolinsk och europeisk stridstaktik 1700–1712* (Gothenburg, 1972).

Artéus, G. Olsson, U. and Strömberg-Back, K. 'The influence of the armed forces on the transformations of society in Sweden, 1600–1945' *Militärhistorisk Tidskrift* 185 (Bihäfte) (1981).

Artéus, G. *Krigsmakt och samhälle i frihetstidens Sverige* (Stockholm, 1982).

Artéus, G. *Till Militärstatens Förhistoria. Krig, professionalisering och social förändring under Vasosönernas regering* (Stockholm, 1986).

Asker, B. *Officerarna och det svenska samhället 1650–1700* Studia Historica Upsaliensia 133 (Uppsala, 1983).

Asker, B. 'Militärstat eller militariserat samhälle. Synpunkter på det karolinska Sverige med anledning av en aktuel debatt' *Historisk Tidskrift* (1987).

Asker, B. 'Åter om det karolinska samhällets "militarisering"' *Historisk Tidskrift* (1988).

Askgaard, F. 'Den korte fred. Mellemkrigstiden 26/2–7/8.1658' *Carl X Gustaf och Danmark. Källkritik och Krigshistoria* Carl X Gustaf-Studier I (Stockholm, 1965).

Askgaard, F. *Kampen om Östersjön på Carl X Gustafs tid* Carl X Gustaf-Studier 6 (Stockholm, 1974).

Askgaard, F. 'Nordisk udenrigspolitik 1660–1675' in F. Askgaard and A. Stade (eds) *Kampen om Skåne* (Copenhagen, 1983).

Askgaard, F. and Stade, A. (eds) *Kampen om Skåne* (Copenhagen, 1983).

Åström, S.-E. 'The Swedish economy and Sweden's role as a great power 1632–1697' in M. Roberts (ed.) *Sweden's Age of Greatness 1632–1718* (London, 1973).

Attman, A. *The Russian and Polish Markets in International Trade 1500–1650* (Göteborg, 1973).

Avtokratov, V.N. 'Pervye komissariatskie organy russkoi reguliarnoi armii (1700–1710)' *Istoricheskie Zapiski* 68 (1961).

Babiński, L. *Trybunał skarbowy radomski* (Warsaw, 1923).

Backlund, J. *Rusthållarna i Fellingsbro 1648–1748. Indelningsverket och den sociala differentieringen av det svenska agrarsamhället* (Uppsala, 1993).

Backus, O.P. 'Mortgages, alienations and redemptions: the rights in land of the nobility in sixteenth century Lithuanian law and practice compared' *Forschungen zur Osteuropäischen Geschichte* 18 (1973).

Baranowski, B. 'Tatarszczyzna wobec wojny polsko-szwedzkiej w latach 1655–1660' in K. Lepszy (ed.) *Polska w okresie drugiej wojny północnej* 4 vols (Warsaw, 1957).

Barfod, J.H. 'Den danske orlogsflåde før 1560' *Historisk Tidsskrift* (1994).

Barudio, G. *Gustav Adolf – der Große. Eine politische Biographie* (Frankfurt/M., 1985).

Bengtsson, F.G. *Karl XII.* T. Baur (tr.) (Stuttgart, 1957).

Besala, J. *Stanisław Żółkiewski* (Warsaw, 1988).

Besala, J. *Stefan Batory* (Warsaw, 1992).

Beskrovnyi, L.G. *Russkaia Armiia i Flot v XVIII veke* (Moscow, 1958).

Beskrovnyi, L.G. 'Strategiia i taktika russkoi armii v poltavskii period Severnoi Voiny' in *Poltava. K 250-letiiu Poltavskogo srazheniia. Sbornik statei* (Moscow, 1959).

Biskup, M. (ed.) *Historia Torunia* II (Toruń, 1996).

Black, J. *A Military Revolution? Military Change and European Society 1550–1800* (London, 1991).

Bobrovskii, P.O. *Istoriia 13-go Leib-Grenaderskago Erivanskago ego Velichestva Polka za 250 let 1642–1892* I *Vybornyi Moskovskii polk soldatskago stroia, izvestnyi pod nazvaniem <Butyrskago>* (St Petersburg, 1892).

Bogoiavlenskii, S.K. 'Vooruzhenie russkikh voisk v XVI–XVII vv.' *Istoricheskie Zapiski* 4 (1938).

Bogucka, M. and Samsonowicz, H. *Dzieje miast i mieszczaństwa w Polsce przedrozbiorowej* (Wrocław, 1986).

Böhme, K.-R. *Die schwedische Besetzung des Weichseldeltas 1626–36* Jahrbuch der Albertus-Universität, Königsberg, Beiheft 22 (Würzburg, 1963).

Böhme, K.-R. 'Geld für die schwedischen Armeen nach 1640' *Scandia* 33 (1967).

Böhme, K.-R. 'Officersrekryteringen vid tre landskapsregementen 1626–1682' in M. Revera and R. Torstendahl (eds) *Bördor, bönder, börd i 1600-talets Sverige* (Motala, 1979).

Böhme, K.-R. 'Schwedische Finanzbürokratie und Kriegführung 1611 bis 1721' in G. Rystad (ed.) *Europe and Scandinavia. Aspects of the Process of Integration in the 17th Century* Lund Studies in International History 18 (Lund, 1983).

Böhme, K.-R. 'Building a Baltic Empire. Aspects of Swedish expansion, 1560–1660' in G. Rystad, K.-R. Böhme and W. Carlgren (eds) *In Quest of Trade and Security: the Baltic in Power Politics, 1500–1990* I (Lund, 1994).

Brambe, R.K. and Kh.E. Palli, 'Dinamika chislennosti naseleniia Estonii i Latvii v XVII–XVIII vv.' *Materialy mezhrespublikanskoi nauchnoi konferentsii po istochnikovedeniiu i istoriografii narodov Pribalitki: Istoriografiia* (Vilnius, 1978).

Brzezinski, R. *Polish Armies 1569–1696* 2 vols (London, 1987).

Buława, J. 'Toruń w okresie potopu szwedzkiego w latach 1655–1660' Unpublished MA dissertation, Nicholas Copernicus University, Toruń (1957–8).

Burleigh, M. *Prussian Society and the German Order: an Aristocratic Corporation in Crisis c. 1410–1466* (Cambridge, 1984).

Buturlin, D. *Istoriia Smutnago Vremeni v Rossii v nachale XVII veka* 3 vols (St Petersburg, 1846).

Carlson, E. 'Slaget vid Poltava och dess krigshistoriska förutsättningar enligt samtida källor' in *Historiska studier. Festskrift tillägnad C.G. Malmström* (Stockholm, 1897).

Carsten, F.L. *The Origins of Prussia* (Oxford, 1954).

Cavallie, I. *Från fred till krig. De finansiella problemen kring krigsutbrottet år 1700* Acta Historica Upsaliensia 68 (Uppsala, 1975).

Cavallie, J. *De höga officerarna. Studier i den svenska militära hierarkien under 1600-talets senare del* Militärhistoriska Studier IV (Lund, 1981).

Chandler, D. *The Art of Warfare in the Age of Marlborough* (London, 1976).

Chernov, A.V. 'Obrazovanie streletskogo voiska' *Istoricheskie Zapiski* 38 (1951).

Chernov, A.V. *Vooruzhennye sily russkogo gosudarstva v XV–XVII vv.* (Moscow, 1954).

Christiansen, E. *The Northern Crusades. The Baltic and the Catholic Frontier 1100–1525* (London, 1980).

Cichowski, J., Szulczyński, A. *Husaria* (Warsaw, 1977).

Cieślak, E. 'Wojskowo-politycne i gospodarcze znaczenie Gdańska w wojnie polsko-szwedzkiej 1655–1660' in J. Wimmer (ed.) *Wojna polsko-szwedzka 1655–1660* (Warsaw, 1973).

Cieślak, E. (ed.) *Historia Gdańska* II (Gdańsk, 1982).

Crummey, R. 'The fate of boyar clans, 1565–1613' *Forschungen zur Osteuropäischen Geschichte* 38 (1986).

Crummey, R. *The Formation of Muscovy 1304–1613* (London, 1987).

Czapliński, W. 'Na marginesie rokowań w Sztumsdorfie w 1635 r.' *Przegląd Współczesny* 17 (1938).

Czapliński, W. *Polska a Bałtyk w latach 1632–1648. Dzieje floty i polityki morskiej* (Wrocław, 1952).

Dahlgren, S. *Karl X Gustav och Reduktionen* Studia Historica Upsaliensia 14 (Uppsala, 1964).

Davies, B. 'Village into garrison: the militarized peasant communities of southern Muscovy' *Russian Review* 51 (1992).

Dembkowski, H.E. *The Union of Lublin. Polish federalism in the golden age* (Boulder, Col., 1982).

Denisova, M.M. 'Pomestnaia konnitsa i ee vooruzhenie v XVI–XVII vv.' *Voenno-Istoricheskii Sbornik* 20 (1948).

Donnert, E. *Der livländische Ordensritterstaat und Rußland. Der livländische Krieg und die Baltische Frage in der Europäischen Politik 1558–1583* (Berlin, 1963).

Dow, J. *Ruthven's Army in Sweden and Esthonia* Historiskt Arkiv 13 (Stockholm, 1965).

Downing, B. *The Military Revolution and Political Change. Origins of Democracy and Autocracy in Early Modern Europe* (Princeton, 1990).

Dukes, P. 'The Leslie family in the Swedish period (1630–5) of the Thirty Years War' *European Studies Review* 12 (1982).

Dunsdorfs, E. *Der Grosse Schwedische Kataster in Livland 1681–1710* (Stockholm, 1950).

Dworzaczek, W. *Hetman Jan Tarnowski. Z dziejów możnowładztwa małopolskiego* (Warsaw, 1985).

Dybaś, B. *Fortece Rzeczypospolitej. Studium z dziejów budowy fortyfikacji stałych w państwie polsko-litewskim w XVII wieku* (Toruń, 1998).

Dybaś, B. 'Dzieje wojskowe Torunia w latach 1548–1660' in M. Biskup (ed.) *Historia Torunia* II (Toruń, 1996).

Ekman, E. 'The Danish Royal Law of 1665' *Journal of Modern History* 29 (1959).

Elmroth, I. *För kung und fosterland. Studier i den svenska adelns demografi och offentliga funktioner 1600–1900* Bibliotheca Historica Lundensis 50 (Lund, 1981).

Englund, P. *Det hotade huset. Adliga föreställningar om samhället under Stormaktstiden* (Stockholm, 1989).

Englund, P. *The Battle of Poltava. The Birth of the Russian Empire* P. Hale (tr.) (London, 1992).

Englund, P. *Ofredsår. Om den svenska stormaktstiden och en man i dess mitt* (Stockholm, 1993).

Esper, T. 'A 16th century anti-Russian arms embargo' *Jahrbücher für Geschichte Osteuropas* NF 15 (1967).

Esper, T. 'Military self-sufficiency and weapons technology in Muscovite Russia' *Slavic Review* 28 (1969).

Fagerlund, R. *Kriget i Östersjöprovinserna 1655–1661* Carl X Gustaf-Studier VII:i (Stockholm, 1979).

Fagerlund, R. 'De finska fänikorna under äldre Vasatid. Forsknigsläge och problem' *Turun Historiallinen Arkisto* 38 (1982).

Filipczak-Kocur, A. *Skarb koronny za Zygmunta III Wazy* (Opole, 1985).

Filipczak-Kocur, A. *Skarb koronny za Władysława IV 1632–1648* (Opole, 1991).

Filipczak-Kocur, A. *Skarb litewski za pierwszych dwu Wazów 1587–1648* (Wrocław, 1994).

Findeisen, J.-P. 'Poltava – Mythos und Wirklichkeit. Einige kritische Anmerkungen zur bisherigen Darstellung dieser welthistorischen Schlacht durch die sowjetische Militärhistoriographie' *Militärgeschichtliche Mitteilungen* 51 (1992).

Floria, B.N. ' "Rossiia, Rech" Pospolitaia i konets Livonskoi voiny' *Sovetskoe Slavianovedenie* (1972).

Floria, B. *Russko-polskiie otnosheniia i baltiiskii vopros v konce 16. – nachale 17 v.* (Moscow, 1973).

Floria, B. *Russko-polskiie otnosheniia i politicheskoie rozvitiie Vostochnoi Evropy ve vtoroi polovinie XVI- nachale XVIIv* (Moscow, 1978).

Floria, B.N. 'Rokosz sandomierski a Dymitr Samozwaniec' *Odrodzenie i Reformacja w Polsce* 26 (1981).

Forsten, G.V. *Baltiiskii vopros v XVI–XVII st. (1544–1648)* 2 vols (St Petersburg, 1893–4).

Fredriksson, B. *Försvarets finansiering. Svensk krigsekonomi under skånska kriget 1675–79* Studia Historica Upsaliensia 81 (Uppsala, 1976).

Friedrich, K. *The Other Prussia: Poland, Prussia and Liberty, 1569–1772* (Cambridge, 2000).

Frost, R.I. *After the Deluge. Poland-Lithuania and the Second Northern War* (Cambridge, 1993).

Frost, R.I. 'The nobility of Poland-Lithuania, 1569–1795' in H.M. Scott (ed.), *The European Nobilities in the Seventeenth and Eighteenth Centuries* II (London, 1995).

Frost, R.I. 'Poland-Lithuania and the Thirty Years War' in K. Bußmann and H. Schilling (eds) *War and Peace in Europe, 1618–1648* I *Politics, Religion, Law and Society* (Münster/Osnabrück, 1998).

Fuller, W.C. *Strategy and Power in Russia 1600–1914* (New York, 1992).

Gajecky, G. and Baran, A. *The Cossacks in the Thirty Years War* 2 vols (Rome, 1969, 1983).

Generalstaben, *Karl XII på slagfältet. Karolinsk slagledning sedd mot bakgrunden av taktikens utveckling från äldsta tider* 4 vols (Stockholm, 1918–19).

Generalstaben, *Sveriges Krig 1611–1632* II *Polska Kriget* (Stockholm, 1936).

Gerbil'skii, G. Iu. 'Russko-pol'skii soiuz i zholkovskii strategicheskii plan' in *Poltava. K 250-letiiu Poltavskogo srazheniia. Sbornik statei* (Moscow, 1959).

Gerlach, J. 'Pospolite ruszenie i obrona za Zygmunta I' *Księga pamiątkowa ku czci Władysława Abrahama* Vol. II (Lwów, 1931).

Gerlach, J. *Chłopi w obronie Rzeczypospolitej. Studium o piechocie wybranieckiej* (Lwów, 1938).

Gierlich, E. *Reval 1621 bis 1645. Von der Eroberung Livlands durch Gustav Adolf bis zum Frieden von Brömsebro* (Bonn, 1991).

Gierowski, J.A. *W cieniu Ligi Północnej* (Wrocław, 1971).

Gieysztorowa, I. 'Zniszczenia i straty wojenne oraz ich skutki na Mazowszu' in K. Lepszy (ed.) *Polska w okresie drugiej wojny północnej* II (Warsaw, 1957).

Glete, J. *Navies and Nations. Warships, Navies and State Building in Europe and America, 1500–1860* vol. I Stockholm Studies in History 43 (Stockholm, 1993).

Goehrke, C. *Die Wüstungen in der Moskauer Rus'. Studien zur Siedlungs-, Bevölkerungs- und Sozialgeschichte* (Wiesbaden, 1968).

Goehrke, C. 'Zum Problem von Bevölkerungsziffer und Bevölkerungsdichte des Moskauer Reiches im 16. Jahrhundert' *Forschungen zur Osteuropäischen Geschichte* 24 (1973).

Grauers, S. 'Den Karolinska feldhärens underhåll 1700–1703' *Karolinska Förbundets Årsbok* (1968).

Grauers, S. 'Den Karolinska fälthärens underhåll 1704–1707' *Karolinska Förbundets Årsbok* (1969).

Gritskevich, A.P. 'Formirovanie feodalnogo sosloviia v Velikom Kniazhestve Litovskom i ego pravovye osnovy (XV–XVI v.)' in *Pervyi Litovskii Statut 1529 goda. Materialy respublikanskoi nauchnoi konferentsii posviashchennoi 450-letiu Pervogo Statuta* (Vilnius, 1982).

Günther, A. 'Das schwedische Heer in Sachsen 1706–1707' *Neues Archiv für Sächsische Geschichte und Altertumskunde* 25 (1904).

Gustafsson, L. *Virtus politica. Politisk etik och nationellt svärmeri i den tidigare Stormaktstidens litteratur* Lychnos-Bibliotek XV (Uppsala, Stockholm, 1956).

Gyllenstierna, E. 'Kampen i Tyskland' in F. Askgaard and A. Stade (eds) *Kampen om Skåne* (Copenhagen, 1983).

Hale, J.R. *War and Society in Renaissance Europe, 1450–1620* (London, 1985).

Hallendorff, C. 'Karl XII och Lewenhaupt år 1708' *Upsala Universitets Årsskrift* (1902).

Hartmann, S. *Reval im Nordischen Krieg* (Bonn-Godesberg, 1973).

Hatton, R. *Charles XII* (London, 1968).

Hellie, R. *Enserfment and Military Change in Muscovy* (Chicago, Ill., 1971).

Hellie, R. 'The Petrine army: continuity, change and impact' *Canadian-American Slavic Studies* 8 (1974).

Hellie, R. 'What happened? How did he get away with it? Ivan Groznyi's paranoia and the problem of institutional restraints' *Russian History* 14 (1987).

Hellie, R. 'Warfare, changing military technology and the evolution of Muscovite society' J.A. Lynn (ed.) *Tools of War: Instruments, Ideas and Institutions of Warfare, 1445–1871* (Urbana, Ill., 1990).

Herbst, S. 'Kampania letnia 1601' *Przegląd Historyczno-Wojskowy* 4:2 (1931).

Herbst, S. *Wojna inflancka 1600–1602* Rozprawy Historycznego Towarzystwa Warszawskiego 19 (Warsaw, 1938).

Herbst, S. 'Wojna inflancka 1603–1604' *Studia Historica. W 35-lecie pracy naukowej Henryka Łowmiańskiego* (Warsaw, 1958).

Herbst, S. 'Trzydniowa bitwa pod Warszawą 28–30 VII 1656 r.' in J. Wimmer (ed.) *Wojna polsko-szwedska 1655–1660* (Warsaw, 1973).

Hill, C.E. *The Danish Sound Dues and the Command of the Baltic* (Durham, NC, 1926).

Hniłko, A. *Wyprawa cudnowska w 1660r.* (Warsaw, 1931).

Hughes, L.J. *Russia in the Age of Peter the Great* (New Haven and London, 1998).

Iakovenko, N.M. *Ukrains'ka shliakhta z kintsia XIV do seredini XVII st. (Volin' i Tsentral'na Ukraina)* (Kiev, 1993).

Janasz, E. and Wasilewski, L. 'Społeczne aspekty rozwoju husarii w latach 1648–1667 na przykładzie chorągwi hetmani wielkiego koronnego Stanisława Potockiego i wojewody sandomierskiego Władysława Myszkowskiego' *Studia i Materiały do Historii Wojskowości* 23 (1981).

Jensen, F.P. *Danmarks konflikt med Sverige 1563–1570* Skrifter udgivet af det Historiske Institut ved Københavns Universitet XII (Copenhagen, 1982).

Jespersen, K.J.V. 'Absoute monarchy in Denmark: change and continuity' *Scandinavian Journal of History* 12 (1987).

Jespersen, K.J.V. 'The rise and fall of the Danish nobility, 1600–1800' in H.M. Scott (ed.), *The European Nobilities in the Seventeenth and Eighteenth Centuries* II (London, 1995).

Jespersen, L. 'The *Machtstaat* in seventeenth-century Denmark' *Scandinavian Journal of History* 10 (1985).

Jespersen, L. '1648 – Magtstat eller minimumsstat? Begreber og udviklingslinier' in L. Jespersen and A. Svane-Knudsen (eds) *Stænder og magtstat. De politiske brydninger i 1648 og 1660* (Odense, 1989).

Johannesson, K. 'Gustav II Adolf som retoriker' in *Gustav II Adolf – 350 år efter Lützen* (Stockholm, 1982).

Johannesson, K. *The Renaissance of the Goths in Sixteenth-century Sweden. Johannes and Olaus Magnus as Politicians and Historians* J. Larson (tr.) (Berkeley, 1991).

Jonasson, G. *Karl XII och hans rådgivare. Den utrikespolitiska maktkampen i Sverige 1697–1702* Studia Historica Upsaliensia 1 (Uppsala, 1960).

Jonasson, G. 'Planläggningen av ryska fälttåget år 1701' *Karolinska Förbundets Årsbok* (1965).

Jonasson, G. *Karl XII:s polska politik* Studia Historica Upsaliensia 27 (Stockholm, 1968).

Kamiński, A.S. 'Przeciwko Szwedom i Leszczyńskiemu. Działania wojsk rosyjskich na terenie Polski w 1705–1706 roku' *Studia i Materiały do Historii Wojskowości* 12 (1966).

Kamiński, A.S. *Konfederacja Sandomierska wobec Rosji w okresie poaltransztadzkim 1706–1709* (Wrocław, 1969).

Kamiński, A.S. 'Piotr I a wojsko koronne w przededniu szwedzkiego uderzenia na Rosję w 1707 r.' *Studia i Materiały do Historii Wojskowości* 15 (1969).

Kappeler, A. *Ivan Groznyj im Spiegel der ausländischen Druckschriften seiner Zeit: ein Beitrag zur Geschichte des westlichen Russlandbildes* Geist und Werk der Zeiten. Arbeiten aus dem Hist. Seminar der Universität Zürich No. 33 (Bern, 1972).

Karlsson, Å. *Den jämlike undersåten. Karl XII:s förmögenhetsbeskattning 1713* Studia Historica Upsaliensia 175 (Uppsala, 1994).

Keegan, J. *The Face of Battle: a Study of Agincourt, Waterloo and the Somme* (London, 1976).

Keep, J.L. *Soldiers of the Tsar. Army and Society in Russia, 1462–1874* (Oxford, 1985).

Kentrschynskyj, B. *Mazepa* (Stockholm, 1962).

Kersten, A. *Stefan Czarniecki 1599–1665* (Warsaw, 1963).

Kirby, D. *Northern Europe in the Early Modern Period. The Baltic World 1492–1772* (London, 1990).

Kirchner, W. *The Rise of the Baltic Question* (Newark, NJ, 1954).

Kivelson, V.A. *Autocracy in the Provinces. The Muscovite Gentry and Political Culture in the Seventeenth Century* (Stanford, Cal., 1996).

Kollmann, N.S. *Kinship and Politics. The Making of the Muscovite Political System, 1345–1547* (Stanford, Cal., 1987).

Kolosov, E.E. 'Artilleriia v poltavskom srazhenii' in *Poltava. K 250-letiiu Poltavskogo srazheniia. Sbornik statei* (Moscow, 1959).

Koroliuk, V.D. *Livonskaia Voina* (Moscow, 1954).

Korzon, T. *Dzieje wojen i wojskowości w Polsce* vol. 2 (2nd edn, Warsaw, 1923).

Kostomarov, N. *Mazepa i Mazepintsy* (2nd edn, St Petersburg, 1885).

Kotarski, H. 'Wojsko polsko-litewskie podczas wojny inflanckiej 1576–1582. Sprawy organizacyjne' I–V *Studia i Materiały do Historii Wojskowości* 16 (1970); 17:1, 17:2 (1971); 18:1, 18:2 (1972).

Krip'iakevich, I. *Istoriia ukrainsk'koho viis'ka* (L'viv, 1936).

Krüger, K. 'Dänische und schwedische Kriegsfinanzierung im Dreißigjährigen Krieg bis 1635' in K. Repgen (ed.) *Krieg und Politik 1618–1648* Schriften des Historischen Kollegs Kolloquein 8 (Munich, 1988).

Kruus, H. *Vene-Liivi sõda (1558–1561)* (Tartu, 1924).

Kubala, L. *Wojna moskiewska* (Warsaw, 1910).

Kumke, C. 'Die Reform der Registerkosaken im Jahre 1638' *Forschungen zur Osteuropäischen Geschichte* 48 (1993).

Kumke, C. *Führer und Geführte bei den Zaporoger Kosaken. Struktur und Geschichte kosakischer Verbände im polnisch-litauischen Grenzland (1550–1648) Forschungen zur Osteuropäischen Geschichte* 49 (Berlin, 1993).

Kungl. Svea Livgardes Historia II *1560–1611* (Stockholm 1938–9) B.C. Barkman (ed.); III *1611–1660* B.C. Barkman and S. Lundkvist (eds) (Stockholm, 1963); IV *1660–1718* F. Wernstedt (ed.) (Stockholm, 1954).

Ladewig Petersen, E. 'From domain state to tax state. Synthesis and interpretation' *Scandinavian Economic History Review* 23 (1975).

Ladewig Petersen, E. and Jespersen, K.J.V. 'Two revolutions in early modern Denmark' in E.I. Kouri and T. Scott (eds) *Politics and Society in Reformation Europe* (London, 1987).

Ladewig Petersen, E. 'Christian IV's skånske og norske fæstningsanlæg, 1596–1622' *Historisk Tidsskrift* (1995).

Łakoczyński, Z. *Magnus Stenbock w Polsce. Przyczynek do historii szwedzkich zdobyczy w czasie Wojny Północnej* (Wrocław, 1967).

Landberg, H. 'Krig på kredit. Svensk rustningsfinansiering våren 1655' in H. Landberg, L. Ekholm, R. Nordlund and S.A. Nilsson (eds) *Det kontinentalna krigets ekonomi. Studier i krigsfinansiering under svensk stormaktstid* Studia Historica Upsaliensia 36 (Uppsala, 1971).

Lappo, I.I. *Velikoe Kniazhestvo Litovskoe vo vtoroi polovine XVI stoletiia. Litovsko-Russkii povet i ego seimik* (Iur'ev, 1911).

Larsson, L.-O. 'Lokalsamhälle och centralmakt i Sverige under 1500- och 1600-talen' in N.-E. Villstrand (ed.), *Kustbygd och centralmakt 1560–1721* (Helsingfors, 1987).

Laskowski, O. 'Wyprawa pod Toropiec. Ze studiów nad wojnami moskiewskimi Stefana Batorego' *Przegląd Historyczno-Wojskowy* 9 (1936–7).

Lassen, A. *1659 da landet blev øde* (Copenhagen, 1965).

Leer, G. 'Petr Velikii kak polkovodets' *Voennyi Sbornik* 3 (1865).

Lepszy, K. (ed.) *Polska w okresie drugiej wojny północnej* 4 vols (Warsaw, 1957).

Lind, G. 'Military and absolutism: the army officers of Denmark-Norway as a social group and political factor, 1660–1848' *Scandinavian Journal of History* 12 (1987).

Lind, G. *Hæren og magten i Danmark 1614–1662* (Odense, 1994).

Lindegren, J. *Utskrivning och utsugning. Produktion och reproduktion i Bygdeå 1620–1640* Studia Historica Upsaliensia 117 (Uppsala, 1980).

Lipiński, W. (Lypyns'kyi, V.) *Z dziejów Ukrainy. Księga pamiątkowa ku czci Włodzimierza Antonowicza, Paulina Święcickiego i Tadeusza Rylskiego* (Kiev, Cracow, 1912).

Lipiński, W. 'Organizacja odsieczy i działania wrześniowe pod Smoleńskiem w r. 1633' *Przegląd Historyczno-Wojskowy* 6 (1933).

Lipiński, W. 'Bój o Żaworonkowe Wzgórza i osaczenie Szeina pod Smoleńskiem (16–30 październik 1633 r.)' *Przegląd Historyczno-Wojskowy* 7 (1934).

Lisk, J. *The Struggle for Supremacy in the Baltic 1600–1725* (London, 1967).

Livgardes Historia See: *Kungl. Svea Livgardes Historia.*

Lockhart, P.D. 'Denmark and the Empire. A reassessment of the foreign policy of king Christian IV, 1596–1648' *Scandinavian Studies* 62 (1992).

Lockhart, P.D. *Denmark in the Thirty Years' War, 1618–1648. King Christian IV and the Decline of the Oldenburg State* (Cranbury, NJ, 1996).

Loewe, K. von 'Military service in early sixteenth-century Lithuania: a new interpretation and its implications' *Slavic Review* 30 (1971).

Loewe, K. von *The Lithuanian Statute of 1529* (Leiden, 1976).

Łowmiańska, M. *Wilno przed najazdem moskiewskim 1655 roku* (Wilno, 1929).

Łowmiański, H. 'Popisy wojska Wielkiego Księstwa Litewskiego XVI wieku jako źródło do dziejów zaludnienia' in Łowmiański, *Studia nad dziejami Wielkiego Księstwa Litewskiego* (Poznań, 1983).

Luber, S. and Rostankowski, P. 'Die Herkunft der im Jahre 1581 registrierten Zaporoger Kosaken' *Jahrbücher für Geschichte Osteuropas* NF 28 (1980).

Lundkvist, S. 'Resurser, skattetryck och fattigdom i 1610-talets Sverige' in M. Revera and R. Torstendahl (eds) *Bördor, bönder, börd i 1600-talets Sverige* (Motala, 1979).

Lynn, J.A. 'Recalculating French army growth during the *Grand Siècle*, 1610–1715' in C. Rogers (ed.) *The Military Revolution Debate. Readings on the Military Transformation of Early Modern Europe* (Boulder, Col., 1995).

Maciszewski, J. *Polska a Moskwa 1603–1618* (Warsaw, 1968).

Mączak, A. *Między Gdańskiem a Sundem. Studia nad handlem bałtyckim od połowy XVI do połowy XVII w.* (Warsaw, 1972).

Mączak, A. 'The structure of power of the Commonwealth of the sixteenth and seventeenth centuries' in J.K. Fedorowicz (ed.) *A Republic of Nobles. Studies in Polish History to 1864* (Cambridge, 1982).

Majewski, W. 'Bitwa pod Prostkami (8 X 1656 r)' *Studia i Materiały do Historii Sztuk Wojennych* 2 (1956).

Majewski, W. 'Wojny polsko-szwedzkie 1600–1629' in L. Sikorski (ed.) *Polskie tradycje wojskowe* I (Warsaw, 1990).

Malec, J. 'Coequatio Iurium stanów Wielkiego Księstwa Litewskiego z Koroną Polską z 1697 roku' *Acta Baltico-Slavica* 12 (1979).

Mal'tsev, A.N. *Rossiia i Belorussiia v seredine XVII veka* (Moscow, 1974).

Mal'tsev, D. 'Voennye deistviia russkikh voisk v Belorussii i Litve letom 1655 g.' *Institut Slavianovedeniia. Kratkie Soobshcheniia* 13 (1954).

Martin, J. 'Economic survival in the Novgorod lands in the 1580s' in L.J. Hughes (ed.) *New Perspectives on Muscovite History* (London, 1993).

Morzy, J. *Kryzys demograficzny na Litwie i Białorusi w drugiej połowie XVII wieku* (Poznań, 1965).

Murdoch, S. 'Scotland, Denmark-Norway and the House of Stuart. A diplomatic and military analysis' unpublished Aberdeen University Ph.D. thesis (1998).

Myshlaevskii, A.Z. 'Ofitserskii vopros v XVII veke. Ocherki iz istorii voennago dela v Rossii' *Voennyi Sbornik* 247 (1899).

Nagielski, M. 'Opinia szlachecka o gwardii królewskiej w latach 1632–1668' *Kwartalnik Historyczny* 92 (1985).

Nagielski, M. 'Społeczny i narodowy skład gwardii królewskiej za dwóch ostatnich Wazów (1632–1668)' *Studia i Materiały do Historii Wojskowości* 30 (1988).

Nagielski, M. *Liczebność i organizacja gwardii przybocznej i komputowej za ostatniego Wazy (1648–1668)* (Warsaw, 1989).

Nagielski, M. *Warszawa 1656* (Warsaw, 1990).

Nilsson, S.A. *Krona och frälse i Sverige 1523–1594. Rusttjänst, Länsväsende, Godspolitik* (Lund, 1947).

Nilsson, S.A. 'Reduktion eller kontribution. Alternativ inom 1600-talets svenska finanspolitik' *Scandia* 24 (1958).

Nilsson, S.A. 'Från förläning till donation. Godspolitik och statshushållning under Gustav II Adolf' *Historisk Tidskrift* (1968).

Nilsson, S.A. *På väg mot militärstaten. Krigsbefälets etabliring i den äldre vasatidens Sverige* Opuscula Historica Upsaliensia III (Uppsala, 1989).

Nilsson, S.A. 'Hemlandet och de stora krigen under Gustav Adolfs tid' in S.A. Nilsson *De stora krigens tid. Om Sverige som militärstat och bondesamhälle* (Uppsala, 1990).

Norberg, A. *Polen i svensk politik 1617–26* (Stockholm, 1974).

Novodvorskii, V. *Bor'ba za Livoniiu mezhdu Moskvoiu i Rechi Pospolitoiu (1570–1582)* (St Petersburg, 1904).

Nowak, T. 'Artyleria polska do końca XIV w. Problematyka i stan badań' *Studia i Materiały do Historii Wojskowości* 9 (1963).

Nowak, T. 'Przegląd polskiego piśmiennictwa z dziedziny fortyfikacji i inżynierii wojskowej w XVI–XVIII w.' *Studia i Materiały do Historii Wojskowości* 11 (1965).

Nowak, T.M. and Wimmer, J. *Historia oręża polskiego 963–1795* (Warsaw, 1981).

Oakley, S. *War and Peace in the Baltic 1560–1790* (London, 1992).

Ochmann, S. *Sejmy z lat 1615–1616* Prace Wrocławskiego Towarzystwa Naukowego Seria A Nr. 141 (Wrocław, 1970).

Ochmański, J. 'Organizacja obrony w Wielkim Księstwie Litewskim przed napadami Tatarów krymskich w XV–XVI wieku' *Studia i Materiały do Historii Wojskowości* 5 (1960).

Ochmański, J. *Historia Litwy* 3rd edn (Wrocław, 1990).

Olden-Jørgensen, S. 'Enevoldsarveregeringsakten og Kongeloven. Forfatnings-spørgsmålet i Danmark fra Oktober 1660 til November 1665' *Historisk Tidsskrift* 93 (1993).

Olejnik, K. *Stefan Batory, 1533–1586* (Warsaw, 1988).

Österberg, E. *Gränsbygd under krig. Ekonomiska, demografiska och administrativa förhällanden i sydvästra Sverige under och efter Nordiska Sjuärskriget* Bibliotecha Historica Lundensis 26 (Lund, 1971).

Österberg, E. 'Local political culture versus the state. Patterns of interaction in pre-industrial Sweden' in E. Österberg, *Mentalities and other Realities. Essays in*

Medieval and Early Modern Scandinavian History Lund Studies in International History 28 (Lund, 1991).

Ostrowski, B. 'Pospolite ruszenie szlachty smoleńskiej w XVII wieku' *Acta Baltico-Slavica* 13 (1980).

Palamets, H. *Liivi sõda 1558–1583* (Tartu, 1973).

Palli, Kh. *Mezhdu dvumia boiami za Narvu. Estoniia v pervye gody Severnoi Voiny 1701–1704* (Tallinn, 1966).

Pałucki, W. *Drogi i bezdroża skarbowości polskiej XVI i pierwszej połowy XVII wieku* (2nd edn, Wrocław, 1974).

Parker, G. (ed.) *The Thirty Years War* (London, 1984).

Parker, G. *The Military Revolution. Military Innovation and the Rise of the West, 1500–1800* (2nd edn, Cambridge, 1996).

Parrott, D. 'The Administration of the French Army during the Ministry of Cardinal Richelieu' unpublished Ph.D. thesis, Oxford University, 1985.

Parrott, D. 'Strategy and tactics in the Thirty Years' War: the "Military Revolution"' in C. Rogers (ed.) *The Military Revolution Debate. Readings on the Military Transformation of Early Modern Europe* (Boulder, Col., 1995).

Pavlenko, N. and Artamonov, V. *27 iunia 1709* (Moscow, 1989).

Perrie, M. *Pretenders and Popular Monarchism in Early Modern Russia* (Cambridge, 1995).

Persson, R. *Rustningar i Sverige under det Stora Nordiska Kriget. Studiar rörande makten över krigsfinansieringen i det karolinska samhället 1700–1709* Biblioteca Historica Lundensis 35 (Lund, 1975).

Picheta, V.I. 'Poverka prav na zemliu vo vladeniiakh korolevy Bony' *Belorussiia i Litva XV–XVI vv.* (Moscow, 1961).

Pisański, G.C. 'Nachricht von dem im Jahre 1656 geschehenen Einfalle der Tataren in Preußen. Aus zuverlässigen Urkunden zusammen getragen' *Mitteilungen der Litterarischen Gesellschaft Masovia* 7 (1901).

Piwarski, K. 'Niedoszła wyprawa tzw. radoszkowicka Zygmunta Augusta na Moskwę w r. 1567–8' *Ateneum Wilenskie* 4 (1927).

Piwarski, K. *Hieronim Lubomirski, hetman wielki koronny* (Cracow, 1929).

Piwarski, K. 'Stosunki szwedzko-brandenburskie a sprawa polska w czasie pierwszej wojny północnej' in K. Lepszy (ed.) *Polska w okresie drugiej wojny północnej* II (Warsaw, 1957).

Plaesterer, A. 'Die Strandpforte und die "Dicke Margarete"' *Beiträge zur Kunde Estlands* 11 (1925).

Platonov, S.F. *Ocherki po istorii Smuty v Moskovskom gosudarstve XVI–XVII vv.* (Moscow, 1937).

Plewczyński, M. *Żołnierz obrony potocznej za panowania Zygmunta Augusta* (Warsaw, 1985).

Plewczyński, M. 'Liczebność wojska polskiego za ostatnich Jagiellonów (1506–1572)' *Studia i Materiały do Historii Wojskowości* 31 (1988).

Plewczyński, M. *Armia koronna 1506–1572. Zagadnienia struktury narodowościowej* (Warsaw, 1991).

Plewczyński, M. *Ludzie wschodu w wojsku ostatnich Jagiellonów* (Warsaw, 1995).

Podhorodecki, L. 'Bitwa pod Warką (7.IV.1656)' *Studia i Materiały do Historii Sztuk Wojennych* 2 (1956).

Podhorodecki, L. *Stanisław Koniecpolski ok. 1592–1646* (Warsaw, 1978).

Podhorodecki, L. and Raszba, N. *Wojna chocimska 1621* (Cracow, 1979).

Pod"iapol'skaia, E.P. 'Voennye sovety 1708–1709 gg.' in *Poltava. K 250-letiiu Poltavskogo srazheniia. Sbornik statei* (Moscow, 1959).

Poe, M. 'The consequences of the Military Revolution in Muscovy: a comparative perspective' *Comparative Studies in Society and History* 38 (1996).

Polska Kriget See: Generalstaben.

Poltava. K 250-letiiu Poltavskogo srazheniia. Sbornik statei (Moscow, 1959).

Poraziński, J. 'Malborska rada senatu w 1703 roku' *Zapiski Historyczne* 44 (1979).

Poraziński, J. *Sejm lubelski w 1703 roku i jego miejsce w konfliktach wewnętrznych na początku XVIII wieku* (Toruń, 1988).

Porshnev, B. 'Sotsial'no-politicheskaia obstanovka v Rossii vo vremia Smolenskoi voiny' *Isoriia SSSR* 1:5 (1957).

Rabinovich, M.D. 'Formirovanie reguliarnoi Russkoi armii nakanune Severnoi Voiny' in V.I. Shunkov (ed.) *Voprosy Voennoi Istorii Rossii XVIII i pervaia polovina XIX vekov* (Moscow, 1969).

Rafacz, J. 'Trybunał skarbowy koronny' *Kwartalnik Historyczny* 38 (1924).

Rasmussen, K. *Die livländische Krise 1554–1561* Københavns Universitets Slaviske Institut. Studier 1 (Copenhagen, 1973).

Renner, U. 'Herzog Magnus von Holstein als Vasall des Zaren Ivan Groznyj' in N. Angermann (ed.) *Deutschland – Livland – Russland. Ihre Beziehungen vom 15. bis zum 17. Jahrhundert* (Lüneburg, 1988).

Rexheuser, R. 'Adelsbesitz und Heeresverfassung im Moskauer Staat des 17. Jahrhunderts' *Jahrbücher für Geschichte Osteuropas* NF 21 (1973).

Ringmar, E. *Identity, Interest and Action. A Cultural Explanation of Sweden's Intervention in the Thirty Years War* (Cambridge, 1996).

Roberts, M. *Gustavus Adolphus. A History of Sweden 1611–1632* 2 vols (London, 1953, 1958).

Roberts, M. 'Gustav Adolf and the art of war', reprinted in M. Roberts *Essays in Swedish History* (Minneapolis, 1967).

Roberts, M. 'Queen Christina and the General Crisis of the seventeenth century' in M. Roberts *Essays in Swedish History* (Minneapolis, 1967).

Roberts, M. 'The Military Revolution 1560–1660', reprinted in M. Roberts *Essays in Swedish History* (Minneapolis, 1967).

Roberts, M. (ed.) *Sweden as a Great Power, 1611–1697* (London, 1968).

Roberts, M. *The Early Vasas. A History of Sweden 1523–1611* (Cambridge, 1968).

Roberts, M. (ed.) *Sweden's Age of Greatness 1632–1718* (London, 1973).

Roberts, M. *The Swedish Imperial Experience, 1560–1715* (Cambridge, 1979).

Roberts, M. 'Charles X and the great parenthesis: a reconsideration', in M. Roberts *From Oxenstierna to Charles XII: Four Studies* (Cambridge, 1991).

Rogers, C.J. (ed.) *The Military Revolution Debate. Readings on the Military Transformation of Early Modern Europe* (Boulder, Col., 1995).

Romański, R. *Cudnów 1660* (Warsaw, 1996).

Rusiński, W. 'Straty i zniszczenia w czasie wojny szwedzkie (1655–1660) oraz jej skutki na obszarze Wielkopolski' in K. Lepszy (ed.) *Polska w okresie drugiej wojny północnej* II (Warsaw, 1957).

Rystad, G. *Johan Gyllenstierna, rådet och kungamakten. Studier i Sveriges inre politik 1660–1680* (Lund, 1955).

Rystad, G. 'Ryssland eller Polen? Karl XII:s planer efter Dünaövergången. Några synpunkter' *Scandia* 27 (1961).

Saarinen, H. *Bürgerstadt und absoluter Kriegsherr. Danzig und Karl XII. im Nordische Krieg* Studia Historica 55 (Helsinki, 1996).

Sahanovich, H. *Neviadomaia Vaina 1654–1667* (Minsk, 1995).

Samuelson, J. *Aristokrat eller föradlad bonde? Det svenska frälsets ekonomi, politik och sociala förbindelser under tiden 1523–1611* (Lund, 1993).

Sauter, W. *Krzysztof Żegocki, pierwszy partyzant Rzeczypospolitej 1618–1673* (Poznań, 1981).

Schuster, O. and Francke, F.U. *Geschichte der Sächsischen Armee von deren Errichtung bis auf die neueste Zeit* (Leipzig, 1885).

Seeberg-Elverfeldt, R. 'Der Tatareinfall in das Amt Johannisburg im Oktober 1656 und 1657' *Mitteilungen der Vereins für Gesellschaft von Ost- und Westpreußen* 8 (1933–4).

Seredyka, J. 'Nowe poglądy na bitwę ze Szwedami pod Gniewem w 1626 r.' *Zapiski Historyczne* 34 (1969).

Seredyka, J. *Sejm zawiedzionych nadziei (1627 r.)* (Opole, 1981).

Shapiro, A.L. (ed.), *Agrarnaia Istoriia Severo-Zapada Rossii XVI veka* 3 vols (Leningrad, 1974–89).

Siekierski, M. 'Landed wealth in the Grand Duchy of Lithuania: the economic affairs of Prince Nicholas Christopher Radziwiłł (1549–1616)' *Acta Baltico-Slavica* 20 (1989), 21 (1992).

Sikorski, J. '"Księgi hetmańskie" Stanisława Sarnickiego na tle piśmiennictwa wojskowego w Polsce XVI wieku' *Studia i Materiały do Historii Wojskowości* 12:2 (1966); 13:2 (1967).

Skrynnikov, R.G. *Rossiia posle oprichniny* (Leningrad, 1975).

Skrynnikov, R.G. *Ivan the Terrible* H.F. Graham (tr.) (Gulf Breeze, Fl., 1981).

Skrynnikov, R.G. *Boris Godunov* H.F. Graham (tr.) The Russian Series vol. 35 (Gulf Breeze, Fl., 1982).

Skrynnikov, R. 'The civil war in Russia at the beginning of the seventeenth century (1603–1607): its character and motive forces' in L.J. Hughes (ed.) *New Perspectives on Muscovite History* (London, 1993).

Smith, D.L. 'Muscovite logistics, 1462–1598' *Slavonic and East European Review* 71 (1993).

Sobik, M.-E. *Polnisch-russische Beziehungen im Spiegel des russischen Wortschatzes des 17. und der ersten Hälfte des 18. Jahrhunderts* (Mannheim, 1969).

Stade, A. (ed.) *Carl X Gustaf och Danmark. Källkritik och Krigshistoria* Carl X Gustaf-Studier I (Stockholm, 1965).

Stade, A. 'Krigsrelationen om Tåget över Bält. Den samtida svenska propagandalitteraturen i källkritisk belysning' reprinted in A. Stade (ed.) *Carl X Gustaf och Danmark. Källkritik och Krigshistoria* Carl X Gustaf-Studier I (Stockholm, 1965).

Stade, A. 'Natten före natten före tåget över Bält. Ett rekonstruktionsförsök' in A. Stade (ed.) *Carl X Gustaf och Danmark. Källkritik och Krigshistoria* Carl X Gustaf-Studier I (Stockholm, 1965).

Stade, A. 'Fältslagen under Skånska Kriget' in F. Askgaard and A. Stade (eds) *Kampen om Skåne* (Copenhagen, 1983).

Stanislavskii, A.L. *Grazhdanskaia voina v Rossii XVII v. Kazachestvo na perelome istorii* (Moscow, 1990).

Staszewski, Jacek *O miejsce w Europie. Stosunki Polski i Saksonii z Francją na przełomie XVII i XVIII wieku* (Warsaw, 1973).

Staszewski, Jacek 'Z listy najczęściej spotykanych błędnych mniemań na temat czasów saskich' *Przegląd Humanistyczny* 1 (1996).

Staszewski, Jacek *August II Mocny* (Wrocław, 1998).

Staszewski, Janusz 'Bitwa pod Trzcianą' *Przegląd Historyczno-Wojskowy* 9 (1937).

Stevens, C.B. 'Belgorod: notes on literacy and language in the seventeenth-century Russian army' *Russian History* 7 (1980).

Stevens, C.B. *Soldiers on the Steppe. Army Reform and Social Change in Early Modern Russia* (DeKalb, Ill., 1995).

Stevens, C.B. 'Evaluating Peter's military forces' in A. Cross (ed.) *Russia in the Reign of Peter the Great: Old and New Perspectives* II Study Group on Eighteenth Century Russia Newsletter (Cambridge, 1998).

Stiles, A. *Sweden and the Baltic 1523–1721* (London, 1992).

Stille, A. *Carl XII:s fälttågsplaner 1707–1709* (Lund, 1908).

Stille, A. 'Bengt Oxenstiernas memorial af den 5 Mars 1702' *Karolinska Förbundets Årsbok* (1914).

Stok, P. 'Bitwa pod Kliszowem w r. 1702' *Studia i Materiały do Historii Wojskowości* 6 (1960).

Storrs, C. and Scott, H.M. 'The Military Revolution and the European Nobility, c. 1600–1800' *War in History* 3 (1996).

Sucheni-Grabowska, A. 'Walka o wymiar i przeznaczenie kwarty w końcu XVI i na początku XVII wieku' *Przegląd Historyczny* 54 (1965).

Sucheni-Grabowska, A. 'Losy egzekucji dóbr w Koronie w latach 1574–1650' *Kwartalnik Historyczny* 80 (1973).

Svensson, S. *Den merkantila bakgrunden till Rysslands anfall på den livländska ordensstaten 1558. En studie till den ryska imperialismens uppkomsthistoria* Skrifter utg. av Vetenskapssocieteten i Lund 35 (Lund, 1951).

Sysyn, F. 'The problem of nobilities in the Ukrainian past: the Polish period, 1569–1648' in I.L. Rudnitsky (ed.) *Rethinking Ukrainian History* (Edmonton, 1981).

Tallett, F. *War and Society in Early-Modern Europe 1495–1715* (London, 1992).

Tarle, E.V. *Severnaia Voina i shvedskoe nashestvie na Rossiiu* (Moscow, 1958).

Teodorczyk, J. 'Wyprawa szwedzka z Meklemburgii do Prus Królewskich wiosną 1627 r.' *Studia i Materiały do Historii Wojskowości* 6 (1960).

Teodorczyk, J. 'Bitwa pod Gniewem (22.IX–29.IX–1.X.1626). Pierwsza porażka husarii' *Studia i Materiały do Historii Wojskowości* 12 (1966).

Teodorczyk, J. 'Wyprawa zimowa Czarnieckiego 1–20.II.1656 r. Bitwa pod Gołębiem' in J. Wimmer (ed.) *Wojna polsko-szwedzka 1655–1660* (Warsaw, 1973).

Teodorczyk, J. and Żygulski, Z. jr. 'Dwugłos o bitwie pod Kircholmem. Historia i ikonografia' *Roczniki Historii Sztuki* 24 (1999).

Tersmeden, L. '"Stormen för Köpenhamn" Planen för det svenska anfallet natten till den 11 Februari 1659 och orsakerna till dess misslyckande' in A. Stade (ed.) *Carl X Gustaf och Danmark. Källkritik och Krigshistoria* Carl X Gustaf-Studier I (Stockholm, 1965).

Tersmeden, L. 'Strategisk defensiv. Carl X Gustaf, Philip av Sulzbach och slaget om Fyn hösten 1659' in A. Stade (ed.) *Carl X Gustaf och Danmark. Källkritik och Krigshistoria* Carl X Gustaf-Studier I (Stockholm, 1965).

Tersmeden, L. 'Carl X Gustafs Armé 1654–1657. Styrka och dislokation' in A. Stade (ed.) *Carl X Gustafs Armé* Carl X Gustaf-Studier VIII (Stockholm, 1979).

Thaden, E. 'Ivan IV in Baltic German historiography' *Russian History* 14 (1987).

Theibault, J. 'The rhetoric of death and destruction in the Thirty Years War' *Social History* 27 (1993).

Tiberg, E. *Zur Vorgeschichte des livländischen Krieges. Die Beziehungen zwischen Moskau und Litauen 1549–1562* Studia Historica Upsaliensia 134 (Uppsala, 1984).

Tidander, L.G.T. *Daniel Rantzaus vinterfälttåg i Sverige 1567–8* (Stockholm, 1886).

Tidander, L.G.T. *Krigsföretagen i Livland under Erik XIV:s regering* (Westervik, 1891).

Tidander, L.G.T. *Nordiska sjuårskrigets historia* (Westervik, 1892).

Tomkiewicz, W. 'Zniszczenie wojenne w dziedzinie kultury' in K. Lepszy (ed.) *Polska w okresie drugiej wojny północnej* II (Warsaw, 1957).

Topolski, J. 'Sixteenth-century Poland and the turning-point in European economic development' J.K. Fedorowicz (ed.) *A Republic of Nobles. Studies in Polish History to 1864* (Cambridge, 1982).

Troebst, S. 'Debating the mercantile background to early modern Swedish empire-building: Michael Roberts versus Artur Attman' *European History Quarterly* 24 (1994).

Tuulse, A. *Die Burgen in Estland und Lettland* Verhandlungen der Gelehrten Estnischen Gesellschaft 23 (Dorpat, 1942).

Tyszowski, K. 'Z dziejów wyprawy Zygmunta III do Szwecji w roku 1598' *Rocznik Zakładu Narodowego im Ossolińskich* I (1927).

Upton, A.F. 'The *Riksdag* of 1680 and the establishment of royal absolutism in Sweden' *English Historical Review* 403 (1987).

Upton, A.F. 'The Swedish nobility, 1600–1772' in H.M. Scott (ed.), *The European Nobilities in the Seventeenth and Eighteenth Centuries* II (London, 1995).

Upton, A.F. *Charles XI and Swedish Absolutism* (Cambridge, 1998).

Urwanowicz, J. *Wojskowe 'sejmiki'. Koła w wojsku Rzeczypospolitej XVI–XVIII wieku* (Białystok, 1996).

Ustrialov, N.G. *Istoriia tsarstvovaniia Petra Velikago* 6 vols (St Petersburg, 1858–64).

Vasar, J. *Die grosse Livländische Güterreduktion. Die Enstehung des Konflikts zwischen Karl XI. und der Livländischen Ritter- und Landschaft 1678–1684* (Tartu, 1930).

Vaupell, O. *Den nordiske syvaarskrig 1563–1570* (Copenhagen, 1891).

Viirankoski, P. 'The impact of military service on Finnish rural society in the 17th century' *Turun Historiallinen Arkisto* 38 (1982).

Viljanti, A. *Gustav Vasas ryska krig 1554–1557* 2 vols (Stockholm, 1957).

Villius, H. *Karl XII:s ryska fälttåg. Källstudier* (Lund, 1951).

Villstrand, N.-E. (ed.), *Kustbygd och centralmakt 1560–1721* (Helsingfors, 1987).

Villstrand, N.-E. *Anpassning eller protest. Lokalsamhället inför utskrivningarna av fotfolk till den svenska krigsmakten 1620–1679* (Åbo, 1992).

Wagner, M. *Kadra oficerska armii koronnej w drugiej połowie XVII wieku* (Toruń, 1992).

Wagner, M. *Kliszów 1702* (Warsaw, 1994).

Waller, S.M. 'Den svenska huvudarméns styrka år 1707' *Karolinska Förbundets Årsbok* (1957).

Wegner, J. 'Warszawa w czasie najazdu szwedzkiego 1655–1657' in K. Lepszy (ed.) *Polska w okresie drugiej wojny północnej* II (Warsaw, 1957).

Weinmann, A. *Reval 1646 bis 1672. Von Frieden von Brömsebro bis zum Beginn der selbständigen Regierung Karls XI.* (Bonn, 1991).

Wernstedt, F. 'Lineartaktik och Karolinsk taktik. Några reflexioner med anledning av framställningen i "Karl XII på slagfältet"' *Karolinska Förbundets Årsbok* (1957).

Westling, G.O.F. *Det nordiska sjuårskrigets historia* C. Silfverstolpe (ed.) *Historiskt Bibliotek* VI-VII (Stockholm, 1879–80).

Wimmer, J. *Wojsko Rzeczypospolitej w dobie wojny północnej* (Warsaw, 1956).

Wimmer, J. *Wojsko polskie w drugiej połowie XVII wieku* (Warsaw, 1965).

Wimmer, J. 'Andrzej Maksymilian Fredro jako projektodawca reform woyskowych' in J. Gierowski (ed.) *O naprawę Rzeczypospolitej XVII–XVIII w. Prace ofiarowane Władysławowi Czaplińskiemu w 60 rocznice urodzin* (Warsaw, 1965).

Wimmer, J. 'Wojsko i skarb Rzeczypospolitej u schyłku XVI i w pierwszej połowie XVII wieku' *Studia i Materiały do Historia Wojskowości* 14:1 (1968).

Wimmer, J. (ed.) *Wojna polsko-szwedska 1655–1660* (Warsaw, 1973).

Wimmer, J. 'Przegląd operacji w wojnie polsko-szwedzkie 1655–1660' in J. Wimmer (ed.) *Wojna polsko-szwedska 1655–1660* (Warsaw, 1973).

Wimmer, J. *Historia piechoty polskiej do roku 1864* (Warsaw, 1978).

Wimmer, J. 'Polskie wojsko i sztuka wojenna w czasie Wielkiej Wojny Północnej' *Studia i Materiały do Historii Wojskowości* 21 (1978).

Wisner, H. 'Wojna inflancka 1625–1629' *Studia i Materiały do Historii Wojskowości* 16 (1970).

Wisner, H. 'Działalność wojskowa Janusza Radziwiłła, 1648–1655' *Rocznik Białystocki* 13 (1976).

Wisner, H. 'Polska sztuka wojenna pierwszej połowy XVII wieku. Wątpliwości i hipotezy' *Kwartalnik Historyczny* 84 (1977).

Wisner, H. *Kircholm, 1605* (Warsaw, 1987).

Wójcik, Z. *Dzikie pola w ogniu. O Kozaczyźnie w dawnej Rzeczypospolitej* (3rd edn, Warsaw, 1968).

Wójcik, Z. 'Czy Kozacy Zaporoscy byli na służbie Mazarina?' *Przegląd Historyczny* 64 (1973).

Wyczański, A. *Studia nad folwarkiem szlacheckim w Polsce w latach 1500–1580* (Warsaw, 1960).

Zechlin, H. 'Die Schlacht bei Fraustadt. Eine militärgeschichtliche Studie' *Zeitschrift der historische Gesellschaft für die Provinz Posen* 11 (1896).

Zechs, E. 'Gustav Adolf und die Belagerung Rigas im Jahre 1621' *Pirmā Baltijas Vēsturnieku Konference, Riga, 16–20.VIII.1937* (Riga, 1938).

Zernack, K. 'Das Zeitalter der nordischen Kriege als frühneuzeitliche Geschicht-sepoche' *Zeitschrift für Historische Forschung* 1 (1974).

Zernack, K. 'Grundfragen der Geschichte Nordosteuropas' in K. Zernack *Nordosteuropa. Skizzen und Beiträge zu einer Geschichte der Ostseeländer* (Lüneburg, 1993).

Zernack, K. 'Schweden als europäische Grossmacht der Frühen Neuzeit' in K. Zernack *Nordosteuropa. Skizzen und Beiträge zu einer Geschichte der Ostseeländer* (Lüneburg, 1993).

Zernack, K. *Polen und Rußland. Zwei Wege in der europäischen Geschichte* (Berlin, 1994).

Zimin, A.A. 'K istorii voennykh reform 50-kh godov XVI v.' *Istoricheskie Zapiski* 55 (1956).

Zobel, R. *Kinduslinn Tallinn* (Tallinn, 1994).

Zutis, J. *Livonijas karš (1558–1582)* (Riga, 1949).

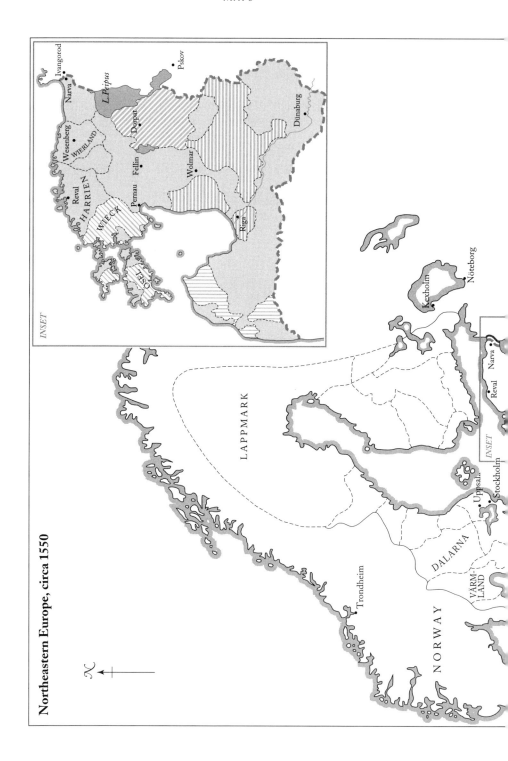

Northeastern Europe, circa 1550

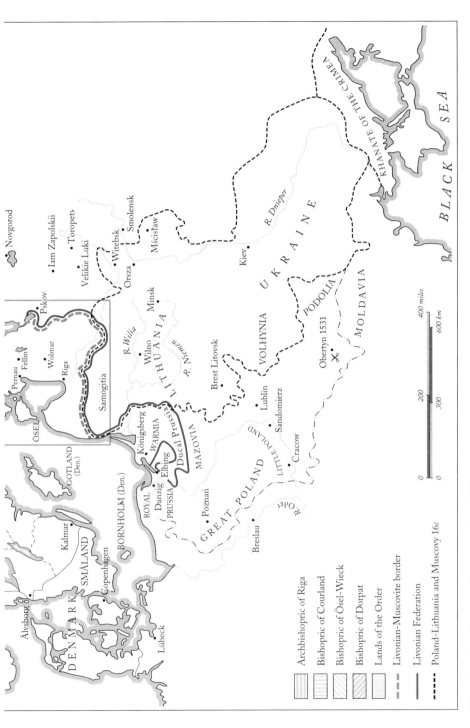

Map 1 Northeastern Europe, circa 1550

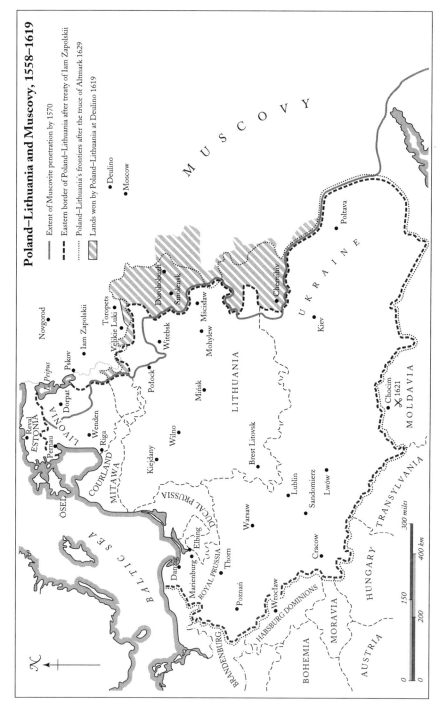

Map 2 Poland-Lithuania and Muscovy, 1558–1619

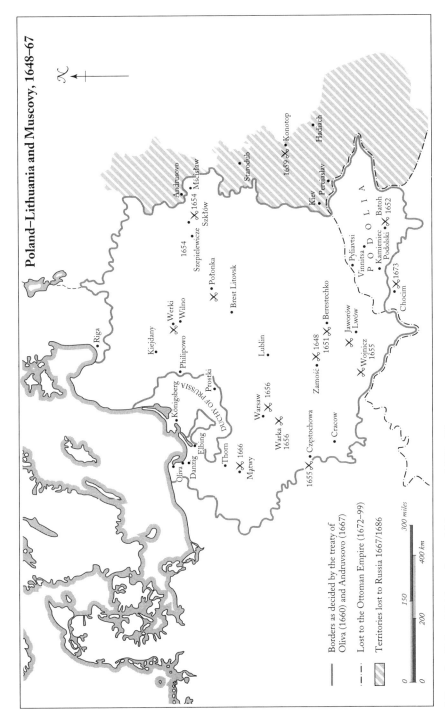

Map 4 Poland-Lithuania and Muscovy, 1648–67

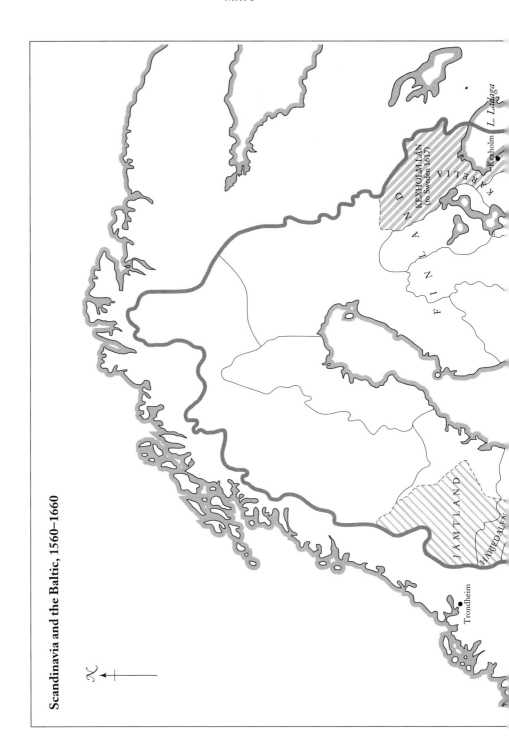

Scandinavia and the Baltic, 1560–1660

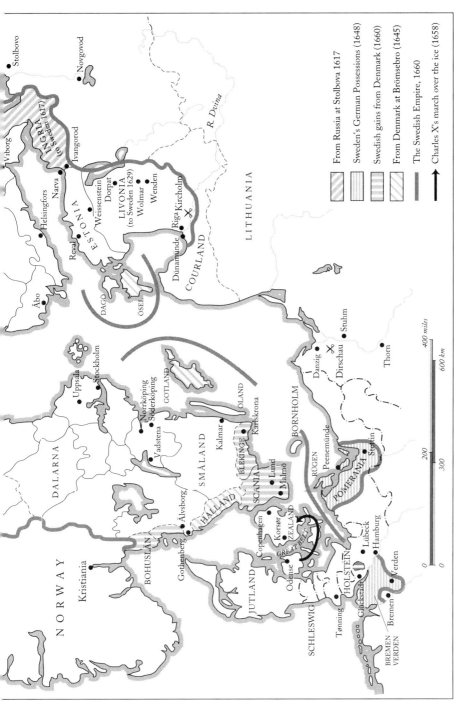

Map 3 Scandinavia and the Baltic, 1560–1660

Stolbovo

Novgovod

R. Dvina

INGRIA
(to Sweden 1617)

Viborg

Narva

Ivangorod

Helsingfors

Weissenstein

Dorpat

ESTONIA

LIVONIA
(to Sweden 1629)

Wolmar

Wenden

Reval

Riga Kircholm

Dünamünde

COURLAND

LITHUANIA

Åbo

DAGO

OSEL

From Russia at Stolbova 1617

Sweden's German Possessions (1648)

Swedish gains from Denmark (1660)

From Denmark at Brömsebro (1645)

The Swedish Empire, 1660

Charles X's march over the ice (1658)

Uppsala

Stockholm

Norrköping

Söderköping

GOTLAND

Vadstena

ÖLAND

SMÅLAND

Kalmar

Karlskrona

BLEKINGE

SCANIA

Lund

Malmö

BORNHOLM

RÜGEN

Peenemünde

Stettin

POMERANIA

Stuhm

Danzig

Dirschau

Thorn

400 miles

600 km

200

300

0

NORWAY

Kristiania

DALARNA

BOHUSLAN

Gothenberg

Älvsborg

HALLAND

JUTLAND

Copenhagen

Korsør

ZEALAND

GREAT BELT

Odense

HOLSTEIN

SCHLESWIG

Tønning

Glückstadt

BREMEN
VERDEN

Bremen

Verden

Lübeck

Hamburg

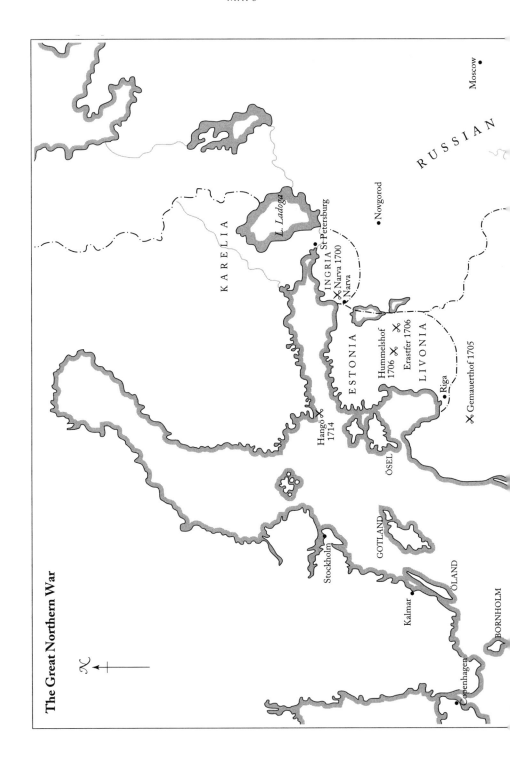

The Great Northern War

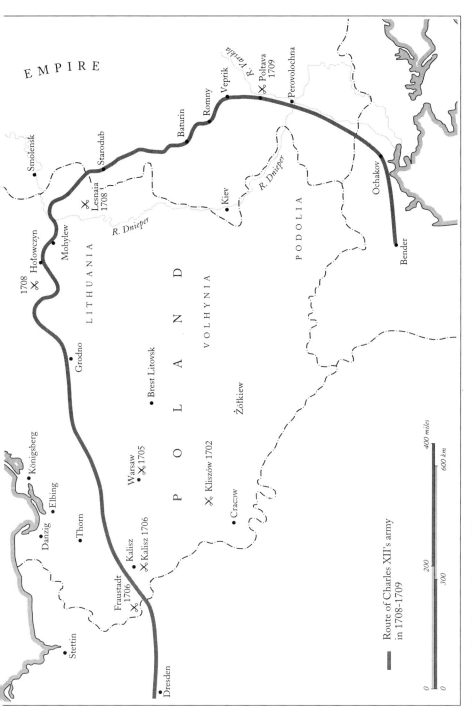

Map 5 The Great Northern War

INDEX